THE DEVELOPMENT
OF COGNITIVE
PROCESSES

THE DEVELOPMENT OF COGNITIVE PROCESSES

edited by

VERNON HAMILTON

and

MAGDALEN D. VERNON

Department of Psychology
University of Reading
England

153

1976

ACADEMIC PRESS

LONDON   NEW YORK   SAN FRANCISCO

A Subsidiary of Harcourt Brace Jovanovich, Publishers

ACADEMIC PRESS INC. (LONDON) LTD.
24/28 Oval Road
London NW1

United States Edition published by
ACADEMIC PRESS INC.
111 Fifth Avenue
New York, New York 10003

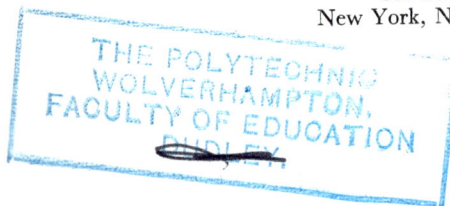

Copyright © 1976 by
ACADEMIC PRESS INC. (LONDON) LTD.

Library of Congress Catalog Card Number: 76 43629
ISBN: 0 12 321750 4

MADE AND PRINTED IN GREAT BRITAIN BY
THE GARDEN CITY PRESS LIMITED, LETCHWORTH, HERTFORDSHIRE SG6 1JS

CONTRIBUTORS

MAX COLTHEART, *Department of Psychology, Birkbeck College, University of London.*

RICHARD F. CROMER, *M.R.C. Developmental Psychology Unit, London.*

MARGARET DONALDSON, *Department of Psychology, University of Edinburgh.*

S. FARNHAM-DIGGORY, *Department of Psychology, University of Texas, Dallas.*

VERNON HAMILTON, *Department of Psychology, University of Reading.*

JOHN HUTT, *Department of Psychology, University of Keele.*

JANE MACKWORTH, *16232 Camellia Terrace, Los Gatos, California 95030.*

PENELOPE H. ODOM-BROOKS and DREW J. ARNOLD, *George Peabody College, Nashville, Tennessee.*

DOUGLASS R. PRICE-WILLIAMS, *Departments of Psychiatry and Anthropology, Center for Health Studies, University of California, Los Angeles.*

HAYNE W. REESE and STEPHEN W. PORGES, *Departments of Psychology, West Virginia University, and University of Illinois.*

PHILIP H. K. SEYMOUR, *Department of Psychology, University of Dundee.*

MAGDALEN D. VERNON, *Formerly Department of Psychology, University of Reading.*

PHILIP E. VERNON, *Department of Educational Psychology, University of Calgary.*

ELIANE VURPILLOT, *Laboratoire de Psychologie Expérimentale, Université René Descartes, Paris.*

RICHARD D. WALK, *Department of Psychology, George Washington University, Washington, D.C.*

PREFACE

This book is intended for all psychologists interested in the various aspects of cognitive development in children, especially as it might be elucidated through the application of the information processing concepts which have recently been extensively employed in the investigation of adult cognition. Readers will be able to judge what are the prospects for future development along these lines in the study of cognitive processes in children. It is hoped that the book may prove to be of special interest to developmental psychologists, but also to other psychologists and to graduate and advanced undergraduate students of psychology. It may also be of relevance to the work of teachers and research workers in the fields of education, pediatrics, neurology and psychiatry.

The book is divided into four parts: Part I discusses information processing in adults; Part II the main aspects of children's cognitive processes; Part III the relation of these to intelligence and motivation, and to cross-cultural variations; Part IV the impairments of normal cognitive processes.

The Editors wish to express their gratitude to the contributors to this volume who have so ably presented the various aspects of the subject which they were invited to discuss.

Reading,
July 1976

VERNON HAMILTON
MAGDALEN D. VERNON

ACKNOWLEDGEMENTS

Acknowledgements for permission to reproduce Figures and Tables are made to the following: Academic Press, Figs 2.2, 3.7, 4.2, 5.6, 9.6, 15.1, 15.2; Allen and Unwin, Table 5.1; American Association for the Advancement of Science, Fig. 6.4; American Medical Association, Fig. 16.3; American Psychological Association, Figs 6.5, 11.1, 14.1, 14.2, 14.3, 16.1 and Tables 11.1, 14.1, 14.4; Cambridge University Press, Figs 4.5, 9.7; Elsevier, Figs 14.10, 14.12; Freeman, San Francisco, Fig. 5.1; Harper and Row, Fig. 9.4 and Table 12.1; Heinemann, Tables 14.2, 14.3; Hemisphere Publishing Corporation, Fig. 11.7; Holt, Blond, Fig. 11.2; Journal Press, Figs 4.1, 6.7, 11.4; McGraw-Hill, Fig. 3.5; The Merrill-Palmer Institute, Fig. 11.5; National Academy of Science, Fig. 3.2; North-Holland Publishing, Fig. 14.5 and Table 14.5; Penguin, Fig. 3.1; Pergamon, Figs 3.3, 3.8, 14.6, 14.7, 14.8; Professor J. Piaget, Fig. 4.7, part of Fig. 5.2; Prentice-Hall, Fig. 16.4; Presses Universitaires de France, Figs 4.6, 4.8, 5.3, 5.10; Psychologie Française, Fig. 5.5; Psychonomic Society, Fig. 3.4; Royal Society of Medicine, Fig. 14.11; Society for Research in Child Development, Figs 3.6, 4.3, 4.4, part of 6.2, 11.3 and Table 11.2.

CONTENTS

PART I

PART II

Introduction

Vernon Hamilton

In planning this volume we have aimed at a possible synthesis between traditional approaches to the study of developmental and experimental child psychology, and the first fruits of cognitive processing theories which have emerged from work on adults. Such a project is patently beyond the resources of a single person and, consequently, we invited each of the present contributors to review his own area of expertise in chapters specially written for this book. Each author had available a tentative set of contents for each of the planned chapters, which reflected our overall aim. Apart from this, our authors were free to decide how to handle their task. In the absence of joint discussion, fully integrated conceptualizations were not expected. Nor was it deemed desirable at this stage to present a consensual set of implications for research on the development of cognitive processes which was elaborated by a small group of theorists.

Cognitive processing theories have emerged as the result of some powerful new models and concepts. Stimuli are signals conveying information to a processing system which has the capacity to code and assign representational status to them. Validation of coding processes depends on a sequence of operations which test the attempted identifications by matching them with additional impressions of external stimuli and with existing coded information in a store of past events. The information processing system has, in each given instance, a finite capacity for handling the input, for passing it into temporary storage components and for analytically selecting and integrating representational data preparatory to a response.

The first iconic store can maintain only a very short-lived record, and because of brief temporal resolution intervals is subject to backward masking from a succession of incoming signals competing for the same available processing time and space. Further interference occurs at the stage of a processing system which can retain stimulus representations for a sufficient length of time to permit their coding.

This is an active process of identification requiring initially the development of a data-signifying operation and subsequently—as in the growing infant and child—the application, by matching and recognizing, of existing codes or data from long-term memory stores.

The difficulty of a process or of a response is defined not only by the maturational level of a system or by the amount of integrated information it has already available for the analysis of input, but by the amount or the categorical complexity of stimuli. These criteria may be further defined by the number of binary decisions required for identification and response selection, where a monotonic logarithmic relationship appears to hold for reaction time to relatively simply defined stimuli.

Difficulty of processing may also be defined by the total amount of *simultaneous* incoming stimuli, either produced by complex demands from the environment, or by self-paced excessive attentional scanning. Responses accompanied by pleasurable, satisfying or desired outcomes contribute to the subsequent development of strategies for operating upon stimulus input by the structuring of economical hierarchies of data-evaluating, identifying and integrating processes. These are considered to involve at least two stages : a search for structure or familiarity and a more detailed search of an event-knowledge memory. Both, but particularly the latter, require access to a correct lexical, semantic or iconogenic entry in appropriate data stores which reflect the development of knowledge of the environment.

Inevitably we are promoting a reductionist approach to the development of perception, conception, reasoning and language which is consistent with analytically derived theories of cognitive processing durations, sequences and capacities. This approach via micro-systems and molecular concepts could lead to new specifiers of developmental events, precocities as well as retardations. It may help, moreover, to institute a new unity for a developmentally oriented behavioural science which, in the past, has suffered substantially from taking up over-compartmentalized positions.

Not all the questions posed by the title of the book or the chapter headings can be answered at present, partly because of inevitable inadequacies in the subsumed analogues. While we must declare our indebtedness to computer science and statistical decision theory, many of our readers may prefer to point to the shortcomings of the models to which they have given rise. It is worth restating, therefore, that human information processing systems may be variably aroused by diverse mechanisms and cognitive events, that they contain dynamically organized goal-seeking programmes, and that they possess an autonomous general capacity and need to continue operations upon inputs and their stores, which elaborate and reorganize their representations long after the event. In other words, the data banks are subject to alterations which are independent of actual external stimuli. Internally instigated stimulation and its processing may thus hold the key to a fuller understanding of the acquisition of, for example, language (Chapter 8), and of the influence of socialization variables, motivation and personality on cognitive behaviour (Chapter 11). These events may similarly strengthen the role of objective and subjective experience in the development of cross-cultural differences in cognitive strategies (Chapter 13), and in the development of abnormal behaviour (Chapter 16). Individual differences in cognitive process development may be seen, therefore, as interactive functions of autonomous and self-driven internal activities, of so-called non-cognitive processes, of the information presented by the total environment, and of the characteristics of the individual's bio-genetic system.

The analytic contributions of Coltheart and Seymour in Part I set the stage for our exercise. Are there processing differences between remembering and identifying? In which conditions is information lost, degraded or distorted? What are the temporal and structural requirements for holding information, for retrieval and comparison operations? How are physical, sensory stimuli transformed in coding operations to permit a situation- and task-relevant correct response to be made? Interesting answers appear to be available from evidence and hypotheses about the capacities of short-term and long-term memory systems, particularly of the roles played by data stores and registers of phonemic, graphemic and semantic information codes. In view of the number of processing stages necessarily traversed by incoming stimuli, and in view of the influence of prior experience on the content of the information stores, the importance of the available processing time as well as the child's development phase may be seen in a new conceptual light.

The perception of form and the identification of objects are readily seen as the development of an increasing capacity to select significant features of a stimulus display. The first internal codes of forms, patterns, faces or their two-dimensional pictorial representations are relatively inaccurate, piecemeal, poorly labelled, and contain redundant information (Chapter 4, M. D. Vernon). Development requires increases in directed scanning, the diminution of stimulus uncertainty and the growth of organized LTM structures. Internal models of the objective environment become progressively less stimulus-bound, and awareness of salience leads to a more restricted sampling of cues, and to the emergence of rules and flexible strategies for the identification of objects (Chapter 5, Vurpillot). The development of the labelling process, and/or rules in the search for salience, must be facilitated by the complementary growth of coding capacity for initially phonemic, graphemic or pictorial data, by the arrival of stimuli in optimal amounts and sequences at the short-term stores, and by the laying down of appropriate past-event stores. For optimal progress, and because of the greater amount of information available to the growing organism, a semantic data store or stores are required. Although rules and strategies in the acquisition of language are beginning to become clearer (Chapter 8, Cromer), the cognitive processes facilitating them remain highly speculative. It is likely, however, that verbal stimuli, whether paired or not paired with forms, objects or pictures, are handled at most processing stages just like other incoming stimuli, even though they constitute a stimulus class of their own. Thus, the findings on the limitations of temporary information storage, of decay, of masking or of compounding, may well apply to them. The recognizer or matching operations may involve, certainly at the pre-language stage, iconogen (see Chapter 2) rather than logogen systems. This may also apply to the development of spatial perception (Chapter 6, Walk), where basic information from ocular convergence, accommodation, motion parallax and texture cues are supplemented ontogenetically by information from the results of actions, and only subsequently by inference, as in the visual constancies.

The data banks which store the representations of the external environment and their individually determined autonomous or motivated elaborations, cannot be accumulated without assigning energy to the scanning and input of stimuli. The energy source for the operation and distribution of attention is finite at any given time and, as we have seen, similar restrictions affect the short-term information storage components of the processing system. Since attention is a prerequisite for input, it is probably the single most important cognitive process. Its two major components, of orienting and selecting or focusing, appear to be controlled by different mechanisms, respectively dealing with signal to noise ratios, and with search for novelty or relevance in the stimulus field. Orientation ontogenetically precedes selection, and scanning only gradually increases in amount, in beam width, in directedness and in the patient selection of situation- and task-relevant cues (Chapter 3, Mackworth). The resulting quality of the data input is determined by the richness of environment stimuli, by the speed and sequencing of registration in a limited capacity temporary storage system, and by the intensity of the attentional energy source or its susceptibility to positive or negative feedback from the results of its activities. Attentional processes need not be driven, however, by these factors only, since a sequence of central decision-making processes can control the strength and direction of external as well as internal scanning and data-gathering operations.

Internal registration of representative stimuli is a prerequisite of concept development, and the processes of abstraction and generalization from discrete stimulus attributes are at its core (Chapter 7, Donaldson). In some respects the integrating and organizing processes leading to efficient perceptual skills are similar to those operating in concept attainment. This is because temporal, structural and functional relationships between stimuli are first coded concretely as single events. As the result of equivalences registering during matching or recognizing operations, or perceptual matches observed on subsequent occasions in respect of outcomes of behaviour, classes of associated stimuli are chunked or re-chunked depending on the degree to which expectancies subsumed by them are confirmed. Little is known about *how* a novel set of conceptualizations emerges from a period of behaviour guided by concrete and discrete schemata, apart from the necessary influence of symbolic—either pictorial or semantic—codes which, by the condensation of separate data, institute a new level of information processing economy.

The neo-Piagetian approach to cognitive development which appears to be emerging embodies new models which can account for the assembly of novel structures. These structures also contain new conceptual categories capable of mediating the feelings of necessity and sufficiency accompanying a correct inferential response (Chapter 9, Farnham-Diggory). Operational algorithms or production system models, or models of operational steps and sequences with in-built logical or binary decision pathways, seem to have considerable utility in the analysis of unobservable operations, and particularly, perhaps, in the understanding of the relationship between optimal development and the mental work load on a processing system and its components.

Intact bio-physiological structures and functioning are required for optimal cognitive development. A system with congenital or acquired damage is subject to autonomous neurological noise or bursts of hyper- or hypo-activity which prevent organized attentional activities and the systematic coding, processing and storing of inputs (Chapter 14, Hutt). Cerebral response levels may also be consistently and systematically abnormal, and show either hyper- or hypo-reactivity or arousal. On this basis, stimulus input may be either excessively high or low, and in the presence of an unadaptable or aversively experienced early environment, weak conceptual classes, idiosyncratic inferential structures or elaborated affectively-loaded representational data may form a substantial part of a long term memory system. Since situation- or task-relevant behaviour depends upon matching and recognizing processes reflecting concepts and experiences shared by children's social reference groups, these historical events may provide a possible basis of neurotic or schizophrenic behaviour (Chapter 16, Hamilton).

The acquisition of socially and personally desirable and valued skills occurs in response to the information content and information transmission strategies of cultures and sub-cultures. Cognitive processes operate upon familiar and salient stimuli which are modal for the reference group, and which reflect its socio-economic system and its institutions (Chapter 13, Price-Williams). Methods of child-rearing and the severity of social norms for precision and achievement will be mirrored in the amount of bio-physiological and cognitively mediated effort which an information processing system will bring to bear on externally available and already internally registered stimula- tion. Western types of logic and standards of evidential verification depend only in part on environmental enrichment. Motivation as well as standards of testing evidence prior to a response may well contribute to the deficiencies in amounts and complexity of information which appear to be available to non-organic subnormal or retarded children (Chapter 15, Odom-Brooks and Arnold). While this points to deficits in assimilation operations, the concept of all-or-none stages of develop- ment appears to be less useful than cognitive processing models. These would tend to stress the adverse effects of a small capacity short term memory, small and not fully representative informational chunks or concepts, and possibly non-correspondence between iconogenic and semantic data stores.

The evidence over the last twenty-five years of favourable changes in the measured intelligence levels and occupational skills of initially subnormal children is consistent with an explanation in terms of slowed development of information processing capacities. It constitutes an important part of the environmentalist rejoinders to genetically biased theories of intelligence and its development. Necessary distinctions between types and factors of intelligence, and their relationship to age, sex and socio-economic or ethic group, are of increasing conceptual importance (Chapter 12, P. E. Vernon). It is now possible to regard the development of intelligence as the development of all perceptual and conceptual skills, and thus as a reflection of the ontogeny and capacity of the cognitive processing system and its separate components.

Despite the dangers inherent in a unilateral conceptual approach to cognitive development, it is possible that the advantages may outweigh the disadvantages. An organism does not respond in the absence of stimulation which it actively seeks, which conveys information, and from which a child constructs the representation of his environment. The development of *consistencies in* and *intensities of* seeking particular types or classes of stimuli reflect the presence of cognitive structures in long term data stores which in their operation and effects are probably indistinguishable from simpler or situation-specific structures. The classification of incoming stimuli in the developing child can sequentially proceed on the basis of stimulus attributes as well as of super-ordinate general strategies concerning the outcomes and implications of behaviour. Thus, attentional, coding and retrieval processes may be validly applied to the development of motivation and personality (Chapter 11, Hamilton).

We may ask whether a cognitive process orientation in the study of behavioural development has implications for the utility and explanatory power of behavioristic, S–R approaches to learning. This is possibly the most carefully investigated area in the field of developmental and experimental child psychology, and well-known studies of classical and operant conditioning, of habituation and discrimination have strengthened rather than diminished the time-honoured concept of association forming (Chapter 10, Reese and Porges). It seems plausible to argue that the role that has been assigned to mediators in the learning process was the first step towards a synthesis with concurrent notions of signal coding, matching processes and theories of STM and LTM functions and capacities in responding to stimuli. It seems equally plausible to suggest that stimulus-response bonds are created and maintained because they constitute a larger conceptual unit which, together with the information concerning probabilistic contingencies, is adaptively available upon retrieval from an LTM store.

It must be noted that we have omitted a full account of the important developmental role of neurotransmitters in the cognitive processes. This is a complex area of study, much of it concerned with the testing of theories in relation to infra-human organisms, which do not always provide a suitable analogue, particularly for cognitive theorizing.

We have been unable also to include a separate chapter on the implications of a cognitive processing approach to educational procedures and strategies. In an epoch of rapidly increasing informational complexity implicit in the emergence of new social and economic structures and institutions, it may be predicted that adequate adaptation to environmental complexity may require a clearer formulation of the cognitive processes and operational stages which determine the development of rules for the acquisition of knowledge (see for example, Broadbent, 1975). This approach, at some future date, will have to be extended to include an informational and cognitive process analysis of the development of social interactions.

REFERENCES

Broadbent, D. E. (1975). Cognitive psychology and education. *British Journal of Educational Psychology, 45,* 162–76.

PART I

CHAPTER 1

Contemporary Models of the Cognitive Processes: I. Iconic Storage and Visual Masking

M. Coltheart

I. INTRODUCTION

My aim in this chapter is to survey what is currently known about early stages in the processing of visual information, from the viewpoint of cognitive psychology rather than of neurophysiology. In the past twenty years, neurophysiologists have discovered an extraordinary amount about the functioning of the visual system—the retina, optic nerve, lateral geniculate, optic radiations and visual cortex. During the same period, cognitive psychologists have learned much about the first few processing stages through which visual information passes when a human being is carrying out such information-processing activities as looking at a scene or reading. At present, the first tentative steps are being taken to relate the neurophysiology to the cognitive psychology—to identify the physiological mechanisms corresponding to the cognitive processes—but this work is still in its infancy and will not be discussed here.

Visual information-processing activities can be divided into two broad classes: those which involve *memorizing* visual stimuli and those which involve *identifying* visual stimuli. Looking at an unfamiliar picture, or the face of a stranger, with the intention of memorizing it so that it could be recognized in the future, is an example of the former class. The visual stimuli here are not being identified, since to identify something means to locate its representation in one's long-term memory, and novel pictures or faces, being novel, have no such representations. Looking at a picture to try to determine who painted it, or scanning a crowd of people looking for one's wife, are examples of the second class of activities : here representations exist in long-term memory (for instance, descriptions of the stylistic characteristics of paintings by particular artists, or a visual specification of one's wife's face), and the activity involves relating visual stimuli in the external world to visual information stored in long-term memory, rather than the memorization of these visual stimuli.

Various kinds of interaction between these two broad classes of visual information-processing activities are possible. For example, if a visual stimulus is presented for a very short time, and if locating its representation in long-term memory, i.e., identifying it, takes a relatively long time, then the duration for which visual data are available will need to be extended, and this can be done by storing these data in some temporary form of visual memory. Conversely, memorizing novel visual stimuli can be assisted by using information held in long-term memory; a picture of an unfamiliar scene is memorized much more efficiently if the objects in the scene are juxtaposed in a plausible way (that is to say, in a way consistent with previous occasions on which one has looked at such objects) than if the objects are disposed at random in the scene. Thus memorizing can assist identification, and identification can assist memorizing.

I shall discuss these issues largely in connection with the memorizing or identifying of linguistic stimuli—letters and words—rather than pictures, simply because nearly all recent work on visual information processing has used such stimuli. As far as is known, however, the two information processing stages I shall discuss (iconic storage and durable storage) are general stages in the sense that *any* visual input, not just words or letters, is dealt with by means of these two stages. Thus what I have to say in this chapter (except for the short section dealing specifically with the perception of words) is meant as a description of the earliest stages in the processing of any kind of visual input.

II.   THE PROCESSING OF BRIEF VISUAL DISPLAYS

(1)   ICONIC AND DURABLE STORAGE

Our inspection of the visual world, whether we are looking at a collection of objects or a page of print, consists alternately of saccadic eye movements lasting some tens of milliseconds and fixations lasting some hundreds of milliseconds. Visual sensitivity is very poor just before, during and after an eye movement (Latour, 1962; Volkmann, 1962); it is when the eye is still that visual information is collected. For this reason, a promising approach to the study of visual information-processing is to try to discover how much information can be collected during a single fixation. This can be investigated in numerous ways: the simplest technically is to present information for a short enough time to ensure that the subject could not fixate in two different places while the information is present. Measurements of the latency of eye movements indicate that, if a display lasts for less than two hundred milliseconds or so, it will not be possible for the subject to collect any new information from it by means of a second fixation. The situation will therefore resemble what happens during a single fixation of a visual scene.

Investigations prompted by these considerations were first carried out in the nineteenth century: electric sparks were used to provide the required brief display times. Little was done along these lines in the twentieth century until the late 1950s. Then Sperling (1960) and Averbach and Coriell (1961) published the results of their work on the processing of brief visual displays. They used the tachistoscope to present alphanumeric displays at durations too short to permit eye movements, and they discovered a considerable amount about the visual information-processing which goes on during a single fixation. Although Sperling's work (1960, 1963, 1967) is better-known, Averbach and Coriell's experiments were also extremely valuable, and since their work is less well known I shall discuss it, rather than Sperling's work, as a basis for describing the essential characteristics of iconic storage and visual masking.

Each display used by Averbach and Coriell consisted of two horizontal rows, each containing 8 letters, and displayed for 50 msec. It has been known for more than a century that, if such a display is presented and a subject is asked to write or speak as many of the letters from the display as he can, he will average between 4 and 5 correct. This figure does not vary much from subject to subject, and is not influenced by varying exposure duration from as low as 15 msec to as high as 500 msec, nor by varying the number of letters in the display from as few as 6 to as many as 18 (Sperling, 1960); these findings are obtained as easily in different countries as they are in different centuries.

Although this limitation on the amount which can be reported from a brief alphanumeric display is thoroughly well-established, its cause remains unknown. However, a number of possible explanations has been ruled out by experimental work. A straightforward explanation would be that the perception of a letter is a process which takes time, and that when time is limited only a small number of letters can be perceived; another is that letter perception is very fast, but subject to some kind of capacity limitation, so that only a limited number of letters can be perceived at any one time. Observers in this kind of experiment deny both of these explanations, and claim that they can perceive *all* the letters well enough; the problem lies somewhere else. Sperling (1960) and Averbach and Coriell (1961) showed experimentally that this claim is correct.

In Averbach and Coriell's experiments, although the subject was always presented with 16 letters in each display, he had to report only one of these letters. Which one, however, was the critical letter was not revealed to him until after the display had been turned off. In the first experiment, this indication was provided by means of a small vertical bar pointing towards the position which had been occupied by the critical letter. The time between the termination of the display and the onset of this bar marker was varied from 0 msec to 500 msec.

When the bar marker occurred immediately after display offset, subjects averaged about 63 per cent correct. Since 63 per cent of 16 is over 10, this shows that, after the display has been terminated, at least 10 of the 16 items are represented in some form of memory. This is in spite of the fact that, if the subject is asked to report all the items he can, he will be able to report only 4 or 5. When Averbach and Coriell investigated the effects of varying the delay between display offset and bar marker onset, they found that as this delay increased performance worsened until, at a delay of about 200 msec subjects were averaging about 32 per cent correct. Further increases in delay, up to 500 msec, did not produce further decrements in performance, which was fairly constant at about 32 per cent (equivalent to 5 letters out of 16) at all delays between 200 msec and 500 msec.

These results have three features and each is important. Firstly, performance is very good at short bar marker delays (at least 10 items from 16 are available). Secondly, performance declines sharply as bar marker delay is increased, until at a delay of 200 msec only 5 items from the 16 are available. Thirdly, performance remains constant at this level with further increases in bar marker delay.

This pattern of results can be interpreted as follows. At display offset, a form of memory has been set up which has high capacity (in fact, as we shall see, it probably holds all 16 of the items in Averbach and Coriell's experimental situation) but rapid decay; it has disappeared completely within 300 msec of the offset of the display. Since a subject takes longer than 300 msec to respond to a display, he could not report anything from it if this were the only form of memory for such displays. We must postulate, then, a second form of memory, not subject to such rapid decay. An item which the subject wishes to report must be registered in this second mode of memory, from which it can be reported at leisure. The first, high-capacity, rapid-decay memory mode was named "iconic memory" by Neisser (1967). The second, non-decaying mode I will refer to as "durable storage", since, compared to the iconic storage mode, it shows negligible decay.

Averbach and Coriell went on to show that loss by decay was not the only way in which information was lost from iconic storage; this storage mode is also susceptible to interference from visual stimuli presented some time after the offset of a display. Such interference is known as "visual backward masking", and one of their many contributions was to show that there are two distinct kinds of visual backward masking, which they called "summation" and "erasure". I shall use these terms, although the equivalent pair of terms "integration" and "interruption" (Kahneman, 1968) is now more common. I will also use the term SOA (stimulus-onset-asynchrony) to refer to the time interval between the onsets of two successively-presented visual stimuli.

At very short SOAs, two successively presented stimuli appear to be simultaneous; in other words, the visual system has imperfect temporal resolution. The iconic storage formed in this situation is a composite one, consisting of the sum of the two stimuli. For example, if a subject is briefly shown an F, and at a very short SOA an L is then presented in the same retinal location, what is seen is an E. This is the process referred to by Averbach and Coriell as "summation". As SOA is increased from a few milliseconds up into decades of milliseconds, this summation effect becomes progressively less frequent. Whenever summation does not occur, erasure does: the second stimulus erases the first from iconic storage, and what the subject sees is either just L, or an extremely brief F followed by an L which lasts much longer than the F. In the conditions of Averbach and Coriell's experiment, summation never occurred at an SOA greater than 100 msec; beyond this point, if there was any visual interference at all it was of the erasure type. Erasure effects occurred at SOAs up to about 250 msec. These effects were demonstrated by using three different kinds of indicator for the critical letter: the bar marker referred to before, a ring which encircled the position formerly occupied by the critical letter, and a circle covered by a cross-hatched pattern which occupied the position formerly occupied by the critical letter.

When summation occurs, only one of these stimuli is harmful: the cross-hatched circle. A letter with a superimposed circle around it, or a bar superimposed and above it, is still legible, but a letter with a cross-hatched pattern superimposed upon it is not legible. When erasure occurs, *two* of these stimuli are harmful, that is to say, they replace the critical letter in iconic storage: the ring and the circle. The bar marker does not produce erasure, because, as it turns out, erasure is *local* in iconic storage; for stimulus A to erase stimulus B, they must be presented to the same or closely adjacent retinal locations. The circle surrounded the retinal location of the critical letter closely, and so could erase it; the bar pointed to this location from some distance away, and so did not erase it. Erasure still occurs even when the erasing stimulus and the display are presented to different eyes. Therefore, at SOAs where the circle produces worse performance than the ring, at least some summation is occurring; at SOAs where the circle and the ring produce equal performance, but worse performance than the bar, erasure but not summation is occurring; and when all three indicators produce equal performance, neither summation nor erasure is occuring.

This analysis of the two forms of visual backward masking produces an unexpected prediction, namely, that, when the circle is used, performance should actually get *worse* as the interval between the display and the circle increases. This is because the circle is harmless when summation occurs; it is only harmful when erasure occurs. As SOA increases, summation becomes less likely and hence erasure more likely; therefore performance worsens. However, as SOA continues to increase, the relevant item is given more and more time in iconic storage before it is erased; this is obviously beneficial, so at these SOAs performance begins to improve as SOA increases. Finally, at still longer SOAs, the item is given so much time in iconic storage that further time is not needed, so further increases in SOA have no effect on performance. Thus there is a detailed prediction about SOA effects on performance using the ring indicator: as SOA increases, performance gets worse and worse, up to some SOA; then it gets better and better up to a second SOA; from then on it remains constant with further increases in SOA. This is precisely what Averbach and Coriell found. Such "U-shaped" (more properly saucepan-shaped) backward masking functions have since been observed by many investigators, for instance, Weisstein and Haber (1965), Fraisse (1966), Turvey (1973), and Bachmann and Allik (1976).

Averbach and Coriell's analysis of backward masking provided them with an invaluable tool for dissecting out various components of the dual (iconic and durable) storage system. For example, it must be the case that some appreciable time is required between when a bar marker is presented and when the indicated letter is safely ensconced in durable storage. This time can be measured by presenting a display and a bar marker simultaneously and then, some time later, erasing the indicated letter with a ring. If the letter can be reported, it must have entered durable storage before the ring arrived. This experiment showed that the time required to appreciate which letter the bar marker is indicating and then to read the indicated letter into durable storage can be up to 270 msec. Consequently, a bar marker presented at display offset is not instantaneously usable; the *real* bar marker delay is somewhere between 0 and 270 msec. Therefore, if ten letters are available in this situation (zero bar marker delay), this is an *underestimate* of the capacity of iconic storage, because some decay has occurred before the critical letter reaches durable storage. When this is taken into account, evidence suggests that iconic storage can hold all sixteen items from a display like Averbach and Coriell's (see Averbach and Sperling, 1961).

The rate at which items accumulate in durable storage can be investigated by using the cross-hatched circle to indicate the critical letter. This removes from iconic storage (either by erasure or by summation) the very letter the subject is required to report: if he gets the letter right, then it must already have reached durable storage before the circle occurred. Thus by varying the SOA of the circle, it is possible to measure the amount of material which has reached durable storage as a function of time since display offset. This, and experiments using similar methods (Sperling, 1963), showed that three or four items reached durable storage rather quickly, in the first 80 msec after display offset. Then something seems to happen; in the next 120 msec, only one more item enters durable storage, and with further time few or no more are added. This is true even if the display is not brief, and is left on for 200 msec. Therefore the cause is not the decay of items from iconic storage; instead, the process recording items into durable storage, or the storage mode itself, jams after dealing with three or four items, and subsequent items are dealt with very slowly, if at all.

Although only four or five items from a large display find their way into durable storage, a subject can choose which items shall do so. In Averbach and Coriell's experiments, the subject records the critical item in durable storage provided it is still available in iconic storage when the bar marker occurs: this is "selective readout", as distinct from "non-selective readout" which is reading items from iconic storage into durable storage during the period between the display and the bar marker. In subsequent experiments, subjects' ability to read selectively from iconic storage into durable storage has been explored in a variety of situations, for instance in reading a particular row from a display, reading all items of a particular hue or brightness or shape (for a review of this work see Coltheart, 1972) or reading all items having a particular direction of movement (Treisman, Russell and Green, 1975).

Subjects can select particular items from iconic storage and record them in durable storage, then, on the basis of the position, hue, brightness, shape, or direction of movement of the items. On the other hand, such selective readout cannot be performed if the subject tries to select the letter items from a mixed set of letters and numbers (Sperling, 1960; von Wright, 1972), nor if the task is to select letters containing the sound "ee" in their names (Coltheart, Lea and Thompson, 1974). This is what would be expected if iconic storage were a purely visual storage mode, since then only purely visual stimulus characteristics could be used to select out certain of the items held in iconic storage.

(2)   "DIRECT MEASUREMENT" OF VISUAL PERSISTENCE

One question about iconic storage which I have not yet mentioned is this : is it visible? If the contents of a visual display are available in a decaying storage mode for some hundreds of milliseconds after display offset, does that mean that an observer continues to "see" the display even after it is turned off? None of the experimental work I have mentioned so far provides an answer to this question, since iconic storage could function as it does in, say, Averbach and Coriell's or Sperling's experiments whether or not it was actually visible. Experiments using rather different methods to study iconic storage have, however, provided various kinds of evidence suggesting that iconic storage is in fact visible, and that therefore it can be studied "directly" (i.e., by having subjects make responses in terms of what they see after the display is terminated) rather than indirectly (as in, e.g., partial-report or backward masking experiments). In fact, in the past five years, five different direct measurement techniques have been used : the rotating radius display, temporal integration of fragmented forms, judgments of onset and offset of visual displays, judgments of apparent continuity of discontinuously presented displays, and viewing through a moving slit.

The rotating radius display has been used by Allport (1970) and Dixon and Hammond (1972); its basis can be illustrated by the following example. Suppose an object is moving from left to right in a dark room. When it gets to position A, it is extremely briefly illuminated. If iconic storage is visible, the observer continues to see the object at position A for some time after the offset of the illumination. During this time the object has continued to move from left to right. Suppose it reaches position B before the iconic storage set up by illuminating it at position A has completely decayed, and suppose that it is illuminated briefly again when it gets to position B. The observer now sees two objects, one at position A (the not-yet-decayed iconic storage of the object illuminated there) and one at B (the actual object, illuminated). In fact, if the object then reaches position C and is illuminated for a third time there before the iconic storage form A has decayed, the observer sees *three* objects. This phenomenon is studied more conveniently with rotary motion than with linear motion; therefore both Allport and Dixon and Hammond used a rotating disc with an illuminated radius drawn on it. Illumination was at brief regular intervals; as the rate of illumination increases, an observer saw one, then two, then three, etc., simultaneous radii arranged like the ribs of a fan, with the whole fan of lines rotating around the centre of the disc. The lines moved because, as the iconic storage of a radius at the trailing edge of the fan decayed to nothing, a new position of the radius was illuminated in front of the leading edge of the fan.

This effect, which is striking and easily observed, demonstrates that an object continues to be visible for some time after its illumination has been terminated. This continued visibility is often referred to as "visual persistence", since many people are unsure about whether it is the same thing as iconic storage. Whether the two are the same has not been conclusively demonstrated; the similarities, however, are highly suggestive, and consequently I shall assume that the direct and indirect techniques are measuring the same thing, and that "iconic storage" and "visual persistence" are synonymous.

If so, we can use the radius display to measure various properties of iconic storage : its duration, for example. If we increase the time interval between successive illuminations of a moving object until only one object is seen, then there must be just enough time between illuminations to allow the iconic storage of position A to decay before position B is illuminated, and so the minimum inter-flash interval at which only one object is seen is equal to the duration of iconic storage. Using this method, Allport and also Dixon and Hammond found that a radius illuminated for less than 1 msec persisted visually for about 200 msec. Allport also discovered two intriguing properties of this visual persistence. Firstly, a dimly illuminated radius persisted for longer than a brightly illuminated radius; one would have expected the opposite result. Secondly, when a comparison was made between two different ways of responding to the display—the difficult task of counting how many radii are visible in the moving fan and the easy task of estimating the angle between the two edges of the fan—Allport found that persistence as measured by the difficult task was longer than persistence as measured by the easy task, even though the stimulus situation was the same for the two tasks. It is tempting to explain these two properties of persistence by proposing that an observer can exert some control over the duration of persistence of a brief visual stimulus, and that if the stimulus is difficult to see (because dim) or difficult to judge (because the task required is complicated), the observer arranges for the persistence to last longer to compensate for the increased difficulty, as compared with bright stimuli or easy judgments.

One virtue of the rotating-radius method of measuring visual persistence is that it is simple and rapid enough to be used with subjects who would find partial report techniques too difficult or too lengthy—children, for example. Even before children can read, they can discriminate between one visible radius and two, and hence this method allows measurements of visual persistence with very young children.

A second method which has been used to study visual persistence could also be used with children. This is the fragmented forms task employed by Eriksen and Collins (1967, 1968). If a meaningful visual stimulus (e.g., a word or a line-drawing) is constructed using dot rows instead of solid lines, it is possible to divide it up into two sub-patterns, X and Y, by randomly choosing half of the dots and calling this sub-pattern X, whilst the remaining half are sub-pattern Y. If an observer looks at X by itself, or at Y by itself, they will look like random scatterings of dots. Only when they are superimposed will the original visual stimulus be detected. Thus, if pattern X is presented briefly and then after a short interval pattern Y, the observer will see a meaningful stimulus only if the visual persistence of X is still available when Y is presented and the stimulus Y and the persistence of X can be added together to reveal the original visual pattern. By varying the interval between the offset of X and the onset of Y, one can investigate how long the persistence of X lasts.

Haber and Standing (1970) used an even more direct method for measuring the duration of visual persistence. An observer viewed a 3 × 3 matrix of letters presented briefly, which he did not have to report. Other kinds of visual stimuli, for instance, pictures, could also be used in this kind of experiment. At the same time he heard a brief click. The time of occurrence of the click relative to the time of occurrence of the display could be varied by the subject. First, he varied the click location each time the visual stimulus was presented until the click appeared to coincide with the onset of the display. Then he varied the click until it appeared to coincide with the offset of the display (in effect, with the disappearance of visual persistence). The time between the two click settings therefore is a measurement of the duration of visual persistence plus the duration of the display. Various durations of the display were used; and Haber and Standing found that the longer the display, the shorter its persistence. For example, when the visual field was light before and after the letter display, a 50 msec display persisted for about 150 msec, a 100 msec display for about 100 msec. a 200 msec display for about 70 msec, and a 300 msec display for about 40 msec. This illustrates again what seems to be a general principle of visual persistence : stimuli which are difficult (because they are dim or short or because the task is complex) persist for longer than stimuli which are easy. Efron (1970) used the same task as Haber and Standing with very clear results : if the stimulus duration was less than 130 msec, the stimulus persisted until 130 msec after its *onset*, that is to say, stimulus duration plus persistence duration always equalled 130 msec. If the stimulus duration exceeded 130 msec there was no persistence at all. Furthermore, if stimulus intensity was varied, Efron found that bright stimuli had shorter persistence than dim stimuli. Briggs and Kinsbourne (1972), using reaction time to display onset or display offset rather than click settings to onset or offset, also found that persistence duration decreased as stimulus duration increased. They compared monoptic and dichoptic presentation: with a stimulus lasting, say, 100 msec, they compared what happens when only one eye is stimulated with what happens when the first 50 msec of the stimulus is presented to one eye and the second 50 msec to the other eye. A 50 msec stimulus produces longer persistence than a 100 msec stimulus. Therefore, if persistence were a retinal process, or a process which occurs in any part of the visual system which receives input from only one eye, the dichoptic presentation should yield longer persistence. In fact, monoptic and dichoptic presentation yielded equal persistence (also found by Haber and Standing, 1969, using a different technique, discussed below). Therefore Briggs and Kinsbourne concluded that the persistence was occurring in some part of the visual system which receives input from both eyes, in which case the persistence must be a cortical effect, since the earliest point in the visual system where binocular combination occurs is in the visual cortex.

A fourth direct technique, which, like the first and second, is simple, quick, and does not require the subject to be able to read or make difficult judgments such as visual-auditory synchronization, is the phenomenal continuity technique used by Haber and Standing (1969). If a stimulus is repeatedly briefly illuminated, and the interval between successive flashes of light is progressively shortened, eventually an observer perceives the stimulus as being present, despite the fact that it is only discontinuously illuminated. This situation can be used to measure visual persistence if we assume that the stimulus seems to be continuously present whenever the visual persistence of a particular display of the stimulus has not decayed completely before the next illumination of the stimulus. Haber and Standing found persistence durations of about 250 to 300 msec using this technique. Once again, dim stimuli produced longer persistences than bright stimuli. Furthermore, persistence times were the same when stimuli alternated between the eyes as when presentation was monocular, suggesting that persistence is a property of some part of the visual system which receives input from the two eyes, and hence is a cortical process.

The final technique, which has also been used with children, involves viewing an object through a narrow vertical slit which moves across the object. The consequences of this have probably been informally observed by most people. For example, if you are walking past a tennis court which is separated from you by a wooden fence with narrow vertical gaps between vertical boards, you find that you can see the match much better if you walk along parallel to the fence than if you stand still, and the faster you walk the more transparent the fence seems to become, until often you can see the whole court, even though at any one instant all you see is some very narrow vertical slices of the scene, separated by broad vertical bands where the fence is blocking your view. Haber and Nathanson (1968) and Haber and Standing (1969) studied the effect of this by using a 3 cm diameter circle as a stimulus and displaying it to the subject through a narrow vertical slit 20 mm wide which oscillated to and fro in a horizontal direction through a sweep of 4 cm. The oscillation rate was increased until the subject reported that the whole circle was visible. The explanation of this phenomenon is the same as that of the rotating radius phenomenon; if the slit is moving from left to right, and it reaches the right edge of the circle before the visual persistence of the left edge has decayed, the circle is visible as a whole. Consequently, by measuring the oscillation rate at which this happens, the duration of visual persistence can be measured. Again, persistence was longer for dimmer stimuli, though in this experiment the effect did not reach significance.

Stanley and Molloy (1975) used this method to measure the duration of visual persistence in adults and 10-year-old children. The children showed shorter persistence than the adults. As has been noted above, when other techniques for measuring visual persistence have been used, adults have shown shorter persistence than children. This discrepancy between the results obtained with slit-viewing and with other techniques remains to be explained.

It should be clear that, provided we assume that visual persistence and iconic storage are the same phenomenon, the use of direct measurement has provided a considerable amount of new information about the properties of iconic storage. The most important result is the suggestion that decay of iconic storage is not as passive and automatic as has been thought in the past (for instance, by Coltheart, 1972), since it appears that subjects have some capacity to adjust persistence times in response to the difficulty of the task they have to perform upon the visual stimulus. A second important result is that the physiological locus of iconic storage appears to be cortical. Engel (1970) was able to show that there are independent monocular and binocular persistence processes, but this should not be taken as evidence for any persistence in the visual system earlier than the visual cortex. Many neurones in the visual cortex, especially those receiving input directly from the retina and lateral geniculate rather than from other cortical neurones, are monocular (see Coltheart, 1973, for a discussion of this), and Engel's monocular persistence could therefore still be purely cortical.

There is an alternative interpretation of the effects of stimulus duration and stimulus intensity on persistence duration which is worth discussing, though it has its problems. Visual processes with brief stimuli exhibit "time-intensity reciprocity": if you double the intensity of a brief stimulus, you can halve its duration, and its visibility will remain constant. The real variable is stimulus *energy*, a product of duration and intensity. For stimuli up to, say, 30 msec, visibility depends on stimulus energy, and a particular degree of visibility can be produced by many different combinations of duration and intensity. Beyond some critical duration this reciprocity breaks down, and stimulus duration becomes important. Now, suppose that there is a process which we might call "read-in to iconic storage" which requires a certain minimum energy; when this has been achieved, iconic storage has occurred, and decay begins. Suppose further that the data operated upon by higher centres are the data held in iconic storage, not the data held in the display. This means that once iconic storage has been achieved, the display can be turned off; it is not contributing to performance. Its only role is to contribute energy, in the first few milliseconds, to iconic storage; the dimmer the display, the more milliseconds of display are needed to reach the critical energy level, but the display duration needed at reasonable intensities will never be more than a few tens of milliseconds.

On this view, decay of iconic storage *is* a passive and automatic process. This apparent relationship between display duration and persistence is illusory; it appears to occur only because persistence is being measured from an inappropriate starting-point (display offset, instead of some short time after display *onset*). Suppose that display intensity is such that 10 msec of display is required to produce sufficient energy for the initiation of iconic storage. Suppose that the duration of iconic storage is 300 msec. Storage will therefore cease 310 msec after display onset. If we vary display duration, and measure duration of persistence after display offset, we may think there is a relationship between display duration and persistence duration : a 100 msec display will have a persistence of 210 msec, a 200 msec display a persistence of 110 msec, and a 300 msec display a persistence of 10 msec. Really, however, persistence duration is 300 msec whatever the display duration, provided that it is long enough (in our example, 10 msec) to contribute sufficient energy for the initiation of iconic storage.

This model makes a rather stringent prediction : at display durations longer than the minimum needed for energy requirements, the sum of stimulus duration and post-stimulus persistence duration must be constant (because the time between stimulus onset and persistence offset is constant according to the model). This is exactly true for the data of Efron (1970). It is a good approximation to the results of Haber and Standing (1969) except for one stimulus condition (dark pre-exposure field, light post-exposure field). In addition, as predicted, the relationship breaks down at short exposure durations, where the sum of stimulus duration and post-stimulus persistence duration decreases as exposure duration decreases. This indicates that, in addition, as predicted, the relationship breaks down at short exposure durations, where the sum of stimulus duration and post-stimulus persistence duration decreases as exposure duration decreases; thus when insufficient energy is available from the stimulus, suboptimal and abnormally short-lived iconic storage is generated.

The effect of stimulus intensity on persistence duration can also be predicted. The time between display onset and the accumulation of the necessary stimulus energy for adequate iconic storage will be longer for a low-intensity display than for a high-intensity display. So the time between display onset and beginning of iconic storage will be longer for weaker stimuli. If, once iconic storage begins, its lifetime is fixed, this means that the time between display onset and the termination of iconic storage will be longer for weaker stimuli. Therefore, if display duration is constant, display intensity is varied and visual persistence duration is measured from display offset, it will look as if weak displays are persisting for longer than strong displays, an effect obtained by Allport (1970), Efron (1970) and Haber and Standing (1969).

This attempt at a model in which there is actually no relationship between persistence duration and such stimulus properties as stimulus duration or intensity seems quite promising, then, and it does emphasize a possibility rarely considered: that even if a display is present, what an observer is analyzing may not be the display itself, but the display's iconic storage, which is decaying away even though the display is present. Thus, provided the display has contributed the required energy, it can be turned off: hence the often-obtained result that, except at very brief display durations and very low display intensities, the amount reported from a brief visual display is independent of display duration. Thus Sperling (1960) varied display duration over the range 15 to 500 msec without influencing the number of items the subject reported from the display. Many unanswered questions are raised here: to take one example, what happens if the display stays on until after iconic storage has decayed away completely? Is the link between the display and durable storage, namely, iconic storage, permanently severed? A factor likely to be important here is eye movements: an eye movement is equivalent to the presentation of a new display, and this will set up a new iconic storage. Since in practice people's eyes do not remain stationary for more than a few hundred milliseconds at a time, even when they are trying to fixate, eye movements will provide a means of renewing iconic storage.

Allport's observation that subjects trying to count the number of radii visible show longer persistence times than those trying to estimate the angle made by the fan of radii has no obvious explanation within this model. Consequently, though persistence duration may be uninfluenced by stimulus characteristics, it seems likely that it is influenced by task difficulty. This is an important question and deserves further investigation.

(3)   SUMMARY

When an observer fixates a new part of the visual field, or when a blank visual field is replaced by a patterned field (for instance, a display of letters or a picture), visual information is rapidly collected from the new visual stimulus and a detailed visual representation of that stimulus is set up in iconic storage. The iconic representation is faithful and capacious, but it is also subject to decay, fading to nothing in a few hundred milliseconds. Aspects of the visual stimulus which are to be reported or which require lengthy processing must therefore be accorded more stable storage, which is achieved by registering selected aspects of the iconically stored material in a more stable storage form which I have called durable storage. Only a small amount of material can be dealt with in this way; the remainder of the iconically-stored material decays away. It is possible, however, for an observer to choose which items of those held in iconic storage will be registered in durable storage, although, since iconic storage is a purely visual memory mode, such selection can be performed only on the basis of purely visual item characteristics (such as position, hue, brightness, shape, or movement), not semantic category, nor any acoustic or phonological characteristic.

The visual nature of iconic storage is emphasized by its vulnerability to subsequently presented visual stimuli. If a display set up in iconic storage is followed by a second display, one of two kinds of interference effects occurs: if the interval is very short, the two displays sum, forming a composite iconic memory; at slightly longer intervals, the second display erases the first from iconic storage and is itself registered in iconic storage.

III.   DURABLE STORAGE

In certain models of visual information-processing, durable storage has been identified as equivalent to the short-term memory system studied in traditional memorizing experiments, that is to say, a system which stores information in a phonological code, even if it was presented visually, and which requires rehearsal to preserve this information. However, this conception of durable storage is clearly inadequate, since it ignores the possibility of registering visuo-spatial information in durable storage, and such registration clearly does occur. For example, suppose that durable storage in Averbach and Coriell's experiment consisted solely of the names of items (thus, exclusively a matter of phonological coding). At bar marker delays greater than the lifetime of iconic storage, the subject would have no way of knowing the original display positions of the items now preserved in durable storage. Thus, even supposing *every* item in the display had reached durable storage, if there is no visuo-spatial (positional) information in this storage mode the subject would simply have to guess at random from amongst the contents of durable storage, and hence his probability of responding correctly would be $\frac{1}{16}$ or about 6 per cent. This is not what happens; at these long delays, performance averages about 32 per cent correct, that is to say, about five letters. This means that, on the average, about five letters are held in durable storage with correct information as to where they had been located in the display. If you simply ask subjects to report as many items as they can from a 50 msec display of sixteen items, they get about five correct; here no position information is needed to respond correctly. Therefore it must be the case if an item's name reaches durable storage, its display position is highly likely also to reach durable storage; that is, this form of storage holds both phonological and visuo-spatial information about each item, and the co-ordination of these two forms of information appears to provide few problems.

These considerations indicate that durable storage is not equivalent to the acoustically-encoded rehearsal-supported STM of memorizing experiments, but is a more general mode of storage which holds and can co-ordinate visuo-spatial and phonological information. It is possible to separate out the two forms of information experimentally. Thus tasks can be employed which require only one kind of information for their correct performance (for instance, asking a subject to say whether a particular display location had been occupied, which requires only visuo-spatial information, *versus* asking him to say whether a particular item had been present in the display, which requires only phonological information). Or tasks can be employed in which one of the two kinds of information would be difficult or impossible to register (for instance, using nonsense shapes or unknown faces, which can be registered visually but not phonologically since verbal description would be impossible, or at least very slow). Or subsidiary interfering tasks can be presented which are designed to interfere selectively with one or other of the two forms of encoding in durable storage.

Perhaps the simplest of these methods is to use stimuli which would be difficult or impossible to store in a phonological code; examples are matrices of black and white squares (Phillips and Baddeley, 1971), free-form outline drawings of nonsense figures (Cermak, 1971), letter-like Gibson figures (Mitchell, 1972) or a single dot whose position relative to the edges of the square display field has to be recalled (Dale, 1973). Such experiments show that a difficult-to-verbalize visual stimulus can be retained in memory faithfully at least for some tens of seconds; that accuracy of performance declines slowly as a function of time since stimulus offset; that this decline can be hastened by various kinds of interpolated tasks during the retention interval; and that visual information in durable storage is not erased by a visual-noise mask. Experiments of this sort make the simple point that there is more to durable storage than a phonologically-encoded list of item names maintained by rehearsal.

Experiments involving selective interference techniques provide more interesting results. Den Heyer and Barrett (1971) used 6 × 4 matrices each containing 8 different letters located in a randomly chosen 8 of the 24 positions in the matrix. Each letter display was presented for 50 msec; after a delay of 10 sec the subject reported the display by filling in a 6 × 4 response matrix. This method enables separate measurement to be made of information about position and information about identity, since the subject is free to fill in a correct position with an incorrect item (indicating that only position is retained), or an incorrect position with a correct item (indicating that only identity of the item is retained). The 10 sec retention interval in this experiment was either unfilled (the control condition), or else filled with one of two interfering tasks: a visuo-spatial task (scanning three dot configurations, two of which were identical, to locate the odd one out), or a verbal task (listening to a sequence of five two-digit numbers and adding them up). Relative to performance in the control condition (no interfering task), the visuo-spatial task reduced position recall by 91 per cent and identity recall by 52 per cent; the verbal task reduced position recall by 53 per cent and identity recall by 64 per cent. Although an item's position could be recorded verbally in durable storage ("second column, three down"), this procedure seems too elaborate for its use to be plausible. On the other hand, an item's *identity* could be registered phonologically (as the item's name) or visually (as the item's shape). This is presumably why the effect of the verbal task on identity recall was not as drastic as the effect of the visuo-spatial task on position recall.

Further insight into this dual registration of identity information was obtained by Scarborough (1972). His idea was to separate out the two methods of registering the identity of items by occupying the phonological system with an irrelevant task (rehearsing a previously presented auditory list), thus leaving only visual registration of identity available for durably storing the contents of a visual display. In Scarborough's first experiment, subjects first heard a sequence of auditory digits. Then they saw a display of six letters or digits, preceded and followed by a visual-noise mask; display duration was 250 msec. Finally, a tone at display offset indicated what to report: a low tone meant report the auditory list, a high tone meant report the display (position in the display did not have to be reported). Control conditions, where displays were reported without an auditory load, and *vice versa*, were run. Report of the display was not significantly influenced by whether or not an auditory list was in memory; report of an auditory list was not significantly influenced by whether or not a display was in memory. It might have been expected that digit displays would have been worse reported than letter displays, because of interference from the auditory items, which were always digits. No such interference occurred. Consequently, the visual and auditory memory systems here were completely independent.

In Scarborough's second experiment, the cue indicating which type of report was required was presented 180 msec before the display, or 350, 500 or 2000 msec after it. With a pre-cue, report of the visual display was not influenced by whether or not there was an auditory sequence to be memorized. With a post-cue, however, report of the visual display was worse when there was an auditory load than when there was not, and the size of this impairment increased as cue delay increased. Another way of describing the same result is to say that, with no auditory load, delaying display report for up to 2 sec had no effect on performance, whereas with an auditory load performance worsened as report delay increased up to 2 sec. The third of Scarborough's experiments showed that, if the display duration were increased (750 msec instead of 250 msec), then even with a report cue at display offset, display report was worse when there was an auditory load than when there was not.

These results can be summarized simply : report of a visual display is unimpaired by a concurrent verbal memory load provided that (a) the display is brief (250 msec rather than 750 msec), and (b) recall is immediate. If the display or the recall interval is lengthened, a concurrent verbal memory load does impair performance. What this tells us about durable storage (following Scarborough, 1972, and Coltheart, 1972) is this : setting up visual representations of the identity of items in durable storage is a fast process, whereas setting up phonological representations is very slow. If the raw data upon which the durable storage process operates is available only for a short time (250 msec, with no iconic storage to prolong it because of the mask), then items are only represented visually in durable storage, and so are not interfered with by phonologically stored items from the auditory list. However, if sufficient time is allowed for some phonological representations of items also to be set up in durable storage, these will be susceptible to interference from the auditory items. Hence an auditory load will impair performance at long display durations but not short ones. Furthermore, even with a short display, auditory load impaired performance when recall was delayed; this suggests that visual representations in durable storage are susceptible to slight decay over a 2 sec period, which a subject can normally counteract by converting some of them to phonological representations during the retention interval. The presence of an auditory load impairs the efficiency of this process, and so allows the decay of visual representations to manifest itself in performance.

Finally, an increase in display duration from 250 msec to 750 msec did not improve performance when there was an auditory load, but did improve performance when there was no load. If visual encoding were still going on 250 msec after display offset, performance should be improved by lengthening the display even if an auditory load is preventing or drastically impairing phonological encoding. Because this did not occur, it seems that the setting up of visual representations of item identity in durable storage is no longer occurring once a display has been present for 250 msec. This would occur if the number of items which could be represented in this way were limited by some property of durable storage, and once this limit was reached no more items could be registered visually. This limiting number can be calculated from Scarborough's data, on the assumption that the two forms of encoding (visual and phonological) are independent: it comes to almost exactly four. Application of these ideas to several other sets of data by Coltheart (1972) yielded roughly similar values for this capacity limitation of the visual representation of item identity in durable storage.

If visual encoding is fast but can cope with only about four items, whilst name encoding is slow, then a plot of the number of letters which can be reported from a brief display (followed by a mask) as a function of display duration should rise steeply up to four letters, and thereafter continue to rise very slowly, since beyond four letters only name encoding is contributing anything to durable storage. This is what happens; moreover, the bend in the curve occurs in the region 50–80 msec, indicating that the visual encoding of four items takes about this time (Coltheart, 1972).

One way of manipulating these two forms of encoding in durable storage is to use deaf subjects. Henderson and Henderson (1973) carried out an experiment with deaf and hearing children aged 12 to 16 years of age. On each trial of this experiment, a seven-letter display was presented for 100, 400 or 1000 msec and was followed by a mask. The subject's task was to write down, on a response sheet, as many letters from the display as he could.

If congenital deafness abolishes or severely impairs phonological encoding in durable storage whilst sparing visual encoding, it would be predicted that at an exposure duration of 100 msec, which allows considerable visual encoding to occur but little or no phonological encoding, the performance of deaf and hearing children should not differ. At longer exposure durations, the hearing children will be able to carry out some phonological encoding, and so their performance should be superior to that of the deaf children. This is what Henderson and Henderson found. A comparison of their Figure 1 (plotting number of items correct as a function of display duration) with comparable figures obtained with adult subjects (see Coltheart, 1972) suggests that the visual code is limited to about four items in both children and adults but that children require more time than adults do to encode four items visually.

It is not only identity information but also spatial information which can be represented visually within durable storage. Sanders

(1968) investigated spatial memory by presenting a series of matrices each with one position indicated in it. Subjects were able to retain about four such positions. Henderson (1972), using exposure durations from 250 to 1000 msec, found that position information was better registered than identity information at the shortest exposure duration, but that identity information benefited much more than position information as exposure duration increased. These results suggest that position information as visually encoded in durable storage resembles visually encoded identity information : encoding is rapid, but the number of items which can be encoded is limited to about four.

In his Experiment III, Henderson (1972) used 150 msec displays consisting of 3 × 3 matrices containing five digits and four empty spaces. Memory was probed by a 3 × 3 matrix containing one red space and one blue space (the rest being blank) and accompanied by two digits. The subject's task in these conditions was to say which of the two probe digits had been in the display and also to name the colour of the matrix cell which had contained a digit in the display. Only one of the digits had been in the display and only one of the coloured cells had been occupied by a digit in the display.

In these conditions subjects are more accurate when the probe is delayed by 2 sec than when it is delayed by 500 msec. Henderson suggested that this was because there was competition between two visual tasks : maintaining a visual code in durable storage and visual processing of the probe stimulus. It is as if a subject needs some time to consolidate a visual representation in durable storage.

> If the subject attends to the probe, which must be processed, he thereby risks losing his grip upon the information maintained in memory. Sometimes a subject will report such success in attending to the memory code that the probe will come and go unattended, leaving him with information that he does not know how to report. (Henderson, 1972, p. 446)

This issue has been investigated directly by Merikle (1976). He used seven-letter displays presented for 100 msec and followed by a probe item, which was one of the digits 1–7. The digit specified the position in the display of the letter the subject was to report; for instance, "one" meant the left-most letter, "seven" the right-most letter. For one group of subjects, the digit probe was auditory; for the other group it was visual, presented about 1° above the position which had been occupied by the central letter in the display. Performance was better with the auditory cue than with the visual cue, even if the visual cue was presented immediately after display offset and the auditory cue delayed by 500 msec. This is not due to interference within iconic storage, since the difference remains even when the display is masked at its offset. This confirms results reported by Lowe (1975). Merikle and Lowe suggest that the processing of the visual cue and the maintenance of non-iconic visual memory compete or conflict, and since this competition does not occur when the cue is in a different modality, performance is better with an auditory cue than with a visual cue. Brooks (1968) describes very similar results from a task involving visual imagery rather than visual memory. If a subject is making responses describing a visual image, his performance is superior if the responses are verbal than if they are visuo-spatial (speaking a series of "yes's" and "no's" *versus* pointing to printed "yes's" and "no's"). If the responses are describing a memorized sentence, the opposite happens, visuo-spatial output produces better performance than verbal output.

This research has yielded information about a number of properties of the visual representation system in durable storage. At least with alphanumeric displays, the registration of visual information (whether it be information about identity—letter shapes—or information about spatial layout) is a process which occurs rapidly, but which seems unable to produce visual representations for more than four or so items. Once visual representations are produced, their maintenance can be disturbed by the subject's having to perform some other visual task such as identifying a visually presented digit or some other visual probe stimulus or judging spatial relationships between dots. The susceptibility of visually encoded information to this kind of disruption is greatest soon after its registration. Scarborough's results suggest that such visually encoded information is subject to slight decay over a period of seconds and that this can be counteracted by recoding some of the information into phonological form. The visual-encoding system is very similar in deaf and in hearing children; when children and adults are compared, the capacity limitations on the system are similar, but the rate at which material is visually encoded is higher in adults than in children.

Many of the characteristics of visual encoding in durable storage can be introspectively observed in dot-counting experiments. Suppose one draws a dot pattern containing, say, nine dots, and presents it briefly to a subject (for, perhaps, half a second), having told him beforehand that his task will be to report how many dots there were. This is not a difficult task, and the subject is likely to be correct or nearly correct. Most people report that, after seeing the dots briefly, they pause to organize their visual memory of the dots into two or three sub-groups before beginning to count; if they do not do this, counting disrupts the visual memory. Thus the visual task of counting must be postponed until a visual representation sufficiently resistant to disruption has been formed. My impression is that one factor involved here is reducing the number of items in the visual memory from nine (ungrouped dots) to four or fewer (each item being a group of one or a few dots), but perhaps the organization is carried out for some other purpose.

I have not discussed the registration of phonological information in durable storage much, since this system is well known from experiments on verbal short-term memory. Its most important property, as far as the processing of brief visual displays is concerned, is that it is slow; to register a single item phonologically in durable storage requires that the item be available in iconic storage for considerably more than 100 msec (Coltheart, 1972; Scarborough, 1972), though once the identities of items have been registered visually in durable storage it appears possible to produce, from these data, phonological representations in durable storage. Just as visual information in this storage system is susceptible to interference from interpolated visual tasks, so phonological information can be interfered with by such tasks as maintaining an auditorily presented memory load, speaking irrelevant material, or listening to and adding numbers.

The question of sex differences in the facility with which these two kinds of representations can be dealt with has received almost no attention, but it seems quite possible that such differences could be demonstrated, especially since sex differences in the ability to *generate* these two kinds of representations have been found. Coltheart, Hull and Slater (1975) showed that females were more accurate than males at counting the number of letters in the alphabet whose names contained the phoneme "ee", a task requiring the generation of phonological representations of the letters. Males were more accurate than females at counting the number of letters in the alphabet containing a curve in their upper-case form, a task requiring generation of visual representations of the letters. Coltheart *et al.* also used two tasks, a visual search task and a lexical decision task, which provide assessments of a subject's facility in converting visually presented words to phonological representations; both tasks indicated that females were more likely than males to carry out such a conversion, which was not required by the nature of the task.

IV.   WORD PERCEPTION

So far, I have discussed ways in which subjects deal with unfamiliar meaningless rows of letters which they were attempting to report. In much experimental work on the processing of brief visual displays, however, the subjects' task is not to store and then report a novel stimulus, but to identify a familiar row of letters—a word. This is quite a different situation, because the subject already knows a great deal about a visual stimulus, even before it is presented, if he knows that it is going to be a word, and it will be possible for him to use this knowledge to short-cut or bypass normal procedures used to transfer items from iconic storage to durable storage.

I wish to use the term "internal lexicon" to refer to a subject's knowledge of the words of his language. Each word he knows is represented in his internal lexicon as a lexical entry; the lexical entry for a word consists of information about the word's spelling, its pronunciation and its meaning.

If a word is briefly presented and the subject is asked to say aloud or write down what he saw, he can of course employ the dual iconic/ durable storage system to do this, just as he would with a non-word; but he has a second option available, which is to collect information from the visual stimulus for the purpose of gaining access to the lexical entry for the word. If this is successfully achieved, the subject knows and can say or write the word even if it did not reach durable storage. Presumably report *via* durable storage and report *via* lexical access are processes which operate independently and in parallel. Over a series of trials involving the report of briefly presented words, sometimes one procedure and sometimes the other is responsible for the report the subject makes.

Allport (1975) demonstrated the major role played by the lexicon in the perception of briefly presented words by showing in a backward-masking experiment that, at an exposure duration which allows a subject to report three letters correctly from a display of random letters, the subject can also report three three-letter words correctly. Thus, if nine letters are displayed, the subject gets three letters correct if the nine letters are unrelated, but he gets nine letters correct if the display consists of three-letter words.

The procedure by which a subject, starting off with a visually-displayed word, eventually gains access to its representation in the internal lexicon, is the subject of a great deal of experimental work at present. Two broad classes of theory concerning the procedure of lexical access can be distinguished. According to one theory, readers used a learned system of letter-to-sound correspondence rules to obtain a phonological representation of a visually presented word, and then use this phonological representation for input to the lexicon.

An alternative and also very popular view is that it is purely *visual* information from the printed word that is used during lexical access. This information could take various forms: individual letter-shapes, the shapes of inter-letter spaces, multiletter visual features such as the curve repetitions in COOP or the angularity of FEET, or overall word-shape (especially with lower-case print). Bower (1970), Kolers (1970) and Smith (1971) are amongst the proponents of the view that reading depends upon visual encoding and not at all upon letter-to-sound translation.

Each of these views apears to face grave difficulties. If the input to the lexicon were solely phonological, how could we discriminate between homophonic words such as SAIL and SALE? English has many such pairs of words, which are phonologically identical but nevertheless easily discriminable; since such words can only be discriminated by using visual information, a purely phonological theory of lexical access seems untenable. A second severe difficulty concerns the rule system which is supposed to be used to convert letters to sounds. No one has actually proposed such a system in any detail, and it is far from clear that this could actually be constructed, because of the irregular relationship between spelling and pronunciation in English. For example, vowel pairs such as EA, OU, IE and AI each have at least four different possible pronunciations in English. Which is correct depends on the word which contains the vowel pair; therefore pronunciation can only be determined *after* lexical access, in which case it would be impossible to generate a correct phonological representation prior to lexical access.

On the other hand, a purely visual theory has its problems too. Firstly, how is it that we can read and understand a word we have only heard before, the first time we see it? Secondly, why is it that in the lexical decision task (requiring discrimination between letter-strings which are words and those which are not), subjects have more difficulty responding NO to non-words which sound exactly like English words (FRAZE, SOAL) than to those which do not (FRUZE, SOAN) (Rubenstein, Lewis, and Rubenstein, 1971; Colheart, Davelaar, Jonasson and Besner, 1975)? If lexical access were purely visual, there is no reason why this effect should occur. If lexical access were purely phonological, subjects would respond YES to FRAZE and SOAL.

No satisfactory resolution of this dilemma has yet been proposed, but some preliminary suggestions can be made. In reply to the objection that phonological encoding could not be used for lexical access during reading because English is so irregular that no system of letter-to-sound rules exists, it can be argued that a system of rules could be devised which would work for *most* English words. For example, although OU has seven possible pronunciations (COULD, THOU, COUGH, MOULDY, SOUP, TOUCH, THOUGHT), in most of the words containing this pair of vowels the pronunciation is as in

THOU. A simple rule which specifies this as the pronunciation of OU would therefore produce the correct pronunciation for most words.

Perhaps, then, for those English words which obey a certain set of pronunciation rules, lexical access can be accomplished in two ways (visually and phonologically); for the exceptions to the rules, only visual access is possible, since application of the rules to these words produces an incorrect phonological representation which is not present in the lexicon. It remains to be seen how well these suggestions will stand up to experimental investigation.

The disorder of reading known as "phonemic dyslexia" (Shallice and Warrington, 1975) is of considerable theoretical interest here. This disorder is produced by certain kinds of damage to the left hemisphere, and its most dramatic symptom is the production of paralexic errors in reading. A subject asked to read single words aloud might produce "PIXIE" when shown GNOME (Marshall and Newcombe, 1966), or "SMALL" when shown LITTLE. Since the erroneous responses are semantically related to the words presented, the patient must be gaining access to some semantic representation of the word he is looking at; so why cannot he utter the word?

When shown simple non-words and asked to pronounce them, these patients cannot do so. When making discriminations between words and non-words, they do not perform worse with non-words like FRAZE or SOAL than with non-words like FRUZE or SOAN, and consequently, unlike normal subjects, appear not to make any use of phonological encoding here (Patterson and Marcel, unpublished). These two results suggest that these patients have lost the ability to translate letters to sounds. This explains why they often cannot read the word LITTLE aloud, but does not explain why they produce a semantically related response as their error. Allport (1975), reasoning along these lines and taking the view that letter-to-sound translation is likely to be a rather slow process, studied the report of briefly presented words, using a mask at short intervals after display offset in order to try to destroy iconic storage before much letter-to-sound translation could be completed. He succeeded in producing numerous paralexic responses from normal subjects by these means. This suggests that visual lexical access is very rapid, but prone to paralexic error, whereas phonological encoding of words is slow, but serves to prevent paralexic error.

Perhaps the proneness of the visual route to paralexic error is not so surprising after all. If we came across a person who read " ÷ " as "square root sign", we would not think this paradoxical. If a subject is treating LITTLE as a purely pictorial symbol, having lost his ability to obtain its phonological representation, then is the response "SMALL" to this symbol any more odd than the response "square root sign" to the symbol " ÷ "?

It should be evident that, although some tantalizing suggestions exist about the roles played by the two types of encoding during reading, the most fundamental question which can be asked about the process of reading—the nature of the code in which words are represented for the purposes of lexical access—remains to be answered.

V. SUMMARY

Each time we fixate, a new portion of the visual field is projected to the retinal region of highest sensitivity, the fovea and its surround; hence there is new visual information to be processed. Experiments on iconic memory, whether they use indirect methods such as the partial report techniques of Sperling or Averbach and Coriell or the more direct methods described earlier, indicate that the first image in the processing of such information is the registration of the information in iconic storage. Provided that there is sufficient energy in the stimulus, this registration is accomplished very rapidly, in a few milliseconds. The less the stimulus energy, the longer the time required for adequate stimulus registration in iconic storage.

Iconic storage is an extremely capacious mode of storage, and complicated visual patterns can be faithfully stored in this way. However, iconically stored information is fragile and can be disrupted in at least three different ways: (a) by *decay*, which begins immediately full iconic storage is achieved and which is completed in a few hundred milliseconds; (b) by *integration*, since two successive visual inputs with a sufficiently short delay between them will be summed to form a composite iconic representation; and (c) by *interruption*, since if integration does not occur between successive visual inputs, the second will simply replace the first in iconic storage.

Thus, if information extracted from visual input is to be retained for more than a few hundred milliseconds, some other storage mode is needed. This stable mode of storage I have termed "durable storage"; it can hold visuo-spatial information (for instance, letter shapes or information about display layout) as well as phonological information (for instance, item names). This is an active mode of storage, and hence can be interfered with by irrelevant tasks which compete for use of those cognitive mechanisms which are responsible for the active maintenance of information in durable storage.

When the two storage modes—iconic storage and durable storage —are compared, it is obvious that the amount of information which can be registered in durable storage in typical experimental situations is much less than the amount which can be registered in iconic storage. Thus only a small proportion of the information held in iconic storage can be accorded durable storage; the remainder rapidly decays away. However, the human information-processor can select *which* information is to be given durable storage provided (a) this information does not overload the limitations of durable storage, and (b) the selection of iconically stored material can be carried out on the basis of simple "physical" stimulus characteristics such as location in display, shape, hue, brightness or direction of movement. Selection from iconic storage in terms of "derived" or "higher-order" stimulus attributes such as phonological or semantic features cannot be performed.

Consequently, in situations involving memorizing the contents of a visual display, the earliest information processing stages are: (a) the setting-up of an iconic representation of the display, which is subject to decay, integration and interruption; (b) the recoding of a selected portion of this information into the durable storage mode; and (c) the retention of information in this durable storage mode by some active process such as rehearsal (which includes visual as well as verbal rehearsal).

If instead the task involves *identifying* a visual display (which implies that some representation of the display already exists in the subject's long-term memory), then a different form of information-processing is involved. Information is extracted from the display for use in gaining access to the appropriate representation in long-term memory, rather than for setting up a representation of the display in durable storage. I have considered only one particular case—the identification of words. Here, the internal representations of words make up an internal lexicon, and the subject's task, if he is trying to identify a visually displayed word, is to collect information from that word and to use this information to locate that word's entry in the internal lexicon. How this is achieved is still unknown; the two principal views are: (a) that it is done by converting a visual representation of the display into a phonological representation by making use of letter-sound correspondence rules, and using the resulting phonological representation to gain access to the correct lexical entry, and (b) that it is done solely by means of a visual representation of the display.

REFERENCES

Allport, D. A. (1970). Temporal summation and phenomenal simultareity: experiments with the radius display. *Quarterly Journal of Experimental Psychology, 22*, 686–701.

Allport, D. A. (1975). On knowing the meaning of words we are unable to report: the effects of visual masking. Presented at *Attention and Performance*, VI. Stockholm.

Averbach, E. and Coriell, A. S. (1961). Short-term memory in vision. *Bell Systems Technical Journal, 40*, 309–28.

Averbach, E. and Sperling, G. (1961). Short-term storage of information in vision. In C. Cherry (Ed.), *Information Theory*. London: Butterworth.

Bachmann, T. and Allik, J. (1976). Integration and interruption in the masking of form by form. *Perception* (in press).

Bower, T. G. R. (1970). Reading by eye. In H. Levin and J. P. Williams (Eds.), *Basic Studies in Reading*. New York: Basic Books.

Briggs, G. G. and Kinsbourne, M. (1972). Visual persistence as measured by reaction time. *Quarterly Journal of Experimental Psychology, 24*, 318–25.

Brooks, L. R. (1968). Spatial and verbal components of the act of recall. *Canadian Journal of Psychology, 22*, 349–68.

Cermak, G. W. (1971). Short-term recognition memory for complex free-form figures. *Psychonomic Science, 5*, 209–21.

Coltheart, M. (1972). Visual information-processing. In P. C. Dodwell (Ed.), *New Horizons in Psychology*. Harmondsworth: Penguin.

Coltheart, M. (1973). Colour-specificity and monocularity in the visual cortex. *Vision Research, 13*, 2595–8.

Coltheart, M., Davelaar, E., Jonasson, J. T. and Besner, D. (1975). Access to the internal lexicon. Presented at *Attention and Performance*, VI. Stockholm.

Coltheart, M., Hull, E. and Slater, D. (1975). Sex differences in imagery and reading. *Nature, 253*, No. 5491, 438–40.

Coltheart, M., Lea, C. D. and Thompson, K. (1974). In defence of iconic memory. *Quarterly Journal of Experimental Psychology, 26*, 633-41.

Dale, H. A. (1973). Short-term memory for visual information. *British Journal of Psychology, 64*, 1–8.

den Heyer, K. and Barrett, B. (1971). Selective loss of visual and verbal information in STM by means of visual and verbal interpolated tasks. *Psychonomic Science, 25*, 100–2.

Dixon, N. F. and Hammond, J. (1972). The attenuation of visual persistence. *British Journal of Psychology, 63*, 243–54.

Efron, R. W. (1970). Effect of stimulus duration on perceptual onset and offset latencies. *Perception and Psychophysics, 8*, 231–4.

Engel, G. R. (1970). An investigation of visual responses to brief stereoscopic stimuli. *Quarterly Journal of Experimental Psychology, 22*, 148–60.

Eriksen, C. W. and Collins, J. F. (1967). Some temporal characteristics of visual pattern perception. *Journal of Experimental Psychology, 74*, 476–84.

Eriksen, C. W. and Collins, J. F. (1968). Sensory traces versus the psychological moment in the temporal organization of form. *Journal of Experimental Psychology, 77*, 376–82.

Fraisse, P. (1966). Visual perceptive simultaneity and marking of letters succes-sively presented. *Perception and Psychophysics, 1*, 285–7.

3—CP　*　*

Haber, R. N. and Nathanson, L. S. (1968). Post-retinal storage? Parks' camel as seen through the eye of a needle. *Perception and Psychophysics, 3,* 349–55.

Haber, R. N. and Standing, L. (1969). Direct measures of short-term visual storage. *Quarterly Journal of Experimental Psychology, 21,* 43–54.

Haber, R. N. and Standing, L. (1970). Direct estimates of the apparent duration of a flash. *Canadian Journal of Psychology, 24,* 216–29.

Henderson, L. (1972). Visual and verbal codes: Spatial information survives the icon. *Quarterly Journal of Experimental Psychology, 24,* 439–47.

Henderson, S. E. and Henderson, L. (1973). Levels of visual information processing in deaf and hearing children. *American Journal of Psychology, 86,* 507–21.

Kahneman, D. (1968). Method, findings and theory in studies of visual masking. *Psychological Bulletin, 70,* 404–25.

Kolers, P. A. (1970). Three stages of reading. In H. Levin and J. P. Williams (Eds.), *Basic Studies in Reading.* New York: Basic Books.

Latour, P. (1962). Visual threshold during eye movements. *Vision Research, 2,* 261–2.

Lowe, D. G. (1975). Temporal aspects of selective masking. *Quarterly Journal of Experimental Psychology, 27,* 375–85.

Marshall, J. C. and Newcombe, F. (1966). Syntactic and semantic errors in paralexia. *Neuropsychologia, 4,* 169–76.

Merikle, P. M. (1976). On the disruption of visual memory : interference produced by visual report cues. *Quarterly Journal of Experimental Psychology* (in press).

Mitchell, D. C. (1972). Short-term visual memory and pattern marking *Quarterly Journal of Experimental Psychology, 24,* 394–405.

Neisser, U. (1967). *Cognitive Psychology.* New York: Appleton-Century-Crofts.

Patterson, K. and Marcel, A. J. Some observations on aphasia and dyslexia: Impairment in the phonological representation of written words (unpublished).

Phillips, W. A. and Baddeley, A. D. (1971). Reaction time and short-term visual memory. *Psychonomic Science, 22,* 73–4.

Rubenstein, H., Lewis, S. S. and Rubenstein, M. A. (1971). Evidence for phonemic recoding in visual word recognition. *Journal of Verbal Learning and Verbal Behavior, 10,* 645–57.

Sanders, A. F. (1968). Short-term memory for spatial positions. *Psychologie, 23,* 1–15.

Scarborough, D. L. (1972). Memory for brief visual displays of symbols. *Cognitive Psychology, 3,* 408–29.

Shallice, T. and Warrington, E. K. (1975). Word recognition in a phonemic dyslexic patient. *Quarterly Journal of Experimental Psychology, 27,* 187–99.

Smith, F. (1971). *Understanding Reading.* New York: Holt. Rinehart and Winston.

Sperling, G. (1960). The information available in brief visual presentations. *Psychological Monographs, 74,* No. 11.

Sperling, G. (1963). A model for visual memory tasks. *Human Factors, 5,* 19–31.

Sperling, G. (1967). Successive approximations to a model for short-term memory. *Acta Psychologica, 27,* 285–92.

Stanley, G. and Molloy, M. (1975). Retinal painting and visual information storage. *Acta Psychologica, 39,* 283–8.

Treisman, A. M., Russell, R. and Green, J. (1975). Brief visual storage of shape and movement. In P. M. A. Rabbitt and S. Dornic (Eds.), *Attention and Performance*, V. London: Academic Press.

Turvey, M. T. (1973). On peripheral and central processes in vision. *Psychological Review, 80*, 1–52.

Volkmann, F. C. (1962). Vision during voluntary saccadic eye movements. *Journal of the Optical Society of America, 52*, 571–8.

von Wright, J. M. (1972). On the problem of selection in iconic memory. *Scandinavian Journal of Psychology, 13*, 159–71.

Weisstein, N. and Haber, R. N. (1965). A U-shaped backward masking function in vision. *Psychonomic Science, 2*, 75–6

CHAPTER 2

Contemporary Models of the Cognitive Processes: II. Retrieval and Comparison Operations in Permanent Memory

Philip H. K. Seymour

I. INTRODUCTION

It is now some years since "cognitive psychology" was reinstated as a respectable field of study, following publication of the books by Miller, Galanter and Pribram (1960) and Neisser (1967). Cognitive psychology has as its goal the study of the *mental operations* underlying performance on tasks which, while being simple and well within the capabilities of most adult subjects, are nevertheless thought to be of fundamental psychological significance. The tasks correspond quite well to the *operations* category in Guilford's (1967) model of the structure of human intelligence, in that they involve recognition, retrieval of names from memory, and comparison or evaluation.

The cognitive studies carried out at the turn of the century by Cattell (1886) and the members of the Wurzburg group (Humphrey, 1951) demonstrated that mental operations could be studied through the medium of introspective reports or through more objective measures such as the time required to indicate the outcome of a decision or to produce a vocal response. It became evident that introspections could provide useful information about processes occurring in some complex solving tasks, but that subjects could often say relatively little about the processes underlying elementary cognitive operations, such as recognition and comprehension of a word, naming an object or colour or producing responses in free and constrained association tasks. For this reason, the trend in contemporary cognitive psychology has been towards the development of techniques which allow the investigator to form inferences about underlying mental operations from variations in an observable *indicator*, such as the time of reaction. Most of the research to be reviewed in this chapter falls within this general tradition.

The intention of the chapter is that it should provide a viewpoint on current progress in research and theorizing about adult information-processing capabilities. The models proposed for description of performance of adult subjects in some task situation refer to the operation of a mature information processing system. Since it is the task of developmental cognitive psychologists to reveal the emergence and perfection of such systems during childhood, it may be hoped that mainstream cognitive psychology may provide a useful framework of relevant tasks, inferential methods and theory. Equally, a developmental perspective may often be valuable in the construction of models of adult performance. This is particularly so in studies of lexical and semantic memory, where many of the experimental tasks require retrieval and manipulation of information which has been laid down in permanent memory during childhood.

A major obstacle which now confronts students of cognitive psychology is that much of the research appears fragmented and unstructured (see for instance Newel, 1973). In attempting to present a viewpoint which may be useful to developmental psychologists it has therefore been necessary to try to impose some structure on a rather disorganized field, and to accept the need for some selectivity (or personal preference) in the choice of topics for discussion. It is suggested that a worth-while major division can be stated in terms of the *knowledge domains*, called types of content by Guilford (1967), which are involved in successful performance of a task. Guilford has argued that the research into human abilities conducted in his laboratory supports a division between symbolic, semantic and figural types of content. In general, the distinction between symbolic and figural content reflects a contrast between systems for representation of *lexical* (verbal) information on the one hand, and *pictorial* (or spatial) information on the other. The *semantic* system is concerned with interpretation of linguistic and non-verbal environmental events, and may be thought of as a bridge between the lexical and pictorial systems. A tri-partite scheme of this kind has been used to provide a general organizing framework for the chapter.

For the purposes of presentation it seemed useful to sub-divide the account of the lexical system into discussions of tasks which require only knowledge of symbol sets (for instance, the alphabet and the numerals), and those which require knowledge of the vocabulary of the language and its associated orthographic, syntactic and semantic rule systems. These domains are referred to as *symbolic memory* and *lexical memory* respectively, and are treated in sections II and III of the chapter. The section on lexical memory also includes a discussion of *semantic memory*, but one which has been limited to consideration of semantic operations on lexical content. The non-verbal *pictorial memory* is discussed in section IV, chiefly in relation to pictorial and semantic representation of objects and retrieval of object names.

The experimenters whose work will be reviewed have for the most part been preoccupied with two kinds of theoretical issue. The first of these concerns the nature of the *codes* or internal representations which are manipulated during solution of a problem. The second concerns the nature of the sequence of *operations* which occurs between reception of a signal and production of an indicator response. Two influential views have been that the codes may sometimes be descriptions which are formally related to shapes and sounds of visual and auditory events in the external world, and that processing often involves a series of distinct functions, occurring one after another, like sub-routines of a computer programme. Associated with both of these preoccupations are the methodological problems of finding indicators which will reveal the characteristics of internal codes or mental operations.

II. SYMBOLIC MEMORY

(1) STRUCTURE OF THE SYMBOLIC MEMORY SYSTEM

The capabilities of the symbolic memory system are involved when people recognize, name, write and mentally manipulate letters, digits and elements from other symbol systems. It seems necessary to postulate permanent stores in the brain for retention of phonemic, graphemic descriptions of individual symbols, and for structural aspects of the symbol sets, such as sequential position and subset membership. These can be referred to as the *phonemic, graphemic* and *semantic* data stores. Corresponding to each store there is a register into which symbol descriptions can be entered for matching or other operations. Finally, there are *input channels* which allow externally presented visual information to enter the graphemic register, and auditory information to enter the phonemic register, as well as *output channels* through which the contents of the registers can be translated into overt speech or writing. An interface structure, analogous to the logogen system of Morton (1969), is postulated for maintenance of information in the registers, and for conversions between codes. This contains recognizers which accumulate evidence up to a threshold value when their defining features are present in data sampled from the graphemic or phonemic

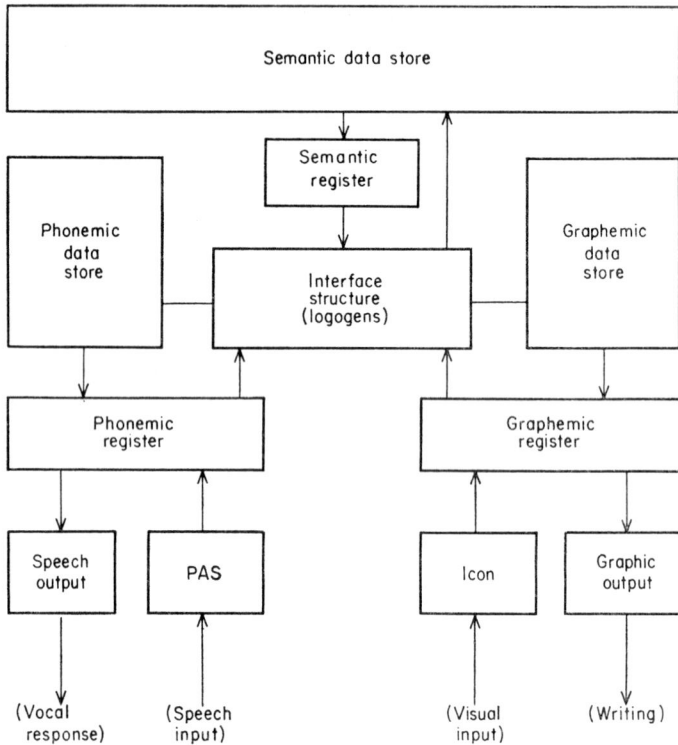

FIG. 2.1. Schematic model for the structure of symbolic and lexical memory.

registers. When the threshold value is exceeded, the addresses of information in the data stores become available, and stored phonemic, graphemic or semantic descriptions can be directly retrieved and entered into the appropriate registers. A schematic representation of this system is shown in Fig. 2.1.

(2) ENCODING

Access to the memory system by external presentation of speech or graphemic signals depends on the occurrence of an operation known as *encoding*. With regard to vision, this can be thought of as an active process involving spatial selectivity in the movements of the head and eyes, and internal attentional processes for selection and scanning of data which have already been superficially encoded. The principal evidence for this comes from studies of accuracy of report of tachisto-scopic exposures by Sperling (1960), Heron (1957) and others. A widely accepted view is that visual input is initially represented in a short-lived buffer memory, called the *icon* by Neisser (1967), and that information must be selected from this sensory memory for further processing if it is to enter short-term memory and emerge as a spoken or written report (Sperling, 1967). The position adopted here is that information sampled from the icon is initially entered as a description of visual characteristics into the graphemic register. Following Coltheart (1972), it is argued that the operations of icon formation and selective encoding are visual processes which are vulnerable to interference by backward masking and other techniques (Spencer, 1969), but that the graphemic description of the input lies at too deep a processing level to be affected by these external factors. This encoded visual description will be referred to as the *graphemic code*. Auditory speech input is also thought to be encoded via a sensory buffer memory called PAS (precategorical acoustic storage) by Crowder and Morton (1969). Processing in this channel will be affected by auditory factors, such as signal-to-noise ratio, and leads to formation of a phonemic description which can be referred to as the *phonemic code*.

The duration of the visual encoding process can be estimated by varying the rate at which symbols are presented, and by determining a point at which identification accuracy begins to deteriorate. For example, Kolers (1970) displayed a succession of letters at a single location, and reported that an interval between symbols of 250 msec or more was needed for correct identification. Rather similar results were obtained by Eriksen and Collins (1969); they presented digits in numerical order but omitted one digit from the sequence; in order to detect where the gap in the sequence had occurred, subjects required an interval of about 200 msec between symbols. These results agree broadly with the findings of experiments using backward masking techniques. Smith and Carey (1966) found that recognition performance was relatively unimpaired when there was a delay in excess of 300 msec following a tachistoscopic exposure of an array of letters, but that there was progressive deterioration as the interval was shortened. This period of 250–300 msec is close to the average duration of fixation pauses in reading (Tinker, 1958), and is probably an approximate indication of the time needed for icon formation and construction of a graphemic input code.

Neisser (1963) introduced a *visual search task* as a technique for studying encoding and recognition processes. In this situation, the subject is given a target symbol, and he then searches for its presence in a column of symbols. By varying the distance down the column at which the target was located, Neisser was able to measure the *rate* of the visual search process. This rate is the slope of the function obtained when total search time is plotted against the position in the column of the target, and it defines the increment in processing time for each symbol that was considered by the subject and rejected as a non-target. As pointed out by Neisser, this index of rate is separated in the analysis from the durations of other processes, such as production of a response when the target is located. An index of the duration of these other processes is given by extrapolating the search rate function back to a list length of zero (referred to as the zero intercept value). Thus visual search rate can be represented by a simple equation: $\mathrm{RT} = T + R(P)$ sec, where R is the time to reject a symbol as a non-target, P is the position of the target in the list, and T represents processes other than the visual search operation. R, the index of the rate of the search process, is a measure of the time needed to encode a symbol up to a point sufficient to determine that it is not a target. The depth to which this encoding process must be taken can be manipulated by altering the target definition. If the subject is instructed to search for the letter Z, it may be sufficient to test data flowing from the icon into the graphemic register for presence of defining features of this character, for instance, horizontal bars, an oblique, etc. Thus, encoding must proceed up to the point of entry to the graphemic register before the decision that no target is present is taken and the search is shifted to the next line of symbols. If the task is changed, so that the subject must search for a line of print which does not contain a Z, he must encode the symbols to a level at which positive identification of Z can be achieved. In Fig. 2.1, the level at which this decision is taken is the interface structure containing recognizers for the individual letters of the alphabet. The task of searching for absence of a letter therefore involves greater *depth of processing*, and this change is indexed by an increase in the value of R, the measure of the search rate.

Since the data flowing from the icon through the graphemic register to the logogens consist of feature list descriptions of some kind (Geyer and DeWald, 1973), visual search rate will also be affected by similarity of the target and non-target symbols. If the subject is searching for a Z in a column of other angular letters, his rate will be slower than if the background letters are curved forms because angular letters will share some featural components with the target definition (Neisser, 1963). The occurrence of visual confusions of this kind is evidence that the search process does indeed operate on visual featural descriptions, and that its locus is the graphemic channel of Fig. 2.1. These confusions also occur in tasks involving the explicit *naming* of symbols. For example, when Kolers (1970) tested subjects on speed of naming letters which had been subjected to geometric transformations, he found that errors occurred within certain subsets of visually confusable letters, such as n, u; a, s; b, p, d, q; t, f. Also Hershberger, Trantina and

Cosgrove (1968) reported that RT to name letters was increased if the symbols used in the experiment were visually similar.

Encoding processes can also be studied in *comparison tasks* in which subjects must indicate whether two simultaneously displayed symbols are "same" or "different". By altering the definition of the concept "same" the experimenter can shift the main focus of the comparison from graphemic to phonemic or semantic properties of the symbols, and thus manipulate the depth to which the symbols are processed. Posner and Mitchell (1967) tested subjects in letter matching tasks in which "same" was defined in terms of *physical identity* (both letters must have the same shape, for instance, AA), *nominal identity* (both letters must have the same name, for instance, Aa), or *rule identity* (both letters must be vowels, or both must be consonants, for instance, AE, BC). The "same" RT increased as a function of the level of comparison that was required, and the difference between *physical identity* and *nominal identity* comparisons was generally found to be 80–90 msec. The effect also occurred for "different" RTs. For example, a pair such as AB can be classified "different" faster under physical identity instructions than under name identity instructions. Thus, the letter matching task can be used to provide an operational definition of depth of encoding analogous to the one formulated by Neisser for visual search processes.

Speed of matching symbols is affected by visual and nominal similarity. If the subject is operating under rule identity instructions the "same" RTs show the ordering $AE > Aa > AA$, illustrating facilitating effects of nominal and physical similarity. For comparisons at the nominal level, a visually similar pair, such as Cc or Kk, will be classified as "same" faster than visually dissimilar pairs, such as Aa, but slower than identical pairs, such as AA, CC, etc. In general, therefore, similarity facilitates the "same" RT. The converse of this is an inhibiting effect of similarity on the "different" RT. Posner and Mitchell found that when subjects were operating under physical identity instructions, visually similar pairs, such as Cc, were classified as "different" less rapidly than dissimilar pairs such as Ac. On the other hand there was no delay attributable to the nominal similarity of pairs such as Aa. This result supports the view that physical identity comparisons involve consideration of graphemic descriptions of the symbols, but not of derived phonemic descriptions. It can be seen from this example that effects of similarity on "different" RT can be diagnostic with respect to the representational codes the subject is using, and can also be helpful in determining the similarity of graphemes (Posner and Mitchell, 1967; Gibson, 1970).

(3) Visual and name codes

The experimental technique employed by Posner can be adapted to study the maintenance and transformation of representations of symbols in short-term memory. This requires a version of the matching task in which the symbols are displayed successively, so that the first must be held in memory for a brief interval before the second is presented. In such an experiment the RT is measured from onset of the second symbol, and the interval between the stimuli (ISI) is often varied in order to study changes in the coding of the memory symbol which occur as time passes.

In experiments reported by Posner, Boies, Eichelman and Taylor (1969), the RT difference between nominal identity and physical identity comparisons (the NI–PI difference) was treated as an index of survival of visual graphemic codes in short-term memory. The subjects were tested under nominal identity instructions, but "same" trials might involve either physically identical pairs, such as A . . . . . . A, or nominally identical pairs, such as A . . . . . . a. The ISI was varied within the range of 0–2.0 secs. If the subject retains a visual coding of the first symbol it is expected that he will respond faster when the second symbol is physically identical to the first than when it is only nominally identical. If, on the other hand, he transforms the memory symbol into a phonemic code during the ISI and discards the graphemic representations, there need be no RT advantage for physical identity matches. Thus, the occurrences of a significant NI–PI difference in "same" RT can be taken as an indication that the graphemic code has been *retained* in short-term memory, whereas the attenuation of this effect indicates that the code has *decayed*. Posner found that subjects retain visual information about a letter if the structure of the experiment encouraged them to do so. The NI–PI difference persisted as the ISI increased provided the subjects were tested in so-called "pure list" conditions in which the case of the test letter was held constant within a block of trials. However, the difference declined to zero as ISI increased when subjects were tested in "mixed list" conditions in which the case of the second letter varied randomly from trial to trial. The latter condition apparently did not encourage subjects to retain a visual code, and therefore this information was allowed to decay and was replaced by a phonemic code.

Cole, Coltheart and Allard (1974) have conducted a rather similar experiment in the auditory modality in which subjects classified successively spoken letter names as "same" or "different". They found that the RT was facilitated when the names of the memory letter and the test letter were spoken in the same voice. This result suggests that the phonemic code preserves information about characteristics of a speech signal, and it appears from the experiment that this information may persist over a period of seconds. Posner, Boies, Eichelman and Taylor (1969) demonstrated that phonemic codes of this kind could also be transformed into a graphemic description of a named letter. They reported that RTs for matching a spoken letter name and a visually displayed letter were slower than physical identity comparisons between two visual letters when the ISI was short, but that this difference disappeared as the ISI was lengthened. Given an ISI of 750 msec or more, audio-visual comparisons were no slower than visual-visual comparisons made under pure list conditions. If it is accepted that pure list visual-visual comparisons are based on a retained graphemic code, the equivalence of audio-visual and visual-visual RT can be taken as evidence that auditory input is transformed to a graphemic code during the ISI.

The general implication of Posner's research is that incoming symbolic information is initially coded in the register corresponding to the modality of input, and that the subject then has the option of maintaining this code, allowing it to lapse, or retrieving and maintaining a code for the other modality. This general proposition is supported by studies in which visual and acoustic similarity have been manipulated. For example, Cohen (1969) reported data for a successive presentation matching task in which the letters were dissimilar, visually confusable, acoustically confusable, or both visually and acoustically confusable. She found that the "different" RT was delayed when the letters were confusable in both modalities but not when they were confusable in only one modality. It seemed likely, therefore, that both graphemic and phonemic codes were formed and maintained during the ISI, and the same–different decision involved consultation of both coding registers, with an option to base the response on the register giving the faster or less ambiguous outcome.

It can be noted that the maintenance of codes in short-term memory is seen by Posner as an optional rather than an obligatory process. Whether a code is maintained or transformed is under the control of the subject who is sensitive to the strategic implications of the structure of the experiment. Code maintenance is a form of rehearsal involving the cycling of information through the coding registers and interface system shown in Fig. 2.1, and as such requires the allocation of some attentional resources. Posner, Boies, Eichelman and Taylor (1969) reported that the NI–PI difference could be eliminated by imposition of a secondary attention demanding task (the addition of numerals) and concluded that maintenance of a graphemic code took up some processing capacity. By contrast, interpolation of a visual masking field between the memory and test letters raised the RT but did not affect the magnitude of the NI–PI difference. This failure to find an effect of visual interference supports the view that the graphemic code is an end-product of visual encoding, and one which cannot be disrupted by backward masking (Coltheart, 1972).

(4) MENTAL ROTATION

Cooper and Shepard (1973) have presented evidence that graphemic codes for symbols may be manipulated by an operation of geometric transformation which they refer to as *mental rotation*. The graphemic code for a letter must contain orientation information which can be related to co-ordinates of the visual field since this information is critical for identification of those letters which alter their identities when rotated. The task used by Cooper and Shepard was one of discriminating between normal and mirror image forms of symbols which had been rotated through various angles from vertical. The basic finding was that the RT to make this discrimination increased as a function of the rotation of the test letter from the normal upright, and was greatest for a 180° rotation, that is, for an inverted symbol. The subjects reported that in order to make the judgment they needed to rotate the symbol to the upright and then check to see whether it was correctly written. This subjective account may be restated in the processing terminology of the model sketched in Fig. 2.1. At the encoding stage a graphemic description of the test character is written into the graphemic register. Features of the symbol, other than orientation, are sampled by recognizers in the interface structure, and a stored graphemic description is retrieved and entered into the register. In the meantime, a rotation operation is applied to the input code; this could be a matter of progressively revising co-ordinate values, although it may be noted that the programme would run most efficiently if the top and base of the character were specified, perhaps as part of the identification process. This revision of values within the graphemic description is, of course, a process rather than an experience, although the contents of the graphemic register may be considered by the system underlying consciousness, giving rise to visual imagery of a rotating letter. When the rotation programme finishes, the description retrieved from permanent storage may be compared with the revised description of the test letter, a positive response being made if they match, and a negative one if they do not.

It may be noted that in this account the delay of reaction occurs because the input code is initially inappropriately structured for matching against a code retrieved from memory. However, on analogy with

Posner's experiments on audio-visual matching, it should be possible to prepare an appropriate code, given advance information and sufficient time to use it. Cooper and Shepard studied effects of presenting subjects with information about (1) the identity of the test symbol, (2) the orientation of the test symbol (indicated by an arrow), (3) identity and orientation separately specified, and (4) identity and orientation specified together by showing the normal form of the test character in the orientation which was about to be tested. It was found that information about identity or orientation alone did not alter the effect of rotation of the test symbol from the upright, although it did result in some overall reduction in the RT. On the other hand, provision of advance information about both identity and orientation, whether given separately or together, reduced RT and eliminated the effect of displacement from the upright, provided that a delay of 1 sec or so was allowed before onset of the test symbol. These results suggest that when information about identity or orientation alone are given, this helps the rotation programme by specifying the top and base positions of the incoming character, but does not eliminate the necessity to run the programme. When both kinds of information are given together, the graphemic description of the symbol can be maintained by a rehearsal process of the kind proposed by Posner. If identity and orientation are specified separately, the rotation programme can be run during the interval before onset of the test stimulus. The decision can then be based on a test for equivalence of the two descriptions in the graphemic register.

(5) MENTAL COMPARISON

The mental rotation task of Cooper and Shepard (1973) and the visual search task of Neisser (1963) were considered in the preceding sections in terms of the inferences they support about the coding of symbols in short-term memory. These tasks also provide information about the overall sequence of *operations* which occurs during the conversion of input to a task-relevant output. For example, it is reasonable to suggest that successful performance in the Cooper and Shepard experiment involved a succession of operational stages, including encoding of the test symbol, rotation of the encoded symbol, and decision and response processes which are dependent on the outcome of a comparison between the rotated symbol and a graphemic description retrieved from permanent memory. The duration of the rotation operation is thought to depend on the orientation of the test symbol, so that the RT can be expressed as a sum of all processes other than rotation (i.e., encoding, decision and response) plus an index of rotation rate in msec per degree: $RT = T + R(A)$ msec, where T is the reaction time for an upright symbol, A is the displacement of the test symbol from the vertical in degrees of angle, and R is the increment of time required for each degree of rotation. This function was not in fact linear in the Cooper and Shepard study, although a linear relation between RT and angle of rotation was found in a similar experiment on rotation of nonsense forms by Cooper (1975).

In support of the argument that encoding, rotation and response are successive and independent stages of processing, Cooper and Shepard point out that effects of rotation of the test form combine additively with effects due to provision of advance information (identity or orientation alone) and effects due to decision outcome. A result of this kind is consistent with the view that mental rotation is an independent "processing stage" since the activity of this stage shows no effect of experimental factors which have their primary influence on other stages. This technique of defining operational stages in terms of the experimental factors which influence their durations has been described in detail by Sternberg (1969). He has applied the method to analysis of the stages or processing which occur in a *memory search* task in which the subject is given a list of symbols to hold in short-term memory, and must then classify a single probe symbol as a member or non-member of the memory set. Sternberg has reported that the RT is typically found to be a linear function of memory set size, the functions being similar for positive and negative responses, although the overall level of the negative RT is often slightly higher than that of positive RT.

Sternberg has expressed this result by the equation: $RT = A + B(M)$ msec, where M is the number of items in the memory set, B is a slope constant and A is a zero intercept value. He argued that the slope constant, B, was an index of the rate of functioning of a comparison process by which the probe item was matched against members of the memory set, and that the intercept value, A, was an index of all those processes which preceded or followed the comparison operation, that is, encoding of the probe, decision and response selection and production. Briggs and his associates have adopted a very similar analysis, but have preferred to relate the index of comparison rate, B, to an information theoretic measure of central processing uncertainty, Hc. This is a logarithmic transformation of memory set size, which expresses the number of distinct outcomes, including a negative decision, which might arise at the comparison stage, and which also takes account of their relative probabilities of occurrence. Thus, $RT = A + B(Hc)$ msec.

Both Sternberg and Briggs have argued that mental comparison is an independent processing stage whose duration can be manipulated by varying the size of the set of symbols held in short-term memory. In support of this view, Sternberg (1967) described an experiment in which the probe item was degraded by visual noise in half of the trials. Degradation of this kind would be expected to delay processing at the stage of icon formation and selective encoding and thus to increase the value of the intercept constant, A. If the visual noise is discarded when the description of the probe is entered into the graphemic register, and comparison is an independent processing stage occurring after encoding has been completed, there need be no effect of stimulus degradation on comparison rate, that is to say, on the value of the slope constant, B. However, if the degradation was preserved, and the comparison involved an operation on the contents of the graphemic register, an effect on rate could be obtained. Sternberg's (1967) results fitted the latter account for the first of two experimental sessions, where degradation of the probe was found to increase the value of the intercept, A, and also to produce a slight increase in the value of the slope constant, B. However, in a second session, the effects of stimulus quality and memory set size were perfectly additive, and this result was also obtained in a replication of the study by Bracey (1969). On the basis of this evidence one may argue that encoding and comparison are separate and successive stages. Sternberg has also reported that the magnitude of the difference between positive and negative responses can be manipulated by varying the relative frequencies of the two classes of response, but that this is independent of a standing difference)etween positive and negative decisions. Since these effects on response processes are additive with the effects of memory set size, a stages model of the kind shown in Fig. 2.2 can be proposed. This consists of stages of encoding, comparison, binary decision and response selection and execution, and is empirically supported by the demonstrations of additivity of effects which Sternberg has presented.

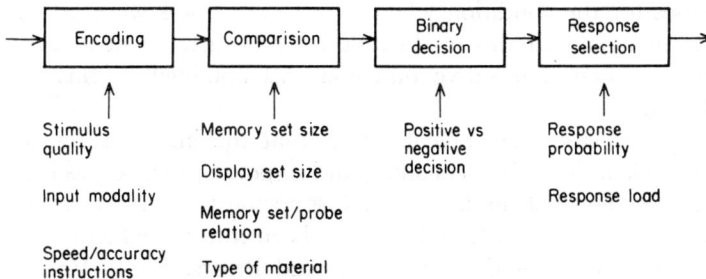

Fig. 2.2 "Processing stages" model for memory search in short-term symbolic memory. Derived from Sternberg (1975 p. 6).

Given this experimental paradigm and its associated assumptions about processing, it is open to the investigator to locate the effects of experimental manipulations by observing whether they influence the intercept or slope of the RT function. Thus, intercept values are lower for auditory than for visual probes, suggesting a difference in access time to the phonemic and graphemic registers; however, the slope of the function is steeper when the memory set and the probe are presented in different modalities than when they are presented in the same modality, suggesting that the comparison stage is complicated by recoding operations in the cross-modal case (Chase and Calfee, 1969). If the number of items on the display is varied as well as the number of items in memory, the subject being instructed to make a positive response if any display item matches any memory item, the main effect of increasing display size is on the slope constant, B, of the RT function. An implication is that the display items may be encoded in parallel, but that increasing the number of items on the display does increase the total number of comparisons which must be made. Briggs and Blaha (1969) plotted the obtained values of B against display size, and found that positive responses yielded a linear function which could also be represented by an equation of the form : $B = C + E(D)$ msec, where D is display size, and C and E are intercept and slope constants. On the basis of this result, Briggs proposed that the comparison stage involved two operations, one of retrieval of an item from the memory set, and the other a comparison of this item against the encoded representation of the display. The intercept value, C, is the index of the retrieval operation, and the slope value, E, is the index of the rate of comparison of a memory item against the display items. This analysis allows Sternberg's original equation to be rewritten as : $RT = A + C(M) + E(D)(M)$ msec, illustrating that the retrieval operation must occur once for each item in the memory, and that the number of comparisons which must be made is the product of D and M. This equation did not fit negative responses, chiefly because responses for the condition where $D = 4$ and $M = 4$ were rather slow. It was thought that this might reflect the occurrence of a rechecking operation when a negative outcome was obtained in this complex condition.

Briggs has also been able to show that the intercept constant, A, can be broken down into encoding and response processes, as is implied in Fig. 2.2. The instruction to give fast responses alters the value of A, but leaves B unchanged, and this has been interpreted as a reduction in stimulus sampling time (Swanson and Briggs, 1969). Variation in *response load* similarly affects the value of A, while leaving the indices of the comparison process unaltered. This point was demonstrated by

Briggs and Swanson (1970) in a study in which the probe letters were presented in varying typographic form. In a first experiment, memory load and display load were varied, as in the Briggs and Blaha study, and subjects in independent groups were instructed to press a negative key on mismatch trials and one, two or three different positive keys on matching trials. The choice between positive keys was contingent on the type face of the probe item. Increasing response load did not alter the relation between memory set size and display size, but did increase the value of A by 84 msec for each additional response. In a second experiment, using single item displays, subjects were tested under response loads of 2, 4 or 8 keys, half positive and half negative. There was no interaction of response load and memory set size, but again the value of the intercept, A, increased by about 90 msec for each additional response.

This discussion should be sufficient to demonstrate how the methodology introduced by Neisser, Sternberg, Briggs and others allows the investigator to study some aspects of the mental operations or "processing stages" which are basic to various simple problem-solving tasks. The technique is to vary the load imposed on a particular processing stage, and then to test whether the effects of change of load are additive with respect to effects of variation in the load imposed on other stages. There is now a fairly complete set of experimental reports on this topic, providing good support for the stages model of information processing shown in Fig. 2.2. One can, of course, distinguish between the hypothesis concerning the independent and successive nature of the processing stages, which is supported by the demonstrations of additivity of effects, and the attempts to provide more detailed analyses of the micro-structure of the comparison stage. Sternberg has consistently favoured a serial exhaustive account of the comparison process, and has defended this position against some viable alternatives (Sternberg, 1975). However, there is a number of experimental results which have proved difficult to reconcile with the serial exhaustive model, such as the occurrence of serial position effects, speeded rejection of unrelated negatives, effects of repetition of memory set items, etc., quite apart from the failure of some experimenters to obtain linear relations between RT and memory set size. There may, therefore, be some advantage in adopting a less explicit account of the events occurring during comparison, such as the one proposed by Briggs. The information theoretic formulation maintains contact with a long tradition in which RT has been related to uncertainty, and treats comparison as an operation of discriminating among a number of possible internal states, without being over-precise about the manner in which this uncertainty reduction is achieved (Briggs and Johnsen, 1972).

(6) Conclusions

The main purpose of this section of the chapter has been to illustrate the techniques which have been developed in recent years for the study of mental phenomena, especially representational codes and operational stages of processing. Most of the research reviewed has been based on the assumption that experimentally induced variations in RT may be interpreted as indices of otherwise unobservable mental processes. The nature of the coding of symbols in short-term memory has been inferred from similarity effects on "same" and "different" RT (Posner and Mitchell, 1967; Cohen, 1969), and from changes in the values of indices such as the rotation effects of Cooper and Shepard (1973) or the NI–PI difference in the experiments by Posner, Boies, Eichelman and Taylor (1969). Operational stages of processing have been defined by looking for experimental factors which selectively influence different stages, and by determining whether their effects on the RT are additive or interactive.

From the viewpoint of the developmental psychologist, this research may be seen as providing a set of techniques and theoretical assumptions which may be adapted to study the emergence of capabilities for visual and memory search, or mental rotation, in symbol processing and other domains (cf. Harris and Fleer, 1974; Hoving, Morin and Konick, 1970). Developmental psychologists will also be concerned with questions concerning the origins and nature of the symbolic memory itself, that is, the system for permanent storage of representations of the written symbols and their names. This is primarily a question about acquisition of basic reading skills, involving the development of a specialized set of feature analyzers for encoding of alphanumeric symbols (see for instance, Gibson, 1965, 1970), and the laying down in memory of highly accessible models of the letter names and their graphic forms. It also seems likely that symbol sets such as the alphabet or the numerals are grouped into higher order structures in permanent memory, perhaps in a form analogous to an ordered array. In a study of comparative judgments of magnitude, Moyer and Landauer (1967) measured the speed with which subjects could indicate which was the larger of two simultaneously displayed digits. They found that the RT was facilitated as the numerical distance between the numerals increased. Since this result paralleled findings for judgments on physical continua, such as choice of the longer of two lines, they argued that judgments about numbers might be made by reference to an internal analogue of magnitude. The findings were confirmed by Parkman (1971). A related effect was reported by DeRosa and Morin (1970) for a version of the memory search task in which the memory sets consisted of ordered sequences of numerals, such as 3-4-5-6. They found that both positive and negative RT were delayed for probes occurring at the boundaries of the memory set, as though the subjects made the discrimination by placing the probe numeral on an internal array and comparing its location against locations of the subset boundaries.

In more general terms it has to be admitted that the symbolic memory is a relatively minor part of the larger permanent memory system in which vocabulary and characteristics of objects and events are stored and represented. If the amount of research effort devoted to symbolic memory has been disproportionate, this is probably because the memory provides experimenters with a convenient set of well-learned stimuli which can be used in experiments designed to examine general issues about human memory and information processing.

III. LEXICAL MEMORY

(1) Sampling of lexical memory

The lexical memory is a system for storage of a person's vocabulary of words. This part of permanent memory is obviously very much larger in scale than the symbolic memory since the number of lexical units it must contain is considerable. Oldfield (1966), for example, estimated that a well-educated young adult may have a vocabulary of perhaps 75,000 words. For this reason, the study of lexical memory raises problems of description which are less evident in symbolic memory. The lexical units differ in length, syllabic structure, frequency of usage, assignment to superordinate classes, and concreteness-abstractness of their referents; and these factors may all have effects on information processing.

A preliminary to the study of lexical memory has therefore been the collection of *normative data* concerning the linguistic behaviour of samples of informants who are considered to be representative of the wider community of language users. These data include word frequency counts, such as that of Thorndike and Lorge (1944), listings of instances of superordinate categories (Battig and Montague, 1969), ratings of the representativeness of category instances (Rosch, 1975) and of the imageability and concreteness of referents (Paivio, Yuille and Madigan, 1968). In some instances experimenters have been interested in determining the effects of these variables on rates of information processing, for instance, the differences between words of high and low frequency of usage, or of words which are good and poor examples of their superordinate categories. If the investigator intends that his results should support general conclusions about lexical information processing, it is important that his statistical analysis should be appropriate for generalization from a sample of lexical units to a larger population. This point has been stressed by Clark (1973), who has shown that many investigators have committed a "language as a fixed effect" error by failing to treat contrasting sets of words as random effects in their analyses of variance. In other cases the lexical variables merely constitute potential sources of unwanted variation, and here experimenters resort to the normative tables in the hope of constructing sets of words which are equated with respect to these variables. These problems of sampling and control of lexical variation are considerable (cf. Landauer and Meyer, 1972), but have to be faced if a broad study of lexical memory is to be attempted.

(2) LOGOGEN MODEL OF LEXICAL MEMORY

For purposes of exposition the assumption will be made that lexical memory has the same general structure as was proposed for symbolic memory, including facilities for graphemic, phonemic and semantic representation of words, an interface structure for conversions between codes, data stores, and input and output channels. The structure of the memory is therefore as sketched in Fig. 2.1, although a very much larger interface is assumed, and the amount of data in permanent store is far greater than for symbolic memory. Indeed, the symbolic memory can properly be viewed as a small subsystem within the larger lexical memory.

It seems possible to identify three major functions of the lexical memory system. Firstly, it can operate as a short-term or *working memory* when information is held in the registers and maintained there by recycling and recoding processes of various kinds. Secondly, it functions as a *permanent memory* in that characteristics of spoken and written forms of words and their meanings are retained in store, and defined together in the interface which functions as an addressing system in retrieval. Thirdly, activation of lexical units in specific situations may lead to the formation of *episodic memories*, indicating, for example, that some more or less arbitrary set of words was included on an experimenter's list. It will be apparent that the operation of the system as a permanent memory is fundamental, and that the short-term and episodic functions are built on the capabilities for addressing, retrieval, recoding, etc., of the permanent system.

The permanent component of lexical memory functions as a *word recognition* device. In Fig. 2.1 word recognition is seen as an operation of sampling of features from the graphemic and phonemic registers by the recognizers in the interface structure. The interface contains a huge number of recognizers, called *logogens* by Morton (1969, 1970), one for each morphemic unit in the individual's vocabulary. Thus, separate units will exist corresponding to the distinct senses of homographs, but syntactic variants on a particular root morpheme may all be handled by a single unit. Each logogen unit is characterized at any given instant by a base level of activation, and this level increases when evidence accepted by the unit flows into the system. Morton (1968) postulates that each unit may also be characterized by two threshold levels. When the activation level exceeds the first threshold, addresses of stored semantic descriptions become available, and these descriptions may be directly accessed and entered into the semantic register. When a second threshold is exceeded, the address of a phonemic description is obtained, and a plan for pronunciation of a word can be entered into the phonemic register. Essentially the same process operates when evidence flows from the semantic register into the logogen system. When a particular unit exceeds threshold, a name or verbal explanation of the concept will be made available for output. It can be noted that, quite apart from the semantic store (which is the individual's knowledge of his world), the account postulates stores in which phonemic and graphemic models of the person's whole vocabulary are permanently held, and that all the problems of referencing and retrieving this information are side-stepped by postulating logogens which carry the addresses in memory of the stored data. Thus, the logogen system is properly viewed as the heart of the lexical memory structure.

According to Morton (1969) the threshold settings in the logogens depend on the frequency with which the unit has been activated in the past history of the individual. Hence, word frequency counts which are based on large samples of text provide a gross indication of relative threshold settings throughout the system. Morton (1969) and Broadbent (1967) have presented detailed mathematical arguments to support the view that the well-known effect of word frequency on identification accuracy in both visual and auditory recognition tasks depends on just such variation in threshold settings. Thus, when the description in the graphemic register is only partial, this inadequate evidence is more likely to bring a high frequency logogen above threshold than a low frequency one, and it is expected that visual errors will occur, and also occasional semantic errors. A semantic error will occur when the threshold for semantic access in a logogen is exceeded, whereas the threshold for phonemic retrieval is not.

Apart from these more or less permanent effects of frequency of usage on threshold settings, the logogens are subject to transitory changes which will also have effects on performance. It is proposed by Morton (1968, 1969) that whenever the threshold for phonemic access of a logogen is exceeded, the threshold is adjusted downward, but drifts back to a level somewhat below its original value over a relatively long time interval. As support for this view he cites his own finding (Morton, 1964) that in tachistoscopic recognition tasks responses which have been given earlier often recur as errors to new stimuli. In a more recent study, Murrell and Morton (1974) trained subjects with a list of words prior to a tachistoscopic recognition test. The words presented for recognition were either new words, words which were visually similar but morphemically distinct from a list word (e.g., if READS had been studied, READY might be presented), or words which were visually and morphemically similar to a list word (for instance, READS followed by READING). It was found that recognition performance was facilitated when a morphemically related variant had been studied, but not when a visually similar form had been studied. This result illustrates the threshold adjustment principle, and supports the contention that the logogens are recognizers corresponding to the morphemes of the language.

The logogens are also affected by more transitory and short-lived forms of semantic priming. As stated earlier, when evidence accumulates in a logogen unit, a threshold may be surpassed which allows semantic data to be retrieved from permanent store. It will be assumed that these semantic descriptions are briefly held in the semantic register, the contents of which are continuously and unselectively sampled by the logogen system. Logogens which find members of their defining semantic sets will be incremented, generally to sub-threshold levels, so that their evidence requirements for retrieval of the phonemic codes have momentarily been reduced. Empirical support for this notion has been given by Morton (1964) in a study demonstrating effects of linguistic context on tachistoscopic recognition threshold, and the mathematical analysis has been developed in his 1969 paper. If the simple vocalization of a visually displayed word involves retrieval of a phonemic code following incrementation of the logogens by data sampled from the graphemic register, it should be possible to facilitate this conversion by presenting an associated word shortly beforehand. That this is so has been demonstrated by Jacobson (1973), and by Meyer, Schvaneveldt and Ruddy (1974) who both found that the RT to name a word was speeded when the word was preceded by a common associate.

Thus, according to the logogen model, the time to retrieve a semantic description for a word, or to find a word to correspond to contents of the semantic register, will depend on the threshold settings of the relevant logogens, and on the degree to which they may have been primed. A second factor of importance is the rate of input of relevant information to the logogens. In general, a reduction in input rate (achieved by visual degradation, tachistoscopic exposure, imposition of load on processing capacity, or whatever means) will tend to magnify effects which are attributable to differences in the evidence requirements of the logogens (that is, the difference between the current threshold setting and the current level of activation in the logogen). This principle has been illustrated in Fig. 2.3, which shows idealized functions for high and low rates of input into two logogens which differ

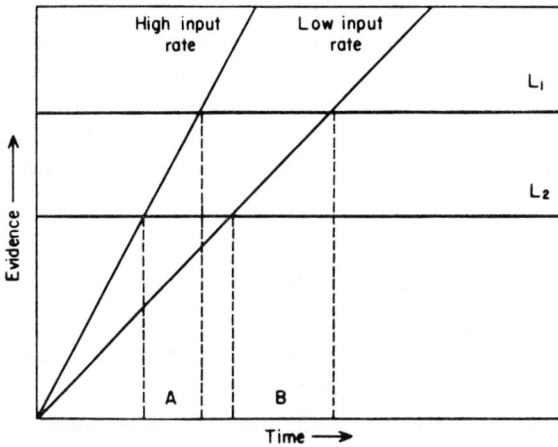

Fig. 2.3. Illustration of relation between input rate and variation in the evidence requirements of logogens. L_1 and L_2 refer to two levels of evidence requirement, reflecting permanent or temporary differences in threshold setting, or presence/absence of priming. With high rate of input of evidence into the system the difference in requirement gives rise to a difference of A msec in processing time. Reduction in the rate of input, due to stimulus degradation or some other factor, increases this difference to B msec and also increases time needed to exceed L_1 and L_2.

in their evidence requirements. It can be seen that at a night rate of input the difference in sampling time attributable to the threshold difference between the logogens is relatively small, but that as the input rate is reduced, the effect is magnified. Thus, a prediction of the model is that interactions will be found between factors which influence evidence requirements in the logogens and factors which affect the rate at which evidence is sampled. For example, Fraisse found relatively little effect of frequency of usage or manipulations of ensemble size in studies of naming supra-threshold visually displayed words, although such effects are obtained when the words are presented tachistoscopically (Fraisse, 1964; Pollack, 1963). Similarly, Meyer, Schvaneveldt and Ruddy (1974) found that the facilitating effect of associative priming on word naming VRT increased in magnitude when the word was visually degraded. Interactions of this kind are considered, according to the logic of Sternberg's additive factor method, to indicate that an experimental manipulation influences two processing stages. According to the structural model proposed in Fig. 2.1 the task of naming a visually displayed word might be thought to involve stages of : (1) Encoding of the word as a graphemic description; (2) logogen incrementation and retrieval of a phonemic description; and (3) transmission of the phonemic description to the speech output system. It is expected that factors such as word frequency, size of the ensemble of experimental materials, recency with which a word has been encountered, and associative priming, will all influence the duration of stage 2. Stimulus quality has an effect on stage 1, as in Sternberg's (1967) experiment, but will also influence the duration of stage 2, on account of the effect on the logogens of a reduction in input rate.

(3) Access to lexical memory

Various tasks have proved useful in studying the operation of gaining access to the lexical memory, including tachistoscopic display of words, visual search, and certain kinds of categorization task. In the lexical version of the *visual search* task, the subject is instructed to scan a column of words for a target which may be visually defined, for instance, a particular word or a word containing a particular letter, or which may be semantically defined, for instance, the name of a member of a large category, such as ANIMALS. Neisser and Beller (1965) found that scanning rates for visually defined targets were faster than for semantically defined targets, and concluded that they had distinguished operationally between two depths of processing, which they called *stimulus examination* and *memory examination*. It can be seen from Fig. 2.1 that visual target definition allows for testing of input at the level of the graphemic register, whereas semantic definition requires that processing should proceed through the logogens to a point where some semantic data are retrieved, so that testing occurs at the level of the semantic register. Nonetheless, the consideration of meaning was probably quite minimal in Neisser's experiments, since his subjects reported that they did not really read the words through which they scanned, and were shown to remember little about them afterwards.

The *memory search* task which was discussed in the preceding section may also be adapted to study access to lexical memory. It has been shown by Clifton and Tash (1973) that the comparison rate constant, B, has about the same value for words as for isolated symbols, but that the intercept constant, A, does show a small effect of syllabic complexity of the probe word. This is consistent with Spoehr and Smith's (1973) suggestion that syllabic parsing occurs during the operation of encoding a visual word. Variation in the level at which the comparison is to be made appears to affect the slope constant rather than the intercept. For example, Juola and Atkinson (1971) obtained a function of $RT = 617 + 26(M)$ msec for decisions about membership of a list of words. When the memory set consisted of a list of category names and the subject was instructed to determine whether a probe word was a member of any one of the categories, the function was $RT = 653 + 111(M)$ msec. On the face of it, this task could be carried out by increasing the depth of encoding of the probe, so that it was transformed to a category name which could then be matched against the names in memory. However, this would have produced a large increase in intercept and relatively little change in slope, whereas Juola and Atkinson's results show the opposite. Rather similar findings have been reported by Burrows and Okada (1973) for an auditory version of the memory search task in which subjects decided whether a probe was a member of a memory set, or whether it was a synonym of a member of the memory set. The functions obtained were: $RT = 390 + 52(M)$ msec and $RT = 302 + 146(M)$ msec. It may be noted that the intercept values are much lower than those obtained in visual experiments with words, confirming that auditory encoding is a faster operation. However, the main effect of involvement of semantic criteria is again on the slope of the RT function. Possibly the memory set and probe are both represented at the graphemic/phonemic level, but are recoded semantically during the comparison stage. The recoding process would have much the same function as the retrieval operation in Briggs and Blaha's (1969) analysis of memory search, and might be investigated by a study varying memory set size and display size.

In a system of the logogen type it is expected that speed of access to the permanent memory will be affected by word frequency, which influences threshold settings in the logogens, and by repetition of words in the experimental situation, which leads to a temporary threshold reduction. These expectations are broadly supported by data reported by Smith (1967), who found effects of both frequency of usage of the test word and repetition in tasks in which the memory sets were lists of words or lists of categories. The frequency effect appeared to be additive with that of memory set size, supporting the view that its locus is the encoding operation, but was greater for the category than for the word list task, and was reduced in magnitude by repetition. Kirsner and Craik (1971) obtained strong recency effects in an experiment in which the memory set contained eight words and the subject indicated whether or not a probe word was a member of it. The RT declined progressively across serial positions within the memory set, as might be anticipated if encoding of the memory set items resulted in brief adjustments to the logogens.

Slightly different tasks are required for investigation of access to lexical memory without the involvement of search and comparison processes in the short-term or working memory system. One useful situation is a *lexical decision* task in which the subject is presented with arrays of letters and must indicate for each one whether or not it is a word in his vocabulary. Successful performance on this task might require that the test word should be encoded to a level at which its logogen has been incremented up to the threshold for semantic access, and some evidence of meaningfulness has been retrieved from the semantic store. The time needed for this graphemic-semantic conversion should be related to frequency of usage of the test word. That this is so has been confirmed by Rubenstein, Garfield and Millikan (1970), who reported that the average RT to classify high-frequency words was about 740 msec, whereas the RT for low-frequency words was over 900 msec. Such an effect would be expected if thresholds for semantic access varied with frequency of usage, as proposed by Morton (1968), and this interpretation is considered preferable, in the context of the present discussion, to Rubenstein's own account, which is stated in terms of a sequential scanning and matching process which proceeds down a memory stack in which higher frequency words are placed nearer the top. There are additional predictions of the logogen model which may not have been adequately tested as yet. One of these is that a reduction in the quality of the probe word, whether by imposition of visual noise or by tachistoscopic presentation, should increase the magnitude of the frequency effect, since this will reduce the rate of input of evidence to the system, and will tend to exaggerate an effect due to logogen threshold differences. A second prediction is that speed of categorization of words should decrease with repeated presentations, as in the memory search study by Smith (1967), and this has recently been confirmed by Forbach, Stanners and Hochaus (1974).

It should also be possible to facilitate lexical decision by presentation of an immediately prior semantic context. If a probe word is preceded by an associate, semantic feedback to the system will result in some priming, reducing the evidence requirements of the unit. Priming effects of this kind have been demonstrated by Meyer in studies in which pairs of words are presented, either simultaneously or successively, for lexical categorization. For the simultaneous case, he found that pairs of associated words were classified as being both words faster than pairs of non-associated words (Meyer and Schvaneveldt, 1971), and comparable results were obtained when the words were presented serially for classification (Meyer, Schvaneveldt and Ruddy, 1972). Meyer has also tested for the effects of degradation of the test word on the magnitude of this *association effect*. In line with the predictions of the logogen model, he found that the association effect increased in magnitude when the test word was visually degraded (Meyer, Schvaneveldt and Ruddy, 1974), and that degradation also raised the general level of the RT. Thus, lexical decision may involve two major processing stages, which can be called (1) *graphemic encoding*, and (2) *lexical access*. Stage 2 involves incrementation of the logogens, and its duration is affected by semantic priming. Stage 1 involves icon formation and construction of a graphemic code, and its duration is affected by stimulus quality. Stimulus quality will have a secondary effect on Stage 2 by reducing the rate of flow of information into the logogens, giving rise to the interaction reported by Meyer.

The decision that a word exists in the subject's vocabulary could be based solely on lexical access, such that a positive response is made if any logogen is incremented above a threshold value. The negative response could be made if this condition was not met within some interval, which would be consistent with the finding that RTs for non-words which are pronounceable are generally found to be greater than RTs for words. However, negative RT does become faster as the non-words become progressively less word-like, or as the frequencies of occurrence of their orthographic elements are reduced (Stanners and Forbach, 1974; Rubenstein, Lewis and Rubenstein, 1971). It seems likely, therefore, that the decision that an array of letters is not a word can depend on the failure of an attempt at syllabic parsing (cf. Spoehr and Smith, 1973), or on failure of lexical access. Novik (1974) has proposed that both types of test are applied in parallel, since he found that non-pronounceable letter strings which were meaningful, such as LBJ, JFK, were rejected as non-words less rapidly than meaningless consonant trigrams. Additional evidence that pronounceable non-words are assigned a phonemic interpretation comes from Rubenstein's finding that homophones such as BURD, BOTE, MUNK, etc., are rejected less rapidly than non-words which are not homophones of actual words. However, since these displays are classified as non-words, is seems likely that the subject considers a graphemic representation of the stimulus, and that this response is primarily contingent on the adequacy of the graphemic code. Further experiments demonstrating phonemic coding have been reported by Meyer, Schvaneveldt and Ruddy (1974). The decision that two letter' strings were both words was delayed when they were graphemically similar but phonemically distinct, e.g., FREAK/BREAK, COUCH/TOUCH. Again, the subject's decision is eventually based on the graphemic code, but there appears to be some parallel consideration of phonemic representations.

These studies suggest that the encoding stage in lexical decision results in the construction of both graphemic and phonemic codes, and includes a grapheme-phoneme conversion operation which is automatically applied to orthographically regular arrays. The second stage of lexical access would then normally involve the sampling of data from the graphemic and phonemic coding registers. James (1975) has suggested that the duration of this sampling process may be sensitive to the nature of the non-words used in the experiment. He found that RTs for positive responses increased when the distractors were homophones of real words, relative to RTs obtained when the distractors were pronounceable non-words. In addition, a semantic variable, the concreteness of the test word, was found to influence the positive RT for low frequency words when the distractors were word-like, but not when they were unpronounceable. These results imply that thresholds throughout the logogen system may be raised when word-like distractors are used, and that, with this increased depth of processing, semantic information is retrieved and may be utilized in lexical decisions about low-frequency words.

(4) SEMANTIC CATEGORIZATION

It has been argued in this section that a main function of lexical memory (the logogen system) is to mediate two-way conversions between physical codings of words (the phonemic and graphemic codes) and the representations of meaning which are held in permanent memory. In the model shown in Fig. 2.1 incrementation of a logogen above the threshold for semantic access leads to retrieval of data from the semantic store, and placement of an entry in the semantic register. Characteristics of the register, or of the descriptions which it may contain, can be indirectly studied by RT measurements in tasks involving decisions about semantic aspects of words.

A widely used situation has been a *categorization task* in which the subject is given the name of a semantic category followed by the name of an instance, e.g., BIRD . . . ROBIN. The instruction is to make a positive response if the instance is a member of the specified class, and a negative response if it is not. It is on the face of it possible that such decisions could be taken at a lexical level, if, for example, presentation of the category name resulted in marking of logogens, for instance names. Another possibility is that determination of category membership depends on a genuinely semantic comparison, that is on a comparison of descriptions of the category and instance names which have been entered into the semantic register.

The principal evidence in favour of the semantic comparison hypothesis comes from studies which demonstrate effects of *semantic relatedness* on positive and negative RTs. The speed with which an item is accepted as a category member depends on the closeness of its associative relation to the category name. This point was demonstrated by Wilkins (1971) in a study showing that words having a high frequency of occurrence in the Battig and Montague (1969) category production norms were accepted faster than words having low production frequencies. Since these results were obtained with general frequency of usage controlled, there was evidence that the *frequency of co-occurrence* of the category and instance names, sometimes referred to as conjoint frequency, was an important factor influencing speed of categorization. Loftus (1973) has suggested that frequency of co-occurrence should also be defined in terms of the probability that a given category name will occur as a superordinate for a particular instance, and Loftus and Scheff (1971) have tabulated category name production norms for a sample of instances. Thus, any pair of words, consisting of a category name and an instance name, can be characterized by two measures of associative strength, *instance dominance* (the likelihood that the instance will be listed as a member of the class), and *category dominance* (the likelihood that the class label will be listed as applicable to the instance). Loftus measured RTs to accept an instance as a member of a category, and a category as a class name for an instance. Pairs having high instance and category dominance, such as TREE–OAK, were classified faster than pairs having low instance and category dominance, such as CLOTH–ORLON, irrespective of order of presentation. Low instance dominance raised the RT when the instance was presented second, but not when the instance was presented first. Conversely, low category dominance raised RT when the category occurred second, but not when it occurred first.

These effects of conjoint frequency on categorization RT parallel findings obtained in sentence verification tasks. Collins and Quillian (1969) found that statements asserting class membership and possession of a property, for instance, A CANARY IS A BIRD, A CANARY IS YELLOW, were verified less rapidly as the "semantic distance" between the subject and predicate terms increased. Conrad (1972) presented data indicating that, for statements about properties, these effects were related to production frequencies of predicates when subjects completed sentence frames of the form : A CANARY IS ——, A CANARY HAS ——, etc. There is, therefore, substantial agreement that positive RT in semantic categorization tasks is affected by the strength of the associative relation between category and instance names, where strength is operationally defined in terms of the number of subjects in a representative sample generating a particular response.

Collins and Quillian and Loftus have argued that these results reflect the operation of a search process within an associatively structured lexical memory. The memory contains nodes, which are internal representations of words, and associative connections between words, so that verification RT depends on the distance through the network which must be traversed in order to find a legitimate connection between two nodes. Loftus, for example, argues that category and instance dominance effects occur because the first of the two words presented activates a node in the memory and then, by spread of activity through the network, nodes of other associated words. If the test word corresponds to one of these, a fast decision can be taken. Otherwise, a more elaborate process will be required, perhaps involving inferential steps of the kind postulated for shifts between hierarchical levels by Collins and Quillian (1969). The effect can also be accommodated by a category search model of the kind described by Landauer and Meyer (1972), if it is assumed that high probability exemplars are scanned before low probability exemplars. However, a compatible alternative explanation which seems closer to the assumptions of the logogen model of lexical memory is that the effect depends on priming of the logogens at presentation of the category name. This can be referred to as a *lexical access* account, and distinguished from the various search process models.

Rosch (1973) has proposed a slightly different interpretation of dominance effects, arguing that certain items are good or prototypical examples of a category, just as different hues may vary in their approximation to one's notion of the typical colour corresponding to a colour name. She obtained ratings of "typicality", and showed that these predicted the RT in a categorization task. However, the typicality ratings correlated quite highly with the Battig and Montague production frequency measures, suggesting that the typical category members are likely to occur to subjects early in listing tasks as well as being accepted faster in the categorization task. Thus, typicality effects can also be accounted for both by the search and the priming or lexical access models. One prediction of both accounts seems to be that there should be no effects of dominance or typicality on speed of rejection of items which are not members of the designated category. Yet

Millward, Rice and Corbett (1975) have recently reported that negative RT is facilitated when the instance is a good example of its own category. This is difficult to account for in models which assume only a search of the designated category, or only priming of logogens for names of good examples of the designated category. However, it could occur if the Yes/No decision depended on retrieval of categorial information concerning the probe word and a comparison of this semantic information against a comparable representation of a category name. The assumption here is that speed of retrieval of categorial features of an instance name is influenced by dominance or typicality.

Support for the view that dominance affects time for categorial recoding of the probe word can be drawn from a study of McFarland *et al.* (1974). They used a lexical-semantic version of Sternberg's memory search task in which subjects were given 1, 2 or 3 category names as a memory set followed by a probe which was to be classified as positive if it was a member of one of the categories, and as negative if it was not. The dominance of the probe words was varied, using the data from the Battig and Montague (1969) norms. The results obtained for positive trials were fitted by the equations: $RT = 674 + 124(M)$ msec for high dominance probes, and $RT = 775 + 156(M)$ msec for low dominance probes. The slope values are of the same order of magnitude as was found for semantic comparisons by Juola and Atkinson (1971) and Burrows and Okada (1973). However, the effect of dominance was on the intercept value, A, the index of encoding processes, and not on the slope, B, the index of central comparison operations. This pattern also occurred for negative RT, where the equations were: $RT = 608 + 202(M)$ msec for high dominance probes, and $RT = 708 + 210(M)$ msec for low dominance probes. For negatives, dominance was defined relative to a category which was not in the memory set, so that the implication that this is an effect on speed of categorial recoding is quite strong.

Additional evidence which seems to point in the same direction has been presented by Rips, Shoben and Smith (1973). They obtained ratings of semantic distance between instances of the categories of BIRDS and ANIMALS, and between the instances and their category names, and the data were analysed by multi-dimensional scaling procedures (Carroll and Chang, 1970). The analysis suggested that the ratings of similarity depended on values assigned to each instance on underlying dimensions of size and predacity (see also Henley, 1969). Subjects were tested in a task in which pairs of instance names were presented, a positive response being required if both were members of the same category (i.e., both birds, or both animals) and a negative response if they came from different categories. This task corresponds to the "rule identity" level of classification in the experiments by Posner and Mitchell (1967). It was also shown by Schaeffer and Wallace (1969) that subjects classified pairs of names as "both living" or "both non-living" faster when the items were members of the same category than when they were members of different categories. Positive RT was correlated with indices of distance between the instance names and their category names, and between the instances alone. It was found that the best predictor of the RT was the distance between the first word of the pair and its category name, again suggesting that the RT depends on speed of retrieval of categorial properties.

Rosch (1975) has recently presented evidence that priming by means of a category name may both facilitate recognition of good examples of the category and assist retrieval of categorial properties. She first identified the major category names used for classification of concrete objects in English, using the Kucera and Francis (1967) word frequency count, and then selected the fifty to sixty instances of each category listed by ten or more subjects in the Battig and Montague (1969) sample. A group of about 200 subjects rated each instance on a 7-point scale regarding the extent to which it "represented their idea or image of the meaning of the category term". In the category BIRDS, for example, subjects rated ROBIN and SPARROW as very good or typical instances, and EMU, PENGUIN and BAT as poor or atypical instances. The gradient of typicality which is revealed by these ratings is referred to as the *internal structure* of the category by Rosch. A reaction time experiment was then carried out in which subjects were presented with pairs of instance names which were to be classified as "same" if they were physically identical or if they belonged to the same superordinate category, and as "different" if they belonged to different categories. Instances were selected from each category at three levels of typicality. In half of the trials the words were preceded by a priming stimulus, the spoken name of the superordinate category of the instances forming "same" pairs, or one of the instances of "different" pairs. Both priming and level of typicality significantly affected the RT to classify pairs of instances as members of the same category, and these effects were additive. Priming and typicality effects were also obtained for "different" pairs, although of a markedly smaller magnitude. A further experiment established that these results for "same" category and "different" category responses could also be obtained when the prime was presented simultaneously with the pair of words. These findings appear generally consistent with the view that determination of category membership depends on retrieval of categorial properties, and that this operation can be facilitated by item typicality and by priming.

In the case of physically identical pairs Rosch (1975) reported an interesting interaction between priming and level of typicality. Although these pairs might on the face of it be matched at a graphemic level the comparison RT showed effects of typicality and an effect of priming which was facilitating for good examples but retarding for poor examples. The interaction occurred when the prime was presented 2 sec before the stimuli, but not when it was presented simultaneously with the stimuli. A further experiment demonstrated that the interaction could be obtained if the prime preceded the stimuli by 400–500 msec. This result indicates that presentation of a category name both facilitates retrieval of categorial properties and evokes some representation of typical category instances which is useful in processing names of good instances while being at the same time disruptive of processing of names of poor instances. It appears that this is not a straightforward matter of facilitation of lexical access, since, in that case, the interaction between priming and typicality would also be found for same category RTs. The effect is therefore difficult to interpret within an additive stage model in which graphemic analysis precedes retrieval of semantic information.

A number of studies has shown that, in contrast to these facilitating effects on "same" RTs, semantic similarity may retard the "different" RT. Collins and Quillian (1970) reported that subjects were slower in rejecting plant names as non-instances of the category ANIMALS than names of inanimate substances, and argued that this was because the superordinates shared properties concerned with denotation of living things. Smith, Shoben and Rips (1974) have presented further evidence of a gradient within a category which is related to the target category: for instance, when the target category is VEGETABLES, names of some fruits take longer to reject than others, and this effect can be predicted by ratings of semantic relatedness. This point has also been made by Schaeffer and Wallace (1970) in an experiment in which subjects decided whether two successively displayed words were both names of instances of any one of four specified categories. Semantically close pairs, such as OAK/TULIP, took longer to classify as "different" than semantically more distant pairs, such as OAK/TIGER. These effects of relatedness on "different" RT are not easily handled in models of categorization which postulate the scanning of an array of exemplars of the target category (Landauer and Meyer, 1972), and were seen by Schaeffer and Wallace as being inconsistent with the hierarchical network model of Collins and Quillian (1969). However, the effect can be accommodated in models which emphasize the role of a semantic comparison process. In such models it is assumed that categorization is achieved by comparing representations of meaning of the category and instance names, and that relatedness influences the decision processes involved in this comparison.

Smith, Shoben and Rips (1974) have developed a model of semantic comparison which is in many respects similar to the Atkinson-Juola model for lexical recognition (see Atkinson and Juola, 1973). They have assumed that instance and category names are internally represented as arrays of semantic features. A feature is seen as a value, or permissible range of variation, on a descriptive dimension, such as size or colour. When a word is presented the relevant dimensions and values are retrieved from permanent store, and may be placed in a *semantic register* (see Fig. 2.1). The occurrence of effects of semantic similarity on "same" and "different" judgmental processes can be regarded as an experimentally useful index of the involvement of this coding register, just as visual and acoustic confusion effects have been treated as indices of graphemic and phonemic coding. Smith, Shoben and Rips represent similarity of meaning in terms of feature overlap, that is to say, the degree to which two word concepts are defined on common semantic dimensions and have similar values on those dimensions. With respect to determination of category membership, it is argued that features vary in their criteriality, some being essential for assignment to a category (the defining features), whereas others are descriptive of non-essential properties (the characteristic features). It is proposed that each feature is given a weighting defining its criteriality, and that these weightings can be used to isolate a subset of criterial dimensions.

The processing model outlined by Smith, Shoben and Rips postulates two stages of semantic comparison. At a first stage the overall similarity of the category and instance name concepts is determined, probably by computing the number of common dimensions and the proximity of values on those dimensions. It can be noted that this stage includes the time to encode the probe word, to retrieve a semantic description and enter this into the semantic register, to transform the contents of the register into a similarity value, and to match this value against two criterion settings. If the similarity value is below one threshold a decision that the item is not a category member is directly taken, and a negative response is made. If it is above another higher threshold, an immediate decision in favour of category membership is taken, and a positive response is made. Thus, an internal scale of semantic similarity is postulated to play the same role in the decision process as the familiarity scale in the Atkinson-Juola (1973) model. When intermediate values of semantic similarity are obtained, a second comparison process is started which involves the isolation of the dimensions which are criterial for determination of category membership, and matching of the two concepts on these defining features only. It follows that reductions in semantic relatedness will raise the "same" RT by increasing the probability that the similarity value obtained at Stage 1 falls in the intermediate range and that the focused comparison operation of Stage 2 is required. Equally, an increase in semantic relatedness for negative items will result in an increased probability that second stage processing will occur, producing a relatedness effect on "different" RT. The major source of errors in categorization is the occasional occurrence of similarity values for atypical positives and related negatives which lie outside the intermediate range. Smith, Shoben and Rips reported that most errors were made to atypical instances or related negatives, and that error RT was generally fast relative to correct RT for these cases.

Schaeffer and Wallace (1970) also described a two-stage model of semantic comparison for interpretation of similarity effects on "same" and "different" RT. The two stages are quite similar to those described by Smith, Shoben and Rips, since the first involves retrieval of semantic data and a global assessment of similarity, whereas the second involves a focused comparison operating on a criterial subset of features. However, categorization always involves both stages, and assessment of similarity at the first stage is used to alter the duration of the second stage. The mechanism proposed for this is one of threshold adjustment, such that the threshold for a "same" decision is lowered as the similarity value passed from Stage 1 increases, while the threshold for a "different" response is raised. Conversely, detection of a low similarity value results in a rise in the "same" threshold and a lowering of the "different" threshold. This reciprocal adjustment principle can provide a general account of similarity effects in domains other than semantic decision-making, and can also accommodate situations where overall similarity does not provide a sufficient basis for positive or negative decisions.

(5) Conclusions

This section has discussed some recent research concerned with the processing of lexical information. It has been assumed that word stimuli gain access to stored semantic information via a system of recognizers, called the logogen system by Morton (1969). Speed of processing lexical input depends on the evidence requirements of the individual logogens, and these requirements are determined by general frequency of usage, repetition and semantic priming. It is therefore necessary to take account of these factors in any experiments concerned with lexical or semantic categorization.

Experiments on lexical memory share with the studies of symbolic memory a reliance on categorization tasks in which the level of abstraction at which the subject makes his decision can be varied. It was considered that decisions at a *lexical level* were involved when subjects indicated whether a word was a member of an arbitrary memory set stored in short-term or long-term (episodic) memory, and when they classified letter arrays as words or non-words. Decisions at a semantic level are implicated when subjects must make judgments about category membership, and the truth or falsity of simple assertions. A third *logical level* can probably be distinguished, and this becomes important when the response is contingent on consideration of effects on truth value of set relation, quantification and negation.

The results of the experiments on lexical and semantic categorization appear broadly consistent with a "processing stages" model of the kind shown in Fig. 2.4. The encoding of visual words is thought to involve a

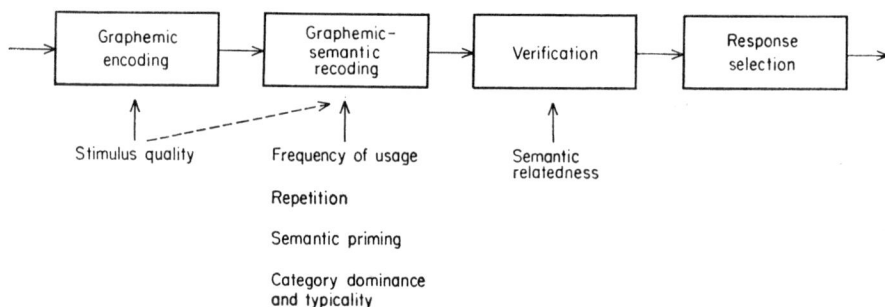

FIG. 2.4. "Processing stages" model for semantic categorization.

stage of graphemic encoding (perhaps supported by phonemic recoding), followed by a stage of retrieval of semantic information. The duration of the graphemic encoding stage is influenced by the quality of the stimulus. Semantic retrieval is achieved via the logogens, and is affected by permanent and transitory changes in the logogen units. Further, by altering rate of input of information to the logogens, stimulus quality has a secondary effect on the semantic retrieval stage. The verification stage operates on retrieved semantic descriptions and determines their equivalence with respect to some task definition. A major factor influencing the duration of this stage is the similarity of the concepts under consideration.

For the developmental psychologist the research poses questions about the origins of the lexical memory system. Pre-school children have a poorly developed notion of "sameness", as is shown in Vurpillot's (1968) study of matching of complex visual figures, but come during primary schooling to acquire the flexible and well-articulated notions of equivalence which are applied so readily by adult subjects in experiments of the kind which have been described. The broader question of acquisition of lexical memory is a very large one, including development of capabilities for speech recognition and interpretation, and acquisition of reading skills. In terms of the model of Fig. 2.1, this involves the formation of specialized feature analysis systems in the auditory and visual input channels, the development of the logogen system, and the establishment of phonemic and graphemic models of words in the data stores. If Murrell and Morton's (1974) proposal that the logogens are morphemically based is correct, it may well follow that the lexical memory is built on to the semantic system, and is, so to speak, an outgrowth of that system.

IV. PICTORIAL MEMORY

(1) Structure of the pictorial memory system

The final section of the chapter is concerned with a system for representation of non-verbal, spatial information which will be called the *pictorial memory*. Research on pictorial information processing has been less extensive and less systematic than the work on symbolic and lexical information processing. This may reflect a verbal bias in the research community, or, more probably, the greater convenience of lexical stimuli as experimental materials. For example, much of the research on semantic categorization which was reviewed in the preceding section has been concerned with object classes and perceptual properties of objects. Yet these experiments have almost exclusively involved tests on processing of word stimuli, and the explanatory models have often treated semantic memory as a network of connections among internal representations of words.

In the feature comparison models of Smith, Shoben and Rips (1974) and Schaeffer and Wallace (1970) it was assumed that semantic representations of names of objects and categories of objects consisted of sets of features, each defining a range of values on an internal dimension. These dimensions must often be definitions of perceptual characteristics, such as colour, size, shape, location of parts, etc., as well as of capabilities and functions, so that, for concrete nouns, the information held in the semantic store may contain a substantial perceptual component.

In the following discussion the term *pictorial memory* will therefore be taken to refer to a semantic system for description of properties of the perceptual world plus a more peripheral system for analysis of visual characteristics of objects and accessing of stored semantic data.

The incorporation of pictorial memory into the scheme shown in Fig. 2.1 involves the postulation of a second visual input channel. This may share with the graphemic channel a sensory buffer memory (the icon), and a register for maintenance of spatial descriptions, to be called the *pictorial register*. It is likely that the graphemic and pictorial registers are part of a single system for spatial representation, so that the graphemic/pictorial distinction is primarily one of content. However, the graphemic channel is a specialized system developed during acquisition of reading skill, and includes the feature analysers needed for identification of letters and words which may differ in various respects from those needed for identification of objects (Gibson, Gibson, Pick and Osser, 1962). Also, it will be argued that graphemic feature descriptions may access the logogen system relatively directly, whereas pictorial descriptions cannot. It is likely, therefore, that there are important functional distinctions between graphemic and pictorial encoding processes, and a separation of graphemic and pictorial codes is proposed in order to emphasize this point.

The second major postulate is that pictorial memory is organized around an interface structure, analogous to the logogen system. This could be called the *iconogen system*. Its function is to mediate the identification of objects, and this is achieved by sampling components of feature descriptions in the pictorial register. It may be assumed that there are object recognizers, or iconogen units, and that stored semantic information becomes accessible when the threshold of one of these units is exceeded. This semantic store is thought to be the same semantic system that was discussed in relation to lexical memory. Its contents might consist primarily of quite abstract descriptions of perceptual and functional characteristics common to members of object classes. Once retrieved, these descriptions can be entered into the semantic register for further processing.

Since people can produce concrete representations of object classes in the form of drawings, models or images, one would probably wish to argue that the iconogens also function to transform semantic input to relatively specific descriptions in the pictorial register. This is analogous to the generation of images of words in the lexical memory, and implies the existence of a permanent store of detailed descriptions of particular objects. These descriptions could define a canonical form for each object, with alternative orientations and viewpoints being constructed by application of rotation programmes to contents of the pictorial register. Thus, a third proposal is that the pictorial memory contains a *pictorial data store*, and that the contents of this store may be accessed when relevant semantic properties occur as input to the iconogen system.

(2) Pictorial encoding

The encoding and internal representation of pictorial information may be studied by the same experimental methods as have been outlined in the section on symbolic memory. Firstly, the proposal that object identification involves formation of an icon and pictorial description followed by accumulation of evidence in an object recognizer (iconogen) can be supported by tachistoscopic experiments which demonstrate masking effects, familiarity effects and context effects on report accuracy. Wingfield (1968) has reported that the visual duration threshold for object identification is influenced by post-stimulus masking, and by familiarity (defined in terms of the frequency of usage of the object name). A recent study by Palmer (1975) has also demonstrated an effect of pictorial context on object identification. Following an experiment on lexical recognition by Morton (1964), Palmer displayed pictures of objects briefly to subjects following a 2 sec exposure of a pictorial scene. The context might be appropriate or inappropriate for the target object; in the latter condition, the object shown might be quite unrelated to the scene, or might be visually similar to an object which would fit the context. There was also a control condition in which no context picture was shown. Palmer reported that the probability of a correct report was raised by an appropriate context but depressed by an inappropriate context, these effects being most marked for objects of average or low recognizability.

Palmer's results may be interpreted as evidence that semantic analysis of a contextual scene results in priming of iconogen units, and that this additional semantic evidence facilitates identification. If the semantic data are also accessible from the lexical system, it should be possible to demonstrate comparable priming effects with a verbal context. Some experiments relating to this prediction have been reported by Rosch (1975). She presented pairs of pictures of objects (simple line drawings) to subjects who were instructed to make a positive response if both objects were members of the same superordinate class (furniture, fruit, weapon, vegetable, etc.), and a negative response if they were not. Displays were preceded by a category name priming signal, or by the word "blank". On "same" trials the pictures might be physically identical, or might be two different objects from the same class. The examples were stratified at three levels of typicality, so that the experiments enable one to see whether the interactions of typicality and priming reported by Rosch for lexical stimuli also occur for pictorial stimuli. Her results for pictures turned out to be qualitatively very similar to those found for words. The speed of decision that two different objects belonged to the same category was affected by rated typicality and by priming, and these two effects were additive. However, for physically identical pictures, the effect of typicality interacted with presence/absence of a priming signal; priming facilitated responses to good category examples, but inhibited responses to poor examples. When the verbal priming signal was presented simultaneously with the pictures, the effect on "same" RT for different members of the category persisted, but the effect on physically identical pairs was eliminated. Further, when the subjects were instructed to respond "same" only to physically identical pairs, the effects of priming and typicality were no longer significant.

These findings suggest that encoding processes for pictures can be described by the same "depth of processing" account as was proposed for lexical stimuli. Under physical identity instructions the comparison can be focused on contents of the pictorial register, and there is no necessity for retrieval of semantic information, and hence no effect of semantic priming. Under rule identity (same category) instructions the decision is based on retrieved semantic information concerning category membership. Speed of retrieval depends on typicality, and is facilitated by immediately prior presentation of the category name. A prediction deriving from the "levels of analysis" account of episodic memory (Craik and Lockhart, 1972) is that incidental memory for pictures should be greater for rule identity than for physical identity instructions. Rosch has shown that this is so, and also that cueing of recall with the category names is effective for rule identity but not for physical identity instructions. The general level of recall was slightly higher for picture than for word stimuli. Incidental recall was also measured in a study by Gellatly and Gregg (1975) in which single pictures of objects were classified as instances or non-instances of verbally designated categories. The size of the category did not influence recall, but pictures classified as congruent with the category name tended to be better recalled than those which were rejected as non-instances. This effect of decision outcome implies that semantic analysis and positive categorization may be the major conditions determining whether information is transferred to a pictorial event-knowledge store.

The finding that typicality and priming effects are so similar for word and picture stimuli is consistent with the view that the lexical and pictorial memories are linked to a single central semantic system, and that the two memories have structurally comparable methods for interfacing with this system. However, the argument that the semantic component of the model contains abstract descriptions of perceptual properties of objects may imply that decisions about category membership should be taken more rapidly for picture than for word stimuli.

This would follow because pictorial codes are congruent with the semantic codes, whereas graphemic codes are not. Such a prediction is difficult to verify since word and picture stimuli might differ with respect to peripheral encoding processes occurring prior to semantic retrieval. Nevertheless, Rosch's data show a consistent RT advantage for picture over word stimuli. This is in agreement with the results of a study of rule identity classification of geometric shapes and their names reported by Seymour (1973d). The stimuli consisted of the shapes SQUARE, CIRCLE, ELLIPSE and rectangular OBLONG and their names; subjects were instructed to classify pairs of shapes or pairs of names as "same" if both were compact (square and circle combinations) or if both were elongated (ellipse and oblong combinations). These decisions were taken faster for shape stimuli than for name stimuli, except for physically identical pairs, where word stimuli were classified faster than shape stimuli.

Some further evidence on this point has recently been presented by Paivio (1975). He obtained ratings of the sizes of animals and other objects, and then tested subjects in a *comparative judgment* task in which they were required to indicate which of two simultaneously displayed names referred to the larger object. He found that the RT for this judgment decreased as the size difference between the two objects increased. This result is in agreement with the findings of Moyer and Landauer (1967) and Parkman (1971) for judgments of numerical magnitude, and replicates an earlier study of judgments of sizes of verbally designated animals by Moyer (1973). Paivio also found that judgmental RT was faster for pictures of objects than for the names of objects. Further, the RT was inhibited if the objects were displayed to show a size difference which conflicted with their actual relative sizes, for instance, a LAMP and a ZEBRA, with the lamp drawn as the larger of the two. On the other hand, variation in the sizes of word stimuli had no effects on RT.

Paivio has argued that these and other results reported in his paper are inconsistent with models of permanent memory which are stated in terms of verbal networks (Collins and Quillian, 1969) or abstract propositional representations (Anderson and Bower, 1973; Clark and Chase, 1972). This is because RTs are faster for picture than for word stimuli, and because the internal size dimension appears to be analogue rather than digital in form. It seems clear that representation of sizes of objects is not in general part of what has here been called the pictorial code (that is to say, a description of physical characteristics of a picture or object) but belongs to the semantic level at which significant properties of objects are stored. Rips, Shoben and Smith (1973), for example, suggested that size was one of the basic dimensions for differentiation among members of the class of animals, and thought of this as a semantic dimension. Thus, what is called the image system by Paivio corresponds to the pictorial memory in the present account, which includes both the pictorial register and the semantic memory system. Since the semantic memory codes object properties, its contents are more easily accessed by picture than by word stimuli.

Additional evidence on this point is contained in Rosch's (1975) paper. She found that a category name prime generated a typicality × priming interaction for physical identity comparisons at shorter prime-display intervals for picture stimuli than for word stimuli. Further, given an adequate interval, the effect occurred for both word and picture stimuli when the two types of display were mixed together in a series of trials. She concluded that the category name generated a representation of prototypical category members which influenced both the pictorial and the lexical recognition systems; however, the development of this expectancy seemed to occur slightly faster in the pictorial than in the verbal system. This is consistent with the view that the semantic representation of a name of an object class is often pictorial in nature.

(3) PICTORIAL AND VERBAL CODES

The argument of the preceding section has been that pictures are encoded by a process of formation of a pictorial description followed by retrieval of a more abstract semantic description of object properties and functions. Once retrieved, this semantic description can be entered into the semantic register of Fig. 2.1. If components of the description are sampled by units in the logogen system some units will be primed and others will exceed their threshold levels, so that phonemic or graphemic representations of names can be retrieved and placed in the lexical registers. Conversely, if a written or spoken object name is analysed in the logogen system, stored semantic properties will be retrieved and placed in the semantic register; this representation can, in turn, be used for retrieval of an object description which can be entered into the pictorial register. It is therefore in principle possible for a verbally or pictorially designated object to be represented in working memory in terms of one or more among four types of code.

Hypotheses about coding of objects in short-term memory can be investigated by adapting the methods for study of symbol representation used by Posner and his colleagues. In a simultaneous matching task two pictures, or a word and a picture, are displayed for classification as "same" or "different". Picture-picture comparisons can take place at the level of the pictorial register when the instructions define "same" in terms of physical identity. The data reported by Rosch (1975) suggest that such comparisons do not involve semantic retrieval, since the RT was not affected by typicality or priming. However, it is expected that the RT will be influenced by the similarity. Evidence on this point can be taken from various studies of same–different judgments for pairs of geometric forms which vary with respect to a small number of dimensions, e.g., size, colour, shape, orientation of a bar, etc. (Hawkins, 1969). In general, the "different" RT increases as the number of dimensions on which the shapes have same values increases. A *pictorial confusability* effect of this kind was also found by Seymour (1973b) in a study in which subjects matched outline geometric shapes: the "different" RT was delayed when the shapes were both rectangular (a square and a rectangle) or were both curved (a circle and an ellipse); however, the RT was not affected if both were elongated (rectangle and ellipse) or if both were compact (square and circle).

When the stimuli presented for comparison consist of a name and a shape, matching could involve the transformation of one stimulus to the input code of the other, or transformation of both stimuli to an abstract semantic code. The experiments on sentence-picture comparison by Clark and Chase (1972), Olson and Filby (1972) and Carpenter and Just (1975) appear to involve comparisons of abstract propositional codes, that is to say, matching at the level of the semantic register. This interpretation is supported by the relative success of the constituent comparison models in accounting for the verification RTs. Additional evidence comes from studies of word-shape comparison in which similarity has been varied. For example, Seymour (1973b) found that there were pictorial similarity effects when subjects matched geometric shapes and their names. These effects were similar to those obtained for shape-shape matching, but not identical. In particular, the property of "elongation" produced confusability effects in the name-shape comparison task but not in the shape-shape task. It is possible that this change in the pattern of confusability effects depends on the consideration of more abstract pictorial descriptions in name-shape comparisons. Another line of research which is consistent with this view is the "axis match" effect reported by Kreuger (1972) and Seymour (1973c). In Seymour's study subjects were shown a dot and the word "above", "below", "left" or "right" located above, below, left or right of it. In one condition of the experiment they were instructed to report "Yes" if the word correctly specified its own location relative to the dot, and "No" if it did not do so. The "No" RT was delayed when the word occupied the wrong position on the correct dimension, for instance, "left" written to the right of the dot. An effect of this kind could occur if the comparison involved matching of semantic representations of location which included a dimensional property and an indication of direction on that dimension (see for instance, Leech, 1969). Finally, Seymour (1973a) has discussed data obtained by Hutcheon (1970) in an experiment in which names were presented together with pictures of objects for comparison. The negative RT was delayed when the designated and displayed object were perceptually similar, for instance the name of one kind of dog with a picture of another kind, and when they were functionally similar, for instance the name of one piece of furniture combined with a picture of another.

Taken together these results suggest that comparisons between simultaneously displayed words and pictures occur in an abstract or semantic mode which nevertheless includes a substantial perceptual component. This formulation is, of course, in line with the assertion that the semantic system functions to encode perceptual properties of objects and their spatial interrelations.

If word and picture stimuli are presented successively for comparison it becomes possible to adapt the methods of Posner, Boies, Eichelman and Taylor (1969) to the study of maintenance and transformation of pictorial and verbal codes for objects. For example, Tversky (1969) taught subjects a set of eight schematic faces and a nonsense name for each face. The faces were produced by combining alternative values on three dimensions, that is to say, shape (fat or narrow) eyes (filled or unfilled) and mouth (straight or curved). The names were CVCV pseudo-words created by combining alternate values for first consonant (D or G), second consonant (M or L), and vowel (I and O), for instance, GOMO, DILI, etc. This procedure generates varying degrees of similarity within the picture and name sets, and Tversky assigned names to pictures in a way which minimized the correlation of similarity within the two sets. The subjects were tested on RT to indicate whether successively displayed name-name, face-face, name-face or face-name combinations were "same" or "different", the RT being measured from onset of the second display. The first display appeared for 1 sec, and was followed by a 1 sec offset-onset ISI. Tversky manipulated the subject's expectancy as to the form of the test stimulus by means of a modification of Posner's "pure list" design. Within a given block of trials 79 per cent of tests were in one modality and 21 per cent were in the other. The modality of the first stimulus was held constant. Thus, subjects might be shown a name as the memory stimulus followed by a face on the majority of trials and a name on the minority of trials. Tversky found that "same" and "different" RTs were always faster when the test stimulus was in the expected modality. The conclusion that subjects maintained or generated a code corresponding to the expected form of the test stimulus was strengthened by the finding that "different" RT was influenced by similarity of the display and the code supposedly set up in memory. In trials where name-face comparisons predominated, "different" RT was lengthened when the face designated by the name differed on only one dimension from the test face, and comparable effects were obtained when words were test stimuli. Tversky's experiment therefore provides good evidence that subjects can retain graphemic codes for words and pictorial codes for shapes, and that they can also generate a pictorial code from a name or a graphemic code for the name of a picture.

The time course for decay and generation of these codes has been investigated in studies by Scheerer-Neumann (1974). He obtained RTs for name-name, picture-picture, name-picture and picture-name comparisons at ISIs of 0–2000 msec, using outline drawings of common objects and their names as stimuli. In a "pure list" design, he demonstrated that word-word comparison RT remained constant as ISI was lengthened; this was also approximately true for picture-picture comparisons. Taken in conjunction with Posner's findings for comparisons of symbols, this result is suggestive of retention of visual graphemic or pictorial codes over this range of intervals. For word-picture and picture-word comparisons, RT was greater than for word-word and picture-picture comparisons with ISIs of 500 msec or less, but the four conditions were equivalent at ISIs in the range 750–2000 msec. These findings clearly support the notion that subjects can generate pictorial or graphemic codes for stimuli presented in the opposite modality. In a second experiment, Scheerer-Neumann used a "mixed list" design in which the modality of the second stimulus varied within a block of trials while the modality of the first was held constant. In these circumstances the level of picture-word and word-picture comparison RTs remained relatively stable over the range of ISIs, and RT for word-word and picture-picture comparisons increased as a function of ISI. This is suggestive of decay of the visual graphemic and pictorial input codes, and of their replacement by more abstract codes, that is to say, descriptions held in the semantic register.

Gellatly and Gregg (1975) have recently presented evidence that relatedness effects of the kind reported by Seymour (1973a) are also obtained when subjects match successively presented names and pictures. In this study, subjects were given a question of the form: "Is this a CHAIR?", and a test picture was presented after a delay of 1 sec. Semantic relatedness was manipulated as a between-subjects factor. Subjects serving in an "unrelated negatives" condition were always shown mismatching pictures which were semantically remote from the object class mentioned in the question. Their RT data showed very similar performance for "Yes" and "No" responses, and a small effect of the level of abstraction of the class name. Subjects responded slightly more slowly to questions about superordinate classes, such as FURNITURE, than to questions about object classes, such as CHAIR. This replicates an effect also obtained by Hutcheon (1970). For subjects receiving "related negatives", for instance, "Is this a CHAIR?" tested by a picture of a table, the level of the "No" RT was raised relative to "Yes" RT and relative to the results for the "unrelated" group. In addition, presence of related negatives also affected the level of the "Yes" RT. It can be noted that an effect of this sort can be accommodated by the Schaeffer and Wallace model of the verification process since there might be a precautionary upward adjustment on both the positive and negative decision thresholds under conditions of discrimination difficulty. It could also be explained in terms of Rips's (1975) model for verification of quantified statements by assuming an adjustment in the placing of upper and lower criteria which increases the probability of Stage 2 analytical processing of both positives and negatives.

The finding that there are effects of semantic relatedness on "different" RT in successive word-picture comparisons tends to argue against Scheerer-Neumann's conclusions concerning generation of pictorial codes. However, there is a difficulty here in separating semantic from pictorial similarity which was dealt with only informally by Gellatly and Gregg. Bartram (unpublished) has described a study in which photographs of objects were selected to be pictorially and semantically confusable with the referent of a previously given name (for instance, violin and guitar), semantically confusable only (violin and tuba), or non-confusable (violin and apple). Name and picture displays were presented successively, at ISIs falling in the range 0–2 sec. Contrary to Scheerer-Neumann's findings, Bartram found that RT increased as a function of ISI. At the shorter ISIs "different" RT was delayed for pictorially similar displays relative to those which were pictorially different but conceptually similar but this effect disappeared at the longer ISIs. Conversely, there was an effect of semantic similarity, defined as the RT difference between non-confusable pairs and visually dissimilar but semantically similar pairs, at the longer but not at the shorter ISIs. This result is the opposite of what might be expected if subjects spent the ISI in generating a well-formed pictorial code. It may be that matching is achieved by maintaining an object description at the level of the semantic register, and that perceptual features are lost from the register at the longer ISIs.

(4) Operations on pictorial codes

Information established in the pictorial coding register can be subjected to spatial transformations, such as rotation or change of size. This can be demonstrated in studies of same–different judgments about pairs of pictures, and by adapting the methods of Cooper and Shepard (1973). Using the same–different method, Bundesen and Larsen (1975) obtained RTs for judgments of physical identity of pairs of random forms which differed in size. They found that the RT was linearly related to the ratio of the sizes of the two shapes, and considered that this effect might be an index of a process of size transformation. Determination of pictorial equivalence may, therefore, depend on prior normalization of size discrepancies rather than on direct extraction of size-invariant properties. Bundesen and Larsen's finding that the size ratio effect occurred for both "same" and "different" judgments is consistent with this conclusion. However, this result conflicts with some findings of Besner and Coltheart (1976) which demonstrate that "same" RT to match random forms is affected by size difference but that "different" RT is not. It is possible, therefore, that size difference is a form of pictorial dissimilarity which influences threshold adjustment in the "same" and "different" decision-makers, as proposed in the Schaeffer and Wallace model for semantic comparisons (see for instance, Seymour, 1975).

With regard to orientation, Shepard and Metzler (1971) obtained RTs for matching relatively complex forms (representations of three-dimensional objects made up of cubical blocks) which had been rotated relative to one another through angles of 0°–180° in the picture plane or in depth. The RT to indicate that two forms were "same" was found to be a linear function of the angular difference between them, the slope of the RT function being about 17 msec per degree. It seems very likely that this is an index of the occurrence of a mental rotation process of the kind described by Cooper and Shepard (1973), and this conclusion was supported by the introspections of the subjects. Cooper (1975) has described a further experiment in which subjects were taught to regard certain random polygons as standard forms and to discriminate these from their mirror images. The subjects then participated in a reaction time study in which the forms were displayed at angles of 0°, 60°, 120° or 180° displacement from the upright. Cooper reported that RT for identification of both normal and reflected forms was a linear function of angular displacement with a slope of just over 2 msec per degree. This estimate of rate of mental rotation is considerably faster than the one obtained by Shepard and Metzler, but is quite similar to that obtained by Cooper and Shepard for well-learned symbols. In a second experiment, Cooper recorded the time which subjects required to prepare for a rotated form which was presented when the subject signalled that he was ready. Preparation time was found to be a linear function of the angle of rotation but, following preparation, RTs to classify forms as normal or mirror image showed no effect of displacement from the upright.

Cooper and Shepard (1975) have recently reported an experiment in which subjects discriminated between pictures of left and right hands presented palm uppermost or back uppermost in various orientations; the subjects were to imagine that the hand was one of their own, held up in front of the face. In the absence of advance information, the left/right discrimination was made fastest for hands with the fingers pointing upwards, and least rapidly for hands with the fingers pointing downwards, producing non-linear function of the kind obtained by Cooper and Shepard (1973) for symbols. It appeared that the subjects made the discrimination by manoeuvering a "phantom" of their preferred hand into the orientation of the test picture. The difficulty encountered with inverted hands may, therefore, relate to the physical awkwardness of placing one's own hand in a fingers down position. As in the other studies, Cooper and Shepard were able to show that subjects could prepare a model of a hand in a particular orientation. On trials in which advance information was given, they were shown a thumbless and featureless outline of a hand in the orientation in which the test stimulus would appear. They were instructed to imagine a particular view (palm or back) of a particular hand (left or right) in the orientation given, the four possible hand views being tested in different trial blocks. When the test hand was in the expected form, classification was rapid and unrelated to orientation. However, when the presented hand differed from the expectation in terms of identity, side, or both, the level of the RT was raised, and the effect of orientation was reinstated.

Additional evidence of occurrence of manipulatory operations on pictorial information is given by Shepard and Feng (1972) in a study in which subjects were shown pictures of arrangements of six squares which could be folded to make a cube. The subjects were instructed to fold the cube mentally, and to determine in doing so whether arrows printed on the sides of two squares would meet point to point. The arrows were placed so that the number of mental folding operations required to determine this question varied. Shepard and Feng reported that the RT to decide whether or not the arrows would touch was an approximately linear function of the number of mental folding operations required to bring the sizes containing the arrows into conjunction. A second factor influencing the RT was the size of the structure of squares which was also involved in each folding operation; and Shepard and Feng found that the best prediction of the RT was given by weighting each folding operation by the number of squares to be shifted, and by taking a total of these scores as an index of the difficulty of a particular problem.

In these experiments by Shepard and his associates the inference that variations in RT reflect the occurrence of operations on pictorial information is quite compelling, since the tasks are those traditionally used to study spatial abilities, and since it is generally difficult to formulate non-pictorial accounts of the processing underlying successful performance. Converging evidence has been provided by Brooks (1968), who has demonstrated that spatially-based response processes may disrupt operations on pictorial codes. He has used a serial categorization task in which the subject is required to classify points on a memorized diagram, reporting, for example, whether or not each point is at the upper or lower extreme of the figure. The responses may be verbal, that is, a sequence of "Yes" and "No" reports, or may require spatial monitoring, as when the subjects must point successively to "y" and "n" symbols which appear at varying positions in the rows of a matrix. Brooks reported that the task was more difficult with spatially monitored than with verbal report. By contrast, classification of the words in a memorized sentence was more difficult with verbal than with spatially monitored report. This finding can be cited as support for the general distinction between pictorial and lexical memory which has been proposed by Paivio and others. It also appears consistent with the suggestion made in Fig. 2.1 that output and representational codes may compete for space in a single modality-specific register. In fact, Anderson and Bower (1973) quote some unpublished evidence which suggests that Brooks' visual interference effect may derive from incongruity in eye-movements required in scanning the response sheet and implicit or overt eye-movements involved in maintenance and inspection of a visual image.

When a scene containing a number of spatially-related objects is coded in the pictorial register the subjects may carry out an operation of shifting attention from one object to another. This can be informally demonstrated by sitting in a familiar room with eyes closed and visualizing the part of the room towards which the eyes are pointing; if the eyes are shifted, the imagery alters to show objects in the new line of potential regard (Berlyne, 1965). These alterations in the focus of imagery appear analogous to the changes of fixation occurring during visual search and to the attentional scanning processes postulated for retrieval from the icon (Heron, 1957; Sperling, 1960; Mewhort, Merikle and Bryden, 1969). Their rate of functioning can be

estimated from RT measurements in tasks which require shifts of attention across locations on a complex pictorial representation. For
example, Kosslyn (1973) showed subjects line drawings of fairly complex objects, such as a speedboat or aeroplane, and ten of these were
committed to memory. In the experimental task the names of the
objects were presented auditorily, followed after 5 sec by the name of
a part or property. The subject pressed a "yes" key if the property was
part of the object, and a "no" key if it was not. Subjects in different
groups were instructed to prepared a verbal description or an imaginal
representation of each object, either holistic in form or with focus on
a particular part of the description or image. The properties to be
verified were all located at the centre or at the extremities (upper,
lower; left, right) of the objects. Kosslyn reported that there were no
effects of position under the holistic instructions, but that, under focus
instructions, RT increased as a function of the distance of the named
property from the point of focus. This occurred for both imagery and
verbalization instructions, but the slope relating RT to distance was
much steeper for subjects in the verbal condition (399 msec per step
vs. 168 msec per step). Kosslyn concluded that the RT was an index
of the time required to shift attention from the point of focus to the
probed position.

An alternative technique of making the same kind of measurement
has recently been described by Lea (1975). Subjects were shown how to
use the method of loci in remembering a list of concrete nouns. This
is a classical mnemonic technique by which items are committed to
memory by attaching them, often through use of imagery, to a series
of familiar locations (Bower, 1970). Lea used campus buildings which
were well known to his subjects in one experiment, and a picture of a
circular array of twelve objects set in a park-like scene for two others.
When the subjects had learned to associate a word with each location
they were tested on speed of naming either the location or the word
which lay a specified number of steps from a starting location. It was
found that the RT was a linear function of the number of intervening
locations, the slope being 643 msec per step in the campus experiment,
and 960 msec per step and 1139 msec per step for the experiments
on a memorized circular array. The RT functions for location retrieval
and retrieval of the word associated with a location were parallel, but
word retrieval was slower by a constant amount, 373 msec in the first
experiment, and 972 msec in the third. Lea argues that these results
are consistent with a "processing stages" model in which an operation
of shifting serially from one location to the next precedes an operation of retrieving the word associated with the target location.

(5) OBJECT NAMING

It has been argued in this section that pictorial memory and lexical memory are functionally distinct systems, at least at the level of representation implied by the graphemic/phonemic registers on the one hand, and the pictorial register on the other. The experimental evidence for this proposition can be found in the demonstrations of pictorial and verbal coding, and of the occurrence of rotation and scanning operations on pictorial codes. The memories are also supposed to be distinct at the level of the interface structures, referred to as the logogen and iconogen systems, but not at the level of a pictorially-based semantic system. The semantic codes are accessible via the logogen and iconogen systems, and can serve as input to both systems in retrieval of speech or graphic codes. For this reason it is possible for the semantic system to function as a "bridge" between the lexical and pictorial memories.

This bridging function is most evident in verbal-pictorial comparison tasks and in tasks which require conversion of an input to one memory system to an output from the other. Some discussion of verbal-pictorial comparison was included in section IV (3), and it was concluded there that equivalence of words and pictures is often determined by matching semantic codings of values on various dimensions, many of which concern perceptual properties. Conversion between the memory systems occurs in naming tasks, where the input is a picture and the output is a spoken name or description, and in construction tasks, where the input is a spoken or written sentence and the output is a drawing, image or other construction. The present discussion will focus on the pictorial-verbal conversion involved in naming, since this topic has been more thoroughly investigated than construction.

In an earlier paper the author suggested that the naming of an object might involve the processing stages shown in Fig. 2.5 (Seymour, 1973a). At a first stage a description of visible characteristics of the object is formed in the pictorial register, following extraction of information from the icon. The duration of this preliminary encoding operation should be sensitive to visual variables, such as exposure duration, picture quality, etc. At a second stage a semantic description of the picture is retrieved and placed in the semantic register. This pictorial-semantic conversion depends on input of pictorial information to the iconogens. It is expected, therefore, that the duration of the stage will be influenced by factors which determine the evidence requirements of the iconogen units such as familiarity of the object. Also, it should be possible to magnify these effects by reducing the rate of flow of information into the system, either by reducing stimulus

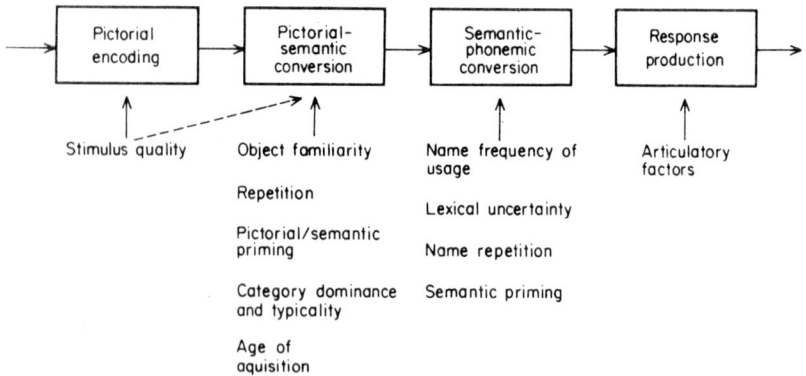

Fig. 2.5. "Processing stages" model for object naming.

quality or by presenting an object in a non-standard orientation or viewpoint. At a third stage, semantic features flow from the semantic register into the logogen system until the threshold for phonemic retrieval in a particular unit is exceeded and a speech code is placed in the phonemic register. The duration of this stage should, in its turn, be affected by the rate at which relevant evidence enters the logogen system, and by factors influencing the evidence requirements of the logogens, such as name frequency of usage, recency of name production, and semantic priming. These effects should also be enhanced if the rate of input of relevant semantic features is reduced. Finally, at a fourth stage, the contents of the phonemic register are sent to a speech output system, and the name of the object is produced as an audible vocalization.

Unfortunately all the experiments which would be required to determine the validity of this model have not yet been undertaken. The model merely provides some guesses about the manner in which object naming might be accommodated in a system of the logogen type (Seymour, 1973a). However, there appear to be two major aspects of the model which can be discussed in relation to the available research. The first of these is the assumption that retrieval of semantic information is a necessary stage occurring between visual analysis of an object and choice of an appropriate name. The second is the view that a name for an object can be directly retrieved from a content-addressable store (the phonemic data store) as soon as the evidence level in a logogen unit exceeds a threshold value. Both of these assumptions are in conflict with the conclusions about object naming reached by Oldfield (1966). He referred to an experiment by Wingfield in which subjects named line drawings of objects the names of which varied in frequency of usage. It was found that the RT was linearly related to the logarithm of the frequency of the object name (Oldfield and Wingfield, 1965). In attempting to explain this relationship, Oldfield proposed a two-stage model in which the general familiarity of the object was assessed at a first stage, and a search through an array of names of the appropriate frequency class was conducted at the second stage. The model fits the data quite well, because it can be shown that if object names are sorted into some arbitrary number of classes with respect to their Thorndike-Lorge frequency of usage the size of the ensemble of names in each class is inversely related to its frequency level (see Zipf. 1935). Oldfield made a count of the number of object names occurring in each of seven frequency classes, and plotted object naming RT in relation to $\log_2$ of the ensemble size for each frequency class. If the AA and A frequency classes are disregarded, this yields a linear relation between RT and log ensemble size, such that $RT = 373 + 58(\log_2 N)$ msec, where N is the estimated size of the set of object names in each frequency range. It can then be supposed that the intercept value of 373 msec represents, among other things, the time needed to assess the familiarity of the object, and that the slope value of 58 msec is the time for each of a succession of binary decisions required to isolate the one appropriate name in an ensemble of N possibilities.

Oldfield's formulation can be criticized on two counts: firstly, it treats name retrieval as a serial search process, whereas much of the evidence considered in Section III suggests that lexical memory may be a content-addressable system; secondly, the model contains no interpretative stage mediating between visual analysis and name selection, so that there is an implicit assumption that there is one definite name for each object. However, it is well-known that the manner in which an object is named or described depends on the act of reference which is being undertaken (Olson, 1970), and that each object can be labelled by a variety of names or descriptions; for instance, a picture of a tulip might be called "tulip", "flower", "plant", "green", "red", "beautiful", "drooping", etc. In the earlier paper, Seymour (1973a) suggested that these conceptual arguments in favour of a semantic conversion process in object naming were supported by well-established findings concerning RT differences between naming and reading. It has been known since the time of Cattell that subjects can vocalize names for objects, shapes or colours less rapidly than they can read the printed names of those stimuli (Fraisse, 1964, 1969). An effect of this kind is consistent with the structural model proposed in this chapter, since phonemic codes for word stimuli are retrieved directly by input of graphemic features to the logogen system, whereas naming of an object involves the more complex operations of retrieval of semantic descriptions, and input of semantic features to the logogens.

Fraisse's investigations have demonstrated that the naming-reading difference is related to uncertainty (size of the ensemble of stimuli used in an experiment) and to word frequency, and that it occurs in part because both of these variables have much greater effects on naming than on reading RT (Fraisse, 1964; Gholson and Hohle, 1968). Fraisse has also presented evidence which helps to exclude accounts of the naming-reading difference which are stated in terms of peripheral processes of response production or stimulus encoding. In an experiment in which RT to read object names is compared with RT to name the objects the response processes are common to the two tasks, indicating that the effect arises at a stage prior to response production. However, Fraisse has also shown that visual duration thresholds are similar for words and pictures, and that the two classes of stimuli produce comparable simple RTs when subjects press a key to indicate that the display has been identified. He has also held stimulus analysis processes constant by obtaining RTs to name a single shape, the circle, as a member of sets of digits, letters, or geometric shapes. The circle was named as "oh" or "zero" consistently faster than as "circle", although the production times for these responses were shown to be approximately equivalent in control experiments. It seems likely, therefore, that the naming-reading difference is a central effect, and Seymour's (1973a) proposal was that it indexed the occurrence of a semantic retrieval stage.

If this proposition is accepted it becomes necessary to reconsider Oldfield's interpretation of the word frequency effect in object naming. In the Seymour model, an effect of object familiarity might be expected to occur at the stage of pictorial-semantic conversion, and an effect of name frequency at the stage of semantic-phonemic conversion. If object familiarity and name frequency are correlated (see for instance, Wingfield, 1966), it follows that the whole of the frequency effect cannot be attributed to the operation of a lexical search process. Indeed, subsequent research has suggested that name frequency is a less important factor in determining object naming RT than Oldfield had thought. For example, Carroll and White (1973) obtained naming RTs for a sample of ninety-four pictures of objects, and correlated the RT against two measures of name frequency (Thorndike and Lorge, 1944; Kucera and Francis, 1967), length of the object name in letters or in syllables, and two estimates of the *age of acquisition* of the object name, obtained from a rating study and from word counts of children's vocabulary. Carroll carried out a multiple regression analysis of the correlation between naming RT and each of these variables. This indicated that frequency of usage and word length were relatively unimportant as predictors of the RT, but that the RT was related to the measures of age of acquisition, RT being fastest for the names which had resided longest in memory. As Carroll has commented, Oldfield's lexical search model might be preserved in face of this finding if it could be shown that acquisition of new vocabulary becomes increasingly extensive with advancing age. However, he doubts this and is therefore inclined to reject the lexical search model. The alternative he suggests is that the vocabulary store is a structure in which old words are stored at the centre with newer words being added around the peripheries; if retrieval was a search process which worked outward from the centre of the store, an age of acquisition effect on naming RT could be obtained. Another possibility is that the age of acquisition measures indicate the age at which a usable semantic description of an object class was first constructed. This could involve the selection of relevant semantic dimensions for description of the appearance and function of the object, and also the formation of a unit in the logogen system and an associated entry in the phonemic data store. The age of acquisition effect might then reflect ease of retrieval of well-established semantic configurations, and perhaps the strength of the components of this description as input evidence for the logogen corresponding to the object's most common name.

This latter statement raises the problem of selectivity and variability in naming. In the studies by Oldfield, Fraisse and Carroll an attempt was made to select pictures which were likely to be named in the same way by most subjects. However, Carroll and White (1973) found some cases of disagreement among subjects as to the appropriate name for a picture; for instance, a parrot was named as "bird" by half the subjects in the sample, and a bugle was named as "trumpet" by thirteen out of thirty-seven subjects. Lachman (1973) has suggested that the variability in the names provoked by pictures may be estimated from normative studies in which subjects indicate their choice of a best name for each picture. Variability can be quantified as an information theoretic measure of uncertainty which expresses the number of different names given to a picture, and their relative frequencies of occurrence. This uncertainty measure will be high for pictures which attract a variety of names (for instance, a picture of the Parthenon is named as "parthenon", "temple", "ruin", "building", etc.), and low for pictures which attract a single name with high regularity (for instance, "apple", "camera", etc.), When object naming RTs are obtained for pictures which differ in lexical uncertainty, a discontinuity is found at a level of approximately two bits of information, and the RT increases as a function of uncertainty (Lachman, 1973; Lachman, Shaffer and Hennrikus, 1974).

In assessing effects of name frequency and age of acquisition Lachman has used the subjects' own ratings of the experimental series of pictures in addition to the objective measures employed by Carroll and White (1973). In general, objects showing low lexical uncertainty have names which are rated as being frequently used and as being acquired early in life (at 6–7 years of age on average). Nevertheless, if these differences are controlled in *post hoc* analyses of the data of each individual subject, there remains a strong effect of lexical uncertainty on the RT. It appears, therefore, that this is an additional factor which must be taken into account in formulating a model of the naming process. One possibility is that objects which yield high lexical uncertainty scores in the normative studies are objects having semantic descriptions which are somewhat equivocal in their effects on the logogens. Such descriptions might be partitioned into a number of subsets of properties with each subset providing evidence for a different logogen; this would contrast with semantic descriptions for objects of low lexical uncertainty, where it could be supposed that most components of the description are accepted as input evidence by the one logogen corresponding to the object's most frequently used name. This suggestion is slightly different from Lachman's own proposal, which is that an extra operation of internal construction (possibly equivalent to re-arrangement of parts of a semantic description) is required for high uncertainty objects, but not for low uncertainty objects which have the addresses of their names written in semantic memory system (referred to as the "encyclopaedia" by Lachman). However, if contents of the semantic register are sequentially sampled by the logogens, as proposed in the present model, it is expected that the duration of the semantic-phonemic conversion stage will be affected by the degree of partitioning of semantic components among different logogens. It is tentatively suggested, therefore, that the lexical uncertainty effect arises at this stage.

Bartram (1974) has suggested that some characteristics of the pic-torial/semantic codes involved in object naming can be determined by tests of transfer of training. If, for the sake of argument, the code is a description of properties of an object class, such as chairs, tables, etc., and it is the operation of forming this description which is facilitated by practice, it would be expected that training with single or varied pictures of a particular object would assist naming of another object from the same class. If, on the other hand, the pictorial/semantic code is object-specific, training in naming a particular object might not transfer to naming another object from the same class. The data reported by Bartram suggest that the second of these possibilities is the more nearly correct. He found that if subjects named identical pictures of objects over six blocks of trials and were then switched to naming different viewpoints of these same objects, the level of their RTs was very similar to that of subjects who named varying viewpoints through-out the experiment. Thus, practice in the same picture condition does transfer positively to the varied picture condition, suggesting in-volvement of a code which is specific to a particular object, but not to a particular viewpoint of that object. By contrast, when subjects were trained in the same picture condition and were then switched to naming new members of the same class, the RT initially increased to a level close to that observed at the start of practice, and remained somewhat higher than that of subjects who named different class mem-bers throughout the experiment. These effects also occurred if the subjects were trained to name different viewpoints of single objects. It appears, therefore, that practice in naming a particular object is not helpful for naming new objects from the same class, and leads to some negative transfer.

A final question which will be considered concerns the relationship between the end product of this stage, that is, the description entered into the semantic register, and the name generating units in the logogen system. In general, if the subject is asked the question: "What is this?" and is then shown a picture, the first answer he gives when pressed for time probably identifies the logogen which is maximally affected by the most readily formed semantic description for that object. Objects of low lexical uncertainty typically evoke one name in preference to others which may be equally applicable. For example, a picture of a carnation will be most readily named as "flower", although subjects could use the more specific name "carnation" or the more general name "plant" if asked to do so. From research carried out in Fraisse's laboratory it is known that the RT to produce the name which is typically given as an answer to the question: "What is it?" is gener-ally faster than RTs for more specific or more general names (Fraisse, Lanati, Regnier and Wahl, 1965; Segui and Fraisse, 1968). Fraisse pointed out that members of classes containing perceptually similar objects, such as flowers, trees, fish, birds or breeds of dog, were typic-ally named by the class label rather than by their more specific names; by contrast, members of functionally defined classes, such as weapons, furniture, clothing, tools or musical instruments were more often given a specific name, such as pistol, chair, shirt, in preference to the class name. Seymour (1973a) suggested that in both cases the preferred name was a label for a perceptually homogeneous object class, which he referred to as a *category name*. In the replication of Fraisse's experiments carried out by Hutcheon (1970) it was confirmed that RT for production of the category names "dog", "flower", "hat", "glove", "table" and "bed" was faster by about 80 msec than RTs for more specific names of dogs and flowers, and faster by about 238 msec than RT for production of the superordinate names "clothing" and "furniture" (see Seymour, 1973a; Gellatly and Gregg, 1975).

These findings point to the conclusion that the semantic description of an object will normally contain a predominance of properties which are common to members of the object class. This is at first sight difficult to reconcile with Bartram's results, which suggested that the representation was specific to a particular object. However, Bartram's experiments involved practice with single objects, and it is likely that this led to adjustments at the iconogen level which facilitated semantic retrieval without necessarily changing the content of the description which was retrieved. The importance of object class descriptions has recently been confirmed by Rosch and her associates (Rosch, *et. al.*, 1976. She obtained listings of attributes for class names differing in level of abstraction, for instance, furniture, table, kitchen table. As might be expected the object class name "table" tended to evoke much the same attribute list as did the names of particular types of table, but relatively few of these attributes were also listed for the superordinate "furniture". This was true of other categories of the functional type (musical instruments, tools, clothing, vehicles) and also for "fruit". However, the category names "tree", "fish" and "bird", which Rosch had initially classified as superordinates, had many attributes in common with names of instances; thus "fish", "trout" and "rainbow trout" all provoke much the same attribute list. Rosch has suggested that these perceptually homogeneous object classes might be referred to as *basic objects*. She has presented additional evidence to show that the shapes of objects in such classes are indeed very similar, and that people use a particular set of "motor programmes" in interacting with them.

Object naming in a free situation may, therefore, be thought to involve perceptual analysis of the major visual characteristics of the picture (pictorial encoding) followed by retrieval of an object class description (pictorial-semantic conversion). The object class description appears, from Rosch's data, to be a listing of parts of the object, actions it can perform, and uses to which it can be put. The components of this description approximate the semantic definition of the logogen for the object class name, and converge preferentially on this unit until the name is evoked (semantic-phonemic conversion).

(6) Conclusions

This section has described some research relating to the pictorial component of permanent memory. It has been suggested that codes used in representation of objects can be studied through experiments on pictorial and semantic confusability (Tversky, 1969; Seymour, 1973a); selective visual interference (Brooks, 1968); selective preparation for pictorial events (Scheerer-Neumann, 1974; Cooper and Shepard, 1975); and demonstrations of the occurrence of rotation, scanning or other operations on pictorial content (Cooper, 1975; Lea, 1975; Shepard and Feng, 1972). The major theoretical proposal has been that pictorial memory is functionally distinct from the lexical and symbolic memories but that the two systems are related at the level of a semantic memory system. In agreement with Paivio (1975) and Rosch (1975) it is suggested that the semantic memory is a system for coding characteristics of object classes and modes of interaction with objects, and that it is for this reason sensible to view the semantic memory as having its origins in the pictorial system. The pictorial and semantic memories are related to lexical memory via the logogen system which mediates retrieval of names of object classes as well as allowing words to be interpreted in terms of their referents. It was suggested that the task of naming objects provides a useful situation for the study of semantic coding of objects and name retrieval (Seymour, 1973a; Bartram, 1974).

Developmentally the pictorial system and its semantic structures constitute the oldest and possibly most fundamental part of the human permanent memory. The system derives from the child's earliest conceptualizations of the objects in his environment and presumably provides the semantic base for development of the logogen system.

V. GENERAL CONCLUSIONS

In this chapter an attempt has been made to review a part of a large body of recently conducted research concerned with the information processing capabilities of adult subjects. It has been necessary to be selective in choice of experiments and theoretical issues, and much important work on topics such as short-term memory, episodic memory, problem solving, reading skills, psycholinguistics and hemispheric specialization of function has been omitted. The work which has been discussed illustrates the contemporary preoccupation of cognitive psychologists with questions about information processing stages on the one hand, and internal representational codes on the other.

With respect to "processing stages" the key ideas are to be found in

Sternberg's use of slope and intercept parameters as indices of encoding, comparison and response stages, and in the additive factor method of determining characteristics of stages and their independence one from another. Within the limited domain of short-term symbolic memory the research reported by Sternberg and Briggs has provided impressive demonstrations of additivity of effects, and these constitute the evidence for the model shown in Fig. 2.2. The assumption is made that the stages of encoding, comparison, decision and response selection are distinct mental events which occur in succession and that the duration of each stage can be independently influenced by experimental factors, such as stimulus quality, display and memory set size, response probability and response load.

Researchers working in the fields of lexical, semantic and pictorial memory have also made extensive use of processing stage models. It seemed possible to apply Sternberg's model directly to versions of the memory search task in which arbitrary lists of words or pictures have been used as memory sets, and also to tasks in which the probe is related to the memory set by a semantic rather than a physical association. This suggested that the short-term or "working memory" functions may be similar in symbolic, lexical and pictorial memory. In addition, the work of Shepard and others provides good evidence for the occurrence of spatial operations on pictorial and graphemic codes, and it is likely that these operations may define a processing stage which combines additively with the encoding and response stages.

Where information is stored in long-term or permanent memory theorists have preferred two-stage models of the decision process in which the occurrence of second stage processing is contingent on the outcome of first stage processing. In the Atkinson-Juola model for recognition of members of word lists stored in long-term memory the first stage involves an assessment of the general familiarity of the test word. If the familiarity of the word falls in some intermediate range a second stage process of scanning a list structure held in an event-knowledge store is undertaken; for higher or lower familiarity values positive or negative decisions are made directly on the basis of Stage 1 processing.

The author's own view, which has been expressed at various points throughout the chapter, is that stages in information processing may be thought of as transformations of internal codes. A coding change involves retrieval of information from one of the permanent data stores, and it has been assumed that retrieval is mediated by interface systems, such as the logogen system and the iconogen system. In a model of this kind small RT variations arise from threshold adjustments and priming. A prediction is that factors which influence states of units in the interface systems and the rate of flow of information through these systems will give rise to interactive rather than additive effects. Some evidence to support this conclusion has been presented, and the manner in which the model might be applied to object naming was considered. With respect to classification tasks, the model is closest to Schaeffer and Wallace's (1970) threshold adjustment model (see also, Seymour, 1975). It must be accepted, however, that the implications of the coding change and threshold adjustment model have not yet been rigorously worked out, and this remains a task for the future.

On the question of representational codes, the important ideas concern the techniques for identification of internal codes which have been developed by Posner and others. In the present discussion it has been assumed that there are data stores for permanent retention of symbolic, pictorial and semantic codes, as well as registers into which a currently active code may be entered following sensory input or memory retrieval. The coding registers and their contents are operationally defined in terms of similarity effects on "same" and "different" RT, and in demonstrations of selective preparation or interference effects. It is argued that the experimental findings support a division of permanent memory into independent lexical and pictorial systems which are inter-related by an overlying semantic system. The semantic component is viewed as a system for classification of characteristics of objects and object classes and, as such, relates more closely to the pictorial than to the lexical memory.

REFERENCES

Anderson, J. R. and Bower, G. H. (1973). *Human Associative Memory.* Washington: Winston.

Atkinson, R. C. and Juola, J. F. (1973). Factors influencing speed and accuracy of word recognition. In S. Kornblum (Ed.), *Attention and Performance, IV.* New York and London: Academic Press.

Bartram, D. J. (1974). The role of visual and semantic codes in object naming. *Cognitive Psychology, 6,* 325–56.

Bartram, D. J. Coding strategies in picture-name and name-picture comparisons. University of Hull (unpublished paper).

Battig, W. F. and Montague, W. E. (1969). Category norms for verbal items in 56 categories: A replication and extension of the Connecticut category norms. *Journal of Experimental Psychology Monograph, 80,* 3.

Berlyne, D. E. (1965). *Structure and Direction in Thinking.* New York: Wiley.

Besner, D, and Coltheart, M. (1976). Mental size scaling examined. *Memory and Cognition* (in press).

Bower, G. H. (1970). Analysis of a mnemonic device, *American Scientist, 58,* 496–510.

Bracey, G. W. (1969). Two operations in character recognition; a partial replication. *Perception and Psychophysics, 6,* 357–60.

Briggs, G. E. and Blaha, J. (1969). Memory retrieval and central comparison times in information processing. *Journal of Experimental Psychology, 79,* 395–402.

Briggs, G. E. and Swanson, J. M. (1970). Encoding, decoding, and central functions in human information processing. *Journal of Experimental Psychology, 86,* 296–308.

Briggs, G. E. and Johnsen, A. M. (1972). On the nature of central processing in choice reactions. *Memory and Cognition, 1,* 91–100.

Broadbent, D. E. (1967). Word frequency effect and response bias. *Psychological Review, 74,* 1–15.

Brooks, L. R. (1968). Spatial and verbal components of the act of recall. *Canadian Journal of Psychology, 22,* 349–68.

Bundesen, C. and Larsen, A. (1975). Visual transformation of size. *Journal of Experimental Psychology: Human Perception and Performance, 1,* 214–20.

Burrows, D. and Okada, R. (1973). Parallel scanning of semantic and formal information. *Journal of Experimental Psychology, 97,* 254–7.

Carpenter, P. A. and Just, M. A. (1975). Sentence comprehension: a psycholinguistic processing model of verification. *Psychological Review, 82,* 45–73.

Carroll, B. and White, M. N. (1973). Word frequency and age of acquisition as determiners of picture-naming latency. *Quarterly Journal of Experimental Psychology, 25,* 85–95.

Carroll, J. D. and Chang, J. J. (1970). Analysis of individual differences in multi-dimensional scaling via an n-way generalisation of "Eckart-Young" decomposition. *Psychometrika, 36,* 283–319.

Cattell, J. M. (1886). The time it takes to see and name objects. *Mind, 11,* 63–5.

Chase, W. G. and Calfee, R. C. (1969). Modality and similarity effects in short-term recognition memory. *Journal of Experimental Psychology, 81,* 510–14.

Clark, H. H. (1973). The language-as-fixed-effect fallacy: A critique of language statistics in psychological research. *Journal of Verbal Learning and Verbal Behavior, 12*, 335–59.

Clark, H. H. and Chase, W. G. (1972). On the process of comparing sentences against pictures. *Cognitive Psychology, 3*, 472–517.

Clifton, C. and Tash, J. (1973). Effect of syllabic word length on memory-search rate. *Journal of Experimental Psychology, 99*, 231–5.

Cohen, G. (1969). Some evidence for parallel comparisons in a letter recognition task. *Quarterly Journal of Experimental Psychology, 21*, 272–9.

Cole, R. A., Coltheart, M. and Allard, F. (1974). Memory of a speaker's voice: reaction time to same- or different-voiced letters. *Quarterly Journal of Experimental Psychology, 26*, 1–7.

Collins, A. M. and Quillian, M. R. (1969). Retrieval time from semantic memory. *Journal of Verbal Learning and Verbal Behavior, 8*, 240–7.

Collins, A. M. and Quillian, M. R. (1970). Does category size affect categorization time? *Journal of Verbal Learning and Verbal Behavior, 9*, 432–8.

Coltheart, M. (1972). Visual information processing. In P. C. Dodwell (Ed.), *New Horizons in Psychology, 2*. Harmondsworth: Penguin Books.

Conrad, C. (1972). Cognitive economy in semantic memory. *Journal of Experimental Psychology, 92*, 149–54.

Cooper, L. A. (1975). Mental rotation of random two-dimensional shapes. *Cognitive Psychology, 7*, 20–43

Cooper, L. A. and Shepard, R. N. (1973). Chronometric studies of the rotation of mental images. In W. G. Chase (Ed.), *Visual Information Processing*. New York and London: Academic Press.

Cooper, L. A. and Shepard, R. N. (1975). Mental transformations in the identification of left and right hands. *Journal of Experimental Psychology: Human Perception and Performance, 104*, 48–56.

Craik, F. I. M. and Lockhart, R. S. (1972). Levels of processing: A framework for memory research. *Journal of Verbal Learning and Verbal Behavior, 11*, 671–84.

Crowder, R. G. and Morton, J. (1969). Precategorical acoustic storage (PAS). *Perception and Psychophysics, 5*, 365–73.

DeRosa, D. V. and Morin, R. E. (1970). Recognition and reaction time for digits in consecutive and nonconsecutive memorized sets. *Journal of Experimental Psychology, 83*, 472–9.

Eriksen, C. W. and Collins, J. F. (1969). Visual perceptual rate under two conditions of search. *Journal of Experimental Psychology, 80*, 489–92.

Forbach, G. B., Stanners, R. F. and Hochhaus, L. (1974). Repetition, and practice effects in a lexical decision task. *Memory and Cognition, 2*, 337–9.

Fraisse, P. (1964). Le temps de réaction verbale: I. Dénomination et lecture. *L'Année Psychologique, 64*, 21–46.

Fraisse, P. (1969). Why is naming longer than reading? *Acta Psychologica, 30*, 96–103.

Fraisse, P., Lanati, L., Regnier, J. and Wahl M. (1965). Le temps de réaction verbale. II. Réponses specifiques et categorielles. *L'Année Psychologique, 65*, 27–32.

Gellatly, A. R. H. and Gregg, V. H. (1975). The effects of negative relatedness upon word-picture and word-word comparisons and subsequent recall. *British Journal of Psychology, 66*, 311–23.

Geyer, L. H. and DeWald, C. G. (1973). Feature lists and confusion matrices. *Perception and Psychophysics, 14*, 471–82.

Gholson, B. and Hohle, R. H. (1968). Verbal reaction times to hues vs hue names and forms vs form names. *Perception and Psychophysics*, *3*, 191–6.

Gibson, E. J. (1965). Learning to read. *Science*, *148*, 1066–72.

Gibson, E. J. (1970). The ontogeny of reading. *American Psychologist*, *25*, 136–43.

Gibson, E. J., Gibson, J. J., Pick, A. D. and Osser, H. (1962). A developmental study of the discrimination of letter-like forms. *Journal of Comparative and Physiological Psychology*, *55*, 897–906.

Guilford, J. P. (1967). *The Nature of Human Intelligence*. New York: McGraw Hill.

Harris, G. J. and Fleer, R. E. (1974). High speed memory scanning in mental retardates: evidence for a central processing deficit. *Journal of Experimental Child Psychology*, *17*, 452–9.

Hawkins, H. L. (1969). Parallel processing in complex visual discrimination. *Perception and Psychophysics*, *5*, 56–64.

Henley, N. M. (1969). A psychological study of the semantics of animal terms. *Journal of Verbal Learning and Verbal Behavior*, *8*, 176–84.

Heron, W. (1957). Perception as a function of retinal locus and attention. *American Journal of Psychology*, *70*, 38–48.

Hershberger, W. A., Trantina, P. R. and Cosgrove, K. (1968). Letter-naming time as a function of set familiarity and symbol distinctiveness. *Quarterly Journal of Experimental Psychology*, *20*, 395–9.

Hoving, K. L., Morin, R. E. and Konick, D. S. (1970). Recognition reaction time and size of the memory set: a developmental study. *Psychonomic Science*, *21*, 247–8

Humphrey, G. (1951). *Thinking: An Introduction to its Experimental Psychology*. London: Methuen.

Hutcheon, E. G. (1970). An investigation into stimulus classification under varying instructions. Dundee University (unpublished M.A. Thesis).

Jacobson, J. Z. (1973). Effects of association upon masking and reading latency. *Canadian Journal of Psychology*, *27*, 58–69.

James, C. T. (1975). The role of semantic information in lexical decisions. *Journal of Experimental Psychology: Human Perception and Performance*, *104*, 130–6.

Juola, J. F. and Atkinson, R. C. (1971). Memory scanning for words versus categories. *Journal of Verbal Learning and Verbal Behavior*, *10*, 522–7.

Kirsner, K. and Craik, F. I. M. (1971). Naming and decision processes in short-term recognition memory. *Journal of Experimental Psychology*, *88*, 149–57.

Kolers, P. A. (1970). Three stages of reading. In H. Levin and J. Williams (Eds.), *Basic Studies on Reading*. New York: Basic Books.

Kosslyn, S. M. (1973). Scanning visual images: some structural implications. *Perception and Psychophysics*, *14*, 90–4.

Kreuger, L. E. (1972). Sentence-picture comparison: a test of additivity of processing time for feature matching and negation coding. *Journal of Experimental Psychology*, *95*, 275–84.

Kucera, H. and Francis, W. N. (1967). *Computational Analysis of Present-day American English*. Providence R.I: Brown University Press.

Lachman, R. (1973). Uncertainty effects on time to access the internal lexicon. *Journal of Experimental Psychology*, *99*, 199–208.

Lachman, R., Shaffer, J. P. and Hennrikus, D. (1974). Language and cognition: effects of stimulus codability, name-word frequency, and age of acquisition on lexical reaction time. *Journal of Verbal Learning and Verbal Behavior*, *31*, 613–25.

Landauer, T. K. and Meyer, D. E. (1972). Category size and semantic memory retrieval. *Journal of Verbal Learning and Verbal Behavior*, *11*, 539–49.

Lea, G. (1975). Chronometric analysis of the method of loci. *Journal of Experimental Psychology: Human Perception and Performance*, *104*, 95–104.

Leech, G. N. (1969). *Towards a Semantic Description of English*. London: Longman.

Loftus, E. F. (1973). Category dominance, instance dominance, and categorization time. *Journal of Experimental Psychology*, *97*, 70–4.

Loftus, E. F. and Scheff, R. W. (1971). Categorization norms for 50 representative instances. *Journal of Experimental Psychology*, *91*, 355–64.

McFarland, C. E., Kellas, G., Klueger, K. and Juola, J. F. (1974). Category similarity, instance dominance, and categorization time. *Journal of Verbal Learning and Verbal Behavior*, *13*, 698–708.

Mewhort, D. J., Merikle, P. M. and Bryden, M. (1969). On the transfer from iconic to short-term memory. *Journal of Experimental Psychology*, *81*, 89–94.

Meyer, D. E. and Schvanevcldt, R. W. (1971). Facilitation in recognising pairs of words: Evidence of a dependence between retrieval operations. *Journal of Experimental Psychology*, *90*, 227–34.

Meyer, D. E., Schvaneveldt, R. W. and Ruddy, M. G. (1972). Activation of lexical memory. Paper presented at the meeting of the Psychonomic Society, St. Louis, Missouri, November 1972.

Meyer, D. E., Schvaneveldt, R. W. and Ruddy, M. G. (1974). Functions of graphemic and phonemic codes in visual word-recognition. *Memory and Cognition. 2*, 309–23.

Miller, G. A., Galanter, E. and Pribram, K. H. (1960). *Plans and the Structure of Behavior*. New York: Holt, Rinehart and Winston.

Millward, R. B., Rice, G. and Corbett, A. (1975). Category production measures and verification times. In R. A. Kennedy and A. L. Wilkes (Eds.), *Studies in Long Term Memory*. London: Wiley.

Morton, J. (1964). The effects of context on the visual duration threshold for words. *British Journal of Psychology*, *55*, 165–80.

Morton, J. (1968). Grammar and computation in language behavior. Progress Report No. 6, Centre for Research in Language and Language Behavior, University of Michigan, May 1968.

Morton, J. (1969). Interaction of information in word recognition. *Psychological Review*, *76*, 165–78.

Morton, J. (1970). A functional model for memory. In D. A. Norman (Ed.), *Models of Human Memory*. New York and London: Academic Press.

Moyer, R. S. (1973). Comparing objects in memory: evidence suggesting an internal psychophysics. *Perception and Psychophysics*, *13*, 180–4.

Moyer, R. S. and Landauer, T. K. (1967). Time required for judgements of numerical inequality. *Nature*, *215*, 1519–20.

Murrell, G. A. and Morton, J. (1974). Word recognition and morphemic structure. *Journal of Experimental Psychology*, *102*, 963–8.

Neisser, U. (1963). Decision time without reaction time: experiments in visual scanning. *American Journal of Psychology*, *76*, 376–85.

Neisser, U. (1967). *Cognitive Psychology*. New York: Appleton-Century-Crofts.

Neisser, U. and Beller H. (1965). Searching through word lists. *British Journal of Psychology*, *56*, 349–58.

Newell, A. (1973). You can't play twenty questions with nature and win. In W. G. Chase (Ed.), *Visual Information Processing*. New York and London: Academic Press.

Novik, N. (1974). Parallel processing in a word-nonword classification task. *Journal of Experimental Psychology, 102*, 1015–20.

Oldfield, R. C. (1966). Things, words and the brain. *Quarterly Journal of Experimental Psychology, 18*, 3–16.

Oldfield, R. C. and Wingfield A. (1965). Response latencies in naming objects. *Quarterly Journal of Experimental Psychology, 17*, 273–81.

Olson, D. R. (1970). Language and thought: aspects of a cognitive theory of semantics. *Psychological Review, 77*, 257–73.

Olson, D. R. and Filby, N. (1972). On the comprehension of active and passive sentences. *Cognitive Psychology, 3*, 361–81.

Paivio, A. (1975). Perceptual comparisons through the mind's eye. *Memory and Cognition, 3*, 635–47.

Paivio, A., Yuille, J. C. and Madigan, S. (1968). Concreteness, imagery and meaningfulness values for 925 nouns. *Journal of Experimental Psychology Monographs, 76* (1, Pt. 2).

Palmer, S. E. (1975). The effects of contextual scenes on the identification of objects. *Memory and Cognition, 3*, 519–26.

Parkman, J. M. (1971). Temporal aspects of digit and letter inequality judgments. *Journal of Experimental Psychology, 91*, 191–205.

Pollack, I. (1963). Verbal reaction times to briefly presented words. *Perceptual and Motor Skills, 17*, 137–8.

Posner, M. I., Boies, S. J., Eichelman, W. H. and Taylor, R. L. (1969). Retention of visual and name codes of single letters. *Journal of Experimental Psychology Monograph, 79*, 1–16.

Posner, M. I. and Mitchell, R. F. (1967). Chronometric analysis of classification. *Psychological Review, 74*, 392–409.

Rips, L. J. (1975). Quantification and semantic memory. *Cognitive Psychology, 7*, 307–40.

Rips, L. J., Shoben, E. J. and Smith, E. E. (1973). Semantic distance and the verification of semantic relations. *Journal of Verbal Learning and Verbal Behavior, 12*, 1–20.

Rosch, E. (1973). On the internal structure of perceptual and semantic categories. In T. M. Moore (Ed.), *Cognitive Development and the Acquisition of Language*. New York: Academic Press.

Rosch, E. (1975). Cognitive representations of semantic categories. *Journal of Experimental Psychology: General, 104*, 192–233.

Rosch, E., Mervis, C. B., Gray, W., Johnson, D. and Boyes-Braem, P. (1976). Basic objects in natural categories. *Cognitive Psychology*.

Rubenstein, H., Garfield, L. and Millikan, J. A. (1970). Homographic entries in the internal lexicon. *Journal of Verbal Learning and Verbal Behavior, 9*, 487–94.

Rubenstein, H., Lewis, S. S. and Rubenstein, M. A. (1971). Evidence for phonemic recording in visual word recognition. *Journal of Verbal Learning and Verbal Behavior, 10*, 645–57.

Schaeffer, B. and Wallace, R. (1969). Semantic similarity and the comparison of word meanings. *Journal of Experimental Psychology, 82*, 343–6.

Schaeffer, B. and Wallace, R. (1970). The comparison of word meanings. *Journal of Experimental Psychology, 86*, 144–52.

Scheerer-Neumann, G. (1974). Formation and utilization of the visual and verbal codes of pictures and words. *Psychological Research, 37,* 81–106.

Segui, J. and Fraisse, P. (1968). Le temps de réaction verbale, III: Réponses specifiques et réponses categorielles à des stimulus-objets. *L'Année Psychologique, 68,* 69–82.

Seymour, P. H. K. (1973). A model for reading, naming and comparison. *British Journal of Psychology, 64,* 35–49. (a).

Seymour, P. H. K. (1973). Semantic representation of shape names. *Quarterly Journal of Experimental Psychology, 25,* 265–77. (b).

Seymour, P. H. K. (1973). Stroop interference in naming and verifying spatial locations. *Perception and Psychophysics, 14,* 95–100. (c).

Seymour, P. H. K. (1973). Rule identity classification of name and shape stimuli. *Acta Psychologica, 37,* 131–8. (d).

Seymour, P. H. K. (1975). Semantic equivalence of verbal and pictorial displays. In R. A. Kennedy and A. L. Wilkes (Eds.), *Studies in Long Term Memory.* London: Wiley.

Shepard, R. N. and Metzler, J. (1971). Mental rotation of three-dimensional objects. *Science, 171,* 701–3.

Shepard, R. N. and Feng, C. (1972). A chronometric study of mental paper folding. *Cognitive Psychology, 3,* 228–43.

Smith E. E. (1967). Effects of familiarity on stimulus recognition and categorization. *Journal of Experimental Psychology, 74,* 324–32.

Smith, E. E., Shoben, E. J. and Rips, L. J. (1974). Structure and process in semantic memory: a featural model for semantic decisions. *Psychological Review, 81,* 214–41.

Smith, F. and Carey P. (1966). Temporal factors in visual information processing. *Canadian Journal of Psychology, 20,* 337–42.

Spencer, T. J. (1969). Some effects of different masking stimuli on iconic storage. *Journal of Experimental Psychology, 81,* 132–40.

Sperling, G. (1960). The information available in brief visual presentations. *Psychological Monographs, 74,* 11.

Sperling, G. (1967). Successive approximations to a model for short-term memory. *Acta Psychologica, 27,* 285–92.

Spoehr, K. T. and Smith E. E. (1973). The role of syllables in perceptual processing. *Cognitive Psychology, 5,* 71–89.

Stanners, R. F. and Forbach, G. B. (1974). Analysis of letter strings in word recognition. *Journal of Experimental Psychology, 98,* 31–5.

Sternberg, S. (1967). Two operations in character recognition: some evidence from reaction time measurements. *Perception and Psychophysics, 2,* 45–53.

Sternberg, S. (1969). The discovery of processing stages: extensions of Donders' method. *Acta Psychologica, 30,* 276–315.

Sternberg, S. (1975). Memory scanning: new findings and current controversies. *Quarterly Journal of Experimental Psychology, 27,* 1–32.

Swanson, J. M. and Briggs, G. E. (1969). Information processing as a function of speed versus accuracy. *Journal of Experimental Psychology, 81,* 223–9.

Thorndike, E. L. and Lorge, I. (1944). *The Teacher's Word Book of 30,000 Words.* New York: Columbia University Press.

Tinker, M. A. (1958). Recent studies of eye movements in reading. *Psychological Bulletin, 55,* 215–31.

Tversky, B. (1969). Pictorial and verbal encoding in a short-term memory task. *Perception and Psychophysics, 6,* 225–33.

Vurpillot, E. (1968). The development of scanning strategies and their relation to visual differentiation. *Journal of Experimental Child Psychology*, *6*, 632–50.

Wilkins, A. J. (1971). Conjoint frequency, category size and categorization time. *Journal of Verbal Learning and Verbal Behavior*, *10*, 382–5.

Wingfield, A. (1966). The identification and naming of objects. University of Oxford (unpublished D.Phil. Thesis).

Wingfield, A. (1968). Effects of frequency on identification and naming of objects. *American Journal of Psychology*, *81*, 226–34.

Zipf, G. K. (1935). *The Psychobiology of Language*. Boston: Houghton Mifflin.

PART II

CHAPTER 3

Development of Attention

Jane F. Mackworth

I. INTRODUCTION

Arousal and attention are neurophysiological states which interact with each other, but are very different in nature. Arousal is a global state which increases from deep unconsciousness to manic excitement or terror. Attention is a selective function with an inverted U-shaped relation to arousal. Arousal depends on the overall level of the organism, but is also affected by incoming stimuli. A new or unexpected stimulus will evoke an orienting response if the state of arousal is suitable. Changes in arousal arise from the reticular activating system of the brain stem. The arousal reaction is therefore very primitive, serving the fight-or-flight mechanism. The orienting reaction is found in very simple organisms. Selective attention, on the other hand, can be considered to be a capacity or quantity of electrochemical energy that is available to be directed by the higher levels of the brain. The frontal lobes in particular can inhibit activity in unwanted areas of the brain, so that attention can be focused on the important event (Pribram, 1971 : N. Mackworth, 1975). Yet attention is only partially controllable, and it is often very difficult to focus on a difficult problem for any length of time. The necessary energy is soon depleted.

Luria (1973) has discussed in detail the work of the Russians on the relationship between the development of attention and the brain. He has pointed out that the frontal lobes develop more slowly than the rest of the brain (see Fig. 3.1). They reach almost full development by about 7 years of age, but continue to increase slowly up to adulthood. Orientation and habituation in early life are biological in origin, arising in the lower regions of the brain, such as the reticular formation and the hippocampus. But voluntary selective attention to a given task is a social act, developed as a result of training.

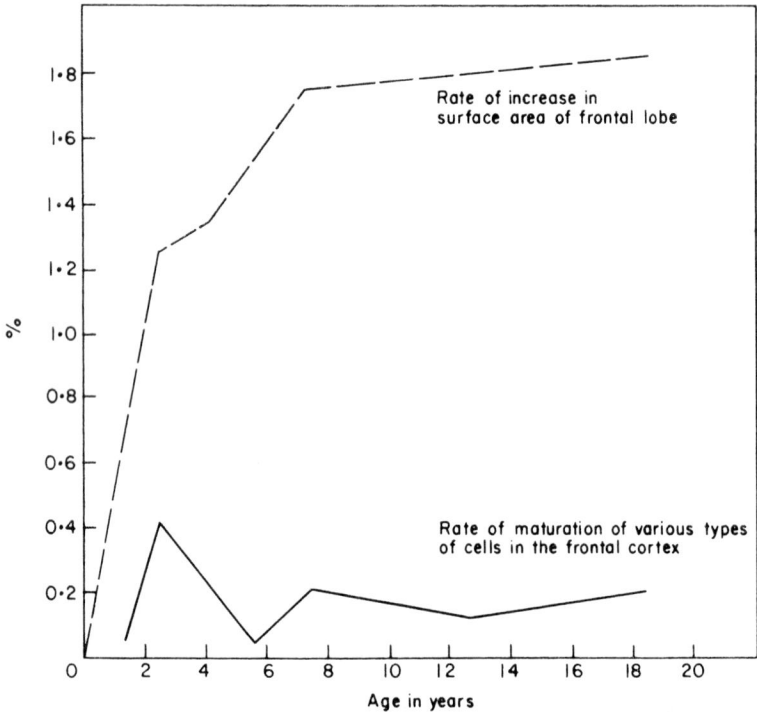

FIG. 3.1. Rate of increase in area of the frontal lobes and rate of increase in size of nerve cells in ontogeny. (*After* Luria, 1973, p. 87.)

It becomes efficient and stable by about 7 years of age, concomitant with the development of the frontal lobes. These are particulary concerned with such voluntary attention. They construct programmes of action and modify them according to the results of actions. During the later stages of development of the lobes, the neurophysiological changes such as the evoked potential become more stable, with the final level of efficiency being reached around 12 years of age.

In additon to active seeking for required information the frontal lobes also control inhibition of attention to unwanted stimuli. Defective frontal lobes lead to impulsive behaviour with restless hyperactivity and an inability to focus attention on the task which is to be attempted. Thus the frontal lobes are the master planners of the brain, instigating attention to the important stimuli and actions, while inhibiting distraction. In addition, they control and coordinate the activities of the rest of the brain, particularly by the use of language. Patients with defective frontal lobes find it impossible to follow instructions.

The young infant, with his infantile frontal lobes, demonstrates the basic reflex of the orienting response and its habituation. The function of the orienting response is to examine the new or unexpected event, and to store it in memory as a model or schema (Sokolov, 1963). Once the internal model has been achieved, habituation to its renewed presentation is rapid.

The energy required to maintain selective attention may be shared between the various attributes of a stimulus in space and time. A stationary object such as a picture will be examined by successive eye fixations so that the brain can construct a composite image of the stimulus. A series of successive inputs, as in reading, may be stored spatially, so that the image of the first input is still present while later stimuli are processed. It seems likely that the initial visual trace or icon can be strengthened by matching with stored memory images. J. F. Mackworth (1963, 1966) has suggested that attention can be divided between the different aspects of a task. For instance, in a memory span task attention must be divided between holding the earlier items in memory and processing later items into store. The amount of attentional energy required to process the visual item into store depends on the familiarity of the relationship between the visual input and the name of the item, and also on the familiarity of the relationship between successive items. Redundancy and the ability to chunk items, as with letters that form words, will greatly increase the number of elementary items that can be stored. This is true for tachistoscopic material as well as for memory experiments.

Attention can be used either as a selective beam (a searchlight focusing on one small area of the input at a time) or as a means of obtaining an overall view of the surroundings. This is true even when the input is auditory. Broadbent (1958, 1970, 1971), Treisman (1960, 1969) and Moray (1959, 1969) have carried out a number of experiments on auditory selective attention. This type of test has recently been used with children by Maccoby and co-workers (see section III, 4). Broadbent (1958) put forward a theory that there is a filter in the brain which allows attention to be paid to one channel of input while attention to other channels in inhibited. This filtering is probably controlled by the frontal lobes as well as by lower areas of the brain (Pribram 1971). The filter can switch between channels (ears) but requires a certain minimum time to make the switch.

Treisman (1960) suggested that there are neural units that respond to single words. When a word is heard, the appropriate neural unit will fire. When a unit fires, the threshold of other units, related in some way to the first, may be lowered, so that these unwanted units may also fire, when the words are heard on the unwanted channel.

Thus she suggested that the brain does not have an absolute filter that completely blocks out unwanted material, but rather there is a relative filtering effect, which allows other material to be attended to in an attenuated fashion. Broadbent (1970) has suggested that there is a difference between stimulus set, the selection of the appropriate channel, and response set, which may incorporate some material from the unwanted ear. Stimulus set affects d', while response set affects *beta*. (See J. F. Mackworth, 1970, for an extended discussion of these measures.) The sensitivity of the observer is measured by d', which indicates the detectability of the signal by the observer; that is, the proportion of signals that are detected. *Beta* measures the criterion, the level of errors that the observer will risk in order to detect as many signals as possible.

Moray and O'Brien (1967) carried out an experiment on the detection of increments in tone bursts. When the subject was asked to listen to both ears simultaneously, it proved to be almost impossible. Moray (1969) commented that discontinuous sampling may be an important factor in aural attention, just as it is in visual processing. He considered that Treisman's model does not deal with this situation. The brain recodes the input in different aspects, such as loudness and pitch. These aspects are then cross-correlated for similarity. The similar aspects are then recoded into a single message. This cross-correlation is assumed to take place well below the level of conscious perception. Selection, competition and integration are included in the final analysis of the encoded material. This model is assumed to be applicable to visual material as well as aural. The model assumes pattern recognition at the highest level, which involves many components or recognizers with different variable thresholds. Conscious awareness may be a response to the output of the recognizers (Deutsch and Deutsch, 1963).

II. THE DEVELOPMENT OF VISUAL ATTENTION IN THE INFANT

(1) STAGES IN DEVELOPMENT

Piaget (1950, 1961) discovered a wide range of developmental and cognitive processes that take place at successive stages of growth of a young child. Bower (1974) has discussed and investigated these processes, in which the attention of a child is directed by his level of cognitive understanding. As the child develops his *object concept* he alters the focus of his attention, predicting what will happen next. The *Stage I infant* (from birth to 2 months of age) looks at an object, but he does not follow it when it moves out of his field of view. The *Stage II infant*, aged 2–4 months, tracks the object as it moves, even when it goes behind a screen. He moves his gaze towards the edge of the screen where he expects to see the object emerge. However, he is not disturbed when a totally different object appears from behind the screen. He defines the identity of a moving object solely in terms of its movement. If the object does not reappear, he demonstrates surprise, as indicated by the cardiac reaction. Since he defines an object in terms of its movement, he sees an object that moves, and then stops, as two different objects. If it then returns to its origin, he sees a further two objects. If it now moves in the opposite direction, he does not track it, but continues to look to the right, hoping to catch it when it stops in the usual place. He simply ignores the object now sitting at his left rather than at his right hand.

The *Stage III infant* (4–6 months) can pick up an object, unless the object is covered by a cloth, Yet he can not understand that a hidden object is still present; he shows surprise when it is found to have disappeared, when the screen is removed. He can co-ordinate place and movement. When presented with a moving object that stops, he stops tracking and remains stopped. Similarly he can follow a stationary object wherever it goes. The *Stage IV infant* (6–12 months) will search for an object under a cloth, but if the object under the cloth is moved to the opposite side, he will keep looking under the flat cloth that has replaced it in the original place. However, he does know that an object can move from place to place, and that two identical objects seen side by side are different objects. The *Stage V infant* (12–15 months) can find an object that has been hidden in two positions successively if he sees the operations of hiding, but not if he does not see the actions. The *Stage VI infant* (15–18 months) can find an object however it is hidden. He has also arrived at a rule that two objects cannot be in the same place simultaneously *unless* one is hidden inside the other.

Bruner (1969) presented a developmental schedule for visual attention in infants. The neonate is attracted by objects and movement, but is easily distractible. By 6 weeks he is "stuck" to the target. He is unable to stop looking at a figure with good figure-ground properties. Later he will begin to anticipate what will occur. His schemata or internal models are developing, and allow him to guess what is coming next. If this expected event does not occur, he will demonstrate the orienting response of surprise, rather than the elementary startle reaction of the neonate, seen when an unexpected event occurs (Charlesworth, 1969). At a month, the infant will move his head in pursuit of an object. At 15–16 weeks (Stages II–III) the infant will actively search for what he expected to find. At 7 months (Stage IV) his eyes will lead or track the hand movements, and at 1 year (Stage V) his eyes will look ahead more often, and are freed from his hand. Now he begins to have biphasic attention : he can register object cues and anticipate other objects. Later still, his visual activity will be increasingly guided by language.

Fantz (1970) has described the various stages that he has found in the development of infants with regard to visual choice. The infant begins well above the minimal complexity level. For instance, premature and full-term infants of about 3–4 days old showed significant preferences (Miranda, 1970). They preferred a dotted pattern over an irregular one and a sharply defined pattern over one in shades of

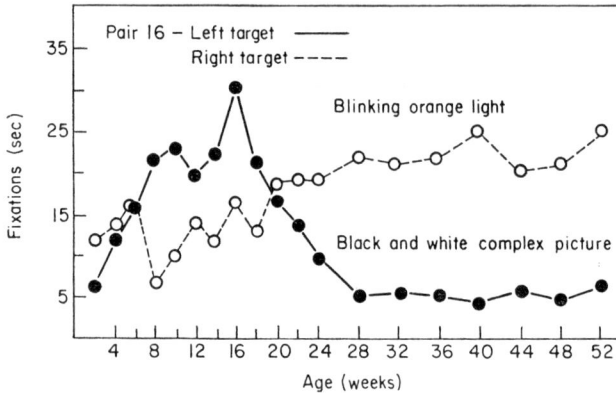

Fig. 3.2. Fixation time for each target of a pair presented for a total of 40 sec, averaged for the same ten infants at each age. (*After* Fantz, 1970.)

grey. The visual system was capable of functioning at least a month before the usual time of birth.

As the child grows older, he chooses more complex, subtle, detailed and novel patterns. Later he prefers solid objects, flashing lights and moving targets (Fig. 3.2). By the end of the first year he pays little attention to patterns, however complex. But interference with the early wide-ranging visual exploration may seriously interfere with later development.

The Stage V–VI child (12–18 months) uses his vision to guide his motor activities. He grasps the object when possible, usually conveys it to his mouth, and manipulates it as much as possible. Now he is building up his schemata into multisensory models. Later on, he returns to an interest in two-dimensional stimuli, but now they are fully meaningful to him. He can link a picture with his internal model of the three-dimensional original. He also attempts to produce his own pictures by scribbles, which may appear meaningless to the onlooker. These scribbles will later develop into the arts of drawing, reading and writing.

Kagan (1971) also carried out a longitudinal study of the behaviour of infants from 4 months to 27 months (Stages III onward). He commented that somewhere between 8 and 12 weeks of age, the degree of discrepancy between the event and a schema or model begins to dominate the effect of the physical parameters of the event. Towards the end of the first year, the density of hypotheses activated to assimilate a discrepant event becomes a primary determinant of fixation time. Kagan pointed out that girls show a greater stability in fixation behaviour than boys. He recorded the total time that the girls and boys spent looking at black-and-white faces at 8 months of age, and compared these times with those spent looking at clay faces at 13 months of age. The fixation times for the girls at 8 months predicted their fixation times at 13 months, but the boys showed very little consistency between the two age levels.

(2) HABITUATION IN INFANCY

Sokolov (1963) has pointed out that the function of the orientation response is to allow the organism to form a scheme or model of a novel event. The very young infant has to develop a great many of these models. He shows the visual orienting response at birth, provided that his eyes are open, but habituation at that early period may be very prolonged. The infant has to construct his visual models from scratch, absorbing every detail, for he has nothing in his brain with which to compare them.

Friedman, Nagy and Carpenter (1970), presented 2×2 and 12×12 black and white checkerboards to forty newborn infants. The male infants showed more rapid habituation than the females when looking at the 2×2 boards, but the females habituated more rapidly than the males to the complex boards.

Habituation of the fixation response has been demonstrated by a number of other workers. Caron and Caron (1968) presented the same pattern repeatedly, and found that there was a decrease in fixation duration with exposures. This habituation was interrupted when a novel stimulus was presented. The rate of habituation was reliably greater for a simple pattern than for a complex one. Cohen, Gelber, and Lazar (1971) presented a pattern twelve times to 4-month-old infants. Then the pattern appeared with a different colour.

Alternatively, a novel pattern was shown in a different colour. The infants showed habituation to the original pattern, some recovery with the novel colour and more recovery with the novel form. Girls showed less habituation than boys, but both showed about the same amount of dishabituation with novelty.

McCall and Melson (1969) predicted that attention should be an inverted U-shaped function of discrepancy. They measured the response in terms of *duration of first fixation*, and found that there were no differences in duration when 4-month-old infants were looking at one of five different patterns of black items. The standard pattern was presented many times, but the other patterns were presented once only. Each group received only one of the discrepant patterns. However, there was a difference in the *cardiac deceleration*. Maximal deceleration was found with the simple transposal from a vertical line to a sloping line of items. Deceleration was minimal with the pattern judged to be maximally different, differing in both vertically and linearity. Habituation in terms of first fixation predicted the response to discrepancy both in terms of first fixation and cardiac deceleration, but habituation in terms of the cardiac response did not predict the response to discrepancy for either measure.

Super, Kagan, Morrison, Haith and Weiffenbach (1972) also found that visual attention to a stimulus bears an inverted U-shaped relationship to discrepancy between stimulus and schema. With maximum discrepancy, the child is not interested, but with intermediate discrepancy he detects something suggestive in the strange picture. So he is stimulated to try to disentangle what he sees in order to relate it to an already developed schema. These authors presented mobiles and flashing lights to children from 2 to 6 months old. The infants were exposed daily to the stimuli in their homes. Then they were shown a standard mobile in the laboratory. Their attention to the standard mobile depended on the degree of discrepancy between it and the mobiles to which they had become accustomed. Maximum attention was paid to the mobile when the child had been exposed to one somewhat similar. The same function was found between the temporal and spatial unpredictability of sequential flashing light patterns and the suppression of limb movement in 4-month-old infants. Welch (1974) paired novel and familiar stimuli for 4-month-old children, and found that there was increased visual attending when the novel stimulus differed from the familiar one by two or three dimensions, but not when only one dimension was different.

Foster, Vietze and Friedman (1973) studied forty-eight 8–14-week-old infants, looking at a moving stimulus. Habituation of fixation was observed, but when the children had to make a motor response to see the stimulus, no habituation was observed. Attention was maintained as long as the stimulus was contingent on the motor response. Schaffer, Greenwood and Parry (1972) studied infants from 6 to 12 months of age, presenting them with objects. No effect of familiarity or incongruity on touching latency was observed until 8 months, when the children were very slow to touch unfamiliar objects.

Greenberg, Uzgiris and Hunt (1970) presented a pattern repeatedly to infants from 1 month old. At 2 months of age, the child showed preference for the familiar pattern, but after two more weeks of exposure the unfamiliar pattern was preferred.

(3) DEVELOPMENT OF ATTENTION TO COMPLEXITY

Greenberg and O'Donnell (1972) presented dot, striped and checkerboard patterns to 6-week and 11-week-old infants. The older infants spent more time looking at the complex and less at the simple patterns than the younger infants. Greenberg (1971) tested children at 8, 10 and 12 weeks of age. After the initial test the infants were divided into three groups; one group had the 4 × 4 checkerboard, at 8–10 weeks of age, in their homes, to look at all the time, followed by the 6 × 6 at 10–12 weeks; the second group had the most complex checkerboards, while the third group had grey stabiles. This third group looked much less at the most complex 24 × 24 checkerboard when it was shown to them than did the other two groups. As a whole, the infants at 8 and 10 weeks showed a preference for the 8 × 8 checkerboard, while at 12 weeks they preferred the 24 × 24. It was concluded that cognitive development can be trained even at this early age. A similar conclusion was presented by Kagan, when he found that institute children were slower to develop visual preferences than home-reared ones.

Horowitz (1969) also carried out a longitudinal study of children's visual preferences from 3 to 14 weeks of age. She found that there was considerable habituation of the response to the simpler checkerboard patterns between 3 and 14 weeks of age, while the response to the more complex patterns showed less habituation. A further study used different infants at each of three ages : 3, 8 and 14 weeks of age. Here the older infants showed a linearly increasing preference for increasing complexity, while the 8-week-old infants preferred the 4 × 4 patterns. Horowitz suggested that a visual response is a double stimulus-response. The first stimulus is the sight of the object, with a response of a visual fixation, often coupled with reaching out towards the object. This first stimulus-response is the orienting response. The second stimulus-response involves paying attention to the object, in order to form a schema or model of the event. When this has been formed, then habituation occurs. Horowitz found that there was considerable difference between infants in rate of development, and she suggested that grouping together curves of development might be misleading (see also Zeaman and House, 1963).

(4) OTHER INDICES OF AROUSAL AND ATTENTION

Kagan (1971) included several indices of arousal and attention in his detailed longitudinal study. These indices included fixation times, vocalization, cardiac deceleration, tempo of play, smiling, irritability and activity. He concluded that positive vocalization represents a diffuse state change, indicating excitement or arousal. It does not correlate with the different stimuli, in contrast to fixation data. Cardiac deceleration indicates surprise, and it is closely related to length of fixation during the first half year. The two indices become more independent around the end of the first year. At 4 months large cardiac decelerations and long fixations are produced by regular and scrambled faces, but at 8 months there is a sharp decrease in deceleration. The large decelerations are accompanied by decrease in motor activity, and probably represent vagal excitation. They also indicate cognitive activity, as the child tries to make sense of what he sees. Even at 2 years of age, over half the children showed marked deceleration when looking at a slide that showed a woman with her head in her hand. At this age, most deceleration responses were related to non-speech sounds, such as a dog barking. Kagan suggested that the cardiac response is much more specific at 2 years than it was earlier.

Berg (1972) also studied habituation of the cardiac response in infants. He indicated that the response shifts from monophasic acceleration at birth to deceleration by 4 months. Four-month-old infants showed marked deceleration at onset and offset of 10 sec tones, but this habituated during six trials. When the frequency was changed, dishabituation occurred. Berg (1974) also found that 6-week-old infants showed the same marked deceleration to the stimulus offset. The orienting response depends on both the sympathetic and the parasympathetic neural systems. Which of these two mechanisms dominates the orienting response must depend to some extent on the nature of the stimulus. If the stimulus change is more surprising than threatening, the vagal response that allows pause for thought may be more powerful than the sympathetic (see also Graham and Clifton, 1966).

(5) State or level of arousal

The response of an organism to a stimulus will depend not only on the nature of the stimulus, but also on the state of the organism. Wolff (1959) developed a five-point scale of levels of arousal in neonates. This work was continued by Prechtl and Beintema (1964). The states were based on observational criteria. The levels ranged from deep sleep (described as eyes closed, regular respiration, no movements except sudden generalized startles), through the normal waking state of open eyes, with or without movements, to "crying". Hutt, Lenard and Prechtl (1969) describe the physiological correlates of these states. They point out that no one physiological variable can be used to describe a state. Heart rate tends to increase with higher states, reaching a maximum during crying. The EEG of neonates consists mainly of slow waves both in sleep and in quiet wakefulness. Rapid eye movements are seen in irregular sleep and in wakefulness. These states are somewhat similar to those observed in adults (Lindsley, 1960), but the duration and occurence of each state is quite different. The neonate spends 70 per cent of his time asleep, and 75 per cent of this sleep is irregular sleep, though naturally there are large differences between babies. From the point of view of testing the child and recording his orienting responses, preferences and habituation, it is essential that the child is in the state of quiet wakefulness, the maximum point of the U-shaped curve relating attention to levels of arousal.

Brackbill and Fitzgerald (1969) have discussed in detail the relation between levels of arousal and responses to stimulation. They describe the work on the inhibition of the sucking reflex that began in Russia (Bronstein and Petrova, 1952). Premature infants will stop sucking when they hear a sound, and will continue to give this orienting response without habituation. However, Brackbill and Fitzgerald report that premature infants (aged 1–63 days) do habituate to a repeated sound, taking about twenty-six trials to do so. Normal infants, matched for chronological age and for state, took about nineteen trials to habituate. Brackbill and Fitzgerald suggested that the differences may be due to the fact that the Russians make less use of drugs during birth than the Americans. They emphasize that it is essential to take account of the infant's state or level of arousal during the experiment. Other experimenters have found somewhat contradictory results, with the OR or the measurement of inhibition of sucking. Haith (1966) found that neonates 1–3 days old showed inhibition of sucking when they observed a moving light, but not when a stationary light was shown. Keen (1964) found inhibition of sucking with a tone in infants 3–5 days old. Yet Kaye and Levin (1963) found no difference in sucking rate whether a tone was given or not, in infants of 3–4 days old. Kaye (1967) reported that he was unable to duplicate the Haith results. He emphasized the importance of states of arousal, which change very fast in young infants. He found that it took five days before the children of mothers, who had received high level of drugs, reached the same rate of sucking as the children of mothers who had received low levels of drugs.

(6) CONCLUSIONS

The major finding in this research on development of attention in infants during the first year of life is that the child is born with the ability to orient visually, and to habituate when he has developed his internal model of the pattern or sound. Even premature infants have this ability. There is less development of attention than one might think. What does develop is the nature of the preferences indicated by the infants as they grow older. From birth the child is using all possible information in order to make sense of this strange world in which he finds himself.

The second finding is that there is a change from preferences for simple patterns to preferences for more complex ones. Yet much of the research indicates that this change may be dependent to a considerable extent on the previous experience of the child. The environment plays a vital part in his cognitive development, and children need to be given as much information as possible. There are also preference changes from bright, flashing patterns and lights to black and white patterns. By the age of a year, the child loses his interest in patterns and prefers solid objects.

The effort to develop a schema of what he is seeing leads the child to pay attention to small differences rather than to large ones. At 4 months old he shows maximal cardiac deceleration when he is observing two patterns which show only slight differences; the 4-month-old also shows suppression of movements, which is maximal when there is only a slight difference between two flashing light patterns. Both these responses indicate the cognitive effort required to notice small differences. However, the 4-month-old may demonstrate increased visual attention when two patterns differ by more than one dimension. By this age discrepancies between event and schema become important.

Around 1 year of age, the cardiac deceleration is no longer such an important indication of attention. Yet even at 2 years of age, it may be seen when the child is shown a picture that contains a serious discrepancy. At this age the cardiac change becomes highly specific, indicating that the child has developed detailed expectancies, and reacts to a conflict between expectancy and event.

Finally, the all-important effect of individual differences must be noted. Children may differ because of their genetic make-up and because of their experience. These differences may show up in delayed performance of as much as three to four months. When children have been exposed to complex patterns in a longitudinal study, they show earlier preference for complexity than children who have had less exposure. Children who have been reared in an institution show slower cognitive growth than those reared in the home.

III. THE DEVELOPMENT OF ATTENTION IN THE SCHOOL-AGE CHILD

(1) THE STUDY OF EYE MOVEMENTS

Bruner and Potter (1964) showed children a series of pictures, which at first were too blurred to recognize, and gradually became clearer until the child could recognize what was represented. The mean recognition time decreased with increasing age from 4 years to 19. The greatest improvement in recognition occurred between the ages of 4 years to $5\frac{1}{2}$ years. The 4-year-old children needed considerable prompting to keep their mind on the task. Mackworth and Bruner (1970) made a study of the way in which 6-year-old children and adults searched these pictures. The position of the gaze on the display was recorded by an eye camera. One group of children and one group of adults were shown the most blurred picture first, followed by a less blurred one, with the clear picture shown last. They were asked to announce the subject of the series when they recognized it. Similar groups of adults and children were shown the pictures in the opposite order, beginning with the clear picture. Now they were just inspecting the pictures, since they knew what they were seeing from the beginning.

The children showed less visual coverage of the display than the adults. Their eye-tracks averaged only two-thirds of the total eye-tracks of the adults, partly because they showed many more very short movements. Adults were more skilful at selecting the informative areas in the blurred pictures, and they also demonstrated many more long leaps covering more than 3 inches on the display than did the children. The adults thus appeared to be able to make better use of their peripheral vision than the children. The mean fixation times for both groups were longer when the task was to recognize a blurred picture than when the nature of the picture was already known.

The difference between the duration of fixations for adults and children was quite small. With the recognition series both averaged 400 msec, while with the inspection series the average was 316 msec for the adults and 337 msec for the children. These figures are quite different from those found in reading; the average fixation of the adult is about 250 msec, while for the 6-year-old child it ranges from 500 msec to 1 sec. By 6 years of age the young child has reached practically adult skill in looking at pictures.

Levy-Schoen and Pouthas (1971–2) studied the eye movements of pre-school children looking at two bright spots projected together on a white field. Each spot contained a drawing, and the children were asked to identify the drawings. The ages of the children ranged from 2.9 to 5.3 years. The pictures were more likely to be looked at if the second one was near the first, and also if the spot was higher in the field. The 5-year-olds were more likely to look at the right spot than the left. There was a progressive decrease in reaction time with age. It was concluded that an object has a greater chance of attracting visual attention when it is near the previous fixation.

Pribram (1971) has discussed the finding that in monkeys the stimulation of a single cell in the frontal lobe can increase the acceptance angle of that cell. The frontal lobes develop quite slowly in the human child (Luria, 1973, see Fig. 3.1) and this may be the reason why young children seem to have rather small fields of view.

Vurpillot (1968) recorded the eye movements of children aged 4–9 years while they were making comparisons between two pictures of houses. Each house had six windows, with varying details. The children were asked to decide whether the two houses were exactly the same or not. The younger children seldom checked all the windows in each house, but made up their minds that they were the same if the first few windows inspected were the same. The older children were more systematic in their search, and checked every window before they decided that the two houses were identical. Olson (1970) carried out a similar experiment in which children aged 4–7 years were shown a picture of a house. They were asked to look carefully at all the details of the house, because they were going to be asked to find it in a group of different houses. In every case the various houses differed from the standard in only one feature. When looking at the model, four out of five of the older children examined every one of the four critical features, whereas only one of the eight younger children made an adequate study of the model. The older children scored 65 per cent correct matches on the first test, and 85 per cent on the second run through. The younger children only succeeded in selecting the correct house 19 per cent of times.

Here again the slow development of the frontal lobes may play a part, since these lobes also control sequencing activities (Pribram, 1971). However, the mistakes were also due to forgetting. The increase in memory span with age is a well-known phenomenon. The young children, for instance, focused on the chimney when it was present, but when it was absent, they did not check the space where it should have been. The three children who did look at the empty space on the roof recognized that there was a difference. Clearly the search was dictated to some extent by the memory model or schema that had been developed and maintained by inward attention. The older children had developed this ability to maintain inward and outward attention simultaneously, and so could compare their short-term memory model with the picture that they were looking at.

Fixation times varied from about 0.1 sec to 5.4 sec. The very long fixations usually occurred when an anomaly had been detected. There might be a lengthy period of scanning between two windows, when the central window was missing. The child recognized that something was wrong, but had difficulty in recalling the original in detail. Even the younger children were able to make a systematic search when they had been trained.

Olson concluded that the child learns by and through his own acts. No amount of verbal instruction will give skill in an activity. The child has to work it out for himself; however, he can be taught. If he is told where to look he soon becomes able to do a task that was previously too difficult for him. We have as yet only begun to scratch the surface of what a child can be taught in his early years. We do know that when those formative years are impoverished, the cognitive ability of the child may never develop up to its fullest potential.

Wilton and Boersma (1974) studied eye fixations and other physiological measures in conservation experiments. They tested normal and retardate children with mean ages of 7 and 10 years respectively. Each group of forty-five children was subdivided into three groups, normal conservers, trained conservers, and non-conservers. The physiological measures included Galvanic Skin Response (GSR), blood flow and heart rate. The surprise reaction was defined as an increase in GSR and blood flow, with a decrease in heart rate. The groups showed reliable differences in surprise reactions. Normal and retarded conservers gave 53 per cent and 40 per cent surprise reactions when conservation was apparently violated by the display. Non-conservers gave 20 per cent or fewer surprise reactions. Children who had been trained in conservation tasks gave

43 per cent surprise reactions. These data indicate clearly how the physiological response to a stimulus is dependent on the internal model that the child has developed about the task. When his expectation is violated, then he will show increased arousal, together with the slowed heart rate that we have already seen to be characteristic of active thought in younger children.

Boersma and Muir (1975) have described looking behaviour in normal and retarded children during directed search tasks and discrimination learning. The work was undertaken to test the Zeaman and House (1963) theory of discrimination learning, which is based on the concept that the child must first discover which dimension of the task he should pay attention to. Boersma and Muir (1975) defined attention as looking behaviour, measured by eye fixations. The major hypothesis of the study was that retarded children would be less efficient than normal children in selecting areas in pictures which had high information value. The children were all about 8–12 years of age. A secondary hypothesis was that verbal information about the solution of a discrimination task would not help the retarded children to select the important information, but that normal subjects would respond with increased attention to the visual cues. Both hypotheses were confirmed by the results, and it was concluded that the retardates did show a visual attention deficiency, in the sense that they could not select the important cues in the display.

The assessment of the importance of the information in each square inch of the pictures was carried out by the technique described in Mackworth and Bruner (1970). The picture was cut up into square inches and ten judges were asked to rate the informativeness of each segment on a six-point scale. The mean of their ratings for each segment was taken as the informative value for that segment. The highly informative areas often showed a discrepancy that the normal child soon noticed. The retarded children were less likely to notice these important areas. They also showed shorter fixations than the normal children.

In the second task the children were asked to select the rectangle containing either one or three dots. Each card also contained a square or a diamond. Fixations on relevant cues were significantly greater with the normal children, while the retarded children showed significantly more unscorable frames, due to looking right off the display. Thus the retarded children clearly demonstrated lack of attention to the correct dimension.

We have already seen how the development of a schema can be observed in the infant by recording eye fixations and their habituation. When the schema is disrupted by an unexpected event, the fixations regain their former intensity. Mackworth and Otto (1970) carried out a study of eye fixations of children, and demonstrated orientation and habituation. The interesting finding was that there was no difference in the visual behaviour of normal children whose ages ranged from 2 to 7 years. They were shown a set of white geometrical symbols for ten 3-sec trials. Then on the eleventh trial, one of the symbols, a circle, suddenly changed to red. Immediately, the percentage of fixations on this circle shot up from 4 per cent to 65 per cent. In the following twenty 3-sec trials, the fixations on the red circle fell off rapidly, but the children were still looking at the red circle for 25 per cent of the time in the twentieth trial. There were no significant differences between the age groups in either the slope or the intercept of these data. It is clear that with such a simple display schema formation proceeds as rapidly with 2-year-old children as with 7-year-old children.

Quite a different pattern was found when aphasic children were tested (Mackworth, Grandstaff and Pribram, 1973). These aphasic children ranged from 5 to 9 years old. They could be clearly divided into two groups, those who had high non-verbal IQ scores, and those who had low non-verbal IQ scores (seven children). The former group showed a more severe form of aphasia. These three children fixated the red circle very strongly (65 per cent) the instant that it first appeared; during the following twenty trials they showed a slight decrease to 55 per cent of all eye fixations, followed by a renewed rise to 62 per cent. Thus they showed almost no habituation during the whole twenty trials. It appears that these children were unable to form an adequate schema for the red circle, perhaps because they were unable to name it. The other group of *mildly* retarded aphasics was quite different. Like the retarded children discussed above, they looked much less at the red circle, looking at it only 30 per cent of the time in the first five trials. For the next fifteen trials they showed the same habituation as the normal children (Fig. 3.3). Thus the high IQ severe aphasics oriented excessively, with little habituation, while the retarded aphasics oriented inadequately. These retarded children also showed a significantly higher number of occasions when they looked right away from the display, while the severe aphasics spent significantly less time looking away from the display than did the normals.

(2) PREFERENCES

Baltes, Schmidt and Boesch (1968) studied the preferences of subjects aged from 8 to 20 years, for light flashes of different rates. The 8-year-

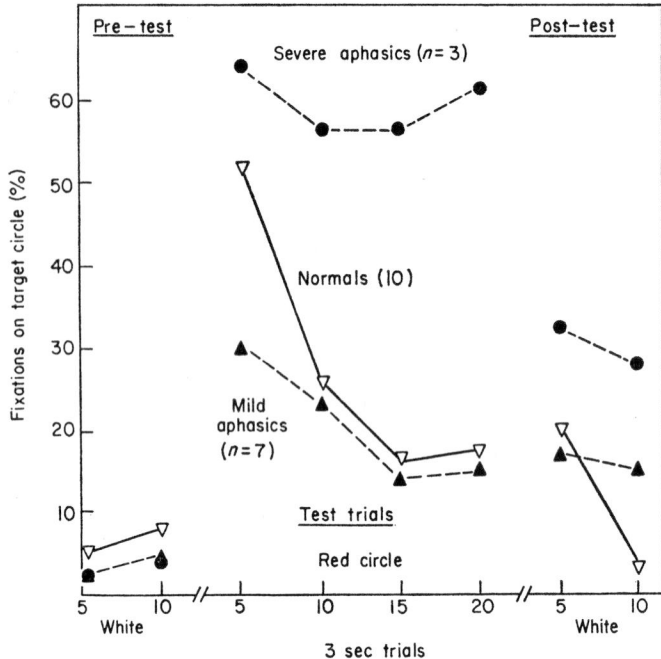

FIG. 3.3. The percentage of time that normal and aphasic children looked at a certain circle in a display of sixteen white geometric symbols. The circle was white in the pre- and post-test trials, but red during the test trials. Each trial lasted 3 sec. (*After* Mackworth, Grandstaff and Pribram, 1973, p. 446.)

olds preferred the fastest flash rate of ten per sec; with increasing age the preference shifted towards the slower rate. Adults preferred the rate of five flashes in 10 sec. Auditory stimuli gave the same result (Boesch, Baltes and Schmidt (1968), see Fig. 3.4). Do these data result from the fact that time seems to pass so much more rapidly as one grows older?

Munsinger, Kessen and Kessen (1964) tested the preferences of subjects from 7 years of age to adult, with pairs of objects. With random black shapes, most subjects indicated a preference for the intermediate complexity of ten angles. The youngest 6-year-olds preferred the most complex ones, while the adults preferred those with fewer turns than the average choice. When the subjects were given letter sequences ranging from random sets, through words to repetitions of one letter, most subjects selected the words.

Bartol and Pielstick (1972) showed slides in pairs to children aged 7 and 12 and to adults. One slide was ambiguous, and the other was unambiguous. The younger children looked at the ambiguous slides

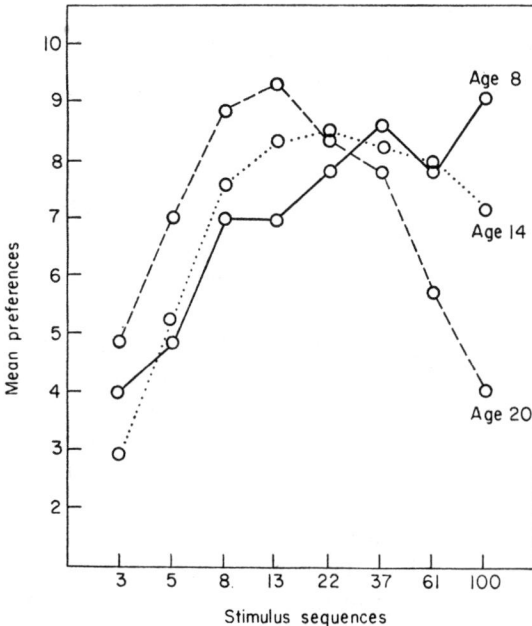

Fig. 3.4. Mean preferences of three age groups for eight stimulus sequences. (*After* Boesch, Baltes and Schmidt, 1968, p. 205.)

less than the older ones did. The girls showed increased attention to the ambiguous slides with increasing age. Their attention to the unambiguous slides was very low at all ages. The boys looked longer than the girls at both kinds of figures, with maximum attention at 12 years; at all ages the boys paid more attention to the ambiguous than to the unambiguous figures. Clearly the looking time was controlled by the effort after meaning. Perhaps the younger ones felt that the ambiguous figures were meaningless.

(3) Selective dimensional attention

Zeaman and House (1963) put forward a theory of the importance of attention in discrimination learning, which has been influential in many studies. It is based on a task in which the child is required to select one of two objects or patterns, on the basis of one attribute. For instance, the child may be rewarded for selecting a red triangle; next time he may select a green triangle, since he does not know which dimension is "right". Now there is no reward. He has sufficient data to give him the correct answer, but naturally the young child cannot achieve this logical conclusion so rapidly. Zeaman and House suggested that there are two separate stages in discrimination learning. First the child must discover by trial and error which is the appropriate dimension. This first stage involves an attentional process. Once he has learned the appropriate dimension, his performance improves rapidly.

Zeaman and House pointed out that the smooth curves obtained from a group of children really conceal a completely different relationship between trials and success. The individual curve for each child consists of a varying length of time during which the curve is more or less flat, around the chance level, and then suddenly a rise to success, though not all the children achieved this final break-through. If the *final* points on the learners' curves are superimposed, it appears that the shapes of all the curves are similar. This method of representation is called a backward learning curve (see Figs. 3.5 a, b, c). It was concluded that the initial flat part of the curve represents learning what to pay attention to, while the sharply rising final portion indicates instrumental discriminative learning. We see that the ability to select the correct dimension by attention is the critical factor in learning to do the task. The length of the flat part varies with intelligence. Two groups of retardates with CA of 140 months had mental ages of 2–4 and 4–6 years respectively. In each group there were some children who never reached the second stage (non-learners). The learners with MA 4–6 learned the task within a

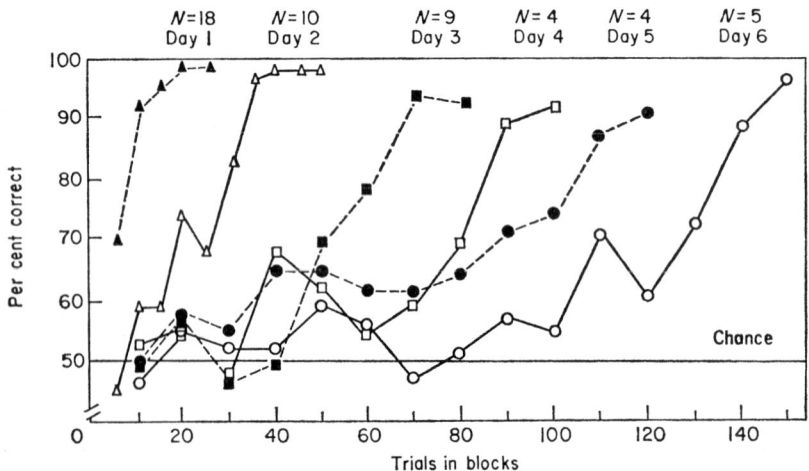

Fig. 3.5a. Forward learning curves of sub-groups requiring various numbers of training days to reach criterion. The number of subjects in each group appears at top. (*After* Zeaman and House, 1963, p. 161.)

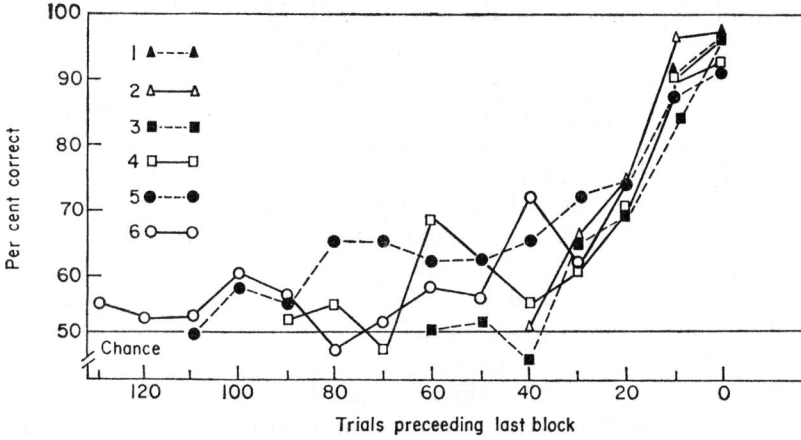

FIG. 3.5b. The functions of Fig. 3.5a have been regrouped prior to averaging for a backward learning curve. The contrast in form of backward and forward learning curves (Fig. 3.5a) is marked. (*After* Zeaman and House, 1963, p. 162.)

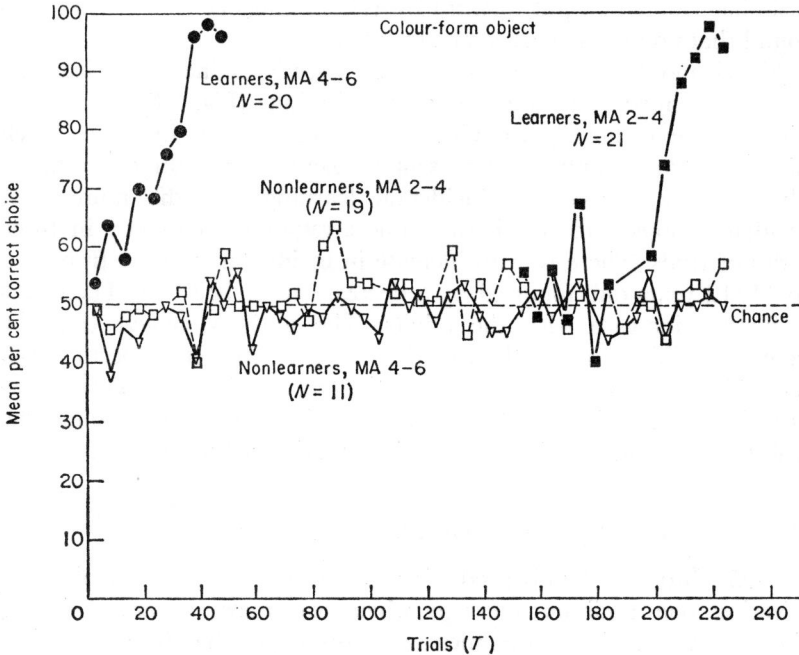

FIG. 3.5c. Effects of intelligence on discrimination learning are shown in the average performances of four groups classified by mental age and achievement. Backward curves are plotted for the two groups of learners. (*After* Zeaman and House, 1963, p. 163)

mean of fifty trials, while the learners with MA 2–4 took about 220 trials, with the final rise occuring around 200 trials.

It is clear that this concept of selective attention is quite different from any of the physiological measures we have discussed. Our only clue to which dimension is being attended to lies in the response. Similarly, in the vigilance experiment we can see the eyes pinned to the tip of the rotating pointer, yet the subject misses the signal that is right before his eyes. He is looking without seeing. We also listen without hearing, and may suddenly return to awareness with the echo of the last few spoken words still lingering in the mind. The higher centres that extract meaning develop more slowly and tire more quickly than the sensory areas.

Schell (1971) found that children aged 4–5 years can be trained to pay attention to the correct dimension in a card sorting task, and can shift quickly to another dimension when required. Schell suggested that Piaget's theory that young children lack cognitive capacity is erroneous. Performance is a question of experience, and the child who is shown what he must attend to quickly gets the idea. We have seen a similar conclusion put forward by Wilton and Boersma (1974), who found that non-conservers can be trained.

Siegel and Stevenson (1966), made a study of incidental learning in subjects aged 7, 12 and 14 years and adults (Fig. 3.6). They were given a three-choice successive discrimination task in which each discriminative stimulus was presented together with three additional objects. The measure of incidental learning was the number of incidental objects to which the subject responded correctly in three series of trials. There was an increase in incidental learning from 7/8 to 11/12 years old, followed by a decrease from 12 to 14. There was a further increase with the adults. The authors suggest that the younger children had little attention to spare from the specific task. The 11-year-olds spread their attention more widely, while the 14-year-old children ignored the irrelevant objects. The adults found the task too easy, and so they took in information about all the objects.

(4) Selective attention in listening

In 1952 Broadbent published his work on the problems involved in selecting one auditory message when two messages are delivered simultaneously. When the messages are spoken by different voices they are easier to disentangle than when they are both spoken by the same voice. He concluded that the brain could filter the messages according to some such characteristic, so that only the message wanted was attended to. Treisman (1960) put forward the theory that

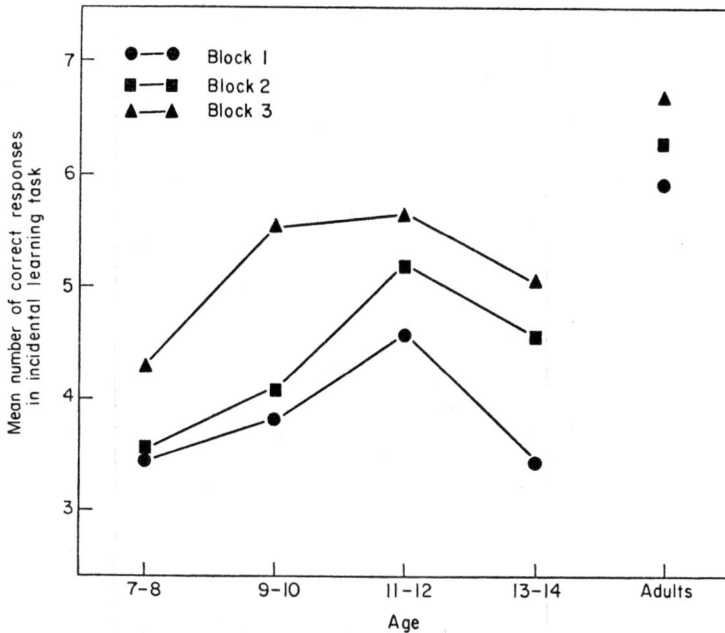

FIG. 3.6. Mean number of correct responses in incidental learning task. (*After* Siegel and Stevenson, 1966, p. 815.)

the filter was not absolute. The material which does break through from the unwanted message may have certain kinds of significance for the listener, such as his own name; or if the unwanted message was in a different language but had the same meaning (Moray, 1959; Treisman, 1964).

Maccoby (1967, 1969) studied the same phenomenon in children, and found that the ability to filter one message developed rapidly in young children. She presented two two-word phrases simultaneously to children aged from $5\frac{1}{2}$ to 12 years. One phrase was spoken by a man, and the other by a woman. The phrases were of high or low probability. The children were informed by a signal which message they should report; this signal was presented either before or after the message. When the child knew beforehand which message he should listen to, even the 5-year-olds were able to get more than half the message correct. But when the signal was presented after the two messages, these very young children chose the messages at random, getting less than half correct. There was a marked improvement between kindergarten and second-grade chilldren (see Fig. 3.7). The older children were able to recall more of both messages when they did not know which they would have to report. Since this involved

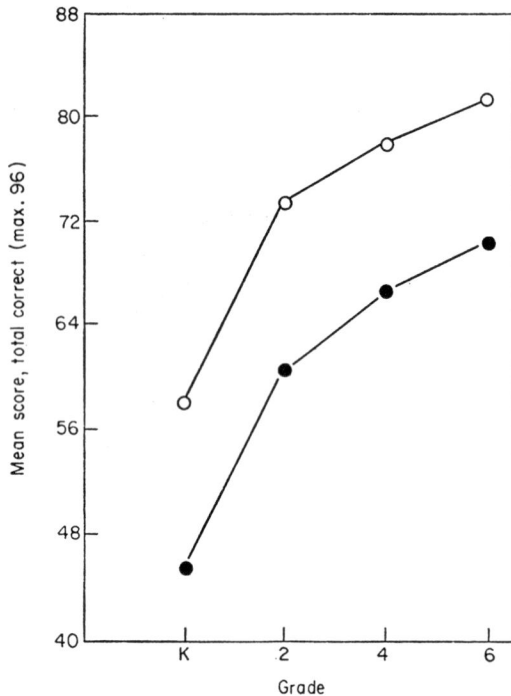

FIG. 3.7. Selective listening for two word phrases: number correct, by grade and before and after signal (○ = before signal; ● = after signal). (*After* Maccoby, 1967, p. 117.)

recalling only four words, it was well within the memory span of the older children.

Maccoby and Konrad (1967) tested children aged from 8 to 12 years with strings of mixed letters and numbers. They were asked to report either the letters or the numbers; this instruction was given either before or after they heard the strings of varying lengths. This involves the idea of "response set". Broadbent (1970) has defined response set as being related to the criterion that has been established. Maccoby and Konrad found that performance was nearly perfect with the four-item strings, even if the children were not told beforehand what to report. The advantage of foreknowledge increased as the length of the strings increased. The age effect on the difference between instruction before or after the string was quite small. The main conclusion was that selective attention to one type of input enhances recall of that material, provided that the length of the message is beyond the memory span of the child. The importance of attention in short-term memory has already been discussed.

Next Maccoby and Konrad asked children aged from 5 to 12 years to listen to two voices coming from different speakers. Again the children were told which voice they were to report either before or after listening to the message. Now there was a clear effect of age. In both cases there was a dramatic increase in recall from 5 to 12 years, and in each age group listening was more accurate when the children knew beforehand which message they should listen to. The improvement with fore-knowledge was about the same in each grade, being about 12 per cent. But even with after-knowledge scores were well above 50 per cent, reaching about 68 per cent with the 12-year-olds. It is therefore clear that the older children could pay attention to both voices at once when they had to. More messages were recalled at all ages when they were highly probable than when they were of low probability. The effect of age was greater when the message to be recalled was of high probability.

Doyle (1973) carried out a similar experiment on 100 children aged from 8 to 14. Again there were two auditory messages, in male or female voices. The presence of two messages was regarded as distraction. The young children were hindered by two voices more than the older ones. Target retention increased linearly with age, but distraction retention remained constant. It was concluded that the superior selective performance of older children is due to their ability to inhibit intrusions during selection. Maccoby and Konrad also found that intrusions decreased with age. The older children can focus their attention more accurately. The ability to focus on one auditory input rather than another depends to some extent on the level of arousal of the hearer. The sleepy or tired listener may forget to pay attention to the required input, and so will be less selective.

(5) DURATION OF ATTENTION AND PHYSIOLOGICAL MEASURES

One of the characteristics of learning-disabled children is that they have difficulty in maintaining attention to the task in hand. This is particularly true of hyperactives. They respond to irrelevant stimuli faster than do normal children (Anderson, Halcomb and Doyle, 1973). Such children may fail to detect the signal light in a pattern of lights, and they may have difficulty in locking on to particular speech when other auditory stimuli are present. In this matter of selective attention, they do not behave like younger normal children, but demonstrate a different pattern of wandering attention. The very young normal child may be able to concentrate for long periods on a particular game that he is playing.

Douglas and Cohen (see Douglas, 1974) carried out a series of

6—CP * *

experiments on hyperactive children. Cohen and Douglas (1972) studied the skin conductance orienting response in hyperactive and normal children aged 6 to 11 years. First they presented thirty non-signal tones to both groups. There was no difference between the groups with regard to orienting and habituation. There was however a difference when the task required an active response to discrete stimuli in a delayed RT task. The control normal children showed significant increases in OR measures, while the hyperactive children were relatively unresponsive. The authors suggest that the alerting signal did not in fact alert the hyperactive children. The term hyperactive suggests over-arousal, but in fact these children can be helped by a stimulating drug such as Ritalin. It has been suggested that they are less alert than the normal child, and therefore the overriding inhibitory action of the frontal lobes is not effective. Thus an increase in arousal activates the inhibitory effect and allows the child to concentrate his attention on the task.

Sykes, Douglas and Morgenstern (1973) also tested these hyperactive children on a discrete reaction time task. In addition to a warning signal, the experimenter made sure that he had the attention of the child before he presented the actual signal. In this case the hyperactive children were able to react as efficiently as the normal ones. In a serial reaction time task both groups made the same number of correct responses, but the hyperactive children made more false responses than the normals. The most sensitive task was found to be one in which twelve different letters were presented at regular intervals. The task was to press the button when an X appeared immediately after an A. This was a modified vigilance task. The hyperactives made fewer correct and more incorrect responses than the normals. We may note that when normal subjects are given a depressive drug while performing in a vigilance task, they will miss more signals and make more false responses than normal (J. F. Mackworth, 1969).

Douglas discusses the concept of a range of personality from impulsive to reflective. The hyperactives are impulsive, and make a response without first pausing to see if it is correct. Impulsivity decreases with age (Kagan, 1966), yet the two tempos can be clearly seen at a very early age. This personality range is not significantly correlated with verbal intelligence, but it is related to errors of commission (false alarms) in a serial learning task, and to reading errors. The problem of the hyperactive is a serious one. He may be unable to focus his attention long enough to perform any task well, and he soon becomes a serious misfit in the school owing to his restlessness and general misbehaviour.

The inability of the hyperactive child to inhibit unwanted activity may be related to inadequate development of the frontal lobes. Luria (1973) has described how the patient with frontal or prefrontal damage is seriously disturbed by disinhibition of his mental processes, which leads to uncontrollable impulsiveness and fragmentation, so that he cannot carry out planned and organized intellectual activity, even though his intellectual processes remain potentially intact. He is unable to concentrate upon any activity long enough to achieve his aim. This account describes the hyperactive child. However, that as he grows older, his impulsivity and hyperactivity improves (Weiss *et al.*, 1972).

When the hyperactive child is given constant verbal encouragement, he may show a marked improvement in reaction time, and an increase in basal skin conductance. However, he does not show any increase in the orienting response, as shown in the GSR, in contrast to normal children. Douglas has shown how the hyperactive will deteriorate more rapidly in a prolonged task than the normal child. Reinforcement should be specifically directed towards the demands of the task. Douglas (1974) has pointed out that a generally accepting and approving attitude does not help the child to perform the task any better, whatever it may do for his general wellbeing.

It has been suggested that the hyperactive indulges in his activity in order to keep himself awake, because he is in fact normally in a state of low arousal. He performs best when given tests individually and does not do well on a group test. Attentional and perceptuo-motor skills seem to go together.

Such decreased physiological reactivity is also found in MBD (minimally brain damaged) children. Dykeman, Ackerman, Clements and Peters (1971) studied MBD children aged 6–12 years, and found that they showed reduced reactivity of the heart rate. They also had low amplitudes of the Contingent Negative Variation (CNV). The CNV is related to the cognitive aspects of the task, and is specially seen when an initial stimulus signals that a second one will occur shortly. The MBD children were less able than normal children to maintain response readiness with a longer foreperiod.

The reversal rate of the Necker cube is also believed to be an index of arousal. Fountain and Lynn (1966) found that the rate decreased with increasing age. There was a minimum at 11 years of age, followed by an increase in active reversal from 11 to 20 years of age (Fig. 3.8). The authors suggested that the decrease in reversal rate was related to the development of the inhibitory effect of the frontal cortex, while the later increase was related to the ability to generate eye movements consciously. The frontal lobes reach maturity at about 12 years of age. Taylor and Henning (1963) have shown that there is the usual exponential decrease of habituation in a number of studies. They asked

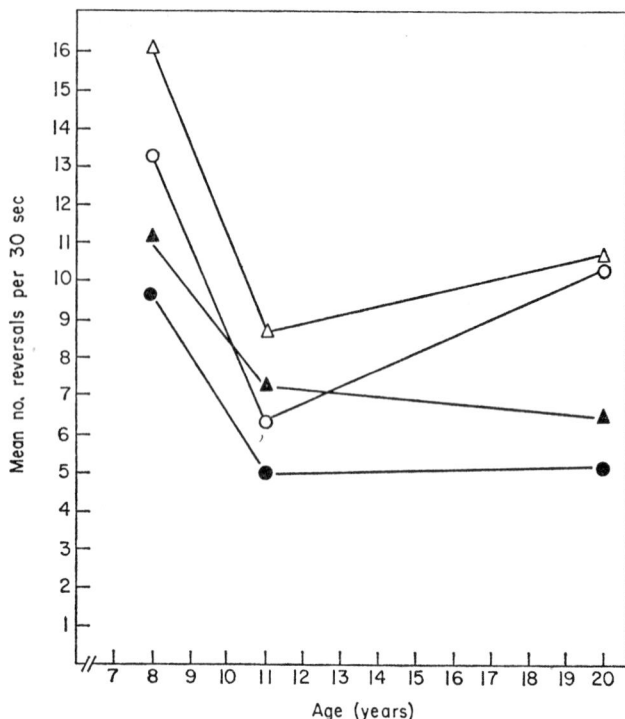

Open triangles=active reversal, small cube. Open circles=active reversal, large cube. Closed triangles=spontaneous reversal, small cube. Closed circles=spontaneous reversal, large cube.

FIG. 3.8. Reversal of Necker Cube in relation to age. (*After* Fountain and Lynn, 1966, p. 215.)

the subjects to describe their perceptions in relation to after-images, meaningless auditory input or various visual monotonous displays. In every case the number of percepts reported by the subject in a given time period was reduced proportionately with the square root of time on task since the beginning of the task. These very simple tasks might be suitable for studies of children.

Jennings (1971) investigated the cardiac reactions of children in various tasks. He found that there was less deceleration in cognitive tasks than in perceptual ones. He tested 5–8-year-old children and found that the cardiac reactions were a joint function of attention and cognitive operations. The perceptual tasks produced deceleration in all subjects, while in the cognitive tasks there was deceleration followed by acceleration. There was increased acceleration with higher levels of cognitive performance in conservation of length and in a verbal form of class inclusion. The skin conductance was not related to cognitive level.

Kaplan (1970) also made a study of the development of cognitive and psychophysiological measures. He tested children from 5 to 7 years of age, giving them the word association test, or the Peabody Picture Vocabulary. The children were divided into two groups, those who gave less than 40 per cent of acceptable responses, and those who were able to do the task better. Most of the younger children were in the first group. The less successful children showed higher skin conductance levels in the test, but there was no difference in heart rate between the two groups. The better subjects showed lower skin conductance, related to inhibition of the first response. Young children tend to give the word that would follow normally in a sentence. In tasks requiring inhibition of first response, low arousal is best. Presumably these more controlled children had somewhat more advanced development of the frontal lobes (Luria, 1973). The young children may have been on the descending curve of the inverted U relating arousal and performance; being too aroused they were unable to inhibit the automatic response. These younger children resemble the hyperactive ones discussed earlier.

(6) ATTENTION AND PREDICTION

Bogartz (1966) studied 4- and 5-year-old children on a task of prediction. They were asked to guess the colour of the next marble in an alternating series of two colours. He considered that errors in prediction would be caused by lack of attention to the stimulus, or to forgetting what had been seen last. If the child fails to pay attention to the stimulus, he may predict an alternating sequence which is out of phase with the actual events. If he forgets his last prediction, he will guess at random. Bogartz (1969) outlined a model of predictive behaviour, suggesting that if the child is attending to the stimulus, he will enter it into his store as a memory trace, and then apply either a transformation or a guessing rule. The new stimulus will erase the previous one from the store, freeing it to receive the new trace. If, however, the child is not paying attention to the stimulus, but to some other distractor, he will forget what he has just been shown, and if he has also forgotten what he had predicted, his only alternative is to guess.

Some children, however, may observe the stimulus, and if it is black, they may then begin immediately to say to themselves, out loud, "white, white". In other words, they are preparing to make their next prediction, and filling in the interval by repetition so that they will not forget. Thus they succeed in maintaining the memory trace by reinforcing it, until they can give their prediction at the right time. Even

4-year-old children can maintain an alternating sequence of verbal responses, e.g., "red-green", even when they are not given any visual stimulus. It was found that when the interval between one stimulus and the signal to predict the next one was 3 sec, the children made fewer errors than when the interval was 10 sec. Errors increased throughout the run with both intervals, but more rapidly with the longer interval. When given a 2-min rest and then a slightly different form of the test, the children showed considerable improvement at the beginning of the second run, but again deteriorated more rapidly with the 10 sec interval.

Jones (1972) examined a similar task with 5- and 6-year-old children. They were told to predict which light would come on by placing a white card in a slot under the predicted light. Both lights were red Sequences with repetition probabilities of 0.1 and 0.9 were chosen. In the first, there was an almost perfectly alternating pattern, while the second produced long runs of each event. Half the subjects were trained on the first and half on the second kind of sequence. For the transfer trials, half of each group was given the opposite system. Jones found that the theory of Bogartz was supported, and could be extended to situations where the children must change the rules. The 6-year-old children made fewer errors than the 5-year-olds in working with the alternating sequence, while the younger children were slightly more accurate than the older ones in working with the long runs.

Craig and Myers (1963) had suggested that nursery school children would be more likely to employ a repetition response tendency, while the older children would be more likely to employ an alternating response sequence. This fits in with the findings by Jones (1972). The Bogartz model fits most accurately with those children who had received the same test sequences with which they had been trained. Bogartz had suggested that children learn rules rather than probabilities. When they must change the rule, they run into difficulty. The kindergarten 5-year-olds made twice as many errors with the long-run sequence as they did with the alternating one, even when they were working with the same sequence on which they had been trained. This indicated that their response tendency was stronger than their ability to learn the rule. It would appear that they paid less attention to the task than to their ideas about the task.

Balling and Myers (1971) presented a similar task to children aged 4 and $5\frac{1}{2}$ years. In addition to the stimulus lights, they were given pegboards on which to record what they had seen. The lights appeared in a double alternation sequence. The children were given either ten or two pegs to make their record. The nursery school children improved in performance when they were given ten pegs, and asked to name each one. The kindergarten 6-year-old children showed considerable improvement with the ten-pegboard, even if they were not asked to name the pegs. The authors concluded that gross attentional deficits have disappeared by $5\frac{1}{2}$ years old. It was clear that the fact of paying attention to the sequence, by reconstructing what had already happened, fixed the material in memory, and allowed cognitive processes to take place.

(7) ATTENTION AND READING

The child who is learning to read has to be taught first of all to pay attention to the sounds of speech. He has to learn that each word is built up from a series of sounds. Though he has learned to imitate those sounds more or less adequately, he often does not realize that there are in fact separate sounds within a word. Next he has to learn how these sounds are represented in the written language. This final stage of learning to read will occupy him for a good many years. In fact, the idiosyncrasies of the English written language are such that pronunciation must be checked for almost any new word.

The child must also learn to pay attention from left to right on the printed page. This is a totally new concept for him. Always he has searched for the informative regions in his world. Now he must painstakingly plod his way letter by letter across the page. It is remarkable how rapidly the average child acquires the new idea, that letters make up words which correspond to the spoken word. But we can learn more about the process by watching the child who does have difficulty. He mixes up letters within a word, and may show great difficulty with the small words, "the, who, when" and so on. These words he uses in speech without noticing them, and he is unable to hear that what he is "reading" from the printed page is not making sense. Similarly, he does not store the words in a visual form with accuracy, and his spelling will always be poor. The poor reader confuses "left" and "felt", "month" and "mouth". He may guess at words from the first and last letters, regardless of the sense, because he is so immersed in the effort to puzzle out the letters that he has no spare attention for recording the meaning.

N. H. Mackworth (1975) carried out a study of the way in which children attempt to locate a word that is missing from a sentence. The eye fixations of the children were photographed while they were doing this task. A sentence such as "He could not carry the ..." was written along the bottom of the slide. In the upper left-hand corner was a column of three nouns; "Sun, Books, Year". In the upper right-hand corner was a similar list of three verbs. Children aged 8, 10, and 12 years were tested. The children were taught by instruction and practice where to look for each part of speech. They were selected from groups assigned by the teachers as good or poor readers.

It was found that the time to find a missing noun was shorter than the time to find a missing verb. Moreover, the poor readers were twice as likely to look at the noun column as at the verb column, regardless of the nature of the missing word, which was in fact a noun or a verb an equal number of times. Moreover, the children re-read the sentence almost twice as often when a verb was missing than when a noun was missing. It is clear that verbs are less easy for the children to process, and in fact they occur about half as often in prose as do nouns.

Mackworth also found that the Reading Aloud Fixation Time (RAFT) was highly correlated with all other measures of reading performance. The RAFT was the mean fixation time for each child when reading prose (leaving out the long pauses when the child had to be prompted as he was reading the appropriate Gray Oral Reading passage). The 8-year-old good readers showed RAFT scores ranging from 0.7 to 0.9 sec, while the three 8-year-old poor readers showed RAFT scores ranging from 1.7 to 2.5 sec per fixation. These three poor readers had great difficulty in reading the passage. The older children from 10 to 12 years showed a smaller range of RAFT scores, from 0.5 to 1.0 sec. However, they showed just as great a range of times to read the passages as did the 8-year-olds, since the passages had been designed to equalize age effects. The RAFT scores were therefore inversely related to the age of the child and his skill in reading. The young child and the poor reader take longer to process the information taken in during each fixation. The age effect is greater than the effect of reading difficulty. The average adult has a mean fixation time of 250 msec in silent reading; the 12-year-old fast readers averaged 330 msec.

The RAFT score has a close relation to many other measures of reading skill. Figure 3.9 shows the relations between the RAFT score and the Missing Word Test, time to read a passage silently, and the number of errors in matching words by sound. The silent reading passages were appropriate to the age of the child, but the word matching task was the same for all ages. It is clear that the duration of attention in each fixation is a direct indication of reading difficulty.

The duration of the fixation is thus a central factor in reading. J. F. Mackworth (1963, 1972) has suggested that the visual image or Ready Store lasts for about 1.5 sec after the visual input has disappeared. Those children who spend a second on each word will be unable to store two words together in their visual system. The first word will already have faded beyond recognition while the second

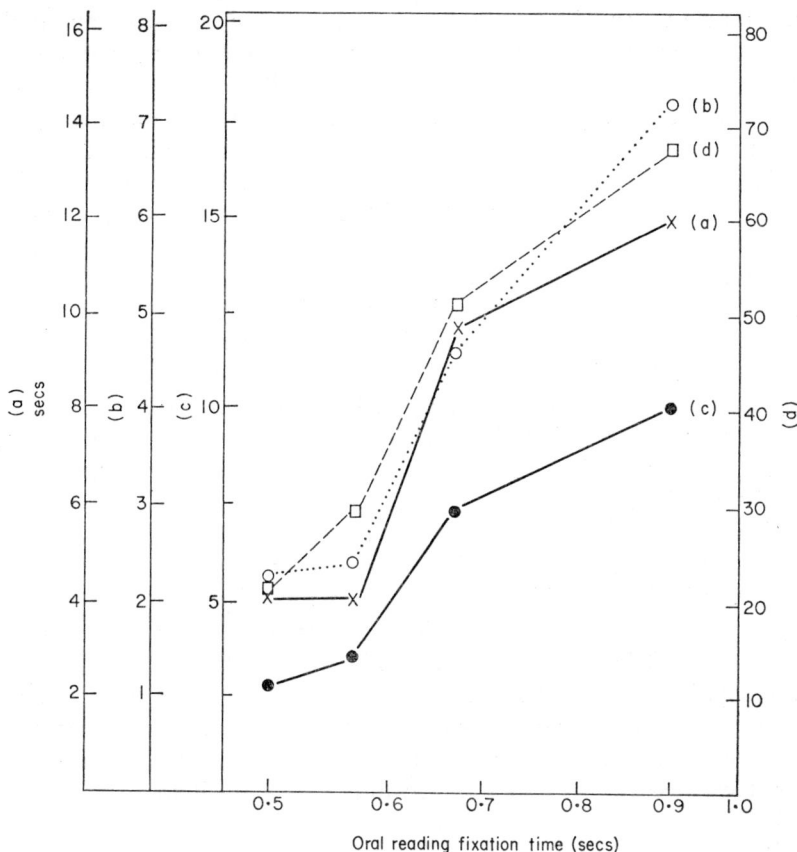

Fig. 3.9. Relation between Oral reading fixation time (RAFT) of sixteen children of 9–10 years, and other reading tasks: (a) errors in coding words into sound; (b) time to find missing word; (c) time spent (by four subjects) on wrong category (verb or noun) in missing word test; (d) time to read silently. (*After* Mackworth and Mackworth, unpublished.)

word is being processed. Yet reading depends on the ability to link two words together visually. Without at least two words in store, the ability to predict what will come next is seriously impaired. This difficulty shows up in the eye fixations as frequent regressions, and in multiple re-readings of the sentence in the Missing Word Test.

Lefton and Spragins (1974) showed that the transfer of pseudo-verbal material from the iconic image to short-term memory was directly related to the experience of the children with the written word. Adults and 7–11-year-old children were shown eight-item pseudo-words of either first or fourth order approximation to English. The results indicated that the 7-year-olds showed little difference between first-

and fourth-order words. By 9–10 years of age, the children had developed normal skills, and were as good as the adults at recalling the letters. At 300 msec the 7-year-olds recalled 30 per cent of the letters, while the 9-year-olds reproduced 50 per cent of the first-order material, and 60 per cent of the fourth-order material. The adults achieved 65 and 75 per cent of the two orders. It was evident that processing took place from left to right, and the last four letters on the right-hand side were reported less accurately than those on the left. This work substantiated the theory put forward by J. F. Mackworth (1963) that the amount reported from a brief flash would depend on the speed at which the items could be coded into speech, which in turn would depend on the familiarity or strength of the relationship between the visual input and the verbal output. It would follow from this theory that young children should report less from a letter task than would older ones. It would also follow that more would be recalled when the relationship between the successive letters was more familiar.

Sheingold (1973) carried out a tachistoscopic experiment with geometric figures. After delay intervals varying from 50 msec to 1 sec, a marker indicated which of the figures the subjects should report. Almost all the children were able to report any form after 50 msec delay, but after 1 sec the 6-year-olds could only report 1.5 items correctly. The 8-year-old children managed 2.5 and the 11-year-olds were the same as the adults, with four forms correct. It was clear that visual input was the same for all ages, but the younger children were less able to recover the fading image and to name the items.

IV. CONCLUSIONS

Attention in the growing child is devoted to learning about his environment, in order to develop cognitive models that will enable him to react effectively with that environment. Attention is believed to be a neural state that is maintained by electrochemical energy. It is normally a selective process, a searchlight that focuses on one neural activity to the exclusion of others. It is divided between the various aspects of an event, such as studying the sensory input, storing the event in short-term memory (possibly as a sequence of events), processing the event cognitively by the activation of long-term memory models, and storing the final synthesis in long-term memory. Since the energy is limited, and must be divided between all these aspects, one aspect may suffer when another requires more processing.

We can distinguish three main stages in the development of attention. First, the very young infant demonstrates selective attention from birth, even when he is premature. His eyes will turn towards movement, or towards patterns or objects that appear at the periphery of his visual field. His task at this time is to construct internal models of the environment, and everything that he sees is new. Throughout life he will continue to construct such models, but as he grows older his attention is devoted more to comparing new experiences with already stored models. Since the neonate has no such stored models, he must spend a great deal of time on assimilating the stimulus, and therefore he shows little or no habituation.

The second major stage of selective attention can be seen in the child up to about 4 or 5 years of age. In his early years he begins to demonstrate habituation to patterns that he has seen before, and to select the novel pattern for study. (Such cognitive behaviour may be delayed when the environment of the child is impoverished.) The young child may show inadequate search of a display. He arrives at a decision after a few quick glances, and may therefore fail to discover a vital point in the display. He may ignore one or more dimensions of the problem, and, for instance, decide that a red circle is the same as a blue circle, because he either ignores the colour or decides that it is unimportant. He may have difficulty in changing this outlook, even when his real task is to respond to colour. When asked to compare more complex patterns, such as houses with many windows, he again makes his decision on an inadequate search. Similarly, 6-year-old children asked to identify a blurred picture show less adequate visual coverage than adults. When, however, young children are asked simply to look at a picture, their rate of detection of a new stimulus and their rate of habituation is the same over a range of different ages. Cognitive processing of such a simple display is achieved by 2-year olds as rapidly as by 7-year-olds.

In the third stage, the cognitive abilities of the child control his attention to a greater degree. Now he can continue to search until he has covered all the available evidence. He also knows how to select the significant details from a display, and how to ignore unimportant dimensions. He can learn to abstract a rule from an on-going sequence of events, and to correct his responses when he is given feedback. He can also change the rule when necessary. Increasing age brings increasing ability to make cognitive decisions about a task, and to absorb more information. Older children can, for instance, listen to two competing auditory messages at once, or pay attention to one and ignore the other, as the task demands. The older child will select the more ambiguous presentation, driven by his desire to make sense of what he sees. Maccoby (1969) has pointed out that the change in the degree to which perceptions are selective in the normal course of events without explicit instructions may be the most important developmental change of all.

The cognitive content of attention is also shown by changes in physiological responses such as heart rate, the surprise reaction, the Contingent Negative Variation and changes in skin conductance. Such changes may indicate that the event was unexpected. The ability to predict begins to develop early in life, and increases in complexity with age. When the prediction is falsified by the event, then the various arousal responses will be seen. Maximum attention is paid to something that contradicts expectancy, that does not fit in with an activated internal model. Thus the child who understands about conversation will show surprise when it is apparently violated, while the child who does not understand the concept will not show surprise. Yet the young or retarded child can be taught the concept, and then he will react in the same way as the older child. The great importance of previous experience is gradually beginning to be realized, and we now recognize that the Intelligence Quotient or IQ is not necessarily measuring something that is purely genetic or innate, it is also measuring the experience of the child.

The cognitive abilities of the child depend to a large extent on the development of the frontal lobes, which develop very rapidly up to 7 years of age. Pribram (1971) had suggested that the frontal cortex increases redundancy by chunking information. In the human this chunking is greatly helped by the use of language. Stimulation of the frontal lobes increases the number of nerve fibres that are available to process one particular stimulus. The child is enabled to pay concentrated attention to the vital aspect of a stimulus, ignoring competing distractions. The hyperactive child or the young child may show inability to concentrate on a task, and may give up before the problem has been fully completed. The hyperactive child may be helped by giving him a stimulant, which will activate his frontal lobes and so allow him to inhibit distractions. The frontal lobes also control the ability to sequence events. This is vital in language and in reading, as well as in mathematics. Many poor readers have difficulty in such sequencing. Stimulation of the temporal lobes has the reverse effect on stimulus processing. Now the focus is broadened, allowing a wider input (Pribram, 1971).

Attention is the crucial requirement for learning and problem solving of all kinds. It concentrates the necessary energy at the point where it is needed. The neural stimulus is heightened and increased in duration as it passes through the different systems of the brain. When a stimulus enters the brain, its very brief duration in the retina and optic nerve is increased as it traverses the visual pathways, and it is recognized by being compared with a stored model that corresponds. This activation of a model from a long-term memory strengthens the incoming trace.

All this activity depends on attention. The moment that we cease to rehearse an input, it disappears from memory, unless it has been sufficiently strengthened. In a task such as reading, which is highly redundant, the memory model of the next word or phrase is usually activated before the word is actually read. If the next word turns out to be different from expectation, there will be a double-take or regressive eye movement as the unexpected word is rechecked and assimilated (J. F. Mackworth, 1972). Bannatyne (1973) has described how the recycling of an input or thought by the use of attention maintains the input in short-term memory. He points out that short-term memory involves the holding in attention of bits, chunks, images, percepts, concepts, and relational programs; this he calls data-matching short-term memory. From this preliminary process the material is gradually incorporated into long-term memory by the activation of associations and relational programs.

The amount of attention required to deal with a stimulus is increased when the stimulus is unfamiliar. Therefore there is less attention available for processing the stimulus or holding it in short-term memory. Young children have fewer and less well developed models of the outer world than older children have; therefore when the young child meets a new situation, he needs to observe it as a whole, before he stops to consider details. Thus he may fail to observe small differences in detail, and will make a decision on the basis of inadequate evidence.

In conclusion, attention is the basis for almost all learning, and it can be studied by recording physiological orienting responses, eye fixations, auditory discrimination, and sudden changes in performance that indicate a new understanding of the task, in addition to cognitive achievements indicating that a problem has been solved.

148   THE DEVELOPMENT OF COGNITIVE PROCESSES

REFERENCES

Anderson, R. P., Halcomb, C. G. and Doyle, R. B. (1973). The measurement of attentional deficits. *Exceptional Children, 39*, 534–6.
Balling, J. D. and Myers, N. A. (1971). Memory and attention in children's double-alternation learning. *Journal of Experimental Child Psychology, 11*, 448–60.
Baltes, P. M., Schmidt, L. R. and Boesch, E. E. (1968). Preference for complex stimuli as an index of diversive exploration. *Psychonomic Science, 11*, 271–2
Bannatyne, A. (1973). *Language, Reading and Learning Disabilities.* Springfield, Illinois: C. C. Thomas.
Bartol, C. R. and Pielstick, N. L. (1972). The effects of ambiguity, familiarization, age and sex on stimulus preference. *Journal of Experimental Child Psychology, 14*, 21–9.
Berg, W. K. (1972). Habituation and dishabituation of a cardiac response in 4-month old alert infants. *Journal of Experimental Child Psychology, 14*, 94–107.
Berg, W. K. (1974). Cardiac orienting responses of 6 and 16 week old infants. *Journal of Experimental Child Psychology, 17*, 303–12.
Boersma, F. J. and Muir, W. (1975). *Eye Movements and Information Processing in Mentally Retarded Children.* Rotterdam University Press.
Boesch, E. E., Baltes, P. B. and Schmidt, L. R. (1968). Preference for different auditory stimulus sequences in various age groups. *Psychonomic Science, 10*, 205–6
Bogartz, R. S. (1966). Test of a theory of predictive behavior in young children. *Psychonomic Science, 4*, 433–4.
Bogartz, R. S. (1969). Short-term memory in binary prediction by children: Some stochastic information processing models. In G. H. Bower and J. T. Spence (Eds.), *The Psychology of Learning and Motivation*, Vol. 3. New York and London: Academic Press.
Bower, T. G. R. (1974). *Development in Infancy.* San Francisco: Freeman.
Brackbill, Y. and Fitzgerald, H. E. (1969). Development of the sensory analyzers during infancy. In L. P. Lipsitt and H. W. Reese. (Eds.), *Advances in Child Development and Behavior*, Vol. 4. New York and London: Academic Press.
Broadbent, D. E. (1952). Listening to one of two synchronous messages. *Journal of Experimental Psychology, 44*, 51–5.
Broadbent, D. E. (1958). *Perception and Communication.* London: Pergamon Press.
Broadbent, D. E. (1970). Stimulus and response set: two kinds of selective attention. In D. Mostofsky (Ed.), *Attention: Contemporary Theories and Analysis.* New York: Appleton-Century-Crofts.
Broadbent, D. E. (1971). *Decision and Stress.* London: Academic Press.
Bronstein, A. I. and Petrova, E. P. (1952). An investigation of the auditory analyzers in neonates and young infants. Reprinted in Y. Brackbill and G. Thompson (Eds.), *Behavior in Infancy and Early Childhood: A Book of Readings.* New York Free Press.
Bruner, J. (1969). Eye, hand and mind. In D. Elkind and J. H. Flavell (Eds.), *Studies in Cognitive Development.* Oxford University Press.
Bruner, J. and Potter, M. C. (1964). Interference in visual recognition. *Science, 144*, 424–5.

Caron, R. F. and Caron, A. J. (1968). The effect of repeated exposure and stimulus complexity on visual fixation in infants. *Psychonomic Science, 10,* 207–8.

Charlesworth, W. R. (1969). The role of surprise in cognitive development. In D. Elkind and J. H. Flavell (Eds.), *Studies in Cognitive Development.* Oxford University Press.

Cohen, L. B., Gelber, E. R. and Lazar, M. A. (1971). Infant habituation and generalization to differing degrees of stimulus novelty. *Journal of Experimental Child Psychology, 11,* 379–89.

Cohen, N. J. and Douglas, V. I. (1972). Characteristics of the orienting response in hyperactive and normal children. *Psychophysiology, 9,* 238–45.

Craig, G. J. and Myers, J. L. (1963). A developmental study of sequential two-choice decision making. *Child Development, 34,* 483–94.

Deutsch, J. and Deutsch, D. (1963). Attention: some theoretical considerations. *Psychological Review, 70,* 80–90.

Douglas, V. I. (1974). Sustained attention and impulse control: implications for the handicapped child. In J. A. Swets and L. L. Elliott (Eds.), *Psychology and the Handicapped Child.* U.S. Department of Health, Education and Welfare, Office of Education.

Doyle, A. B. (1973). Listening to distraction: A developmental study of selective attention. *Journal of Experimental Child Psychology, 15,* 100–15.

Dykeman, R. A., Ackerman, P. T., Clements, S. D. and Peters, J. E. (1971). Specific learning disabilities: An attentional syndrome. In H. R. Myklebust (Ed.), *Progress in Learning Disabilities.* New York: Grune and Stratton.

Fantz, R. L. (1970). Visual perception and experience in infancy. In F. A. Young and D. B. Lindsley (Eds.), *Early Experience and Visual Information Processing in Perceptual and Reading Disorders.* Washington, D.C.: National Academy of Sciences.

Foster, M., Vietze, P. and Friedman, S. (1973). Visual attention to non-contingent and contingent stimuli in early infancy. *Proceedings of the 81st Annual Convention of the American Psychological Association, Montreal, 8,* 93–4.

Fountain, W. and Lynn, R. (1966). Change in level of arousal during childhood. *Behavior Research and Therapy, 4,* 213–17.

Friedman, S., Nagy, A. N. and Carpenter, G. C. (1970). Newborn attention: Differential response decrement to visual stimuli. *Journal of Experimental Child Psychology, 10,* 44–51.

Graham, K. K. and Clifton, R. K. (1966). Heart rate change as a component of the orienting response. *Psychological Bulletin, 65,* 305–20.

Greenberg, D. J. (1971). Accelerating visual complexity level in the human infant. *Child Development, 42,* 905–18.

Greenberg, D. J. and O'Donnell, W. J. (1972). Infancy and the optimal level of stimulation. *Child Development, 43,* 639–45.

Greenberg, D. J., Uzgiris, I. C. and Hunt, J. (1970). Attentional preferences and experience. III. Visual familiarity and looking time. *Journal of Genetic Psychology, 117,* 123–35.

Haith, M. M. (1966). Response of the human newborn to movement. *Journal of Experimental Child Psychology, 3,* 235–43.

Horowitz, F. D. (1969). Learning, developmental research and individual differences. In L. P. Lipsitt and H. W. Reese (Eds.), *Advances in Child Development and Behavior,* Vol. 4. New York and London: Academic Press.

Hutt, S. J., Lenard, H. G. and Prechtl, H. F. R. (1969). Psychophysiological studies in newborn infants. In L. R. Lipsitt and H. W. Reese (Eds.), *Advances in Child Development and Behavior*, Vol. 4. New York and London: Academic Press.

Jennings, J. R. (1971). Cardiac reactions and different development levels of cognitive functioning. *Psychophysiology*, *8*, 433–50.

Jones, S. (1972). Test of Bogartz' model of binary prediction by children. *Psychonomic Science*, *27*, 77–9.

Kagan, J. (1966). Reflection-impulsivity: the generality and dynamics of conceptual tempo. *Journal of Abnormal Psychology*, *71*, 17–24.

Kagan, J. (1971). *Change and Continuity in Infancy*. New York: Wiley.

Kaplan, B. E. (1970). Psychophysiological and cognitive development in children: The relationship of skin conductance and heart rate to word association and task requirements. *Psychophysiology*, *7*, 18–26.

Kaye, H. (1967). Infant sucking behavior and its modifications. In L. P. Lipsitt and C. C. Spiker (Eds.), *Advances in Child Development and Behavior*, Vol. 3. New York: Academic Press.

Kaye, H. and Levin, G. R. (1963). Two attempts to demonstrate tonal suppression of non-nutritive sucking in neonates. *Perceptual and Motor Skills*, *17*, 521–2.

Keen, R. (1964). Effects of auditory stimuli on sucking behavior in the human neonate. *Journal of Experimental Child Psychology*, *1*, 348–54.

Lefton, L. A. and Spragins, A. B. (1974). Orthographic structure and reading experience affect the transfer from iconic to short-term memory. *Journal of Experimental Psychology*, *103*, 775–81.

Levy-Schoen, A. and Pouthas, V. (1971-2). Experimental study of the field of ocular activity in the pre-school child. *Bulletin de Psychologie*, *25*, 888–96.

Lindsley, D. B. (1960). Attention, consciousness, sleep and wakefulness. In J. Field (Ed.), *Handbook of Physiology*, Section I, Vol. III. Washington, D.C.: American Physiological Society.

Luria, A. R. (1973). *The Working Brain: An Introduction to Neuropsychology*. Harmondsworth: Penguin Books.

Maccoby, E. E. (1967). Selective attention in children. In L. P. Lipsitt and C. C. Spiker (Eds.), *Advances in Child Development and Behavior*, Vol. 3. New York: Academic Press.

Maccoby, E. E. (1969). The development of stimulus information. In J. P. Hill (Ed.), *Minnesota Symposium of Child Psychology*, Vol. 3. University of Minnesota Press.

Maccoby, E. E. and Konrad, K. W. (1967). The effects of preparatory set on selective listening: developmental trends. *Monographs of the Society for Research in Child Development*, *32*, 4, Whole No. 112.

Mackworth, J. F. (1963). The relation between the visual image and post-perceptual memory. *Journal of Verbal Learning and Verbal Behavior*, *2*, 75–85.

Mackworth, J. F. (1966). Perceptual coding as a factor in short-term memory. *Canadian Journal of Psychology*, *20*, 18–33.

Mackworth, J. F. (1969). *Vigilance and Habituation*. Harmondsworth: Penguin Books.

Mackworth, J. F. (1970). *Vigilance and Attention*. Harmondsworth: Penguin Books.

Mackworth, J. F. (1972). Some models of the reading process: learners and skilled readers. *Reading Research Quarterly*, *8*, 710–33.

Mackworth, N. H. (1975). The line of sight approach to children's reading and comprehension. In S. Wanat, H. Singer and M. Kling (Eds.), *Extracting Meaning from Written Language.* Delaware: International Reading Association.

Mackworth, N. H. and Bruner, J. S. (1970). How adults and children search and recognize pictures. *Human Development, 13,* 149–77.

Mackworth, N. H. and Otto, D. A. (1970). Habituation of visual orientation response in young children. *Perception and Psychophysics, 7,* 173–8.

Mackworth, N. H., Grandstaff, N. W. and Pribram, K. H. (1973). Orientation to pictorial novelty by speech-disordered children. *Neuropsychologica, 11,* 443–50.

McCall, R. B. and Melson, W. H. (1969). Attention in infants as a function of discrepancy and habituation rate. *Psychonomic Science, 17,* 317–19.

Miranda, S. B. (1970). Visual abilities and pattern preferences of premature infants and full-term neonates. *Journal of Experimental Child Psychology, 10,* 189–205.

Moray, N. (1959). Attention in dichotic listening: affective cues and the influence of instructions. *Quarterly Journal of Experimental Psychology, 9,* 56–60.

Moray, N. (1969). *Attention: Selective Processes in Vision and Hearing.* London: Hutchinson.

Moray, N. and O'Brien, T. (1967). Signal detection theory applied to selective listening. *Journal of Acoustic Society of America, 42,* 765–72.

Munsinger, H., Kessen, W. and Kessen, M. (1964). Age and uncertainty: developmental variation in preference for variability. *Journal of Experimental Child Psychology, 1,* 1–15.

Olson, D. R. (1970). *Cognitive Development: The Child's Acquisition of Diagonality.* New York and London: Academic Press.

Piaget, J. (1950). *The Psychology of Intelligence.* New York: Harcourt Brace.

Piaget, J. (1961, 1969). *The Mechanisms of Perception.* Tr. G. N. Seagrim. London: Routledge and Kegan Paul.

Prechtl, H. and Beintema, D. (1964). The neurological examination of the full-term newborn infant. *Clinics in Developmental Medicine,* No. 12. London: Heinemann.

Pribram, K. H. (1971). *Languages of the Brain.* Englewood Cliffs, New Jersey: Prentice-Hall.

Schaffer, H. R., Greenwood, A. and Parry, M. H. (1972). The onset of wariness. *Child Development, 43,* 165–75.

Schell, D. J. (1971). Conceptual behavior in young children: Learning to shift dimensional attention. *Journal of Experimental Child Psychology, 12,* 72–87.

Sheingold, K. (1973). Developmental differences in intake and storage of visual information. *Journal of Experimental Child Psychology, 16,* 1–11.

Siegel, A. W. and Stevenson, H. W. (1966). Incidental learning: a developmental study. *Child Development, 37,* 811–17.

Sokolov, E. N. (1963). *Perception and the Conditioned Reflex.* New York: Pergamon Press.

Super, C. M., Kagan, J., Morrison, F. J., Haith, M. M. and Weiffenbach, J. (1972). Discrepancy and attention in the five-month infant. *Genetic Psychology Monographs, 85,* 305–31.

Sykes, D. H., Douglas, V. I. and Morgenstern, G. (1973). Sustained attention in hyperactive children. *Journal of Child Psychology and Psychiatry and Allied Disciplines, 14,* 213–20.

Taylor, M. M. and Henning, G. B. (1963). Transformations of perception with prolonged observation. *Canadian Journal of Psychology, 17,* 349–60.

Treisman, A. M. (1960). Contextual clues in selective listening. *Quarterly Journal of Experimental Psychology, 12,* 242–8.

Treisman. A. M. (1964). Verbal cues, language and meaning in selective attention. *American Journal of Psychology, 77,* 206–19.

Treisman, A. M. (1969). Strategies and models of selective attention. *Psychological Review, 76,* 282–99.

Vurpillot, E. (1968). The development of scanning strategies and their relation to visual differentiation. *Journal of Experimental Child Psychology, 6,* 632–50.

Weiss, G., Minde, K., Werry, J. S., Douglas, V. and Nemeth, E. (1972). Studies on the hyperactive child: five year follow-up. In S. Chess and A. Thomas (Eds.), *Annual Progress in Child Psychiatry and Development.* New York: Brunner and Mazel.

Welch, M. J. (1974). Infants' visual attention to varying degrees of novelty. *Child Development, 45,* 344–50.

Wilton, K. and Boersma, F. J. (1974). *Eye Movements, Surprise Reactions and Cognitive Development.* Rotterdam University Press.

Wolff, P. H. (1959). Observations of newborn infants. *Psychosomatic Medicine, 21,* 110–18.

Zeaman, D. and House, B. (1963). The role of attention in discrimination learning. In N. Ellis (Ed.), *Handbook of Mental Deficiency,* New York: McGraw-Hill.

CHAPTER 4

Development of Perception of Form

Magdalen D. Vernon

I. INTRODUCTION

From recent discussions of the perception of form and pattern by adults (see for instance Corcoran, 1971), it would appear that there is a generally accepted view that the parts of these are processed by separate "analyzers", which extract distinctive features. Appropriate analyzers, normally selected by previously established attentional sets, are switched on to process particular types of stimuli. The separate parts are then actively synthesized and a whole figure constructed which is identified as a rule as one of a class of similar figures, previously encountered, and which may incorporate information coming from other sources. From this class a "schema" may be encoded on the basis of a set of commonly related characteristics (Evans, 1967). Subsequent examples are then perceived in terms of the initial schema together with certain corrections appropriate to the particular instance. Thus a schema or prototype could be extracted from variations in a simple dot pattern (Posner and Keele, 1968). According to Jones and Holley (1970), in the case of very complex patterns a schema could be constituted and learnt even when individual features were not perceived.

The characteristics of form to which much consideration has recently been given are those of information content, in terms of uncertainty *v*. redundancy. Complex randomly generated figures have the greatest amount of uncertainty; simple, regular and symmetrical figures the highest degree of redundancy. Though phenomenal complexity is not necessarily the same as information theory complexity, they are highly correlated (Zusne, 1970). More attention is given, and the duration of eye fixations increases, with increase in complexity of forms; and these are longest at the points of maximum information, that is to say where direction of contour changes (Baker and Loeb, 1973). Adults can differentiate complex and less redundant forms more accurately, though in longer time. Redundant forms are more accurately identified and reproduced, though there is an optimum degree of complexity. Thus randomly generated polygons having six to eight turns exhibit the minimum errors of identification in brief tachistoscopic exposures.

However, Michels and Zusne (1965) considered that perceptibility might be a function of the organization of forms, as well as of their information content. Probably redundancy was the most important characteristic determining discrimination and identification, as exhibited in the Gestalt qualities of symmetry, good continuation, proximity and closure. However, other important secondary variables were curvature v. rectilinearity of outline, jaggedness, compactness and elongation.

But in identification as involving allocation of a form to a particular class, or as instancing a particular schema, the size and variability of the class may be important. Garner (1962) considered that forms regarded by the Gestalt psychologists as "good" were readily identified because they belonged to a small sub-set of forms containing few alternatives; indeed, the circle and the square may be regarded as unique. The number of names that can be given them is also small (Clement, 1964).

Now it cannot be assumed that children, especially infants and young children, are capable of the same perceptual processes as adults, nor that their perceptions are determined by the same factors. It may, however, be possible to trace the early or gradual development of these processes as age and intelligence increase.

II. PERCEPTION OF FORM AND PATTERN BY INFANTS

(1) Physiological factors

Clearly the perception of forms and patterns is impossible unless the visual mechanisms in the retina and nervous system are functioning effectively. However, the evidence is that in the main the visual mechanisms are operative at birth, though in some cases they may continue to mature during the first 2 or 3 months of life. Thus the infant at birth or soon afterwards possesses the physiological capacity to perceive visual form in the external environment. Reese and Lipsitt (1970) considered that although the retinal cells are not fully differentiated at birth, they do not differ greatly from those of adults. Hershenson (1967) cited evidence to show that rods and cones are structurally differentiated very early in life. The differential functioning of photopic and scotopic vision is also apparent in the electroretinograms. The structure and functioning of the eye is adequate physiologically to provide differential responses to most parts of the field. Visual evoked responses appear in the EEG at birth, though more slowly than in adults; and relatively intense stimulation may be required to produce them (Hershenson, 1967; Eichorn, 1970).

Sensitivity to brightness differences has been measured by means of the optokinetic response to a moving target of black and white stripes. The reflex response occurs soon after birth, but is gradually replaced by following responses under voluntary control. There is also a gradual increase in sensitivity over the first 2 or 3 months, infants responding to decreasing brightness contrast of the stripes (Doris et al., 1967). Acuity is lower than that of adults at birth and also increases with age. Fantz et al. (1962) cited Gorman et al. (1959) as obtaining the optokinetic response soon after birth to stripes subtending a visual angle of 33.5 min. Miranda (1970) found that newborn infants differentiated stationary stripes from plain targets when the angle subtended by the stripes was 66 min. This improved to 40 min at 1 month, but the differentiation was not stable until over 2 months (Fantz et al., 1962). However, it would appear that visual acuity is adequate for the discrimination of the targets normally employed in investigating the perception of young infants.

There has been some argument as to the development of accommodation. Haynes et al. (1965), employing the method of dynamic retinoscopy to observe modifications in the image reflected from the lens, found that infants did not adjust accommodation to target distance before 1 month, but maintained it at about 19 cm. Accommodation began to adapt to target distance during the second month, and was comparable to that of adults at 3 months. However, it is possible that the target of black marks and dots they employed was an inadequate stimulus (Hershenson, 1967). Moreover, Fantz et al. (1962) found that striped targets were preferred to plain even when the target distance was varied.

Young infants exhibit some degree of binocular co-ordination in orientating their gaze towards a single stimulus, but convergence of the eyes may be inaccurate and intermittent for the first few weeks. Wickelgren (1967) found that in newborn infants there might be considerable divergence of the eyes when a single stimulus was presented; or the eyes might be directed towards different parts of the stimulus. But convergence was better with a striped target, and became accurate by 7–8 weeks. Before that it is possible that information from one eye is suppressed by that from the other and vision is therefore reasonably clear (Hershenson, 1967).

(2) Perception of the sensory characteristics of the field

A number of investigations of the eye movements and fixations of infants has been carried out to demonstrate the manner in which they scan the visual field, and what parts of it they fixate. Scanning begins at birth or soon after, and is particularly noticeable when the infant is propped into a more or less upright position (Korner and Grobstein, 1966), or held against the shoulder (Frederickson and Brown, 1975). Infants then become relatively quiescent in body while looking (Stechler *et al.*, 1966). There is more steady fixation of patterned than of plain fields (Salapatek, 1968); and eye movements are more dispersed in the horizontal than in the vertical dimension of the field. Fixations are therefore dispersed when a horizontal black edge on a white field is presented, but cluster about a vertical edge (Kessen *et al.*, 1972). This might result from a natural tendency for eye movement to be easier in the horizontal than in the vertical dimension.

If shapes are presented, there may be a characteristic direction of gaze, towards smaller rather than larger shapes and to solid rather than to outlined figures (Salapatek, 1968). When a large triangular shape was shown, fixations tended to cluster near the vertices (Salapatek and Kessen, 1966). Usually a single vertex was selected, but there were individual variations in the vertex chosen (Salapatek and Kessen, 1973). Moreover, some infants scanned quite extensively; others scanned sides rather than vertices. It is interesting to note that even in adults fixations made in scanning complex geometrical shapes tended to cluster round the angles of these, presumably because they are the points giving the greatest amount of information (Baker and Loeb, 1973).

Scanning becomes more extensive and varied as infants increase in age. By 4–5 weeks they appeared to possess well organized and coordinated patterns of head and eye movements, with alternating fixations and saccades, which operated when they looked about the field (Tronick and Clanton, 1971). In older infants of 14–15 weeks there was wider exploration of the field, with longer eye movements, than in younger infants who tended to focus on a central area. Whereas scanning was at first confined to small segments of the contours of shapes such as a square, triangle, etc., later the whole contour was scanned; and by 8–10 weeks the centres also (Salapatek and Kessen, 1973). When geometric patterns containing interior features were presented, infants of about 10 weeks fixated the latter as well as the external contour. The peripheral field covered also increases with age (Tronick, 1972). When a peripheral stimulus was presented shortly after a central stimulus, infants looked from the latter to the former.

At 2 weeks the peripheral stimulus had to be within 15° of the central stimulus. But from 6–10 weeks the peripheral field expanded until it covered 35°, and even more if the peripheral stimulus was moving.

One cannot of course assume that an infant perceives everything he fixates. Nevertheless when he fixates a particular area repeatedly, such as the vertex of a triangle, it would seem probable that this feature attracts his attention and is salient in his perceptions. At 2 months areas of high brightness are important in determining the direction of gaze (Fantz, 1970). It would appear that in early infancy attention is captured and held by certain impressive features in the stimulus pattern (Hershension, 1967). In later infancy attention becomes increasingly controlled by centrally organized perceptual processes. It is possible that this begins as the peripheral field expands, from 6 weeks upwards. At this stage it would seem that perception is not determined wholly by the salient sensory characteristics, but also by the information content of the stimulus. The infant then begins to explore it in order to discover its nature and characteristics. Directed looking between various objects in the field occurs at 2–3 months (Woodward, 1971). But there is a sharp decrease in amount of visual attention rather before then when the infant begins to look at his own hands (White, 1971). Further increases at a later age may depend on the complexity and variation of the surroundings.

(3) INFORMATION SEARCH IN PATTERN PERCEPTION

The gradual transition from response to sensorily salient features to the search for information is demonstrated in the considerable number of observations made on infants' fixation preferences between two stimuli. Fantz (1958) was the first to report these preferences, finding by observing the direction of gaze that quite young infants looked longer at a square containing a checked pattern than at a plain square. In a later study (Fantz, 1963), he showed that newborn infants exhibited the same preference. Miranda (1970) found that both full-term and premature newborn infants preferred figured to plain fields, and more clearly defined to less clearly defined patterns. The premature infants, somewhat older than the full-term since birth though younger since conception, preferred a single square to a 4-square check pattern. The full-term infants preferred the latter. But Jones-Molfese (1972) found that some full-term and premature infants preferred the plain field to the 4-square pattern; others preferred the latter. However even if there are individual differences, it does appear that the ability to discriminate figured from plain fields may arise before full-term.

Other studies have demonstrated the transition to determination of direction of gaze by the search for information in the increasing fixation of complex rather than simple patterns. There has been some disagreement between findings, possibly because different methods of observation and assessment have been employed by different experimenters. However, the main trend is fairly clear. Thus for instance Brennan *et al.* (1966) presented check patterns with 4, 64 and 576 squares, and found that the total fixation duration in infants of 3 weeks was longer for the simplest pattern than for the more complex. At 8 weeks the 64-square pattern was fixated longest, and at 14 weeks the 576-square pattern. It would appear therefore that as age increases there is an increase in the capacity for perceiving and processing patterns providing a greater amount of information.

There are, however, individual differences between different infants which may related to their previous experience as well as to their maturation. Thus Horowitz *et. al.* (1972) obtained different results in cross-sectional groups at 3, 8 and 14 weeks, and in longitudinal studies over the same period. For the 3-week infants in the cross-sectional studies there were no differences in looking time at patterns of varying complexity. At 8 weeks a 4-square check pattern was looked at less than were the more complex patterns; and at 14 weeks a 16-square pattern was looked at less. But in the longitudinal group, the 4-square and the 16-square patterns were looked at less than the more complex patterns at all ages, suggesting that previous experience had increased the ability to process information. The effects of previous experience were also demonstrated in a study by Greenberg (1971), who found that infants of 8–12 weeks, after exposure in their homes to check patterns, advanced more quickly to the stage of preferring 576-square to 64-square patterns than did infants exposed to a homogeneous grey square. Again, those exposed to a slightly more complex pattern (144 or 256 squares) than that to which they had previously responded (64 squares) looked more at the 576-square pattern than did those exposed to a similar pattern (64 squares). It would seem that patterns slightly more complex than those which could be comprehended stimulated attention and information-processing.

But factors other than the number of checks in patterns may be important in determining response, for instance, the size of the checks; large checks are sensorily more salient than small ones. Thus Harter and Suitt (1970) found that cortical evoked responses were more variable in amount to checks of different sizes until about 5 weeks; but thereafter progressively smaller checks evoked the greatest response. Karmel *et al.* (1974) also claimed that the cortical evoked response varied with the sizes of the elements in check patterns, the size which evoked the maximum response decreasing between 8–10 weeks and

13 weeks. Variation in fixation duration had been found to vary in the same manner (Karmel, 1969a). However, Greenberg and Blue (1975), varying contour and number of elements in rows and columns of black dots on a white screen, found no significant change in preference as measured by duration of fixation, between 2 and 4 months. But when both contour and number of elements were increased, there was a significantly greater preference in the older infants for the more complex patterns. Greenberg and Blue therefore concluded that perception of increasing complexity depended on both contour and number of elements; but it did not seem to be affected by the size of the latter. However, in infants of 4 months the latency of turning towards a pattern appeared to be determined by the size of the checks, but duration of fixation by the number of checks (Cohen, 1972). Thus at this age attraction of attention may still be to some extent a function of the sensory characteristics of the stimulus, whereas maintenance of attention is related to information-processing.

The complete regularity and high degree of redundancy of the check patterns which have been employed so extensively may obscure the effects of factors other than the number and size of elements. Thus Friedman (1972) found that newborn infants fixated patterns with a high degree of regularity and redundancy, such as check patterns, stripes and bullseyes, for longer than irregular patterns such as randomly arranged lines. Karmel (1969b) showed that older infants of 9–21 weeks also preferred redundant to random patterns of squares, though there was no variation in fixation time with variation in complexity. Redundancy may also be assessed in terms of the number of "turns" (changes of direction of outline) in irregular solid black figures. Newborn infants were found to fixate figures with ten turns rather than figures with five or twenty turns; that is to say, they selected those with a moderate degree of redundancy (Hershenson et al., 1965).

It would appear from these findings that, at least in younger infants, search for information may not be the main determinant of fixation time, since redundant patterns afford less information than random patterns. Thus it seems possible that in some cases the over-all appearance of certain patterns may attract infants, such as regularity and symmetry, characteristic of "good" Gestalt configurations. Other types of appearance may be significant. Thus Fantz (1958) found that in the majority of cases infants under about 8 weeks looked longer at a striped pattern than at a bullseye; but at that age preference changed and they looked longer at the bullseye.

It is difficult to decide what characteristics of these patterns are involved in these preferences. However, that certain other general form characteristics may be significant in perception is suggested in a study by Bower (1967). He observed that there was a decrease of non-nutrient sucking in infants of 5 weeks in response to a novel stimulus. When a triangle divided by a horizontal space was replaced by a complete triangle there was a decrease in sucking, suggesting that the infants perceived the latter as a new configuration. But there was no similar decrease when a triangle with a horizontal bar across it was presented first. Therefore it was concluded that the infant perceived the latter, but not the former, as an integrated whole, in accordance with the Gestalt principle of "good continuation".

These observations would seem to indicate that infants may perceive patterns as wholes, rather than their separate elements. It is not possible of course to conclude from investigations of looking preferences and fixation duration whether infants are seeing whole patterns or their separate elements (Hershenson, 1967). The evidence from eye movements in scanning suggests that at least the younger infants are likely to perceive figures piecemeal. However, it is possible that as they shift their gaze they may see several pieces in succession which combine together to produce a rather vague general impression; this is sufficient to enable them to differentiate between patterns of simple structure.

(4) IDENTIFICATION OF FORM AND PATTERN

It has been shown that infants are able to differentiate a figure from the ground and certain figures from one another, either as a whole or in terms of their parts. Moreover, ability to process these improves with increase in age. What is less certain is the degree to which they are able to identify them. Identification necessitates not only fairly accurate perception but also the matching of current perceptions against memory traces of previous percepts. It is claimed by some experimenters that such traces begin to be laid down soon after birth, but they must be very rudimentary. Certainly they develop and improve in extent and permanence with increase in age, as has been demonstrated in the numerous studies of habituation. Again, the nature of early identification is doubtful. It is possible that the infant is merely aware of a vague familiarity with the repeated stimulation employed in habituation, and that genuine identification does not develop until the latter part of the first year.

The characteristics of habituation are that response to a stimulus gradually decreases in amount if it is presented repeatedly; and if a stimulus differing to some extent from the repeated stimulus is then presented, response is restored. Thus the process depends on a decline in attention to a stimulus which is remembered, and a renewal of attention to a novel stimulus. From the duration between repetitions and between the repeated and the novel stimulus, it is possible to determine how long memory persists. And from the amount and types of dissimilarity between the repeated and the novel stimulus, some information may be obtained as to the manner in which the infant relates stimuli together, and identifies or fails to identify an existing stimulus in terms of stimuli previously perceived.

Friedman *et al.* (1970) have claimed to have obtained evidence of habituation, that is to say response decrement, even in newborn infants, to repeated presentations for 60 sec of 4 and 144-square check patterns, with an inter-stimulus interval of 5–10 sec. Fixation durations began to decrease after the third or fourth trial. However, though the decrement occurred in infants over 66 hours of age, there was very little in infants under 48 hours (Friedman and Carpenter, 1971). When infants were shown the 4-square pattern 5–10 sec after a series of eight or more presentations of the 144-square pattern, there was a significant increase in response; and the same for presentation of the 144-square pattern after a series of 4-square patterns (Friedman, 1972b). But response was variable.Some infants did not habituate at all; others did not show an increased response to the novel stimulus; and in fact only 32 per cent of the infants displayed both responses. In a further experiment, Friedman *et al.* (1974) found that although both male and female newborn infants responded to a novel stimulus showing a large discrepancy with the repeated stimulus (4-square *v.* 144-square), only female infants responded to a moderate discrepancy (4-square *v.* 16-square); just as, in an earlier experiment (Friedman and Carpenter, 1971), female infants were shown to habituate more to a 144-square pattern, male infants to a 4-square pattern. Thus it was argued that differentiation was more advanced in female than in male newborn infants. However, even if momentary memory traces are established soon after birth, these do not appear to be universal.

Jeffrey and Cohen (1971) on the other hand considered that habituation to any form of visual stimulation is not established until 2–3 months, and that recovery and response to a novel stimulus may develop even later. This of course depends both on the type of pattern and the inter-stimulus interval. Wetherford and Cohen (1973) obtained no trace of habituation in infants of 6–8 weeks to a series of coloured geometrical shapes presented at 8 sec intervals. But habituation began to appear at 10 weeks. Caron and Caron (1968) found a steady decrease in fixation duration at 14–16 weeks to check patterns presented immediately after one another with no inter-trial interval, which decrease was less for a more complex 144-square pattern than for a simpler 4-square pattern. Fixation time then increased on presentation of a novel pattern of dots, lines or irregular shapes. But even at 4 months, although there was an increase of response to a novel stimulus presented immediately, there was none with a delay of 5 min (Pancratz and Cohen, 1970).

As regards the effects of complexity of pattern : Brown (1974) obtained habituation to 4-square and 576-square check patterns at 8 weeks, followed by increased response to a different pattern; but there was no decrement and no subsequently increased response to a 64-square pattern. The latter was the preferred pattern, as assessed previously from fixation preferences. Thus perhaps interest in and attention to it was prolonged and habituation did not occur. However, there are individual differences in response. Greenberg *et al.* (1973) found that infants of 11 weeks who habituated quickly to a pattern of four black dots showed relatively longer fixations of complex 576-square patterns than of simpler 4-square patterns; whereas those who habituated slowly showed a greater response to the simpler patterns. These differences may be due to differences in maturation.

One of the determinants of response to a novel stimulus after habituation was its degree of unlikeness to the repeated stimulus, related presumably, at least in part, to accuracy of differentiation. Thus Cohen *et al.* (1971) obtained habituation in 4-month infants to a repeated simple geometrical shape, a red or a green circle or triangle. They then presented a novel stimulus which differed in form or colour or both form and colour from the repeated stimulus. There was some recovery of response to change of either form or colour alone, but greater recovery to change of both. Welch (1974) also found that at 4 months there was an increase of fixation duration to a novel stimulus according as it differed from the repeated stimulus in one, two or three dimensions of shape, colour and arrangement of elements. Super *et al.* (1972) showed that there was a maximal increase in fixation time to a novel complex mobile which was moderately discrepant from a mobile to which infants had been exposed for three weeks at home. The effect was less for minimally and maximally discrepant mobiles. It should be noted that minimally and moderately discrepant mobiles involved merely different arrangements of the same shapes, whereas the maximally different had five quite different shapes of different colours (Fig. 4.1). Therefore it was not surprising if the latter was regarded as a totally different class of stimulus. The minimally discrepant was presumably not readily discriminated. However, McCall and Melson (1969) found that in infants of 5 months the amount of cardiac deceleration, which is considered to indicate interest and surprise, decreased with increase in discrepancy between repeated and novel complex stimuli (see Fig. 4.2). Degree of discrepancy had been estimated

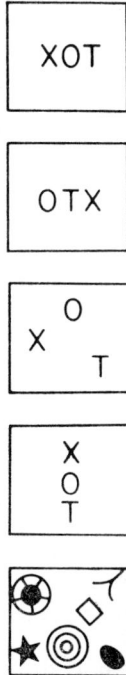

Fig. 4.1. Repeated and novel stimuli. (*After* Super *et al.*, 1972, p. 311.)

by adults (McCall and Kagan, 1967). It is difficult of course to compare the degree of discrepancy involved in these different types of stimuli. Possibly the maximally discrepant were regarded here also as belonging to a different and non-comparable category. But the perceptual features determining differentiation and identification are obviously numerous, including form and complexity. Also individual variations in the maturation, experience and interests of the infants may be significant.

It appears that at about 4 months infants begin to show some discrimination between the whole and parts of patterns with interior detail. Thus Miller (1972), having ascertained the relative saliency of the parts of Fig. 4.3 from the relative duration of fixation, presented the whole pattern repeatedly. After habituation to this, the parts were presented separately. Fixation duration then decreased for the more salient parts but increased for the less salient. It was concluded that the infants had perceived the more salient parts as well as the wholes during habituation, but not the less salient parts. However, Bower (1974) trained infants in a conditioned response to the whole figure of Fig. 4.3a. Infants below 4 months then responded to any of the parts;

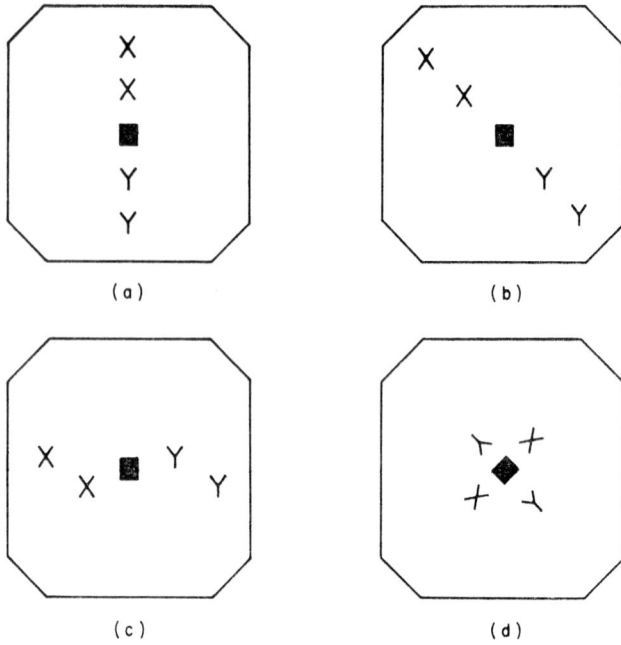

FIG. 4.2. Repeated (a) and novel (b, c, d) stimuli. (*After* McCall and Kagan, 1967, p. 383.)

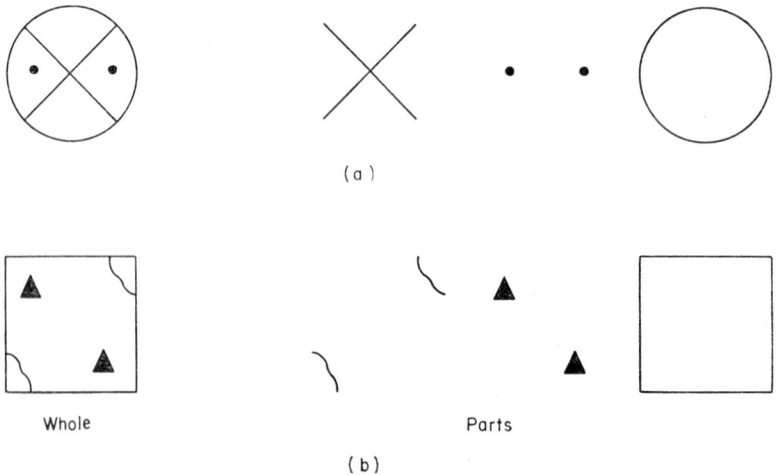

FIG. 4.3. Response to parts after habituation to whole. (*After* Miller, 1972, p. 484.)

but infants of 4 months responded only to the whole figure. Thus although there is some disagreement between these findings, possibly due to the difference in experimental method, it does appear that at about 4 months infants are beginning to discriminate certain parts of whole patterns instead of identifying the former with the latter.

(5) PERCEPTION AND IDENTIFICATION OF PICTURES OF FACES

Some light is thrown on the differentiation and integration of parts of patterns within the whole by studies of the development in response to pictures of faces. The problems which have been investigated mainly relate to the ability to discriminate pictures of faces from other complex patterns and to identify the former; and whether parts of the face, notably the eyes, are perceived independently of the face as a whole On the first question, a number of experiments has been performed to show whether, and when, infants fixate realistic photographs of faces longer and more frequently than stylized or "schematic" drawings of faces and drawings with the features "scrambled", that is to say arranged at random. There appeared to be no discrimination between these at the age of $2\frac{1}{2}$ months (Koopman and Ames, 1968). Wilcox (1969), presenting photographs of faces and schematic, scrambled and incomplete faces to infants of 4, 10 and 16 weeks, found that fixation time increased with the complexity of the stimuli as measured by the number of facial features. There were no differences between types of stimulus for the younger infants; but the older infants looked longest at the photographs. Again, Haaf and Bell (1967) found that at 4 months infants, shown pairs of stimuli with four degrees of resemblance to a face and four degrees of complexity, fixated the most face-like for longest, but were not affected by complexity (see Fig. 4.4). Lewis (1969) also found that with infants of 12, 24, 36 and 57 weeks the order of preference as assessed from the duration of the first fixation was the same at all ages; namely, regular, schematic, one-eyed and scrambled faces. Thus, when differentiation begins, it is mainly in terms of complexity; but older infants seem to perceive the face as such.

It has been suggested that while the face is perceived in terms of the complexity of its pattern and before it is perceived as a face, infants respond preferentially to particular features. Early experiments (Ahrens, cited by Gibson, 1969) seemed to indicate that infants under 2 months of age smiled at pairs of eyes presented alone, and dot patterns resembling eyes. However, Salzen (1963) found that at this age smiling could be elicited by a variety of stimuli such as flashing lights. It may be that smiling is aroused by stimuli of high brightness contrast; and we know that they also stimulate fixation. Caron *et al.* (1973) studied the differ-ences in fixation of facial features in 4-month infants by means of the habituation technique. Infants were shown repeated presentations of pictures of a variety of distortions of the face : faces with no eyes, dis-placed eyes, no nose and mouth, displaced nose and mouth. After eight repetitions of one of these they were shown the picture of a normal face. The largest increase of fixation time in response to this was after

Fig. 4.4. Varying degrees of similarity to face. (*After* Haaf and Bell, 1967, p. 895.)

the face without eyes and with displaced eyes. There was no increase with nose and mouth distortions. Thus it appeared that these infants attended more to the eyes than to the nose and mouth, and the former were discriminated and recognized earlier. This again may have been due in part to their high brightness contrast. But at 5 months there was no difference in response to the eyes and the nose and mouth; thus presumably the latter were perceived also. Again, whereas the younger infants responded more to an inverted head than to an inverted face, the older infants responded more to the latter. This suggested that they had become aware of the face as such, as well as its features.

It has been hypothesized that during the first few months of life infants were attracted to particular facial features, notably the eyes which stood out by virtue of their brightness contrast. They also fixated more complex patterns for longer, but did not discriminate pictures of faces from meaningless patterns. But at about 4 months they began, by studying the realistic photographs of faces, to acquire a "schema" of the face as a whole (Lewis, 1969), which enabled them to identify faces as such. Some degree of familiarity may have been involved, since it was found that infants smiled especially at realistic photographs. But even if the infants were pleased by this familiarity, this hardly warrants the assumption that they perceived them as representations of real faces. Fixation might have been prolonged by attempts to gain information and to understand complex and unfamiliar patterns, as well as to establish a facial schema.

As age increased, infants paid increasingly less attention to realistic photographs of faces. At first they looked most at stimuli which resembled faces fairly closely; but later, during the second year of life, at increasingly discrepant pictures (Kagan, 1971). They were presumably attempting to establish the limits of the facial schema and speculating at length as to what could be included within it, and what must be excluded and classified in a different category. However, the latter was sometimes ignored altogether if it was too discrepant. Similar processes were found to occur in children of 2 years to incongruous pictures such as those of a man with three heads and a man with his head upside down (Lewis et al., 1971). But also fixation duration was greater for more complex than for simpler pictures—three men v. one man. Thus search for information as related to complexity was still a significant determinant of fixation.

After the infant had acquired the generalized facial schema, he began to discriminate differences between pictures of faces and thus to identify particular pictures. This was shown by Cornell (1974), using the habituation procedure. He presented repeatedly to infants of 19 and 23 weeks pairs of pictures of different male and female faces; pairs of the same face; and pairs of the same face looking in different directions. The decrease in fixation time was greatest with the same faces, and less with the same face looking in different directions; but there was no decrease with different faces. However, when a novel pair was subsequently presented, the older infants showed an increase in fixation time, but not the younger. These findings suggest that at about 5 months the generalized facial schema begins to be diversified to include variations in facial appearance.

7—CP * *

(6) CONCLUSIONS

It is perhaps unfortunate that the picture of the face is the only complex pattern identifiable as such the perception and identification of which has been extensively investigated at successive ages. It is possible, though not proven, that the infant's attempts to identify this type of pattern are in fact motivated by interest in human faces, and the endeavour to relate it to the real faces of people he perceives. But this factor, and also the complications arising in the differentiation and classification of slightly different faces, make it difficult to determine the exact manner of operation of the perceptual processes as such, especially in relation to configurational characteristics. Neither is it certain what part is played in identification by the discrimination of distinctive features. Gibson (1969) considered that the establishment of the facial schema postulated by Lewis (1969) follows the discrimination of individual facial features which are then retained and function as invariants in subsequent identification. However, it would seem that only the eyes are differentially discriminated, and these particularly because of their high brightness contrast in pictures. Thus it may be that the identification of the face as a whole pattern is established independently. But it is likely that the distinctive features, especially the nose and mouth, play an important part in enabling the infant to differentiate between different faces.

Considering the evidence from all types of form and pattern, it would appear that when the young infant is presented with simple forms he fixates and perceives them piecemeal, regarding first particular points of strong constrast. Some unsystematic exploration of contours then occurs, but there is at first no perception of over-all form. Thus Fantz (1958) found that infants under 14 weeks did not discriminate between a circle and a cross; or at least did not show any preference for either. The piecemeal perception of repetitive patterns such as the check pattern may engender a general impression which enables differentiation in terms of complexity, or possibly of density. However, infants increasingly explore the more complex patterns and seek to derive information from these. There is some differentiation in terms of redundancy, though it is not certain whether this is a function of differences in uncertainty or of differing general appearance. According to Cohen (1972), the aspects which initially attract attention may not be the same as those which maintain it. Thus it is possible that attraction may result from general appearance, maintained attention from uncertainty. It is true that Lewis et al. (1966) considered that 24-week infants, once they had begun to look at an interesting stimulus, tended to continue to do so. But these stimuli were mainly pictures of faces which probably both aroused and maintained attention.

Development in diversification of memorization follows the same line as that of discrimination. However, this does not perhaps constitute real identification, at least in the early stages. But it does appear in the identification of particular faces.

It would appear that in some cases parts of patterns are perceived before the whole pattern, especially if they contrast strongly with the background, and may be retained as invariants. It is more doubtful if they are perceived with great accuracy and precision; still more that they are systematically integrated together in an organized perception of the whole. Thus in the perception of pictures of faces, the identification of the facial schema may follow in time the differentiation of particular features, especially the eyes. But it should not be inferred that the facial schema is directly constructed by relating together these distinctive features. Again, in other cases the perception of parts may seem to follow the perception of the whole pattern; but there is no systematic analysis of the latter into its constituent parts. This is not established until considerably later in life.

III. PERCEPTION OF FORM BY CHILDREN

(1) PERCEPTION OF FORM CHARACTERISTICS

Not many investigations have been made of the perception of form by quite young children who have just emerged from infancy. The method most often used in such investigation as there are has been is that of the discrimination and matching of simple shapes; though copying has also been employed. It may, however, have been difficult to obtain satisfactory performances in the youngest children; negative results may have been due to inattention or failure to understand the task. From the latter part of the first year, according to Fantz (1970), children exhibit increasingly less interest in the perception of meaningless forms and patterns, and are concerned predominantly with the identification of objects. Indeed Fantz (1961) found that as early as the third month infants looked longer at a solid sphere with a textured surface than at a flat disc. At 6 months they differentiated between a real object which they could grasp and a "virtual" object produced by a stereoscopic shadow caster, which they could not (Bower et al., 1970). At this age they are concerned with solid objects which possess distinguishing characteristics other than those of two-dimensional form.

It has frequently been stated that young children, if they perceive forms at all, do so globally, obtaining vague impressions of the forms as wholes without perceiving their precise characteristics; though, as we saw, some differentiation of parts of complex patterns seemed to begin in infancy. But Venger (1964) and Babska (1965) found that, whereas below 3 years matching of simple geometrical shapes, such as circles, squares and triangles, was purely a matter of chance, some matching could be performed at 3–4 years, even from memory. Performance on the Terman-Merrill test suggested that simultaneous matching is well advanced by 4 years. Birch and Lefford (1967) found that matching of the standard geometrical forms could be performed by 5 years. They considered that form perception does not develop as a single continuous function, but involves three levels of functioning, the first of which is this gross figure discrimination. It is followed by discrimination involving selective response to certain aspects of the whole figure; and lastly by analysis and reconstruction of sub-wholes within the whole.

That children, as their age advances, first observe mainly the general configuration, then the internal parts and lastly both together, appears in the findings of Tampieri (1974). He required children of 3–5 years to sort figures consisting of one of two types of element (small squares or stars) arranged in one of three types of configuration (circle, triangle or stair-like line). Critical figures followed which could be sorted either according to the elements or to the configuration. Tampieri found in general that at 3 years sorting was predominantly according to the configuration, and at 4 years according to the elements. But the 5-year-olds apparently took both features into account, since they exhibited hesitation and difficulty in sorting the critical figures. However, performance varied to some extent with the different types of figure; sometimes the type of configuration tended to dominate, sometimes the type of element.

Some general characteristics of forms as wholes are perceived at an early age. Thus at 4–5 years children were capable of making quite fine discriminations between forms with different numbers of sides; and in terms of symmetry and asymmetry (Gaines, 1969). Children of the same age were also able to recognize randomly generated shapes which had been presented to them, though the more complex, with twenty independent turns, were less well recognized than those with only five independent turns (Munsinger, 1965). Symmetrical forms were discriminated more quickly than asymmetrical (Gaines, 1969). Symmetrical forms of five and ten turns were better recognized than asymmetrical by children of 6 years (Munsinger and Forsman, 1966). But when there were twenty turns, the symmetrical were less well recognized, presumably because there was a reduction in information with redundancy.

Characteristics other than symmetry were also observed. Thus Aiken and Williams (1973) required children of 6–10 years and adults to select which of three irregularly shaped eight-sided polygons was different from the other two. The one and the two had been derived from two different prototypes (which were not exhibited to the subjects). Both children and adults employed both the over-all appearance of the figures in discrimination and also certain particular individual features. Among the latter were the size of the smallest interior angle and the ratio of the horizontal to the vertical extent, that is to say, the elongation. The same criteria were used at all ages, though the younger children were slightly less proficient in discrimination. Owen (1971) also found that the criteria employed in matching an irregularly shaped eight-sided polygon to one of twenty-five other polygons were much the same in a 5-year-old boy as those of adults, though the child was much slower. The principal criteria were elongation $v.$ compression, and jaggedness.

In several earlier studies the nature of children's perceptions of shapes and their characteristics was inferred from the manner in which they copied these. Since copying was often grossly inaccurate, it was concluded, notably by Maccoby and Bee (1965), that shape characteristics were not perceived at all exactly by younger children. Thus they found that children of 3–5 years could not copy a circle or a triangle with even approximate correctness, although they could discriminate between them. There was a rapid improvement in copying geometrical shapes between 5 and 6 years (Birch and Lefford, 1967). However, even at this age children who could discriminate correctly between geometrical shapes and small distortions of these made gross mistakes in copying them (Cutler et al., 1973). But the correlation between the two performances was not very high, indicating that abilities other than discrimination were required for copying. One important ability may be the motor skill of the children, which at this age may be inadequate for drawing certain characteristics of shape at all exactly, particularly geometrical characteristics. Thus Wise (1968) found that complete inability to copy with matchsticks a series of shapes increasing in complexity was uncommon by 4–5 years.

Difficulty in accurate drawing might account in part for the finding of Piaget and Inhelder (1956) that "topological" characteristics such as inside and outside, open and closed, were copied correctly at an earlier age than were geometrical characteristics, even of simple shapes such as the square and the triangle. Reproduction of straight-sided shapes was equally incorrect when they were copied with matchsticks. But Lovell (1959) found that matchstick reproduction was easier than drawing. With the former, even the youngest in a group aged 3–6 years did not ignore geometrical characteristics, though topological characteristics were more frequently reproduced correctly.

Piaget and Inhelder considered that topological characteristics were copied earlier than geometrical because the former were more easily perceived by touch than the latter. But it is doubtful if visual perception of form is facilitated by tactile perception at this age. Thus Millar (1971) found that children under 4 years performed at chance level in tasks involving successive matching by touch of irregular shapes, though they were able to match these visually. Even at 4 years, though matching by touch was facilitated by simultaneously presented visual cues, visual matching was unaffected by tactile cues. Again, when matching is employed, topological shapes are not apparently more readily noticed than geometrical. Thus Cousins and Abranavel (1971) presented to children of 4–5 years figures which were to be matched to one of two variables, one of which was topologically similar, the other geometrically similar (Fig. 4.5). They found that at all ages geometrical matches were more frequent than topological, though the latter were relatively more common with complex irregular figures, especially in the younger children. Thus it may be simply that topological characteristics are easier to copy than geometrical.

However, certain specific characteristics of form of a topological nature may be perceived and copied at an early age. Graham *et al.* (1960) presented forms varying from lines and pairs of lines to geometrical shapes to children of $2\frac{1}{2}$–5 years, and found that by 4 years the majority of children could copy correctly the characteristics of open

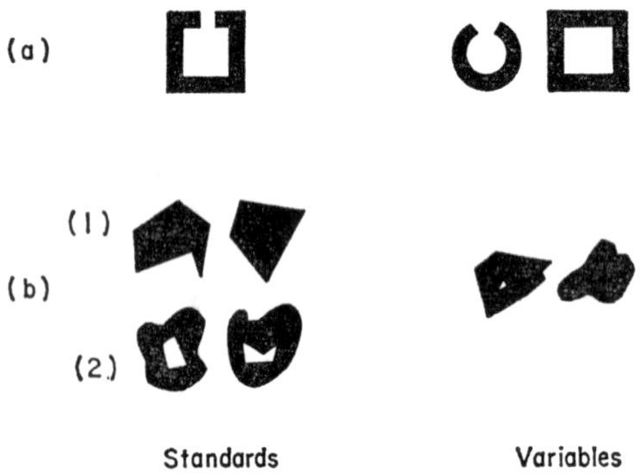

Standards   Variables

(a) Standard can be matched for rectilinearity or solidity.
(b)(1) Standards can be matched for rectilinearity or solidity.
(b)(2) Standards can be matched for hollowness or curvilinearity.

FIG. 4.5. Topological and geometrical matching. (*After* Cousins and Abranavel, 1971, p. 477.)

v. closed and linear *v.* curved. At about the same age Gaines (1969) and E. J. Gibson *et al.* (1962) showed that the same characteristics were readily discriminated in matching tasks. Gibson *et al.* investigated this discrimination very thoroughly in children of 4–8 years using "letter-like" forms, which were rather more complex than those of Graham *et al.* Each of twelve standard forms had to be matched against one of twelve "transformations", which employed changes of straight and curved lines and broken and closed lines; and changes of tilt, rotation, inversion and reversal. Errors of break and close were few throughout (though by contrast Rosca (1959) found that children of 3–4 years did not detect the gaps in incomplete figures). With Gibson's figures, errors of straight and curved lines, of rotation and reversal were high at 4 years but rapidly decreased with age; and errors of tilt were high throughout. From 5 years upwards some definite analysis of the standard forms into their parts seems to have occurred, since performance was improved by drawing them in red (Silver and Rollins, 1973).

But perception of these characteristics depended on direct comparison of the forms. When transformations were presented after the standards, not simultaneously, children even of 7 years made more errors than did the younger children with direct comparison (Trieschmann, 1968). Thus these distinctive features were relatively easy to discriminate but much harder to memorize and identify subsequently. In this respect these forms differed from simple geometrical shapes which are readily identifiable even by young children.

This identifiability of geometrical shapes as such probably accounts at least in part for the findings of Ricciuti (1963). He required children of 3–8 years to judge the similarity between a standard form and variations which possessed either the same general shape (e.g. a square) or the same details, such as outlines of full lines, dashes, dots, particular thicknesses, etc. Figures with the same general shape were judged most similar at all ages, though a sizeable proportion of those with the same details were judged most similar, especially by the younger boys. Thus, even in immediate discrimination, the over-all form of the simplest geometrical shapes stands out clearly.

(2) FORM CHARACTERISTICS NOT EASILY PERCEIVED

There are some particular characteristics of forms which children seem to have special difficulty in perceiving correctly. Graham *et al.* (1960) found that copying of angles was often incorrect; only about 40 per cent even of 5-year-olds could copy these correctly. At 6 years the majority of children reproduced the angles of the Bender test figures inaccurately (Snyder *et al.*, 1971). Such errors often seem to operate in copying the diamond (Beery, 1968). These errors may be due in part to difficulties in the actual drawing of geometric characteristics; but Piaget and Inhelder (1956) found the diamond to be equally difficult to reproduce with matchsticks.

Again, the spatial orientation of forms is not always readily perceived. It is true that, according to Wohlwill and Wiener (1964) children of $4-4\frac{1}{2}$ years showed little tendency to confuse upright and inverted forms, though this discrimination was not made by 3-year-olds. However, Landers *et al.* (1971) showed that correctness in making judgments of upright or inverted, with triangular forms, increased from 4–8 years. But reversals from left to right seem to be a much more frequent cause of difficulty, as Wohlwill and Wiener found. Gibson *et al.* (1962) also noted frequent confusions between standards and reversals with their letter-like forms in children of 4–5 years, but these rapidly decreased with age. The majority of children were able to discriminate between mirror-image pairs of triangles at 5–6 years (Robinson and Higgins, 1967). These were probably simpler to discriminate than the letter-like forms. But even when discrimination between reversed forms is correctly performed, children may find it difficult to remember and recognize orientation correctly. Gummerman and Gray (1972) showed that when a patterned mask was interposed between presentation of a T-figure and the same figure rotated to left or right, even 7–8-year-olds had difficulty in remembering its orientation. They considered that these children were slower than older children to transfer orientation information to iconic storage. It may be, however, that this information is difficult to encode, as Bryant (1969) supposed. He found that children of 5 years who could discriminate between mirror-image oblique lines could not recognize them afterwards. However, this does not appear to have been due to a tendency to encode obliques in terms of their orientation to the edges of the page, as Bryant suggested. Stein and Mandler (1974) found the same errors with a diamond-shaped framework. However, they also showed that 5-year-olds, but not 4-year-olds, could code and retain the orientation information related to the shape ⌐ and its reversed form. The 4-year-olds could only remember ⌐ and its inverted form. Thus it would appear that forms are coded as such in the upright position before other orientations are precisely encoded. However, a later study by Stein and Mandler (1975) showed that information as to all types of orientation was fairly well retained by 6 years, but possibly in so far as it was labelled and therefore remembered verbally.

(3) Differentiation and integration of parts of complex forms

When children are shown complex structures made up of a number of parts, they may perceive the latter before the former, especially when the parts are relatively simple and easy to isolate (Reese and Lipsitt, 1970). But the relation of the parts to each other and to the whole are more difficult to perceive. It is true that Graham *et al.* (1960) found that the majority of 5-year-old children could relate the parts of simple figures together. However, when children of 5–10 years were required to copy the figure shown in Fig. 4.6a, the younger children reproduced some of the parts in isolation, but not the whole structure (Stambak and Pêcheux, 1969). At about 6 years the general structure began to appear, though inexactly. From 7 years the inter-relations of the parts were reproduced, correctness increasing with age.

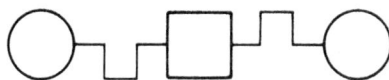

(a)

(1)   (2)   (3)   (4)

(b)

Fig. 4.6. Complex figures: (a) (*After* Stambak and Pêcheux, 1969, p. 58). (b) (*After* Verba, 1973, p. 10).

Thus it seemed that a concept of the structure as a whole developed gradually from 6 years upwards. Children of $3\frac{1}{2}$–7 years, required to copy the figures shown in Fig. 4.6b, at first produced circles and lines dotted about at random, and then connected them in pairs (Verba, 1973). Later, a row of four circles was drawn, with a line running through them. Some indications of the positions of the connecting lines then appeared. But (1) and (2) were copied correctly before (3) and (4), presumably because the former were perceived as continuously connected wholes whereas the latter had to be analysed into parts with connecting lines in different positions. This study therefore indicates also that the parts of complex forms are first perceived, but that some apprehension of the general structure develops at 5–6 years. However, relating the parts accurately within the whole is not achieved until 6–7 years. But the structures of the figures employed in these studies were comparatively simple ones. Osterrieth (1945), who presented a much more complex figure (Fig. 4.7), found that the exact shape of parts and their relationship within the whole were not accurately copied until 11–12 years. This may have been due in part to difficulty in drawing this very complex figure. However, when the children were required to recognize in the figure certain parts presented to them separately, the youngest could identify the outstanding details and the 7–9-year-olds, less outstanding details. But the main outlines of the structure were not recognized until 9–10 years. This

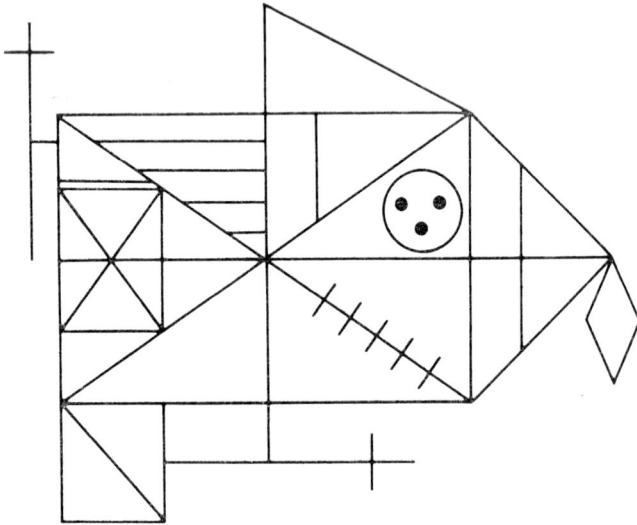

FIG. 4.7. Complex figure with interior parts. (*After* Osterrieth, 1945, p. 212.)

seems to indicate a considerable delay in perceiving structure in an adult manner.

However, it is also very difficult for children to perceive parts within a complex form when these are continuous with each other and with the contour, as in Gottschaldt's "embedded" figures (1926). Vurpillot and Florés (1964) showed that 30 per cent of children of 4–6½ years could trace out parts of whole figures when these were merely juxtaposed and retained the initial identity (see Fig. 4.8a and b). But when the parts were completely articulated and continuous with each other and with the whole, as in Fig. 4.8c and in Gottschaldt's original figures, only a very small number could trace the former even at 6 years. However, rather more could perform the task when they were required to colour in the part (Silver and Rollins, 1973); they were able to add to

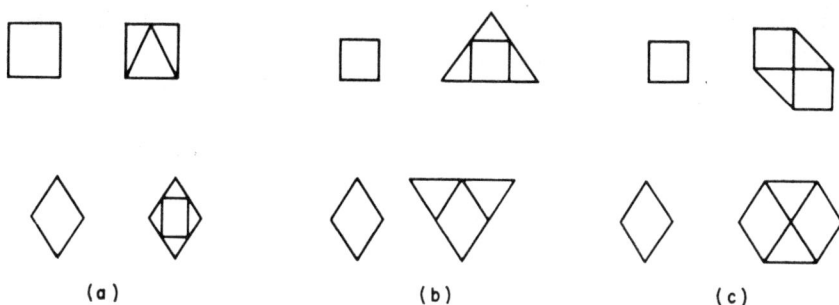

FIG. 4.8. Simple figures contained in complex figures. (*After* Vurpillot and Florés, 1964, p. 390.)

the latter bit by bit until it was complete, at the same time of course obscuring the confusing lines. Thus the parts became sub-wholes in themselves.

One explanation of some of the visual illusions is that it is difficult to analyse whole figures into their parts and perceive the latter independently of the former. Though adults are subject to visual illusions, these are in some cases stronger in children. This is particularly noticeable with the Müller-Lyer illusion (Vurpillot, 1963), but it appears also in the majority of illusions except the Oppel-Kundt and possibly also the Ponzo (Robinson, 1972). Piaget (1961) considered that the Oppel-Kundt illusion increased in magnitude with age because younger children perceived the figures globally as wholes without observing the dividing cross-lines which produce the illusion.

Difficulties in integrating separated parts of figures into inclusive wholes are also encountered in young children. Bender (1938) found that children under 7 years did not relate together the parts of even the simplest two-part figures; and with the more complex the parts were not related until 11 years. Poor integration of the parts was also observed by Keogh (1968) at 5 years, but it improved by 7 years. A somewhat similar difficulty was demonstrated by Piaget and Stettler-von Albertini (1954) in the completion of incomplete and mutilated figures. Figures with large parts of the outlines missing were seldom identified before 6 years; the younger children were unable to do this because they could not envisage the whole figure.

Even simple geometrical figures such as a square, a cross and an E, were difficult to recognize when their parts were presented separately, either in a sequence of exposures (Girgus and Hochberg, 1970) or by viewing each part of the figure in turn through a narrow aperture (Girgus and Hochberg, 1972). The latter was the easier procedure, presumably because children could control the rate and sequence of views.

Children of 3–4 years could not recognize the cross and the E in the first procedure, though at $4\frac{1}{2}$ years some did so in the second procedure. There was improvement in the processing of this sequential information with repetition in older children, but children of 5 years were not helped to process effectively by practice (Girgus, 1973).

It is not surprising therefore that children have considerable difficulty in constructing whole patterns from isolated parts. Birch and Lefford (1967) required children to select which of four sets, each of four lines, would make up a whole triangle or a diamond, which were also shown. They found that very few children of 5 years could do this; about one-quarter of the 7-year-olds; and about half of the 9-year-olds. It was more difficult to integrate isolated parts into a whole figure than to analyse the whole figure into parts.

(4) THE FUNCTIONS OF PERCEPTUAL ACTIVITY

It would seem that in general children under about 6 years have more difficulty than older children and adults in perceiving precisely the exact characteristics of complex figures and the inter-relationships of the parts of these to each other and to the whole figure. This may be associated with what Piaget (1961) has termed "centration"—a tendency for attention to become fixed upon certain aspects of the field, especially those which are sensorily striking such as size and brightness contrast; and to ignore those features which are essential for accurate perception and identification of form. However, at about 6 years of age children develop the capacity for "perceptual activity", which involves decentration and the systematic exploration of the field. Figures are analyzed and their essential characteristics extracted; moreover, in a series of "couplings" between "encounters", features are compared and related together so that their relations to each other and to the whole figure are correctly determined.

This exploration and analysis may be studied by recording the eye movements over the field and the points in the field which are fixated. But it should be noted that decentration is a movement of attention which does not depend solely on eye movement; it can occur in tachistoscopic exposures. Moreover, on some occasions observers may fixate parts of the field without perceiving them. However, the contrast between the eye movements of children under 6 with those of older children does indicate that scanning the visual field is more systematic in the latter than in the former, more adapted to the figures it contains and more capable of providing the essential information as to its significant parts. Thus Yendovitskaya (1971) found that eye movements were few and fixations prolonged in children of 3–4 years; movements wandered about and did not always follow the contours of the figure. At 4–5 years movements were more numerous and fixations were directed towards the more important features of the figure, though not systematically. At 5–6 years, eye movements followed the figure contours, but certain features were centrated and others ignored. Finally, eye movements decreased in number and the relevant and informative features were mainly fixated. This study related, however, to the scanning of pictures, as did also that of Mackworth and Bruner (1970). They found that 6-year-old children in trying to identify blurred pictures made a large number of small movements and often fixated relatively unimportant features. Adults began by making large movements, locating significant characteristics of the field, and then fixated mainly these.

Now the procedure of effective scanning may be more difficult with shapes and patterns than with pictures, since it may not be clear what are the essential features of these. But the same type of behaviour may occur even with comparatively simple patterns. Thus Whiteside (1974) presented to children of $5\frac{1}{2}$ years patterns of luminous dots which they were required to recognize subsequently. Wide scanning and wandering eye movements occurred, with scattered fixations sometimes outside the pattern altogether. Adults, whose recognition was more accurate than that of the children, scanned a comparatively small area in the middle of the pattern.

Again, Nodine and Simmons (1974) presented to children of about 6 and 8 years pairs of simple irregular shapes made up of straight and curved lines, requiring them to say whether the members of each pair were the same or different. The total numbers of eye fixations and cross-comparisons between the members of the pair were less for the older than for the younger children; but a larger proportion of the fixations for the former than for the latter were on areas containing the features which distinguished the two shapes from each other. It appeared that the older children, utilizing peripheral vision, extracted the essential distinctive features and concentrated on comparing them; whereas the younger children scanned feature by feature.

Eye movements may also be related to the child's ability to reason out the essentials of a task, as was indicated by the studies of O'Bryan and Boersma (1971) and Boersma and Wilton (1974). They found that in viewing diagrams of conservation tests, such as pouring liquid from a wide to a narrow vessel, children who had achieved conservation exhibited fewer and more systematic movements between the two figures than did those who had not, with greater decentration and more couplings and orderly comparisons between related parts. Those who had not achieved conservation wandered about, fixating irrelevant cues, and centrated on the perceptually dominant parts of the figures. It should be noted also that children of 6–7 years who performed better on the embedded figures test, exhibiting more decentration and perceptual activity, were also better at achieving conservation (Fleck, 1972).

It would seem therefore that as children's age and intelligence increase, they become capable of deliberately analyzing forms and directing attention systematically towards their significant features. They are also able then to inhibit attention and ignore unimportant and irrelevant aspects. Thus Gibson (1969) required children to learn the names of nine capital letters printed in different colours, and subsequently to identify them when they were printed in black. It was found that 5-year-old children remembered as many colours as letters; but 9-year-old children remembered few if any colours, since they had disregarded the irrelevant feature of colour. When children were required to learn to match stimuli in terms of form, colour and/or size, the inclusion of irrelevant as well as relevant dimensions made the task more difficult (Osler and Kofsky, 1965). Four-year-old and 6-year-old children could perform the task only when there were no irrelevant dimensions; 8-year-olds when there was one. Those who failed to perform the task were distracted by the irrelevant cues.

Piaget's theory of the modifications of simple immediate perception produced by perceptual activity may appear somewhat dated, but nevertheless it still seems relevant to the perceptual development of children. He considered that perceptual activity involves relating together not only the perceived characteristics of form which are actually present to view, but also those which may be displayed over a period of time in sets of similar forms. Presumably these operate when forms are classified in schemes, and new examples identified in terms of these schemes. But also anticipations are derived from these as to the characteristics of new instances. In the case of the common geometrical shapes anticipations and expectations are so firmly established in adults that distortions may be overlooked. Thus in the figure in which Müller-Lyer arrow-heads are attached to the corners of a square—extruding arrow-heads above, receding ones below—children may see the sides of the square approaching each other by virtue of the illusion. But adults tend to perceive an undistorted square. So also with mutilated and incomplete figures and when parts are presented sequentially; adults can anticipate the missing parts, whereas children may not.

(5) CONCLUSIONS

It may be concluded that in early childhood, although perception of form has advanced beyond the primitive nature it exhibited in infancy, it is not very accurate or well focused. Simple forms such as the familiar geometrical shapes are perceived as wholes, since little analysis is required to discriminate them from each other. They are, moreover, easily identified and classified, either as unique forms or as members of well-defined familiar categories which indeed may be named. Though identification does not seem to create such strong expectations as in adults, they may be directly perceived as early as Piaget's topological shapes, even if they cannot be reproduced correctly. It should not be assumed that Piaget's findings that topological shapes are more easily copied than geometrical shapes applies to perception of form generally.

The perception of other types of shape with less obvious and familiar characteristics may not therefore follow the same lines as perception of simple geometrical shapes. It is true that the characteristics of redundancy and uncertainty may operate, even in young children, in perceiving irregular shapes such as Attneave's (1957). Somewhat older children may also perceive elongation and certain angular characteristics (Owen, 1971; Aiken and Williams, 1973). With the type of form employed by Graham *et al.* (1960) and Gibson *et al.* (1962), characteristics such as open *v.* closed, complete *v.* incomplete, straight *v.* curved lines, were significant. However, the effects of these were to some extent dictated by the type of shape and the shape variables presented. The same is true of the topological shapes employed by Piaget and Inhelder (1956). Thus it may be true that what these children perceived was not simply a global impression, as hypothesized by Birch and Lefford (1967), but those distinctive features which enabled them most easily to match and copy shapes. It seems therefore that at quite an early age children may be able to select from the particular types of material presented, and in accordance with the particular task they are required to perform, those features which to them are the most obvious and significant. These are not necessarily perceived with complete accuracy, but with sufficient clarity to enable the children to discriminate and identify them as invariant with at least approximate correctness and efficiency.

We noted that in adults it was considered that the processing of distinctive features was performed by analysers selected through the operation of previously established attentional sets; and that their synthesis into whole figures might take place in terms of schemas based on previously perceived related variations in particular forms and patterns. It would seem that the latter begin to operate at an early age with simple and familiar forms; and it appears also that the types of distinctive feature selected are the same in children as in adults. However, this form of perception is too imprecise, and the amount of information processed too limited, to enable children to gain a veridical grasp of the nature of the environment. Attentional sets are rudimentary, and schemas are based on inadequate differentiation and are insufficiently generalized to cover all related instances. Thus to supplement and refine simple initial perception, ability must be acquired to analyse percepts into their constituent parts, selecting for attention those parts which are relevant and significant, and discarding those which are not; and to employ multiple cognitive operations for integrating into comprehensive schemas what is immediately perceived with what is known from previous experience. But as Donaldson (1972) has pointed out, there may be a period round about 5 years of age when children are beginning to realize the inadequacy of primitive perception, but have not yet acquired the more efficient type of cognition. At this time errors in performance, for instance in conservation tasks, may be more numerous than at an earlier age.

REFERENCES

Aiken, L. S. and Williams, T. M. (1973). A developmental study of schematic concept formation. *Developmental Psychology, 8*, 162–7.

Attneave, F. (1957). Physical determination of the judged complexity of shapes. *Journal of Experimental Psychology, 53*, 221–7.

Babska, Z. (1965). The formation of the conception of identity of visual characteristics of objects seen successively. In P. H. Mussen (Ed), European Research in Cognitive Development. *Monographs of the Society for Research in Child Development, 30*, No. 2.

Baker, M. A. and Loeb, M. (1973). Implications of measurement of eye fixations for a psychophysics of form perception. *Perception and Psychophysics, 13*, 185–92.

Beery, K. E. (1968). Form reproduction as a function of angularity, orientation of brightness contrast and hue. *Perceptual and Motor Skills, 26*, 235–43.

Bender, L. (1938). *The Visual Motor Gestalt Test and its Clinical Use.* New York: American Orthopsychiatric Association.

Birch, H. G. and Lefford, A. (1967). Visual differentiation, intersensory integration and voluntary motor control. *Monographs of the Society for Research in Child Development, 32*, No. 2.

Boersma, F. J. and Wilton, K. M. (1974). Eye movements and conservation acceleration. *Journal of Experimental Child Psychology, 17*, 49–60.

Bower, T. G. R. (1967). Phenomenal identity and form perception in an infant. *Perception and Psychophysics, 2*, 74–6.

Bower, T. G. R. (1974). *Development in Infancy.* San Francisco: Freeman.

Bower, T. G. R., Broughton, J. M. and Moore, M. K. (1970). The coordination of visual and tactual information in infants. *Perception and Psychophysics, 8*, 51–3.

Brennan, W. M., Ames, E. W. and Moore, R. W. (1966). Age differences in infants' attention to patterns of different complexities. *Science, 151*, 354–6.

Brown, C. J. (1974). The effects of preference for visual complexity on habituation of visual fixation in infants. *Child Development, 45*, 1166–9.

Bryant, P. E. (1969). Perception and memory of the orientation of visually presented lines by children. *Nature, 224*, 1331–2.

Caron, R. F. and Caron, A. J. (1968). The effects of repeated exposure and stimulus complexity on visual fixation in infants. *Psychonomic Science, 10*, 207–8.

Caron, A. J., Caron, R. F., Caldwell, R. C. and Weiss, S. J. (1973). Infant perception of the structural properties of the face. *Developmental Psychology, 9*, 385–99.

Clement, D. E. (1964). Uncertainty and latency of verbal naming responses as correlates of pattern goodness. *Journal of Verbal Learning and Verbal Behavior, 3*, 150–7.

Cohen, L. B. (1972). Attention-getting and attention-holding processes of infant visual preferences. *Child Development, 43*, 869–79.

Cohen, L. B., Gelber, E. R. and Lazar, M. A. (1971). Infant habituation and generalization to differing degrees of stimulus novelty. *Journal of Experimental Child Psychology, 11*, 379–89.

Corcoran, D. W. J. (1971). *Pattern Recognition.* Harmondsworth: Penguin.

Cornell, E. H. (1974). Infant's discrimination of photographs of faces following redundant presentations. *Journal of Experimental Child Psychology, 18*, 98–106.

Cousins, D. and Abranavel, E. (1971). Some findings relevant to the hypothesis that topological spatial features are differentiated prior to Euclidean features during growth. *British Journal of Psychology*, *62*, 475–9.

Cutler, C. M., Cicirelli, V. G. and Hirshoren, A. (1973). Comparison of discrimination and reproduction tests of children's perception. *Perceptual and Motor Skills*, *37*, 163–6.

Donaldson, M. (1972). Preconditions of inference. In J. K. Cole (Ed.), *Nebraska Symposium on Motivation, 1971*. University of Nebraska Press.

Doris, J., Casper, M. and Poresky, R. (1967). Differential brightness thresholds in infancy. *Journal of Experimental Child Psychology*, *5*, 522–35.

Eichorn, D. (1970). Physiological development. In P. H. Mussen (Ed.), *Carmichael's Manual of Child Psychology* (3rd ed.). New York: Wiley.

Evans, S. H. (1967). A brief statement of schema theory. *Psychonomic Science*, *8*, 87–8.

Fantz, R. L. (1958). Pattern vision in young infants. *Psychological Record*, *8*, 43–7.

Fantz, R. L. (1961). A method for studying depth perception in infants under 6 months of age. *Psychological Record*, *11*, 27–32.

Fantz, R. L. (1963). Pattern vision in newborn infants. *Science*, *140*, 296–7.

Fantz, R. L. (1970). Visual perception and experience in infancy. In F. A. Young and D. B. Lindsley (Eds.), *Early Experience and Visual Information Processing in Perceptual and Reading Disorders*. Washington, D. C.: National Academy of Sciences.

Fantz, R. L., Ordy, J. M. and Udelf, M. S. (1962). Maturation of pattern vision in infants during the first six months. *Journal of Comparative Physiology and Psychology*, *55*, 907–17.

Fleck, J. R. (1972). Cognitive styles in children and performance on Piagetian conservation tasks. *Perceptual and Motor Skills*, *35*, 747–56.

Frederickson, W. T. and Brown, J. V. (1975). Posture as a determinant of visual behavior in newborns. *Child Development*, *46*, 579–82.

Friedman, S. (1972). Newborn visual attention to repeated exposure of redundant *v.* "novel" targets. *Perception and Psychophysics*, *12*, 291–4. (a).

Friedman, S. (1972). Habituation and recovery of visual response in the alert human newborn. *Journal of Experimental Child Psychology*, *13*, 339–49. (b).

Friedman, S., Bruno, L. A. and Vietze, P. (1974). Newborn habituation to visual stimuli: a sex difference in novelty detection. *Journal of Experimental Child Psychology*, *18*, 242–51.

Friedman, S. and Carpenter, G. C. (1971). Visual response decrement as a function of age of human newborn. *Child Development*, *42*, 1967–73.

Friedman, S., Nagy, A. N. and Carpenter, G. C. (1970). Newborn attention: differential response decrement to visual stimuli. *Journal of Experimental Child Psychology*, *10*, 44–51.

Gaines, R. (1969). The discriminability of form among young children. *Journal of Experimental Child Psychology*, *8*, 418–31.

Garner, W. R. (1962). *Uncertainty and Structure as Psychological Concepts*. New York: Wiley.

Gibson, E. J. (1969). *Principles of Perceptual Learning and Development*. New York: Appleton-Century-Crofts.

Gibson, E. J., Gibson, J. J., Pick, A. D. and Osser, H. (1962). A developmental study of the discrimination of letter-like forms. *Journal of Comparative Physiology and Psychology*, *55*, 897–906.

Girgus, J. S. (1973). A developmental approach to the study of shape processing. *Journal of Experimental Child Psychology, 16,* 363–74.

Girgus, J. S. and Hochberg, J. (1970). Age differences in sequential form recognition. *Psychonomic Science, 21,* 211–12.

Girgus, J. S. and Hochberg, J. (1972). Age differences in shape perception through an aperture in a free-viewing situation. *Psychonomic Science, 28,* 237–8.

Gottschaldt, K. (1926). Über den Einfluss der Ehrfahrung auf die Wahrnehmung von Figuren. *Psychologisiche Forschung, 8,* 261–317.

Graham, F. K., Berman, P. W. and Ernhart, C. B. (1960). Development in preschool children of the ability to copy forms. *Child Development, 31,* 339–59.

Greenberg, D. J. (1971). Accelerating visual complexity levels in the human infant. *Child Development, 42,* 905–18.

Greenberg, D. J. and Blue, S. Z. (1975). Visual complexity in infancy. *Child Development, 46,* 357–63.

Greenberg, D. J., O'Donnell, W. J. and Crawford, D. (1973). Complexity levels, habituation and individual differences in early infancy. *Child Development, 44,* 569–74.

Gummerman, K. and Gray, C. R. (1972). Age, iconic storage and visual information processing. *Journal of Experimental Child Psychology, 13,* 165–70.

Haaf, R. A. and Bell, R. Q. (1967). A facial dimension in visual discrimination by human infants. *Child Development, 38,* 894–99.

Harter, M. R. and Suitt, C. D. (1970). Visually-evoked cortical responses and pattern vision in the infant. *Psychonomic Science, 18,* 235–7.

Haynes, H., White, B. L. and Held, R. (1965). Visual accommodation in the human infant. *Science, 148,* 528–30.

Hershenson, M. (1967). Development of the perception of form. *Psychological Bulletin, 67,* 326–36.

Hershenson, M., Munsinger, H. and Kessen, W. (1965). Preference for shapes of intermediate variability in the newborn human. *Science, 147,* 630–1.

Horowitz, F. D. Paden, L., Bhana, K., Aitchison, R. and Self, P. (1972). Developmental changes in infant visual fixation to different complexity levels among cross-sectionally and longitudinally studied infants. *Developmental Psychology, 7,* 88–9.

Jeffrey, W. E. and Cohen, L. B. (1971). Habituation in the human infant. In H. W. Reese (Ed.), *Advances in Child Development and Behavior,* vol 6. New York: Academic Press.

Jones, E. C. and Holley, J. R. (1970). Schema utilization in pattern perception. *Psychonomic Science, 18,* 197–8.

Jones-Molfese, V. J. (1972). Individual differences in neonatal preferences for planometric and stereometric visual patterns. *Child Development, 43,* 1289–96.

Kagan, J. (1971). *Change and Continuity in Infancy.* New York: Wiley.

Karmel, B. Z. (1969). The effect of age, complexity and amount of contour on pattern preference in human infants. *Journal of Experimental Child Psychology, 7,* 339–54. (a).

Karmel, B. Z. (1969). Complexity, amount of contour and visually dependent behavior in hooded rats, domestic chicks and human infants. *Journal of Comparative Physiology and Psychology, 69,* 649–57. (b).

Karmel, B. Z., Hoffman, R. F. and Fegy, M. J. (1974). Processing contour information by human infants evidenced by pattern-dependent evoked potentials. *Child Development*, *45*, 39–48.

Keogh, B. K. (1968). The copying ability of young children. *Education Research*, *11*, 43–7.

Kessen, W., Salapatek, P. and Haith, M. (1972). The visual response of the human newborn to linear contour. *Journal of Experimental Child Psychology*, *13*, 9–20.

Koopman, P. R. and Ames, E. N. (1968). Infants' preferences for facial arrangements. *Child Development*, *39*, 481–7.

Korner, A. F. and Grobstein, R. (1966). Visual alertness as related to soothing in neonates: implications for maternal stimulation and early deprivation. *Child Development*, *37*, 867–76.

Landers, W. F., Cogan, D. C. and Hunt, R. R. (1971). Developmental changes in the perception of inverted triangular forms. *Perceptual and Motor Skills*, *32*, 587–92.

Lewis, M. (1969). Infants' responses to facial stimuli during the first year of life. *Developmental Psychology*, *1*, 75–82.

Lewis, M., Kagan, J. and Kalafat, J. (1966). Patterns of fixation in the young infant. *Child Development*, *37*, 331–41.

Lewis, M., Wilson, C. D. and Baumel, M. (1971). Attention distribution in the 24-month-old child: variations in complexity and incongruity of the human form. *Child Development*, *42*, 429–38.

Lovell, K. (1959). A follow-up study of some aspects of the work of Piaget and Inhelder on the child's conception of space. *British Journal of Educational Psychology*, *29*, 104–17.

Maccoby, E. E. and Bee, H. L. (1965). Some speculations concerning the lag between perceiving and performing. *Child Development*, *36*, 367–77.

Mackworth, N. H. and Bruner, J. S. (1970). How adults and children search and recognize pictures. *Human Development*, *13*, 149–77.

McCall, R. B. and Kagan, J. (1967). Stimulus-schema discrepancy and attention in the infant. *Journal of Experimental Child Psychology*, *5*, 381–90.

McCall, R. B. and Melson, W. H. (1969). Attention in infants as a function of magnitude of discrepancy and habituation rate. *Psychonomic Science*, *17*, 317–19.

Michels, K. M. and Zusne, L. (1965). Matrices of visual form. *Psychological Bulletin*, *63*, 74–86.

Millar, S. (1971). Visual and haptic cue utilization by preschool children. *Journal of Experimental Child Psychology*, *12*, 88–94.

Miller, D. J. (1972). Visual habituation in the human infant. *Child Development*, *43*, 481–93.

Miranda, S. B. (1970). Visual abilities and pattern preferences of premature infants and full term neonates. *Journal of Experimental Child Psychology*, *10*, 189–205.

Munsinger, H. (1965). Tachistoscopic recognition of stimulus variability. *Journal of Experimental Child Psychology*, *2*, 186–91.

Munsinger, H. and Forsman, R. (1966). Symmetry, development and tachistoscopic recognition. *Journal of Experimental Child Psychology*, *3*, 168–76.

differentiation of letterlike symbols. *Journal of Experimental Psychology*, *103*, 21–8.

O'Bryan, K. G. and Boersma, F. J. (1971). Eye movements, perceptual activity and conservation development. *Journal of Experimental Child Psychology*, *12*, 157–69.

Osler, S. F. and Kofsky, E. (1965). Stimulus uncertainty as a variable in the development of conceptual ability. *Journal of Experimental Child Psychology*, *2*, 264–79.

Osterrieth, P. A. (1945). Le test de copie d'une figure complexe. *Archives de Psychologie*, *30*, 205–353.

Owen, D. H. (1971). Developmental generality of form recognition. *Journal of Experimental Child Psychology*, *11*, 194–205.

Pancratz, C. N. and Cohen, L. B. (1970). Recovery of habituation in infants. *Journal of Experimental Child Psychology*, *9*, 208–16.

Piaget, J. (1961). *Les Mécanismes Perceptifs*. Paris: Presses Universitaires de France. (Translated as *The Mechanisms of Perception*. London: Routledge and Kegan Paul, 1969.)

Piaget, J. and Inhelder, B. (1956). *The Child's Conception of Space*. London: Routledge and Kegan Paul.

Piaget, J. and Stettler-von Albertini, B. (1954). Observations sur la perception des bonnes formes chez l'enfant par actualisation des lignes virtuelles. *Archives de Psychologie*, *34*, 203–42.

Posner, M. I. and Keele, S. W. (1968). On the genesis of abstract ideas. *Journal of Experimental Psychology*, *77*, 353–63.

Reese, H. W. and Lipsitt, L. P. (1970). *Experimental Child Psychology*. New York: Academic Press.

Ricciuti, H. N. (1963). Geometric form and detail as determinants of comparative similarity judgments by children. In *A Basic Research Program on Reading*. Cooperative Research Program No. 639, U.S. Office of Health, Education and Welfare.

Robinson, J. O. (1972). *The Psychology of Visual Illusion*. London: Hutchinson.

Robinson, J. S. and Higgins, K. E. (1967). The young child's ability to see a difference between mirror-image forms. *Perceptual and Motor Skills*, *25*, 893–7.

Rosca, M. (1959). The perception of incomplete pictures in normal and mentally retarded children. *Studia Universitatis Babes-Bolyai*, *3*, 71–96. (*Psychological Abstracts*, 1965, *39*, 4557.)

Salapatek, P. (1968). Visual scanning of geometric figures by the human newborn. *Journal of Comparative Physiology and Psychology*, *66*, 247–58.

Salapatek, P. and Kessen, W. (1966). Visual scanning of triangles by the human newborn. *Journal of Experimental Child Psychology*, *3*, 153–67.

Salapatek, P. and Kessen, W. (1973). Prolonged investigation of a plane geometric triangle by the human newborn. *Journal of Experimental Child Psychology*, *15*, 22–9.

Salzen, E. A. (1963). Visual stimuli eliciting the smiling response in the human infant. *Journal of Genetic Psychology*, *102*, 51–4.

Silver, J. R. and Rollins, H. A. (1973). The effects of visual and verbal feature-emphasis on form discrimination in preschool children. *Journal of Experimental Child Psychology*, *16*, 205–16.

Snyder, R. T., Holowenzak, S. P. and Hoffman, N. (1971). A cross cultural item-analysis of Bender-Gestalt protocols administered to ghetto and suburban children. *Perceptual and Motor Skills*, *33*, 791–6.

Stambak, M. and Pêcheux, M.-G. (1969). Essai d'analyse de l'activité de réproduction de figures géométriques complexes. *L'Année Psychologique,* *69*, 55–66.

Stechler, G., Bradford, S. and Levy, H. (1966). Attention in the newborn: effect on motility and skin potential. *Science, 151*, 1246–8.

Stein, N. L. and Mandler, J. M. (1974). Children's recognition of reversals of geometric figures. *Child Development, 45*, 604–15.

Stein, N. L. and Mandler, J. M. (1975). Development of detection and recognition of orientation of geometric and real figures. *Child Development, 46*, 379–88.

Super, C. M., Kagan, J., Morrison, F. J., Haith, M. and Weiffenbach, J. (1972). Discrepancy and attention in the five-month infant. *Genetic Psychology Monographs, 85*, 305–31.

Tampieri, G. (1974). How does the weight of the "parts" change in the visual perception of pre-school children? Unpublished Report from the Laboratory of Child Psychology of the University of Trieste.

Trieschmann, R. B. (1968). Undifferentiated handedness and perceptual development in children with reading problems. *Perceptual and Motor Skills, 27*, 1123–34.

Tronick, E. (1972). Stimulus control and growth of the infant's effective visual field. *Perception and Psychophysics, 11*, 373–76.

Tronick, E. and Clanton, C. (1971). Infant looking patterns. *Vision Research, 11*, 1479–86.

Venger, L. A. (1964). The development of visual matching of form in preschool children as a function of experience in handling objects. *Voprosy Psikhologii, 1*, 114–26. (*Psychological Abstracts*, 1965, *39*, 1289.)

Verba, M. (1973). Construction de l'espace graphique chez l'enfant. *L'Année Psychologique, 73*, 7–21.

Vurpillot, E. (1963). *L'Organisation Perceptive: Son Rôle dans l'Évolution des Illusions Optico-Géométriques.* Paris: Vrin.

Vurpillot, E. and Florés, A. (1964). La génèse de l'organisation perceptive. I. Rôle du contour et de la surface enclose dans la perception des figures. *L'Année Psychologique, 64*, 375–95.

Welch, M. J. (1974). Infants' visual attention to varying degrees of novelty. *Child Development, 45*, 344–50.

Wetherford, M. J. and Cohen, L. B. (1973). Developmental changes in infant visual preferences for novelty and familiarity. *Child Development, 44*, 416–24.

White, B. L. (1971). *Human Infants: Experience and Psychological Development.* New Jersey, Englewood Cliffs: Prentice-Hall.

Whiteside, J. A. (1974). Eye movements of children, adults and elderly persons during inspection of dot patterns. *Journal of Experimental Child Psychology, 18*, 313–32.

Wickelgren, L. W. (1967). Convergence in the human newborn. *Journal of Experimental Child Psychology, 5*, 74–85.

Wilcox, B. M. (1969). Visual preferences of human infants for representations of the human face. *Journal of Experimental Child Psychology, 7*, 10–20.

Wise, J. H. (1968). Stick copying of designs by pre-school and young school age children. *Perceptual and Motor Skills, 27*, 1159–68.

Wohlwill, J. F. and Wiener, M. (1964). Discrimination of form orientation in young children. *Child Development, 35*, 1113–25.

Woodward, W. M. (1971). *The Development of Behavior*. Harmondsworth:
    Penguin.
Yendovitskaya, T. V. (1971). Development of sensation and perception. In A. V.
    Zaporozhets and D. B. Elkonin (Eds.), *The Psychology of Pre-School
    Children*. Cambridge, Mass: M.I.T. Press.
Zusne, L. (1970). *Visual Perception of Form*. New York and London: Academic
    Press.

CHAPTER 5

Development of Identification of Objects

Eliane Vurpillot

I. INTRODUCTION

(1) What is meant by identification?

To identify an object means to consider it as being the same as one or several other objects. An identity response, therefore, will especially depend on the definition given to the word "the same", which can vary for the same objects according to the situations and people involved. It follows then that the term identification is rarely lacking in ambiguity and that the criteria of decision are more or less arbitrary.

Identification can be relative to objects present simultaneously, directly perceptible and comparable. Those objects are considered to be the same which are equivalent in some way. The equivalence required can be total, in which case the objects must be perfectly capable of substitution and therefore alike from every point of view. Only those objects physically identical fulfil these conditions. Thus, before giving an identity response, we must be sure that there is an absence of any difference. In this case, the criterion of decision is the rule of logical identity. If the equivalence required is only partial, then the objects are capable of substition on condition that they have a certain number of properties in common. Two objects can therefore be the same, while presenting certain differences. The criteria of decision are relative to the nature and number of differences permitted, and the level of equivalence can be extremely variable.

Identification can also concern a single object which is compared to objects previously perceived. The comparison is indirect and takes place by means of memories, schemas, concepts, that is to say, psychological structures built up in the course of previous encounters with the environment. These structures play the role of standards, points of reference, against which are measured the actual perceptions of the object to be identified. Identification may be individual : Is this object the same as the one encountered previously? Has it remained the same in spite of changes due to use, growth of style? It can also be a judgment concerning total or partial equivalence; in the latter case, we are speaking about categorial identification.

(2) Preliminaries to identificaton

Except in very particular circumstances, we agree to describe the physical world in terms of individual objects qualified by intrinsic properties or measurable values on dimensions of variation and of spatial relations between these objects, measurable in a system of reference. When objects are moved, the observer being only one among others even if he has a particular role, these spatial relations are modified while the intrinsic properties of the objects remain invariable. We cannot ignore the fact that in order to perceive his environment, to obtain knowledge that will permit him to make judgments of identity or non-identity of the objects which compose it, the observer has only two sources of information at his disposal. The first is found at the level of excitations resulting from the arrival at the sensory receptors of physical energy coming from the environment. For each state of the environment, there is a corresponding pattern of energy or proximal stimulus, the form of which depends on the intrinsic properties of the objects in the perceptual field and on their position in space. The sequence of patterns contains information which is rich, but ambiguous. The second source of information is the action that the observer can apply to his environment, action which is qualified by its form, amplitude and point of impact; it introduces changes of state into the environment and in the observer, which result in a variation in the pattern of excitation.

The identification of objects, therefore, is based on a comparison of multiple patterns of excitation; an arrangement, the organization of which is indispensable.

(i) *Figure-ground segregation.* All the sensory excitations resulting from each proximal stimulus are organized into individualized units. The phenomenon of figure-ground segregation was demonstrated in an indirect way by the analysis of the distribution of ocular fixations. These concentrate preferably on a picture rather than on a homogeneous field (Fantz, 1963); the dispersion of the fixations varies with the size of the picture (Salapatek and Kessen, 1966; Salapatek, 1968).

(ii) *Distinction between modification of the object and modification of its position.* As has been clearly shown by J. J. Gibson (1950, 1966), when the observer has received a sufficient series of sensory inputs and when there is covariation between his own action and the contents of the proximal stimulus, he has sufficient information to distinguish between a change caused by the modification of the object itself and a change caused by a simple displacement of the object. In fact, variations in proximal stimulus, the result of the observer or the objects having moved, take place according to certain rules, each of which specifies a type of displacement.

To be in possession of the necessary information and to be capable of using it are not synonymous. Therefore, we have wondered at what age the human infant responds differently to the modification of intrinsic properties of a physical object, and to its simple displacement. The little research available on the constancy of size or shape in infants provides us with some information on this point. Since perceptual constancy will be dealt with in another chapter (Chapter 6), I shall simply point out that when a comparison between objects is made, it is said that constancy exists when identity is based on the intrinsic qualities of an object (size or shape), rather than on the variations in their retinal projection, linked to their position in relation to the observer (distant or slanted).

With an operant conditioning of head-turning, Bower (1964, 1965) found the constancy of size to appear in infants of $2\frac{1}{2}$ months. Using a completely different method, the measurement of visual fixation time and the reaction to novelty after habituation, Day and McKenzie (1973) obtained constancy of form from the age of 2 months. In both cases, the authors insisted on the fact that responses of constancy were observed only with real, three-dimensional objects.

Infants of 2 to 3 months treated photographs of the same object, taken from different distances or at different angles, as distinct objects. The infant can modify the perceptual aspect of real objects by moving his head, which is not possible with photographs. At that age, the distinction between a change in state and a change in position is only possible if the parallactic movement permits the introduction of a real covariation between the modification of the aspect of the object and the individual action of the child.

(iii) *The hypothesis of permanence and invariance.* It is easy to demonstrate (Vurpillot, 1974) that the invariance and permanence of any physical object are temporary. However, when an object ceases to be perceptible, the first hypotheses of an adult in our culture are that this object continues to exist in a precise place; that its disappearance is the result of other objects intervening; that it will become perceptible again when these blocking objects have been taken away; and, therefore, that it will have the same intrinsic properties as at the moment of disappearance. Such hypotheses are not astonishing, for whatever the real nature of the physical world, the model that we built of it can be useful for survival only if it includes a certain stability, thus certain invariants, and predictability in the form of rules of change. Like his elders, the human infant expects to find permanence and invariance in his environment, but permanence is rather a persistence of sensory pictures and invariance is only concerned with certain of their properties.

In ceasing to be perceptible, an object may or may not lose all existence for an infant; that depends on the manner in which its disappearance has come about (Bower, 1967). A red and white striped ball can become invisible, either by putting a mobile screen between it and the child (perspective transformation) or by the progressive diminution of lighting until total darkness prevails, followed by a progressive increase in lighting (non-perspective transformation).

During the period of non-perceptibility of the object, the experimenter may take away the object, so that its disappearance may or may not be followed by its reappearance. The reappearance of the object surprises the infant when it follows a non-perspective change, but not when it follows a perspective change. On the contrary, the infant is surprised when the ball does not reappear after the screen is taken away, but not after a non-perspective change. From the age of 7 weeks, an infant acts as if the object were destroyed by a non-perspective change, but expects to see the object again when there is a simple temporary eclipse by a screen. These facts confirm the results of experiments done in constancy (Bower, 1965): from the age of 2 months, an infant is capable of responding to relational invariants in sensory inputs and of distinguishing between several types of changes in them. Infants also give evidence of a belief in the permanence of elements in their environment, however short in duration and gross they may be.

It appears then that at a very early age, infants are capable of responding to invariants and rules of change in sensory inputs which they receive and to make differentiations and identifications in their environment. This capacity does not seem to be acquired but is inscribed in the central nervous system; in fact, its appearance at the age of 2 months coincides with that of good accommodation and sufficient visual acuity, the progress of which is directly linked to that of nervous maturation.

(3) THE PROCESS OF IDENTIFICATION

The identification of an object puts into play a series of intellectual operations, each of which ends in a choice.

(i) *Choice of the object on which identification will be fixed.* We have seen that a set of sensory excitations is organized at a very early age by the infant, but this can be done in several ways. Thus, the same physical object can be perceived as a single large unit, or else as a large unit composed of smaller units or parts, each one made up of even smaller units, etc. (hierarchical organization); or else, as a set of small juxtaposed units. The level of organization used is important in the task of identification, for it determines the object involved in identification. Let us take the case of two necklaces made of assorted beads. The instructions given to the child require him to say if these two necklaces are quite the same or not. They determine a certain level of organization and state precisely the object to identify. If the instructions are followed, the general form of the necklace and the relative place of the beads are intrinsic properties of the object, and must be taken into consideration in the identification. But the child may consider the necklace as a collection of beads; the level of organization becomes something different, that of juxtaposed units, and the objects of identification become the beads. The general form of their configuration, that of the necklace, as well as the relative place of the beads, cease to be intrinsic properties of the object, and become relational properties. They, therefore, can be ignored during the identification. In the majority of cases, the answer is liable to vary according to the level of perceptual organization chosen.

(ii) *Choice of the type of identification involved.* The role of differences changes according to whether it is a question of recognizing objects as equivalent or as perfectly identical. Where partial equivalence is concerned, some differences can be permitted. The essential matter is to verify whether the objects have common features when we make piles of things that go together, to find out if an object possesses those critical characteristics of a category previously determined, when the task consists in recognizing them as a chair, a snail or a triangle (categorial identity), or as my dog, Flok (individual identity). On the other hand, when it is a question of total equivalence, no differences can be permitted.

To decide on one or the other level of identification implies a choice of different rules of response. This also has an effect on the strategy of comparison. When an identification by partial equivalence is made, the strategy is based on comparing common features. To apply the rule of logical identity, the strategy would be based on the search for differences.

(iii) *Relevance or irrelevance of a dimension of variation.* Theoretically, identification is made on the basis of the intrinsic properties of objects, and the relational properties are considered as irrelevant. A triangle remains identical no matter how many times we turn it round. This is not true when we apply the same rotations to the letters of the alphabet, such as "p", "d", "q" and "b"; orientation, a relational property, is here a critical feature. When it is a question of equivalence, the invariant of the category determines the critical features for which no distortion can be permitted; the example of the letters of the alphabet shows that these features can be relational as well as intrinsic. In turn, any intrinsic property is capable of becoming irrelevant, in real life as well as in the laboratory. All living creatures are semi-rigid, which permits them to move about but which brings about a continual deformation of their bodies; the same is true for numerous objects in the environment, such as clothing, cushions, etc. Only certain spatial relations between their different points are invariant, their shape being an intrinsic property of which certain modifications—but not others—may be permitted, without their identity being affected.

In short, whatever the form of identification involved, there is no rule applicable in all circumstances. Each time a decision must be made, based on the information at hand and on one's previous experience.

(iv) *Measurement of the characteristics of objects.* The methods of measurement and the systems of reference possible are varied, and do not always give the same value to the same object. To choose one or the other can bring about different results. I would like to borrow two examples from Bryant (1974). The first concerns the "relative codes" used by a young child to judge the identity or the non-identity of two lines going in different directions. The most simple "relative code" is a match–mis-match code: if the two lines are parallel, they are identical; if they are not parallel, their absolute direction is unimportant; they are different. The code works perfectly when the two lines are presented simultaneously; such is no longer the case when they are presented successively, or when the positive orientation must be discovered through discrimination learning. Another code consists in choosing a fixed standard in the environment which is parallel to one of the lines; the identity or the non-identity of the other is deduced by means of matching or mis-matching it against the standard.

To judge the identity of numbers involved in two lines of identical tokens, three methods, at least, are possible. The surest way consists in counting the tokens in the first line, then that of the second, and comparing the two figures. We can also set up a one-to-one correspondence between the tokens, which is as sure as the first method, if it is possible to handle them. On the other hand, this could work only in exceptional cases where the elements are placed in a regular and parallel formation. The last solution is to compare the two lines from the point of view of the quantity of space they take up, but this is hardly trustworthy.

(v) *Strategies.* To identify objects, information must be gathered and compared. The strategy of research, made effective by moving the sensory receptors about, and interiorized by scanning the stock of categorial invariants or the dimensions of differentiation, plays an important role.

This brief review of the numerous choices involved in the process of identification shows that, if the performances of children are different from those of adults, which is quite obvious, the causes are manifold. Commensurate with the passing of time, beginning with birth, is the progress of nervous maturation, bringing about a refinement in sensory sensitivity, an increase in memory span and the achievement of biological growth. At the same time, the encounters between the child and his environment multiply and grow in variety. The interaction of these two factors, biological development and acquired experience, brings about intellectual development, exemplified by the building up of a stock of invariants, of systems of reference and rules for decision-making. This stock can only become richer and change with age.

When the child's identity response is the same as the adult's, it is called correct; the proportion of these correct answers is the measure of his performance, the other answers being called errors. Rather than errors, they are witness to the fact that the child uses other systems of reference, other rules for making decisions, than the adult. The performance of a child tells us only about the degree to which these rules and systems of reference are different from ours. Analysis of the nature of these errors, an infinitely richer measure, allows us to a certain degree to infer which rules, which references or which strategies the child has used to resolve the problems which we have given him in the tasks of identification. It is with this in mind that we have chosen the examples which will be discussed in the following pages.

II. INDIVIDUAL IDENTIFICATION

(1) PERMANENCE AND INVARIANCE OF THE OBJECT IN AN INFANT

We have seen that from the first few weeks of life, the human infant expects to see the reappearance of an object temporarily hidden by a screen. What common characteristics does he expect to find in the initial object and in that which reappears, so that he can treat them as a single object? Research on that question has been carried out in two situations, that in which a stationary object is progressively hidden by a mobile screen, and that in which a mobile object moves behind a fixed screen. Three types of reactions have been recorded: visual tracking; surprise measured by a modification in sucking and cardiac rhythm; mimicking and hand-reaching. The latter is used only after 3 or 4 months, when co-ordination between prehension and vision has come about.

(i) *Identification of a stationary object*. While the screen is occluding the object, the infant keeps his eyes fixed on the spot where the object had initially been placed; he expects to see it reappear where it had ceased being visible. This behaviour is observed as soon as the infant is 4 to 6 weeks old. If tachistoscopic devices are used to make two physically different objects appear successively in the same place, which for us corresponds to substituting one object for another, the infant continues to look towards the same place, without showing any surprise. This behaviour is observed until the end of the first year, with unfamiliar objects. It disappears towards the age of 5 months when the object is very important, such as the baby's mother (Bower, 1974). In this case, the infant is disturbed and tries to find out where his mother has disappeared to. Her identity is linked to the presence of precise physical characteristics; this does not seem to be true as yet for other objects.

With the same tachistoscopic device, a particular object can be made to appear successively in two different places, which does not surprise infants of 5 to 6 months, who fix their gaze on the visible object irrespective of place. On the other hand, infants of 3 to 4 months look back and forth between the two locations. It must be added that the simultaneous appearance of multiple images of the same object does not disturb an infant of 3 to 4 months, while one of 5 months is very upset if he suddenly sees three images of his mother at the same time (Bower, 1974).

Bower concludes from these diverse observations that for the first 4 or 5 months of his existence an infant identifies a stationary object with the place that it occupies and not with a set of characteristics such as its form, colour, size, etc., variations in which he is perfectly capable of perceiving. As can be expected, the mother, an object which is particularly familiar and important, is the first to be identified by her intrinsic properties.

(ii) *Identification of a mobile object.* The infant tracks a moving object visually and anticipates its reappearance on the other side of a screen. From the age of 8 weeks, he turns his eyes towards that side, as if he were continuing to follow the path of movement of the object that has become invisible. If the object stops just before reaching the screen, thereby remaining visible, the infant holds his gaze on the stationary object for a fraction of a second and then goes back to tracking on the same path of movement (Bower, Broughton and Moore, 1971). This behaviour can be observed even without a screen, until the age of 5 months (Bower, 1974). A little train with blinking lights can be run on rails in front of the infant (Fig. 5.1). At first the train remains stationary, in place A, for 10 sec, then moves towards the right, to place B, where it remains for 10 sec, then comes back to A, where it stops for 10 sec, goes back to B, etc. These comings and goings between A and B, interspersed with stops, continue and the infant rapidly adapts himself to following the movements of the train with his eyes. After ten of these, the experimenter intervenes, and instead of going from A to B, the train now goes in the opposite direction, towards another place, C. Instead of following it with his eyes, the infant will look towards B where there is now nothing (Bower and Paterson, 1973).

In another experiment, inspired by the work of Michotte (1962), Michotte, Thinès and Crabbé (1964) and Bower, Broughton and Moore (1971) substitute one object for another while it is hidden behind a screen. The child therefore sees the first object (two superimposed circles) change place, disappear, and then another object physically different (a square) appear at the other end of the screen. It is only after twenty weeks that this substitution disturbs the infant's visual tracking. Before that age, the infant continues to follow the moving object with his eyes without any sign of surprise. A complementary experiment consists in making an object reappear that is physically identical to the one which disappeared, but on another path of movement. The second suddenly appears on the right side of the screen as soon as the first has disappeared behind the left side. The 5-month-old infant makes a rapid eye-movement to catch the moving

8—CP * *

FIG. 5.1. Test trial in Bower's experiment. (From top to bottom) (1) Infant looks at the train stopped in A. (2) Infant tracks the train visually between A and B. (3) Infant tracks the train back from B to A. (4) The train moves to C, the infant looks to B. (*After* Bower, 1974, p. 193.)

object. Younger infants, however, return to the side of the screen as if they were still waiting for the first object to come out.

Out of all of these experiments, only the essentials of which have been discussed here, Bower (1974) draws the following conclusions as to the identification of objects by infants of 2 to 5 months (Stage 2 of the permanence of the object, in Piaget, 1937). All objects which occupy the same place are examples of the same object; there cannot be two objects in the same place. That is to say, if the physical object keeps its intrinsic properties but changes place, it becomes another object for an infant of 2 to 4 months; again, if an object having entirely different properties is substituted in the same place, the infant will consider it as the same but with a different aspect. In short, for Bower, the individual identity of an object, at this age, is uniquely defined by its habitual place. Moreover, all mobile objects on the same path of movement, defined by a certain direction and speed of movement, are considered to be the same object, whether they have the same intrinsic properties or not. Two distinct objects cannot follow the same path. The individual identity of a moving object is uniquely defined by its path of movement. These definitions of identity for fixed objects and mobile objects have a certain number of consequences.

Before the age of 5 months, the intrinsic properties of objects do not come into play in individual identity. The latter is concerned only with relational spatial properties, such as habitual or initial place, or the pathway of movement. The world of these infants contains a multitude of objects, since a stationary object which changes its place becomes another object, as well as a mobile object which changes its pathway of movement. Thus, in the experiment with the train, there are two stationary trains for the infant, one at A the other at B; and two moving trains, one in the direction A→B, the other in the direction B→A. Therefore, there are four distinct objects which dematerialize and rematerialize in turn. Fortunately, the memory span of the infant is very short.

The world of the tiny baby is rather different from ours; thus we must have some reservations in accepting all the conclusions of Bower. They are especially based on a certain interpretation of the oculo-motor activity of the infant, so that we wonder if the author has not placed too much emphasis on it. Nevertheless, I should be ready to follow him if the ocular behaviour in question were as clear and easy to demonstrate as he believes. To me, this does not seem as yet to be completely proved.

Can it be said that for an infant over 5 months an object is henceforth a thing that can retain its identity independently of the place it fills and the displacement to which it is submitted? Is there a "group of displacement", and at the same time true conceptual permanence and invariance? This does not seem to be the case. If another kind of response is used, such as hand reaching instead of visual tracking, and if some modification of the experimental situation is added, then errors similar to those observed during the first months of life appear. Such is the case when the vertical screen is replaced by a cloth, a cushion or a cup, when the number of screens increases, or when delays are introduced between the disappearance of the object and the response. In such circumstances, at 6 months an infant will make no attempt to search actively for something; he is content to look at the screen under which the object has disappeared. Beginning at 8 months, he will do some searching, but very often elsewhere than in the place that the object has been hidden.

These errors can be of a conceptual nature; such is the interpretation of Piaget. During the first six to eight months of an infant's life, objects have only a general, practical and subjective permanence. The world does not contain objects but provides sensory pictures, open to perpetual destruction and rematerialization.

> "Permanence is affective or subjective, without localization or substantialization; the disappearing picture remains, for all intents and purposes, at his disposal, although spatially it can nowhere be found" (Piaget, 1937) . . . "The object does not constitute the permanent element . . . but the act itself . . . therefore, the whole of the situation" (Piaget, 1937).

Identity does not concern the object, but the schema of action. The sensory picture is identified with reference to the total schema; the infant expects to see the object rematerialize after destruction in the place where it had been linked to the action of the infant.

Very recently, several authors (Miller, Cohen and Hill, 1970; Landers, 1971; Evans and Gratch, 1972; Webb, Massar and Nadolny, 1972; Harris, 1974; Butterworth, 1975, etc.) have wondered if the errors in localization observed between 8 and 15 months could not be interpreted as faulty memorization, defective strategy or use of inadequate systems of spatial references, etc., rather than as due to conceptual insufficiency. In this connection, the object would be substantial, permanent and invariant, but the infant would not code its place in memory or would use inappropriate spatial references. He would simply have forgotten where the object had gone to, or would be lacking the cues necessary to identify its place. Since the permanence of the object is taken up in Chapter 7, the results of these researches will not be discussed here.

(2) Individual identity in pre-school children

Very little research has been done in this field, but we should take note of some very interesting work done by Piaget and his colleagues (Piaget, Sinclair and Vinh-Bang, 1968).

(i) *Identity of objects in the course of reversible transformation.* Piaget and Voyat presented a child with a simple object such as a piece of wire, a small ball of plasticine or a jar of red liquid. Then, in front of the child, they changed the shapes of the object : they curved the wire; they made a frankfurter or a flat cake with the plasticine, or poured the liquid into a wider or narrower jar. Then they asked the child questions about the objects. For example, concerning the conservation of individual identity : "Is it still the same object?"; on conserving quantity : "Is the wire still the same length? Is there as much plasticine or liquid as before?"

The authors noted four steps in the development of answers between the ages of 3 and 8. In the first stage, the children accepted individual identity, basing their answers on the invariability of a perceptible property such as colour or the nature of the object, and flatly stated that nothing had changed. Piaget saw in these answers both the demonstration of a principle of identity as a regulator of knowledge (Piaget *et al.*, 1968, p. 2) and that of identification by semi-generic assimilation. In other words, we are not sure if a child of 3 years thinks that it is the same object at two different moments and in two different forms, or if there are two equivalent objects. Equivalence for Piaget, in this case, would be based on the schema of action applicable to the object.

At the second stage (4 years), the child is centred on the differences in appearance of the object. Thus, R., looking at the wire, straight at first, then bent into a curve, said, *"It's not the same wire"*. The experimenter tries to suggest that "perhaps we can say the same, but a little changed or transformed", but the child answers, *"No ... another"*. It is clear from the responses that for this child, from the moment a property has been modified, the object has become another; individual identity has not been preserved. The authors did not find these two steps in all children or in all the experiments. As a matter of fact, these findings point out a very general characteristic of the nature of judgment in young children; they use only a part of the available information. Either they take into consideration only the property that has been modified and conclude that the object has become another. Or they consider only the property or properties which remain constant, and conclude that the object has not changed.

At the third stage, towards 5 or 6 years of age, identity is affirmed;

it is the same object, but a modification in shape brings about a change in the other properties. A curved wire is still the same piece of wire as in the beginning, but it has become shorter. For Piaget, an object gives two kinds of cues : those which are qualitative and can be perceived, such as shape or colour; those which are quantitative, and can be appraised only through operational composition, such as number and physical and spatial qualities. At this third stage, identity is still only qualitative; it is only at the fourth stage, around the ages of 7 or 8, that identity becomes quantitative. The transition from third to fourth stage in identification is a sign of the appearance of new operations in the child.

(ii) *Identity of organisms in development.* The same development can be seen when identification concerns a plant or a growing, living creature.

The child is asked to draw himself as he is now, then when he was younger, and then, younger still; he is then asked to draw how he will be when he is older; then, even older. He must make the same series of drawings for the experimenter and for a plant. Questions concern the comparison of drawings within each series. The individual identity of the child himself is accepted from the age of 4 for the drawings relative to his past, but not for those relative to the future. When the experimenter asks J. if it is he on the drawings, J. answers *"Not always"*. The experimenter (E.) asks "What do you mean, not always? That is Jack (name of the child), isn't it? (J.) *"No"*. (E.) "Which drawing is not Jack?" (J.) shows the largest of the drawings. (E.) "Who is that?" (J.) *"A father"*. (E.) "But the others are you, aren't they?" (J.) *"Yes"*.

In general, from 5 to 6 years of age, there is a conservation of individual identity during growth for all human beings, for the experimenter as well as for the child. Piaget sees in the precocity of identity of the self proof that identification is an assimilation to schemas of action, the self constituting the convergence of all the schemas of action of an individual. The conservation of identity of an object exterior to the subject results from being able to return to the first state before change took place (the curved wire can be straightened), by a simple action. The impossibility of such a return makes the conservation of identity of a lighted candle much more difficult to accept than that of a ball of plasticine or of a curved piece of wire. The candle cannot stay the same when it burns because it becomes smaller without any possibility of returning to its original size. However, this is a weak argument, inasmuch as the child of 5 years cannot become smaller either, and yet he does not conclude that he was another child at 3 or 4 years old.

(iii) *Individual identity and categorial identity.* Another experiment in the same series (Piaget *et al.*, 1968) is particularly interesting, because it brings up the point of relations between individual and categorial identity, and the role of spatial relational properties in identification. The experiment concerns the conservation of identity of a piece of cardboard, cut into a square, which is first presented on its base (two sides are horizontal and two are vertical in relation to the child), and then on its point (with a rotation of 45°). Questions concern individual and categorial identity : "Is it still a square? Is it still the same square? Is it still the same piece of cardboard?"

The authors distinguish three stages in the development of answers. Between 4 and 5, no identity is preserved. By being rotated 45° the object stops being a square; it is no longer the same piece of cardboard and it has changed in size. The modification of a relational property, its orientation, has destroyed both categorial identity and individual identity. We may even ask if a change in categorial identity is not the cause of the non-preservation of individual identity. For young children, squares on their points form a single category together with diamonds and certain triangles; squares on their bases are another category and the only ones that can rightfully be called "squares". Going from one category to another involves the loss of individual identity, based on the principle—respected until 7 or 8 years of age—that one object cannot belong to two categories at the same time.

At the second stage (6 to 7 years of age), the child continues to classify square geometrical shapes into two categories, squares and diamonds, but a change in categorial identity does not prevent him from saying that it is still the same object, the same piece of cardboard and the same size. It is only at 8 or 9 that a child becomes capable of making a complete dissociation between relational and intrinsic properties. As J. said: *"Well, it's still a square. Its place has been changed."* Or P.: *"A square, no, not a square. It's not like that. A square is . . .* (draws a square on its base with his finger). *There, it's on its point. Oh, it's a square anyway. A square on its point, then."*

III. IDENTIFICATION BY REFERRING TO A FIGURATIVE MODEL OF THE OBJECT

(1) THEORETICAL APPROACH

(i) *Referents and modes of representation.* All knowledge of the world is a model of nature, representative of events which have taken place or will take place. It is with reference to these models that we identify sensory inputs. A system of representation can be defined by ". . . a set of rules in terms of which one conserves one's encounters with events" (Bruner, 1973). Even the term "representation" can have a different meaning for different authors. Some, like Piaget, refuse to use it for an infant or an animal, since they are devoid of symbolic function. Whatever the names used, psychologists agree that the identification of an object can be made in relation to three large categories of referents: an action, an image and a concept. Piaget speaks of sensori-motor schemas, of figurative structures and of operatory structures, while Bruner prefers the terms of enactive, iconic and symbolic representation, and the Russian psychologists use practical activity, ideal activity and conceptual imagery (Zaporozhets and Zinchenko, 1966).

All agree on a certain number of points. The three types of referents appear in the course of development in chronological order. The object is first known by the action that can be applied to it. According to Piaget (1936, 1937), until the middle of his second year, an infant identifies a sensory picture by the sensori-motor schema that it evokes and of which it is an integral part. During this period, the signifier (the percept) is not detached from the signified (the schema). Beginning at 15 to 18 months, symbolic imagery becomes possible, the signified is detached from the signifier, but the figurative schemas remain centred on the successive states of the environment. They are therefore static, rarely reversible and indivisible. It is only towards 6 to 8 years of age, with the appearance of operational thought, that the child has cognitive structures at his disposal, centred on transformations which can be composed and reversed such as logical classifications.

Experiments confirm the essentials of this development except on one point. Well before the end of his first year the infant is capable not only of responding differentially to two visual targets presented simultaneously, but of recognizing a toy or a target as one he has already seen or as equivalent to others. Unless we consider that seeing is a sensori-motor schema, we must admit that the identification of sensory inputs not included in a schema of action is possible for the infant.

(ii) *Schematas or distinctive features.* Models for visual pattern recognition belong to two large categories: matching of the object to a prototype, or identification by the scanning of a property list (Minsky, 1961). Theoretical models for perceptual identification of objects can also be classified according to one or the other categories.

According to certain authors, repeated encounters by an individual with his environment result in his setting up a series of representative models called "schemata" (Bartlett, 1932; Vernon, 1955, etc.); prototypes, categories (Bruner, 1957; Bruner, Goodnow and Austin, 1956). When identification takes place, the object is compared with the different prototypes previously set up and the best fitting template is kept. A perfect fitting is not required and a certain margin of distortion is permitted, depending on the observer and the situation. These schemata have two functions : they direct selection from among the multitude of cues presented by the stimulus at the time of perception, and they permit us to make an inference as to the signification of the percept.

According to others (E. J. Gibson, 1969), the encounters with the environment bring about a growing refinement in perceptual differentiation and the discovery of a growing number of possible dimensions of differentiation, as well as the extraction of relational invariants. Any object can be described by a unique bundle of features, only some of which are critical for identification. On this subject, Gibson insists on the fact that the same response can be given to different objects, either because of non-perception of differences (primary generalization) or because of a distinction between critical and non-critical dimensions. Complex objects are identified by critical features. Within the same set, such as phonemes or letters of the alphabet, a limited number of distinctive features can be found, each of which forms a binary opposition. These define either the polar qualities of the same dimension (for example, open/closed) or the presence or absence of a quality (for example, the intersection of lines). Each letter of the alphabet is assigned a value on each of these dimensions. The set of these values, specific for each letter, constitutes an invariant. The other dimensions of variation, such as size or compression, for example, can be ignored because they are not critical. This invariant permits us both to identify a letter and to differentiate it from others.

Identification of an object first consists of determining the set to which it belongs, which in the laboratory depends on the information provided by the experimenter, or from the series of stimuli which have preceded the stimulus-test. Then, the subject sequentially explores the list of distinctive features particular to that set, eliminating at each step a certain number of possibilities.

At first glance, the difference seems great between these two types of models of identification,* one having reference to a prototype and the other, reference to a list of distinctive features. Identification takes place either by overlapping an object and a series of prototypes considered as wholes, or by an ordered sequence of differentiations. Emphasis is put on the feature that objects of the same category have

---

* These are so well known and have appeared in so many publications that only a very summary explanation has seemed necessary here. For a more detailed discussion, see M. D. Vernon, 1955, Minsky, 1961 and E. J. Gibson, 1969.

in common (prototypes) or on those which distinguish them from other objects, belonging to another category (distinctive features). Perceptual learning concerns prototype learning or distinctive feature learning. It is more specific for prototypes; more general, and more capable of a better transfer, in so far as distinctive features are concerned.

A close examination of the two models leads us to believe that what separates them is not as great as the authors would have us believe. For example : perceptual learning is interpreted by M. D. Vernon as an "increasing refinement of the categories, and hence, a narrowing of the limits of permissible variation from the 'standard form' which determines that category" (Vernon, 1954, p. 14); and by E. J. Gibson (1969) as an "increase in specificity of response to a set of stimuli" (E. J. Gibson, 1969, p. 77) "due to the discovery of critical dimensions of differentiation" (p. 108). Would it not be better to speak of complementarity rather than opposition ? Perhaps we should suggest that in all identification emphasis is alternately placed on that which permits the assimilation of the object in question to certain objects, and on that which permits its differentiation. The process of identification is more successful when the relation between the processes of assimilation and differentiation are more harmonious.

Ingenious and well-known experiments have not succeeded in demonstrating that either model gives a better explanation of reality than the other. These experiments, conceived by A. D. Pick (1965), Pick, Pick and Klein (1967), Caldwell and Hall (1970), consist in having the children perform a multi-discrimination learning task with letter-like forms. In the first phase, the children learn by a matching procedure to recognize standard shapes in a group of comparison shapes which differ from the standard according to three types of transformations. Then, for half of the children (Group I), the transfer task consists in identifying these same standard shapes among comparison stimuli which are different from the standard according to three other types of transformations. For the other half (Group II), identification in the transfer task is concerned with three new shapes the comparison stimuli of which differ according to the same types of transformation as in the first task. Pick advances the hypothesis that if the child learns to identify the standard shapes by forming a prototype, the transfer will be better in Group I; but if the initial learning consists in discovering the critical dimensions of differentiation between the standard and the comparison stimuli, the transfer will be better in Group II. This second hypothesis seems to be verified in the first experiment. However, in the transfer task, the two groups seem to be much superior to a control group. Differences between the two experimental groups can be eliminated by varying the experimental conditions which do not touch the fundamental structure of the design. Children of 5 years, therefore, learn both the specific characteristics of shapes (prototypes) and the dimensions which permit their differentiation (distinctive features).

(2) PERCEPTUAL ORGANIZATION AND IDENTIFICATON

(i) *Syncretism.* For a long time, a controversy has raged among developmental psychologists as to the origin of the poor performance of young children in tasks of identification and differentiation. Some, faithful to classical associationist theory, said that children essentially concentrate on the small details of objects and are more sensitive to differences than to resemblances. Others said that the children showed syncretic behaviour and treated objects as wholes that were more or less confused and unstructured. The first group tried to show that children identify an object starting from a detail, while the latter wished to show that they start from the whole. As more and more information was obtained and experimental controls became more rigorous, it became apparent that the opposition between globalism and pointillism was false. Children identified objects in both ways; their inferior performance in relation to older children resulted from their incapacity to consider several features at the same time. According to circumstances, they based their response on one or the other.

When both a picture as a whole and also the elements composing it represent familiar objects, the structural properties of the stimulus will determine the perceptual level of organization chosen by the child, which, for him, will constitute the object or objects to identify. Thus, Dworetzki (1939) designed pictures representing persons made up of diverse fruits, and observed that between the ages of 3 and 5, identification in 80 per cent of the cases was uniquely based on the persons; i.e., on the whole. Using the same principle of picture design, Elkind, Koegler and Go (1964) observed the contrary; that at the same age, in 71 per cent of the cases, identification was exclusively made on the basis of details. An examination of the drawings (Fig.5.2) shows that in the experiment of Elkind and his colleagues, the details are very often a short distance away from each other, while in Dworetzki's, they are contiguous. In addition, the representation of details is more realistic than in Dworetzki's. If we remember that the identification of pictures with incomplete figures is particularly difficult for young children (Rey, 1947; Piaget and Stettler-von Albertini, 1954; Gollin, 1960, etc.), it seems clear that a perceptual organization based on wholes has been favoured by Dworetzki, while that based on individual units has been given preference by Elkind and his colleagues. The most

FIG. 5.2. Identification in reference to the whole or to details. (*After* Dworetzki, 1939, p. 260 and Elkind, Koegler and Go, 1964, p. 84.)

important conclusion that can be drawn from these experiments is that identification by the whole or by details are mutually exclusive for children under 8 years of age. The same part of a picture cannot at one and the same time represent a banana and the body of a cyclist. On another level, this can well be the result of a rule acquired by the infant in his first year: that two objects cannot occupy the same place in space (Bower, 1974).

The influence of the level of perceptual organization chosen by the child is also shown when pictures are being compared and judgments made as to "the same" or "not the same". As regards the configuration of discrete elements, representing objects familiar to the child (flowers or leaves), it is the nature of the elements which determines identity rather than the shape of the configuration, even though its modification can be perceived by the children, as can be seen in Fig. 5.3. From $4\frac{1}{2}$ to $6\frac{1}{2}$ years the pairs of drawings AB and CD, in which the shape of the configuration is the same but the elements differ, are more often judged different than the pairs AC and BD, in which the same elements constitute configurations of a different shape (Pineau, 1969).

(ii) *Perceptual organization and identification in the infant.* Diverse cues are used to show the identification of stimuli in an infant : global or specific motor behaviour; affective demonstrations such as smiles, tears, vocalizations; a differentiated orientation of attention measured by visual fixation time; and modification in cardiac or respiratory rhythm. The method most frequently used is habituation, followed by novelty reaction. An infant is repeatedly presented with one or more stimuli, for a certain amount of time. When the infant's attention decreases over a certain period of time, habituation is said to have taken place. A new stimulus is then presented. If the infant's attention increases, it is considered that this stimulus is perceived differently from the preceding ones; if on the other hand, the curve

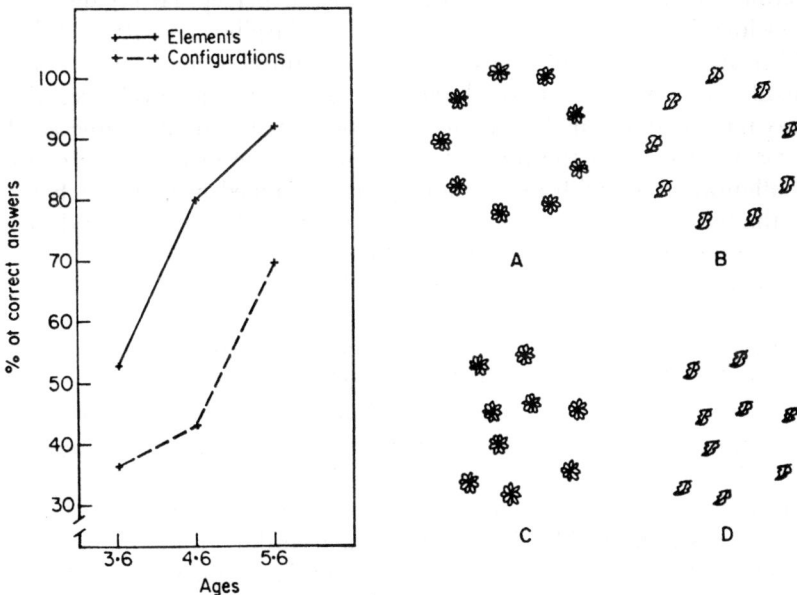

Fig. 5.3. Percentage of correct answers "different" given by children aged 3:6 to 5:6 years, to pairs of drawings differing by the shape of the whole configuration (pairs AC and BD) or by the shape of the elements (pairs AB and CD). (*After* Vurpillot, 1972b, p. 147.)

representing changes in his attention is not modified, it is considered that, for the infant, the new stimulus is equivalent to the preceding ones; they are identical for him. This method gives good results providing that, (1) distinct habituation has taken place, which is very difficult and often impossible to obtain in very young infants with complex stimuli; (2) the stimuli in question have nearly the same power of eliciting attention before habituation; and (3) a reasonable certainty exists that the stimuli are capable of being perceptually differentiated.

A variant of this technique consists in familiarizing an infant with a stimulus over a long period of time, for example, by putting it in front of him in his crib for half an hour each day for several weeks. At the beginning of the experiment, it must be made certain that the two objects receive the same amount of attention. The child is then made familiar with one of them; then the two are again presented together. A novelty reaction is considered to take place when one of the two objects at that moment clearly receives more attention than the other. The appearance of a novelty reaction has been interpreted as a sign that the infant has set up an internal model based on the object or the set of objects presented during the period of familiarization.

The method of habituation followed by a novelty reaction has permitted the study of the relations between perceptual organization and identification in infants of 4 months (Vurpillot and Ruel, 1975). After habituation took place to a visual stimulus made up of nine small crosses arranged into a large cross (Fig. 5.4), the novelty reaction was measured when the infants were presented with the same small crosses arranged in the form of a square (change in the shape of the configuration) or with nine small squares arranged in a cross (change in the form of the elements). We made sure that the elements and their separation were above the threshold of visual acuity and that the infants were well able to discriminate between a little square and a little cross presented individually. Two sizes of stimulus were used.

Infants of 4 months reacted to modification in the configuration when the stimuli were small but not when they were large; and to modification of elements when the stimuli were large, and not when they were small. The authors concluded that infants at that age are capable of organizing the nine elements into one single unit when the entire configuration does not cover too large an area (small stimuli). In this case, infants identify the stimulus according to the shape of the whole and treat the differences in shape of the elements as irrelevant. When they cannot perceptually organize the elements into a single unit (large stimuli), the elements constitute perceptual units and identification then takes place according to their form. As in the experiments of Dworetzki (1939) and Elkind and his colleagues (1964), the level

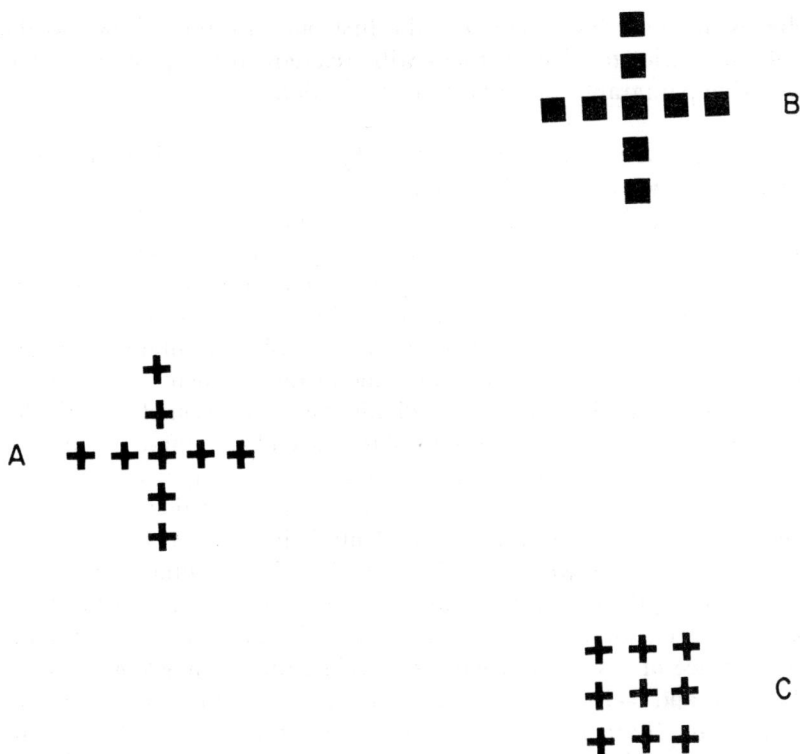

Fig. 5.4. Perceptual organization in infants and identification: A habituation stimulus; B and C stimulus tests. (*After* Vurpillot and Ruel, 1975.)

of perceptual organization (the whole or the elements) chosen by the infant is a result of the structural properties of the stimulus and determines the object to be identified in an exclusive way.

(3) CHARACTERISTICS OF FIGURATIVE INVARIANTS OF VERY FAMILIAR MEANINGFUL OBJECTS

The characteristics of figurative invariants in young infants have been studied in two kinds of situation, which are important to distinguish. In the first, very familiar objects are chosen, and the experimenter tries by various means to find out what the essential characteristics of these objects are for children of different ages. In the second situation, non-familiar objects are repeatedly presented to the infant, who is supposed to construct a prototype of the series, in the laboratory. Unfamiliar objects, more or less resembling the first ones are then shown to the child who tries to identify them with relation to the prototype. The following paragraph concerns the first situation.

(i) *Identification of the human face by an infant.* It is unnecessary here to review the extensive literature that has already appeared on the subject of the infant's reactions to the presence of a human face, since this has been done many times (by Gibson, 1969; Vurpillot, 1972a; Bond, 1972, among others). It should be noted that much of this investigation has been carried out with *pictures* of faces (which is described in Chapter 4). But it seems improbable that infants' reactions to pictures of faces follow the same line of development as their reactions to real faces. Furthermore, individual identification of a particular face, especially that of the person taking care of the infant (mother or mother substitute), should be differentiated from categorical identification of the human face as such. In recognizing a particular person, it seems doubtful whether a single modality is implicated. Identification of the mother could well be made at first by odour, contact or a certain way of taking the infant in her arms, but unfortunately, these variables have not been studied. At 4 months, the baby smiles more in response to the voice of his mother, who is invisible, than to a stranger's voice (Laroche and Tcheng, 1963). At 7 months, the same situation brings about tears (Laroche and Tcheng, 1963), and so does a "montage" which makes his mother's face and a stranger's voice appear in the same spot, or *vice versa* (Cohen, 1974). It seems that at that age the infant has formed a multisensory schema of his mother which has integrated both visual and auditory attributes.

(ii) *Characteristic detail and privileged orientation.* Most of the research done on the identification of very familiar objects by an infant date from the high point of syncretism; their methodological faults are numerous, but their great merit has been to bring to light through careful and patient observation certain characteristics of the representation that very young children make of their daily environment (Segers, 1926a, Decroly, 1929, Meili, 1931, among others). Modern research, more rigorous, has especially been involved in verifying and extending their conclusions.

For each category of familiar object, young children seem to have at their disposal a figurative invariant, which is simple and unambiguous, composed of a few characteristic details the presence or absence of which determines identification. Cramaussel (1924) and Segers (1926b) point out that before the age of 7 children have a tendency to identify an object or its representation according to a single cue, neglecting to verify the truth of their first hypothesis by examining other parts of the picture. An experiment permitted me to confirm these observations (Vurpillot, 1962). Two pictures were first used, one which represented a sheep and the other a rabbit (Fig. 5.5). The parts constituting the sheep (head, woolly body, horns, legs) and those of the rabbit (head, bare body, ears, tail) were then combined by 1, by 2, by 3, by 4, by 5 and by 6—which gave fifteen sheep and fifteen rabbits, more or less incomplete, and twenty-four monsters. Children of 4 to 11 (twenty-five at each age) were asked to put the pictures into the categories of sheep or rabbits by a forced choice. At each age, the twenty-five responses given to each picture (one by each child) were put into one of the three following categories : identified sheep, identified rabbit, non-identified. The non-identified were the pictures for which responses were distributed randomly between sheep and rabbit.

For 4-year-old children, a rabbit necessarily has ears and cannot have

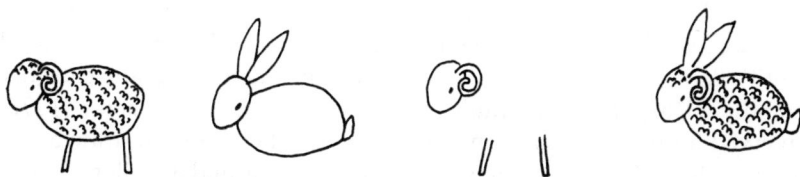

FIG. 5.5. Critical features for identification of familiar objects. Sample of stimuli: complete sheep, complete rabbit, one incomplete sheep, one monster. (*After* Vurpillot, 1962, p. 149.)

wool; in the same way, a sheep must have wool and no ears. Among the non-identified drawings there were as many incomplete animals as monsters. Identification is therefore nearly exclusively based on a characteristic detail; the other details are not taken into account. As the child grows, he takes more features into account, which permits him to identify the incomplete pictures, even if a characteristic detail is missing, and to reserve the category of non-identified for the monsters.

Analysis of children's spontaneous drawings has shown the existence of systematic preferences for certain orientations in the objects represented. A human being is first drawn from a frontal view, and animals in profile; a house is shown by its gabled side. Three-quarter views, either of houses or of faces, appear much later. The figurative schema of a familiar object seems to correspond to a privileged aspect, linked to a certain position in space relative to the observer. A measure of preference verifies this hypothesis (Vurpillot and Brault, 1959). After having seen a familiar object for 30 sec on a turn-table, children of 5 to 9 years were asked to look at a series of photographs of that object, taken at different angles, and to pick out the one which was most nearly the same as the model. The choices confirmed the results of the spontaneous drawings; between the ages of 5 and 7, the photograph deemed most to resemble a doll was the one with a frontal view; then came the three-quarter frontal-view (face visible), the profile, then the three-quarter back view and the back view. At 9 years, the three-quarter frontal view is said to have the greatest resemblance; then the front and the profile. The photographs of a house with two visible sides are said to have the greatest resemblance at all ages, but the view of only the gabled side, often selected at 5 years, is chosen less and less. The figurative schema represents the object with a certain orientation, which varies with age. For the smaller children, the privileged orientation seems to be that which gives the clearest information, while for the older children, it is that which gives the most complete information.

The object in question can have both the cues characteristic of the category, such as the handle of a cup, and those specific to a particular object of the category, such as a floral motif on the cup. In this case, smaller children give pre-eminence to the specific cue (floral motif), and the older children, to the cue which determines the category (handle) (Vurpillot and Brault, 1959). Freeman and Janikoun (1972) observed an opposite reaction when they asked children to draw a cup from reality, the handle of which was invisible and the floral motif visible. The children from 5 to 7 drew the cup without a floral motif but with a visible handle; they retained from the model only the quality of "cup-ness", and drew an ideal cup conforming to their figurative scheme and ignoring information which was actually present.

(4) IDENTIFICATION ACCORDING TO A PROTOTYPE FORMED IN THE LABORATORY

(i) *Salience and relevance of the dimensions or components of a set of objects, in the infant.* Much research has been devoted to attempts made to establish a hierarchy of salience in the dimensions of description of a set of stimuli. The question of the relative preference for shape or colour has been of considerable interest over the years. At present, there is more concern with the relations between relative or absolute salience, and the relevance of a dimension in discrimination learning or in a matching task.

Whatever the method used to measure the relative salience of the dimensions of description of a series of stimulus objects, a certain number of coherent facts has resulted from present research. Before the age of 7, children very often select a single component from a series of objects. The prototype they form is therefore very incomplete (Hale and Morgan, 1973; Hale and Lipps, 1974; Odom, 1972; Odom and Corbin, 1973; Lasky, 1974, etc). The dimension or the component retained by a child is that which is the most salient for him. We should not be surprised if a task of perceptual differentiation or identification produces satisfactory results when the dimension relevant for the experimenter is also the most salient for the child (Odom, 1972; Odom and Lemond, 1974). If, after having measured the relative salience of several dimensions, we train the child to concentrate his attention on one of them, the initial differences in salience can be neutralized. In a transfer task, performance is best when the relevant dimension has been trained; and worse when training has taken place on an irrelevant dimension. The initial degree of salience of a dimension then ceases to intervene (Rollins and Castle, 1973). It therefore seems that a child from 4 to 7 takes only one dimension into account when he makes an identification. The focusing of his attention on a particular dimension can result either from marked salience, defined by the degree to which the perceptual system is sensitive to it (Odom and Guzman, 1970), or from specific training. If a child's attention can be diverted from one component to another, it nevertheless remains fixed on one only. The figural invariant of a series of objects is always poor, limited to some of the properties, and, most important, liable to change in content in relation to direction of attention. Identification of the same object is therefore open to much variation, at least in the experimental conditions of the laboratory.

The same approach in terms of orientation of attention and analysis of stimuli in components characterizes much research done with infants.

Jeffrey (1968) puts forward the hypothesis that in the course of repeated presentations of one or many stimuli (objects or pictures) an infant of several months constructs a schema or object percept which integrates the attending responses furnished by diverse cues present in the stimulus. His hypothesis of serial habituation and Miller's (Miller, 1972) attempt to verify it experimentally have been discussed in Chapter 4.

Miller's experiment shows very well that habituation does not take place uniformly with all the cues present in a stimulus, and that the schema constructed by the infant varies according to the relative salience of the cues.

(ii) *Identification and composition of a series of stimuli of familiarization.* To differentiate between two orientations of the same object (0° and 180°) seems possible, precociously, at the age of 2 months (McGurk, 1970) or at 3 months (Watson, 1966). Recent research by

McGurk (1972) shows that the orientation of the test stimulus is or is not taken into account at the time of their identification, depending on the composition of the series of stimuli of familiarization. Infants from 3 to 12 months were divided into twelve groups according to age and three experimental conditions. In each condition, the infant first saw a series of four stimuli of familiarization, then a first stimulus test, then again the series of familiarization, followed by a second stimulus test. The stimulus tests were the same in all conditions; one differed from the stimulus of familiarization by its shape, and the other by its

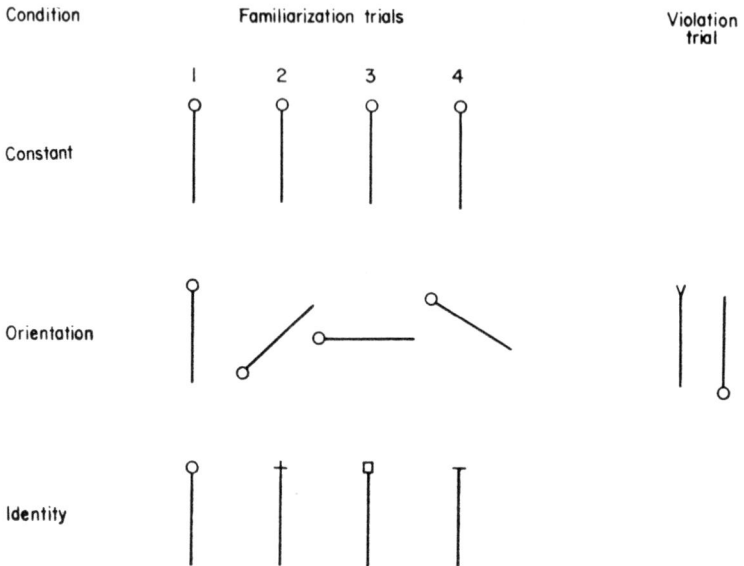

FIG. 5.6. Relevance of shape and orientation for infants. Composition of the series of four habituation tests in three conditions: constant, orientation, identity. On the right, the two stimulus tests presented in the violation trials. (*After* McGurk, 1972, p. 154.)

orientation (Fig. 5.6). In condition 1, the stimuli of familiarization all have the same shape and the same orientation; in condition 2, they have the same shape but different orientations; in condition 3, they have the same orientation but different shapes. The author was not able to obtain habituation in any of the conditions with infants of 3 months; and he found no differences between those of 6, 9 or 12 months, who became habituated in all the conditions. In conditions 1 and 2, the infants had a clearly defined novelty reaction to the stimulus test which differs in form from the stimulus of familiarization; they only have a novelty reaction to the stimulus test which differs in orientation from the stimuli of familiarization in condition 1. It is clear, then, in this experiment, that from the age of 6 months, infants perceive differences of orientation as well as of shape. It may be said that habituation takes place for the cues present in all the stimuli of the series of familiarization; for shape and orientation in condition 1, for shape only in condition 2. There is only a novelty reaction when there is a modification of habituated cues. These results are in line with Jeffrey's hypothesis : habituation takes place selectively with certain cues and is not immediate. When orientation changes from one stimulus of familiarization to another (condition 2), habituation cannot take place.

(iii) *Can we speak of figurative invariants in an infant?* Various authors have raised the possibility that an infant of several months could construct figurative schemas during longer or shorter periods of familiarization. Thus, Kagan (1967) speaks of a representative visual structure, Jeffrey (1968) of a schema or an object percept; and, for Cohen, Gelber and Lazar (1971) habituation of a response to a stimulus repeatedly presented implies the existence of some sort of representation of the stimulus. It seems evident that around 5 months the infant is capable of individually identifying his mother, and, generically the human face. In these cases, it seems legitimate to speak of the existence of a figurative invariant. However, it must be made clear that such an invariant was constructed in the period of familiarization of several months, over numerous encounters, and in varied contexts.

In the laboratory, after a quarter of an hour of familiarization and sometimes even less, infants of four months react in different ways to stimuli which present varying degrees of discrepancy with the original object. In general, the reaction, which is weak when the new stimulus differs from the familiar in only one dimension, is stronger when modifications are made in many dimensions, regardless of the dimensions in question : form, colour, arrangement of elements, orientation (McCall and Melson, 1969; Cohen, Gelber and Lazar, 1971; Super, Kagan, Morrison, Haith and Weiffenbach, 1972; Welch, 1974; Cornell, 1975). These experiments, like those of Miller (1972) and McGurk (1972), seem to show that an infant takes several cues into account. Can we conclude that he has constructed a figurative invariant of the series of familiarization which incorporates several cues, 1 to 3 according to Miller, 1 to 2 according to McGurk? Research on children of 5 to 7 has shown that they seem to form figurative invariants in the laboratory, but only incorporate a part of the cues, and most often only 1. It is very difficult to believe that infants of 4 to 6 months can do better than children of 5 to 7. The construction of a figurative invariant by infants in a quarter of an hour seems hardly likely.

In effect, experiments with infants give us information only as to the degree of attention elicited by visual targets. This attention varies with the physical properties of the targets involved and with the nature of encounters that the infant previously had with his environment. So that, presented at different times and in different circumstances, one and the same object can elicit different degrees of attention; and two objects that are physically different may or may not elicit the same degree of attention. To use the terms "differentiation" and "identification" with regard to infants by defining them operationally as to whether they elicit equal or unequal degrees of attention is not very dangerous, but it becomes so when inferences are drawn from information on the duration of relative fixation times of an infant while referring to representative invariants similar to the adult's.

(5) IDENTIFICATION ACROSS MODALITIES

Older children and adults are very capable of recognizing an object visually which they had previously encountered only tactilely, and *vice versa*. We may conclude that the representation of the object with which they compare their sensory inputs has a certain independence of the sensory modalities involved. In the same cross-modal tasks, young children perform very badly. Thus numerous authors have hypothesized that in an early phase of development, sensory inputs furnished by different sensory modalities are dealt with independently by the central nervous system, and it is only little by little that information of different sensory origins is co-ordinated. Such an interpretation produces the following predictions: (1) Performance in cross-modal problems improves with age : (2) In young children, performance in inter-modal problems is worse than in intra-modal problems (presentation and recognition in the same sensory modality); (3) The infant is incapable of succeeding in a cross-modal task. The first prediction was rapidly verified by numerous authors (Birch and Lefford, 1963, 1967; Blank and Bridger, 1964; Abravanel, 1968, etc); but the second prediction was not. When experimenters presented inter-modal and intra-modal problems of identification of forms to children of the same age, the tactile-tactile condition appeared much more difficult than the visual-visual condition, and more difficult than the two cross-modal conditions, visual-tactile and tactile-visual to children between 4 and 7 years of age (Hermelin and O'Connor, 1961; Rudel and Teuber, 1964; Milner and Bryant, 1970; Millar, 1971; Rose, Blank and Bridger, 1972, etc.). In effect, the difficulty increases with the introduction of the tactile modality.

The recognition of a shape depends on the comparison of the actual sensory inputs and a representative model of the shape previously perceived, stored in the memory. The construction of a representative model of a form presented tactilely, as well as the identification of tactile sensory inputs, requires an efficient strategy of exploration to be used and the information recorded sequentially to be integrated. These requirements are much less important when the construction of a model and the identification of inputs are based on the visual modality. Progress with age in cross-modal tasks can essentially be attributed to progress in the strategies of exploration and in information processing, this progress having an effect on all tasks concerning the tactile modality.

By means of a very clever experiment, Bryant *et al.* (1972) showed that infants of less than 12 months are capable of recognizing visually an object previously presented tactilely, thus invalidating the third prediction. The integration hypothesis of Birch and Lefford (1963) therefore does not seem to be confirmed.

IV.   IDENTITY OR NON-IDENTITY OF TWO OBJECTS SIMULTANEOUSLY PRESENT

(1) METHODS OF JUDGING IDENTITY

The identity of two objects can be measured either by a procedure of matching a model with comparison stimuli or by a judgment of "same" or "different". In the first case, the series of comparison stimuli always contains one which is physically identical with the model; in the second case, pairs of stimuli are presented, the members of which are sometimes physically identical and sometimes different.

The task of the child involves comparison. The final response is based on the application of a rule and on a strategy of information gathering and of comparison of the two objects. The rule defines the conditions which the two objects must fulfil in order to be judged "the same". In the conditions in question, an adult in our culture would choose the rule of logical identity. Two objects are said to be identical, the same, when they both have all the same properties (positive definition), and when they show no differences (negative definition). As a result, before declaring two objects as identical, it must be ascertained that they have no differences; thus, a thorough scanning becomes necessary. The slightest difference becomes relevant and requires the answer, "not the same". In the laboratory, the stimuli are very often pieces of cardboard with a picture; the position, the orientation of the picture with reference to the edges of the cardboard are considered to be properties of the stimulus. On the other hand, the position of the cardboard with respect to the observer is not a property of the stimulus, and its variations are not relevant for an identity judgment. The necessary strategy is a one to one correspondence between all the cues (global properties of details) present in the two objects. Until the age of 8 or 9, the child does not use the rule of logical identity but rules of equivalence, which are more or less strict, and allow him to take into account only a part of the information available. On the one hand, certain properties of the stimulus are neglected and their variations considered as irrelevant; on the other hand, the child is content with examining and comparing only a part of the objects. Even with good criteria of decision-making, a child can give an erroneous answer because he has adopted a strategy inadequate for obtaining information, or a faulty system of reference for determining the relative place of the elements or details within the stimulus.

A series of experiments with children of $3\frac{1}{2}$ to 10 years tried to show the relation between a change in performance and the factors which have just been cited : definition of identity, relevance of differences, extent of scanning, strategy of information-gathering, criteria of localization. In these experiments, the child was asked to carry out a limited number of paired-comparisons, fourteen at a maximum, most often with black-and-white pictures or slides, and instructed to say if the two pictures of a pair were completely alike or not. The experimenter also asked the child to justify each of his answers, but never discussed the correctness of his responses. In the absence of reinforcement and of correction of responses it may be hoped that the performances were a result of an application of personal rules of decision-making in the child. In certain experiments, oculo-motor activity was recorded during the comparison of the stimulus.

(2) IDENTITY DETERMINED BY GLOBAL SIMILARITY OR BY THE PERCEPTION OF RELEVANT DIFFERENCES

In the first experiment, forty-five children of 3 years 4 months to 5 years : were asked to compare pairs of three-dimensional toy-houses, each having four windows. According to the pairs, the number of differences varied between 0 (identical pair) and 4; one difference consisted in putting a different window in the same place in the two houses (difference by substitution). By having the child point out each window with his finger before giving his response, the experimenter was sure that the exploration of the stimulus had been thorough (Berthoud and

Vurpillot, 1970). A second experiment used the same design with other children, and houses with one, two or three windows; thirty-six children of 4 years were involved (Vurpillot, 1972b). Out of eighty-one children participating in those two experiments the performance of twenty-eight was "entirely correct". Twenty-three answered "the same" to all pairs, without our knowing whether they gave a stereotyped response because of a simple perseveration, or because the word "same" had no meaning for them, in proportion to the increasing number of differences in a pair (Table 5.1). For these children, identity or non-

TABLE 5.1

Percentage of correct "not the same" responses as a function of the total number of windows and of the number of differences

Number of differences	1	1	1	1*	2	2	2*	3*	4*
Number of windows	1	2	3	4	2	3	4	4	4
Percentage of correct responses	83.3	63.3	43.3	36.7	70.0	63.3	53.3	73.3	93.3

This table regroups the results of fifteen children from Berthoud and Vurpillot's (1970) experiment and fifteen children from the subsequent experiment. The columns marked with an asterisk relate to the results from Berthoud and Vurpillot's experiment. (*After* Vurpillot, 1975, p. 304.)

identity of two objects seems to be linked not to the presence or absence of relevant differences but to an evaluation of their global similarity. If two objects have more points in common than differences, they are declared to be "the same"; if on the contrary, they have more differences than similarities, they are declared "not the same". There is a sort of rough categorization, by dichotomy, between the alikes and not-alikes, as can be observed between large and small objects at the same ages. This level of judgment by global similarity ends at an age when an experiment with a verbal response, like our own, becomes possible. The kind of behaviour corresponding to such a rule (global similarity) is not found in the majority at 4 years (44.4 per cent of the children) or at 5 years (33 per cent).

(3) RELEVANCE OF DIFFERENCES

A child of 3 to 4 years considers that two pictures are not the same when a detail, such as a snowman's hat or a donkey's foot is found in one and not in the other (Vurpillot, 1972b). The presence of two differences by substitution in the pictures of houses with six windows produces the response "not the same" in half of the children of 4, and in nearly all of the children of 5 (Vurpillot and Moal, 1970). The displacement of one element out of nine arranged in a circle changes the shape of the configuration. This modification is perceived very early, but does not bring about a response of "not the same" in any child of $3\frac{1}{2}$ years, and does so in only one-third of those of $4\frac{1}{2}$. The same modification (displacement of an element) applied to an irregular configuration is even less effective (Vurpillot et al. 1971).

As the child grows, more and more types of difference become relevant and are taken into account in identity responses. The relevance of differences is linked to their degree of salience. Until the age of 6, a child will often say that two objects are identical if all the elements or details found in one are also present in the other. It matters very little to him if the experimenter has introduced permutations between the elements, or that one of them, A for example, is shown twice in one of the pictures, but only once in the other, while for element B, the reverse has occurred (Vurpillot and Moal, 1970; Vurpillot and Taranne, 1974, 1975).

Some very recent research by Vurpillot has demonstrated the process of change that takes place in children as regards the relative place of elements taken into account in responses of identity. Fifty-six children were asked to respond "the same" or "not the same" to eight pairs of pictures of necklaces. Each necklace was made up of six round beads, each bead having a picture of a familiar object on it (Fig. 5.7). In one necklace, the six beads were different, but all the necklaces were made of the same beads. Two pairs (I) were identical. In the six others, none of the beads were in an identical place in both pairs of necklaces. Thus in two pairs (M) the same bead always had a symmetrical place, the necklace thereby acting as mirror images of each other; in two pairs (P), no bead was found either in a symmetrical or

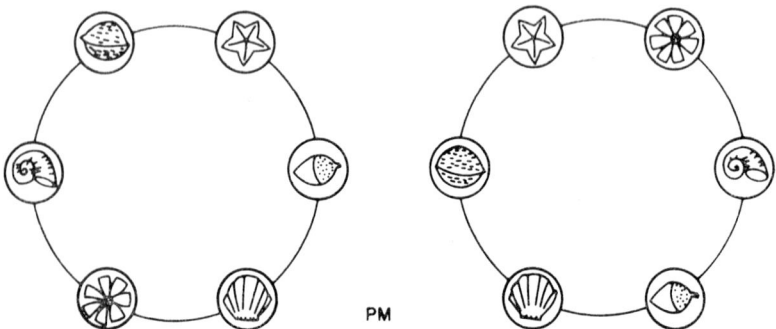

FIG. 5.7. Sample of stimuli used by Vurpillot in a differentiation task. With this pair of necklaces (PM), three beads are in symmetry and three are different.

identical place; and in two pairs (PM), three of the beads were found in symmetrical places, and the three others were not identical. Eye-movements were recorded during the task.

A limited number of patterns of response became apparent from the series of responses "the same" or "not the same" made by the child, and from the way he justified them. As a result of this experiment, in the age-group considered (5 to 9 years), five levels in the evolution of rules of response could be discerned. On the first level, no coherent rule seemed evident, either in the distribution of responses according to the pairs, or in the justifications given to them. On the second level, the rule of response became clear and could be stated as such : "Two objects are the same when the elements present in one are also found in the other." The place of a bead was never mentioned and the eight pairs of necklaces were declared to be alike. On the third level, the children began to take both the place and the nature of the beads into account, but not all the time. The same child said in succession that two (PM) necklaces were different : "They are the same but the nut is not next to the star ... They are a little alike but not too much ... no they're not completely the same." Then about two (P) necklaces he said that "they are the same, but the shell isn't on the right side". The hesitations showed that the differences in place were noticed, but the children did not as yet have a rule by which to define their relevance. On the fourth level, there was no longer any doubt as to the relevance of place and nature, but the determination of what constitutes "the same place" for two beads was made according to in-adequate criteria. It was only when we came to the fifth level that the problems of localization were resolved and only those necklaces which were physically identical were judged to be "the same". Three-quarters of the children of 9 attained this level in the experiment in question.

(4) CRITERIA OF LOCALIZATION

An analysis of the response of children at level 4 of the previous experiment shows that a change took place in the determination of what constitutes "the same place".

The first system used was that of a one-to-one correspondence be-tween the beads located in a horizontal line when the two objects are placed side by side. For children who use such a system of reference, two beads are in the same place when they are on the same horizontal alignment. The necklaces of identical and mirror-image pairs (I and M) are thus judged to be the same since the same beads are found in the same alignment. The fact that they are found in identical (I) or symmetrical places (M) is of little importance. On the other hand, the necklaces (P) and (PM) are not the same because all or a part of the beads are found in different horizontal lines. Displacement from one horizontal to another constitutes a difference in place.

Other children can distinguish identical places from symmetrical places very well, but cannot decide where the "same places" are located. Thus, sometimes they say that two identical necklaces (I pair) are "the same" and sometimes "not the same" and the same contradictory responses occur with mirror-images. When a child has passed the period of hesitation, the "same place" becomes the identical place. None of the fifty-six children in the experiment considered the possibility that the mirror image necklaces were the only ones completely "the same".

(4) EXTENT OF EXPLORATION

Much research done on the analysis of visual scanning while objects are being compared for identification has shown that, under 6 years of age, the child does not consider it necessary to explore two objects thoroughly in order to judge whether they are completely alike or not (Vurpillot, 1968; Vurpillot, 1972b; Vurpillot, Castelo and Renard, 1975; Vurpillot and Baudonnière, 1975).

The number of thorough children (who have entirely scanned the stimulus before responding "the same") greatly increases between 5 and 6. In one experiment (Vurpillot, Castelo and Renard, 1975), there was only one thorough child out of thirty-six at 5 years of age, but sixteen out of thirty-six at $6\frac{1}{2}$. Nearly all the children at 4 and 5 years and half at 6 were content with taking a small sample of the available information from a stimulus and using it to make a judgment on the whole. This behaviour has been well known since the outset of research done on syncretism. It is certainly responsible for a number of errors observed in tasks of recognition and identification, and for some of those appearing in the measurement of identity or non-identity of objects also.

The size of the sample varies, but two factors seem to have an influence on it. The first is the interest evoked by the intrinsic properties of the stimulus or by its novelty. For the child as well as for the infant certain objects have a greater power of attraction and are looked at more than others. Not only are they looked at longer, but the surface explored and number of elements examined are also greater. At all ages, the number of ocular fixations on a series of pairs of pictures of houses diminishes from the presentation of the first picture to the last. At the same time, at 7 and 9 years of age, the average number of windows looked at does not change; only the redundant fixations have been eliminated. Children of 4 and 5, however, look at fewer and fewer windows (Fig. 5.8), thereby obtaining less and less information before giving a response (Vurpillot, 1972b).

A second factor involved in the extent of exploration is the quantity of information available in a stimulus. With pairs of houses having either 6, 8 or 10 windows, the size of the sample is proportional to the number of existing windows. That size increases with age. Before answering "the same", children of 5 look at half the windows, while those of $6\frac{1}{2}$ look at three-quarters; and this is true for houses with ten windows as well as for those having eight or six (Vurpillot, Castelo

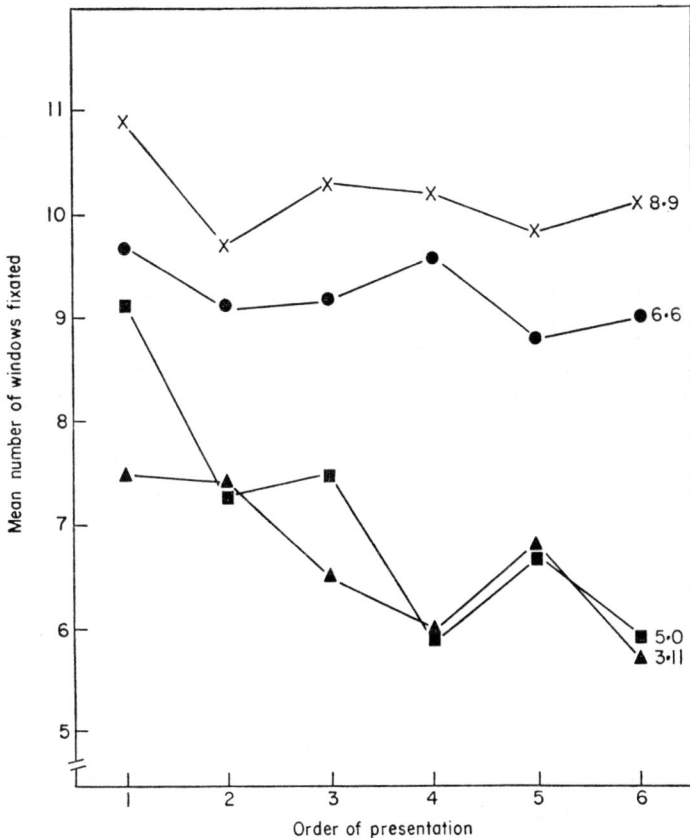

FIG. 5.8. Evolution with time of the extent of visual scanning in a differentation task. The four curves are for ages: 3:11, 5:0, 6:6 and 8:9 years. Each point is the mean number of windows fixated on the pair of drawings presented at the first, second, third, fourth, fifth and sixth rank in the series. (*After* Vurpillot, 1972b, p. 245.)

and Renard, 1975). It would be imprudent to infer from this that
the proportion would be maintained in all cases, regardless of the
number of elements and the type of stimulus. Current research has
shown that the sample examined is smaller with houses of twelve windows, arranged in four rows and three columns (tweny-four elements
in all), than with houses with ten windows, arranged in five rows and
two columns (twenty elements).

(5) STRATEGIES OF INFORMATION-GATHERING

The manner in which visual scanning is organized, is, to a certain
extent, informative as to the strategies of exploration. In children of
less than 6, oculo-motor exploration is not random; a certain organization exists, but it does not yet seem linked to any rules of decision-
making. Analysis of hundreds of scan-paths in children of 5, recorded
during tasks of comparison involving pictures of necklaces or houses,
has permitted us to distinguish certain common characteristics. Ocular
displacements are made more often between neighbouring elements
(effect of proximity) and are inclined to follow horizontal lines. The
centre and the top of the visual field receive more ocular fixations than
other parts of the field. In short, the localization of the fixations and
the direction of the movements seem determined mainly by the structural characteristics of the stimulus and their relative power to attract
attention. At the same ages, the extent of exploration depends to a
large degree on the interest that the child has for the stimulus. Ought
we therefore to conclude that before the age of 6 scanning is totally
independent of the task to be accomplished? This would be going too
far. The child takes the instructions he has received into account in
the sense that he looks first at one and then at the other object before
answering. A good part of the ocular displacements (30–40 per cent
at 4 and 5 years of age) connect an element in one object to an element
in the other, whether they are placed side by side (horizontal vector of
comparison) or one above the other (vertical vector of comparison).
The direction of the ocular displacements is influenced by this and
the relative proportion of horizontal and vertical movements is not
the same for both forms of presentation (Fig. 5.9). An adaptation
of scanning to the task exists even if it is limited by the privileged
role of the horizontal axis (Vurpillot and Baudonnière, 1975). But
the influence of the task does stop there. No correlation can be shown
to exist between performance as measured by the percentage of correct
verbal responses, and the extent of organization of exploration, before
6 years of age.

Beginning at 6, the relation between the scan-path and the rule

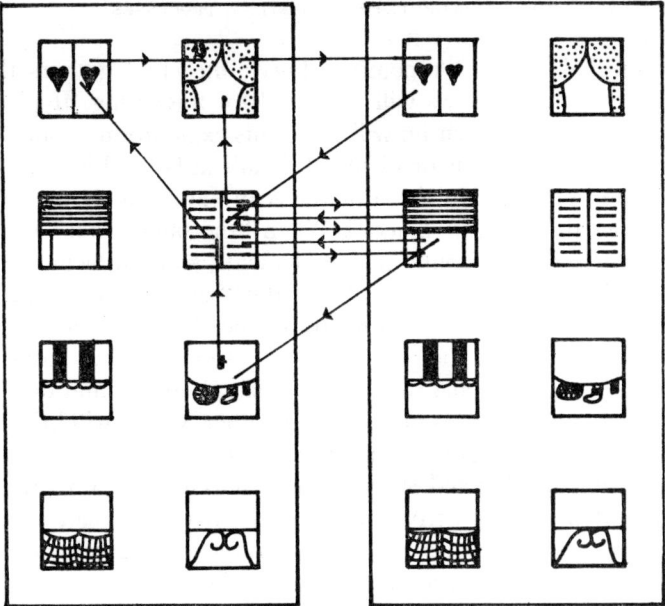

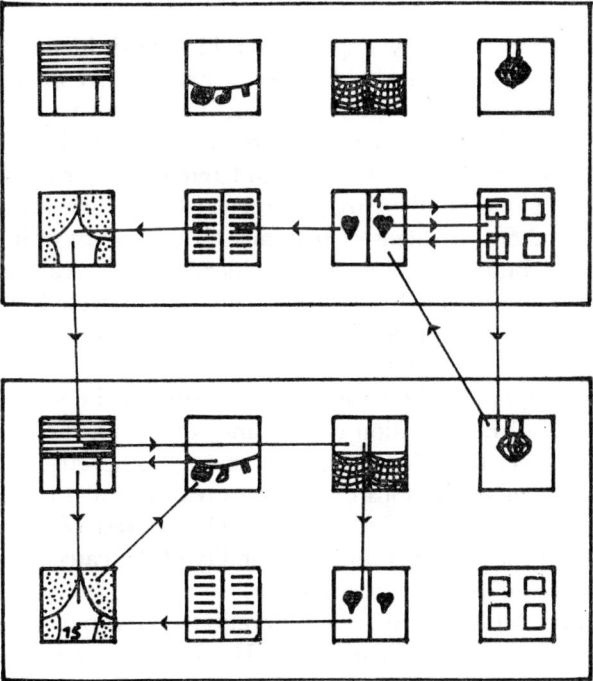

FIG. 5.9. Scan paths of 5-year-old children on pairs of drawings in a differentiation task.

of decision-making used becomes defined; the child gathers that information which he knows will be useful for answering. If place is a relevant cue for him, then he will direct his exploration in such a way as to see if those elements or identical details in both objects are really in "the same place". The form of the scan-path will show a connection between these "same places". When "the same place" is defined with reference to a horizontal line of elements, scanning will essentially be done by horizontal movements. If the "same place" is identical, the proportion of movements directly connecting the identical places will be greater than in the preceding case. On the other hand, if the place is not a relevant cue, the child will simply try to find out if each element of an object is also present in the other, which will bring about a greater number of comparisons, and therefore a greater number of ocular movements, directed obliquely as well as horizontally (Fig. 5.10). The amount of ocular activity and the form of the scan-path gives evidence of real strategies of information-gathering which directly depend on criteria of decision-making in the child.

V   CONCLUSIONS

The poor performance of young children in tasks of identification and the progress observed with development are illustrative of certain well-known characteristics of their behaviour. The passage from stimulus-bound to goal-directed behaviour can be observed. Little by little, categories, rules of decision-making and references formerly used independently of one another are incorporated into logical hierarchical classes and authentic systems of reference. The amount of information taken into account increases in identification and real stategies in problem-solving of defined tasks appear and are perfected. A primitive rigidity gives way to a flexibility of choice and strategies according to given instructions and material.

In the young child, the structural properties of the stimulus determine the level of organization chosen and, therefore, the definition of what is the object to be identified. These same properties elicit a concentration of ocular fixations on certain areas and a privileged direction of ocular movements in scanning. The interest of the child has more effect on the scanning and accessibility of the categories than the instructions given by the experimenter.

The young child takes into consideration only a part of the available information at a given moment. He makes a comparison of the objects on only one of their dimensions, preferably the most perceptually salient. He identifies them according to a critical characteristic. His scanning is limited to a small number of details or elements. His

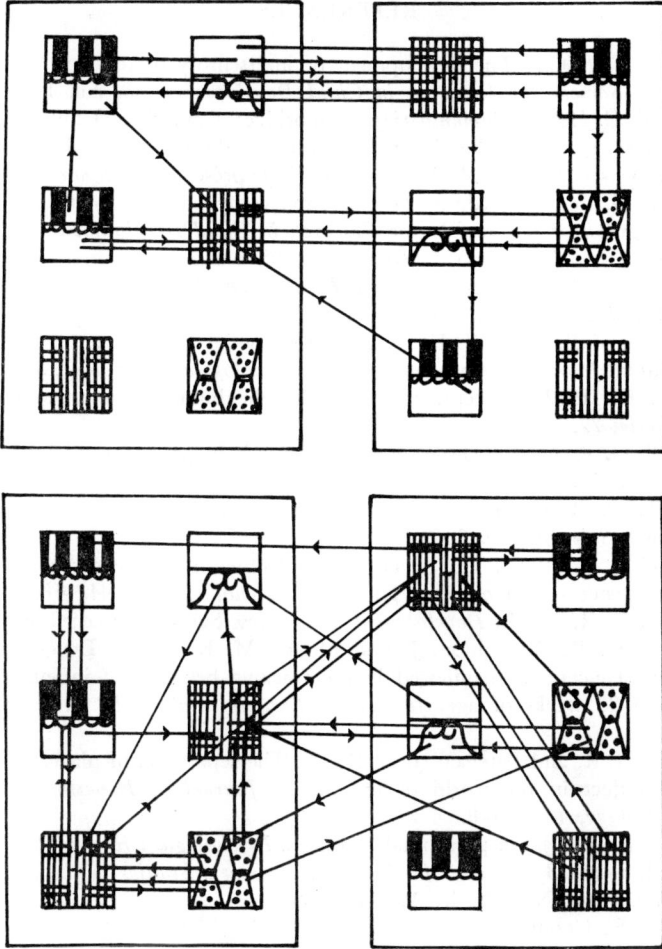

FIG. 5.10. Scan paths of two children of 6 years who differ by their rule of decision: the place of a window is relevant for the child on the top display, but not for the child on the bottom display. (*After* Vurpillot and Taranne, 1974, pp. 90 and 91.)

responses fluctuate and are often contradictory from one moment to the other because he focuses his attention first on one detail, then on another; or refers first to one dimension and then to another; or uses one cue and then another to localize or identify. Thus, his greatest weakness lies in an absence of co-ordination between all the cues he is capable of perceiving and the rules he is capable of using.

REFERENCES

Abravanel, E. (1968). The development of intersensory patterning. *Monograph of the Society for Research in Child Development, 38*, No. 118.

Bartlett, F. C. (1932). *Remembering*. Cambridge: Cambridge University Press.

Berthoud, M. and Vurpillot, E. (1970). Influence du nombre de différences sur les réponses "pas pareil" chez l'enfant d'âage préscolaire. *Enfance, 23*, 23–30.

Birch, H. G. and Lefford, A. (1963). Intersensory development in children. *Monograph of the Society for Research in Child Development, 28*, No. 5.

Birch, H. G. and Lefford, A. (1967). Visual differentiation, intersensory integration and voluntary motor control. *Monograph of the Society for Research in Child Development, 32*, No. 2.

Blank, M. and Bridger, W. H. (1964). Cross-modal transfer in nursery school children. *Journal of Comparative and Physiological Psychology, 58*, 277–82.

Bond, E. K. (1972). Perception of form by the human infant. *Psychological Bulletin, 77*, 225–45.

Bower, T. G. R. (1964). Discrimination of depth in premotor infants. *Psychonomic Science, 1*, 368.

Bower, T. G. R. (1965). Stimulus variables determining space perception in infants, *Science, 149*, 88–9.

Bower, T. G. R. (1967). The development of object-permanence: some studies of existence constancy. *Perception and Psychophysics, 2*, 411–18.

Bower, T. G. R. (1974). *Development in Infancy*. San Francisco: Freeman.

Bower, T. G. R., Broughton, J. and Moore, M. K. (1971). Development of object concept as manifested in the tracking behavior of infants between 7 and 20 weeks of age. *Journal of Experimental Child Psychology, 11*, 182–93.

Bower, T. G. R. and Paterson, J. G. (1973). The separation of place, movement and object in the world of the infant. *Journal of Experimental Child Psychology, 15*, 161–8.

Bruner, J. S. (1957). On perceptual readiness. *Psychological Review, 64*, 123–52.

Bruner, J. S. (1973). *Beyond the Information Given. Studies in the Psychology of Knowing*. New York: W. W. Noton.

Bruner, J. S., Goodnow, J. J. and Austin, G. A. (1956). *A Study of Thinking*. New York: Wiley.

Bryant, P. E. (1974). *Perception and Understanding in Young Children. An Experimental Approach*. London: Methuen.

Bryant, P. E., Jones, P., Claxton, V. C. and Perkins, G. M. (1972). Recognition of shapes across modalities by infants. *Nature, 240*, 303–4.

Butterworth, G. (1975). *Mapping the self into the world in infancy*. Paper presented to the International Society for the study of behavioral development. Guildford: University of Surrey.

Caldwell, E. C. and Hall, V. C. (1970). Distinctive features versus prototype learning reexamined. *Journal of Experimental Psychology, 83*, 7–12.

Cohen, L. B., Gelber, E. R. and Lazar, M. A. (1971). Infant habituation and generalization to differing degrees of stimulus novelty. *Journal of Experimental Child Psychology, 11*, 379–89.

Cohen, S. E. (1974). Developmental differences in infants' attentional responses to face-voice incongruity of mother and stranger. *Child Development, 45*, 1155–8.

Cornell, E. H. (1975). Infants' visual attention to pattern arrangement and orientation. *Child Development, 46,* 229–32.

Cramaussel, E. (1924). Ce que voient des yeux d'enfant. *Journal de Psychologie Normale et Pathologique, 21,* 161–9.

Day, R. H. and McKenzie, B. E. (1973). Perceptual shape constancy in early infancy. *Perception, 2,* 315–20.

Decroly, O. (1929). *La Fonction de Globalisation et l'Enseignement.* Bruxelles.

Dworetzki, G. (1939). Le test de Rorschach et l'évolution de la perception. Étude expérimentale. *Archives de Psychologie, 27,* 233–396.

Elkind, D., Koegler, R. R. and Go, E. (1964). Studies in perceptual development. II. Part-whole perception. *Child Development, 35,* 81–90.

Evans, W. F. and Gratch, G. (1972). The stage IV error in Piaget's theory of object concept development: difficulties in object conceptualization of spatial localization. *Child Development, 43,* 682–8.

Fantz, R. L. (1963). Pattern vision in newborn infants. *Science, 140,* 296–7.

Freeman, N. H. and Janikoun, R. (1972). Intellectual realism in children's drawings of a familiar object with distinctive features. *Child Development, 43,* 1116–21.

Gibson, E. J. (1969). *Principles of Perceptual Learning and Development.* New York: Appleton-Century-Crofts.

Gibson, J. J. (1950). *The Perception of the Visual World.* Boston: Houghton Mifflin.

Gibson, J. J. (1966). *The Senses Considered as Perceptual Systems.* Boston: Houghton Mifflin.

Gollin, E. S. (1960). Developmental studies of visual recognition of incomplete objects. *Perceptual and Motor Skills, 11,* 289–98.

Hale, G. A. and Lipps, L. E. T. (1974). Stimulus matching and component selection: alternative approaches to measuring children's attention to stimulus components. *Child Development, 45,* 383–8.

Hale, G. A. and Morgan, J. S. (1973). Developmental trends in children's component selection. *Journal of Experimental Child Psychology, 15,* 302–14.

Harris, P. L. (1974). Perseveration search at a visibly empty place by young infants. *Journal of Experimental Child Psychology, 18,* 535–42.

Hermelin, B. and O'Connor, N. (1961). Recognition of shapes by normal and subnormal children. *British Journal of Psychology, 52,* 281–4.

Jeffrey, W. E. (1968). The orienting reflex and attention in cognitive development. *Psychological Review, 75,* 323–34.

Kagan, J. (1967). The growth of the "face" schema: theoretical significance and methodological issues. In J. Hellmuth (Ed.), *Exceptional Infant,* Vol. 1, *The Normal Infant.* Seattle: Special Child Publications.

Landers, W. F. (1971). Effect of differential experience on infant's performance in a piagetian stage IV object-concept task. *Developmental Psychology, 5,* 48–54.

Laroche, J. L. and Tcheng, F. (1963). *Le Sourire du Nourrisson: la Voix comme Facteur Déclenchant.* Louvain: Publications Universitaires.

Lasky, R. E. (1974). The ability of six-year-olds, eight-year-olds, and adults to abstract visual patterns. *Child Development, 45,* 626–32.

McCall, R. B. and Melson, W. H. (1969). Attention in infants as a function of magnitude of discrepancy and habituation rate. *Psychonomic Science, 17,* 317–19.

McGurk, H. (1970). The role of object orientation in infant perception. *Journal of Experimental Child Psychology, 9,* 363–73.

McGurk, H. (1972). Infant discrimination of orientation, *Journal of Experimental Child Psychology, 14,* 151–64.

Meili, R. (1931). Les perceptions des enfants et la psychologie de la gestalt. *Archives de Psychologie, 23,* 25–44.

Michotte, A. (1962). *Causalité, Permanence et Réalité Phénoménale.* Louvain: Publications Universitaires.

Michotte, A., Thinès, G. and Crabbé, G. (1964). *Les Compléments Amodaux des Structures Perceptives.* Louvain: Publications Universitaires.

Millar, S. (1971). Visual and haptic cue utilisation by pre-school children: the recognition of visual and haptic stimuli presented separately and together. *Journal of Experimental Child Psychology, 12,* 88–94.

Miller, D. J. (1972). Visual habituation in the human infant. *Child Development, 43,* 481–93.

Miller, D. J., Cohen, L. B. and Hill, K. T. (1970). A methodological investigation of Piaget's theory of object concept development in the sensory-motor period. *Journal of Experimental Child Psychology, 9,* 59–85.

Milner, A. D. and Bryant, P. E. (1970). Cross-modal matching by young children. *Journal of Comparative and Physiological Psychology, 71,* 453–58.

Minsky, M. (1961). Steps toward artificial intelligence. *Proceedings of the Institute of Radio Engineers, 49,* 8–30.

Odom, R. D. (1972). Effects of perceptual salience on the recall of relevant and incidental dimensional values: a developmental study. *Journal of Experimental Psychology, 92,* 285–91.

Odom, R. D. and Corbin, D. W. (1973). Perceptual salience and children's multidimensional problem solving. *Child Development, 44,* 425–32.

Odom, R. D. and Guzman, R. (1970). Problem solving and the perceptual salience of variability and constancy: a developmental study. *Journal of Experimental Child Psychology, 9,* 156–65.

Odom, R. D. and Lemond, C. M. (1974). Children's use of component pattern of faces in multidimensional recall problems. *Child Development, 45,* 527–31.

Piaget, J. (1936). *La Naissance de l'Intelligence chez l'Enfant.* Neuchatel: Delachaux & Niestlé.

Piaget, J. (1937). *La Construction du Réel chez l'Enfant.* Neuchatel: Delachaux & Niestlé.

Piaget, J., Sinclair, H. and Vinh-Bang (1968). *Epistémologie et Psychologie de l'Identité.* Paris: Presses Universitaires de France.

Piaget, J. and Stettler-von Albertini, B. (1954). Observations sur la perception des bonnes formes chez l'enfant par actualisation des lignes virtuelles. *Archives de Psychologie, 34,* 203–42.

Pick, A. D. (1965). Improvement of visual and tactual form discrimination. *Journal of Experimental Psychology, 69,* 331–9.

Pick, H. L., Pick, A. D. and Klein, R. E. (1967). Perceptual integration in children. In L. Lipsitt and C. Spiker (Eds.), *Advances in Child Development and Behavior,* Vol. 3. New York and London: Academic Press.

Pineau, A. (1969). Organisation perceptive et identification chez le jeune enfant (quoted in E. Vurpillot, *Le Monde Visuel du Jeune Enfant,* 1972).

Rey, A. (1947). *Étude des Insuffisances Psychologiques. I. Méthodes et Problèmes.* Neuchatel: Delachaux et Niestlé.

Rollins, H. and Castle, K. (1973). Dimensional preference, pretraining, and attention in children's concept identification.*Child Development, 44*, 363–6.

Rose, S. C., Blank, M. S. and Bridger, W. H. (1972). Intermodal and intramodal matching of visual and tactual information in young children. *Developmental Psychology, 6*, 482–6.

Rudel, R. G. and Teuber, H. L. (1964). Cross-modal transfer of shape discrimination by children. *Neuropsychologia, 2*, 1–18.

Salapatek, P. (1968). Visual scanning of geometric figures by the human newborn. *Journal of Comparative and Physiological Psychology, 66*, 247–58.

Salapatek, P. and Kessen, W. (1966). Visual scanning of triangles by the human newborn. *Journal of Experimental Child Psychology, 3*, 155–67.

Segers, J. E. (1926a). *Les Perceptions Visuelles et la Fonction de Globalisation chez les Enfants.* Bruxelles: Lamertin.

Segers, J. E. (1926b). Recherches sur la perception visuelle chez des enfants âgés de 3 à 12 ans et leur application à l'éducation. *Journal de Psychologie Normale et Pathologique, 23*, 608–36; 723–53.

Super, C. M., Kagan, J., Morrison, F. J., Haith, M. M. and Weiffenbach, J. (1972). Discrepancy and attention in the five month infant. *Genetic Psychology Monographs, 85*, 305–31.

Vernon, M. D. (1954). *A Further Study of Visual Perception.* Cambridge: Cambridge University Press.

Vernon, M. D. (1955). The functions of schemata in perceiving. *Psychological Review, 62*, 180–92.

Vurpillot, E. (1962). Détails caractéristiques et reconnaissance de formes familières. *Psychologie Française, 7*, 147–55.

Vurpillot, E. (1968). The development of scanning strategies and their relation to visual differentiation. *Journal of Experimental Child Psychology, 6*, 632–50.

Vurpillot, E. (1972a). Quelques données sur les structures visuelles du nourrisson. In H. Hecaen (Ed.), *Neuropsychologie de la Perception Visuelle.* Paris: Masson.

Vurpillot, E. (1972b). *Le Monde Visuel du Jeune Enfant.* Paris: Presses Universitaires de France. *The Visual World of the Child.* London: Allen & Unwin, 1975.

Vurpillot, E. (1974). Les débuts de la construction de l'espace chez l'enfant. In *De l'Espace Corporel à l'Espace Écologique,* Symposium de l'Association de Psychologie Scientifique de Langue Française, Paris: Presses Universitaires de France.

Vurpillot, E. and Baudonnière, P. M. (1975). Étude génétique des stratégies d'exploration en fonction du vecteur, horizontal ou vertical, de comparaison. *Le Travail Humain.*

Vurpillot, E. and Brault, H. (1959). Étude expérimentale sur la formation des schèmes empiriques. *Année Psychologique, 59*, 381–94.

Vurpillot, E., Castelo, R. and Renard, C. (1975). Extension de l'exploration visuelle et nombre d'éléments présents sur des stimulus, dans une tâche de différenciation perceptive. *Année Psychologique, 75.*

Vurpillot, E., Lecuyer, R., Moal, A. and Pineau, A. (1971). Perception de déplacements et jugements d'identité chez l'enfant d'âge préscolaire. *Année Psychologique, 71*, 31–52.

Vurpillot, E. and Moal, A. (1970). Évolution des critères d'identité chez des enfants d'âge préscolaire dans une tâche de différenciation perceptive. *Année Psychologique, 70*, 391–406.

Vurpillot, E. and Ruel, J. (1975). Organisation perceptive et identification de forme chez le bébé de 4 mois (unpublished data).

Vurpillot, E. and Taranne, P. (1974). Jugement d'identité ou de non identité entre dessins et exploration oculo-motrice chez des enfants de 5 à 7 ans. *Année Psychologique, 74*, 79–100.

Vurpillot, E. and Taranne, P. (1975). Pertinence de différences et fréquence d'occurrence d'un élément particulier dans un jugement de non identité chez des enfants d'âge préscolaire. *Enfance, 28*, 151–64.

Watson, J. S. (1966). Perception of object orientation in infants. *Merrill-Palmer Quarterly, 12*, 73–94.

Webb, R. A., Massar, B. and Nadolny, T. (1972). Information and strategy in the young child's search for hidden objects. *Child Development, 43*, 91–104.

Welch, M. J. (1974). Infants' visual attention to varying degrees of novelty. *Child Development, 45*, 344–50.

Zaporozhets, A. V. and Zinchenko, V. P. (1966). Development of perceptual activity and formation of a sensory image in the child. In *Psychological Research in the USSR*. Moscow: Progress Publishers.

CHAPTER 6

Development of Spatial Perception*

Richard D. Walk

I. INTRODUCTION

When we watch a mosquito as it circles a room, avoids objects and perhaps lands on our leg where we try to swat it, we do not wonder at the insect's marvellous spatial sensitivity. The bees in our garden are more dramatic, and usually less threatening, as they hover over flowers, perhaps stop to gather pollen, and then fly off to some unknown hive. Minnows can easily be observed in the shallow part of a pond as they manoeuvre effortlessly through the three dimensional watery medium. Small birds swoop through the air and capture insects or they may evade larger birds of prey in a scene reminiscent of aerial combat in World War II, Korea or Vietnam. Countless species have mastered spatial perception—in the air, in the water or on the ground.

At the human level, however, space perception has often been a matter of philosophical speculation. Few of the philosophers or early psychologists ever, so far as we can tell from their writings, watched the spatial feats of the birds and the bees and related them to man. If evolution had had to wait on the deductions of these wise men our evolutionary forebears would still be mired in the ooze. Hochberg (1962) has discussed the early history of the study of space perception. Perhaps we are still prisoners of some of that background in the way we approach the topic. If at times the discourse seems weighty, remember the admonition—space perception is natural, requiring no intellectual capacities of any higher order than those possessed by the gnat

* Research on visual depth discrimination was supported by grants from the following sources: the National Science Foundation, the National Institute of Mental Health, and a NIH Biomedical Sciences Support Grant to George Washington University.

or the housefly. Not that we perceive space as they do with their compound eyes, but we certainly perceive it just as naturally.

A second admonition concerns the multimodal nature of space perception. You avoid a hole. It does not matter whether you did this by seeing it or because your foot felt that empty space. You may have even been alerted by a peculiar smell. No matter. You avoided the hole and survived. Nature has permitted us many spatial senses, or ways of reacting to and locating objects at a distance: seeing, hearing, smelling and the "feeling" senses—the proprioceptive-vestibular senses—sensitivity of the skin to touch from objects or wind currents, or to hot and cold. Most of the research reviewed will concern vision, but the senses work together and interact in ways we do not yet understand.

II. WAYS OF PERCEIVING SPACE

We have two eyes and the most natural way to perceive space is through both of them. Figure 6.1 shows how the different views produced by the two eyes (retinal disparity) might be used to discriminate the difference in depth or distance between Object A and Object B. The eyes must turn more inward for close objects but this convergence cue does not seem to be important. Recently, neurophysiological evidence has shown that cells in the visual cortex respond differently when an object at a particular distance stimulates both eyes with the correct amount of overlap. Different cells respond optimally at different distances in the cat (Barlow, Blakemore and Pettigrew, 1967) and in the monkey (Hubel and Wiesel, 1970). Selective adaptation experiments seem to show similar "disparity detecting neurons" in man (Blakemore and Hague, 1972).

Another method of discriminating depth is the result of the apparent expansion of an object as it gets closer. Only one eye is needed for a response to approach or recession. This expansion pattern is that of "looming" (Schiff, Caviness and Gibson, 1962) and cells in the visual cortex responsive to "looming" or "zooming" have been found in man (Marg and Adams, 1970) and in the monkey (Zeki, 1974). The expansion pattern or visual looming can serve as a cue to depth because the approaching object projects a larger image as it gets closer and the closer it gets the higher the *rate* of expansion, a sudden explosion of visual expanse that fills the field at very close ranges.

Parallax comes from a Greek word meaning to change. Motion parallax is thus a change due to motion, just as binocular parallax is the change due to binocular vision. In that sense visual looming is also motion parallax, but motion parallax is usually reserved for changes due to lateral and complex motion.

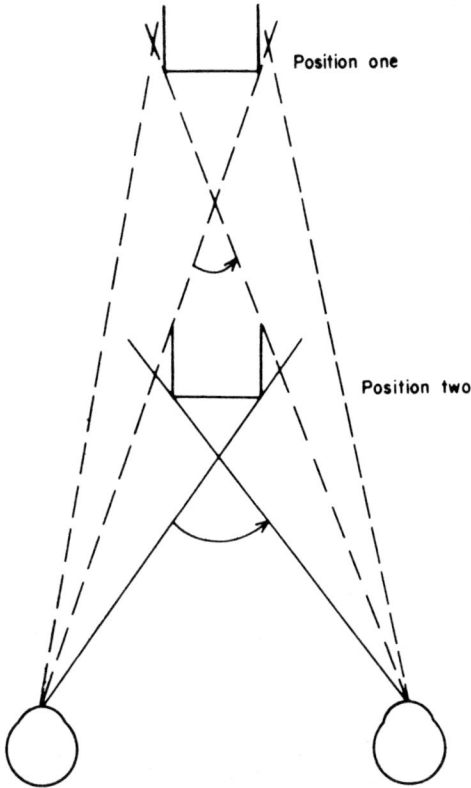

FIG. 6.1. Stereopsis. Each eye obtains a different view of the same object, seeing the front and one side of the object. Both eyes together see both sides. When the object is closer (Position two as compared to Position one), the eyes converge more.

The usual use of motion parallax is from motion produced by the observer, although the same effects are produced as we ride in an automobile or on a train. In addition to looming, three kinds of motion will be discussed : motion of the observer with different points of fixation, motion of the observer around a pinhole and motion of an observer around a hub or point.

The usual type of motion discussed under motion parallax is that where the observer fixates a point at some distance from him and then moves the head laterally, keeping the distant point fixated. Figure 6.2 shows several possibilities of such motion. The observer, however, is usually not aware of the motion produced beyond the point of fixation. The overwhelming impression is that of much greater movement of near compared with distant objects. It is actually difficult, and a little dizzying, to fixate a point 6 ft away and move the head and eyes too

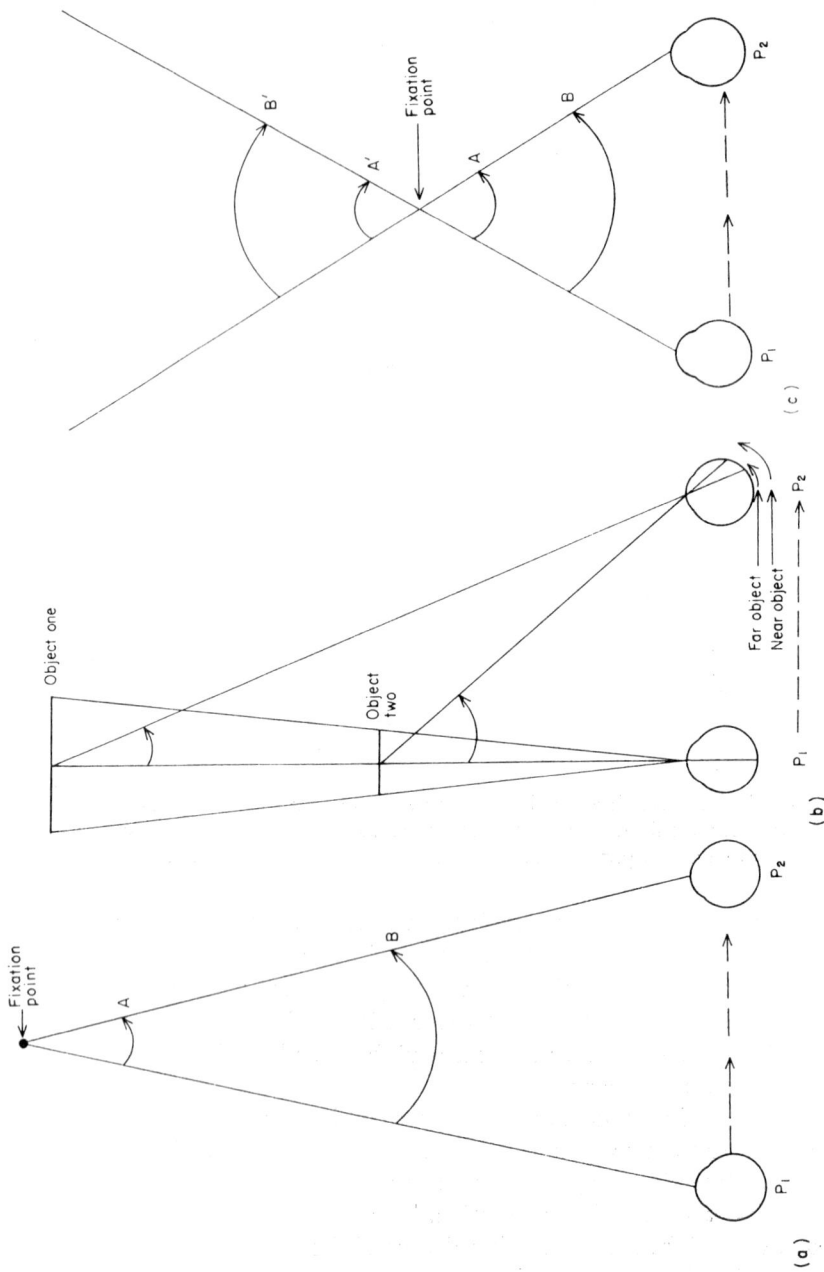

FIG. 6.2. Motion and point of fixation. (a) The eye fixates a distant point and motion is greater for near than for distant objects (Object B as compared with Object A) as the eye goes from P_1 to P_2. (b) Two objects project the same size on the retina but in moving from P_1 to P_2 the motion produced by the near object (Object two) is greater on the retina than the motion produced by the far object (Object one). True size can be discriminated from projected size. (c) An intermediate fixation point demonstrates that motion beyond the fixation point may be greater than motion from the nearer point (A as compared with B').

much. The best impression of motion is when a point at least 20 or 30 ft away is fixated. Very little movement is needed to give a strong impression of the rapid motion of near objects and the much slower change of more distant ones.

The pinhole type of motion change is illustrated in Fig. 6.3, which shows motion of the observer around a stationary point. Without lateral

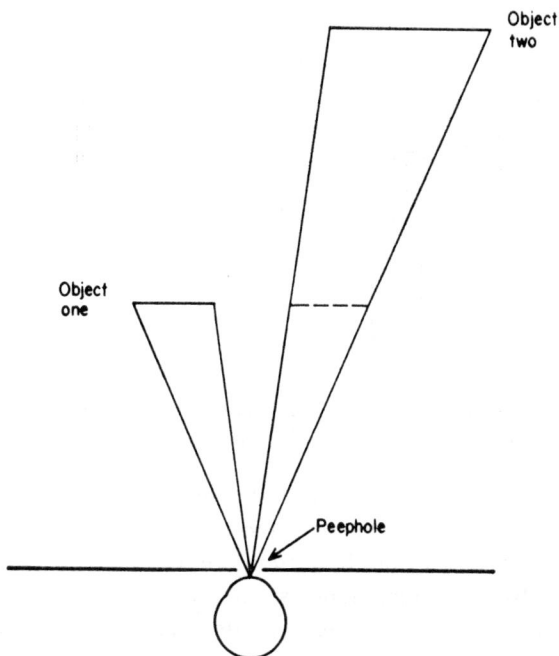

FIG. 6.3. The peephole. Despite motion as the observer looks from Object one to Object two, the restricted observation point prevents the observer from learning that the objects are of different sizes and at different distances. True size cannot be discriminated from projected size.

or to and fro movement no particular change is produced so that in Fig. 6.4 the motion of the observer does not discriminate two objects that project the same retinal angle but are at different distances. The distant one must be larger. This distinction, and the way motion parallax can distinguish the objects in terms of true size, not retinal angle, is a classic one in the study of size constancy. Figure 6.1 shows how lateral motion can easily make the distinction because the closer object moves more. The Ames rooms, constructed to look like normal rooms despite the greater distance of one wall, make use of a stationary viewing point (Ittelson and Kilpatrick, 1951). Because of the constraints of the single point, motion cannot disentangle this type of deception.

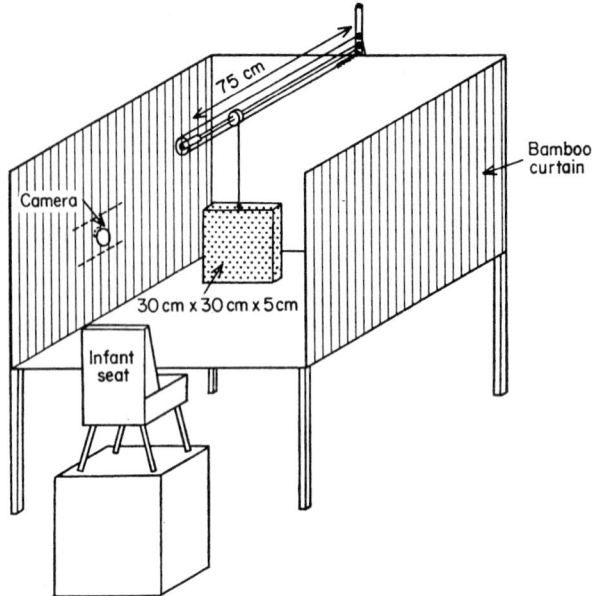

FIG. 6.4. Visual looming apparatus. The cube can approach or retreat from the infant's eyes. (*After* Ball and Tronick, 1971, p. 819.)

The motion of an observer around a single point can be illustrated by a person at the hub of a merry-go-round. Distant objects actually move faster than closer ones because more distance is covered, a classic problem in physics. Ballet dancers experience this type of motion as they spin around and they minimize its effects by a sort of selective perception, trying to fixate on one point and ignoring the rest of the environment and its rapid motion. If you try this you will note that the eye actually does not experience much speed; you experience only a few selective points of fixation at a distance and are just as affected, if not more so, by the slower motion for the circumference closer to you.

For the discrimination of distance by motion parallax the first type of motion is the most useful. It depends for its effects on the point of fixation.

Movement *per se*, when properly utilized, can lead to the discrimination of depth. But movement, by itself, is not enough without considering the relation of the observer to the environment. Motion parallax does not distinguish between a tunnel and a gorge. In both situations, with the eyes fixed on some distant point, near surfaces move more rapidly than distant ones. The vertical environment, represented by a cliff or gorge, is fearful in a way that similar stimulation from an environment straight ahead is not. Why? What visual cells discriminate up and down from straight ahead? Perhaps the horse, for which covered bridges were developed to prevent panic, has special receptors in its ramp retina for distance downward. Since motion parallax cannot distinguish down from straight ahead, something else must. The role of the vestibular system in vision has not been investigated by psychologists and yet all of us who have been made dizzy by a merry-go-round are aware that there is a relation between vision and the vestibular system. Sometimes, in such situations, closing the eyes can give a respite from the wrong kind of visual stimulation.

The analysis so far has ignored the stimulation from the environment. From what has been written one might believe that visual acuity was not affected by distance. Gibson (1950) has pointed out that texture density increases with distance. Larger or grosser textures are close to the observer and smaller and denser textures are more distant. Any environment projects, on the average, smaller objects from longer distances and larger ones from shorter distances, but an environment of the same type of texture makes the point more clearly. One example of this might be the view from the centre of a cobblestone street in Georgetown. Another example is my neighbour's lawn which looks dense from my lawn while my own lawn is full of gaps and imperfections. If I look at my own lawn from across the street, the improvement is immense and the embarrassment somewhat lessened.

Another important distinction is that between produced motion and imposed motion. We ordinarily walk and bob up and down and scarcely notice it. The same motion in a rowing-boat, where the motion is imposed, can lead to seasickness. If an observer approaches a wall, the wall expands in size on the retina at close ranges at an alarming rate. This is produced by motion. The same motion imposed on the retina by someone trying to strike us with a fist can lead to quick evasive action. The visual patterns on the retina may be the same in both instances but the action of the individual very different. Both von Holst (1954) and Held (1965) have discussed this difference at length.

Accommodation is the focus of the eye on near or distant objects. Convergence, mentioned before, is the manner in which the eyes turn inward at some object that is near us. These are mechanisms; their role with adults in helping determine distance is in dispute. As mechanisms, however, they are necessary; without accommodation the eye cannot focus at different distances. Without convergence the eyes cannot work together at close ranges.

The pictorial cues are the painter's cues. They are size, aerial perspective, linear perspective, interposition, height of an object on a plane and direction of illumination. Texture density, already discussed, is a size cue, but size, as a depth cue, involves depicting objects close to the observer as larger than those more distant. Linear perspective, also a size cue, is the perspective of lines as in looking at a road or at railroad tracks where the distant road or rails seem to converge to a point. In interposition close objects block out more distant ones. In aerial perspective close objects are more distinct than distant ones; blurring objects is usually a cue reserved for objects at great distance unless the painting depicts a fog or snowstorm. In the plane of the picture, and of our gaze, higher objects are farther away and nearer objects are closer. From direction of illumination, which produces shadows, we assume that light comes from above and that is why craters can look like mounds if we turn the picture upside down. The direction of illumination is one cue that will help distinguish up from down.

These basic ways of perceiving space will be related, where appropriate, to the development of the space perception of the human infant and other species.

III. BASIC VISUAL PROCESSES OF THE HUMAN INFANT

Investigations of early visual behaviour in the human infant have shown how some of the basic processes develop. Accommodation, convergence, conjugate eye movements, pattern vision, visual acuity and a large enough visual field are all necessary for visual behaviour related to space perception. In addition, certain optimal textured pattern relationships are important for space perception.

Wolf and White (1965) observed visual pursuit with conjugate eye movements alone immediately after birth. By four days after birth the infant rotated its head, along with conjugate eye movements, to increase the size of the visual field. Fantz (1963) observed that newborns fixated patterned stimuli (such as faces, circles, or newsprint) more than unpatterned white, yellow or red. Dayton et al. (1964) investigated visual acuity using the technique of optokinetic nystagmus (for optokinetic nystagmus a striped pattern is moved past the eyes and the infant follows the pattern involuntarily; the eyes are drawn for a short time, then return, producing a jerky motion). They found visual acuity of 20/150 in the day-old infant, a positive response to 7.5 min of visual angle (1 min for adults) or 0.032 in. wide lines at a distance of $14\frac{1}{2}$ in. Like Wolf and White (1965) they also observed conjugate eye movements. Fantz, Ordy and Udelf (1962) used a preference test to find whether infants would fixate stripes over grey, a voluntary response. The newborn fixated $\frac{1}{8}$ in. stripes in preference to grey at a 10 in. distance, somewhat inferior to the findings of Dayton et al. (1964) but still excellent vision. Over the course of the next six months the infant's acuity improved to a preference for $\frac{1}{64}$ in. stripes over grey.

Accommodation was investigated by Haynes, White and Held (1965). They found that the newborn's eye was focused at about 8 in. (19 cm) and did not adjust to target distance. About the middle of the second month accommodation became more flexible and adult accommodation was present by 4 months of age. But Wickelgren (1967) did not find convergence of the eyes towards a near object present at birth. A textbook in clinical neuroophthalmology describes it as present at 4 to 5 months of age and well established by 6 months (Walsh and Hoyt, 1969). White, Castle and Held (1964), however, describe the 2- to $2\frac{1}{2}$-month-old as occasionally converging on objects as close as 5 in. from the eyes; and the $2\frac{1}{2}$- to 3-month-old converging on objects 3 in. from the eyes.

Tronick (1972) studied the growth of the infant's effective visual field. The infant fixated a small object and a small light was moved in from the periphery towards the centre until the light was noticed. He found that the initial visual field of the infant was no more than 15–20° on each side of the line of regard. It did not begin to expand until 2–6 weeks of age and then gradually expanded to 40–50° on each side by 10 weeks of age. The 2-week-old has only an 8 in. pattern 10 in. from the eye, but this expands to as much as 24 in. at 10 weeks. Eye movements and head movements can considerably increase the size of the visual field and acuity drops off rapidly from the line of fixation, so size of the visual field is probably not a serious limitation for most study.

The discussion so far has shown some unexpected strengths for early vision (conjugate eye movements, visual acuity) and some weaknesses (poor accommodation, no convergence, small visual field). Despite possible conjugate eye movements, many investigators photograph only one eye; the other eye does tend to wander in very young infants. Also, while Haynes et al. (1965) found no accommodation in newborns, Fantz et al. (1962) showed that visual acuity did not differ with pattern distances ranging from 5–20 in.; but of course a constricted pupil from bright light can increase focal distance. Visual acuity and the preferred level of visual stimulation are not the same. Brennan, Ames and Moore (1966) showed infants two patterns 6 in. square side by side and recorded the amount of looking at each. The patterns were checkerboards, 3 in. squares, $\frac{3}{4}$ in. squares or $\frac{1}{4}$ in. squares, and a grey surface. The 3-week-olds looked more at the 3 in. checks, the 8-week-olds most at the $\frac{3}{4}$ in. checks and the 14-week-old children looked the longest at the $\frac{1}{4}$ in. checks. Yet both the 3- and 8-week-olds preferred (looked more at) the fine $\frac{1}{4}$ in. checks to the plain grey surface. Karmel (1969a, 1969b) presented to 13- and 20-week-old infants both checks and patterns where the contour of the checks was more randomly determined. He found that looking behaviour could be described as based on the total amount of contour in a pattern. Like Brennan *et al.* he found a peak for an optimal level of complexity which was around the equivalent of a $\frac{1}{4}$ in. checked pattern. One can say, then, that infants look at some optimal amount of contour and this is not the same as visual acuity.

IV. PRE-LOCOMOTOR SPACE PERCEPTION

As an introduction to the discussion of pre-locomotor space perception, consider this passage from Brazelton *et al.* (1969) as they describe the behaviour of two newborn infants of the Zinacanteco Indians in Mexico :

> ... they lay quietly on the blanket looking around the room for the entire hour after delivery. In addition to quiet motor activity, they demonstrated a striking sensory alertness ... in the first week ... they alertly looked at the red ball visual stimulus and followed it back and forth as it was moved; on one occasion, a baby followed for 60 seconds without interruption ... We noted frequent head movement to augment such pursuit, and only rarely would startles or jerky motor activity interrupt this attentive state. (p. 279)

The above passage is not proof of the early development of visual space perception, but it does show that many of its components are represented by the alert following of the ball with head movement to assist the tracking.

(1) VISUAL LOOMING

Bower, Broughton and Moore (1970c) studied the response of infants 6 to 20 days of age to an approaching object. The infants were supported in a sitting position and an object approached the infant. The infants seemed to avoid the object by pulling the head back and putting the hands up as if to avoid the object, a foam rubber cube. The optimal condition for eliciting this reaction was a slow approach of the cube, around 5 cm per second, and very little reaction was observed at 25 cm per second. They also studied a shadow or visual looming pattern. The infant faced a screen and a point source of light projected on to it from behind. A small object was between the screen and the light. Movement *towards* the light, away from the screen and the infant, makes the shadow expand and produce an impression of looming. The opposite motion gives an impression of contraction. The infants responded with avoidance reactions to the looming stimulus but the reaction was somewhat reduced compared to that to the real object (see Fig. 6.4). Ball and Tronick (1971) conducted a similar experiment with infants 2 to 11 weeks old. They also moved the point source of light to one side of the path travelled by the cube. The shadow produced was asymmetrical and the impression was of an object on a miss path rather than a hit path. With a symmetrical looming shadow (hit path) the infants moved their heads back and raised their arms. The asymmetrical shadow (miss path) produced no avoidance responses but, rather, tracking behaviour, as the infant watched the shadow. Contraction of the shadow, as if the object were retreating, produced neither avoidance nor tracking. Ball and Tronick did not observe any age differences in the reaction to the looming sequence. These experiments show dramatic examples of space perception at a very young age but they may not be easy to reproduce. We have tried informally in our laboratory to observe these reactions without much success. Sometimes the infants smile, but that is about all. However, Clarence Walters and I had an infant monkey a few weeks old that exhibited very similar reactions. One of us held the monkey and if a hand was brought "threateningly" towards the monkey's face it would scream and give a classic avoidance reaction with arms and legs flailing. It was rather like Cannon's "sham rage" reaction, as if a button had been pushed to elicit behaviour that would go away as suddenly as it came. The monkey liked to have its head patted and it had no visual placing reaction since raising in a chair delays the visual placing reaction, one that usually appears at 5 days of age in the normal monkey (Sechzer et al., 1971).

The looming reaction is related to two other reactions to the approach of a surface or object. One is the eye blink, the shutting of the eyes to an approaching object, and the other is the visual placing reaction. The eye blink is rather like a conditioned reaction, a protective reaction to guard the eyes that appears after some experience with approaching objects or surfaces. This has been studied most extensively by White (1971). The visual placing reaction is one where the arms are placed forward as if to break a fall. The infant is held horizontally, face downward, and the reaction does not appear until months after birth. Placing of the hands in front of the face as if to ward off a blow, however, appears soon after birth as Bower et al. (1970c) and Ball and Tronick (1971) have shown. It is similar to a vertical placing reaction.

(2) SOLIDITY

Fantz (1961) studied the preference for solidity of infants of 1 to 6 months of age. They were shown a textured sphere and a textured circle. The preference was for the sphere, and it was stronger for the monocular infants (who wore an eye patch) than for the binocular ones. Solidity or three dimensionality appears over and over again as a discriminated dimension. Fantz (1958) found that baby chicks without visual experience pecked at hemispheres in preference to flat circles. Tinbergen and Kruyt (1938) found a preference for solidity among his homing wasps. Cott (1940) gives many examples of countershading, the method which animals have evolved to make solids appear flat. That Gross, Rocha-Miranda and Bender (1972) have found a neuron which seems to respond to solidity, monocularly, is entirely in accord with behaviour observed in a variety of species. Solidity may even be amodal. The brilliant experiments of Cooper (1957) on how the larva emerges from cells showed that the Eumenine wasp leaves a code to her offspring. Walls leading to the exit from the nest are rough and convex; those pointing away, where the larva would die, are smooth and concave. The offspring avoids concave walls and smooth walls and approaches roughly textured walls (the preference for convexity is slight).

(3) VISUAL REACHING

Reaching towards an object is a natural response to an object that is near. The infant, if accurate, must assess all the co-ordinates in space, left-right, up-down and near-far. Such reaching does improve with age, and the reach becomes one where the whole response to the designated co-ordinate is rapid, with the hand opening in anticipation as it approaches the object. Visual reaching has been studied by a great many investigators. If we begin with some more recent research, with its stress on younger infants, we must remember that it built on the foundation of the earlier work.

Bower, Broughton and Moore (1970a, b) studied visual reaching with very young infants. Bower et al. (1970a) showed that infants 6 to 11 days old reached out in the direction of a visual object. They were presented with an object in five positions, and the accuracy of a reach measured towards an orange foam rubber sphere 19 cm from the infant. The infants averaged a reach within $5°$ (1.5cm) of the object. To assess intention they presented both real objects and virtual objects to another group of infants 8 to 31 days old. The virtual object was produced by making the infant wear goggles with polaroid filters. A point source of light was projected through polaroid filters on to a real object through a screen to produce a virtual object (as long as the goggles were worn) in front of the child. Infants began to reach when the virtual object appeared to be about 20 cm (8 in.) in front of them. When no object could be touched, all infants became very upset, while none of the infants who reached towards a real object cried. From this Bower et al. deduced that not only had the infants "intended" to reach towards a tangible object, but that from soon after birth they expected visual objects to have actual properties. Bower et al. (1970b) employed the same theme. Infants presented with virtual images of objects reached towards them with anticipatory shaping of the hand (infants up to 5 months of age also cried when no object was there). Only at 5 to 6 months of age did the infants pause on touching the apparent position of the object, leaving the hands open because there was nothing to grasp. In contrast, when the infants had an object placed in their hands they did not shape their hands to the object. They did not even look at the object until they were 3 months of age. Bower et al. concluded that vision is dominant over touch and that the adjustment of the hands is much easier when the object can be viewed than when it can just be felt. Bower (1972) conducted several further studies related to visual reaching. He found that infants 7 to 15 days of age would reach towards a solid object but not to a photograph of it; they thus distinguished, as did Fantz's infants, between solidity and flatness, but in a more definite form than with a looking preference since they reached for the object, not the photograph. The infants also reached for an object close to them far more often than to one further away that projected the same retinal angle; but the accuracy of reaching was the same for both when it did in fact occur. The infants also distinguished by their finger-thumb separation between objects of different size, with a larger separation for large objects than for smaller ones.

Bruner and Koslowski (1972) also studied reaching towards large and small objects. Their infants were 10 to 22 weeks of age and many had not developed satisfactory reaching. They sat in an infant seat at a 45° angle and were presented with an object about 4 in. in front of them. Interest of the experimenters was not so much in grasping as in the activity prior to grasping. The infants looked for about the same amount of time at large and small objects, but grasping at the midline occurred more frequently with the small, graspable, object than with the large one. The type of activity that occurred most often with the large object was described as "forward swiping" or moving the hands and arms forward and away from the body. They thought this type of behaviour was appropriate for an object that was large enough (10 in. in diameter) to be perceived as a surface rather than as something to be grasped. The experiments show different types of behaviour in the presence of the two different sized objects prior to the time the infants actually engaged in successful reaching activity.

An intensive study of visually directed reaching was conducted by White, Castle and Held (1964). They investigated the reactions of infants 1 to 6 months of age to a multicoloured object, a fringed party toy with many colours and contours. From the first the object was tracked visually although visual pursuit improved for the next couple of months. The infants did not swipe at the object until 2 to $2\frac{1}{2}$ months of age; the infant began to look at both the hands and the object at about this time. The first true reaching occurred at about 4 months of age and the infant could only grasp the object awkwardly. Not until almost 5 months of age did the infant show "top level reaching" or the capacity to approach the object with the hand held in an anticipatory position. These were institutionalized infants, and a subsequent study where some of these infants were given various types of "enrichment" reduced the acquisition of the top level reaching to 89 days or 3 months. These studies show a much later development than does Bower, apparently, but they are in agreement with much prior research. Baruk *et al.* (1953), for example, studied visual reaching towards objects and made extensive motion picture records. They confirmed the interest of infants of 1 month of age in following the object with the eyes, but success in hitting the object did not occur until the fifth month, and the advanced type of reaching with anticipatory finger-thumb motion not until about $7\frac{1}{2}$ months of age.

Clearly, then, the Bower studies show fairly advanced reaching, including anticipatory finger-thumb separation, at 7 to 15 days of age, behaviour that does not appear in any other study for several months. What is the reason for the discrepancy? What do the discrepancies tell us about visual space perception? Perhaps future research can clear up these discrepancies.

(4) DISCRIMINATION OF DISTANCE

Another demonstration of the discrimination of distance by young infants 6 to 20 weeks old was made in an experiment by McKenzie and Day (1972). They used habituation of visual fixation as their measure. In the first experiment objects were presented at 90 cm and again at 30 cm. The infants spent far more time fixating the near object, a small cube. A second experiment presented the cubes at four different distances in random order, and showed that time spent looking varied as a function of distance, with more looking time at the nearer object. Was accommodation a factor in visual looking? Mature accommodative focusing was noted for 4-month-olds by Haynes *et al.*

(1965). Both older and younger infants in the Day and McKenzie study behaved similarly, with more looking at near objects.

The eye blink response to an approaching object is a response preparatory to a blow. The eyelid closes as protection against damage to the delicate eye. White (1971) conducted a normative study with human infants and found that the eyeblink began developing at about 2 month of age and was consistent at 3 to 4 months of age. His "enrichment" condition did not accelerate the acquisition of this response although some measures of visual-motor behaviour were accelerated. Bower (1974) is critical of the blink response as not being adaptive; the eye widening and the hand raising he observed in younger infants would be a more adaptive reaction to an approaching object. He considers that the eyeblink may protect the eye, but a closed eye is of no help in avoiding danger. Whatever its adaptive significance, we all have the protective eyeblink and have had it most of our lives. My own research has not studied this response intensively, but it does seem to develop at around the same time for kittens, puppies and monkeys as it does for human infants, around the age of 2 to 3 months.

(5) SIZE CONSTANCY

Bower (1964, 1965) investigated size constancy in infants 1 to 2 months old (Bower, 1965) and 2 to 3 months old (Bower, 1964). The infants were presented with a 12 in. cube as a conditioned stimulus. The infants learned that pushing the head to the left closed a microswitch and produced a reinforcement—the experimenter jumped up and played peek-a-boo with the child. With training, presentation of the cube was not accompanied by a "peek-a-boo" on every trial. This meant the infant learnt to tolerate some uncertainty, postponing extinction. The extinction phase consisted of presentation of the same-sized cube at the same distance, the same-sized cube at a greater distance, or a larger cube at a greater distance that produced the same projected retinal angle as the original small cube. The infants gave very few head turns to the cube of equal retinal size (the large cube at a distance) and responded moderately well to the same-sized cube at a greater distance. By rejecting the large cube at a distance the infant was, in effect, indicating that this cube was not like the other one, despite its equal retinal size. By responding well to the same cube at a greater distance the infant might be inferred to be indicating that it was the same cube as for training but now far away. Bower (1965) also showed that monocular infants reacted like binocular ones. Thus motion parallax is the remaining cue for the children, since binocular parallax is eliminated for the monocular infants. The infants have demonstrated size constancy based on information produced by motion parallax.

The visual placing response is transitional between the pre-locomotor and the locomotor child. The infant extends its arms forward in approach to a visual surface just beneath a transparent sheet of glass or plastic. If the surface is placed some distance below the glass surface the infant fails to extend the arms and may bump its head (Walters and Walk, 1974). Unpublished research by C. P. Walters and myself indicates that the response develops around the age of 6 to 7 months, an advance of $1\frac{1}{2}$ to 2 months over similar norms published by Paine and Oppé (1966) for the "parachute reflex". The unpublished research of C. P. Walters shows that older infants place more in all situations (with or without visual depth) than younger ones. The infants also place to a homogeneous non-patterned surface occasionally and older infants place more than younger ones, whether there is a visual depth or not. This is somewhat different from the results for the visual cliff with locomotor infants.

V. LOCOMOTOR SPACE PERCEPTION

(1) VISUAL CLIFF DEPTH DISCRIMINATION

The visual cliff has been used extensively in the investigation of the development of space perception for locomoting subjects—animals and human infants. The general principle of the visual cliff is that of the simulation of a visual drop, abyss or cliff. A piece of glass covers a table, for example, and a patterned surface is placed under the glass on one side of a centre board. The patterned surface is some distance below the glass on the other side of the board. The subject placed on the board has its choice of descent towards a nearby pattern, the "shallow side", or a pattern some distance away, the "deep side". Figure 6.5 shows the apparatus. The type of pattern and the depth of the pattern below the glass surface can easily be varied. Is this response innate or learned? Many species, e.g., the ungulates (sheep, goats, pigs, etc.) and precocial birds such as chickens and ducks, locomote at birth or very soon after. The Yorkshire veterinarian, James Herriot, writes:

> All young animals are appealing but the lamb has been given an un-
> fair share of charm. The moments come back; of a bitterly cold
> evening when I had delivered twins on a wind-scoured hillside; the
> lambs shaking their heads convulsively and within minutes one of them
> struggling upright and making its way, unsteady, knock-kneed, towards
> the udder while the other followed resolutely on its knees. The shep-
> herd ... gave a slow chuckle. "How the 'ell do they know?" He had

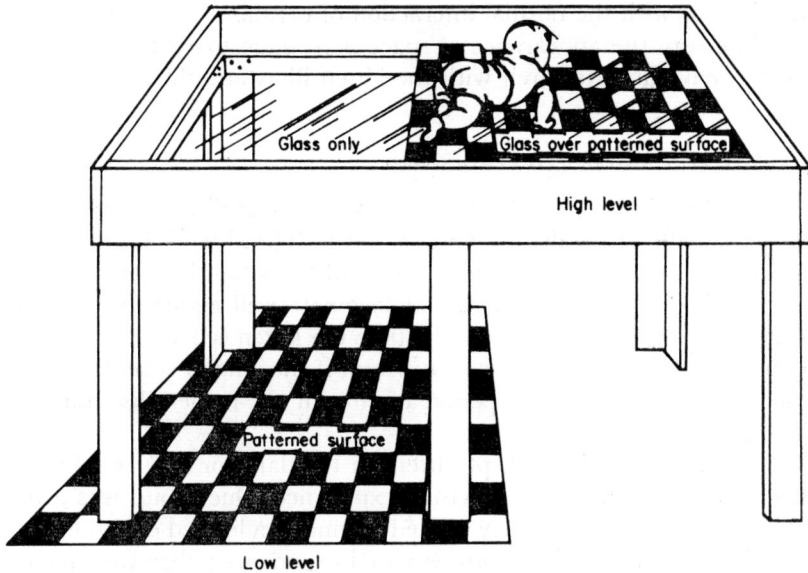

FIG. 6.5. The visual cliff. The infant is called by the mother from the "shallow" side, where the pattern is directly under the glass, and also from the "deep" sides where the pattern is far below the glass. (*After* Walk and Gibson, 1961, p. 8.)

seen it happen thousands of times and he still wondered. So do I. (Herriot, 1972, p. 147)

Lambs can discriminate depth on the visual cliff at birth. So can pigs, goats and probably all other ungulates. A baby chick emerges from the shell and within a short time will avoid the deep side of the visual cliff. A rat is small, hairless and helpless when born, but the mother and the litter can be placed in the dark for several months and the helpless young are now adults. These animals have had no visual experience and yet, when placed on the visual cliff, they choose the shallow side almost unerringly. Like James Herriot, I have seen thousands of young animals; in my case they have demonstrated visual depth perception with no or minimal visual experience. As James Herriot wonders how the lambs find the udder, so I wonder how the lambs or the chicks or the rats find the shallow side. As the Yorkshireman said, "How the 'ell do they know?" I don't know either. We do know, however, that, empirically, the evidence favours innate mechanisms in many species (Walk and Gibson, 1961).

What about the others? The human infant, as we have seen, seems capable of rudimentary space perception soon after birth. In early development mechanisms are very delicate for some species and interference with the normal interaction of organism and environment may interrupt the appearance of space perception together with many other behaviours. Research with the kitten illustrates this.

(2) ACTIVITY AND DEPTH PERCEPTION

A kitten kept in the dark for four weeks no longer discriminates depth on the visual cliff (Walk and Gibson, 1961). The kitten is born with its eyes closed and the eyes do not open until the kitten is about 10 days old. At this time the kitten cannot locomote well enough to demonstrate depth discrimination. By the time the kitten is 4 weeks old locomotion is adequate, but, as we have seen, if the animal is kept without visual experience for that period of time it no longer discriminates depth.

Held and Hein (1963) kept kittens in the dark for *eight* weeks and then gave them two kinds of visual experience. One group was given *active* visual experience : they walked around in a lighted environment; the other group was given *passive* visual experience : they were pulled through the identical environment by the active kittens, but they were restrained, in holders, so they could not locomote and they could not see their paws. After approximately ten days of such experience, three hours a day (the remainder being spent in the dark), both groups were tested on the visual cliff. The active animals discriminated depth, the passive ones did not. From this, Held and Hein concluded that self-produced movement was necessary for the development of depth discrimination.

Whereas the animals in the Walk and Gibson (1961) experiment had been kept in the dark for only four weeks, the Held and Hein (1963) animals were kept in the dark for twice as long, eight weeks. Perhaps the long visual deprivation had affected the animals. Miller and Walk (1975) repeated the Held and Hein (1963) experiment with 4-week-old animals and added both light-reared and dark-reared control groups. The active and passive animals were raised in the dark until 18 days old and then given 3 hrs light exposure a day. The active animals locomoted around a patterned visual environment, and the passive animals were kept in holders that allowed a view of the same environment but they could not locomote or see their own limbs. At 4 weeks of age all groups were tested on the visual cliff, and, in addition, they were called by the experimenter from the shallow and deep sides of the visual cliff. Active animals discriminated depth better than the passive ones on the first visual cliff test, yet, thereafter, performed similarly. Light-reared animals were superior to any others, even the active ones, showing that deprivation of the active animals had some effect. The dark-reared animals were much worse than any other group. Paradoxically, when called from the shallow and deep sides all groups, even the dark reared, descended to the shallow side much more rapidly than to the deep side. This test was given 15 min after the first visual cliff test. The evidence favours unlearned mechanisms, and the initial impairment of the passive group might be the confusion of animals that have never locomoted in the light before. The different measures give slightly different results, showing the advantage of more than one measure. The "calling test" stressed similarities among groups. The regular visual cliff test demonstrated an impairment for the passive animals that was not present on any subsequent visual cliff tests. On the regular visual cliff test the passive animals were 15 to 30 min impaired but the dark-reared did not discriminate depth with this test until after 6 hr light exposure. Primitive depth discrimination seems to be unlearned. Its refinement requires both light exposure and, perhaps, visual-motor activity. The experiments of Hein, Held and their co-workers (summarized in Hein, 1972) are a series of ingenious demonstrations of the fragility of visual-motor behaviour in that it can be disrupted by unusual kinds of experience. Future research should help clarify the role of motor experience in perceptual behaviour.

(3) PERCEPTION OF DEPTH DOWNWARD

Theories of space perception give no special role to depth downward. Motion parallax is the same, as was mentioned, for a tunnel and a gorge, yet the behaviour of the individual may be very different for the two situations. Some individuals, and some species, react to a cliff with a strong emotional response; others are relatively indifferent.

Individual differences in visual depth perception have been studied in two ways: (1) visual depth discrimination, and (2) reactions to an apparent void. The first category includes mainly visual cliff discrimination along with other measures. The second includes placing the subject on the glass over the apparent void of the visual cliff or near to the apparent void. A selection of studies will have to illustrate the main points.

The main generalization from studies of different species is this: visual depth discrimination is related to an animal's way of life. Yerkes (1904) observed long ago that aquatic turtles crawled off high places, and they would have been injured had he not caught them in a net. Land turtles do not fall off platforms as frequently. Routtenberg and Glickman (1964) found aquatic turtles much more careless on the visual cliff than land turtles. A snow leopard lives in the mountains and the tiger in the flatlands. Leopards discriminate depth on the visual cliff better than tigers (Routtenberg and Glickman, 1964). Horner (1954) investigated the behaviour of many species of deer mice (*Peromyscus*). The semi-arboreal animals tended to stay on a small platform for a 5 min observation period while the animals from beach country, prairie desert or sandhill tended to fall off. The chick and the duckling can discriminate depth well on the visual cliff though the duckling tends to be careless; the domestic duckling, an aquatic species, walks off 6 ft high platforms with little hesitation (Walk, 1972). Kear (1967) tested many species of ducklings. The species that hatched in holes above the ground were more careless on the visual cliff than were the species that hatched in the ground; leaving the hole and jumping to the ground is part of the life pattern, and an animal that remained in the nest, afraid to jump, might starve. Emlen (1963) studied cliff nesting and plateau nesting herring gull chicks. The cliff nesting chicks were more hesitant to jump from a platform than plateau nesting chicks. Eggs were cross-fostered and some chicks were reared in an environment opposite the one in which eggs were laid. The hesitancy to jump came from the rearing situation; plateau eggs hatched and reared on the cliff were non-jumpers and *vice versa*.

Walk and Gibson (1961) placed a number of species on the glass over the deep side. The most dramatic reactions were observed in the ungulates : pigs and lambs became rigid while goats backed up. Kittens tended to circle backward and puppies trembled and backed. In an attempt to quantify this behaviour, Walk (1965) placed several species successively on the shallow and deep sides and clocked the time until forward movement. The goats, cocker spaniels, little river duck dogs and albino rabbits froze on the deep side and walked forward on the shallow side. Chicks were very hesitant on the deep side but did walk forward, ducklings less hesitant and kittens and hooded rats much less so. Schiffman (1968, 1970) placed animals on the deep side but close enough to the shallow side so that it was within easy reach. Chicks and pigmented rabbits moved towards the shallow side while albino rabbits, guinea pigs, kittens, mice, rats, gerbils and hamsters had little reaction to the void; about half stayed on the deep side.

Human infants have had their reactions to visual depth tested by being placed on the deep side. Three investigations agree that apprehension matures, being less present in the younger child. Walk (1963) placed infants 7 to 13 months of age on the shallow and deep sides of the visual cliff. Refusal to crawl forward over the glass of the deep side to the mother occurred most frequently in infants over 10 months of age. In a study of the development of various kinds of fear during infancy Scarr and Salapatek (1970) used the visual cliff as one of the indices of fear. The percentage of infants showing fear in a variety of visual cliff tests increased linearly from less than 7 months of age, where only 20 per cent showed fear to 13 months and over when 100 per cent were fearful. Schwartz, Campos and Baisel (1973) placed 5- and 9-month-old infants on the shallow and deep sides of the visual cliff. The heart rate of the 5-month-olds *decelerated* on the deep side while that of the 9-month-old infants *accelerated*. They interpreted the cardiac deceleration of the younger infants as showing attention or orienting and the acceleration of the older infants as indicative of fear.

(4) THE SIGNIFICANCE OF SURFACE TEXTURE

The first visual cliff studies investigated the visual stimulus for this type of depth discrimination. These are summarized in Walk and Gibson (1961). If one places a textured pattern on the deep side of the visual cliff and a similar pattern on the shallow side, the subject will have two main cues to distance : the near textured pattern projects a larger texture than the more distant one and the distance of the far pattern involves a motion parallax difference between the two sides. The subject may prefer either the larger textured surface or may discriminate on the basis of the differential visual motion. A natural control for the effect of texture is to make the texture on the far surface larger so that the projected texture to the eye of the subject is the same for both the shallow and the deep sides. Walk and Gibson (1961) used this control with rats, chicks, goats and sheep and found no difference; the animals chose the shallow side with the same frequency as they did when both texture and motion parallax were available as cues. Walk (1966) conducted the same experiment with human infants and found, similarly, no difference in the choice of the shallow side. The experiments thus showed the importance of motion parallax.

The importance of texture can be illustrated in several ways. A grey, untextured, surface can be placed directly under the glass or it can be placed some distance below it. Animals, hooded rats, confronted with this choice could not distinguish depth from no-depth (Walk and Gibson, 1961). About one-third remained on the centre board and the remainder divided themselves equally between the shallow and the deep sides. When the homogeneous grey was directly under the glass and a textured pattern was also directly under the glass, the hooded rats descended to the textured pattern. Studies with human infants confirmed these results (Walk, 1966). With a choice of texture or homogeneous grey the children went to the textured pattern. Some could be coaxed across the grey pattern, however. About one-third could be coaxed to the mother. The grey stimulus for the human infants, as it had for the hooded rats, gave no cues to depth so that the grey was crossed to the coaxing mother about the same percentage of times if the grey was directly under the glass, 10 in., 20 in. or 40 in. below it. A similar experiment that varied texture had very different results: almost all of the infants went to the mother with the textured surface directly beneath the glass, somewhat fewer at 10 in., many fewer at 20 in. and almost none when the textured pattern was 40 in. below the glass surface. This is shown in Fig. 6.6. The grey was crossed by more

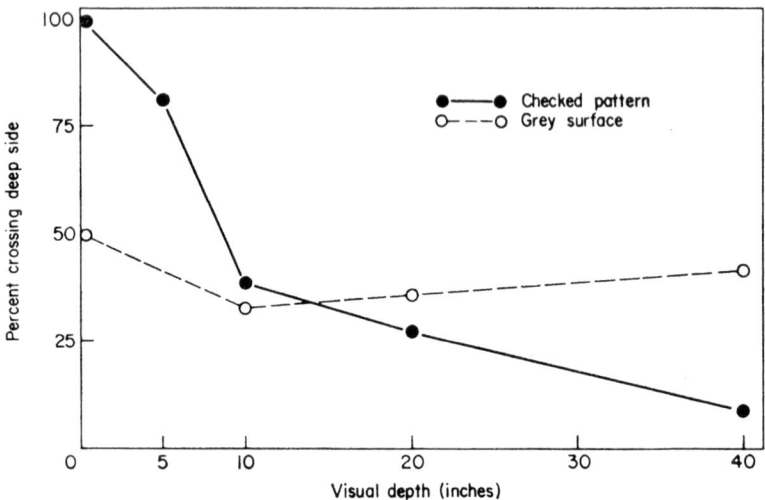

Fig. 6.6. Per cent of infants crossing to the mother across the deep side as a function of visual depth and type of stimulus pattern.

young infants than older ones. If crossing it makes it equivalent to a visual surface then the results are opposite to visual placing where older infants (not younger) place more to an indefinite surface. The apparent equivalence of homogeneous surfaces as capable of some optical support in both the visual placing and visual cliff situations is very interesting, but the age difference is puzzling.

The experiments so far are fairly straightforward. The texture is important; without it the subject cannot discriminate depth. Motion parallax is also important since, with equal projected texture, motion parallax must determine the choice, and this is overwhelmingly to the shallow side. Some doubts as to this formulation were introduced when small textured patterns ($\frac{1}{4}$ in. red and white checks) were used on the shallow side. With a definite pattern 36–40 in. below on the deep side and the small checks on the shallow side, about 34 per cent of the infants could be coaxed to the mother as against less than 10 per cent when the larger $\frac{3}{4}$ in. checks were on the shallow side. Since more younger infants were affected by this change, with about half of the 7- to 9-month-old ones coaxed to the mother as against about 20 per cent of the 10- to 12-month-old children, the results seemed explicable in terms of some type of acuity weakness in the younger infants.

An experiment that confuted this easy explanation of these anomalous results was performed by Doris DeHardt (1969). She used rats, and placed a 3 in. checked pattern on the shallow side along with a similar pattern on the deep side, 10 in. below the glass. The deep side 3 in. checked pattern projects to the eye as about the equivalent of a 1 in. pattern on the shallow side. Her animals apparently disregarded motion parallax and 83 per cent chose the deep side. When she altered the experiment by placing 1 in. checks instead of 3 in. checks on the shallow side the results reversed; now, the choice was 65 per cent choice of the shallow side. She interpreted her results as indicating that the animal was not affected by motion parallax but, rather, by retinal angle; that the animals simply went to a preferred texture, the 1 in. checks or about an 11° retinal angle. We repeated the experiment almost immediately in the hope that some procedural difficulty underlay her results. The results held. While the experiment was not published for some time because of the many variations we added (Walk and Walters, 1974), the "DeHardt effect" began to change our thinking on the effective stimulus for depth discrimination.

The DeHardt (1969) hypothesis was that animals approached a preferred retinal angle. This is not literally true. When she had a "preferred" retinal angle on both sides (the 1 in. checks shallow and the 3 in. checks deep), the animals should have no preference according to the preferred retinal angle hypothesis since the retinal angles are the same. Actually, the animals went to the shallow side as, indeed, had been shown before in the "equal density" experiments of Walk and Gibson (1961) and many others. As a further test of the preferred retinal angle hypothesis Walk and Walters (1974) kept the non-preferred 3 in. checks on the shallow side and varied depth, keeping the retinal angle the same, at 11° (6 in. checks for a visual depth of 20 in., 9 in. checks for a visual depth of 40 in.). Fewer animals descended to the deep side as depth increased. While this disconfirmed the preferred retinal angle hypothesis, about half of the animals still went to the deep side at these increased depths. When two surfaces were directly under the glass the rats had no preference for the 3 in. checks compared to grey while they markedly preferred 1 in. checks to grey. Was it some aversion to the 3 in. checks? A one-sided cliff was constructed where the animal could descend or not descend to the side with a pattern 10 in. below the glass. With a 1 in. pattern very few came off the centre board (confirming a similar experiment in Walk and Gibson, 1961), but when the 3 in. checks were below almost all descended. The 11° retinal angle may not have met all of the conditions for a "preference" that the DeHardt hypothesis demanded, but retinal angle had a powerful effect on behaviour and one that showed a certain weakness in motion parallax.

Similar experiments with chicks with the 11° angle on the deep side and the large 33° angle on the shallow side showed that they, too, were influenced by a projected 11° pattern from the deep side (Walk and Walters, 1974). However, increased visual depth resulted in few deep side choices. A preferred retinal angle of 4° elicited even more deep side descents from the chicks, but as depth increased, their choice of the deep side decreased rapidly. This shows the chick's greater sensitivity to visual depth. Davidson and Whitson (1973) conducted the same type of experiment with chicks, but the shallow side had a very fine non-preferred pattern of $\frac{1}{32}$ in. checks rather than the large 3 in. checks we had used. They also found more choices of the deep side than normal when the deep side had a retinal angle of about $2\frac{1}{2}°$; with 10 in. of visual depth 24 per cent went to the deep side, whereas our 4° visual angle (along with the large checks on the shallow side) produced 50 per cent shallow side choices at the same depth.

The importance of these experiments can be understood in terms of the apparent preference that human infants have for checks of certain sizes, mentioned previously. Karmel (1969a) had found that rats prefer check sizes of about $\frac{1}{2}$ in. to $\frac{3}{4}$ in., rejecting very small checks or very large checks in favour of checks in the $\frac{1}{2}$–1 in. range, a retinal angle of about 6° to 11°. Schiffman (1968, 1969) and Karmel (1969a) found that the chick preferred a retinal angle of about 2°; but Schiffman used a much higher lighting level than ours, so the maximum effect we found at 4° is not in disagreement with his results.

With this as background, it was interesting to use human infants in the same conditions. Preliminary experiments showed that large checks on the shallow side had little effect on the human infants, so that the direct analogy to the DeHardt (1969) experiment was not employed. The use of $\frac{1}{8}$ in. checks on the shallow side, however, had the desired effect. Many more infants went to the deep side, a highly significant difference as compared to the 2 in. checks on the shallow side (Walk, Walters and Rosner, 1972). With increasing visual depth fewer infants crawled to the deep side. We can, however, be criticized for not keeping the retinal angle as constant on the deep side as we should have. One might wonder about the $\frac{1}{8}$ in. checks. Could they really see those $\frac{1}{8}$ in. checks? More and more infants "chose" the $\frac{1}{8}$ in. checks on the shallow side as depth increased, but we needed better evidence than that. The $\frac{1}{8}$ in. checks and the large checks were placed directly under the glass. The infant was given, essentially, a choice, and they choose the large checks about 75 per cent of the time. The $\frac{1}{8}$ in. checks were then placed directly under the glass along with a homogeneous grey. The hooded rats, it will be remembered, had no preference for a grey as compared to the 3 in. checks on the shallow side. The infants, however, clearly chose the $\frac{1}{8}$ in. checks—81 per cent of them went to the small pattern, a significant preference as compared to the grey.

The data on human infants, along with the data on the animals, clearly show the importance of optimal texture and minimize the importance of motion parallax. Both the infants and the animals go to the deep side when there is some sort of optimal retinal stimulation from there. The condition, however, is that of inadequate stimulation from the shallow side; either large checks outside the range of the visual acuity, as for rats and chicks, or very small ones, as for human infants and chicks. In addition to a demonstration of the importance of some kind of optimal stimulation, the experiments also show that the animal or infant must actively compare the two sides. In some cases the experimenter can see the subject look from one side to the other and then make a choice, but, often, active comparison is not obvious. The human infant, in particular, orients towards the mother and may seem to be looking only towards her from a position on the centre board where he can see only the side where she stands. Nevertheless, the other side must have an active interest. How else can we explain the fact that the infant may actively avoid deep side checks with one shallow side pattern, and then crawl to the same deep side checks when another pattern is placed on the shallow side?

The results where the optimal check sizes on the deep side are contrasted with an unsatifactory shallow side stimulus agree with those of other experiments. The results with the stripes are not so easily explained.

Stripes, rather than checks, were used for visual cliff research because it seemed that stripes parallel to the centre board would offer less of an opportunity for binocular fixation than would stripes perpendicular to it. Still, the human infant moves its head around so much that whatever the experimenter thought was being presented might not in fact be effective. The experiment was performed with the idea there *might* be such a difference.

The experiment used a bright pattern of $\frac{7}{8}$ in. (2.2 cm) red and white stripes, a very definite and contrasted pattern (Walk, Samuel and Mann, 1973). Half of the infants had the stripes parallel to the centre board on both sides and half of them had the stripes perpendicular to the centre board. The results were totally unexpected. With 10 in. (25 cm) of visual depth, 81 per cent were coaxed to the mother across the deep side. The pattern on the deep side was lowered to 14 in. (35 cm) and the experiment repeated. The same number (84 per cent) were coaxed to the mother when she stood at the deep side. The same number of infants was also coaxed to the mother when the stripes were parallel to the centre board (78 per cent) as were coaxed there when the stripes were perpendicular to it (87 per cent). Checked patterns were then used as the visual stimulus. A checked pattern was first woven out of the 2.2 cm stripes, but this has the effect of doubling the amount of contour; 2 in. (5 cm) checks, on the other hand, have slightly less overall contour than the $\frac{7}{8}$ in. (2.2 cm) stripes. The results were similar for both sizes of checks : 42 per cent were coaxed to the mother on the deep side for each condition. While it is true that quite a few infants were coaxed to the deep side with the checks, something expected at these low visual depths, the fact remains that twice as many infants were coaxed to the deep side for the stripes as for the checks, and contour cannot explain the difference.

Two other experiments are possibly related to these results. MacKay and Jeffreys (1973) and James and Jeffreys (1975) report that the visually evoked response for adult subjects is much less for stripes than it is for checks or similar patterns that have a sharp corner or bend in them. Greenberg and O'Donnell (1972) found that infants looked less at stripes than at checks of equal contour, although his experiment was criticized by Karmel (1974) for not computing the amount of contour correctly.

Recently Greenberg and Blue (1975) presented to 2- and 4-month-old infants black dots on a white background. Looking behaviour was determined by contour and number of elements, not just the amount of contour alone. They found no age factor related to acuity, even indirectly, since that would predict the 4-month-olds would look at smaller element sizes. They did not so look and the authors suggested that "perceptual cognitive" factors are involved.

Let us sum up the visual stimulus studies. They have found :

1. The strength of a patterned stimulus as compared to no pattern;
2. The influence of visual depth, other factors equal;
3. An influence of optimal patterns of some kind, the dimensions of which are not yet completely specified;
4. The surprising weakness of motion parallax when certain pattern relationships compete.

Hubel and Wiesel (1965) found that away from the primary projection area, area 17, of the visual cortex and in more central areas 18 and 19, simple and complex cells, responding to straight lines in an optimal orientation, gave way to an increasing number of "hyper-complex" cells. These cells respond best to stopped lines, lines that change direction.

The optimal stimulus for depth perception, thus, is not just one that reproduces the contours of the natural environment, but also one that reproduces their irregularity. Not just contour, but also the way the contour is arranged is important. Presumably this interacts in some way with motion produced by depth and this relationship is one that varies among species. The chick, for example, is more sensitive to motion, the rat more responsive to optimal pattern.

The "code" for visual depth discrimination is being broken. Data from studies of infant looking behaviour, electrophysiological processes, single cell processes and the visual cliff all converge. More research is needed, obviously. One important area is research with different species and their reaction to depth downward under different stimulus conditions. Such research will begin to probe a fairly undefined area, the relation of vision to the vestibular, proprioceptive, kinaesthetic system.

(5) Visual proprioception

We all know that if we close our eyes it is much more difficult to stand on one foot than it is with our eyes open. This may be due to the lack of visual support, but there are other possibilities such as some general increase in tension. Lee and Aronson (1974) have studied the way in which the visual environment controls the standing of human infants. The infants were 13 to 16 months old and they stood inside a small room the walls of which could move independently of the floor. When the room was moved either towards or away from the infants, they swayed, staggered or fell in the direction the room was moving. All infants fell at least once. Lee and Aronson believed that their experiment investigated the "visual proprioceptive" system, showing the dependence of proprioceptive standing on vision. Witkin (1959) showed that young children are more dependent on the visual cues of a room than adults in that when subjects were placed in a chair that could be moved with respect to the vertical and surrounded by a room that could be similarly displaced, young children were more apt to be influenced by the skewed position of the room, and less likely to be influenced by gravitational cues than older children and adults. A study of the moving room with adults by Lishman and Lee (1973) showed that adults were also affected by the motion of the room but less so than were the infants.

10—CP * *

VI. PERCEPTION OF DEPTH IN PICTURES

The pictorial cues to perception have already been mentioned. They were : size, interposition, height of an object on a plane, direction of illumination, linear perspective, texture density and aerial perspective. Without discussing each "cue" separately, one can still ask : in what respect is there perceptual development with respect to the pictorial cues? The answer to this question will be interwoven with a more general discussion of picture perception and of certain controversies about pictures.

We are all familiar with the Western way of painting pictures. There is an assumption of a fixed point with everything in the scene projected to that point. A camera takes such a picture. We are so used to such pictures that we feel no other way would be natural.

Two-dimensional pictures assume a certain reality for psychologists interested in space perception because of an old fallacy. This is the fallacy that space must somehow emerge from a two-dimensional retinal image. There is no evidence of the two-dimensional retinal image : the retinal image of the moving organism is never static. If we are freed of the notion of the two-dimensional retinal image, we can begin to understand perceptual development as it applies to picture perception.

First, we must ask : what are the differences between the real world and a Western picture? A large difference between the perceptions of the real world of the active, moving organism and the perceptions of the static picture can be expressed in two words : the constancies. We see the man up close and the man at a distance as being the same height. In a picture the man who is close is large and the man who is far away is a midget. We see that table-top as a rectangle. In a picture it appears as a trapezoid. We see the expanse of colour remaining the same colour. In the picture it changes with every shadow.

A famous experiment by Hudson (1960) illustrates the point. This picture (see Fig. 6.7) showed an elephant in the distance, a man with a spear in the foreground, and an antelope in the foreground. The elephant, somewhat small because of the assumed distance, was between the man and the antelope. Projection lines between the foreground and the background gave a linear perspective impression of depth. Natives of Africa, and many schoolchildren, reported the elephant to be closer than the antelope to the man. Hudson called them "two-dimensional perceivers", an ironic twist since they were not two-dimensional perceivers, but true three-dimensional perceivers who were unfamiliar with the Western way of depicting depth on a two-

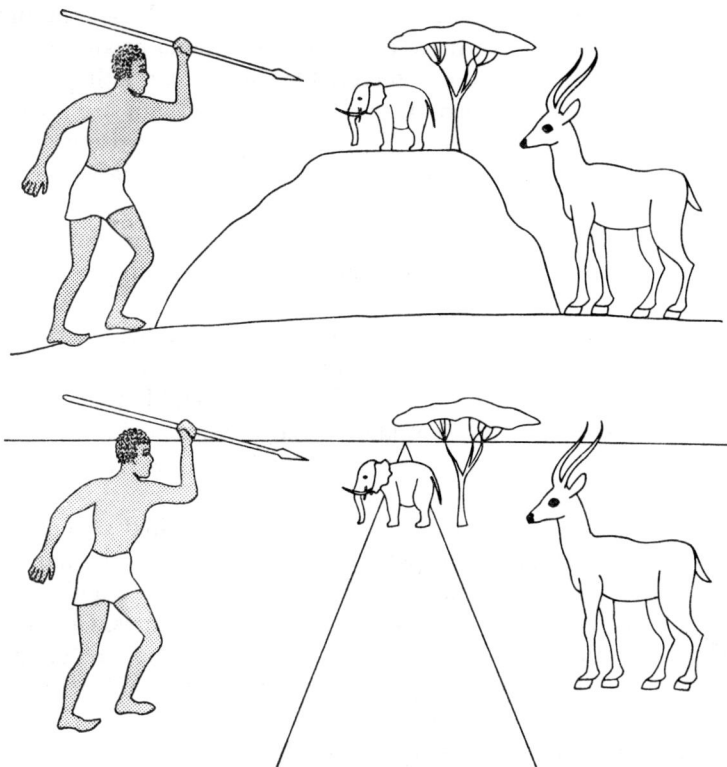

FIG. 6.7. Two of the pictures used by Hudson in his cross-cultural study of the cues to space perception in pictures. The first picture shows the elephant on a "mountain" or "hill" (hence high in the picture plane and more distant) and small in size (also a distance cue). The second picture has added projective lines (linear perspective) together with size to show that the elephant is farther from the man than the antelope (the elephant is also higher in the picture plane). (*After* Hudson, 1960, p. 186.)

dimensional flat surface. He called them two dimensional perceivers as if they somehow saw the world as flat, when they simply did not know our code.

Gibson (1954, 1960, 1971) is usually cited as a staunch defender of the necessity of creating pictures as projections to a common point, an invention that Gombrich (1961) likens to the invention of flying. To break away from his original espousal of the point-projection theory, with its limitations, Gibson (1971) proposed a modification that is based on the pick-up of information. Noting that artists have always been dissatisfied with the point-projection theory, Gibson proposed that a picture should provide the same *information* as the real world. A picture should depict the *invariants* of the real world. But the invariants discovered by his own research were invariants produced by the motion of the object or the observer. One may ask : Is it possible to produce invariants on a two-dimensional plane without using conventions? No. A simple example will make this clear. Two men are the same size and yet are at different distances. In our ordinary perception we see them as of the same size yet at different distances. In a picture we can make them the same size, but, if we do, how can we show distance? Some methods of pictorial representation simply place one man on a higher plane, keeping the images the same size. The Western method is to make the distant man smaller and higher on the page, then add projective lines so that the ratio of each object to its surroundings is the same. The problem here is that children and individuals from other cultures do not know what the perspective lines mean (or, indeed, the size changes), since in "daily life" we are not aware of these relations.

Goodman (1968) and Arnheim (1954) are often cited as representative of the symbolic school of pictorial representation. Goodman wrote that "reality" is simply a convention for a given culture at a given point of time, that there is no "real" way of depicting pictures. Goodman is particularly critical of Gibson's (1954, 1960) espousal of point-projection theory, writing, "the artist who wants to produce a spatial representation that the present-day Western eye will accept as faithful must defy the 'laws of geometry' " (Goodman, 1968, p. 16). Arnheim (1954) is often quoted for his statement that only a shift in viewpoint is needed "to make the Picassos, the Braques, or the Klees look exactly like the things they represent" (Arnheim, 1954, p. 93). Neither of these authors is quite as radical as he sounds. Arnheim, an heir to the Gestalt tradition, described at length the organizational forces (presumably unlearned) that are used in pictures. Goodman did not advocate the position that the meaning of a picture depends on cultural traditions.

A way out of this difficulty is to look at the history of painting and also to investigate the way in which animals, children and individuals from other cultures respond to pictures. We have no difficulty in recognizing the objects in the Lascaux cave paintings of 10,000 to 15,000 B.C. (see Leroi-Gourhan, 1967, for example). Horses, bison, mammoths, deer are just a few of the objects represented. What of the method of representing space? Usually four legs of the animals are visible, as we perceive them in daily life, but there may be some slight use of the cue of interposition (overlap). Size does not seem to diminish with distance, but position on the page (wall) may represent distance, height indicating greater distance. Light and shade may help to give some solidity to the figures, though we can debate this. Occassionally animals seem to be running; the cave painters must have had a way of showing *activity* in pictures.

The amount of developmental research on picture perception is vast, and I have no intention of citing much of it. The evidence is, however, that children, individuals from other cultures, and, even, some animals (such as pigeons or monkeys) have no difficulty recognizing common objects in pictures. Sackett's (1966) experiment with monkeys reared in isolation illustrates this nicely. These animals were reared in isolation and yet they not only recognized pictures of other monkeys, without experience, they also responded appropriately to a picture threat by another monkey, an interpretation of a pictured emotion which they had not seen before. But what of space perception? Space perception in pictures is the difficulty. A recent experiment by Duncan *et al.* (1973) pitted the cues of size against position on the page. The Bantu were very accurate in judging that the lowest position on the page was close, while the Europeans were much more affected by size (houses of the same size above one another on the page were very confusing to them). Does this mean that position on the page is a more "natural" cue than is size? Perhaps, but even the Bantu showed a developmental trend for position on the page, with older children utilizing it more than younger ones.

The difference between real size constancy and pictured size can be illustrated from basic research. Richards (1967) found that the size constancy mechanisms of the eye operate in central vision, but not in peripheral vision. That the eye has size constancy mechanisms, considering the importance of size constancy for survival, is not strange. No such mechanisms are available for size constancy in pictures. Bower (1965), who demonstrated size constancy with real objects in young infants, also showed them pictures in which size constancy could also be demonstrated. None was demonstrated; these were pictures and without motion parallax no size constancy operated. The conclusion, then, is that the constancies of size and shape can be represented in pictures only by conventions.

Are some depth cues more "natural" than others? The use of light and shade for concealment and attraction by animals (Cott, 1940) would argue for a relatively unlearned basis for this cue. Research by Benson and Yonas (1973) on the ease with which young children learn to employ light and shade would also argue for its relative primacy. Perhaps position on the vertical dimension, as on a wall, is also relatively primary.

Future research will help to clear up the basis of some of the difficulties for children and those of other cultures in the representation of depth and distance in pictures. The position taken here is that picture perception is not all "symbolic" and that the "point-projection" theory is erroneous, too. There is no one solution as to how to represent depth and space in pictures; the notion that there is such a solution has handicapped flexibility in visual communication. If we recognize the lack of any one answer we can be a little more humble and less dogmatic in viewing the way other cultures (or periods of Western civilization) represent a space in pictures. The artists were trying to solve a problem, one that has no finite solution, because the active three-dimensional medium can be represented in the static two-dimensional only by artificial means.

The difficulty young children and those of other cultures have in recognizing depth cues in pictures (Hudson, 1960; Duncan *et al.*, 1973) is evidence enough that conventions, not immutable laws, are the basis for our way of representing depth in a two-dimensional medium.

VII. COGNITIVE MAPS AND OTHER RESEARCH

The person moves around in the environment. To what extent is a "cognitive map", to use a term coined by E. C. Tolman, built up? Pick (1972) studied this experimentally by investigating whether the child understood the spatial layout of the home. He found that from 4 to 5 children improved markedly in their understanding of what was on the other side of the walls of a room. Kosslyn, Pick and Fariello (1974) required 5-year-old children and adults to judge from memory the distance between various toys the location of which they had learned. The environment had transparent barriers (a low fence) or opaque ones (a blanket). Objects separated by transparent or opaque barriers were judged by children to be farther apart than toys the same distance apart not separated by barriers. Adult judgments for distance were increased only for opaque, not transparent, barriers. Thus, judged perceptual distance is affected by barriers, particularly for children.

Piaget's mountains task (Piaget and Inhelder, 1956) has inspired a wealth of research. The child is shown a scene with three mountains of different colours. A doll is placed at various points in the display and the child is asked to reconstruct the scene as seen by the doll. This was difficult, and not until age 9–10 did the child show accurate spatial awareness of the viewpoint of another, the doll. Huttenlocher and Presson (1973) found that the child could imagine the display rotating and could judge what could be seen then. The difficulty was for the child to imagine himself in another position and then to predict what would be seen.

These are just a sample of more complex spatial tasks. We all remember the tasks on intelligence tests where we had to find the same pile of outlined blocks from a display where all choices had been rotated in some way as compared to the example. This type of space perception, the ability to rotate objects accurately in memory, is very important for the architect or the mechanical engineer.

VIII. CONCLUSION

The naturalness of space perception was stressed in the introduction. Examples were cited of insects, fish and birds as species that had mastered spatial perception. Where does space perception fit into a book on cognitive processes?

First, knowledge about space perception and its development helps us to understand where this important capability fits into the broad ecology of the organism. The stress on the naturalness and relatively unlearned nature of space perception is only possible as a result of recent research, particularly that of T. G. R. Bower. To show that space perception is present early is not to deny that its full development may take many months and years. My own research, for example, shows weaknesses in the space perception of 12-month-old infants; they will crawl towards an apparent void with proper visual stimulation. This helps us to understand the basis of space perception, but we also must wonder why it takes a long time for spatial capablities to develop fully. The perceptual weaknesses, along with the slow rate of motor development, must have some utility. What survival value is there in such late development? The answer must be : language development. Man's noblest unique faculty and its attendant cognitive development requires time. A fully developed organism is not a natural pupil, but an organism with perceptual and motor weaknesses will stay close to the family or group unit to survive, and in so doing will acquire the language and cognition necessary for long-term survival. Thus, our study of space perception helps to put space perception into its proper niche as related to cognition.

Second, the study of space perception and its many facets shows a continuum from early development to spatial abilities for survival that few of us may possess. Think of the hunter, the sure-footed avoider of real cliffs and obstacles. The hunter needs to locate the prey by means of minimal perceptual cues, then to gauge the direction and distance of the prey in order to hit it. The hunter then finds the way back to camp using a "cognitive map" few of us could follow. The same hunter may even paint pictures of the prey on a two-dimensional cave wall and we may still recognize it, thousands of years later. Is it perception or cognition which is necessary to track an animal, then wait to intercept its path, and, at the right moment, to leap and plant the primitive spear in the prey's heart? The infant reaches out with accuracy. Is this perception or cognition? The boundary between perception and cognition cannot be drawn.

REFERENCES

Arnheim, R. (1954). *Art and Visual Perception*. Berkeley, California: University of California Press.

Ball, W. and Tronick, E. (1971). Infant responses to impending collision: optical and real. *Science, 171*, 818–20.

Barlow, H. B., Blakemore, C. and Pettigrew, J. D. (1967). The neural mechanism of binocular depth discrimination. *Journal of Physiology, 193*, 327–42.

Baruk, H., Leroy, B., Launay, J. and Vallancien, B. (1953). Les étapes du développement psycho-moteur et de la préhension voluntaire chez le nourrisson. *Archives Françaises de Pediatrie, 10*, 425–32.

Benson, K. and Yonas, A. (1973). Development of sensitivity to static pictorial depth information. *Perception and Psychophysics, 13*, 361–6.

Blakemore, C. and Hague, B. (1972). Evidence for disparity detecting neurones in the human visual system. *Journal of Physiology, 225*, 437–55.

Bower, T. G. R. (1964). Discrimination of depth in premotor infants. *Psychonomic Science, 1*, 368.

Bower, T. G. R. (1965). Stimulus variables determining space perception in infants. *Science, 149*, 88–9.

Bower, T. G. R. (1972). Object perception in infants. *Perception, 1*, 15–30.

Bower, T. G. R. (1974). *Development in infancy*. San Francisco: W. H. Freeman.

Bower, T. G. R., Broughton, J. M. and Moore, M. K. (1970a). Demonstration of intention in the reaching behavior of neonate humans. *Nature, 228*, 679–81.

Bower, T. G. R., Broughton, J. M. and Moore, M. K. (1970b). The coordination of vision and tactual input in infancy. *Perception and Psychophysics, 8*, 51–3.

Bower, T. G. R., Broughton, J. M. and Moore, M. K. (1970c). Infant responses to approaching objects: an indicator of response to distal variables. *Perception and Psychophysics, 9*, 193–6.

Brazelton, T. B., Robey, J. S. and Collier, G. A. (1969). Infant development in the Zinacanteco Indians of Southern Mexico. *Pediatrics, 44*, 274–83.

Brennan, W., Ames, E. W. and Moore, R. W. (1966). Age differences in infants' attention to patterns of different complexities. *Science, 151*, 354–6.

Bruner, J. S. and Koslowski, B. (1972). Visually preadapted constituents of manipulatory action. *Perception, 1*, 3–14.

Cooper, K. W. (1957). Biology of Eumenine wasps. Part V. Digital communication in wasps. *Journal of Experimental Zoology, 134*, 469–514.

Cott, H. B. (1940). *Adaptive Coloration in Animals*. London: Methuen.

Davidson, P. W. and Whitson, T. T. (1973). Some effects of texture density on visual cliff behavior of the domestic chick. *Journal of Comparative and Physiological Psychology, 84*, 522–6.

Dayton, G. O., Jr., Jones, M. H., Aiu, P., Rawson, R. A., Steele, B. and Rose, M. (1964). Developmental study of coordinated eye movements in the human infant. I. Visual acuity in the newborn human: a study based on induced optokinetic nystagmus recorded by electro-oculography. *Archives of Ophthalmology, 71*, 865–70.

DeHardt, D. C. (1969). Visual cliff behavior of rats as a function of pattern size. *Psychonomic Science, 15*, 268–9.

Duncan, H. F., Gourlay, N. and Hudson, W. (1973). *A Study of Pictorial Perception Among Bantu and White Primary School Children in South Africa.* Johannesburg: Witwatersrand University Press.

Emlen, J. T., Jr. (1963). Determinants of cliff edge and escape responses in herring gull chicks in nature. *Behavior, 22,* 1–16.

Fantz, R. L. (1958). Depth discrimination in dark-hatched chicks. *Perceptual and Motor Skills, 8,* 47–50.

Fantz, R. L. (1961). The origin of form perception. *Scientific American, 204* (5), 66–72.

Fantz, R. L. (1963). Pattern vision in newborn infants. *Science, 140,* 296–7.

Fantz, R. L., Ordy, J. M. and Udelf, M. S. (1962). Maturation of pattern vision in infants during the first six months. *Journal of Comparative and Physiological Psychology, 55,* 907–17.

Gibson, J. J. (1950). *The Perception of the Visual World.* Boston: Houghton-Mifflin.

Gibson, J. J. (1954). A theory of pictorial perception. *Audio-visual Communication Review, 1,* 3–23.

Gibson, J. J. (1960). Pictures, perspective and perception. *Daedalus, 89,* 216–27.

Gibson, J. J. (1971). The information available in pictures. *Leonardo, 4,* 27–35.

Gombrich, E. H. (1961). *Art and illusion: A Study in the Psychology of Pictorial Representation.* Princeton, New Jersey: Princeton University Press.

Goodman, N. (1968). *Languages of Art: An Approach to a Theory of Symbols.* New York: Bobbs-Merrill.

Greenberg, D. J. and Blue, S. Z. (1975). Visual complexity in infancy: contour or numerosity? *Child Development, 46,* 357–63.

Greenberg, D. J. and O'Donnell, W. J. (1972). Infancy and the optimal level of stimulation. *Child Development, 43,* 639–45.

Gross, C. G., Rocha-Miranda, C. E. and Bender, D. B. (1972). Visual properties of neurons in inferotemporal cortex of the macaque. *Journal of Neurophysiology, 35,* 96–111.

Haynes, H., White, B. L. and Held, R. (1965). Visual accommodation in human infants. *Science, 148,* 528–30.

Hein, A. (1972). Acquiring components of visually guided behavior. In A. D. Pick (Ed.), *Minnesota Symposia on Child Psychology,* Vol. 6, pp. 53–68. Minneapolis: University of Minnesota Press.

Held, R. (1965). Plasticity in sensory-motor systems. *Scientific American, 213* (5), 84–94.

Held, R. and Hein, A. (1963). Movement-produced stimulation in the development of visually-guided behavior. *Journal of Comparative and Physiological Psychology, 56,* 872–6.

Herriot, J. (1972). *All Creatures Great and Small.* New York: St. Martin's Press.

Hochberg, J. E. (1962). Nativism and empiricism in perception. In L. Postman (Ed.), *Psychology in the Making,* pp. 225–330. New York: Knopf.

Holst, E. v. (1954). Relations between the central nervous system and the peripheral organs. *British Journal of Animal Behaviour, 2,* 89–94.

Horner, B. E. (1954). Arboreal adaptations of Peromyscus, with special reference to use of the tail. *Contributions from the Laboratory of Vertebrate Biology* (University of Michigan), *64,* 1–84.

Hubel, D. H. and Wiesel, T. N. (1965). Receptive fields and functional architecture in two nonstriate visual areas (18 and 19) of the cat. *Journal of Nenrophysiology, 28,* 229–89.

Hubel, D. H. and Wiesel, T. N. (1970). Cells sensitive to binocular depth in area 18 of the macaque monkey cortex. *Nature*, *225*, 41–2.

Hudson, W (1960). Pictorial depth perception in sub-cultural groups in Africa. *Journal of Social Psychology*, *52*, 183–208.

Huttenlocher, J. and Presson, C. C. (1973). Mental rotation and the perspective problem. *Cognitive Psychology*, *4*, 277–99.

Ittelson, W. H. and Kilpatrick, F. P. (1951). Experiments in perception. *Scientific American*, *185* (2), 50–5.

James, C. R. and Jeffreys, D. A. (1975). Properties of individual components of pattern-onset evoked potentials in man. *Journal of Physiology*, *249*, 57–8.

Karmel, B. Z. (1969a). Complexity, amounts of contour and visually-dependent behavior in hooded rats, domestic chicks, and human infants. *Journal of Comparative and Physiological Psychology*, *69*, 649–57.

Karmel, B. Z. (1969b). The effect of age, complexity and amount of contour on pattern preferences in human infants. *Journal of Experimental Child Psychology*, *7*, 339–54.

Karmel, B. Z. (1974). Contour effects and pattern preferences in infants: a reply to Greenberg and O'Donnell (1972). *Child Development*, *45*, 196–9.

Kear, J. (1967). Experiments with young nidifugous birds on a visual cliff. *Wildfowl Trust 18th Annual Report*, 122–4.

Kosslyn, S. M., Pick, H. L., Jr. and Fariello, G. R. (1974). Cognitive maps in children and men. *Child Development*, *45*, 707–16.

Lee, D. N. and Aronson, E. (1974). Visual proprioceptive control of standing in human infants. *Perception and Psychophysics*, *15*, 529–32.

Leroi-Gourhan, A. (1967). *Treasures of Prehistoric Art*. New York: Harry N. Abrams.

Lishman, J. R. and Lee, D. N. (1973). The autonomy of visual kinaesthesis. *Perception*, *2*, 287–94.

MacKay, D. M. and Jeffreys, D. A. (1973). Visually evoked potentials and visual perception in man. In R. Jung (Ed.), *Handbook of Sensory Physiology*. Vol. VII/3. *Central Processing of Visual Information*, Part B, pp. 647–78.

Marg, E. and Adams, J. E. (1970). Evidence for a neurological zoom system in vision from angular changes in some receptive fields of single neurons with changes in fixation distance in the human visual cortex. *Experientia*, *26*, 270–1.

McKenzie, B. E. and Day, R. H. (1972). Object distance as a determinant of visual fixation in early infancy. *Science*, *178*, 1108–10.

Miller, D. R. and Walk, R. D. (1975). Self-produced movement is unnecessary for the development of visually-guided depth discrimination. Paper presented at Meetings of the Eastern Psychological Association, New York.

Paine, R. S. and Oppé, T. E. (1966). *Neurological Examination of Children*. Clinics in Developmental Medicine Nos. 20 and 21. Lavenham, Suffolk: The Lavenham Press.

Piaget, J. and Inhelder, B. (1956). *The Child's Conception of Space*. New York: Norton.

Pick, H. L., Jr. (1972). Mapping children—mapping space. Paper presented at the meetings of the American Psychological Association, Honolulu, Hawaii.

Richards, W. (1967). Apparent modifiabilty of receptive fields during accommodation and convergence and a model for size constancy. *Neuropsychologica*, 5, 63–72.

Routtenberg, A. and Glickman, S. E. (1964). Visual cliff behavior in undomesticated rodents, land and aquatic turtles, and cats *(Panthera)*. *Journal of Comparative and Physiological Psychology*, 58, 143–6.

Sackett, G. P. (1966). Monkeys reared in isolation with pictures as visual input: evidence for an innate releasing mechanism. *Science*, 154, 1468–73.

Scarr, S. and Salapateck, P. (1970). Patterns of fear development during infancy. *Merrill-Palmer Quarterly*, 16, 53–90.

Schiff, W., Caviness, J. A. and Gibson, J. J. (1962). Persistent fear responses in rhesus monkeys to the optical stimulus of "looming". *Science*, 136, 982–3.

Schiffman, H. R. (1968). Texture preference in the domestic chick. *Journal of Comparative and Physiological Psychology*, 66, 540–1.

Schiffman, H. R. (1969). Texture preference and acuity in the domestic chick. *Journal of Comparative Physiology and Psychology*, 67, 462–4.

Schiffman, H. R. (1970). Evidence for sensory dominance: reactions to apparent depth in rabbits, cats and rodents. *Journal of Comparative and Physiological Psychology*, 71, 38–41.

Schwartz, A. N., Campos, J. J. and Baisel, E. J., Jr. (1973). The visual cliff: cardiac and behavioral responses on the deep and shallow sides at five and nine months of age. *Journal of Experimental Child Psychology*, 15, 86–9.

Sechzer, J. A., Faro, M. D., Barker, J. N., Barsky, D., Gutierrez, S. and Windle, W. F. (1971). Developmental behaviors: delayed appearance in monkeys asphyxiated at birth. *Science*, 171, 1173–5.

Tinbergen, N. and Kruyt, W. (1938). Uber die Orientierung des Bienenwolfes *(Philanthus triangulum* Fabr.) III. Die Bevorzugung bestimmter Wegmarken. *Zeitschrift für vergleichende Physiologie*, 25, 292–334. (Available in translation in N. Tinbergen (1972), The *Animal in its World*, Vol. 1. *Field Studies*. Cambridge, Mass: Harvard University Press).

Tronick, E. (1972). Stimulus control and the growth of the infant's effective visual field. *Perception and Psychophysics*, 11, 373–6.

Walk, R. D. (1963). Chronological age as a determinant of responsiveness to visual depth in human infants. *American Psychologist*, 18, 424.

Walk, R. D. (1965). The study of visual depth and distance perception in animals. In D. S. Lehrman, R. A. Hinde and E Shaw (Eds.), *Advances in the Study of Behavior*, Vol. 1, pp. 99–153. New York and London: Academic Press.

Walk, R. D. (1966). The development of depth perception in animals and human infants. *Monographs of the Society for Research in Child Development, 31*, (No. 107), 82–108.

Walk, R. D. (1972). Visual depth preferences of the domestic duckling. *Journal of Comparative and Physiological Psychology*, 78, 14–21.

Walk, R. D. and Gibson, E. J. (1961). A comparative and analytical study of visual depth perception. *Psychological Monographs, 75* (15, Whole No. 519).

Walk, R. D., Samuel, J. M. F. and Mann, B. N. (1973). Contours and corners as stimuli for the depth perception of human infants (unpublished paper).

Walk, R. D. and Walters, C. P. (1974). Importance of texture-density preferences and motion parallax for visual depth discrimination by rats and chicks. *Journal of Comparative and Physiological Psychology, 86,* 309–15.

Walk, R. D., Walters, C. P. and Rosner, W. (1972). Influence of texture preferences on the depth discrimination of human infants (unpublished paper).

Walsh, F. B. and Hoyt, W. F. (Eds.) (1969). *Clinical Neuro-Ophthalmology,* Vol. 1, 3d Ed. Baltimore: Williams and Wilkins.

Walters, C. P. and Walk, R. D. (1974). Visual placing by human infants. *Journal of Experimental Child Psychology, 18,* 34–40.

White, B. L. (1971). *Human Infants: Experience and Psychological Development.* Englewood Cliffs, New Jersey: Prentice-Hall.

White, B. L., Castle, P. and Held, R. (1964). Observations on the development of visually-directed reaching. *Child Development, 35,* 349–64.

Wickelgren, L. W. (1967). Convergence in the human newborn. *Journal of Experimental Child Psychology, 5,* 74–85.

Witkin, H. A. (1959). The perception of the upright. *Scientific American, 200* (2), 50–6.

Wolf, P. H. and White, B. L. (1965). Visual pursuit and attention in young infants. *Journal of American Academy for Child Psychiatrists, 4,* 473–84.

Yerkes, R. M. (1904). Space perception of tortoises. *Journal of Comparative Neurology and Psychology, 4,* 17–26.

Zeki, S. M. (1974). Cells responding to changing image size and disparity in the cortex of the rhesus monkey. *Journal of Physiology, 242,* 827–41.

CHAPTER 7

Development of Conceptualization

Margaret Donaldson

I. THE NATURE OF CONCEPTUALIZATION

The concept of a concept is not a particularly simple one, and there is room for disagreement about what is to be understood by "conceptualization", so it may be as well to spend some time at the outset on questions of interpretation.

There exists a tradition whereby a person is held to give evidence of possessing a concept if he responds in like manner to each member of a set of non-identical stimuli. The subject is then assumed to have abstracted some common feature from these stimuli and to be responding to this feature, whether or not he has any awareness of what the feature may be, and indeed whether or not he has any awareness of anything whatever. According to this tradition, the development of conceptualization could be nothing other than the development of responses to new—and in some sense more complex—groupings of stimuli.

Even when no such extreme behaviourist position is maintained, however, there is a fairly widespread tendency to think of conceptualization in a way that has been much influenced by the numerous studies of "concept learning" and "concept attainment" in which the concepts to be studied have been exemplified by a limited range of small objects that can be readily manipulated in a laboratory.

There is much that is of interest to be said about these studies and they are of course relevant to a discussion of conceptualization, however that term is interpreted. But I do not propose to interpret it in such a way as to be limited to them. I shall take it as a matter of definition that the process of "conceptualizing" is the process of constructing complex representations of the world (including oneself) and using these representations for the purpose of directing behaviour.

And I shall consider it appropriate to be concerned with the degree to which consciousness accompanies this process—consciousness of the world thus represented and ultimately of the representations themselves.

It is evident that we do not all represent the world in precisely the same way. Yet there is much that normal adults hold in common. We come to conceive of a world that is distinct from us, yet able to be affected by us and to affect us in turn. We conceive of this world as enduring through time yet undergoing change through time; and in the world's independent being we recognize certain distinct entities or "chunks"—that is, we develop what has come to be called the "object concept". Some of the entities that we distinguish are animate, some inanimate: another person, a bird, a rock, a forest, an ocean. These units have more or less well-defined boundaries. They also have location in space which may or may not be likely to change across an interval of time. Birnam Wood does not usually come to Dunsinane.

We conceive of these chunks of our world as having attributes which enable us to compare them one with another, judging them the same or different. So we can group them on the basis of likenesses of various kinds and organize them according to classificatory systems. Across time we also recognize sameness and difference in the recurrence or variation in patterns of events. So we come to conceive of the world as predictable at least to some degree: we develop expectancies.

The entities which have location in space, even if only vaguely bounded, are the ones we usually call "concrete". But we also conceive of "things" of other kinds which do not exist in a place that can be pointed to: a plan, a meaning, a value, a number, a possibility. We tend to call our representations of these things "abstract"—though in another sense all our representations are abstract.*

Among the abstract concepts the notion of possibility is of rather special importance. For consideration of possibilities and making decisions about whether two world states can possibly both occur—that is, whether they are compatible or incompatible with one another—are at the root of inferential thinking. And it is one of the distinguishing characteristics of the human intellect that it is a system capable of inference. We conceive of the world as a place where, given certain information, we can be sure of other things of which we have no immediate knowledge, things which we have not verified in any direct way.

* The words "abstract" and "concrete" are used in many different ways, and much confusion is liable to attend them. For a discussion of their uses see Pikas (1966).

II. THE DEVELOPMENT OF THE SEARCH
FOR INFORMATION

It is hard to get clear evidence about the earliest origins of an apprehension of possibility. We must distinguish first of all between a conscious concept of "the possible" and the intuition of some possibility, unreflectingly and perhaps quite fleetingly apprehended. The former is a relatively late development; the latter may be very early and quite primitive, corresponding to the recognition of being in a state of uncertainty, of wanting to know.

There can be little doubt that we want to know from an early age.* We actively seek information about the world, and it is a fact of some significance that in this search we are not only active but also selective, that is, we ask questions (not all of them articulated in verbal form). We ask questions of other people but we also ask them of ourselves, setting ourselves the task of finding the answers. It is characteristic of us that we approach the world as questioners.

The nature of the questions that we typically ask repays close study. Many of them are what Frege (1956) would call "sentence-questions". That is, they take the form : "Is it x ?" rather than merely : "What is it ?" Questions of the latter type are called by Frege "word-questions". He calls the former type sentence-questions because they contain a complete thought which could be asserted in the corresponding indicative sentence. The question form expresses the thought without asserting it. That is, it embodies a hypothesis.

Considerable attention has been paid to children's word-questions, or wh-questions as they are usually called in the psychological literature, and it is a common observation that young children ask many of these. But from an early age they also ask many sentence-questions (see Donaldson, 1971), which fact shows very clearly that they formulate hypotheses and try to get them verified. Or, if the word "hypothesis" is thought to suggest too high a degree of formalization or generalization, we may at the very least say that they have notions about which they are uncertain and that they try to check whether these are sound. This is certainly true for the age at which sentence-questions are expressed in verbal form. It is almost certainly true much sooner. R. Brown (1973) suggests that the semantics of sentence-questions—or "yes-no" questions—would seem to be available to "Stage 1" children (Mean Length of Utterance between 1.0 and 2.0 morphemes)

---

* It must also, however, be recognized that children can be in a state of what looks like very obvious "uncertainty" and yet not seem to be aware that they lack the knowledge that would justify a conclusion. See, for instance, Pieraut-Le Bonniec (1974) and Donaldson (1971).

even though the appropriate grammatical forms are still beyond them.

Among the wh-questions, one sub-set is of special interest in the context of this discussion. This is the set of questions which constitute requests for the names of things—or at least which adults normally interpret in this way. At an early age (indeed once more at Stage 1; see R. Brown, 1973) children typically begin to ask: "What's that?" And one may argue that this is a kind of landmark in the child's conceptual and linguistic progress; for the question "What is that?" is a tool through the use of which he can rapidly expand his ability to communicate and hence to acquire further information. But it is noteworthy that there is another closely related question which would be at least equally useful for this purpose yet which is not normally asked until much later, namely: "What does that mean?"

What this amounts to is that the young child, starting from objects, can ask to be informed about the words that refer to them. But he does not, with comparable readiness, start from words and ask questions about the things to which the words refer. We shall return later to some discussion of the significance of this asymmetry.

Meanwhile emphasis on the child as a questioner leads on to a consideration of what he does with the answers to his questions when he gets them. Presumably he does his best to fit them together to form a coherent and integrated model of the world, for an incoherent or scrappy model is not likely to be of much use. If we assume that a major adaptive function—if not *the* major function—of a representational system is to make it possible to anticipate events and be ready to deal with them (and this basic notion is to be found in the work of theorists as diverse as Hull and Piaget), then it is clear that the model must not yield contradictory predictions and that the more unified it is the better. There is very wide agreement that incoherence or conflict in our representational system is something we try hard to eliminate. Berlyne (1965), for instance, believes that the attempt to resolve this kind of conflict is the principal motive power underlying cognitive advance. And this is certainly at the core of Piagetian theory.

III. THE EFFECTS OF EGOCENTRISM

(1) PIAGET'S HYPOTHESIS

According to Piaget, however, the young child's efforts at constructing a unified and co-ordinated representation of the world are greatly hampered by one very important limitation: he is egocentric. This notion has been so influential and has such far-reaching implications that it will be worth while to spend some time examining the validity of the claim. In spite of all the developments in Piagetian theory over the years, the concept of the egocentric child remains in one form or another at the heart of many of his arguments. Let us look briefly at some of the things that are maintained.

The child is held to be initially so profoundly egocentric that he recognizes no distinction between himself and a universe external to himself. This "complete and unconscious egocentrism of the early stages" (Piaget, 1955) is overcome gradually in the course of the sensori-motor period as a concept of enduring objects with independent existence is formed. But egocentrism continues to manifest itself in many ways. For a long time the child has great difficulty in adopting any point of view other than his own. This is held to be true in the literal sense, so that the child fails to appreciate what another person sees where this differs from what he himself sees. It is also held to be true in the metaphorical sense that he fails to appreciate another person's knowledge or lack of it and so cannot communicate effectively. But this is not all. Most important of all, it is argued that the inability to shift flexibly from one point of view to another results in an inability to make deductive inferences of the kind that characterize concrete operational thinking. For these inferences call for an ability to "decentre", both with respect to the structuring of the immediate perceptual situation and with respect to the co-ordination of relations between situations or states of affairs. Failure to decentre in the immediate situation means failure to understand, for example, how changes in two dimensions can compensate for one another, and so cancel out one another. Similarly, failure to decentre over time is closely related to the inability to handle reversible transformations, which is the hallmarks of pre-operational thought.

How, then, does an egocentric child conceive of the world, when he has freed himself sufficiently from his primitive profound egocentrism to conceive of it at all? Clearly his picture of it must be very scrappy and disjointed. The pieces of his model cannot fit well together. His representations must be at once rigid and unstable. They must be rigid because of the way he is pinned down, as it were, in the position of the moment. They must be unstable because, as that position happens to shift, he cannot co-ordinate the changes into any system that can represent the relationships between them. Piaget argues that rigidity and instability of precisely this kind characterize the thinking of the pre-operational child. But is it really so? The data on which he bases his interpretation are certainly sound. They are easy to replicate, and they have been replicated many times. Yet on the other hand a number of findings has been reported in recent years which are not at all easy to reconcile with his claims and which can be put together to form a picture of a substantially different kind. I shall now try to give some indication of what the shape of the emerging alternative may prove to be.

(2) The significance of the object concept in infancy

The place to begin is clearly with the "object concept"—the concept of a world of separate, enduring objects, distinct from ourselves and existing independently of us. For it is on claims as to the absence of any such concept in the first eight months or so of life that Piaget rests his arguments about the initial profound egocentrism which has then slowly to be overcome.

I shall not recapitulate in any detail the well-known Piagetian evidence or the stages which he postulates (see Piaget, 1955). The central finding is that if an object is covered by a cloth or a box in the child's presence, he will not attempt to retrieve that object until he is about 8 months old. Out of sight, it is then argued, really *is* out of mind.

There is one important consequence of this interpretation of the failure to search. If the object ceases to exist for the child when it is no longer seen then it clearly should not matter how the disappearance is effected. One way of vanishing should be equivalent to any other. It appears that this is not so.

Bower and his collaborators, in a series of important studies (see Bower, 1974) have experimented with different modes of disappearance. For their behavioural data they rely mainly on eye movements, sometimes in conjunction with "startle" reactions or indices of surprise, in very young infants; and on hand search patterns in older babies. One example is sufficient to make the main point. They report that if an object is made to vanish from sight by the device of plunging the room into total darkness, a child who has been playing with that object will reach out in the appropriate direction to find it again (Bower and Wishart, 1972).

Bower believes that, at least from the age of about 8 weeks, the child does not fail to comprehend object permanence (Bower, 1974). But in this case, we clearly need another explanation of why he does not remove the cover from the object in the classical Piagetian situation. I. Brown (1973) argues that the true difficulty in this task lies not in conceiving of a separate universe but in understanding the spatial relation "inside". For she finds that children who do not search *under* a cloth will nevertheless commonly search behind a screen. She concludes that when they fail in the classical task, they do so because they do not understand how two objects can occupy the same part of space simultaneously. They do not see how it is *possible* that when a

DEVELOPMENT OF CONCEPTUALIZATION

cup is placed over a small toy, the toy can still be there inside it. Brown's conclusion is strengthened by evidence of considerable surprise on the child's part if the cup is lifted away and the toy is again revealed. On this view of the matter one would have to say that the child does indeed think an object is no longer there when it has been covered by another one; but the disappearance puzzles him, and his acceptance of it is specific to the situation, not wholly normal and general as Piaget's interpretation would imply.

It is too soon yet to claim that this explanation is fully adequate, and that we really understand what is going on. Brown herself (personal communication) doubts that we do. And other recent work (for instance, Evans and Gratch, 1972; Harris, 1974; Webb, Massar and Nadolny, 1972) indicates that there is still a great deal to discover about the exact nature of the child's difficulties in constructing a mature concept of objects and their relations to one another in three-dimensional space. What is clear, however, is that Piaget's claims concerning the extent of early egocentrism are called radically into question by evidence of the kind that Bower and his colleagues have obtained.

(3) THE DEVELOPMENT OF CONCEPTS OF PERSONS

These same claims are called in question by another body of evidence of a different, though not unrelated, kind. In the world around us, other people constitute a class of objects of very special significance. But are they of special significance for infants? Or does early egocentrism admit of no such discrimination? What is the capacity of very young children for response of a genuinely social kind? These questions are important in a discussion of the development of conceptualization not only because of the interest which attaches to so fundamental a concept as that of another person but because of the issue of the role of other people in furthering the progress of conceptual thought.

Recently some powerful opposition to the notion of the profoundly egocentric infant has come from research workers who have been studying interpersonal responsiveness at what they believe to be its origins. Bruner (1975) reports observations which suggest that genuine sharing of attention and communication of intention between adult and child are very early phenomena; and he argues that without this basis in "mutuality", language learning as we know it could not take place. Trevarthen (1974) makes the claim that infants of even a few weeks of age respond differently to people and to things; and he too regards these first responses to people as constituting a sort of prelinguistic conversation. He believes his data indicate that human intelligence is interpersonal from the start and that the source of the meanings and intentions later expressed in language lies in the early encounters between persons. Newson (1974) agrees closely.

An interesting piece of evidence concerning the early capacity for social response was obtained by John Tatam, working in Trevarthen's laboratory (Tatam, unpublished). Tatam used an arrangement of mirrors and lights to devise a situation in which a mother, who had previously been "conversing" with her young baby, remained visible to the child and appeared still to be looking in his direction although she could no longer see him. An experimenter then asked the mother to reply to questions written on cards for her to read. This meant, of course, that she ceased entirely to respond to the child or to behave in a manner to which the child was accustomed. Tatam found that children of 8 to 10 weeks were very troubled by this experience. They seemed to try hard to win back the mother's attention, and some became markedly depressed and withdrawn when after a little while they had failed to do so.

There is no doubt that findings such as these are hard to reconcile with Piaget's views. A profoundly egocentric infant could not be capable of social response. Piaget certainly allows that by 7 or 8 months "another person constitutes a more lively centre of actions than any object whatsoever" (Piaget, 1955, p. 252), and he adds: "It is enough to observe the subject's expression to realise this difference". On the other hand, this is a very limited admission, for he goes on almost immediately to say ". . . as yet nothing contrasts him (another person) in principle with the rest of that universe".

It would, however, be quite false to suppose that Piaget takes no account of the role of other people—specifically as persons—in the later development of conceptual thinking. For Piaget, conceptual thinking proper begins only as the sensori-motor period is completed and left behind. He makes explicit the point that conceptual thought, as distinct from sensori-motor intelligence, is "collective thought obeying common laws" (Piaget 1955, p. 360), developed by collaboration between persons. But then he comes back again to his recurring theme: our attempts to achieve this are for a long time limited by our egocentrism.

(4) Egocentrism in pre-school and school children

So we turn now to the question of egocentrism in the pre-school and early school years. And once again there is new evidence which seems to force a reconsideration of Piaget's claims.

In a very interesting recent study, Hughes (1975) has concentrated on children's ability to estimate what another person can see, in the literal sense. Hughes considers it important to make a distinction between the ability to calculate "*what* another person is looking at" and "how that thing looks to the other person". He calls the former "projective ability" and the latter "perspective ability". Each of these clearly requires a basic awareness that differences in viewpoint are possible; each also involves the ability to carry out certain computations. But tasks which demand perspective abilities would appear to call for computations that go beyond those needed for projective tasks. Hughes carried out a series of experiments which led him to conclude that children as young as three years can readily use projective skills in many situations, and can even perform well on tasks which require them to co-ordinate two or three lines of sight. The last conclusion is based on two studies in which the task was to hide a boy doll behind one of a number of walls so that "the policeman (or policemen) can't see him". As many as three "policemen" were used in the most difficult task, yet on this task 90 per cent of the 4-year-old children and 70 per cent of the 3-year-olds were successful.

The issues concerning perspective abilities proved, like these abilities themselves, to be more complex. But Hughes was able to show that, if steps were taken to remove ambiguity from the instructions and from the pictorial conventions that were being used, then very high proportions of both 3- and 4-year-old children could succeed on tasks which required them to select pictures showing another person's point of view of a three-dimensional scene. Hughes pointed out that a question such as "Which picture shows what X sees?" admits of two interpretations which he called the *object interpretation* and the *view interpretation*. Clearly there is a sense in which "what is seen" does not alter as an observer moves around an object (object interpretation) and another sense in which "what is seen" does change as this movement occurs (view interpretation). For the child to succeed it is essential that he understand that the view interpretation is that one intended. Huttenlocher and Presson (1973) observe that even sophisticated adults show some tendency to make an "egocentric choice" in a task of this kind and then promptly to add "but seen from here", pointing to the position of the other viewer. Huttenlocher and Presson add that children sometimes make a gesture which is the counterpart of the phrase "but seen from here" but that the children, unlike the adults, continue to insist that the egocentric choice—the thing as seen from their own position—is just what the other viewer would see. In Hughes's terms one would say that they hold to the object interpretation.

Hughes used material consisting of three coloured dolls (red, blue and yellow) mounted on a triangular base, so that each doll faced outwards from one corner. The child looked directly at the face of the doll nearest him. The experimenter faced one of the other dolls. The standard question asked by the experimenter was: "Which picture shows what I see?" And it evoked typical egocentric responses. However, dramatic improvement in performance resulted if this question was preceded by questions of two other kinds: questions about the array, with no pictures shown; and questions about a series of pictures of the array. In the first series there were questions like: "Which doll's face do you see?", "Which doll's face do you see now?" (after rotation of the array) "Which doll's face do I see?" and (again after rotation) "Which doll's face do I see now?" The second series contained the question: "Which doll's face do you see in this picture?" repeated for three pictures giving a direct view of the face of each doll in turn.

When these questions preceded the standard question Hughes found that very high success rates were obtained. He held that the first set helped the children to understand the language of the instructions and that the second set helped the child to understand the pictorial conventions that were being used and to avoid, for instance, choosing an incorrect picture yet pointing on that picture to the doll whose face the experimenter was indeed looking at (the side view of that doll being of course visible).

Hughes' studies seem to show very clearly that no radical inability to calculate how something looks to another person was present in his 3- or 4- year-old subjects. Articles by Masangkay et al. (1974), Fishbein, Lewis and Keiffer (1972) and Light (1974) are in general agreement with Hughes' findings.

There is, then, good reason to doubt that 3- and 4-year-old children are incapable of appreciating another point of view. It turns out that their ability to recognize another *cognitive* point of view may also be greater than has been supposed. Here the question turns on their skill as communicators—their ability to appreciate what information another person may need, or may be able to provide.

Lloyd (1975) has carried out a number of studies of the communicative capacities of young children. In some of these studies pre-school children gave information to one another, in some they gave and received it in conversation with an adult or with a talking toy panda. (The voice of the panda was provided by an adult experimenter from within a sound-proof cubicle.) Lloyd concludes that previous work has considerably underestimated the communicative skills which children possess. Particularly relevant to the discussion of egocentrism is the fact that the panda was presented as a creature who could not speak very well and who might need help. Most of the children were able to respond to this situation effectively, giving evidence of understanding that the panda might know less than they did and of making allowance for his incompetence in what they said.

From Lloyd's research as a whole it emerges that one of the main weaknesses of young children as communicators is that they are poor at spontaneously indicating that a message which they have received is inadequate. But in the talking panda situation when the children were explicitly encouraged to ask the panda for more information if they thought he had not given them enough, many of them proved able to do this competently. And when the children were speakers rather than listeners nearly all of them could provide additional relevant information if they were asked for it.

So once again we find there is evidence to suggest that Piaget's picture of the egocentric child is, at the least, too firmly drawn. But if the flexible shifting of point of view is not in fact beyond the power of a pre-school child, then the whole Piagetian account of the change from pre-operational to concrete operational thinking must be reconsidered.

IV. CONCEPTUALIZATION IN CLASS INCLUSION AND CONSERVATION

There is no doubt that the shift in patterns of response to such tasks as class inclusion and conservation genuinely takes place. The data stand firm, as usual. How, then, are they to be explained?

Recent work by McGarrigle* has yielded some very interesting suggestions about what may be going on. McGarrigle (unpublished) discovered that the presence or absence of a single adjective in the formulation of a class-inclusion question could dramatically affect the responses made to that question by children of 4 or 5. His material was somewhat analogous to that used by Piaget in the famous question which asks the child whether he can make a longer necklace with the brown beads or with the wooden beads in a situation where some (but not all) of the wooden beads are brown (Piaget, 1955). In McGarrigle's task there were four red discs and two white ones. These were referred to as steps, forming a straight path along which a teddy bear had to walk to get either to a chair (placed beside the fourth red disc) or to to a table (placed beside the sixth disc). McGarrigle then asked the following questions:

---

* James McGarrigle was a young research student of great promise who died tragically, a short time after this work was completed.

1. Are there more red steps to go to the chair or more steps to go to the table?

2. Are there more steps to go to the chair or more steps to go to the table?

There was a significant difference between these questions, question 1 being the more difficult. (McGarrigle controlled for order effects between questions and for order of mention within questions. Neither of these made any difference.) Around 37 per cent of a group of thirty-two children between $3\frac{1}{2}$ and 5 years answered question 1 correctly. Around 65 per cent succeeded with question 2.

As McGarrigle realized, these results admit of at least two possible kinds of explanation. On the one hand, it is possible to argue that the inclusion of the word "red" somehow makes it harder to decentre and thus to achieve "operational reversibility". On the other hand, one might explain the effect as relating to the manner in which children interpret utterances, and as not relating to decentration or reversibility.

To test these possibilities, McGarrigle carried out a number of further studies including one in which there was no overlap, or inclusion of one set within another, so that reversibility could not be involved. This was achieved by having two paths set at an angle to one another. One path led from the teddy to the chair and was composed of four red discs. The other led from the teddy to the table and was composed of three red and two white discs. The questions were formulated exactly as before, namely (1) Are there more red steps to go to the chair or more steps to go to the table? (2) Are there more steps to go to the chair or more steps to the table? And, as before, the inclusion of the adjective "red" led to a significant increase in difficulty.

On the other hand, McGarrigle was able to find circumstances in which the inclusion of an adjective made the question easier. In this case, the adjective qualified the whole set (rather than one of the sub-sets). Thus if three black toy cows and one white toy cow were laid on their sides, the question: "Are there more black cows or more sleeping cows?" was significantly easier than the question: "Are there more black cows or more cows?"

Research reported by Isen et al. (1975) relates interestingly to McGarrigle's class inclusion studies. Isen et al. used two classes (A and B) each divided into two sub-classes (A_1 and A_2; B_1 and B_2) and found that questions calling for comparison of A_1 with A (that is, traditional class inclusion questions) were no different in difficulty, over the age range 5 to 9, from questions calling for comparison of A_1 with B. In the latter comparison, as in one of McGarrigle's studies, the notion of reversibility has no relevance and cannot be invoked to explain errors.

Isen *et al.* propose an information processing model to account for their findings. Their model incorporates the notion that the main source of difficulty in these problems lies in achieving a correct interpretation of the experimenter's intended referent when he speaks of the class with which the sub-class is to be compared.

McGarrigle likewise concluded from his series of studies that only an explanation which took account of the ways children interpret language could possibly account for his findings. However, the class inclusion work left him convinced that the question the child answers depends not just on what the experimenter says (important as his precise words may often be, as McGarrigle's own work had shown) but also on what the experimenter *does*, even when this is formally irrelevant. This notion led to a study of conservation of length and number (McGarrigle and Donaldson, 1975) in which, in one condition, the transformations were carried out by a "naughty teddy bear" who tried to "spoil the game". Thus the changes were not presented as part of the experimenter's intended behaviour. And in this condition a very large proportion of pre-chool children conserved their initial judgments that the length and the number were the same.

Evidence of this kind has implications that go beyond the interpretation of responses to one particular task. Of these implications perhaps the most important is that we must no longer ignore the social or interpersonal aspects of the situations in which we endeavour to study children's concepts. If, as it now seems, the child's main purpose when we test him is to discover what *we* mean rather than what our words mean (in some formal sense) then we shall grossly distort our view of his cognitive skills if we fail to recognize what he is doing. Another way to put this is to say that one of the things which is conceptualized by the child is the experimenter*—and yet another is the experiment. If we do not take account of the complications thus introduced we cannot hope to make successful inferences from the child's responses to his conceptual capacities.

V. FURTHER DEVELOPMENT OF CONCEPTUALIZATION

(1) INTERACTION WITH LANGUAGE

Considerations such as these lead on to two main questions. The first is: how can we improve our methods of study?—a question which is of great importance, but which is outside the scope of this essay. The second is: how in the meantime are we to re-interpret the data that

* See J. R. Hayes (1972) for a discussion of this which deals specifically with class inclusion and accords well with the argument presented here.

we have, in the light of such understanding of the situation as we now possess? In particular, if the notion of the egocentric pre-school child has to be considerably modified, then what may have to take its place in a theoretical account of the shift from pre-operational to operational responding?

A first point to notice is that the position arrived at by McGarrigle is interestingly related to recent claims as to the ways in which younger children begin to learn languages. Among the strongest statements of these new claims is a paper by Macnamara (1972). In this paper Macnamara stands on its head the Chomskian argument that children have a capacity for language acquisition which is highly specific and in advance of the general level of their cognitive capacities. He proposes that, on the contrary, they are able to learn language because they possess a relatively developed capacity for interpreting situations. In situations of direct and immediate human interaction a child frequently apprehends the sense of what is going to be said before the words are uttered. He can then use his understanding of the speaker's meaning to crack the linguistic code.

In a more recent paper, Nelson (1974) pursues some of the implications of this way of thinking. She argues that traditional models of concept formation bear on the question: How does a child form a concept to fit a word?—whereas the question which we need to ask if we are to understand both conceptual and linguistic development in the early years is rather: How does a child match words to his concepts? Nelson emphasizes by italics the following sentence: "Thus while it can be stated that naming is dependent upon the existence of concepts, the existence of concepts need not lead directly and easily to naming them". For the child may form concepts based on relations that are salient to him yet not coded by the adult language.

The emphasis on "relations" is important in Nelson's model. She believes that we first categorize entities on the basis of the dynamic relationships into which they enter—relations to self, to others, to places, to actions. Only after this do we abstract static attributes, and proceed thence to the learning of names.

The main point that is common to the arguments of Macnamara and of Nelson is that children are able to begin to learn language because—and to the extent that—they are able to organize and interpret situations. If we link this with McGarrigle's studies we may postulate that, for a long time after the child has begun to crack the linguistic code, he continues to use his knowledge of situations and his sense of the probable meaning of the speaker to help him interpret what he hears.

There is indeed no doubt that we all continue to do this to some extent through the whole of our lives in ordinary everyday settings. But children do it more extensively than adults presumably because their cracking of the code is not complete. And it seems there is one other relevant difference. As adults we have learned, some of us at least, that there are certain situations—in particular the formal situations of mathematics or verbal reasoning—where it is not appropriate to take extralinguistic cues into account, where it is the meaning of statements with which we must be concerned. But it would hardly be surprising if young children failed to appreciate that this was expected of them (leaving aside for the moment the question of whether they are capable of exercising the control which it requires); for even fairly sophisticated adults appear to have a rather uncertain grasp of it. For example Taplin and Staudenmayer (1973) suggest that their findings concerning the performance of groups of undergraduates on tasks involving implication (if p then q), can best be interpreted by supposing that small and strictly irrelevant differences in task presentation can affect the way in which subjects assess the experimenter's intention, and hence the way in which they respond.

Donaldson (1963), working with children between the ages of 9 and 14, found that many of their errors in reasoning seemed to stem from a failure to adhere strictly to "the meaning" of the premises given; and that while errors of this kind grew less over time they did not by any means disappear. If we postulate two modes of reasoning—a formal mode, which confines itself to the given, and a "common-sense" mode, which does not—then many of the children seemed to alternate between one and the other even within a single problem, as if unsure of what was expected of them. Thus a child called Flora, aged 12, said: "I did have a temptation (*sic*) to choose 5 (the formally correct solution) but I thought 2 was more common-sense"—as indeed it was!

So we may perhaps conclude that, if children fail to confine themselves to interpreting "the meanings" of the statements used in the tasks we set them, this is at least partly because the basic human mode of dealing with language is to interpret it within a whole context of meaning arrived at in non-linguistic ways. It is then by a curious irony that the concern with the speaker's intention, which is a feature of this basic mode, gets our subjects into difficulty. It does so because of the paradoxical nature of a situation where it is the speaker's intention that his listeners should ignore his intention, except in so far as it is expressed in explicit verbal form. And it is noteworthy that research workers in cognitive development do not commonly try to communicate the strange nature of this situation to their subjects before they begin.

We shall return later to the topic of whether, if they only knew what they were meant to do, the children could do it; for this is important in relation to the way in which conceptual thinking develops to its most advanced levels. Meanwhile, however, there is more to be said on the subject of the influences which may shape a child's interpretation of the words he hears.

(2) THE EFFECTS OF CHILDREN'S EXPECTATIONS

So far the emphasis has been on attempts to arrive at speaker's meaning. However it seems on present evidence that the child also attends to non-linguistic cues of a different kind. These cues appear to be related to powerful expectations and predispositions which the child brings to the tasks we set him and which operate with some degree of independence (how great a degree is not yet clear) of anything which the experimenter may do or say.

I am not talking here about expectations which depend on a moment-to-moment fluctuating prediction of events about to take place, like the expectation that something will be said about food when a knife and fork are being laid on the table. The expectations in question are of a more stable and enduring kind. What I am suggesting is that the child is inclined to particular ways—among others that are in principle equally possible—of structuring his experience and that in consequence of this he has a number of predispositions to act in particular ways and attend to particular features of his environment. Some things are salient for him; and he expects to be spoken to about these things. These expectations are expressions of the ways in which the child is himself prone to interrogate the world. They indicate the nature of his thinking as well as the ways in which he acquires language. The argument concerning language is fully compatible with that proposed by Nelson (1974), namely that the child will most readily master those bits of language which express meanings compatible with the ways in which he is already disposed to structure or interpret the world. Indeed, if it is true that he is predisposed to structure or interpret the world in certain ways, how can it be otherwise?

Evidence pointing to the existence of expectations of the kind in question has come from a number of recent studies. Donaldson and Lloyd (1974) report research in which children between the ages of 3 and 5 were asked to make true/false judgments about the sentences "All the cars are in the garages" and "All the garages have cars in them" in two situations: one where there were three cars in a joined row of four garages and one where four cars occupied the four garages and a fifth car sat in full view outside. Systematic patterns of error occurred, the most common being to judge both of the sentences true when the garages were all filled (irrespective of whether or not there was a fifth car outside) and to judge both false otherwise. A powerful impression was given by the pattern of the children's behaviour that they expected to be asked whether each garage was occupied. Further studies (Donaldson and Lloyd, unpublished) confirmed the idea that what the children had been looking for and attending to was the fullness of the garages; for when different material was used—material where the notion of fullness had no relevance—different patterns of error were obtained.

Donaldson and McGarrigle (1974) report other evidence of a closely related kind. They showed their subjects an array consisting of two rows of cars arranged in one-to-one correspondence on display shelves placed one above the other. On one shelf there were five cars, on the other four. When the children were asked : "Are there more cars on this shelf or more cars on this shelf?" they normally chose the more numerous sub-set, as would be expected. However, when each row of cars was enclosed by a joined set of garages (which had no floors and so could be added or removed without disturbing the rows of cars in any way) a substantial number of the children changed their judgments. The crucial feature that accounted for this change appeared to be that the four cars were now enclosed by a structure of four garages, which was thus full, whereas the five cars were enclosed by a structure of six garages so that one garage was empty. The children's verbal comments made it clear that when subjects changed judgment and decided that there were now more cars in the row containing four than in the row containing five, it was fullness that was determining the change. And closely related results, using the same arrays of cars with garages present or absent, were obtained when the question was : "Are all the cars on this shelf?" When the garages were present, about one-third of the subjects denied that the row of five cars contained "all the cars" yet agreed to this statement for the row of four cars, that is for the garage structure that was full.

Clark (1973) reports studies of the comprehension of the prepositions "in", "on" and "under", by subjects aged between 1 year and 5 years. In her study the task was not to make a true/false judgment but to carry out an instruction. The main finding was that when the referential context was of such a kind that "in" was a reasonable interpretation—that is, when any kind of container was present—"in" was the interpretation which tended to be given to all three terms by children under $2\frac{1}{2}$. In circumstances where there was no container but there was a supporting surface, the preferred interpretation was "on". "Under" was never preferred. Thus responses to "in" tended to be most often correct, those to "under" least often correct.

What clues do findings like these provide about the nature of the systems which young children use to interpret language? On the face of it, they seem to show that certain words have a wider variety of possible meanings for children than for adults. Thus "more cars" can apparently be interpreted as "cars which fill a garage" or as "cars which form a longer row" and so on, with ready shifting from one interpretation to the other. And likewise "in" can be interpreted as "in" or "on" or "under". If this shifting were random we could simply postulate a relatively undifferentiated lexicon and leave the matter there. But since the shifts in interpretation are related in highly systematic ways to the referents of the utterances, such an account will not do. The explanation seems rather to be that there are non-linguistic rules interacting with the linguistic ones to produce the highly systematic response patterns that we obtain. This same conclusion was reached independently by Clark and by Donaldson and her colleagues. Donaldson and McGarrigle (1974) suggest the general name "local rules" for non-linguistic rules of this kind since they have to do with circumstances locally obtaining and since they determine a kind of "local meaning" for the language.

So if considerations of speaker's intention—that is, features of the interpersonal context—interact with the child's linguistic knowledge to affect his interpretation of utterances, so also, it seems, do certain features of the impersonal context. It appears that some features of situations are salient and compelling for children and will, as it were, pull the interpretation in their own direction. What is not at all clear as yet is how powerful this pull may be—that is, just how far the distortion of "the meaning" of the language can go. What *is* clear is that the closer an utterance comes to the child's expectancies—both the expectancies that derive from his own modes of interrogating and structuring the world and those that derive from his reading of the experimenter's behaviour—then the more likely he is to interpret that utterance as the adult intends.

It is interesting in this connection to note a finding reported by Bloom (1974) to the effect that children between 19 months and 3 years produced far fewer utterances in response to what someone else had said than they produced spontaneously; and—more important for the present discussion—that communicative effectiveness* was greater for "utterances that were not responses to adult utterances, that is utterances that originated with what the child was thinking about, or did, or saw". For in such cases conflict between the structure of the language and the structure of the child's experiences will not arise.

In summary, then, the argument is this: there is now a considerable

---

* Bloom does not say how this was assessed.

amount of converging evidence which suggests that the shift from "pre-operational" to "concrete operational" responding is less important in overcoming the rigidities and the irreversibilities of an egocentric conceptualization of the world than is the emerging ability to respond with close attention to "the meaning" of utterances *even when this meaning is an unexpected one*, not supported by context in any way. But in speaking here of *"emerging ability"* we must not forget the issue of whether the child realizes that responding with close attention to linguistic meaning is the appropriate thing to do.

VI. THE EFFECTS OF CONSCIOUS AWARENESS

What, then, causes this ability to emerge, or brings the child to this realization? It seems likely that the change is closely linked to the process of becoming literate. Support for this notion comes from a variety of sources (cf., for instance, de Laguna, 1927; Bruner, 1974; Olson, 1975). Oral language is always language embedded in some kind of a context (though its referents may or may not be in the here and now). Written language endures unchanging across space and time, and by virtue of this there is pressure for it to become explicit, self-sufficing, context-free; so that ultimately, as Olson puts it, "the meaning is in the text". Olson regards written language as a necessary means for "the particular mental achievements we designate as conceptual intelligence".

Now clearly it is an essential characteristic of strict logical reasoning that only what is stated in the premises—and all of what is stated there—must be used in deducing the conclusions. For this kind of activity, the meaning must be in the text. One might argue, then, returning to the interpretation of pre-operational behaviour, that as literate adults we have come to assume that the meaning is in the spoken utterance as well, whereas the children we test do not entertain any such unnatural notion. Similar arguments can likewise be used to interpret certain cross-cultural findings (see Cole and Scribner, 1974).

However, it would be a major error to suppose that literacy can guarantee logic. Studies of adult subjects by Henle (1962) and Wason and Johnson-Laird (1972), for instance, make this very clear. And it is worth noting that Wallington (1973), working with pre-school children, found that some of her subjects, on certain tasks calling for deductive reasoning, responded in very much the same manner as a control group of adults, both groups showing the well-established tendency to handle implication as if it were equivalence.

Thus there is no reason to think that the shift to concrete operational

11—CP * *

thinking and the further changes which take place thereafter, can be accounted for entirely by reference to the growing recognition that utterances have what Grice (1968) calls "timeless meaning". This is clearly not sufficient. At the very least there is also the issue of growth in what we may call cognitive control : growth in the ability to direct attention voluntarily, resisting irrelevance, and to manipulate systematically considerations of compatibility and incompatibility, possibility and impossibility, which are crucial for the processes of inference. The question is how closely these may all be inter-related in the actual course of development.

One suggestion is that the change underlying them all is growth in the awareness of one's own thinking : the expansion of the conceptual system in the direction of increasing ability to represent itself. What might help to bring this about? And what might the consequences of such an expansion be?

We do not have much hard knowledge as yet about the growth of awareness. Most psychologists have been nervous of the subject for too long. But Piaget, who has opened up so many pathways in the past, has begun also to blaze this trail for us.

On the basis of a series of studies of the ability of children to give accounts of their own actions, in situations ranging from crawling on hands and knees to solving problems like the Tower of Hanoi, Piaget (1974) builds a theoretical account of what he calls "la prise de conscience". His main point is that consciousness is not just like a light that is suddenly turned on. Rather it is the result of a process of conceptualization—a process involving the reconstruction of what it brings into awareness, hence often producing retroactive change, so that the things of which we become conscious are altered by the very fact of our awareness of them.

Since "la prise de conscience" is a process, there are degrees of awareness. These, Piaget suggests, are a function of different degrees of integration—that is, of the extent to which one mental state is integrated with those that precede or follow it within some system of representation. At an elementary level there is transient consciousness, linked to immediate perception and fading with it. At a higher level perception is interpreted or conceptualized, and one moves from action to the representation of action, from "action schemas" to genuine concepts. This movement implies the growth of an enduring awareness. Typically this awareness develops as the subject engages in a more active consideration of possibilities of action; and it can be furthered, Piaget suggests, by the attempt to talk about what one is doing. Speaking of the activity of crawling on hands and knees, he says that when the child attempts to describe this he is led to hesitate between various possibilities before putting a hand or a knee forward and this forces him to choose, thereby bringing the formerly automatic and unreflecting action into the realm of consciousness, and by the same token increasing voluntary control.

If we apply this to mental acts then "stopping to think" and talking about our thinking would be critical for progress. It is well-known that pre-school children often disappoint experimenters who hope to get "verbalizations" and "justifications" from them. Blank (1974), however, suggests that children will talk more effectively about their responses if they are not asked to do so in the presence of some visually perceptible array relevant to the task. She claims that when the child is dealing with immediate visual experience he does not rely on language; he does not bring his linguistic powers fully into use. If, however, the test objects are removed from view and he is then asked to talk about his responses he does so much more effectively. It could be that it would encourage children to become conscious of their thinking if we were to put them in this kind of situation more often.

Now these considerations bring us once more, though by a different path, to the significance of the contrast between spoken and written language. It may be that the acquisition of literacy has unique significance for the expansion of the conceptual system in the direction of self-awareness. For it seems likely that learning to study the written word is particularly apt to promote conscious reflection about at least one very important act of thought—namely the apprehension of meaning. If it is through hesitation between possibilities that awareness grows, then clearly growth of awareness of the processes of interpreting utterances is more likely to take place with a written text. It is more likely both because of the context-embedded way in which we learn spoken language in the first instance, with the whole context shaping the sense of the words for us, so that questions of choice hardly arise; and because of the external and enduring character of the printed page. There is quite simply time to pause. Or there ought to be, if those who teach us will allow it. One may assume that the extent to which the learning of reading promotes conscious reflection about meaning will depend greatly on modes of teaching. And this is true not just for the early stages of learning. One need only think of "rapid reading courses" and contrast these with the advice given by I. A. Richards in his book *How to Read a Page* (Richards, 1943).

In a most intriguing study called "Learning to think about reading", Reid (1966) explored concepts of the reading process as they developed in children during their first year in school. Reid found that the children started off with very little idea of what reading *was*, and that they were very ill-equipped to talk of the activity, being much confused as to the meanings of "numbers", "letters", "words", "names" and so on. Yet as the year went on some of them became able to speak in illuminating ways about their own efforts to decode the written text. A child called Tommy made the following comment on his learning of the word "kitten".

> "When I get half the other half goes half off. I get 'n' in the first half when it's supposed to be last. I get it jumbled up. I say 'ket-nin'."

Then, speaking of his ultimate triumph :

> "The day after I got it like anything, 'cos I seen the 'i' and the 'n'."

Reid concludes that if a child is helped to talk about reading, this should help him to learn to read and even help "his general logical thinking and the more sophisticated thinking about language he will be required later to do".

We should not, of course, assume that learning to "reflect on one's own reflections", as Coleridge put it, can come *only* through literacy. But if learning to read is particularly effective in encouraging movement in the direction of increased reflective self-awareness while at the same time it helps us to develop the kind of conception of "timeless meaning" which both logic and mathematics require, then Reid's claim certainly does not go too far.

The ability to reflect on one's own reflections is placed by Piaget at the heart of his account of mature adult thought. The formal operational thinker is one who can engage in "second-order operations"— that is, he can operate on the operations that constitute his own thinking. And at the formal stage this is held to involve a high degree of awareness. The processes of "reflective abstraction", by which we abstract the properties not of objects but of our own actions, develop into "reflected abstraction" (Piaget, 1974) and we can then, for example, consciously and systematically compare alternative strategies and consider what they have in common and how they differ. This yields great advance in deliberate control.

Not everyone would agree, however, that mature adult thought is most adequately to be conceived of in this way. Lunzer, for instance, doubts it (Lunzer, 1973). He accepts as the hallmark of *concrete* operational thinking awareness of the criteria that one is using to guide one's actions; and he cites as an outcome of the growth of this awareness the ability to classify a set of objects according to one criterion and then, by an act of deliberate choice, to break up that classification and re-sort the objects in another way.* But it is one thing to be aware of using a plan. It is another to think about the nature of a plan considered as a type of mental phenomenon, or to reflect on the means by which plans are formed. It is as to the significance of this latter kind of activity in the thinking of ordinary adults that Lunzer appears to have doubts. Lunzer argues that, just as we can speak very well without being conscious of the rules which govern our speech production, so we can think very well without consciousness of the means by which we do it. He further points out that when we bring the rules of grammar into awareness we do not necessarily speak the better for it; and he suggests that, similarly, consciousness of what he calls "the system as a whole"—that is, the conceptual system—need not necessarily make our thinking any more effective.

What really concerns Lunzer, however, when he uses this argument is the risk of too close an identification between effective thinking and "the rules of logic". In the context of a discussion of conceptualization it is hardly possible to question the importance of the fact that we ultimately can become conscious not only of objects and events in the external world but also of our own thinking about these things. To illustrate the kind of effect this can have we may return to the issue of the apprehension of possibility that was raised at the beginning of this chapter. A quite young child, as we saw then, certainly had some intuition of possible states of affairs in the sense that he is aware, at least fleetingly, of uncertainty about particular external happenings and tries to resolve this uncertainty. But it would seem to be a very different matter to conceive of "possibility".

One way to focus on what may be the most significant aspect of the difference is to contrast the attitude that sees a possibility as something to be converted to a certainty with all possible speed, and the attitude that "entertains" a possibility, regarding it as something to be played with. A possibility is always a mental event. But it is only when it can be represented and attended to as a mental event that it can be played with. And there is a strong case to be made for the claim that playing with possibilities is one of the very important features of developed forms of creative thinking.

Awareness of the act of entertaining possibilities may be relevant to what Lunzer regards as one important characteristic of mature thought (though he is careful not to claim that it plays a part in all advanced thinking). This is what he calls "acceptance of lack of closure", or the ability to tolerate, for a while, unresolved doubt. Per-

* This is well established as an important turning-point in the development of classificatory ability. See, for instance, Inhelder and Piaget (1963), Werner (1948), Vygotsky (1962).

haps it is through becoming aware of possibilities as mental events that we can learn to tolerate them for a time in the course of a sustained and directed problem solving endeavour.

VII. CONCLUSION

It seems fitting to end this chapter by acknowledging that, in the attempt to understand conceptual development at the present time, a considerable ability to accept lack of closure is called for. Yet I believe that real—and in some ways surprisingly rapid—progress has been made over the last few years, with many different lines of research converging in ways which suggest that a new pattern is taking form. It has been my main purpose to give some idea of what the shape of this emerging pattern may prove to be.

REFERENCES

Berlyne, D. (1965). *Structure and Direction in Thinking.* New York: Wiley.

Blank, M. (1974). Cognitive functions of language in the pre-school years. *Developmental Psychology, 10,* 229–45.

Bloom, L. (1974). Talking, understanding and thinking. In R. L. Schiefelbusch and L. L. Lloyd (Eds.), *Language Perspectives: Acquisition, Retardation and Intervention.* New York: Macmillan.

Bower, T. G. R. (1974). *Development in Infancy.* San Francisco: Freeman.

Bower, T. G. R. and Wishart, J. (1972). The effect of motor skill on object permanence. *Cognition, 1,* 165–72.

Brown, I. (1973). The development of the object concept—inside is not behind. University of Edinburgh (Final Honours thesis).

Brown, R. W. (1973). *A First Language.* London: Allen and Unwin.

Bruner, J. S. (1974). *The Relevance of Education.* Harmondsworth. Penguin.

Bruner, J. S. (1975). The ontogenesis of speech acts. *Journal of Child Language, 2,* 1–19.

Clark, E. (1973). Non-linguistic strategies and the acquisition of word meanings. *Cognition, 2,* 161–82.

Cole, M. and Scribner, S. (1974). *Culture and Thought: A Psychological Introduction.* New York: Wiley.

De Laguna, G. A. (1927). *Speech: its Function and Development.* Indiana University Press.

Donaldson, M. (1963). *A Study of Children's Thinking.* London: Tavistock.

Donaldson, M. (1971). Preconditions of inference. In J. K. Cole (Ed.), *Nebraska Symposium on Motivation, 1971.* Lincoln, Nebraska: Nebraska University Press.

Donaldson, M. and Lloyd, P. (1974). Sentences and situations: children's judgments of match and mismatch. In F. Bresson (Ed.), *Problèmes Actuels en Psycholinguistique.* Paris: Centre National de la Recherche Scientifique.

Donaldson, M. and Lloyd, P. (unpublished). Cognitive development in pre-school children: the comprehension of quantifiers. Final Report to the Social Science Research Council.

Donaldson, M. and McGarrigle, J. (1974). Some clues to the nature of semantic development. *Journal of Child Language, 1,* 185–94.

Evans, W. F. and Gratch, G. (1972). The Stage IV error in Piaget's theory of object concept development: difficulties in object conceptualisation or spatial localization? *Child Development, 43,* 682–5.

Fishbein, H. D., Lewis, S. and Keiffer, K. (1972). Children's understanding of spatial relations: co-ordination of perspectives. *Developmental Psychology, 7,* 21–33.

Frege, G. (1956). The thought: a logical inquiry. *Mind, 65,* 289–311.

Grice, H. P. (1968). Utterer's meaning, sentence-meaning and word-meaning. *Foundations of Language, 4,* 225–42.

Harris, P. L. (1974). Perseverative search at a visible empty place by young infants. *Journal of Experimental Child Psychology, 18,* 535–42.

Hayes, J. R. (1972). The child's conception of the experimenter. In S. Farnham-Diggory (Ed.), *Information Processing in Children.* New York: Academic Press.

Henle, M. (1962). The relationship between logic and thinking. *Psychological Review, 69,* 366–78.

Hughes, M. (1975). Egocentrism in preschool children. University of Edinburgh (unpublished Doctoral Thesis).

Huttenlocher, J. and Presson, C. C. (1973). Mental rotation and the perspective problem. *Cognitive Psychology, 4,* 277–99.

Inhelder, B. and Piaget, J. (1963). *The Early Growth of Logic in the Child.* London: Routledge and Kegan Paul.

Isen, A. M., Riley, C. A., Tucker, T. and Trabasso, T. (1975) How does a child understand part-whole relations? *Child Development,* (in press).

Light, P. (1974). The role-taking skills of four-year-old children. University of Cambridge (unpublished Doctoral Thesis).

Lloyd, P. (1975). Communication in preschool children. University of Edinburgh (unpublished Doctoral Thesis).

Lunzer, E. A. (1973). Formal reasoning: a reappraisal. Keynote paper presented to the 2nd Conference of the Jean Piaget Society, Philadelphia.

Macnamara, J. (1972). Cognitive basis of language learning in infants. *Psychological Review, 79,* 1–13.

McGarrigle, J. (unpublished). Language interpretation in studies of cognitive development.

McGarrigle, J. and Donaldson, M. (1975). Conservation accidents. *Cognition, 3,* 341–50.

Masangkay, Z. S., McFluskey, K. A., McIntyre, C. W., Sims-Knight, J., Vaughn, B. E. and Flavell, J. H. (1974). The early development of inferences about the visual percepts of others. *Child Development, 45,* 357–66.

Nelson, K. (1974). Concept, word and sentence: interrelations in acquisition and development. *Psychological Review, 81,* 267–85.

Newson, J. (1974). Towards a theory of infant understanding. *Bulletin of the British Psychological Society, 27,* 251–7.

Olson, D. (1975). The language of experience: on natural language and formal education. Invited address to the British Psychological Society, Nottingham.

Piaget, J. (1955). *The Child's Construction of Reality.* London: Routledge and Kegan Paul.

Piaget, J. (1974). *La Prise de Conscience.* Paris: Presses Universitaires de France.

Pieraut-Le Bonniec, G. (1974). *Le Raisonnement Modal.* The Hague: Mouton.

Pikas, A. (1966). *Abstraction and Concept Formation.* Cambridge, Mass.: Harvard University Press.

Reid, J. F. (1966). Learning to think about reading. *Education Research, 9,* 56–62.

Richards, I. A. (1943). *How to Read a Page.* London: Routledge and Kegan Paul.

Taplin, J. E. and Staudenmayer, H. (1973). Interpretation of abstract conditional sentences in deductive reasoning. *Journal of Verbal Learning and Verbal Behavior, 12,* 530–42.

Trevarthan, C. B. (1974). Conversations with a two-year-old. *New Scientist,* 2nd May, 230–5.

Vygotsky, L. S. (1962). *Thought and Language.* Cambridge, Mass.: M.I.T. Press.

Wallington, B. (1973). Some aspects of the development of reasoning in preschool children. University of Edinburgh (unpublished Doctoral Thesis).

Wason, P. and Johnson-Laird, P. N. (1972). *Psychology of Reasoning—Structure and Content.* New York: Batsford.

Webb, R. A., Massar, B. and Nadolny, T. (1972). Information on strategies in the young child's search for hidden objects, *Child Development, 43,* 91–104.

Werner, H. (1948). *The Comparative Psychology of Mental Development.* New York: International Universities Press.

CHAPTER 8

Developmental Strategies for Language

Richard F. Cromer

I. INTRODUCTION

Two decades ago, Bruner, Goodnow and Austin (1956) posed the question, "How do people achieve the information necessary for isolating and learning a concept?" In the course of analyzing the data from a series of experiments on concept attainment, these authors arrived at the conceptualization of "strategies" to account for the behaviour of individuals in various laboratory experiments. A strategy describes regularities observed in decision-making. In a concept attainment task, subjects were first shown a positive instance of a concept on a card. They were then allowed to choose cards for testing, one at a time, and were told whether or not they were positive instances of the concept. Particular strategies were inferred from the patterns of decisions made on successive cards. These strategies included simultaneous scanning (testing hypotheses to see which were still tenable and which had been eliminated), successive scanning (limiting new choices to those instances that provided a direct test of a particular hypothesis), conservative focusing (finding a positive instance of the concept to serve as a focus, and then making a sequence of choices in which one attribute at a time was altered), and focus gambling (in which more than one attribute value was changed at a time). The authors were careful to point out that such strategies did not necessarily represent conscious plans by people for achieving and utilizing information. They were merely inferred by the experimenters from the pattern of decisions actually observed.

During the twenty years since the publication of the work on strategies, there has been a renewed interest in the acquisition and development of language. This has partly resulted from the theoretical attack on traditional theories of learning as being incapable of explaining language acquisition (Chomsky, 1959), and from a number of empirical studies which indicate that the child is engaged in a very active process in acquiring language rather than passively responding to differential frequencies of language input and reinforcement (see, e.g., Bellugi-Klima, 1969; Brown, 1973; McNeill, 1970; and Miller and McNeill, 1969). It is this change of emphasis to the child as an active organism which has sparked an interest in the methods by which he goes about acquiring his native language, and has led to the increasingly frequent use of the term "strategy" to describe observed developmental language behaviour. In this chapter, a number of different strategies which have been proposed to account for language behaviour will be explored. First, a number of strategies apparently used by very young children will be reviewed. Some of these strategies may help the child to "get into" the linguistic system, although such a notion is also open to dispute. At some point, it appears that certain perceptual strategies become relatively more important than the earlier action-based strategies. Experiments on these perceptual strategies, particularly those concerned with word order, will be discussed in some detail. As part of that discussion, the problem of individual differences will be raised, and some strategies used by some children will be reviewed. In a fifth section, the emphasis will be changed to one in which broader cognitive strategies associated with language are considered. The sixth section will raise the issue of whether there are any specifically linguistic grammatical strategies which are used in the acquisition of language. Finally, the entire notion of "strategy" as applied to language acquisition will be examined, and we can ask whether we have learned anything about that mysterious process, language acquisition, from such an approach.

II. SOME EARLY STRATEGIES

It has often been assumed that children at a very early age acquire the word order of the grammar of active declarative sentences. It is said that the extension of this word order to other grammatical forms leads to misinterpretations of such forms as the passive, in which the first noun is mistakenly believed to be the actor. For example, children about 4 years of age will often interpret sentences like "The black cat was chased by the white cat" as it if it meant "The black cat chased the white cat". As part of a study of this phenomenon, Strohner and Nelson (1974) discovered that the usual assumption that very young children understand the word order of *active* sentences may be false. They presented various sentences to children of age 2 to 5 years. The child's task was to carry out the action of the sentence with various puppets and toys which were provided. As will be seen in a later section, several investigators have examined the differences between what are called reversible and non-reversible passives. The example just mentioned with the cats, in which either noun could logically serve as the actor, is a reversible passive, but sentences like "The marble was rolled by the boy" cannot be reversed and still make sense. Strohner and Nelson, however, extended their testing to active sentences as well. Thus, they included not only the various types of passives, but also reversible active sentences and what they called improbable active sentences. An example of the latter would be, "The fence jumps the horse", for which the "probable" form would be "The horse jumps the fence". A reversible active sentence, of course, would be one in which either noun could serve as the actor, as in "The boy hit the girl". The results on the 4- and 5-year-olds show strong evidence for a word order strategy, but the results from the younger children present quite a different picture. The 2-year-olds were not tested on passive sentences, but the 3-year-olds were 100 per cent wrong on improbable passive sentences, which is not surprising since such a result is predicted by both a word order strategy and by a strategy based on the probability of the event. However, the 2- and 3-year-olds, while 100 per cent correct on probable active sentences, were nearly always wrong on improbable active sentences (83 per cent wrong by 2-year-olds, 90 per cent wrong by 3-year-olds). Strohner and Nelson interpret this as evidence of a "probable event strategy" used by the younger children, which leads them to interpret sentences describing improbable events as if they referred to probable events. Furthermore, they point out that although by the age of 5, a child knows even more about event probabilities, such information only occasionally leads the older child to make errors in interpreting improbable sentences. It is also of note that the younger children, when they are not able to extract information about the actor and the object of sentences from syntactic structure, nevertheless do not behave randomly. Instead, they are likely to apply extra-syntactic strategies such as the probable event strategy in order to interpret sentences.

It is even possible to affect the "probability" of some sentences by the surrounding linguistic context. In one interesting experiment, Hazel Dewart (1975) studied the comprehension of passive sentences by twenty children aged 3 years and 5 months to 4 years and 10 months. Some sentences were given without any context. For example, children had to act out with hand puppets sentences like "The duck is bitten by the monkey". But some sentences were embedded in an "appropriate context" ("Poor duck. The duck is bitten by the monkey." and "Bad monkey. The duck is bitten by the monkey."), while others were given an "inappropriate context" ("Bad duck. The duck is bitten by the monkey." and "Poor monkey. The duck is bitten by the monkey.") When the children were divided into those who knew passives and those who did not (as judged from the no context condition), significant differences emerged. Of the group of thirteen children who failed no-context passives, the inappropriate context condition led to 90 per cent errors (against 63 per cent errors on the appropriate context condition). In other words, sentence comprehension in $3\frac{1}{2}$- to $4\frac{1}{2}$-year-olds can be affected by a short linguistic context which bears on the appropriateness or likelihood of the action. But again this appropriateness affects mainly those children who do not otherwise know how to interpret the structure, and has very little affect on children with adequate syntactic knowledge. This matches the results of Strohner and Nelson on event probability.

Recent research is beginning to explore the use of other extra-linguistic strategies by young children to interpret certain kinds of sentences. Margaret Donaldson and her associates have been looking at the development of the understanding of certain relational terms such as "more" and "less" (Donaldson and Balfour, 1968; Donaldson and Wales, 1970). She has recently proposed (Donaldson and McGarrigle, 1974) that lexical and syntactic rules, in some situations, do not provide enough guidance for assigning truth values for such terms. Instead, the child applies a number of what are called "local rules", which, while not linguistic in any narrow sense, interact with the lexical and syntactic rules when the child is interpreting the sentence. As Donaldson and McGarrigle put it, these local rules determine which features of the referent will be selected as criteria for the assignment of meaning when the child's linguistic rules leave the matter vague. In their experiment, children were presented with differing numbers of cars on two shelves, five cars on one shelf, and four on the other. They were asked, "Are there more cars on this shelf or more cars on this shelf?", with the experimenter indicating the two shelves in turn. Then, a set of garages was placed over the cars. The set of garages placed on the shelf with five cars, had six garages so that one garage remained empty. The other garage set consisted of four garages, so that every car on the other shelf had a garage over it. The children were then asked the same question again. Of the forty children aged 3 years to 5 years and 2 months, twenty-one were consistently correct both with the cars alone and with the garages, as adults presumably would be. Another five children consistently chose the less numerous subset as being "more", with or without the garages in place. But fourteen children changed their choice when garages were introduced or removed. Of these, thirteen correctly chose the greater number of cars as being "more" in the absence of garages, but chose the smaller subset as being "more" when the garages were in place. They would point at the shelf with four cars and say such things as "There's more on that shelf because there's enough to go in there". Donaldson and Mc-Garrigle suggest that instead of assuming that the "meaning" of an utterance changes frequently for the young child, it is more likely that the child is guided by local rules which determine that an utterance be interpreted first one way and then another. There are "more" cars in the garage structure which is full although shorter, yet "more" cars in the longer row when the garages are not there. Only as children grow older will purely linguistic constraints on the interpretation of such utterances become stronger, and the local rules correspondingly come to have a reduced part to play in interpretation. It is not yet clear what these various local rules may be that influence the interpretations of sentences by young children. Perhaps the probable event strategy mentioned earlier is one type of local rule. Other rules, such as the judgment of differing amounts, would presumably be based on broad developmental cognitive strategies which would be observed in non-linguistic behaviour as well.

Some local rules may be highly specific. Eve Clark (1973b) has proposed two rules for the interpretation of prepositions and has suggested that such rules may interact with the child's linguistic hypotheses about the meanings of words. In one experiment, seventy children between the ages of 1 year and 6 months and 5 years were given toy animals and asked to place them "in", "on", or "under" six reference points. Two of these six items, a box on its side and a tunnel, allow either "in" or "on". Two more, a dump truck and a crib, allow "in" or "under", and the last two, a table and a bridge, allow "on" or "under". The child had to place twenty-four items, i.e., eight for each of the three prepositions. Each preposition occurred twice with each of the four reference points it was allowed by. The results appeared to show that even the youngest children knew the meaning of "in". "On" appeared to be of intermediate difficulty, and "under" was the developmentally latest acquisition. However, Clark proposed that two strategies for placing the materials could account for the results. One rule says that if the reference point is a container then X is *in* it. The second rule says that if the reference point has a horizontal surface, then X is *on* it. These non-linguistic rules are strategies used by young children in a comprehension test in the virtual absence of comprehension. If one looks carefully at what possibilities are allowed by each of the six reference points, it becomes clear that the use of these two rules would lead to results in which the child would appear to know the meaning of "in", to have no knowledge of "under", and to perform intermediately on "on". It is also apparent however, that such an analysis tells us nothing about how the child acquires language. It merely tells us how he answers questions about the meaning of sentences when he does not yet possess the linguistic structure (semantic or syntactic) necessary for correct interpretation. But Clark proposes that such non-linguistic strategies may play a role in the acquisition of language. Clark cites the suggestion by Slobin (1973) that the main determinant of linguistic acquisition is cognitive complexity. One problem with such a proposal, however, is the difficulty of quantifying or measuring cognitive complexity. Clark proposes that non-linguistic strategies may provide the basis for the child's linguistic hypotheses about such phenomena as the meaning of words, and as such could be used as a kind of cognitive measure. For example, if a strategy coincides with semantic knowledge, there is nothing for the child to learn. But when a strategy does not coincide, the child has much to learn in order to acquire the meaning. In terms of Clark's experiment, "in" is cognitively simpler than "on" or "under" because it requires minimal adjustment of the child's hypothesis about its meaning. Clark also mentions the possibility of additional non-linguistic strategies which might explain the order of acquisition of other linguistic behaviours. A strategy such as "Always pick the greater amount" would lead to children treating the word "less" as if it means "more" as Donaldson and Balfour (1968) and Donaldson and Wales (1970) have found. A strategy of retaining the description of a series of events in time in the order in which they occurred might lead to the linguistic hypothesis that the order of mention reflects actual order. This has been observed by several investigators (Clark, 1971, 1973a; Cromer, 1968, 1974b; Ferreiro, 1971).

More recently, Wilcox and Palermo (1975) have challenged Clark's explanation of the acquisition of "in", "on", and "under". Rather than specific rules about "in" and "on" as Clark proposed, they considered that the results she obtained might be due to the objects she used in her experiment, and that a more general explanation was possible. With three age groups whose mean ages were 1 year and 9 months, 2 years and 3 months, and 2 years and 9 months, Wilcox and Palermo tested comprehension of the same terms, but using different materials. Furthermore, they used sentences which were what they called congruent or incongruent with the materials. For example, with a toy truck and a toy road, they might give a congruent sentence ("Put the road under the truck") or an incongruent one ("Put the road in the truck"). It can be seen that these terms are used in the way "probable" and "improbable" events were used in the Strohner and Nelson study, and "appropriate" and "inappropriate" context were used in Dewart's experiment. The results using this material were very different from

Clark's. Many children now treated "in" as if it meant "under" or "on", and they treated "on" as if it meant "under". Wilcox and Palermo suggest two reasons for these results. One is the tendency to put objects in their most congruent contextual relationship. This was most pronounced in the older children and may be due to their know-ledge of what relations objects should be in. Notice that these older groups are ages 2 years and 3 months and 2 years and 9 months and are thus equivalent to Strohner and Nelson's youngest groups. Here is more evidence then of children aged approximately 2 and 3 years using a probable event strategy. However, the youngest group in Wilcox and Palermo's experiment actually did better on the incongruent (improb-able) tasks. It was the older children who were affected by congruency (probability). This too represents a development. Children below 2 years old use a different strategy. Wilcox and Palermo suggest that the youngest children are following a tendency to make the simplest motor response. Their errors are motor errors, and this leads them to make such responses as putting the road "in" rather than "under" the truck.

Huttenlocher and her associates have also studied the motor respon-ses of children and the effect they may have on performance with some types of verbal material. In one test of children's comprehension of relational statements of the type, "The red block is on top of the green block" (Huttenlocher and Strauss, 1968), children performed differ-ently depending on which block they had to place. The task was to place a block which they held in their hands in relation to a block fixed to the middle rung of a ladder in such a way as to match the experimenter's verbal description. The results revealed that it was much easier for children to place the block they were holding if it was the grammatical subject of the descriptive sentence than if it was the grammatical object. For example, it was easier to perform the action required by "The red block is on top of the green block" if they were holding the red block (corresponding to the grammatical subject) than if they were holding the green block (corresponding to the grammatical object). Huttenlocher and Strauss suggested that this was so because comprehension is aided by a correspondence between the form of a linguistic description and the extralinguistic state of affairs. Further-more, in this case, the block being held is the "actor" (the block to be moved), and the grammatical subject of a sentence often plays the role of the actor. However, as this was confounded by temporal order of the mention of the two blocks, a second experiment was undertaken (Huttenlocher, Eisenberg and Strauss, 1968). In the second experiment, both active and passive sentences were used. Children had to carry out the action of placing a truck which they held in their hands (the mobile truck) in relation to a fixed truck so that their truck was pulling, push-ing, being pulled by or being pushed by the fixed truck. The results showed that for active statements, it was easier to place the mobile truck when it was the grammatical subject, as the earlier experiment had shown. But for passive sentences it was easier to place the mobile truck when it was the grammatical object (i.e., the logical subject or real actor). In other words, the ease of placing the truck matched the action of the sentence—the logical rather than the surface grammati-cal feature. Children, then, seem to co-ordinate the logical subject and the actor.

The children in the Huttenlocher experiments were 9 and 10 years of age. The kind of motor preference mentioned earlier was said to be a strategy used by very young children, at ages prior to their recogni-tion of the importance of word order. Hazel Dewart (1972) obtained results similar to Huttenlocher's but with somewhat younger children —5 and 6 years old. In later experiments (Dewart, 1975), using 4-, 5-, and 6-year-old children, a strategy based on treating the mobile toy as actor was observed. In this experiment, the child had to carry out the actions described under conditions in which sometimes the *actor* was mobile (the toy to be the actor was placed in the child's hand before the sentence was given), and sometimes the *object* was mobile (the child held the toy to be acted upon). First the child performed six passive sentences holding neither toy (no context condition). This was done to gauge his ability on passive sentences generally. Then a pretest was given consisting of active sentences. The test itself consisted of twelve passive sentences, six with the actor mobile and six with the object mobile. The results were in agreement with the Huttenlocher studies. There were significantly fewer errors in the actor mobile condi-tion, and there were significantly more errors on the object mobile condition than even on the no context condition. Furthermore, the context did not affect the known active sentences at these ages. Since the active sentences were not affected, one may assume that the results are not just due to an assumption by children that they are supposed to move the toy in their hand. Some children consistently used a strategy of treating the mobile toy as the actor for any passive sentence. If one compares children who knew the passive with those who did not (in the no context condition), it becomes apparent that children use a strategy when they do not know how to interpret passive sen-tences. Of children who were correct on the no context passives, none were misled into using the strategy that the mobile toy was the actor. But many children who did not yet know the passive form used that kind of action strategy. Many of these, indeed, had used strategies in answering the unknown passives. For example, thirteen children used a strategy in which they consistently treated the first noun as the actor for all passive sentences in the no context condition (a strategy which will be discussed in the next section). Of these, seven abandoned that word order strategy on the twelve passive test sentences and used the contextual cue of treating the mobile toy as the actor. It appears, then, that a child uses an extra-linguistic strategy when he does not know how to make use of grammatical structure in the adult manner. At the much younger age of about 1 year and 9 months Wilcox and Palermo tested, when children did not know the meaning of "in", "on", and "under", and before they knew or made use of event probabilities, they used a strategy of making the simplest motor response. Similarly, some children of 4 and 5 years of age, who might normally be making use of a word order strategy on structures they do not yet know, use a motor-related strategy of consistently treating the easily mobile toy (the one in their hand) as the actor.

It was noted that the effect in the Huttenlocher studies was not due to position in the sentence as such, but to the role of the item. Thus, if a child was holding a toy, he performed with fewer errors if that toy served in an "actor" role. The actor is the surface grammatical subject in active sentences, but is the surface grammatical object in passive sentences. It has been suggested, therefore, that perhaps performance is related to the role that is played by particular grammatical units, rather than to the grammatical units themselves. This would call for analysis along the lines of a case grammar (Fillmore, 1968) or one of the more semantic grammars (for instance, Chafe, 1970). In a series of experiments, Suci and Hamacher (1972) found some evidence that sentence processing by undergraduate subjects was more affected by the action role of the noun in the sentence (that is, whether the noun was agent or patient) than by the position or grammatical category. In an experiment on 10- and 12-year-old children, Suci and Hamacher investigated whether the effect on processing was indeed that of action role or whether it was based on case grammar units. Suci and Hamacher claim that for Chafe (1970) there are two dimensions to the agent category : the action role of the noun-verb relation and the animateness of the noun. Fillmore's case units (1968) divide the domain somewhat differently. The agentive and instrumental cases are really both agents, but the agentive is an animate agent ("The man opened the door") while the instrumental is an inanimate agent ("The key opened the door"). Similarly, one might say that the dative and objective cases differ in that the dative is an animate patient and the objective is an inanimate patient. Questions about the subject-adjective or object-adjective relations were asked, and the response latencies timed. Adult subjects had been found to be affected by both action role and animacy. Thus, case grammar distinctions seemed to be observed. On the 10- and 12-year-olds, however, it was found that case units by themselves (agentive, instrumental, dative, and objective) did not produce significant differences in processing. But there were effects due to action role. Suci and Hamacher concluded that action role is a psychologically valid concept for children but that the case units were not. It appears, then, that the Suci and Hamacher results show that animacy is important for adults but not for 10- and 12-year-old children. However, there are drawbacks both in the technique that they used and in the fact that the sentences for the children and for the adults were not the same. It is very difficult to interpret their complex results at some points. Other investigators have observed that animacy is a very important variable in the interpretation of sentences by young children. One such study was that carried out by Hazel Dewart (1975) in which younger subjects than those used by Suci and Hamacher were tested for their comprehension of sentences in which the animacy of various nouns was varied in conjunction with various sentence positions.

In Dewart's experiment, twenty children aged 3 years and 3 months to 5 years (median age 4 years and 3 months) were given a total of twenty-four sentences in which one noun was a nonsense word. The child's task was to choose from a pile of toys which one he thought the nonsense word referred to. The toys included six dolls and animals which would be named by animate nouns, and six objects which would be named by inanimate nouns. The sentences were of four types: active voice sentences with either the actor or object being a nonsense word, and passive voice sentences with either the actor or object being a nonsense word. The verbs in these sentences were chosen to include (I) those which required an animate actor (e.g., "fight", "kiss") and (II) those which could take either an animate or inanimate actor (e.g., "wake", "scare"). These two types of verbs (based on requirements of the actor) were cross-classified into three types in terms of the object which they necessitated: animate, inanimate, or either. A concrete example will make this clearer. The verbs "fight", "read", and "send", all require animate actors (Type I). But in addition, "fight" requires an animate object, "read" requires an inanimate object, and "send" can take either an animate or inanimate object. Similarly, "wake", "break", and "hold" can take either animate or inanimate actors (Type II), but "wake", requires an animate object, "break" requires an inanimate object, and "hold" can take either. In the twenty-four sentences of the test, four verbs from each of these six categories were used, one in each of the four sentence types. Although the results of this experiment are complex, the main findings can be easily summarized. Nonsense words functioning as actors were more likely to be replaced by animate nouns if they were in preverb position as in active sentences than when they followed the noun as in passives. Similarly, those functioning as objects were more often replaced by animate responses in passives, again where they were first noun, than in actives, where the object comes second. In other words, children aged 3 and 4 years behaved as if they were using a strategy that the first noun is animate and the second noun is inanimate. However, this tendency was less strong on passive voice sentences. Dewart hypothesizes that perhaps children at this age are progressing from that strategy towards the adult pattern of response.

It has now been seen that young children make use of a variety of strategies in order to perform on tests of their comprehension of linguistic knowledge. One early strategy has been described as a probable event strategy (Strohner and Nelson, 1974), the use of which, by very young children, even appears to lead to incorrect interpretations of active sentences. Others have used the terms appropriate and inappropriate contexts (Dewart, 1975), or congruent and incongruent relationships (Wilcox and Palermo, 1975), in order to describe a similar phenomenon. A second type of conceptualization has used the term "local rules" (Donaldson and McGarrigle, 1974) to describe the way a child may approach sentence and word interpretation in various cognitive tasks. Some of these local rules may be very specific, such as placing things "in" a container but "on" a surface (Clark, 1973b). Even earlier than all these strategies may be one based on the child's carrying out the simplest motor response (Wilcox and Palermo, 1975). Related to this type of strategy may be those based on various features of the action role of the actor. Treating the mobile toy as the actor was observed not only in young children (Dewart, 1972, 1975), but in older children as well (Huttenlocher and Strauss, 1968; Huttenlocher, Eisenberg and Strauss, 1968). In experiments where error scores rather than reaction times were used as the measure, it appears that older children use this strategy only when they do not know the syntactic structure (Dewart, 1975). In other words, the older children fall back on the use of a strategy found in much younger children when comprehension based on grammatical principles fails. Finally, it was noted that, while in adults the action role included the use of animacy for agents and inanimacy for patients (Suci and Hamacher, 1972), younger children, about age 4, used animacy in relation to sentence position, with the first noun being animate and the second noun being inanimate, to some extent independently of grammatical role (Dewart, 1975). This last observation, the importance of sentence position at particular ages, has been noted by many investigators of child language. Sentence position is claimed to be the basis for several strategies used by both children and adults. These strategies are seen as being part of a perceptual processing apparatus which acts on the surface features of language. They are "perceptual" in that they deal with such phenomena as word order, segmentation of the incoming speech sequence, and interruptions of that sequence. It will be suggested that some of these strategies which have been called perceptual may really be part of broader cognitive mechanisms.

II. PERCEPTUAL PROCESSING STRATEGIES

(1) A THEORETICAL BACKGROUND

In the Strohner and Nelson experiment (1974) mentioned in the previous section, young children aged 2 and 3 years old were found to act in accordance with a probable event strategy, even to the extent of performing incorrectly on simple active voice sentences about improbable events. However, children of ages 4 and 5 were also tested, and here the findings were quite different. The 4- and 5-year-olds were no longer greatly influenced by event probabilities. The 4-year-olds often made use of a strategy that the sentence word order corresponded to actor-action-object. They did well on active sentences, but poorly on passive ones. Even some of the 3-year-olds had begun using this type of word order strategy, at least on reversible sentences, i.e., sentences in which either event was equally possible. By the age of 5 years, the child was found to rely mainly on syntactic information, both ignoring event probabilities and no longer using the actor-action-object word order strategy. It is clear, then, that although the youngest children may comprehend the language they hear in terms of what they know about events in the world, there comes a point in development where the structures of language become comprehensible in their own right even if they do not match reality. This is, after all, what we mean when we say that a linguistic structure is acquired—that it will be employable without context, and even in spite of conflicting context. This is the point where "The fence jumped over the horse" is acted upon correctly even though it may appear amusingly silly to the child. It is the basis for the glee with which young, but not too young, children greet :

> Hey diddle, diddle
> The cat and the fiddle,
> The cow jumped over the moon,
> The little dog laughed to see such fun
> And the dish ran away with the spoon.

In order to understand language acquisition and how it occurs, it would appear to be necessary to do more than merely state how language is related to reality. Syntactic structure, however it is acquired, becomes something which is separate from and beyond that reality. This resembles an issue in linguistics which is the subject of much controversy.

For some time certain linguists have been proposing a type of grammatical analysis that differs from Chomsky's particular formulation of transformational grammar. Chomsky's position is usually referred to as "standard theory" (Chomsky, 1965), or in a later modified version, "extended standard theory" (Chomsky, 1972; Jackendoff, 1972). The proposals which disagreed with the standard theory have often been referred to under the broad term "generative semantics" (see, e.g., Lakoff, 1971; McCawley, 1971a,b, 1973; and a collection of reprinted articles edited by Seuren, 1974). It is not appropriate here to give a detailed analysis of the differences between the two types of theory. For our purposes we need only centre attention on what Katz and Bever (1974) have called the issue of absolute notions of grammaticality versus graded ones. The older standard theory of Chomsky paid little attention to the semantic or meaning component of the grammar. This was its weakest point. Furthermore, the generative semanticists claimed that a Chomskyan analysis was inadequate to deal with many sentences, and that this inadequacy was traceable to the lack of consideration given to meaning in the generation of sentence structures. Both the extended standard theory and the theory of generative semantics were reactions to the inadequacies of the earlier view. However, those adhering to the extended standard theory still emphasize the autonomy of the syntactic component. Although they have given more attention to the semantic component and its interaction with the syntax, this semantic component is conceived of as a set of interpretation rules which act on or are applied to the syntax. The followers of that theory have come to be called "interpretive semanticists". By contrast, the generative semanticists claim that the meaning component plays an essential part in the generation of the structures themselves, and cannot be separated from them. They claim that the two components (semantics and syntax) are inextricably entwined and that sentences are generated from a syntactic/semantic base. Indeed, another way of characterizing the two broad schools of thought is to call the theory of the latter "semantic syntax" and to label the Chomskyan position as "autonomous syntax" (Seuren, 1974). Both theories are concerned with specifically linguistic entities. The word "semantics" is not identical to "thoughts", "cognitions", or "meanings". Semantics is concerned with the representation of meaning in language. Many psychologists have shown some confusion about this, and have drawn on the generative semanticists as support for a relatively anti-linguistic view. Bloom (1973) has called attention to this problem of misinterpretation. As she puts it, the semantic versus the syntactic basis for a grammar is an important issue for psychologists only to the extent that the formal correlates of such a difference make different predictions, if any, about cognitive and behavioural aspects of language use. Bloom claims that the more important distinction for those studying child language is not within linguistic categories (grammatical and semantic), but between linguistic categories on the one hand, and cognitive categories on the other.

However, Katz and Bever (1974) point out that aspects of Lakoff's theory of grammatical competence include a number of non-grammatical facts about the world. For Chomsky, a theory of competence relates to the principled knowledge which explains the intuitions that speakers have about sentence structure. For Lakoff, by contrast, well-formed sentences depend in part on knowledge of the world and on the beliefs of the speaker. For example, Lakoff's theory would claim that some sentences like "My frying pan enjoys tormenting me" depend for grammaticality not on a structural notion of "+human", but on whether the speaker considers the subject of the sentence to be sentient. If so, then and only then the sentence just quoted would be grammatical. In other words, the notion of the well-formed sentence is not absolute, but is relative, depending on the belief of the speaker. This may sound sensible as a theory of "acceptability", but as a theory of "grammaticality" this view seems very odd. Surely we can use grammatical sentences to talk about nonsense or about improbable or unlikely occurrences whether we believe them or not. Even 5-year-olds, as well as adults, have been empirically observed to know what to do with the toys when given the sentence "The fence jumped over the horse", and such a sentence is still grammatical even though it violates what we expect about events in the real world. Moreover, as Katz and Bever point out, deviant sentences can be used to make true statements. Furthermore, they claim that Lakoff's view would entail the belief that there is no distinction between a speaker's knowledge of grammatical and semantic properties of language and the speaker's beliefs about the things to which the language refers in the world. In other words, such a theory would claim that there is no distinction between "language" and "cognition". Such a view would, it seems to me, be somewhat of a hindrance when one tries to study the language acquisition of children, and even more so when studying such conditions as developmental aphasia in children and various types of adult aphasia.

Katz and Bever suggest that we need to know precisely what the specifically grammatical relations are, and that many of the problems raised by the favourite examples quoted by generative semanticists should more properly be regarded as being due to considerations which are outside the grammar entirely. An early example of this kind of problem was that raised by the unintelligibility of multiple centre-embedded sentences such as "The rat that the cat that the dog that the cow tossed worried killed ate the malt". Miller (1962) and Miller and Chomsky (1963) dealt with problems of this type by turning to non-grammatical considerations. They argued that centre-embedded sentences may be "grammatical" but perceptually complex. For example, memory limitations put such structurally complex sentences involving recursive features beyond the analytic power of any finite device. Furthermore, severe memory limitations may put any sentence of sufficient complexity beyond comprehensibility even when it lacks properties such as self-embedding. Short-term memory limitations have in fact been implicated in the language deficiencies observed in some mentally retarded children (Graham, 1968, 1974) and in other language deviant groups (Menyuk, 1964, 1969).

In generative semantics, all sorts of performance factors count as a legitimate part of the grammar. Lakoff's theory, for example, insists that anything whatsoever which influences the distribution of observed linguistic forms is to be accounted for in the grammar. However, a Chomskyan type of grammar rejects a conception of grammaticality which is based simplistically on the principles of distributional linguistics. Instead it is based on the notion of explication (Chomsky, 1972; Katz and Bever, 1974). It is meant to explain syntactic behaviour, and although it is based in large part on distributional phenomena, many of the principles which help account for the distribution of linguistic forms are not included in the notion of grammaticality itself. As we will see further on, this is certainly not to say that such principles are unimportant; they are essential to the understanding of child language acquisition. Indeed, the rest of this section will be concerned with a number of perceptual processing strategies used by adults and by young children acquiring language. But it will be necessary to ask later whether these principles *explain* language acquisition, and to examine what they tell us about developing grammatical processes.

(2) Some perceptual strategies

Having said that some aspects of language organization are explicable on the basis of perceptual mechanisms as distinct from grammatical mechanisms, Bever (1970; Katz and Bever, 1974) has comprehensively examined what some of those perceptual processes might be. In this section, some of the strategies he has outlined will be reviewed, and mention will be made of work of a few others which might conceivably be viewed in this framework.

Some of the processing strategies relate to the segmenting of the incoming speech sequence. It has been found that the lexical sequences that are placed together as units correspond to underlying structure. In a series of well-known experiments (Fodor and Bever, 1965; Bever, Fodor and Garrett, 1966; Garrett, Bever and Fodor, 1966) the subject hears a click while listening to a sentence. Subjectively, the click appears to migrate to the clause boundary. For example, in the sentence "Because it rained yesterday, the picnic was cancelled", a click, which in reality occurred either during the word "yesterday" or the word "the", appears to occur *between* the two words. This migration will vary according to the structure of the sentence even when the heard sequence is identical. For example, if the sequence ". . . eagerness to win the horse is quite immature", is preceded by "Your . . ." the click seems to occur just after the word "horse"; but if that same sequence is preceded by "In its . . ." the click is subjectively heard just after the word "win". From this, Bever concludes (1970) that adults have a strategy of perceptually organizing adjacent phrases in the surface structure which correspond to sentence units at the level of internal structure. That is, as Bever puts it, "As we hear a sentence we organize it perceptually in terms of internal structure sentence units with subjects, verbs, objects, and modifiers."

Sometimes perceptual strategies inhibit the understanding of the sense of certain structures and mislead the hearer into an unintended interpretation. Katz and Bever (1974) give the example "The friend of my brother's fiancée left town." It is very difficult to interpret this sentence as meaning that it was the fiancée who left town. This is because of the perceptual attractiveness of N + N (noun plus noun) sequences. However, any aspect of the sentence which would perceptually separate "brother's" from "fiancée", or which emphasizes the word "fiancée" as head noun, would have the effect of making acceptable the interpretation of "fiancée" as subject. Thus, "The fiancée of my brother's friend was discovered to be a cat burglar so the friend of my brother's fiancée left town" (Katz and Bever, 1974), serves to render the meaning of the sentence as something which could be written as "The friend-of-my-brother's fiancée left town", where "friend-of-my-brother's" becomes a phrase modifying "fiancée". In other words, as simply given, the sentence first quoted is ambiguous. Most people would interpret it as meaning "friend" left town, and would find it difficult to see the possible meaning, "fiancée" left town; this is due to what Katz and Bever call a perceptually suppressed sense which is caused by the perceptual attraction of the two adjacent nouns.

Amongst the processing strategies which Bever reviews is one which predicts that sequences which interrupt one another are especially complex. In addition, the complexity of a sequence varies in proportion to the complexity of the intervening sequence. It may be, however, that some of these principles Bever has isolated in this set of related strategies should not be designated as narrowly perceptual. Perhaps they are really broad cognitive strategies that affect not only the perception of language but other human behaviours as well. One theory has been proposed which relates the difficulty of interrupted sequences to the relative difficulty of various motor strategies for handling material objects (Goodson and Greenfield, 1975). It is a theory which has developmental implications as well, and it will be discussed in some detail in the fourth section of this chapter.

One special kind of interrupted sequence was mentioned earlier: self-embedded or centre-embedded sentences. It was suggested that memory limitations may play an important role in the unacceptability of longer sequences of this type. However, it has also been found that some self-embedded sentences are easier than others with the same number of self-embeddings (Fodor and Garrett, 1967; Fodor, Garrett and Bever, 1968). For example, in one of these experiments, it was found that the presence or absence of relative pronouns affected performance on embedded sentences of the same length. Therefore the differences in difficulty cannot be attributed to memory limitations. More recently, Bever (1970) has also proposed that the difficulties of other types of centre-embedded sentences may lie in a perceptual principle and two related word order strategies rather than on memory limitations. Suppose one has the following sentence: "The dog the cat was scratching was yelping". In this sentence, the basic relations can be more clearly shown as:

N_1	N_2	V_1	V_2
The dog	the cat	was scratching	was yelping

The main sentence is "The dog ... was yelping", into which has been embedded the clause "the cat was scratching". Bever proposes two perceptual strategies that yield correct interpretation of this construction. One is that with a V_1–V_2 combination in which both verbs are finite, V_2 is taken to correspond to the main verb of the sentence with V_1 being the subordinate verb. Second, with N_1–N_2–(VP) sequences in the surface structure, N_1 is the internal object of the internal sentence structure unit of which N_2 is the subject. In the example above, N_1, the dog, is the object of an internal sentence, "The cat was scratching the dog", of which N₂, the cat, is the subject. Notice that N₁ thus serves a "double function" as Bever calls it. It is a subject of one sentence (the main sentence), yet an object of the embedded sentence. Bever proposes a general principle that a stimulus may not be perceived as simultaneously having two positions on the same classificatory dimension, i.e., a stimulus can't be perceived in two incompatible ways at the same time. According to Bever, it is this that leads to the difficulties with self-embedded sentences of this type.

This is very similar to a problem posed by some sentences with relative clauses which has been studied by Amy Sheldon (1974). In such sentences, the co-referential nominal may either have the same function in both clauses, or instead there may be a change of function or role. Take, for example, two sentences with subject relatives:

The dog that jumps over the pig bumps into the lion.
The lion that the horse bumps into jumps over the giraffe.

In the first of these, the dog is co-referential nominal. Furthermore, it serves the same function in both clauses. It is the subject who both jumps over the lion and bumps into the pig. In the second sentence, however, the co-referential nominal (the lion) serves different functions in the two clauses. The lion is the object of the first clause (the horse bumps into the lion), but is the subject of the second clause (the lion jumps over the giraffe). The first sentence, where no role change of the co-referential nominal occurs, is referred to by Sheldon as exhibiting "parallel function". Where changes of role occur, as in the second sentence, the term "non-parallel function" is used. The two examples just given are of subject relatives. Sheldon also included object relatives, some of which exhibit parallel function and some of which have non-parallel function of the co-referential nominals:

The dog stands on the horse that the giraffe jumps over.
The pig bumps into the horse that jumps over the giraffe.

With all four sentences, there is the further difference that the two subject relatives have the main clause interrupted, while the two object relative sentences do not. If interrupted sequences are more difficult than uninterrupted ones, the subject relatives should be harder. There are also differences based on whether the relativized noun phrase is a subject or object. For example, in the two object relatives just cited, the horse which is relativized in the first sentence is the object while the horse which is relativized in the second is the subject. Thus, if difficulty is due to word order, then relative clauses in which the subject noun phrase is relativized should be easier to process than relative clauses in which the object noun phrase is relativized, because the underlying word order is preserved in the surface structure of the former, but it is not preserved in the latter.

Sheldon tested thirty-three children between the ages of 3 years and 8 months and 5 years and 5 months, by having them act out the sentences with toy animals. Each child received twelve sentences—three examples of each of the four types of relatives. The results indicated that interruption played no part in difficulty, nor did word order. There were no significant differences between subject relatives and object relatives; and there were no significant differences between sentences in which the subject was relativized and those in which the object was relativized. However, performance on parallel function relative sentences was significantly better than on non-parallel function sentences. Analysis of errors showed that in some sense word order plays a part in that some children used a strategy of identifying the antecedent to the relative pronoun on the basis of treating the relative clause that followed a main clause as if it were an extraposed subject modifier. For example, in "The dog stands on the horse that the giraffe jumps over", many children understood the giraffe to be jumping over the dog, as if the entire relative clause modified the subject (the dog). Sheldon concludes that children use two strategies on relative clause sentences. In trying to find the antecedent to the relative pronoun in object relatives, children rely on an extra-position strategy; in attempting to assign a function to the relativized noun phrase, they use a strategy of assigning parallel function.

Sheldon's discussion is concerned only with linguistic interpretations. Bever's analysis of self-embedded sentences attempts to identify the difficulty in terms of the broader perceptual principle of the same stimulus serving a double function. Perhaps the principle is broader still, and encompasses various cognitive phenomena which go beyond perception. Furthermore, Bever does not relate this particular principle to developmental phenomena. Something very similar to Bever's "double function" can be said to be lacking in what Piaget calls preoperational stage children. When operational thinking is attained, the use of double functions becomes possible. In the well known conservation experiment, the water which is higher is, at the same time, now co-ordinated with being narrower. On seriation tasks, the interposed sticks are now conceptually known to be at one and the same time larger than some and smaller than others. Goodson and Greenfield (1975) have referred to this same type of double function thinking as "role change". For them, role change is a cognitive process in which a single element plays different roles in relation to different parts of a complex structure. The developing ability for employing this process accounts for the developmental changes in sentence interpretation. We will return to the Goodson and Greenfield study in the section on cognitive strategies for language. It is apparent from the Sheldon study that role retention and role change have a part to play in the interpretation of some sentences.

The retention of the same role within a sentence has also been found to be an important principle in the young child's understanding of the referents of certain pronouns. Maratsos (1973) studied sentences of the following type:

John hit Harry and then Sarah hit him.
John hit Harry and then he hit Sarah.

In these sentences, we are concerned with the problem of the referents of the pronouns "him" and "he". In the first sentence, the usual interpretation is that "him" refers to Harry. In the second sentence, "he" refers to "John". Notice that with these interpretations the grammatical relations are the same in both clauses. In the first sentence, "Harry" is the object of the first clause. "Him" is the object of the second clause, and if it is interpreted as referring to Harry, then the grammatical categories for Harry have been maintained. Similarly, in the second sentence, "John" is the subject of the first clause. "He" is the subject of the second clause, and if it refers to John, then John is functioning as the subject in both. However, in conditions of contrastive stress, adult English speakers know that a change has been signalled. If one reads "John hit Harry and then Sarah hit *him*", with special stress on "him", then "him" is taken as referring to "John". Similarly, special stress on "he" in the second sentence leads to the interpretation that it refers to Harry instead of John. In other words, stressed pronouns signify a change in roles. In the first sentence, "John", the *subject* of the first clause becomes "him", the *object* in the second clause. In the second example, "Harry", the *object* of the first clause becomes "he", the *subject* of the second. Maratsos tested 106 3-, 4- and 5-year-olds for their comprehension of sentences of this type. All children performed similarly on the unstressed sentences, retaining the same role from the first clause to the second. However, performance on sentences in which the pronouns received contrastive stress improved with age and language ability (as measured by an imitation task). The youngest group interpreted the stressed pronouns just like the unstressed ones. Maratsos interpreted this as being due to a general heuristic strategy used by young children to interpret pronouns in order to change the grammatical and semantic roles as little as possible. Correct performances on the stressed pronouns requires one to violate this strategy. As mentioned earlier, the nature of the learning that allows one to begin to violate certain strategies remains unclear; it is by no means apparent that the mechanism is a simple one of learning exceptions to rules based on such principles as frequency of occurrence.

Semantic considerations can also affect perceptual strategies. Katz and Bever (1974) claim that one perceptual rule is that relative pronouns usually modify an immediately preceding noun phrase. Sequences which violate this principle may be grammatical, but nevertheless unacceptable due to perceptual complexity. Thus, in the sentence, "The man likes the girl who lives in Chicago", the interpretation that "who" refers to "the man", rather than to "the girl", is unacceptable. However, that such an interpretation is nevertheless allowed by the *grammar* can be seen in a sentence of identical structure, "The man likes your idea who lives in Chicago". In this case, "who" refers to "the man", since semantically, "ideas" can't live in Chicago. In other words, perceptual, not grammatical, features determine the unacceptability of the first sentence.

Similarly, behavioural variables, not grammatical structure, can affect the acceptability of certain sequences with co-referential pronouns. Bever gives the example, "He and he like juice" which is unacceptable. Note, however, that the grammatically identical "He and she like juice" is acceptable. Bever further notes that even "He and he like juice" is acceptable if it is accompanied by appropriate gestures.

It appears that what Bever is arguing is that the usual interpretation of pronoun reference in several different conditions is based on perceptual strategies, mainly relating to word order. However, these perceptual strategies can be overridden by semantic and behavioural factors. In other words, the principles determining interpretation in these cases are not entirely "grammatical". Rather, perceptual phenomena play a major role in interpretation, and these perceptual features are in turn subject to modification by semantic and behavioural variables.

As can be seen, most of the perceptual strategies that Bever has proposed are based on considerations of surface structure word order, and these perceptions can be overridden at times by semantic or behavioural considerations. These basic perceptual strategies are not unlike some kinds of strategy which other experimenters have observed in young children. Carol Chomsky (1969), for example, examined the acquisition of some linguistic structures which violate a more general principle observed in sentences of similar structure. Take the following sentences:

John told Bill to leave.
John wanted Bill to leave.

These sentences are of the form $NP_1 + V + NP_2 + $ Infinitive V. In both of these, NP_2 (Bill) is the subject of the infinitive verb; it is Bill who will be leaving. Some verbs, like "told" in the example above, mandatorily take an object (Bill); "John told to leave" is not a sentence. But with other verbs, like "wanted" in the above example, the object is optional. One can say either "John wanted Bill to leave" or "John wanted to leave". In the first of these, Bill is the subject of the infinitive verb, but in the second, the first NP (John) now becomes the subject of the infinitive. Where the second NP is optional, the description can be written: $NP_1 + V + (NP_2) + $ Infinitive V. In other words, when the second NP occurs, it is the subject of the infinitive; when it is omitted, the first NP becomes the subject. Carol Chomsky described this as the "minimum distance principle" for it is the NP closest to the infinitive verb which is taken as the subject. This works for most verbs in English. However, a few verbs violate this principle. One of these is "promise". In the sentence, "John promised Bill to leave", it is John, not Bill, who will be leaving. Even more complicated is the verb "ask". When used as a request, as in "John asked Bill to sing", the minimum distance principle is applied, and it is Bill who will be singing. But when "ask" is used as a question, as in "John asked Bill what to sing", then the minimum distance principle is violated and it is John who proposes to provide the entertainment.

Chomsky tested children between the ages of 5 and 10 years on sentences of these types by using procedures and materials with which children could cope. For example, to test sentences with "promise", children were given small Donald Duck and Bozo-the-Clown figures. Then, after various practice and warm-up sentences, they were given such test sentences as "Donald promised Bozo to hop up and down. Make him hop". Chomsky found that correct interpretation of sentences with "promise" and "ask", which are exceptions to the minimum distance principle, is a rather late acquisition. Children at the lower end of the age range usually failed, and they did so by consistently applying a strategy based on the perception of word order relations— the minimum distance principle. It is not known when children begin to apply this strategy, but at least at ages when it is applied, it leads to incorrect interpretations until new learning intervenes. Here, then, is a strategy which children, but not adults, apply to perceived surface structure relations. They do so at about ages 5 and 6 (and possibly younger). It gives them a means of performing on comprehension tests set by psycholinguists, but it does not yield a correct interpretation of underlying sentence structure as judged by adult grammatical analysis. Precisely how the exceptions to this strategy are learned is not yet at all clear and some of the complexities associated with the attainment of adult-like performance with the verb "ask" will be mentioned in the final section of this chapter.

Most of Bever's perceptual strategies mentioned earlier were intended by him to account for adult performance on various linguistic structures. However, one strategy in which he has been interested for several years is used primarily by 4-year-olds. It is that noun-verb-noun sequences will be treated as if they refer to actor-action-object. Recently (Bever, 1971), the basic strategy has been conceived more simply as being one in which the first noun is taken as the actor. A good deal of experimental research has been directed at discovering the use and developmental changes of this perceptual, word order strategy.

(3) The strategy that the first noun is actor

It has already been noted that Strohner and Nelson (1974) observed that children aged 2 and 3 years old were likely to make use of a probable event strategy, but that by age 3 some children had begun to change to a strategy based on word order. On reversible passive sentences there were many errors, which is consistent with the strategy of interpreting the first noun in the sentence as the actor. Wetstone and Friedlander (1973) similarly were interested in the degree to which word order carries communicative information for young children. They studied twenty children from 2 to 3 years and 1 month, by presenting them both with questions to be answered and commands to be carried out in three conditions. One condition consisted of normal word order, as in "Show the clown to Mommy". A second condition had a misplaced word order; "Show to clown the Mommy" would be an example of this order. It was formed by reducing the normal form to "telegraphic" speech (as often used by children of this age for sentences of this type) and re-inserting the non-referent words out of their normal order. The third condition was a scrambled word order, as in "Mommy clown to the show". Although children were of about the same age, they were divided into a developmental order which consisted of non-fluent children, who were described as being either at the stage of holophrastic word use and had a mean utterance length (MUL) of 1.75 morphemes, or at the stage of telegraphic word use (MUL = 2.79 morphemes). The developmentally most advanced children were described as fluent children, and they had a MUL of 3.73 morphemes. The children's responses were scored as being either relevant or non-relevant, the latter being a failure to respond, acting outside of the context of the question or command, or showing marked puzzlement, a demand for explanation, and the like. The results showed that for both groups of non-fluent children, there were no differences between normal, misplaced, and scrambled word order. By contrast, the fluent children performed significantly worse on the scrambled word order—significantly worse both from their performance on the other

12—CP * *

two conditions and from the other two groups. Wetstone and Fried-lander conclude that for non-fluent young children word order carries little or no communicative value. But fluent children seem to utilize syntactic as well as semantic information since they did significantly worse when the word order was scrambled. The least developmentally advanced children make do with context and with content words of specific reference. Developmentally more advanced children have en-tered the syntactic system. Studies of this kind show the unsatisfactory nature of theories incorporating only communicative intent and meaning.

In relatively early experimental work on the developmental course of sentence interpretation by young children, Bever, Mehler and Valian (1968) noted a number of stages based on different interpretation strategies. They claim that in stage 1 (age 2 to 3) the child understands simple declarative sentences even when improbable. Performance on passive sentences was found to be near random even when correct interpretation was aided by semantic constraints. Only physically im-possible sentences were responded to incorrectly. It is only in stage 2A (boys: age 3 to 4 years and 4 months; girls: age 3 to 4) that results similar to those later reported by Strohner and Nelson were found. In this stage, semantic probability determined the interpretation on im-probable active and passive constructions. That is, there was poorer performance on improbable active and passive sentences than during the preceding year. Performance on other passive sentences continued to improve until stage 2B (boys: 4 to 4 years and 4 months; girls: 3 years and 8 months to 4). In this stage, sentences without semantic constraints (i.e., reversible passives) were responded to such that any noun-verb-noun sequence was interpreted as actor-action-object. Thus, the children evidenced poorer performance on reversible passives now than at the immediately preceding stage. Finally, in stage 3 (boys: 4 years and 4 months upwards; girls: 4 upwards) performance on all types of sentences improved steadily. In later writing, Bever (1971) has treated the strategy of the noun-verb-noun sequence as a perceptual processing strategy that continues to affect adult interpretation of sentences. He claims that as a processing strategy it allows the listener to shortcut the use of full linguistic rules. Support for this comes from a number of experimental investigations which indicate that when there are no semantic constraints, the passive is harder to understand than the active (see Bever, 1970, 1971 for a review of these experiments).

The strategy affects the interpretation of sentences other than pas-sives. For example, Mehler and Carey (1968) have observed that adults find progressive sentences such as "They are bombarding cities"

easier to verify than participial constructions like "They are performing monkeys". This could be interpreted as being due to the perceptual
expectation of actor-action-object order. Bever reports (1970) that cleft
sentences of the type "It's the cow that kisses the horse", where the
actor is first, are easier for children of about 4 years of age than cleft
sentences such as "It's the horse that the cow kisses", where the object
occurs first.

Hazel Dewart (1975), whose work on the effect on sentence comprehension of such variables as animacy, linguistic context, and
mobility of the object to be moved has already been mentioned, has
also carried out a number of experiments on structures possibly affected by the strategy that the first noun be treated as the actor. In one
of these experiments, sentences containing both direct and indirect
objects (double object constructions) were presented to fifty children
between the ages of 3 years and 1 month and 7 years and 7 months.
The children were given two carts which each contained an animal.
Then they had to carry out instructions which used the double object
construction. Some of these were of the type, "Send the cat to the dog",
which has the direct object first, the preposition "to", and then the
indirect object (IO). This structure can be designated "V-DO-to-IO".
Others, such as "Send the dog the cat" have the indirect object before
the direct object, and in adult English do not contain a preposition.
These are of the form, "V-IO-DO". In order to study the kinds of
strategies children used, however, Dewart also presented a number of
other constructions which are deviant from the adult point of view,
but which are nevertheless comprehensible by adults. These included
sentences such as "Send to the dog the cat" (V-to-IO-DO), "To the
dog send the cat" (to-IO-V-DO), "To the dog the cat send" (to-IO-
DO-V), "The cat to the dog send" (DO-to-IO-V), and "The cat send
to the dog" (DO-V-to-IO). Notice that, given the task, it is the DO
which is to be moved. In a sense, then, the DO is the actor. The
prediction from the strategy that the first noun is the actor would be
that sentences with DO as the first noun should be easier than those
with IO as the first noun. Her results confirm this. Similar findings
have been reported by Cook (1974), Cromer (1975b), Waryas and
Ruder (1973) and Waryas and Stremel (1974). However, Dewart
was more interested in whether children used consistent strategies for
their answers. Possible cues to interpretation included not only order
of mention, but also the proximity of one or the other of the nouns to
the verb, and the presence or absence of prepositional marking. By
making an error-by-error analysis, Dewart found that of thirty-nine
children who made at least one error, sixteen used consistent strategies
for their answers. Eight used the strategy of treating the first noun as

the actor (DO). Six consistently chose as the DO the noun not marked by "to". One child used the strategy that the DO (actor) was the noun nearest the verb, and one child always chose the second noun as the DO (the opposite of the particular hypothesized word order strategy). In other words, at least one child used each of the possible types of strategy, but the most popular was that based on order of mention (nine of the sixteen children who used any consistent strategy at all), and almost all of these (eight out of nine) treated the first noun as actor (DO). Thus, although Bever's notion receives support, it must be qualified by the fact that these eight children are the only children who consistently used the hypothesized strategy. And as Dewart points out, their mean age was 4 years and 6 months, and not 4 years as reported in the Bever studies.

Another structure where the strategy that the first noun is the actor could be employed is called the instrumental structure. In sentences of the form "Hit the X with the Y", Dewart (1975) asked, what cues do children use to determine what is hitting and what is being hit? Sentences were used with equally likely interpretation, such as "Hit the dog with the cat", and fifteen children between the ages of 3 years and 2 months and 4 years and 6 months had to carry out the action described. Again, Dewart used various combinations of word order which result in deviant but interpretable sentences to adults. These included the orders "Hit with the cat the dog", "With the cat hit the dog", "With the cat the dog hit", "The dog with the cat hit", and "The dog hit with the cat". This allows the experimenter to observe whether children's answers are following a consistent strategy. The results indicated that instrumental sentences were very difficult for the children. They actually made more errors on normal word order instrumentals than on the various forms of deviant word order. But again, the interest is on the error analysis and on what, if any, strategies the children consistently employed. Three types of strategy are possible: one based on the order of the two nouns, another based on the noun marked by the word "with", and the third utilizing the position of the noun in relation to the verb. Of the fifteen children, five were found to employ consistent strategies (on the strict criterion of using that strategy for every sentence) for identifying the instrumental noun, i.e., the one to be manipulated in the task. Four of these always chose the first noun as the instrument. The remaining child always used the noun marked by "with". Thus, although one child used a different strategy, the most popular strategy was the one that the first noun be treated as the actor (that is to say, as the instrument in this structure).

Another experiment by Dewart included the cleft sentences mentioned earlier. There are various types of cleft structures, and these include, "It's the wolf that bites the duck", "It's the wolf that the duck bites", and "It's the wolf that is bitten by the duck". Dewart had eighty children between the ages of 3 years and 4 months and 7 years and 7 months carry out these kinds of instruction, but in addition she was interested in the generality of the strategies used. Therefore, in addition to the cleft sentences the children were given a battery of linguistic tests which included passive sentences, the double object constructions, and the instrumental constructions. As before the sentences were given with normal word order and also with various non-English orders. In all, there were twenty-seven sentences on which the child had to perform. Of the eighty children, eight performed correctly on all twenty-seven. An analysis by strategy was carried out. A child was credited with using a strategy if he used that method of answering significantly more often than chance. This meant that if a child answered twenty or more items of the twenty-seven in accordance with the strategy, he was counted as using that strategy (0.05 2-tail binomial test). When this criterion was applied, it was found that twenty-four children had used the strategy that the first noun is the actor across the various sentence types. In fact, eight of these twenty-four children used the first noun as actor on all twenty-seven items. The children had been divided into eight age groups of ten children each. Below are listed the median ages of the eight groups along with the total number of children in each who used the first noun = actor strategy :

3 years and 8 months	3
4 years and 1 month	7
4 years and 4 months	6
4 years and 8 months	6
5 years and 7 months	1
6 years and 4 months	0
6 years and 10 months	1
7 years and 6 months	0

It can be seen that the strategy is mainly used by the 4-year-olds. This confirms Bever's original finding and the later results of Strohner and Nelson, that very young children do not yet use the word order strategy. It is mainly used at about 4 years of age. It can also be seen in Dewart's results that the use of the word order strategy drastically declines after 4 years and 8 months. Note also that Dewart's results show that the more accurate description of the strategy is indeed that the first noun is the actor, rather than the earlier formulation that N-V-N sequences be interpreted as actor-action-object. This is clear from the deviant word order sentences where children treated the first noun as actor in spite of varying noun and verb combinations.

Finally, Dewart makes the important point that the actor in these sentences, in the sense of being the thing moved, serves a number of different functions. In terms of the surface structure, in double object sentences the moved piece or actor is the direct object of the verb. In instrumental sentences, the moved piece is the head noun of the prepositional phrase. In passive sentences, it is the grammatical object of a passive voice verb and is marked by "by". In cleft sentences with the object first and an active verb, it is the grammatical subject of a complement clause. In cleft sentences with passive verbs, the moved piece is the grammatical object of a complement clause and is marked with "by". If instead one looks at the sentences in terms of an underlying case grammar, such as Fillmore's (1968), then in double object sentences the moved piece or actor is the dative; in instrumental sentences it is the instrument; and in passive and cleft sentences it is the agentive case. It is apparent, then, that children use the same strategy, that the first noun is the actor, to identify a number of disparate grammatical functions.

A number of questions can be asked about the development and use of this strategy. For example, does it continue to be used in some form by older children or adults? Although Dewart's data seemed to indicate a sudden decrease in the use of this strategy after the age of 5 years, it may be that children were acquiring enough information about the structures tested to make the use of the strategy unnecessary. She found that both passive sentences and cleft sentences with passive verbs appeared to be acquired by the age of $5\frac{1}{2}$ years, and instrumental sentences were acquired soon after (by about age 5 years and 8 months). On the other hand, performance on cleft sentences with active verbs was mixed to the end of her age range (median age of her oldest group was 7 years and 6 months), and the prepositionless form of the double object construction ("Send the dog the cat") was not acquired by the end of the age range. It could be that knowing the "easier" structures led to a score on strategy use well under that required for significance overall; that is, perhaps some of the older children were making use of the strategy only for the more difficult structures. Or it could be the case that even though they had not yet fully acquired these more difficult structures, they knew enough about them to attempt various answers not based on constant application of the strategy.

Davis and Blasdell (1975) studied the comprehension of centre-embedded relative clauses in both normal hearing and hard of hearing children at ages somewhat older than we have been considering. The hard of hearing group consisted of twenty-three children aged 6 to 9 years, with hearing losses of between 35 and 70 dB in the 500, 1,000, and 2,000 Hz range. These children were congenitally hard of hearing. They were of normal intelligence and attended an American public school at least half the day. The normal group was made up of fifteen children aged 6 to 9 years. When presented with sentences such as "The man who chased the sheep cut the grass", they had to point at pictures of the action. Apparently Davis and Blasdell counted as "correct" only the picture of the man cutting the grass. Normal hearing children did this 78 per cent of the time and the hearing-impaired did so 51 per cent of the time. Pointing to the picture of the man chasing the sheep was said to be evidence of the strategy that N_1–V–N_2 be taken as actor-action-object. This response was made 14 per cent of the time by the normal hearing group, and 23 per cent of the time by the hearing-impaired group. Thus, some older children were said to be using the strategy more typically found in younger children. The hard of hearing did one additional thing. Several of them seemed to shift the strategy to the end of the sentence. They seemed to process only the last few words (". . . the sheep cut the grass"), and in order to use sheep as the actor, would "mis-hear" the verb as "ate", and point to a picture of the sheep eating the grass.

Adults would appear to use strategies either to short-cut full linguistic processing (observable in such measures as response time differences, perceptual suppression of other possible meanings, etc.) or when they do not otherwise know how to perform on a test of their comprehension. It has been emphasized throughout this discussion on strategies, that children use them, not to acquire language, but to interpret structures they do not yet understand. The area in which this might arise for adult speakers is when they are attempting to learn a foreign language. Susan Ervin-Tripp (1973) reports that English speakers who know the passive, nevertheless use the first noun as actor strategy in their first foreign language utterances.

Another question that can be asked about this strategy is whether it is really a perceptual strategy or a purely linguistic abstraction. By the latter is meant merely that the child abstracts a rule from the more common active voice sentences that he hears and generalizes this rule to other types of sentences such as the passive. Bever (1970) appears to argue for a nativistic component in the development of the strategy. He reasons that even if the strategy is an induction from experience, why are certain strategies followed rather than other possible generalizations which would be equally justified by experience? He claims that a nativistic component selects certain possible generalizations but rejects others. Furthermore, he argues that it is not at all clear that all perceptual strategies are based on experience. Whatever the exact status of this strategy's origin, Bever believes that all children pass through a phase of using it.

However, the results of Dewart's study leave a good deal of room for doubt. Many children at all the age ranges did not give any evidence of using the strategy. Of course, it may be that they have not yet entered or are already past the stage of using it. As she suggests, only longitudinal studies can answer this question. In addition, however, her studies showed that many children made no use of any strategy, while others used different, less frequent, strategies for comprehending the various types of structures. A recent study by Margaret Harris (1976) on the cues used to interpret agent-deleted passives such as "The boy got hit" (also called truncated passives) revealed that although children in the two youngest groups she studied (below age 4 years and 5 months, and 4 years and 6 months–5 years and 11 months) could not yet perform passives correctly, they were aided by such cues as non-reversibility and by the lack of an agent in the truncated form. She found that very few children used a consistently inappropriate strategy. In fact, the pattern of cue use for her groups was so mixed that she suggested that the processes involved in comprehending the passive voice are not identical for all children. A more general question can be raised, then, about the use of any strategy for comprehending sentences: Are there consistent differences among children in the strategies they use in their approach to comprehending and acquiring language?

IV. STRATEGIES ACCOUNTING FOR INDIVIDUAL DIFFERENCES

Katherine Nelson (1973) was interested in the language acquisition processes of very young children. Specifically, she wanted to know how the child proceeds from the one word stage to the stage where short sentences begin to be used. To this end, she made a study of eighteen middle-class children in Connecticut, who were between 10 and 15 months old at the beginning of her study. Nelson visited the home once each month for half an hour over a period of about one year, depending on the starting age of the individual child. In addition to this data base, the mothers kept records of the acquisition of the child's first words. The first fifty words of each child were analysed. Mother/child interaction was also recorded and analyzed at two points in time. Some psychological testing was carried out, and the children were seen during a follow-up session when they were approximately 30 months old.

One of the interesting things that emerged from this study was that children differed greatly in their early use of words. For example, one child would have many general nominals or names for objects. In contrast to this, another child would be observed to have a large number of what can be called personal and social words. Nelson found that she could divide the children into two groups on the basis of these differences in language use. One group, which she called the referential group, was object oriented. The other, the expressive group, was self-oriented. This expressive group used many more two word utterances than the referential group. Nelson describes their language as being a very personal, social language for expressing feelings and needs.

Nelson used this division of the children and analyzed the data to see if various features of acquisition were associated with one or the other "strategy" of using language. She found that there was no difference in the ages at which the first ten words were acquired. However, the referential group showed a faster rate of acquisition of words per month and attained a higher vocabulary at age 2 years. But the age at which they acquired their first ten *phrases* was later. In other words, for the referential group, it is the lexicon and not syntactic acquisition which is advanced. The phrases of the referential group were usually two-word telegraph-like utterances (for instance, "more car"), whereas the expressive group's phrases were more complete grammatically (for instance, "Don't do it").

In addition to affecting the size of vocabulary at age 2 years and the content and form of the language acquired, these different acquisition strategies affected the pattern of development as well. Nelson proposed that semantic structure acquisition differs from child to child. Fundamental to all children, however, are some basic distinctions such as that between object and non-object. The object side of the semantic tree is itself divided into animate (which is again subdivided into people and animals) and inanimate (which is subdivided into personal items such as toys, food, and clothing, and impersonal items such as vehicles and furniture). The non-object side of the tree is divided into categories which are person-related (action, expressive) and object-related (action, various object properties). All of these sub-categories on both sides of the tree continue to subdivide. According to Nelson, the manner in which semantic development proceeds differs in the two basic groups. The referential group children show greater development on the object side of the tree, whereas the expressive children develop the non-object side. The manner in which the semantic tree is filled in also differs, with the expressive group children establishing greater diversity in their categories.

In the latter part of her monograph, Nelson elaborates two other dimensions which affect language acquisition. One of these is the relative degree of match between the child's concepts and the environmental linguistic usage. The other relates to mother/child interaction and is characterized as acceptance or rejection on the mother's part of the child's attempts at verbalization. In conjunction with the referential/expressive dimension, eight language learning patterns are shown to be possible. The contribution of the child's linguistic strategies, however, is seen mainly in the referential/expressive distinction.

Other investigators have also drawn attention to differing "strategies". Dore (1974) approached language acquisition from the rather different point of view of studying what are called primitive speech acts, which consist of single words or single prosodic patterns which function to convey an intention. Some of the primitive speech acts he has observed include labelling, repeating, answering, requesting an action, requesting an answer, calling, greeting, protesting, and practicing. Although his empirical data consist of the video-taping of only two children, a girl from the age of 1 year and 3 months to 1 year and 5 months and a boy from 1 year and 3 months to 1 year and 7 months, he observed a distinction which is very similar to that found by Nelson. The girl evidenced what he called the "code-oriented style" which was made up basically of labelling, repeating and practicing words. It consisted mainly of primitive speech acts which were not addressed to other people. This would match Nelson's referential strategy. The other child, the boy, used what Dore called the "message-oriented style", a style which used language mainly to manipulate other people. Of the boy's primitive speech acts, 63 per cent involved other people, compared to only 26 per cent of the girl's speech acts. This message-oriented style would be what Nelson called the expressive strategy.

In another recent study, Susan Starr (1975) visited sixteen children longitudinally from the age of 1 year to $2\frac{1}{2}$ years. Each visit lasted for about an hour and a half, with about $1\frac{1}{4}$ hours of recording made for each session. When the child was observed to have ten or more two-word combinations in a single session, he was said to be in the sentence stage. Analysis was then made of the single words in the session exactly two visits prior to this stage, in order to have a developmentally similar data point for all the children at the single word stage. Similarly, the data from the session two visits after the one which marked the beginning of the sentence stage were analysed for the two-word stage data. Starr found that there was a functional continuity between single words and two-word sentences. She found that children use language either to describe objects or to talk about themselves. Again, these are the same two strategies that Nelson found. Starr noted that whichever strategy the child was observed to use at the one-word stage was the same as that he used at the two-word stage, showing a continuity of strategy use across developmental milestones.

Nelson has also speculated on whether some other observed differences in language use might be described as different individual strategies of acquisition. One of these concerns the comprehension/production distinction. Children who use a comprehension strategy appear to attend selectively to the talk around them, enlarging the number of utterances which are understood. Nelson says that this strategy is especially noticeable in children who talk "all of a sudden" after months or years of little or no verbal response. The reverse is true of children who use a production strategy in which they constantly test their conceptions of words and sentences against their acceptance by the environment. Yet another possible strategy is the use of questioning by some children. Nelson found a positive correlation between the use of questioning at age 2 years and the other language indices, especially vocabulary acquisition. It was not, however, related to the referential/expressive strategy distinction. Nelson points out that since there is merely a correlation, it could be that questioning is an activity which is engaged in by more advanced speakers, rather than being a strategy for acquiring a larger lexicon.

In most of the earlier studies of children's language, more attention has been paid to generalities across children in their methods of acquisition. It may be that a closer analysis will reveal that children use several different paths in the particulars of acquiring the structure of their native language. Some evidence for this has been presented in this section; and we saw in the previous section that slightly older children may use rather different processing strategies from one another on similar linguistic structures; and some children may use no strategies at all. There may nevertheless be some broad similarities in the language acquisition process which may be due to similar cognitive stages through which the normal developing child must pass. If cognitive abilities underlie the language acquisition process, it may be possible to trace a number of strategies used by children of similar cognitive levels to deal with linguistic structures.

V. BROADER COGNITIVE STRATEGIES

After much initial interest in the structural descriptions of child language, a number of psychologists began to turn to underlying conceptual processes and their development to help explain language acquisition (see, for instance, Bloom, 1970; Cromer, 1968; Macnamara, 1972; Slobin, 1973; and reviews of the field by Cromer, 1974b, 1976). The initial impetus for this change in direction came primarily from the Piagetian school of psychology. Piaget's view of language is rather complex. Language obviously plays a major part in the person's internal representation of the world. For example, when language begins in the child, it serves as the major contributor to the interiorization of action into thought. Nevertheless, language is seen as only one part of what is called the symbolic function. Other parts include deferred imitation, mental imagery, symbolic games, and drawing. The symbolic function allows thought to be detached from action, and language is particularly important for this formative process (Piaget and Inhelder, 1969). Piaget's main emphasis, however, is that language builds on and affects a number of cognitive abilities which have already arisen in the sensori-motor period of intellectual growth. In fact language acquisition is said to be able to begin only at the conclusion of the sensori-motor period because it is dependent on some of the intellectual accomplishments of that period.

Hermine Sinclair (1971) has put the Piagetian case most succinctly. She has noted a number of sensori-motor schemes which she considers can account for corresponding linguistic abilities observed in language acquisition. For example, it is the developing ability to put things in spatial and temporal order which would also allow for the linguistic equivalent of being able to concatenate linguistic elements. The child's developing ability to classify actions (such as using entire categories of objects for the same action or applying a whole category of action schemes to one object) also makes possible the linguistic classification ability of placing verbal elements into major categories like noun phrases and verb phrases. The ability to relate objects and actions to one another provides the basis for the functional grammatical relations such as "subject of" and "object of". The achievement of the ability to embed action schemes into one another allows for the kind of linguistic recursive property in which phrase markers can be inserted into other phrase markers, as found in some of the types of sentence mentioned earlier such as centre-embedded structures and relative clauses.

A similar theoretical approach has been proposed by Greenfield, Nelson and Saltzman (1972). They argue that the existence of action structures formally similar to grammatical structures may provide a cognitive base for language learning itself. In order to study action structures, they presented five cups of increasing size to sixty-four children who were between 11 and 36 months of age. The experimenter demonstrated an advanced strategy for seriating the cups. The children were then allowed free play with the cups. In one trial the child was allowed free play with the cups. In another trial, he was handed the smallest cup first; in a third trial he was handed the middle-sized cup first; and in a fourth trial he was given the largest cup first. Any time a seriated arrangement was accomplished by the child, he was handed a cup midway in size between the third and fourth cups and told to put it "where it belongs". Responses were scored in terms of "final structure", defined as the largest cup structure attained before dismantling. Three distinct strategies were identified for handling the cups, and they were associated with different age levels. The strategy which was dominant at 11 months of age was "pairing", where a single cup was placed in or on a second cup. A second strategy, which reached its peak at about 20 months of age when it became the dominant strategy for most children at that age, was the "pot method". Here a stationary cup functions as a pot which holds the mobile cups. In this strategy, the child successively holds a number of cups which move into or on to a single stationary cup. The most advanced strategy, and the one which was used most by the oldest children, is called the "sub-assembly method". In this strategy, a previously constructed structure consisting of two or more cups was moved as a unit into or on to another cup or cup structure. In this method, the stationary cup which was acted upon in the first move becomes the acting cup in the second move. Some cups, then, serve a double function or double role. They change from being acted upon to being the actor. It was also observed that children using a particular strategy did so fairly consistently, using that strategy about 80 per cent of the time. Greenfield *et al.* relate these strategies to particular grammatical constructions. The pairing strategy, for example, is said to be parallel to the subject-verb-object grammatical ordering. That is, the first cup (actor) enters (action) the second cup (acted upon). The second strategy, the pot method, is said to involve multiple actor-action-acted upon sequences which would be similar to conjoined linguistic structures. The first cup (actor) enters (action) the cup acting as the "pot" to hold the other cups (acted upon), and another cup (actor) enters (action) the cup acting as the "pot" (acted upon). Finally, the sub-assembly method is thought to be parallel to the linguistic structures in which the first object in the sentence becomes the subject of the following clause. The first cup (actor) enters (action) the second cup (acted upon object) which then (now becoming subject) enters (action) a third cup (acted upon object). This would be parallel to the kind of relations found in relative clause sentences like "The dog chased the cat that caught the mouse".

Greenfield *et al.* argue that the same human capacities may be responsible for both the action structures and the linguistic structures. That is, both the cup strategies and the language strategies are said to be behavioural manifestations of underlying internal forms of organization. These forms of organization may have other concrete applications as well. There are, of course, problems with such a view. First, although the cup strategies are said to be analogous to certain linguistic features, and although the linguistic features are shown in terms of increasing complexity (and are observed to be acquired in an order which matches the increasing complexity), there is no direct evidence of a link between the two classes of phenomena. Children using the most advanced cup strategy were under 3 years of age in the experiment, but we have seen that much older children have difficulties with relative clauses in which role change occurs. Second, although one may well suppose that the ability to handle certain types of relationships linguistically must depend on an underlying cognitive ability to handle those relationships on a non-linguistic level, such an observation does not explain the language acquisition process itself. But it would tell us that certain cognitive abilities which result in certain strategies for dealing with the non-linguistic world might well be used in attempting to handle linguistic input. We would also expect that the inability to deal with certain structural principles on the non-linguistic level would be paralleled by the inability to use similar principles on a linguistic plane.

In a more recent study, Goodson and Greenfield (1975) have examined three structural principles which are common to linguistic behaviour and manipulative play. They labelled these principles hierarchical complexity, interruption, and role change. Hierarchical complexity occurs when a sub-assembly is constructed and used as part of a larger construction. It occurs in both manipulative tasks and in linguistic constructions, and was the most advanced strategy in the experiment of Greenfield et al. previously discussed. Interruption can be observed in manipulation tasks when one activity is stopped in order to complete an intervening activity before the first activity is resumed and completed. In grammar, the interruption of one sequence by another would be seen in centre-embedded sentences such as "The boy who was sick stayed home", where "who was sick" constitutes the interruption. In both motor activities and grammar, interruption is said to make the sequence more complex. Role change is observable when a single element plays different roles in relation to different parts of a complex structure. The experiments of Amy Sheldon (1974) mentioned earlier, and the similar speculations by Bever (1970) concerning "double functions" in centre-embedded sentences, were examples of the difficulties caused by role change. It will be recalled that role change, or what Sheldon called "non-parallel function" made the largest contribution to the difficulty experienced by the 4- and 5-year-olds that she studied. In the study of Greenfield *et al.* role change occurred in the sub-assembly construction which was also an example of hierarchical complexity. Thus the two principles, role change and hierarchical complexity, were confounded in that earlier study. Goodson and Greenfield, then, designed their experiment in order to study these various principles separately.

The materials used were various blocks, boards, nuts, and bolts, from which various objects could be constructed. Two objects were chosen for study, a bench and a propeller. The bench may be constructed by means of two strategies. In one, the subject can place the board on one support, screw it in, and then move to the other side to attach the second support. In the second strategy, however, one can interrupt the sequence. One can place the board on the two supports, and then move to one side to place the screw, returning to the other side to place the second screw. The first method could be called a simple sub-assembly, while the second would be a sub-assembly with interruption. The propeller can also be constructed by two different strategies. In one, the various pieces are merely piled on to a single piece, the nut or bolt. That is, the nut or bolt always serves as the recipient of the action and defines the locus of the action. This strategy is called "piling" and is similar to the "pot method" of the earlier experiment. A second strategy, however, is much more complex. One can place the two blades of the propeller together and then the nut and bolt through them. This does not involve interruption, but it does require that the pieces which served as actor in the first action become the acted upon pieces in the second action. This strategy was termed sub-assembly with role change. Noting Sheldon's data that role change was more difficult than interruption, Goodson and Greenfield predicted the following order of difficulty of the four strategies : piling (propeller), simple sub-assembly (bench), sub-assembly with interruption (bench) and sub-assembly with role change (propeller).

Thirty-six children who ranged in age from 2 to 7 years were tested. Pilot testing had revealed that all 8-year-olds tested were capable of employing all four strategies. First, a completed bench was shown and the child was asked to build another just like it. In this way, the child's spontaneous strategy could be observed. But Goodson and Greenfield were interested in what a child was *capable* of doing. So as the next step in the experiment, the experimenter took the model apart and asked the child to copy a new method of constructing it. The experimenter then modelled the strategy that the child had not used. If the child had used the advanced strategy spontaneously, he should easily be able to copy the less advanced method. If he had spontaneously used the simpler strategy, then this step would show which children were capable of the more advanced assembly technique, and which were not. In the third step in the experiment, the experimenter took out a completed propeller and asked the child to make one. Finally, as in the procedure with the bench, the experimenter demonstrated the method opposite to that spontaneously used by the child and asked him to make the propeller in that manner. The results corresponded exactly with the predicted order of difficulty. Furthermore, the strategies were scalable; a child could perform up to his most advanced strategy and not beyond it. Only three of the thirty-six children revealed a gap in the strategy order. The increasingly complex strategy use also correlated with age $(r = 0.75)$. Goodson and Greenfield interpreted their results as suggesting two developmental steps in strategy use : the acquisition of complex hierarchical structures, and the acquisition of the ability to deal with role change. An inspection of their table of the individual strategy use of the thirty-six children revealed that interruption itself did not affect competence very much, and this is in line with Sheldon's findings on relative clauses.

Once again, as in the earlier study, one can ask whether there is any direct link to strategies used in comprehending or producing linguistic structures. Goodson and Greenfield argue that one need not find a specific parallel between manipulation and language, due to the differences in the media. Rather, these strategies are really general principles which appear many times in development. But this claim is somehow unsatisfying. A child may need to have the cognitive underpinnings which make him capable of carrying out certain types of operations before they are observed in either action or language. This is essentially what Sinclair's argument, using the Piagetian framework, insists on. It was claimed that in order that language should begin, certain accomplishments of the sensori-motor period had to be achieved. But we are again faced with the problem concerning how these are specifically encoded in a linguistic system. It is one thing to speculate that certain cognitive abilities are *necessary* in order for certain aspects of language acquisition to occur, but it is another to claim that they are *sufficient*. Since these cognitive strategies appear a good deal earlier in manipulative play, what exactly is it about language that "prevents" a child from applying the same strategies to that medium? Dulay and Burt (1974) ask a similar question in a slightly different context. They were looking just at linguistic structure, rather than at the commonalities of structures found in action and in language. But they argue that even if one is solely concerned with linguistic structure itself, a linguistic description only tells one *what* is eventually learned and not *how* it is learned. It may of course be that certain cognitive strategies will be used by the child gradually to re-construct his more primitive linguistic system until it more closely matches the adult system, but these will will have to be more closely specified. The strategies will have to be shown to be directly related to the language acquisition process, and not merely related by analogy.

A number of other important questions also arise. How are these various cognitive mechanisms or strategies thought to be organized in the brain? For example, what is one to say about children who have difficulty acquiring linguistic structures (developmentally aphasic children), but who are otherwise intellectually normal? What about adults suffering from some form of traumatic aphasia, who lose certain grammatical abilities? Would one claim that they also lose precisely the same cognitive structures in their action patterns? In both of these cases one might be tempted to speculate about specific language mechanisms beyond the cognitive ones, although alternatively one could suppose that the impairments are purely in the auditory modality. But in addition, what about unimpaired adults attempting to learn a foreign language? Since they have presumably passed through all the developmental stages and possess all of the necessary cognitive equip-ment, what prevents them from easily acquiring in the second language hierarchically complex forms, embedded structures, structures with interrupted sequences, and structures which incorporate role change? It is possible to accept that specific cognitive underpinnings are neces-sary for language acquisition to occur and yet still assume some speci-fically linguistic mechanisms in addition to these.

VI. SPECIFICALLY LINGUISTIC STRATEGIES

One area of linguistics in which evidence of strategies is available is the study of phonology, and some of the strategies which have been observed appear to be specifically linguistic. Even in studies of the per-ception of language there is strong evidence that speech is analysed differently from non-speech sounds (Liberman, 1970; Liberman, Cooper, Shankweiler and Studdert-Kennedy, 1967; Studdert-Kennedy, 1974). This appears to be the case in infants 2 and 3 months old (see, for instance, Eimas, 1974a). Even infants as young as 4 weeks of age are able to discriminate linguistic and non-linguistic stimuli (see reviews by Eimas, 1974b; Morse, 1974).

In the production of speech, it is becoming generally accepted that the young infant does not acquire his sounds by imitating them. Rather he appears to produce them in accordance with a systematic set of phonological rules. This was the position put forward originally by Jakobson in 1941, but only more recently translated into English

(1968). Basically, his theory proposes that the infant makes a series of discriminations of the features of the language that he hears. These features are represented by phonological contrasts such as vocalic/non-vocalic, voiced/voiceless, nasal/oral, grave/acute, etc. It appears that the child first dichotomizes sounds on the basis of one feature, and begins to classify all sounds on that basis of that feature. Later, new contrastive features are added to his system, and in this way he progressively adds to his differentiations until all the sounds in the language to which he has been exposed have been identified on the basis of the distinguishing features. These features are rules which act across particular sounds. For example, when the child acquires the contrast voiced/voiceless, he creates not one but a number of distinctions based on the voicing feature. There include /g/ versus /k/, /b/ versus /p/, /d/ versus /t/, and /v/ versus /f/. Moreover, Jakobson claims that these contrasts appear in the child's productive speech in a constant order, and this order is said to correspond to the number of languages in the world which contain the particular feature. In other words, the strategies the child uses to discriminate sounds follow a constant order which appears to be some kind of species-specific and language-specific system, and is observable in the universal distributional characteristics of human language sounds. Details of theories of this type can be found in Chomsky and Halle (1968), Jakobson (1968), Jakobson and Halle (1956), and Jakobson, Fant and Halle (1952).

Neil Smith (1973) in a longitudinal study of phonological acquisition mentions several strategies that the child employs in his early productive speech. One of these is consonant harmony, in which a child changes the sound of the adult form so that the consonants of the syllables are identical. An example of this would be the child's producing [keɪki] *or* [teɪti] for "Katy". Another common strategy is systemic simplification in which classes of sounds are reduced to one of their common elements. A third strategy is cluster reduction. Here, certain sound combinations are reduced to simpler sounds. An example would be the child's rendition of "flower" as "fower". Barbara Dodd has found the same types of strategies to be used by deaf children (Dodd, 1976b), and by severely subnormal non-Down's syndrome children (Dodd, 1976a).

The Jakobson type of theory of the acquisition of distinctive features emphasizes the generalities across children in acquisition order. Some deviations from this order are found, however, in individual children. Ferguson and Farwell (1975) claim that some of the differences are attributable to the different strategies adopted by children in acquiring the adult phonological system. Amongst the individual strategies that they mention are : the use of "favourite sounds" (that is to say, the preference for certain sounds, sound classes, or features), extensive use of reduplication, special markers for certain classes of words, preference for either lexical expansion or phonological differentiation at the expense of the other, and persistent avoidance of particular "problem sounds".

If there are certain phonological strategies some of which can be thought to be specific to the language system, one may ask whether there are any strategies which children use in acquiring grammar which may be specifically linguistic. Dan Slobin (1973) calls attention to the cognitive prerequisites for grammar, but he also notes that formal linguistic complexity plays an important role in language acquisition. He points out that cognitive development and linguistic development do not proceed in unison. The child must find the linguistic means to express his intentions and understandings. According to Slobin, it is possible to postulate a number of what he calls "operating principles" which the child seems to apply to language input. These operating principles are inferred from child language acquisition data which have been gathered cross-culturally, and are meant to represent universal strategies used by children. However, most of these strategies would seem to be explicable as linguistic manifestations of broader cognitive strategies. For example, the principle "avoid interruption or rearrangement of linguistic units" has already been discussed by Goodson and Greenfield (1975) as being observable in manipulation strategies used by young children. Similarly, it is not difficult to imagine the broader cognitive strategies of which these language acquisition principles are a part:

Pay attention to the ends of words;
Pay attention to the order of words and morphemes;
Avoid exceptions;
The phonological forms of words can be systematically modified.

Even two principles which at first appear to be slightly more linguistically specific:

Underlying semantic relations should be marked overtly and clearly;
The use of grammatical markers should make semantic sense;

can be seen as part of a number of general, non-linguistic principles for coping with information.

Whatever the exact status of these strategies, whether linguistic or more broadly cognitive, their adequacy for accounting for observed language behaviour has been questioned. Dulay and Burt (1974) ask what is predicted when two apparently conflicting principles are applicable to a certain structure. For example, in utterances like "no Daddy go" and "wear mitten no" the child has avoided the interruption of the main sequence, but he has not paid attention to the proper placement of the negative morpheme. Of course, this could be dealt with by ordering the principles. But Dulay and Burt have other criticisms as well. They point out that some common observations appear to confute certain operating principles. The principle, "pay attention to the ends of words", is violated by English-speaking children who regularly omit functors at the ends of words even after having acquired several prepositions. Also, such a principle would not apply to pre-fixing languages such as Navajo. As Dulay and Burt put it, there is no evidence that Navajo children acquire their morphological structure later than children acquiring suffixing languages such as Turkish.

It is difficult to see what might count as a specifically linguistic strategy, unless it was one which is not applied to other material or which exhibits certain features which are unlike other cognitive strategies. An example of the latter might be the observation that such a strategy is not used beyond some sort of critical period for language acquisition (Lenneberg, 1967). I made a series of studies (Cromer, 1970, 1972a,b, 1974a, summarized in Cromer, 1975a) in which I hypothesized that such a strategy was being used in the acquisition of new linguistic material. The structure used in these experiments was one studied by Carol Chomsky (1969). It is usually rendered by linguists as the contrast pair, "John is eager to please" versus "John is easy to please". In the first, John is the actor of the sentence, but in the second, he is acted upon; someone else finds it easy to please John. Correct interpretation of the second type of sentence is acquired at a rather late age by children. The reason for this appears to be that they must learn to violate their expectation that the surface subject is the actor. The experiments were designed with materials the children could handle and which studied comprehension of a number of examples of the structure. The child had wolf and duck hand puppets and had to act out the meaning of such sentences as "The wolf is happy to bite" and "The duck is glad to bite", in which the surface subject is indeed the actor, as well as sentences such as "The wolf is fun to bite", and "The duck is tasty to bite", in which it is the surface object which is the actor. In all, there were eight sentences which served as a clear test of this structure, four of each of the two types, with appropriate controls for which animal was named first and which animal acted as the biter. The results indicated that young children persisted in the interpretation that the surface subject should be the actor even at an age when they could correctly perform passive sentences of the type "The wolf was bitten". These children could be labelled as being at a "primitive rule stage" since they applied a rule that the named animal was the actor in this particular structure. At about 6 years old, however, they enter what can be called the "intermediate stage". At this stage they no longer always treat the surface subject as the actor, but they do not yet perform correctly. They get some sentences right and others wrong. Furthermore, they are not simply acquiring the semantic markings or syntactical understanding of the particular words like "happy", "glad", "fun", and "tasty" which indicate which deep structure to recover when they are used in this structure. Rather, they are inconsistent from day to day in their answers, and this intermediate period lasts for about three years. Finally, about 9 to 10 years old, they fairly rapidly become capable of performing correctly in the adult manner on all the exemplars of this sentence type. How this learning occurs is a mystery, but an attempt was made to examine it by having them learn new material (nonsense words) which could be used in the structure. For example, it is the case that words like "happy" and "glad", which serve as the cue to the fact that the surface structure subject is the actor in this sentence, are allowable in sentence frames such as "I'm always ———— to read to you". The words like "fun" which indicate that the surface subject is *not* the actor, are excluded from this frame. One cannot say "I'm always *fun* to read to you". Similarly, there are frames which allow the latter types of words, but exclude the former. For example, one can say "Reading to you is *fun*", but it is ungrammatical to say "Reading to you is *glad*". It was suggested that perhaps children learned the structural properties of words such as "glad" and "fun" by hearing them in these and similar transformational frames which serve to differentiate them. In various experiments, normal children at the different stages of acquisition of this structure, subnormal children, and normal adults, were given nonsense words in related differentiating frames, and then asked to perform with the wolf and duck when these same words were used in the test structure. Although the learning hypothesis was not supported, a number of strategies were observed, and these differed in the different groups. In normal children, those using the primitive rule on normal sentences continued to do so on all the sentences with the nonsense words. Of intermediate children, about 50 per cent used a consistent strategy for interpreting all new material. Half of these applied the primitive strategy of treating the surface subject as the actor, but half applied a strategy of treating the surface subject as acted-upon. Amongst children capable of adult performance, about a quarter applied a consistent strategy, but now it was always the strategy of treating the surface subject as acted-upon. This strategy might be loosely characterized as "bending over backwards" to expect a change in the basic grammatical relations. It was hypothesized to be related to a linguistic universal to do with marked and unmarked forms. What is intriguing is that this strategy was never used by adults. More than 40 per cent of the adults used a strategy to interpret all the sentences with the nonsense forms, but they always used the strategy used by the youngest children—treating the surface subject as the actor. Educationally subnormal children behaved just like the normal adults, and it was suggested that this might be because they were 14, 15, and 16 years of age, and thus beyond a critical period when the surface subject equals acted-upon strategy might be likely to be used.

Cook (1973) studied the acquisition of this structure by adults who were learning to speak English. He found that on the normal sentences with real words ("happy", "glad", "easy", "fun", etc.), adults were progressing through the same stages as children. This was inferred both from the average amount of time they had been living in England and from the average amount of time that they had been learning English in their home country. Those who performed on all sentences in accordance with the primitive strategy of treating the surface subject as actor had been in England an average of two months, and had been learning English in their home country for an average of two years and two months. Adults who were intermediate on this structure had been in England seven months, and learning English for three years and five months. Those who were capable of performing in the adult English fashion had been in England an average of one year, and had been learning English an average of four years and eight months. However, on learning new instances (the nonsense words used first in the frames meant to differentiate them), they performed differently from the children. The primitive rule users on real sentences did not use that strategy on the new words. And the strategy of treating the surface subject as acted-upon was not observed in any adults, just as it was lacking in the native English speaking adults in Cromer's experiment. Cook's experiment has two implications. First, these foreign speaking adults can be presumed to have the ability to use adult cognitive operations, but they are observed to go through the same stages as children in learning this structure. Second, the strategies they apply to new instances of the structure are not the same as those applied by children.

It was hypothesized that the strategy used by children who were advanced on this structure was related to an observed linguistic universal concerning marked and unmarked grammatical forms. Since it did not appear in adults, it was further hypothesized that it is the kind of strategy which is somehow tied to a critical period in which language is more easily acquired and by different methods. It was thus concluded that the strategy observed in the advanced children may be a purely linguistic one. But one would like a more direct experimental test of a supposed linguistic strategy. Recently, I subjected a strategy suggested by McNeill, Yukawa and McNeill (1971) to experimental test (Cromer, 1975b). The strategy was that the child would expect overt inflectional marking to indicate the indirect rather than the direct object. Using English-speaking children in a language game in which they had to break codes, one of which was in accordance with the universal expectation and one of which was against it, no differences were observed in the error scores in the two groups. Various possibilities can be suggested for this negative result, but another important question arises instead. How does a strategy allow learning to occur in any case? In a language in which only indirect objects are marked, it would allow for quick and easy acquisition of the form. But most inflectional languages provide special word endings for both the direct and indirect objects (accusative and dative cases). A strategy of treating all marked forms as the indirect object would lead to a high proportion of incorrect comprehensions. Similarly, in the wolf and duck experiments, the strategy of treating the surface subject as the one to be acted-upon led to a 50 per cent error rate. Perhaps the whole notion of "strategy" as applied to language acquisition needs to be examined.

VII. THE NOTION OF "STRATEGY" AS APPLIED TO LANGUAGE ACQUISITION

In an earlier section which dealt with the use of various perceptual processing strategies by children, a complication was observed. Children were seen to differ in their use of some commonly observed strategies, many not using them at all. Yet all the children acquire the adult forms. How does the acquisition occur? This is not necessarily a difficult problem. In the Bruner, Goodnow and Austin experiments on concept formation, individuals used widely varying strategies to learn the same concepts and these strategies were classified into four basic types. Similarly, we saw that there are many strategies that account for individual differences in the language acquisition process. There are further complications with these language acquisition strategies, however. Not only do not all individuals use them, but even those who do, do not apply them to all linguistic input. For example, when 6-year-old children apply the rule that the surface structure is the actor in sentences like "The wolf is fun to bite", they do not apply that strategy to passive sentences such as "The wolf is bitten". What makes the child apply a particular strategy to one structure but not to another? Perhaps they have a broad strategy (such as first noun is the actor) which they apply to many structures and slowly learn the particular structures which are exceptions to it. This kind of explanation would be compatible with the results obtained by Dewart (1975) across a number of different sentence types. But again, this is really a description which in essence says that as the learning of various linguistic structures occurs, particular comprehension strategies which often lead to an incorrect interpretation are no longer applied to them.

Even more complex are cases where the linguistic structure itself seems to determine whether a strategy is to be used or not. Earlier, the minimum distance principle hypothesized by Carol Chomsky (1969) was mentioned. The strategy consisted of treating the noun nearest to the complement verb as the subject of that verb. Verbs like "promise" violate that rule, and children must learn that the first of the two nouns is the actor. Thus, in "John promises Bill to sing", it is not until a rather advanced age (8 or 9) that children begin to realize that it is "John" and not "Bill" who will be "singing". However, in experiments on interpreting "ask", further difficulties were observed. First, it is more complicated for children because it has two meanings. When used as a question, as in "John asked Bill what to sing", the minimum distance principle is violated as with "promise"; it is "John" who will be singing. But when used as a request, the minimum distance principle is observed. Thus, in "John asked Bill to leave the room", in British English, Bill must leave the room. In American English, the sentence is ambiguous, and the context can influence the interpretation. Compare, for example, "The teacher asked the boy to leave the room" and "The boy asked the teacher to leave the room". To Americans, the boy will be leaving in both cases. To British English speakers, the second sentence does not sound quite grammatical. But in both dialects, "ask" as a request is treated differently from "ask" as a question. For both dialects, "ask" as a request observes the minimum distance principle—consistently for the British, inconsistently for Americans.

When Chomsky tested a number of children on their interpretation of "ask", she was surprised to find that many children treated the sentences as if they meant "tell". She therefore changed her study to an investigation of when the child could correctly interpret "ask" as a question instead of using "tell". Two children were seated at a table with various toys and objects. The task was for one child to "ask" and "tell" the other child certain things. Chomsky found that there were three structures in which "ask" could be used, which varied in difficulty. She called these Cases 1, 2, and 3. Examples of these three cases are :

Case 1   Ask Laura what colour this is.
Case 2   Ask Laura the colour of this book.
Case 3   Ask Laura what colour to make the square.

In Case 1, the child merely has to change "what colour this is" to "what colour is that" in order to form the question. Case 2 is slightly more difficult. The child must now supply a question word and a verb in order to form the appropriate question. Thus, "the colour of the book" must be changed to "What's the colour of the book?" In Case 3, the most difficult case, the child must not only supply the auxiliary verb, but must specify the correct subject. In the example, "what colour to make the square" must be changed to "What colour *should I* make the square?" To do this, the child must refer outside the complement clause to retrieve the subject and must essentially choose between NP_1 and NP_2 (i.e., it is not appropriate to say "What colour should you make the square?").

Chomsky found that the children could be divided into five developmental stages on the basis of their answers. Treating "ask" as if it means "tell" is scored as a failure. Treating it correctly to mean asking a question was scored as success. Given these definitions, the five stages were:

Stage A :   Failure on Cases 1, 2, and 3
Stage B :   Success on Case 1; Failure on Cases 2 and 3
Stage C :   Success on Cases 1 and 2; Failure on Case 3
Stage D :   Success on all cases, but wrong subject assignment for Case 3
Stage E :   Success on all cases and correct subject assignment for Case 3

The interesting stages for this discussion are Stages B and C. At these stages, children can be said to know the meaning of "ask" and can perform correctly in the situation—as long as the simplest linguistic structure is used. At all other times they seem to apply the strategy "Treat 'ask' as if it means 'tell'". The moment a slightly more advanced linguistic structure is used, they fall back to the use of that strategy. Here is an example of one Stage C child taken from Carol Chomsky's report:

Experimenter : Ask Joanne what colour this book is. (Case 1)
Laura : What colour's that book?
Experimenter : Ask Joanne her last name. (Case 2)
Laura : What's your last name?
Experimenter : Tell Joanne what colour this tray is.
Laura : Tan.

Experimenter : Ask Joanne what's in the box? (Case 1)
Laura : What's in the box?
Experimenter : Ask Joanne what to feed the doll. (Case 3)
Laura : The hot dog.
Experimenter : Now I want you to *ask* Joanne something. Ask
  her what to feed the doll. (Case 3)
Laura : The piece of bread.
Experimenter : Ask Joanne what *you* should feed the doll. (Case 1)
Laura : What should I feed the doll?

Of the thirty-nine children between the ages of 5 and 10 who took part in the experiment, nine evidenced this kind of behaviour and were classified as being at Stage C. A close inspection of the example dialogue shows that the child understands the meaning of the word "ask". Furthermore, she can form the appropriate questions structurally. What she does, however, is to use a strategy, as it were, of supplying a "tell" interpretation for any linguistic *structure* which is beyond her competence. In order to apply the correct interpretation, she must already know the structure of the sentence. In other words, once again one can observe a strategy which is applied when the child doesn't know what to do. It does not tell us how the child acquires the structural knowledge which determines whether he uses a strategy for interpretation or not. And this is really the central problem of strategies as applied to language acquisition.

At the beginning of this chapter, the work of Bruner, Goodnow and Austin was cited as providing the basis of definition for the concept of "strategies". But the strategies they explored were very different from those now being proposed for language acquisition. Concept formation strategies provide a means for testing hypotheses which are easily disconfirmed. By contrast, young children use strategies sometimes for years to produce utterances they do not hear others producing around them, and which in the linguistic community are being constantly disconfirmed. A more essential difference, however, is that the "strategies" of Bruner *et al.* are *methods for acquiring new information.* The strategies proposed to account for language acquisition do nothing of the sort. As has been repeatedly emphasized throughout this chapter, the various strategies which have been proposed are merely ways of answering a psycholinguist's questions on a comprehension test, or a way of interpreting sentences in the world when their structure is not yet understood. Nelson (1973) recognized this distinction and wrote of the differences between strategies for *acquiring* language and strategies for *processing* language. She characterizes the former as being strategies for adding new elements to the original repertoire, whereas the latter match elements to the existing repertoire. We do not seem to have discovered many acquisition strategies as yet.

The emphasis on "strategy" has had, overall, a beneficial effect. It has made us aware of some of the ways by which the child may possibly "get into" the linguistic system. It has shown us the importance of perceptual mechanisms for interpreting utterances, and how as adult speakers with full linguistic competence we nevertheless rely on a number of short-cuts to understanding. We are even misled at times by some perceptual strategies, as we saw, for example, when some interpretations of a structure are perceptually suppressed. The emphasis on "strategy" has also made investigators much more aware of the individual differences exhibited by children learning language. Psychologists have also begun once again to realize the crucial importance of underlying cognitive operations which are necessary for any language behaviour to occur. Some operations may be specifically linguistic, but little is yet known about them. The concept of language acquisition strategies has told us much—except how the child acquires language.

REFERENCES

Bellugi-Klima, U. (1969). Language acquisition. Paper presented at the Wenner-Gren Foundation for Anthropological Research in the symposium on *Cognitive Studies and Artificial Intelligence Research*, Chicago.

Bever, T. G. (1970). The cognitive basis for linguistic structures. In J. R. Hayes (Ed.), *Cognition and the Development of Language*. New York: Wiley.

Bever, T. G. (1971). The nature of cerebral dominance in speech behaviour of the child and adult. In Renira Huxley and Elisabeth Ingram (Eds.), *Language Acquisition: Models and Methods*. London and New York: Academic Press.

Bever, T. G., Fodor, J. A. and Garrett, M. (1966). The psychological segmentation of speech. Paper delivered at the International Congress of Psychology, Moscow.

Bever, T. G., Mehler, J. R. and Valian, V. V. (1968). Linguistic capacity of very young children. Mimeographed paper.

Bloom, L. (1970). *Language Development: Form and Function in Emerging Grammars*. Cambridge, Mass.: M.I.T. Press.

Bloom, L. (1973). *One Word at a Time*. The Hague: Mouton.

Brown, R. (1973). *A First Language*. Cambridge, Mass.: Harvard University Press.

Bruner, J. S., Goodnow, J. J. and Austin, G. A. (1956). *A Study of Thinking*. New York: Wiley.

Chafe, W. (1970). *Meaning and the Structure of Language*. University of Chicago Press.

Chomsky, C. (1969). *The Acquisition of Syntax in Children from 5 to 10*. Cambridge, Mass.: M.I.T. Press.

Chomsky, N. (1959). A review of B. F. Skinner's verbal behavior. *Language, 35*, 26–58.

Chomsky, N. (1965). *Aspects of the Theory of Syntax*. Cambridge, Mass.: M.I.T. Press.

Chomsky, N. (1972). *Studies on Semantics in Generative Grammar*. The Hague: Mouton.

Chomsky, N. and Halle, M. (1968). *The Sound Pattern of English*. New York: Harper and Row.

Clark, E. V. (1971). On the acquisition of the meaning of *before* and *after*. *Journal of Verbal Learning and Verbal Behavior, 10*, 266–75.

Clark, E. V. (1973a). How children describe time and order. In C. A. Ferguson and D. I. Sobin (Eds.), *Studies of Child Language Development*. New York: Holt, Rinehart, and Winston.

Clark, E. V. (1973)b). Non-linguistic strategies and the acquisition of word meanings. *Cognition, 2*, 161–82.

Cook, V. J. (1973). The comparison of language development in native children and foreign adults. *International Review of Applied Linguistics, 11*, 13–28.

Cook, V. J. (1974). The acquisition of indirect object constructions. Mimeographed paper.

Cromer, R. F. (1968). The development of temporal reference during the acquisition of language. Harvard University (unpublished Doctoral Dissertation).

Cromer, R. F. (1970). "Childern are nice to understand": Surface Structure clues for the recovery of a deep structure. *British Journal of Psychology, 61*, 397–408.

Cromer, R. F. (1972a). The learning of surface feature cues to deep structure by educationally subnormal children. *American Journal of Mental Deficiency*, 77, 346–53.

Cromer, R. F. (1972b). The learning of surface structure clues to deep structure by a puppet show technique. *Quarterly Journal of Experimental Psychology*, 24, 66–76.

Cromer, R. F. (1974a). Child and adult learning of surface structure clues to deep structure using a picture card technique. *Journal of Psycholinguistic Research*, 3, 1–14.

Cromer, R. F. (1974b). The development of language and cognition: The cognition hypothesis. In B. Foss (Ed)., *New Perspectives in Child Development*. Harmondsworth, Middlesex: Penguin.

Cromer, R. F. (1975a). Are subnormals linguistic adults? In N. O'Connor (Ed.), *Language, Cognitive Deficits, and Retardation*. London: Butterworth.

Cromer, R. F. (1975b). An experimental investigation of a putative linguistic universal: Marking and the indirect object. *Journal of Experimental Child Psychology*, 20, 73–80

Cromer, R. F. (1976). The cognitive hypothesis of language acquisition and its implications for child language deficiency. In D. M. Morehead and A. E. Morehead (Eds.), *Normal and Deficient Child Language*. Baltimore: University Park Press.

Davis, J. and Blasdell, R. (1975). Perceptual strategies employed by normal-hearing and hearing-impaired children in the comprehension of sentences containing relative clauses. *Journal of Speech and Hearing Research*, 18, 281–95.

Dewart, M. H. (1972). Social class and children's understanding of deep structure in sentences. *British Journal of Educational Psychology*, 42, 198–203.

Dewart, M. H. (1975). A psychological investigation of sentence comprehension by children. University College London (unpublished Doctoral Dissertation).

Dodd, B. (1976a). A comparison of the phonological systems of mental age matched normals, severely subnormals, and Down's syndrome children. *British Journal of Disorders of Communication*, 11, 27–42.

Dodd, (1976b). The phonological systems of deaf children. *Journal of Speech and Hearing Disorders*, 41, 185–98.

Donaldson, M. and Balfour, G. (1968). Less is more: A study of language comprehension in children. *British Journal of Psychology*, 59, 461–72.

Donaldson, M. and McGarrigle, J. (1974). Some clues to the nature of semantic development. *Journal of Child Language*, 1, 185–94.

Donaldson, M. and Wales, R. J. (1970). On the acquisition of some relational terms. In J. R. Hayes (Ed), *Cognition and the Development of Language*. New York: Wiley.

Dore, J. (1974). A pragmatic description of early language development. *Journal of Psycholinguistic Research*, 3, 343–50.

Dulay, H. and Burt, M. (1974). A new perspective on the creative construction process in child second language acquisition. *Language Learning*, 24, 253–78.

Eimas, P. D. (1974). Auditory and linguistic processing of cues for place of articulation by infants. *Perception and Psychophysics*, 16, 513–21. (a).

Eimas, P. D. (1974). Linguistic processing of speech by young infants. In R. L. Schiefelbusch and L. L. Lloyd (Eds.), *Language Perspectives—Acquisition, Retardation, and Intervention*. Baltimore: University Park Press. (b).

Ervin-Tripp, S. (1973). Some strategies for the first two years. In T. E. Moore (Ed.), *Cognitive Development and the Acquisition of Language.* New York and London: Academic Press.

Ferguson, C. A. and Farwell, C. B. (1975). Words and sounds in early language acquisition. *Language, 51,* 419–39.

Ferreiro, E. (1971). *Les relations temporelles dans le language de l'enfant.* Genève: Librarie Droz.

Fillmore, C. (1968). The case for case. In E. Bach and R. Harms (Eds.), *Universals in Linguistic Theory.* New York: Holt, Rinehart and Winston.

Fodor, J. and Bever, T. (1965). The psychological reality of linguistic segments. *Journal of Verbal Learning and Verbal Behavior, 4,* 414–21.

Fodor, J. A. and Garrett, M. (1967). Some syntactic determinants of sentential complexity. *Perception and Psychophysics, 2,* 289–96.

Fodor, J. A., Garrett, M. and Bever, T. G. (1968). Some syntactic determinants of sentential complexity, II: Verb structure. *Perception and Psychophysics, 3,* 453–61.

Garrett, M., Bever, T. G. and Fodor, J. A. (1966). The active use of grammar in speech perception. *Perception and Psychophysics, 1,* 30–2.

Goodson, B. D. and Greenfield, P. M. (1975). The search for structural principles in children's manipulative play: A parallel with linguistic development. *Child Development, 46,* 734–46.

Graham, N. C. (1968). Short term memory and syntactic structure in educationally subnormal children. *Language and Speech, 11,* 209–19.

Graham, N. C. (1974). Response strategies in the partial comprehension of sentences. *Language and Speech, 17,* 205–21.

Greenfield, P. M., Nelson, K. and Saltzman, E. (1972). The development of rule-bound strategies for manipulating seriated cups: A parallel between action and grammar. *Cognitive Psychology, 3,* 291–310.

Harris, M. (1976). The influence of reversibility and truncation on the interpretation of the passive voice by young children. *British Journal of Psychology, 67,* 419–27.

Huttenlocher, J., Eisenberg, K. and Strauss, S. (1968). Comprehension: Relation between perceived actor and logical subject. *Journal of Verbal Learning and Verbal Behavior, 7,* 527–30.

Huttenlocher, J. and Strauss, S. (1968). Comprehension and a statement's relation to the situation it describes. *Journal of Verbal Learning and Verbal Behavior. 7,* 300–4.

Jackendoff, R. S. (1972). *Semantic Interpretation in Generative Grammar.* Cambridge, Mass.: M.I.T. Press.

Jakobson, R. (1968). *Child Language Aphasia and Phonological Universals.* The Hague: Mouton. (Originally published in 1941).

Jakobson, R., Fant, C. G. M. and Halle, M. (1952). *Preliminaries to Speech Analysis: The Distinctive Features and Their Correlates.* Cambridge, Mass.: M.I.T. Press.

Jakobson, R. and Halle, M. (1956). *Fundamentals of Language.* The Hague: Mouton.

Katz, J. J. and Bever, T. G. (1974). The fall and rise of empiricism. Paper reproduced by the Indiana University Linguistics Club.

Lakoff, G. (1971). Presupposition and relative well-formedness. In D. D. Steinberg and L. A. Jakobovits (Eds.), *Semantics.* Cambridge: Cambridge University Press.

Lenneberg, E. (1967). *Biological Foundations of Language.* New York: Wiley.

Liberman, A. M. (1970). The grammars of speech and language. *Cognitive Psychology, 1,* 301–23.

Liberman, A. M., Cooper, F. S., Shankweiler, D. P. and Studdert-Kennedy, M. (1967). Perception of the speech code. *Psychological Review, 74,* 431–61.

Macnamara, J. (1972). Cognitive basis of language learning in infants. *Psychological Review, 79,* 1–13

Maratsos, M. P. (1973). The effects of stress on the understanding of pronominal co-reference in children. *Journal of Psycholinguistic Research, 2,* 1–8.

McCawley, J. D. (1971a). Meaning and the description of languages. In J. F. Rosenberg and C. Travis (Eds.), *Readings in the Philosophy of Language.* Englewood Cliffs, N. Jersey: Prentice-Hall.

McCawley. J. D. (1971b). Where do noun phrases come from? In D. D. Steinberg and L. A. Jakobovits (Eds.), *Semantics.* Cambridge: Cambridge University Press.

McCawley, J. D. (1973). A review of Noam A. Chomsky, studies on semantics in generative grammar. Paper reproduced by the Indiana University Linguistics Club.

McNeill, D. (1970). *The Acquisition of Language.* New York: Harper and Row.

McNeill, D., Yukawa, R. and McNeill, N. B. (1971). The acquisition of direct and indirect objects in Japanese. *Child Development, 42,* 237–49.

Mehler, J. and Carey, P. (1968). The interaction of veracity and syntax in the processing of sentences. *Perception and Psychophysics, 3,* 109–11

Menyuk, P. (1964). Comparison of grammar of children with functionally deviant and normal speech. *Journal of Speech and Hearing Research, 7,* 109–21.

Menyuk, P. (1969). *Sentences Children Use.* Cambridge, Mass.: M.I.T. Press.

Miller, G. A. (1962). Some psychological studies of grammar. *American Psychologist, 17,* 748–62.

Miller, G. A. and Chomsky, N. (1963). Finitary models of language users. In R. D. Luce, R. R. Bush and E. Galanter (Eds.), *Handbook of Mathematical Psychology* Vol. II. New York: Wiley.

Miller, G. A. and McNeill, D. (1969). Psycholinguistics. In G. Lindzey and E. Aronson (Eds.), *The Handbook of Social Psychology,* 2nd Edition, Vol. 3. Reading, Mass.: Addison-Wesley.

Morse, P. A. (1974). Infant speech perception: A preliminary model and review of the literature. In R. L. Schiefelbusch and L. L. Lloyd (Eds.), *Language Perspectives—Acquisition, Retardation and Intervention.* Baltimore: University Park Press.

Nelson, K. (1973). Structure and strategy in learning to talk. *Monographs of the Society for Research in Child Development, 38* (Nos. 1–2, Serial No. 149).

Piaget, J. and Inhelder, B. (1969). *The Psychology of the Child.* London: Routledge and Kegan Paul. (Originally published in 1966.)

Seuren, P. A. M. (Ed.). (1974). *Semantic Syntax.* London: Oxford University Press.

Sheldon, A. (1974). The role of parallel function in the acquisition of relative clauses in English. *Journal of Verbal Learning and Verbal Behavior, 13,* 272–81.

Sinclair, H. (1971). Sensorimotor action patterns as a condition for the acquisition of syntax. In Renira Huxley and Elisabeth Ingram (Eds.), *Language Acquisition: Models and Methods.* London and New York: Academic Press.

Slobin, D. I. (1973). Cognitive prerequisites for the development of grammar. In C. A. Ferguson and D. I. Slobin (Eds.), *Studies of Child Language Development*. New York: Holt, Rinehart and Winston.

Smith, N. V. (1973). *The Acquisition of Phonology*. Cambridge: Cambridge University Press.

Starr, S. (1975). The relationship of single words to two-word sentences. *Child Development*, *46*, 701–8.

Strohner, H. and Nelson, K. E. (1974). The young child's development of sentence comprehension: Influence of event probability, nonverbal context, syntactic form and strategies. *Child Development*, *45*, 567–76.

Studdert-Kennedy, M. (1974). The perception of speech. In T. A. Sebeok (Ed.), *Current Trends in Linguistics* Vol. 12. The Hague: Mouton.

Suci, G. J. and Hamacher, J. H. (1972). Psychological dimensions of case in sentence processing: Action role and animateness. *International Journal of Linguistics*, *1*, 34–48.

Waryas, C. L. and Ruder, K. (1973). Children's sentence processing strategies: the double-object construction. Parsons Research Center working paper no. 296.

Waryas, C. and Stremel, K. (1974). On the preferred form of the double object construction. *Journal of Psycholinguistic Research*, *3*, 271–80.

Wetstone, H. S. and Friedlander, B. Z. (1973). The effect of word order on young children's responses to simple questions and commands. *Child Development*, *44*, 734–40.

Wilcox, S. and Palermo, D. S. (1975). 'In', 'on', and 'under' revisited. *Cognition*, *3*, 245–54.

CHAPTER 9

The Development of Logical Operations and Reasoning*

S. Farnham-Diggory

I. INTRODUCTION

(1) INFORMAL CRITERIA

The capacity for logical thought is an important distinguishing characteristic of the human animal, and has preoccupied philosophers,
theologians, educators, and psychologists since the inception of their
respective disciplines. Most cultures recognize that reasoning ability
develops with age, and have institutionalized certain chronological
benchmarks. In many American states, for example, 16 marks a cross-
over point for driving an automobile. The 16-year-old is considered
to have reason enough for that (i.e., to be legally responsible for his
decisions). But only 17-year-olds are considered able to make wise
judgments about joining the Navy, and only 21-year-olds are entrusted
with the problem of choosing political representatives.

What do we mean when we say an individual has reached the age
of reason? It is helpful to think, first, of what we do not mean. We do
not mean that an individual is capable of learning particular responses
through endless repetition. We do not mean that he is capable of
ordinary description—of saying what colour an apple is, for instance.
We do not mean that he is capable of simple imitation. We do not

* I am grateful to Elliott Simon for his assistance with research chores; to
Lee Gregg, David Klahr and Robert Siegler for critical readings of the
manuscript; and to Rachel Falmagne (Editor) and Lawrence Erlbaum (Publisher)
for graciously making available page proofs of *Psychological Studies of Logic
and its Development*, an important collation of papers relevant to this chapter
topic.

13—CP * *

mean that he can match up identical stimuli. We do not mean he can perform exact translations, or one-to-one mapping. We do not mean that he is capable of applying rules mechanically, such as saying "Thank you" for a present, or stepping on the brakes when a traffic light turns red.

Instead, we mean that the individual is capable of inventing novel responses that are appropriate to a situation he may never have experienced before, much less practised. We mean that he can make inferences about properties of objects, rather than simply describe them. We mean that he can go beyond imitation and predict unobserved behaviour. We mean that he can detect equivalences among nonidentical stimuli and recognize hierarchical relations among equivalence classes. We mean that he can perform transformations, not merely one-to-one translations. We mean that he can formulate rules, discover patterns, invent organizations and design plans.

Of course these are not all the things we mean by reason or nonreason but they serve to stake out the behavioural domains in question.

(2) FORMAL CRITERIA

The above interpretations of "reasoning" and "logic" are informal. More formally, the terms derive from a philosophical discipline which has many branches (Johnson-Laird and Wason, 1970; Johnson-Laird, 1975). Most commonly, we think of the type of inference illustrated by the nonsense syllogism:

(1) All birds have purple tails
(2) All cats are birds
(3) Therefore all cats have purple tails

Formal syllogisms have a precise structure. The first proposition (1) asserts a relation between the predicate term of (3) the conclusion (have purple tails) and another term (all birds). The first proposition is called the *major premise*. The second proposition (2), known as the *minor premise*, describes a relation between the subject of the conclusion (cats) and the second term, above (all birds).

In reasoning with quantifiers, there are additional rules. First, within each proposition, the orders may be reversed (all things with purple tails are birds). Consequently, the syllogism can be expressed in 4 possible ways (2 orders per premise × 2 premises). These orderings are called *figures*. Secondly, premises are characterized by *quantification* and by *polarity*. They may be quantified as *all* or *some*; that is, as universal or particular. They are polarized as *negative* or *affirmative*.

Quantification and polarization can refer to either the first or second term of a proposition:

All cats have purple tails...
No cats have purple tails...
Some cats have purple tails...
Some cats do not have purple tails...

Since these combinations can be found in either the major or minor premise, there are 16 possible combinations—2 (quantifications) × 2 (polarizations) × 2 (locations) × 2 (premises)—which in turn are multiplied by the 4 possible figures. That means a given syllogism can be expressed in 64 possible ways. Because the same conclusion is always stated, many of the 64 syllogisms will be invalid; exactly 45 of them.

Precise structural formalizations of that type are valuable to psychologists because they provide a way of detecting differences in decision processes. The decision in this case is as to whether a given conclusion is true or false. Suppose a premise contains a negative. Will that affect the speed or accuracy of the decision? If so, it means that processing negative information requires additional mental steps or effort (Just and Carpenter, 1971; Wason, 1959). Does the nature of the quantification make a difference? Is *all* more likely to produce errors of judgment—or slower decision times—than *some*, or *vice vera*? That may depend upon the nature of the empirical facts being examined (Just, 1974).

It is also the case that reality matters—the fact that cats are not birds, for example. Wason and Johnson-Laird (1972) found that college students reasoned poorly on a problem referring to letters and numbers, while they reasoned well on exactly the same problem (formally) when it was presented in terms of natural language and experience (for instance, "If A, then 6" as compared to "If I go to Manchester, I travel by train"). This illustrates the fact that although human reasoning is rule governed, its rules are those of traditional propositional logic alone.

Nevertheless, formal logic like any viable discipline is continually developing, and an appropriate calculus of human reasoning may someday be formulated. "For this reason", Osherson (1975, p. 89) points out, "it is prudent to keep an eye on rapid developments in logic ... Many of these systems have been developed precisely with the idea of capturing our intuitions ... in a superior fashion to that of standard logic" (see Hughes and Cresswell, 1968).*

* I am irresistibly reminded of paleontologist Loren Eiseley's report on his wife's comment on viewing some tree-climbing fish, remnants of our phylogenetic past. "They ought to be watched," she said suspiciously, "they ought to be watched."

(3) RELATIONSHIP BETWEEN FORMAL AND INFORMAL REASONING TASKS

Consider this item from the Binet intelligence scale :

> A man said, "I know a road from my house to the city which is
> downhill all the way to the city, and downhill all the way back home."
> What (the experimenter asks the child) is foolish about that?

In this item, propositions are stated, compared, and conclusions about
them are reached. Theoretically, we could specify a list of possible
ways in which this could be done. On the basis of the list, we could
derive predictions about the speed or accuracy of the child's answer.
And indeed, anyone who has administered the Binet "absurdities" has
been struck by the temporal parameters of the child's response. After
the item has been read, there is a measurable pause before the child
breaks into a grin. That pause is filled with the reasoning processes
we want to understand. If our model of them were sufficiently detailed
and correct, we would be able to predict the length of that pause.

Informal reasoning, like formal syllogistic reasoning, can be evaluated against a theoretical set of logical processes. The nature of the set
will vary, depending upon the problem and upon the background of
the theorist. We are far from knowing if exactly one true and proper
set exists for all forms of human reasoning. We are only just beginning
to recognize some of our theoretical options.

(4) THEORIES OF OPERATIONAL CAPABILITY

Historically, an early theory of reasoning arose from *the mental testing
movement*. A mysterious factor called g was alleged to exist, and to
have been isolated empirically through various statistical techniques
(Spearman and Wynn-Jones, 1951). Partly in opposition to the non-
specific nature of g, Piaget then constructed his own theory of operational development—the major developmental theory of our time
(Piaget and Inhelder, 1969). With the advent of psycholinguistics, these
same operations were approached through the analysis of children's
language acquisition and usage. Simultaneously, the new science of
information processing introduced unique concepts, empirical strategies, and methods of formalization.

These four historical trends have not been mutually exclusive. The
mysterious g is still with us, and still of practical use. Language analyses
and information processing analyses are enriching and extending
Piagetian theory, but by no means supplanting it.

In the sections to follow, we shall survey each major formulation and point out some of their interconnections. Within each section, illustrative studies of formal or informal reasoning will be cited, but it will not be possible to provide an exhaustive review of the literature. Our emphasis will be on modes of research rather than upon empirical facts as such, because the facts are still often a matter of interpretation. The aim of the chapter is to prepare the reader to recognize the significance of new experimental studies for ongoing theoretical positions.

II. REASONING AS GENERAL INTELLIGENCE

(1) PHYLOGENETIC DEVELOPMENT

One way of accounting for the growth of reasoning and logic is to postulate genetic controls. Reasoning is said to develop because it is genetically predisposed to develop in certain populations.

There has been a number of attempts to compare the reasoning ability of different species of animals. Thorndike (1898) originated one line of research with the invention of his famous "puzzle boxes". Animals placed inside a box had to learn how to paw or bite open a door latch in order to escape. More sophisticated apparatus was eventually developed. Warden (1951) described a multiple-plate problem box consisting of a large mesh cage with a small cage inside it. Metal discs or plates were placed around the small cage, and the animal had to learn to step on them in order to open the door to the food cage. Many variations of plate-stepping were possible: the animal might have to step on 1, 2, 3, or more plates, and/or it might have to step on them in a given order. Each animal was trained to the limit of its learning ability. Warden reported: "The limit score for the guinea pig is one plate; for the white rat, two plates; for the cat, seven plates; and some monkeys were able to learn to step on twenty-two plates in the given order. A human child old enough to count presumably could go on indefinitely on such a test" (Warden, 1951, p. 4).

These tests seem clearly a matter of rote memory rather than of reasoning, but it can be argued that the evolution of intelligence depended upon the prior evolution of just such basic skills. Stenhouse (1973) believes that four factors have contributed to the evolution of higher forms of reasoning: (a) increasing memory storage and retrieval capacity; (b) increasing ability to abstract and generalize, which, Stenhouse points out, all animals have to some extent; (c) increasing sensorimotor efficiency (for instance, the ability to see farther); and (d) increasing ability to delay or withhold instinctive responses (fixed action patterns). Those same capacities can be said to underlie ontogenetic development, the mental growth of an individual. But this does not mean "ontogeny recapitulates phylogeny", which it certainly does not. It means only that Stenhouse's critical abilities are very general ones, a fact which poses major problems for a phylogenetic argument.

General abilities are not passed on genetically. There are no genes for "remembering" or "abstracting". Genes control physiological mechanisms which make pieces of complex behaviour possible. For example, we know that the ability to synthesize protein is involved in memory (Agronoff, 1967; Barondes, 1973). Protein synthesis is itself a complex biochemical reaction and there are many ways in which stages of the reaction could be genetically affected. To be able to state with scientific accuracy that "differences in memory ability are inherited", we must be able to demonstrate exactly what those genetic mechanisms are.

Behaviour genetics, in contrast to *biochemical* genetics, is a very crude first step in the search for biochemical mechanisms. Behaviour genetics relies on the administration of tests to groups of individuals, some of whom are more strongly related biologically than others. If test scores are more alike among related than unrelated individuals, we suspect genetic influences. That is all we can do, suspect. Until specific genetic mechanisms are isolated biochemically, we cannot be sure.

To help refine behaviour domains, psychometricians have broken down general tests into subsets of homogeneous skills. This is done statistically by means of factor analysis or other multidimensional scaling techniques. Essentially, a battery of tests is administered, and tests which co-vary are said to define a single psychological factor. By such means, Cattell (1971) has isolated what he calls "fluid v. crystallized" intelligence. Crystallized intelligence is defined by tests which require special knowledge and education, while fluid intelligence is defined by tests of so-called pure reasoning. Two examples are shown in Fig. 9.1. Scores on tests of fluid intelligence are more likely to co-vary with biological relationship than are scores on tests of crystallized intelligence. That seems plausible, since crystallized intelligence is intended to be a measure of what has been provided by the environment,

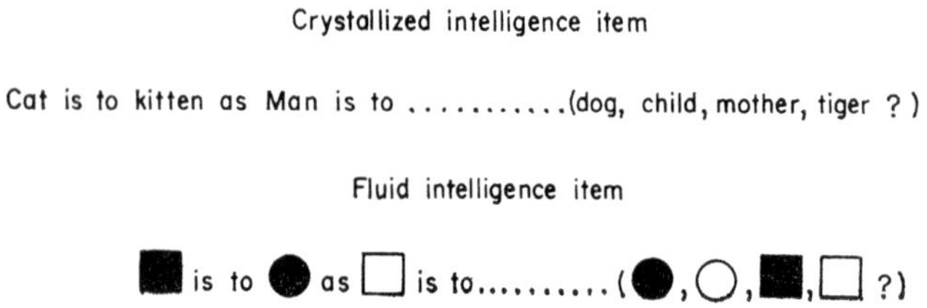

Crystallized intelligence item

Cat is to kitten as Man is to ....(dog, child, mother, tiger ?)

Fluid intelligence item

■ is to ● as ☐ is to.........(●, ○, ■, ☐ ?)

FIG. 9.1 Items from a typical test of human reasoning.

although, of course individuals differ in their capacity to learn from an environment, and some of this difference also has genetic roots.

(2) ONTOGENETIC CHANGE

The distinction between fluid and crystallized intelligence is still a very gross distinction. If we are to make real scientific progress on the genetics issue—that is, if we are to pinpoint biochemical mechanisms —then we must be able to specify exactly how a reasoning task is being performed. Similarly, if genetic programmes control the unfolding of reasoning ability during the life span, then we must understand exactly what unfolds. We must be able to specify how a task that is passed by 50 per cent of a 5-year-old population makes demands that differ from those made by a task passed by 50 per cent of a 3-year-old population. Only if we can discover such task differences shall we know what biochemical factors to look for. For example : On the Stanford-Binet, 3-year-olds and 5-year-olds are expected to put paper fragments together; to make a ball, and to match a rectangle, respectively, as shown in Fig. 9.2.

What psychological factors might be involved in this particular line of development? Attention to colour might govern the 3-year-old response. Attention to form is necessary for a correct 5-year-old response. Perhaps the maturation of form-specific neurons is the crucial genetic controller of this particular reasoning task. But other things are also involved; the 5-year-old task requires a comparison strategy. The child must look back and forth from the pieces to the model, performing certain mental tests each time. That means he must also be able to relate the task instructions to what he is looking at. What genetic mechanisms might underlie the ability to compare or to relate language to perceptual stimuli? These are the kinds of question we must ask in evaluating the contribution of behaviour genetics to the science of mental development.

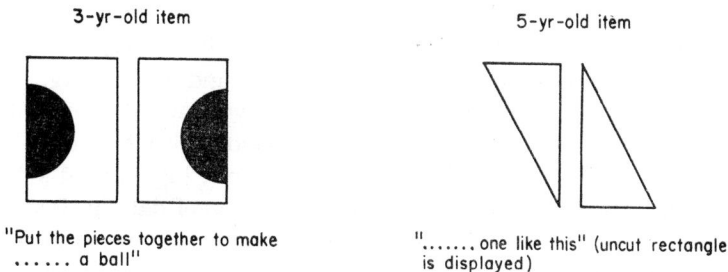

FIG. 9.2 Items from the Stanford-Binet intelligence test.

We must also consider the decline of reasoning abilities. It seems well established by now that fluid intelligence declines with ageing, while crystallized intelligence—what the individual has learned during his lifetime—does not (Cattell, 1971; Schaie, 1965, 1973). But again, without a detailed analysis of the tasks an ageing individual begins to fail, we cannot tell if memory, imagery, attention, knowledge of strategies, or other factors critically mediate the loss of reasoning ability.

(3) NEW RESEARCH TRENDS

The behaviour geneticist's disinterest in mental process is illustrated by the following comment of Vandenberg's (1968). Disappointed by a failure to find substantial concordance on Raven's Matrices in one sample of twin data, he wrote :

> Many reasoning tests allow one to reach the correct conclusion through several different approaches. Identical twins frequently select different routes, one of which may be speedier. Such more or less *accidental differences* in the method used would lower the (twin) concordance on that test (p. 157, italics added)

Individual differences in strategies of reasoning, which to a behavioral geneticist may constitute merely annoying error variance, are the data of primary interest to cognitive and developmental psychologists. In a paper entitled "Quote the Raven? Nevermore!", Hunt (1974) formally modelled as computer algorithms (to be described shortly) two strategies for solving Raven's Matrices, and noted that

> ... Nothing in the psychometric literature leads one to believe that identical general factor scores should be associated with qualitatively different styles of cognition ... what we require are diagnostic tests which tell us a person's cognitive style in intellectual operations, rather than an index of the person's location in a static Euclidean model of mental power (pp. 154–5)

Test research of this type is new, and most of it has been carried out by Hunt and his collaborators (Hunt, Frost and Lunneborg, 1973; Hunt, Lunneborg, and Lewis, 1975). They have found that many basic information processing variables are correlated with scores on a standardized test of verbal intelligence; for example, high verbal subjects (adults) are also "more rapid in the manipulation of data in short term memory, as evidenced by their performance on scanning and simple computation tasks" (Hunt *et al.*, 1975, p. 224). These authors believe that information processing skills are productive of high verbal ability, rather than the other way around. Research on that point is crucial, as is research utilizing test items themselves. Most urgently needed are developmental studies.

(4) SUMMARY

To summarize, we have considered the general proposition that reasoning ability is genetically pre-programmed and must be understood within the biological framework of human evolution. Probably (the biologist would argue) it resulted from the evolution of such basic capacities as the ability to remember, and to notice commonalities of experience. Current research in this area is focused on the search for biochemical mechanisms. Behaviour geneticists contribute to this search by administering tests of reasoning to groups that differ genetically—for instance, twins as compared to siblings—and looking for evidence that a biological relationship is mirrored by a relationship of test scores.

To understand what is being inherited, we must have better theories of the processing involved in answering test questions. Other fields of psychology—notably, cognitive and cognitive-developmental areas—have devised paradigms for analysing these processes. When such paradigms are incorporated into the fields of psychometrics and behaviour genetics, we should move more quickly towards an understanding of genetic influences on human logic.

III. THE STRUCTURES OF PIAGETIAN LOGIC

(1) THE SENSORIMOTOR STAGE OF DEVELOPMENT

As most readers probably know, Piaget once worked with Binet. Because he was displeased by Binet's emphasis on right answers—rather than on the reasoning strategies that could be inferred from wrong answers—Piaget left Binet's group and went on to build his own edifice. (As we have noted above, this difference between psychometricians and cognitive developmentalists is still with us.) The best introduction to Piagetian theory is the 1969 book with his famous collaborator Bärbel Inhelder, *The Psychology of the Child*, from which much of the following summary is taken.

According to Piaget, the earliest developmental stage is the sensorimotor stage. At this stage intelligence begins where the infant begins, with a set of simple reflexive capabilities. Within a few weeks, the infant has brought these action patterns under voluntary control, and soon becomes able to combine and extend them purposefully. Piaget describes the first 18 months to 2 years of life as the *sensorimotor period*, because it is characterized by the infant's discovery and expansion of his abilities to interpret his environment, and to direct his own motor system accordingly. By the end of this period, sensorimotor "know-how" has accumulated, and primitive concepts of space, time, the permanence of objects, and causality have stabilized. In effect, the infant now possesses a *logic of action*. Cognitively, he has moved from simple rhythm-structures and movement patterns to schematic regulations (actually, Piaget says, feedback loops like sucking→satiation →stop sucking), to primitive notions of principles underlying the schemes; for instance, to the notion that one can undo, or reverse, a pattern of activity.

In addition to the data generated by Piaget's own infant study methods (for instance, those in *The Construction of Reality in the Child*, 1954), evidence for infant logic has accumulated with the invention of other special research techniques; for example, habituation paradigms (Jeffrey and Cohen, 1971; Cohen, 1973). Once a stimulus (such as a red square) has "adapted out", as indicated by the infant's loss of interest in looking at it, its subjective nature—for the infant—can be tested by re-administering part of it, say a red blob. If redness was the crucial feature for the infant, his interest will not be reawakened, because from his standpoint the same stimulus has been presented again. If squareness was also a factor, then presenting a red *circle* may reawaken interest. That is, we can infer that *squareness* was registered and habituated if *circleness* does in fact reawaken interest.

This type of research has indicated that infants build up systematic knowledge structures and expectations. For example, S. Cohen (1974) has shown that 5- and 8-month-olds construct auditory-visual expectations that a certain face will be associated with a certain voice. When voices and faces are mis-matched, the infant's interest is markedly stimulated.

From the genetics standpoint, a recent study is of special importance. Matheny (1975) selected items from the Bayley infant tests of mental development that also tapped Piagetian sensorimotor skills. Matheny tested both identical and fraternal twins, and found that the concordance of scores was significantly greater among the monozygotic than among the dizygotic twins. That should encourage us to search for biological, heritable components in the development of sensorimotor logic.

(2) THE PREOPERATIONAL STAGE

About the age of 2, the child becomes able to represent or symbolize experience. Piaget describes this as the onset of the "semiotic function". It first appears—as does any form of intelligence in Piaget's system—as action. Events are symbolized in play and imitation, they are enacted. Later, the child becomes able to represent them in drawings, mental images, and words. All forms of symbolic behaviour are guided by the child's developing system of logic. For example, the difficulty that a 5-year-old has in drawing a diamond occurs, Piaget says, because the child lacks the logical capacity to reverse his drawing motions; to create a second half of a figure that is symmetrical with its first half.

We have obtained some data which are consistent with that proposition. Figure 9.3 is a schematization of eye and hand movements obtained by videotaping a 5-year-old child (Tina) attempting to draw a square and a diamond on a matrix of nine dots. The details of the analytical procedures are in Farnham-Diggory and Simon (1975). Applying the key, we can see that at T1 Tina looks ahead, and her hand, drawing the line, tracks her eye. At T2, the hand has caught up to the eye, and is being monitored by it. The developing square is shown as the solid line being "drawn" behind the wiggly one, at T3. Continuing through the protocol, the entire square has been completed by T14. Beginning at T15, Tina starts to draw the square again, but this time she is drawing it erroneously; she is supposed to draw a diamond. The development of the square, nevertheless, appears to be proceeding normally until T22, where the hand stops at the lower left dot, and the eye looks around "wildly". After that, things settle down, and the square is completed by T28.

The occurrences at T22 have theoretical significance within the framework of Piaget's theory. According to Piaget and Inhelder (1967), 5-year-olds are unable to draw diamonds because they lack the logical capacity to generate a figure that depends upon "reversing the relative order of the parts lying each side of the central axis" (p. 75). Unlike a square, a diamond-drawing programme apparently contains a "symmetry subroutine" which is activated when half the figure has been completed.

If Tina began her diamond in the wrong place (top right instead of top middle of the matrix), she may have noticed her error for the first time at the point where the "symmetry subroutine" would have been fired; the lower left dot where the hand waited at T22. Note that no "wild looks" appeared at T9, when Tina had reached exactly the same point in drawing a square intentionally. This suggests that the "symmetry subroutine" is not part of a square-drawing programme, only of a diamond—drawing programme—in keeping with Piaget's proposition.

Pattern drawing is often thought of as a purely perceptual task.

☐ → ☐   TINA   ◇ → ☐

T1 332   T9 149   T15 515 249   T23 365

T2 1345   T10 879   T16 1709 2141   T24 1145

T3 381   T11 564   T17 830   T25 232 232

T4 1029   T12 1992 979   T18 1211   T26 647

T5 879   T13 365   T19 83 199 249 597   T27 1361

T6 1079   T14 514   T20 315   T28 2091 3303

T7 614   T21 664

T8 1577   T22 83 232 / 83 / 249 365 / 249 664 / 298 315

KEY

Eye waiting hand tracking

Hand waiting, eye looking

Eye monitoring hand

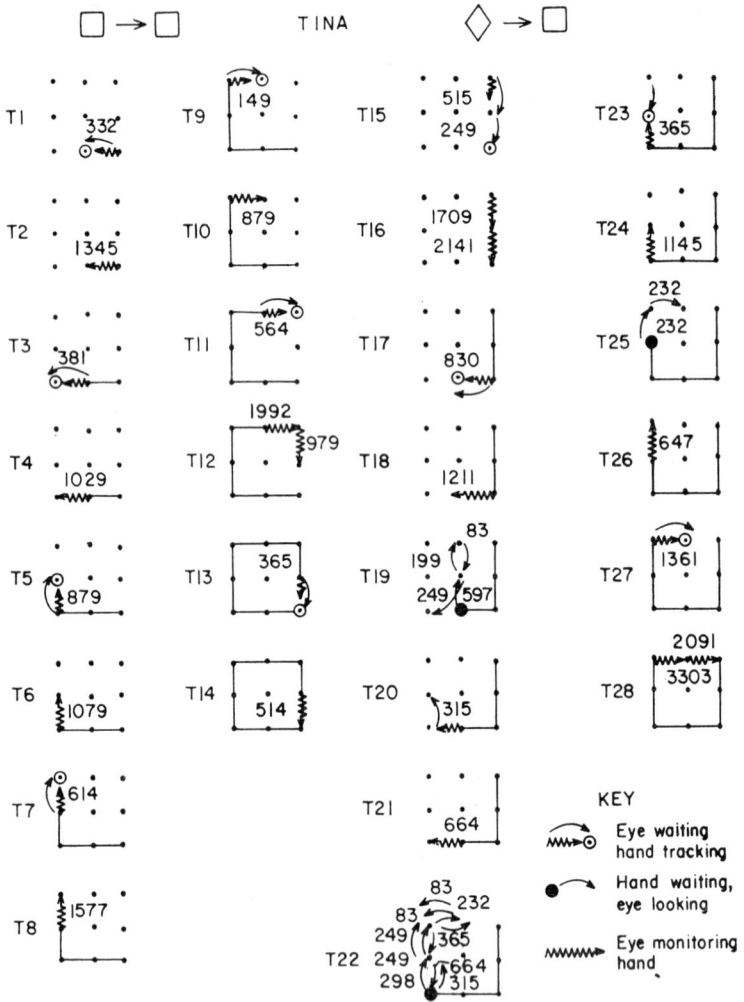

FIG. 9.3 Eye and hand movement protocol: a 5-year-old draws a square and a diamond.

The fact that cognition was found to be involved supports Piaget's belief that perception is governed by operational development. Piaget has studied perception as well as cognition, and has reported research on the *constancies*, on *field effects* similar to those described by Gestalt psychologists, and on what he calls "*perceptual activities*", which we can think of as skills in detecting and integrating featural information.

On the basis of his research, Piaget concluded that logical abilities and perceptual abilities follow different courses of development. Perception is essentially static. If improvements in it seem to occur, they are usually the result of improved guidance from the logical system. "Not ... that intelligence ... replaces perception, but by structuring reality it helps to program the way perceptual data are collected; that is, it helps indicate where to concentrate the attention" (Piaget and Inhelder, 1969, pp. 41–2).

The logical capacities governing semiotic functions also govern memory. The development of memory is, according to Piaget, primarily a matter of schematic organization (Piaget and Inhelder, 1973). Habitual action patterns are not memory. Memory is a result of comprehension or understanding. One implication is that memory will improve over time rather than deteriorate with improvements in intelligence. Piaget and his collaborators have tested that by having children reproduce, say, a seriated pattern of sticks at the age of 5, and then again six months later. In the intervening six months, if the child has discovered rules of seriation (that seriated objects can be organized like stairs going up or down) then his memory of what he saw will be improved; he will recreate the stick pattern more accurately than he did six months before. There is controversy over this experiment (see for instance, Liben, 1975; Dahlem, 1969; Furth, Ross and Youniss, 1974); but it is generally true that improvements in mental organization will improve memory.

As development continues, language plays an increasingly important function because it is flexible and public.

> Unlike images and other semiotic instruments which are created by the individual as the need arises, language has already been elaborated socially and contains a notation for an entire system of cognitive instruments (relationship, classifications, etc.) for us in the service of thought. The individual learns this system and then proceeds to enrich it. (Piaget and Inhelder, 1969, p. 87)

Even the act of learning this system, however, is governed by principles of mental development. In a later section, we shall review some of the research in developmental semantics which supports the proposition that pre-linguistic mental capacities direct language learning, rather than the other way around.

In the task of *predicting alternative directions of travel* (Piaget, 1971b), the child is shown three movable elements, for instance beads threaded on a wire, which disappear successively into a tunnel or behind a screen. He is asked to state the order in which the objects will emerge at the other side and the order in which they will reappear when moving in the opposite direction. The first question is repeated with the child moved to the other side of the table; with the tunnel rotated through 180° and then 360°; and finally half rotated to and fro several times. At Stage I (age 2–5) only the first question can be correctly answered; and at Stage III (age 7 and upwards) all questions are correctly answered. In the intermediate Stage II (age 5–7), questions are gradually answered, and there is some evidence of learning through practice, but the child has not abstracted any general rule. It is interesting to compare the design of this task with the plate-stepping task of Warden's (1951) described earlier. Instead of assuming that the sheer number of tunnel rotations measures the child's developing reasoning capability, Piaget looks for qualitative shifts in the child's strategy: first (Stage I) the child answers on the basis of simple memory; then (Stage II) he becomes able to organize his memory into classes of events, and to test hypotheses about them; and finally (Stage III) he becomes able to represent relations among the classes in the form of an abstract rule.

In the task of *understanding knots* (Piaget and Inhelder, 1967), the child is required to tie various knots, sometimes after demonstration. At Stage I (age 3–5) he cannot at first tie even a simple knot, but gradually acquires the capacity to do this. At Stage II (age 4–6) he can copy some types of knot, but cannot generalize a rule covering all these. Piaget states that the child can achieve a three-dimensional knot concept on the level of action, but not yet symbolically. This is achieved at Stage III (age 6 and upwards).

It is intuitively evident from the study of many such problems that Piaget is describing the emergence of what has elsewhere been called *learning sets* (Harlow, 1949; Gelman, 1969). But Piaget is concerned not merely with the fact of their emergence but also with their set structures.

(3) THE STAGES OF CONCRETE AND FORMAL OPERATIONS

> In my terminology, "operations" are internalized actions which are reversible; that is, they can be performed in opposite directions. Finally, they are co-ordinated into overall structures, and these structures give rise to a feeling of intrinsic necessity. (Piaget, 1971a, p. 2)

It is not easy to understand what Piaget means by *operations*, *internalized actions*, *reversibility*, *co-ordination*, *structures*, or *feelings-of-necessity*. He usually explains them by illustrating them. One illustration concerns a mathematician friend who reported (to Piaget) a discovery that he made as a young child. He was counting pebbles, and discovered that the number of pebbles remained the same no matter which way he was counting and no matter what the pattern of the pebbles (line, square, circle). The activity illustrates the action of counting. How was it then internalized as a counting operation; the reversibility of the operation; the co-ordination of the operations into a set which has certain elegant, quasi-mathematical properties and which also has a logically compelling quality? An adult hearing this anecdote is inclined to say, "Well of *course* the pebbles were the same number no matter which way he was counting!" The point is, the adult was not born with that knowledge. He had to discover it, and in the course of making many such discoveries he formulated principles for thinking logically about everything.

The child who has not yet internalized his actions (as operations which are independent of whatever circumstance gave rise to them) is called *pre-operational*. Even though a 4-year-old can count, he is not likely to discover properties of his own counting actions. He is more interested in properties of the pebbles. The child who can make the above discoveries is operational, but he is *concretely operational* because his discovery depends upon the presence of the pebbles. The mathematician who can discover and describe the formal properties of concrete logic is *formally operational*. He will recognize that the logic of pebble-counting has certain properties in common with the logic of other situations, and will have a "feeling of necessity" regarding the formalization of these commonalities.

The principles which govern mature thought are, in Piaget's model, interlocked and balanced. He has attempted to axiomatize them; to show that logical operations have formal mathematical characteristics. This has not been especially successful, but it is interesting to consider that a craving for elegance, for a logically compelling descriptive system, for a set of generative principles that will account for all thought with no loose ends; this urge on Piaget's part, and on the part of other theorists is in itself the essence of what Piaget means by formal operational development.

(4) THE ROLE OF TEACHING

In general, Piaget believes that the structures of one stage of development make those of the next stage necessary.

> Formal structures become necessary when the concrete structures are complete; concrete structures become necessary when the . . . (pre-operational) structures are complete; and these in turn become necessary when the sensorimotor functions are complete. (Piaget, 1971a, p. 9)

Such growth cannot be hurried. About two years are necessary for the construction of the sensorimotor structures. Six or eight years may be necessary for the construction of the concrete operational structures, the six- to eight-year period being the pre-operational stage. Four to six years are then necessary for the construction of those structures which give birth to formal operational thinking somewhere between the ages of 12 and 14. Nothing can be hurried, nothing can be skipped, nothing can be put into the child from the outside; the child must design and build his own reasoning abilities, in his own way, in his own time, from the inside.

This constraint is disturbing because it seems to imply that teaching may be of no use, that a child will not learn what does not already fit the mental structures he has developed. But this is not strictly true. In Piaget's terms, new knowledge will be *assimilated* to existing structures. If assimilation is not altogether possible, however, the structures may then *accommodate* to the information. The child's ideas about the situation will "stretch". Of course there is a limit to the amount of stretching that will be possible or comfortable, and therein lies the teacher's skill : to begin with a sense of where the child is and what he knows, and then to enlarge that knowledge "just the right amount". This is not yet a science, it is an art, but many teachers practice that art brilliantly.

(5) THE LOGIC OF CLASSES

We can see from the tasks described on pp. 371 and 372 that classes of events are being defined and experienced. Some of these classes, for instance, particular knots, or a small number of tunnel turns, are included in higher-order classes (all knots, all odd numbers of tunnel turns). In these two tasks, because the elements are transitory and consecutive, the formal set structure is not immediately evident. In other tasks, the elements remain at the child's (and the reader's) disposal. The classification task in particular makes the nature of the formalized Piagetian set structure more explicit.

The classification experiments utilize materials of many different kinds; for instance, flat geometrical blocks or pictures of flowers. Basically, the child is asked a series of questions probing his understanding of the logic of classes. The materials to which the questions refer are always present, and the child is often instructed to manipulate them.

The mental developments of interest to Piaget concern the child's discovery of grouping principles. At maturity, this awareness includes the following self-discovered, self-imposed rules of free classification (Inhelder and Piaget, 1964, p. 48):

1. Everything must be classified, with nothing left over.

2. Every class must imply its complement (if the child recognizes animals as a class, he must also be able to recognize that a class of non-animals exists).

3. Classes are defined by particular properties.

4. A class must include only members having those particular properties.

5. Classes must not overlap unless one is included in the other.

6. A complementary class also has its own characteristics.

7. A class is included in every higher ranking class which contains its elements (for instance, dogs are animals, dogs are also living things).

8. Classes should be minimized (fewest possible).

9. Distinguishing criteria should be similar (do not make one group reds, and another squares; make one group reds and the other blues).

10. Hierarchies should be symmetrical (if blues are sub-divided into squares and circles, then reds should be also).

The presence of these rules can be inferred from the child's behaviour and statements. As always, the child is found to progress through stages.

Stage I (age 2–4: Piaget calls this the stage of "graphic collections". The child, in response to the instruction "Put together the things that are alike" creates a collective spatial object, such as a string of squares, or a tower, or a "house with a roof and chimney". Essentially, none of the above rules is discovered. The child does not even feel obliged to use all of the elements (1).

Stage II (age 4+ to 6+): Called the stage of "non-graphic collections". The child spontaneously applies Rules (1), (2), (3), (4), (5) and (6), and may attempt to find symmetries and simplicities (8) and (9). But he completely fails to understand principles of class inclusion (7) and (10).

Stage III (age 7 on): The class inclusion rules now appear.

Several types of experiments have been devised to probe the child's knowledge of class inclusion rules. In one, the child is shown sets like the array in Fig. 9.4, and is asked such questions as: "Are all the squares red?" The probe here concerns the child's awareness that the set of squares is larger than, and includes, the set of red squares.

During Stage I (graphic collections), children concentrate on the meaning of the word *all*. They apparently attempt to formulate mentally a collection "all the squares", and base their answers on the

FIG. 9.4 Sample stimuli used in class-inclusion studies. The solid shading indicates red; the hatched shading indicates blue. (*After* Inhelder and Piaget, 1964, p. 60).

success of that formulation. If anything in the stimulus display is not square, the answer will be "No", and conversely.

At Stage II (non-graphic collections), the child answers as if the question were: "Are *all* of the squares *all* of the reds?" Whereas the question is really (by implication) "Are all of the squares *some* of the reds?" Hence, it can be inferred that class-inclusion is not recognized.

At Stage III, the questions are answered correctly.

Piaget further investigated the child's comprehension of the word "some", and found that it evolved from a vague awareness of a difference between "some" and "all", to an absolute meaning of *small* ("some" = "one or two"), or to an absolute meaning of *a particular subset* ("some" = "all the same colour"), to a final stage of relative meaning ("some" = "part" regardless of the total set size). Neimark and Chapman (1975) have carried these investigations up the age scale and report that although subjects in grades 7 through college interpret "all" and "no" (the universal negative) in accord with logical convention, they still interpret "some" as meaning "some but not all", an interpretation which is not strictly logical.

In another type of experiment, children may be shown a bunch of flowers containing three tulips and seven daisies, and asked: "Are there more daisies or more flowers?" Questions of that form have received a great deal of experimental attention. One line of argument says that the perceptual "pull" of the situation is misleading. The visual salience of seven daisies relative to three tulips is thought to cause the child to respond in terms of a salience effect, rather than logically. Ahr and Youniss (1970) varied the sub-class ratios, and showed that correct inclusion responses increased as the ratio decreased. Another way of approaching this is not to show the child any stimulus materials at all, but merely to say: "I have seven daisies and three tulips. Do I have more daisies or more flowers?" When the task is in that verbal form, it is more likely to elicit correct answers (Wohlwill, 1968). Still a third line of argument is that the question is misunderstood; the child thinks he is supposed to compare subclasses, rather than to compare one sub-class to the higher-order class (flowers) that includes it. Each of these arguments is susceptible to further arguments, which have been forthcoming (Winer, 1974b); Tatarsky, 1974; Kalil, Youssef and Lerner, 1974; Brainerd and

Kaszor, 1974). Klahr and Wallace (1972) summarized the main issues, and concluded that any explanation would be inadequate if it failed to analyze the information processing demands of the task.

There has been some discussion as to whether children can be trained in classification. Using a habituation paradigm, Faulkeneder, Wright and Waldron (1974) found that the looking time of toddlers decreased (habituation occurred) on repeated presentation of pictures from a single conceptual category (for instance animals). When novel pictures from the same category were presented, looking time increased but not as much as it increased for items from a new category (food, for instance). These subjects were quite young, still in what Piaget would consider the stage of graphic collections. Their behaviour indicates that classification skills on naturalistic materials may develop earlier than skills on unfamiliar geometrical materials.

That fact is not inconsistent with Piagetian theory; on the contrary, Piaget has often reported such anomalies. For example, if 6-year-olds are shown the bunch of flowers containing three tulips and seven daisies, and are asked, "Are there more daisies or more flowers?" they are likely to respond, logically enough, "More flowers". However, if they see pictures of three lions and seven tigers, and are asked, "Are there more tigers or more animals?" they are likely to answer, "More tigers, because there are only three lions" (Inhelder and Piaget, 1964, p. 110). As noted earlier, a generally unsolved problem in the study of logical behaviour concerns the effect of personal familiarity on reasoning (see Wason and Johnson-Laird, 1972).

We do know that familiarity improves the ability to discriminate important features of a stimulus. If that is a reason why classification skills improve with familiarity, then other kinds of discrimination training should improve them as well. Studies by Denney and Acito (1974) and by Zimmerman (1974) have shown that discrimination training, especially modelling with verbalization, does improve the classification skills of 3- and 4-year-old children, even with unfamiliar, geometrical materials.

(6) MULTIPLE CLASSIFICATIONS

Like Hunt (1974) and Spearman before him (Spearman and Wynn-Jones, 1951), Piaget also recognized that there are two strategies for solving multiple classification problems, illustrated in Fig. 9.5. The (a) section of the figure shows a three-attribute problem : the correct choice concerns the type of animal, the colour of the animal, and the orientation of the animal. The (b) section shows a two-attribute problem. Despite the fact that the three-attribute problem is more

(a)

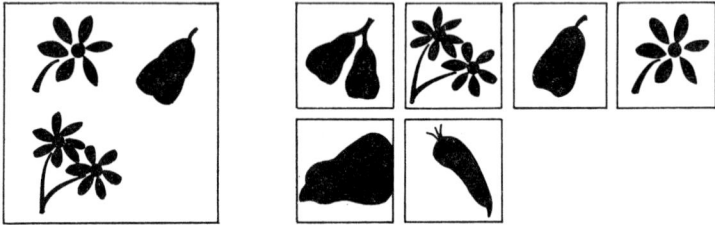

(b)

FIG. 9.5 Two of the items used by Piaget in multiple classification studies. For item (a) and item (b) respectively, the blank in the left box is to be filled in by an item selected from the box on the right. (*After* Inhelder and Piaget, 1964, p. 160 and 161.)

complex, it is easier to solve, because it can be solved on a global perceptual basis; what Hunt calls a "gestalt algorithm", and what Spearman called a "synthetic manner". Piaget likened this to a graphic collection, and showed that young children, still in the stage of graphic collections, could solve some three-attribute problems, although they could not justify their solutions.

The same children, however, could not solve two-attribute problems when they required operational thinking (which both Hunt and Spearman referred to as "analytic"). Spearman believed that only the "analytic" strategy was related to *g*. In Piaget's terms, the operational solution meant that the child was reasoning in terms of classes, rather than in terms of the perceptual "pull" of the display.

Hunt's analytic algorithm is especially interesting in this context, because it provides a way of making Piaget's meaning explicit. Unlike his Gestalt algorithm, which operates on sensory-perceptual data such as images, Hunt's analytic algorithm operates on sets of *features*. The algorithm first notices features of a matrix, represents them as an ordered collection, and then applies transformation rules to that collection. Hunt describes this as a "formal operational algorithm", but actually its rules of operation more closely resemble the concrete classification rules (1) through (10) listed above. Hunt's rules include tests for the presence of an element in each row (class) of a matrix (1) and operations for the production of symmetries and complementarities (2) and (10). His paper should be studied as an example of how simulation techniques force the theorist to be very explicit about how he thinks a reasoning process works.

(7) THE LOGIC OF RELATIONS

Simultaneously with developing classificatory logic, children develop a logic of relations, or orderings. We shall use a child's protocol to illustrate this and to illustrate how Piaget makes theoretical inferences from protocol data.

The child is shown a set of coloured rods that increase in length. The rods are in jumbled order. The child is first asked to draw, with coloured pencils, what the rods will look like when correctly seriated.

> Ang (7; 0) first draws colored lines of equal length, in an arbitrary order. *"I'm going by the colors. The green is here, the red is here,* etc." [The experimenter then says :] "'I'd like you to draw the sticks arranged in order of size (repeating the original instruction) using a black pencil." (Ang looks carefully at the objects.) *"The green one is the first."* (Draws a line, and looks at the objects each time he draws a new line. In this way, he constructs a perfectly regular series.) [The experimenter says :] "Could you make a drawing without looking at the sticks?" *"No"*. (Draws three lines and then stops.) [He is then instructed to seriate the actual sticks, and does so in this order :] 1, 2, 4, 3 (corrected), 6, 5 (corrected), 7, 8 (he compared them), 9, 10. (Inhelder and Piaget, 1964, p. 256).

First of all, the child defines the problem as a colour-matching one, and proceeds to solve it in an organized, methodical manner, in the course of which he forgets the seriation instructions! When given a black pencil, he attends to the seriation requirement but then tries to use colour cues too ("The green one is first . . ."). He attempts to incorporate both colour and length information because he fails to recognize that colour is irrelevant. This is quite characteristic of children who are concretely operational, but not yet formally operational. One of the defining characteristics of formal operations is recognition of how a set of task requirements may or may not comprise an integrated whole. The pre-formal child wants to do everything that he can think of doing, with no "feeling of necessity" regarding the logical interrelationship of all these activities. The protocol also illustrates the child's continuing (pre-operational) tendency to seriate by pairs; Piaget calls this "juxtaposition of couples". It is as if the child were somewhat unstable in recognizing that an ordered element can be simultaneously smaller and larger; smaller than the element on one side, larger than the element on the other. This is an important application of the *reversibility* principle.

Once this principle has stabilized, the child becomes capable of understanding *transitivity*. An outstanding series of experiments on the mechanisms underlying transitivity has been carried out by Trabasso and his colleagues (Trabasso and Riley, 1973; Riley and Trabasso, 1974; Bryant and Trabasso, 1971; Trabasso, Riley and Wilson, 1975). These experiments have shown how verbal representation of both comparative terms ("greater than" and "less than"), spatial imagery, and memory, facilitate transitivity in 4- and 5-year-olds. Their research strategies will be discussed further in our final section on information processing techniques.

(8) THE PRINCIPLE OF CONSERVATION

Implicit in all the logical behaviour previously described is the notion of *invariance*. To adults it is self-evident that an object remains the same object even though one's back is turned, or that a number, quantity, or weight remains the same despite changes in shape or orientation. But it was not always so. The principle of *conservation* in its many forms has to be discovered. Once discovered, its application powerfully increases mental logic.

There are seven types of situation in which conservation may be demonstrated to be incomprehensible to pre-operational children. Thus they consider that : (1) Quantity increases when liquid (or sand, etc.) is poured from a shorter, wider vessel into a taller, thinner one (conservation of quantity : Piaget, 1952); (2) Two pencils of equal length are unequal when they are not in line (conservation of length : Piaget, Inhelder and Szeminska, 1964); (3) Scattered models of houses cover a larger area then when they are close together (conservation of area : Piaget, Inhelder and Szeminska, 1964); (4) Blocks cannot be built into constructions of equal volume on bases of different areas (conservation of volume : Piaget, Inhelder and Szeminska, 1964); (5) Objects placed close together are less numerous than objects spaced apart (conservation of number : Piaget, 1952); (6) There is more clay when a ball of clay is rolled out into a thin "sausage" (conservation of substance : Piaget and Inhelder, 1941); (7) The weight of a ball of clay changes when it is rolled out thin or cut up into chunks (conservation of weight : Piaget and Inhelder, 1941).

Sheppard (1974b) found that training in compensation (learning how a change in one dimension produces a change in another) would facilitate conservation. Zimmerman and Rosenthal (1974) examined the effects of modelling and corrective feedback, and found they were positive. Brainerd (1974b) compared the effects of feedback on conservation, transitivity, and class inclusion. He found positive effects in all cases, but failed to find generalization from one type of training to the other tasks. Most of these studies have had the direct or indirect effect of drawing the child's attention to *features* of stimulus materials. (The discriminability of these features may be one of the factors underlying Piaget's "resistances".) It is clear that pre-operational children are not directing their attention properly, and that they can be trained to do so. The seminal study showing that strategies for direction of attention can be learned by young children was Gelman's (1969). We know from the work of Gibson and her colleagues that strategies of perceptual selectivity develop (see for instance Pick and Frankel, 1974; Gibson, 1969; Lasky, 1974). The problem for the cognitive theorist is to explain why. What are the mechanisms underlying the spontaneous development of the ability to manage one's own attention properly? Once we can answer that question, we shall have gone a long way towards understanding the development of conservation and of subsequent logical skills.

(9) The logic of geometrical intuition and number

The growth of conservation, classification and relational logic makes possible an understanding of number and geometry, but this is not a simple additive process. Our description has been fragmented, referring to reversibility or conservation principles as if each grew up in isolation. In Piaget's theory, what really grows up is a balanced group of logical structures.

Consider what is involved in the development of spontaneous logical measurement (Piaget, Inhelder and Szeminska, 1964). The task is to build a tower that is the same height as another tower. Blocks are provided, but they are of sizes and shapes different from those in the original tower, so one-to-one matching is not possible. Further, the table for the new tower is lower than the table holding the original tower. And finally, a small screen is in the way, so that the new tower cannot be seen from the site of the original, although the latter is readily accessible.

Stage I (age 4–6): Perceptual comparison, which the child trusts implicitly, is the only measurement mechanism. Nothing is moved except the line of vision, nothing is used as a measurement device.

Stage II (age 5–7): Objects are moved in the process of measurement. Sometimes this is one of the blocks being used in the construction, sometimes it is the child's own body, the span of a hand or arm, or the height of a shoulder. This representation is a form of imitation, and serves what Piaget now calls a "semiotic function", or primitive symbolism. Of special importance is the fact that the measurement object must be equal to the tower. If it is smaller or larger it is dismissed as useless, because the child has not yet formulated a concept of standard measurement units.

Stage III (age 7 on): The transitivity and conservation principles make possible the discovery that a third item, a measuring object of any size, can be used as an intermediary. In effect, if a portion of Tower A is equal to a block, and the block is in turn equal to a portion of Tower B, then the portion of Tower A must be equal to the portion of Tower B. This assumes, of course, that length is conserved despite changes in position. Further, the reversibility principle makes possible the discovery of accurate stepping—that a measuring device can be used as a counter. No matter which way the counter is moving, it will still add up to the same number of distance units provided the end-points of each step remain stable. That is, each time the measuring device is moved, it must begin where it previously left off. That is the same principle (reversibility) underlying the development of relational logic as illustrated by the seriation task. An element can be the beginning of something and the end of something at the same time. All these relations among distance, length, counting, etc. must be organized by the child and linked to a system of external reference points. That type of network is what Piaget means by a "logical grouping".

Much current research is directed towards identifying the component skills of number logic. What knowledge must a child have to understand the number system? Piaget considered this knowledge easier for the child to develop, relative to geometrical knowledge. Gelman's "surprise" experiments have shown that 3- and 4-year-olds can distinguish among variables (such as length or density) that do not affect number, and variables (such as adding or subtracting objects) which do (Gelman, 1972a, b; Gelman and Tucker, 1975). Similar findings have been reported by Winer (1974a); Lawson, Baron and Siegel (1974); Smither, Smiley and Rees (1974); and LaPointe and

O'Donnell (1974), among others. Work on ordination and cardination has established a developmental progression here : ordination is understood first (Brainerd, 1974a; Siegel, 1974; Schaeffer, Eggleston and Scott, 1974). Similarly, serial ordering is understood before transitivity (Youniss, 1975). Counting skills, number naming skills, and other number operations have been charted (Gelman, 1972b).

While much of this research is relevant to Piagetian theory, there are two other lines of theoretical work which should help provide an integrative framework for empirical data. Klahr and Wallace (1973), working within the information processing tradition, are constructing a detailed model of quantification skills. They have postulated three main quantification operators : a *subitizing* operator (subitizing is immediate apprehension, without counting, of small quantities), a *counting* operator, and an *estimating* operator. The development of these operators is said to depend upon the tendency of a system to seek consistency and to eliminate redundancy (by re-coding, say). Thus, when two identical objects are represented by two identical symbol-structures, an alternative, higher-order symbol is constructed to represent the redundancy. That is how the same number name comes to refer to qualitatively different sets, for example.

Counting requires such additional skills as direction of attention (for instance, learning to notice things in a particular order, and learning to notice where one stopped in a series). Once these skills are available, the system can begin to apply some of the higher-order rules it derived from subitizing to quantities which are out of the subitizing range. A similar mechanism leads to the refinement of estimating skills.

Schaeffer (1974) and his colleagues (Schaeffer, Eggleston and Scott, 1974) are constructing a theory of number development that is also hierarchical. Schaeffer is concerned with the integration of six number skills : the cardinality rule, the counting procedure, the idea of acquisition or cumulation, judgments of relative numerosity, pattern recognition of small numbers (subitizing), and one-to-one correspondence. He has graphed his hierarchical theory of development as shown in Fig. 9.6.

Schaeffer's growth principle is similar to a redundancy principle. In effect, he suggests how a redundancy principle would work : by automating certain component skills so that attention is freed to make new connections and associations. For example, "As the child practices counting, he appears to use less and less of his processing capacity to form and remember one-to-one correspondences and more and more of it for the ancillary operations of unitizing complex

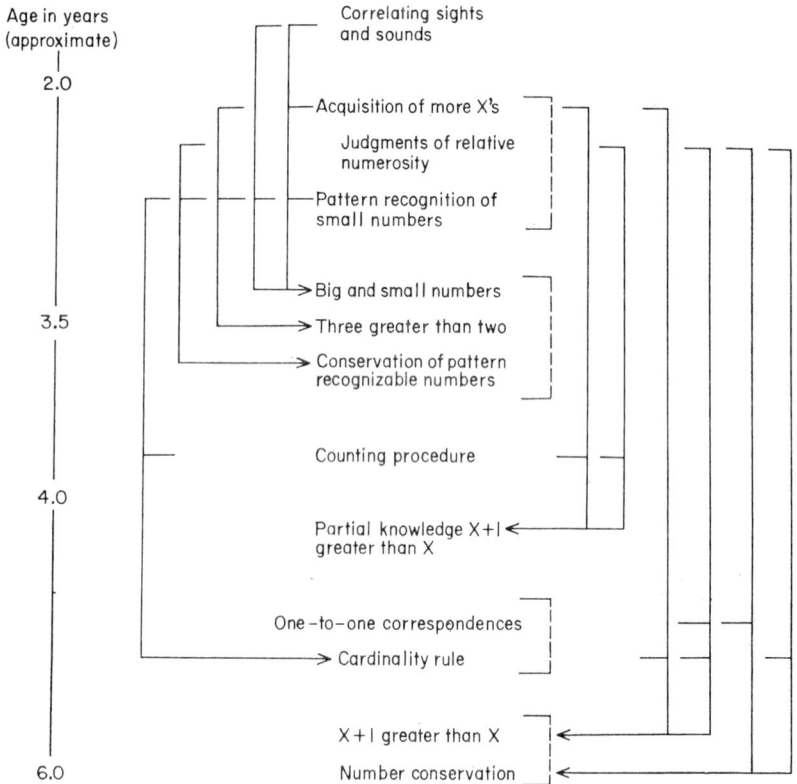

Fɪɢ. 9.6 Summary of hypothesized hierarchic integration during number development shows which old skills (short horizontal lines) are integrated (vertical lines) to form new skills (long horizontal lines with arrows). Two vertical lines connected to the same long horizontal line indicate two ways of forming the new skills. Dashed brackets enclose skills formed at approximately the same time. (*After* Schaeffer *et al.*, 1974, p. 377.)

stimuli and utilizing spatial plans to facilitate systematic counting" (Schaeffer *et al.*, 1974, p. 366). Strategies, in other words, eventually come to function as higher-order components of a counting programme.

The exact relationship of the foregoing work to Piagetian theory is not well worked out, primarily because that is very hard to do. But it is clear that such behaviourally-defined operations as comparing, judging density, and managing attention are compatible with Piaget's concepts. We are probably seeing here an evolution of scientific language and method, rather than a conflict of theoretical belief.

(10) THE EMERGENCE OF FORMAL OPERATIONS

Despite the fact that the concretely operational child is capable of performing abstractions, his ability to manipulate those abstractions mentally is limited. To reason logically, he must manipulate concrete materials. By the age of 12 or 13, this dependence upon the physical world begins to diminish. He becomes capable of "reasoning about reasoning", of testing hypotheses about ideas. This is much closer to formal syllogistic reasoning. The adolescent formulates propositions about reality, and tests the logic of their interrelationship. As we saw earlier, for many kinds of problem a set of logical possibilities can be precisely specified. We can thus evaluate the efficiency of an adolescent's reasoning by determining how many of those possibilities he will spontaneously express. Fifteen relevant experiments are compiled in the Inhelder and Piaget (1958) volume *The Growth of Logical Thinking from Childhood to Adolescence*. The experiments resemble those found in high school science classes, and appear to assess what the child has been taught in school. This appearance is deceptive. Paradigms of scientific reasoning are taught in high school instead of in elementary school because society has discovered that the paradigms will not be understood any earlier. That is exactly what Piaget is interested in investigating—the nature of the mental developments that make such understanding possible. Subjects work on problems that (in Piaget's opinion) are analogues of inner mental states. Their problem-solving protocols are therefore "outpicturings" of a logical system (or its absence) within. One experiment will be described, the pendulum problem (Inhelder and Piaget, 1958).

The child sees a pendulum which is varied in the following ways: it can have different weights attached to it, and it can have different length strings. The child's problem is to specify which variables, weight, length of string, or both, affect the amplitude of the pendulum's swing. It may appear, to the child, that such variables as the height of the release point or the force of the push, are also relevant. Actually, the only relevant variable is the length of the string. Thus the student's problem is to find a way of separating the effects of that variable from the effects of all the other variables, and to exclude the effects of the other variables. Exclusion is an important point here. The experiment can be performed with children of all ages, and it thus provides a convenient summary of Piagetian developmental theory. The pre-operational child never obtains any useful data because he continually interferes with the motion of the pendulum. It is as if he can understand only his own actions, not the independent actions of a piece of apparatus. The concrete operational child, with his grasp of classificatory and relational logic, wants to exercise all these capabilities at once; that is to say, he wants to vary everything at once. Because he *can* seriate weights, lengths, and forces, he has a "feeling of necessity" about doing so. What he lacks, and what the adolescent has, is a sense of interrelationship among these logical capabilities.

The pre-adolescent wants to make all possible combinations simultaneously. The adolescent has an intuitive recognition of the fact that *a set of all possible combinations are implied, and negated, by the exclusion of a variable*. Therefore, by holding one variable constant while manipulating another, he is automatically testing a complete set of possible factors. This intuitive knowledge has been built into such statistical techniques as the analysis of variance. But that does not mean the adolescent knows those particular techniques. It simply means there is a correspondence between certain scientific or statistical or mathematical methods, and the logical state of the (formally operational) minds which invented them. Thus, we have the 15-year-old successfully solving the pendulum problem by the following means:

> Eme (15; 1), after having selected 100 grams with a long string and a medium length string, then 20 grams with a long and a short string, and finally 200 grams with a long and a short concludes: *"It's the length of the string that makes it go faster or slower; the weight doesn't play any role."* She discounts likewise the height of the drop and the force of her push. (Inhelder and Piaget, 1958, p. 75)

The formal relationship between the structures of adolescent reasoning and those of concrete operational reasoning have not yet been well enough worked out to warrant further discussion here. In general, Piaget believes that the child's logic of classes and relations comprises *part* of the total logical programme found in the adolescent and adult. Exactly how the whole system should be axiomatized is too long and detailed an issue to be broached here. Osherson (1975) provides a good introduction and bibliography. Sheppard (1974a), Toussaint (1974), and Weinreb and Brainerd (1975) have provided some recent empirical data on Piaget's axiomatic principles.

Studies of training in formal operations have two values: (1) they provide practical guidance for teachers; and (2) they indicate what some of the underlying mechanisms of development may be. Thus, the transitivity training studies have implicated imagery and particular verbal representations; classification training studies have implicated feature discrimination; and conservation training studies have implicated both feature discrimination, and the more general skill of learning to manage one's own attention.

Relatively little work has been done in the area of formal operational development. The seminal studies are those of Siegler and his colleagues (Siegler, 1975a; Siegler, Liebert and Liebert, 1973; Siegler and Simon, 1975; Siegler and Liebert, 1974). Siegler has analysed several of the tasks in the Inhelder and Piaget volume on adolescent reasoning, as well as some new tasks of his own. His training studies have shown that the following variables are involved in scientific reasoning: knowledge of scientific language and concepts; knowledge of general experimental procedures relevant to a particular type of problem; knowledge of systems for recording data; and training on methods of making inferences from data. A comprehensive theory of how these task-specific behaviours are related to general powers of formal reasoning has not yet been offered. Further work is now being directed towards analysing the cognitive processes actually involved in the above skills, and an overall theory should result. The theory will be especially welcome because of its strong empirical base. Many model-builders, following Piaget, build elaborate structures on little more than illustrative cases.

(11) Evidence for the general growth of logic

We shall briefly note here a sampling of general research on the development of logical thinking. These studies are typical of those appearing in the current literature.

Two studies have investigated the relationship of Piagetian constructs to measures of general intelligence. De Vries (1974) found that Piagetian tasks, achievement tests, and intelligence tests measured different kinds of ability (factors) in elementary age children. Keating (1975) found, however, that a positive correlation existed (as one would certainly expect) between measures of formal operational ability and measures of intelligence among adolescents.

A variety of studies have shown that logical abilities increase with age, but many of these studies were not concerned with underlying mechanisms. Neimark and Lewis (1967) looked at behaviour on a concept-attainment type of game, and showed that logical behaviour increased with age, but offered no model of what was increasing. Offenbach (1974) and Gholson and McConville (1974), both working within the framework of Levine's model (Levine, 1966; Eimas, 1969) have shown that learning to attend to relevant cues—feature selection and direction of attention—facilitate logical hypothesis-testing over the life-span. It seems clear that concept-learning paradigms provide data of interest to Piagetians, but little attempt has been made to integrate the two research traditions.

Conditional reasoning (Kodroff and Roberge, 1975), analogical reasoning (Levinson and Carpenter, 1974), and causal reasoning (Berzonsky, 1975; Siegler and Liebert, 1974; Siegler, 1975b) have all been shown to improve with age, and some work has been done on underlying mechanisms. Siegler and Liebert (1974) showed, for example, that temporal *contiguity* was a critical one for young children, but that the *regularity* of a causal relationship was not. The reason was that young children failed to attend to the regularity. Again, direction of attention was found to be a key development mechanism.

It is interesting to consider some of the ways in which the study of reasoning abilities can be extended to other realms. Kun, Parsons and Rubel (1974) have shown that the capacity to integrate information about another person's ability and effort increases with age. Shultz (1974), Shultz and Horibe (1974) have been investigating the cognitive mechanisms underlying children's appreciation of riddles and jokes. Denney and Connors (1974) examined logical changes on a twenty questions game. Rogoff, Newcombe and Kagan (1974) have been studying the ability to take future time into account in planning present activities, and Collis (1974) has investigated the development of a preference for logical consistency in school mathematics.

There is also a large literature on moral logic, originated by Piaget (1965), and extended theoretically by Kohlberg (1963, 1969). Recent studies include those of Turiel (1974); Tomlinson-Keasey and Keasey (1974); and Damon (1975). This literature is too extensive to discuss here, but it generally demonstrates the existence of stages in moral reasoning, and the fact that a morally simple stance (for instance, "an eye for an eye . . .") is a product of a cognitively simple system. The work has extremely important practical implications for our methods of criminal justice and rehabilitation, as well as for socialization processes (Kohlberg, 1970).

These lines of research point up the tremendous generality of the study of reasoning. It is important in our preoccupation with theoretical details not to lose sight of where it is all going eventually : out of the laboratory and into the real world.

(12) SUMMARY

We have reviewed some of the principles that characterize Piaget's theory of cognitive development including : sensorimotor logic, perceptual development, the semiotic function, memory-as-organization, the role of language, the nature of concrete and formal operations, and the "feeling of necessity" that signals the existence of a structure. We then considered some illustrative Piagetian tasks, and showed how they led to the postulate that certain logical capabilities (classes, relations, transitivity, conservation) provide the foundation for others (geometrical intuition, number concepts). Finally, we reviewed aspects of formal operational development, and considered the relationship between scientific reasoning and Piagetian theory. Throughout, we have sampled from the recent empirical literature.

Because of the scope of Piagetian theory, every other current theory of cognitive development is in some measure a continuation of it, or an attempted departure from some facet of it. For that reason, the theory has comprised the central focus of this article. But in addition to the chronologically prior theory of general IQ development (discussed earlier) there have been two post-Piagetian theoretical positions which are having a strong impact on the developmental field: psycholinguistics, and information processing. We shall now indicate briefly the nature of the contributions these areas are making to the study of human logic.

IV. THE LOGIC OF LANGUAGE

(1) EARLY WORD ACQUISITION

As soon as one begins to analyze reasoning processes, whether in formal or informal tasks, the critical role of language becomes apparent. One may say about a child, for example, "He can *reason* perfectly well. He just didn't understand what the *words* meant". Intuitively, we feel there is a distinction between language comprehension and logical thinking. But in fact there may not be a qualitative distinction, only a difference in degree. Language comprehension is not a trivial matter of learning a word list. It involves such operations as comparing, estimating, and predicting. So does reasoning. The ability to perform these operations may develop separately from their application in either language or thinking, at least according to such theorists as Piaget. We should therefore expect to find that language use and comprehension embody many of the logical principles discussed in the previous section. This proves to be the case.

Let us consider first Piaget's emphasis upon action as the basis of operational growth. Brown (1958) pointed out some years ago that adults teach children class names which index functions of importance to the child. Thus, *chair* is to sit on, but *good chair* is not to sit on, and especially not to let the dog sit on. Nelson (1973) has provided evidence from the first fifty-word vocabularies of eighteen children that action is an important categorical cue and facilitates the formation of sub-classes, from car (for all things that move) to *bus, train, cab,* for example. These early word acquisitions appear to be simple forms of association, but they are not.

> Not only are there numerous names and descriptive terms which can be applied to a single object, but it soon transpires that descriptive terms refer to objects only through the speaker's complicated network of concepts ... The child's success depends on a set of cognitive strategies which function as shortcuts in the task of relating symbols to a speaker's intentions. (Macnamara, 1972, p. 3)

These strategies also govern syntactical growth. Children seek language to fit what they need to say concerning : locations ("there car"), demands ("more milk"), events ("Bambi go"), possessions ("my shoe") and modifications ("pretty dress") among other things. Slobin's (1970, 1973) cross-cultural investigations have shown that these intentions govern syntactical development in all linguistic environments. Further, the acquisition processes are themselves rule-governed. Slobin reports, for example, that children behave as if they are applying such rules as "Pay attention to the ends of words", and "Word stems can take morphological variations (bigger, un-big)". Such behaviour exemplifies the development of feature-discrimination and attention-management skills that are also characteristic of operational growth.

(2) CLASSIFICATION

There is evidence from very early language that children are aware of the fact that words designate classes of things or events. They do not limit the use of a word to a single experience, but generalize rapidly. Eve Clark (1973) has collated diary data on children's early word generalizations. Feature-discrimination skills were apparent, but the looseness of the generalization patterns were consistent with the stage of behaviour that Piaget calls "graphic collections".

A large body of free recall research has shown that verbal concepts are categorically organized in long-term memory, even in very young children (see for instance, Bozinov and Goulet, 1974; Eysenck and Baron, 1974; Goldberg, Perlmutter and Myers, 1974; Halperin, 1974; Hasher and Clifton, 1974; Moely and Jeffrey, 1974; Nelson, 1974; Worden, 1974). Of additional interest has been free association research showing that the organization shifts from relational (functional) classes, known as *syntagmatic*, to classes called *paradigmatic*, which are characterized by common forms (verbs, nouns, etc.). This research was begun by Entwisle (1966; Entwisle, Forsyth and Muuss, 1964). The shift in lexical organization parallels the shift from relational, graphic collections in the classification of geometric forms, to the feature-based classification formats characteristic of concrete operational children.

If words are organized into classes, then classes are probably organized into classes, which is to say that class-inclusion relations must exist in semantic memory. Further, it is probably the case that the relations are directional; one may think of the particular (cat) first, and the general (animal) second. If so, then it should and usually does take longer to make a propositional inference about the animal than about the cat. This line of research began with the attempt to build a computer simulation of semantic memory (Collins and Quillian, 1972a, b) and has extended to more general areas of cognitive psychology (Landauer and Meyer, 1972; Rips, Shoben and Smith, 1973; Loftus, 1973; Loftus and Loftus, 1974). Unfortunately, very little work has as yet been done with children (Loftus and Grober, 1973). It will be important to find out if the onset of class-inclusion abilities on Piagetian tasks is accompanied by changes in accuracy or speed of semantic inference.

(3) PROPOSITIONS

Language is a process of relating propositions. The fact that any native speaker of a language can tell a well-formed sentence from a poorly-formed one means that logical principles of word relationships are being tested. These principles are learned by the native speaker at a very early age. There are many ways of characterizing them. Currently, reliance is being placed on Fillmore's (1968) listing of a small set of categories which appear to account for most of what we say. In a sentence like *The boy hit the ball,* there is an Agent, an Action (verb), and an Object. The same cases are represented in the sentence *Baby eat cookie,* as spoken by a 2-year-old. (There are additional cases, locative, for example.) From the beginning, a formal system of propositional categories can be identified in a child's language.

At a later age, the propositional structure can be demonstrated through the use of a paradigm introduced by Bransford and his colleagues (Bransford and Franks, 1972; Bransford and Johnson, 1972; Bransford, Barclay and Franks, 1972). In this paradigm, a subject hears statements like *The girl looked out the window,* and *The rain was falling.* The subject is then presented with some of

14—CP * *

these same statements, and asked if he recognizes them. Subjects typically say (erroneously) that they recognize such statements as *The girl saw the rain on the window.* In fact, the subject constructed that statement from the pieces of information that he was given. And the construction is, of course, quite logical. These experiments have been extended to children (Paris and Carter, 1973; Paris and Mahoney, 1974), and the same phenomena are found.

It is very easy to demonstrate that verbs and prepositions are governed by rules of logic, by considering sentences like: *The girl walked between the house,* or *The boy dug a whole.* It is much harder to design experiments that will tell us how and when such logical knowledge develops. Eve Clark (1971, 1972) listed the semantic components which (in her judgment) gradually accrue to such words as *before* and *after,* and to certain antonyms. To test her theory, she examined children's comprehension of the terms in play-like settings. Comprehension of the more complex terms appeared at a later age than did comprehension of the theoretically simpler terms.

This same research strategy was adopted by Gentner (1975) in her study of the possession verbs. For example, *give* contains, in Gentner's view, the semantic components, DO, CAUSE, and CHANGE-OF-POSSESSION; while the more complex verb *sell* contains DO, CAUSE, CHANGE-OF-POSSESSION, CON-TRACT, and FULFILLMENT-OF-CONTRACT. Ninety per cent of Gentner's 5-year-olds could enact (with puppets) the meaning of *give,* but only 70 per cent of her 8-year-olds could enact *sell.* Similar work is being carried out by Maratsos and his students with reference to such terms as *front, back,* and *side* (Kuczaj and Maratsos, 1975) and *big* (Maratsos, 1973) which shows a temporary decrease in correct usage with age, as children refine their concept of the distinction between *big* and *tall.*

Logic associated with the development of comparatives and polar adjectives has an especially interesting course of development. Donaldson and Balfour (1968) and Donaldson and Wales (1970) originated this line of research by showing that young children sometimes respond to the word *less* as if it meant *more.* This suggested that an ordinal scale is first represented in terms of its positive or unmarked pole (*more, greater than*). The concept of being non-positive (*less, littler than*) develops later. Using a completely different type of scaling procedure, Palermo (1973) verified this finding. It has also been verified experimentally. Non-positive words are harder for children to learn (Klatzky, Clark and Macken, 1973), and once learned they may not be retained or generalized (Holland and Palermo, 1975).

More generally, H. Clark (1969, 1970) examined the linguistic structure of such formal problems as :

Mary is taller than Betty.
Betty is taller than June.
Who is tallest?

These problems are of special interest to developmentalists because Piaget used them in characterizing operational development. Piaget's point was that pre-operational children have difficulty in thinking of Betty as both taller than and shorter than—a reversibility principle. Clark's point was that "Developmentally, the ability to judge membership in comparative statements arrives earlier than the ability to judge relations" (1969, p. 399). The child first learns that *Mary is tall* and that *Betty is tall*, and may answer on the basis of that information alone—what Piaget calls "transductive reasoning" (Knifong, 1974). The operation of making the comparison may not be in a young child's repertoire.

Generally, this line of research has fathered a whole new generation of research strategies relating linguistic analyses to processes of thinking. Sentence comprehension (or production) is broken up theoretically into a small set of functions or stages, each of which takes time (measured in milliseconds), and each of which may be associated with particular response characteristics or errors.*

Developmentally, much work of this type needs to be done. The major questions will be : Do children have different models from adults? Or are their models fragments of the adult models? Is the construction of the adult model a gradual process? Or does the adult form suddenly emerge, as from a chrysalis?

The final topic of this section concerns linguistic mechanisms for combining ideas together—causally, conditionally, conjunctively, disjunctively, and so forth. Piaget (1928) originally postulated three stages in children's use of the term *because* : a pre-logical stage, where "because" connects clauses on the basis of vague notions of motivation; a causal stage, where the event in one clause produces the event in the other one; and a logical stage, containing the adult notion of implication. Corrigan (1975) has recently published a more extensive scalogram analysis, looking at the affective, physical, and logical usage of the term. She found that affective motivation was under-

---

* There are now hundreds of stage model papers in the literature. The general theory and methodology will be summarized in a forthcoming text by Herbert and Eve Clark. In the meantime, a good recent paper which spells out the approach is the one by Clark and Lucy (1975), "Understanding what is Meant from What is Said: A Study in Conversationally Conveyed Requests".

stood at the youngest age (3 years); then physical causation; and then logical implication (7 years), much as Piaget would have predicted.

Other studies have examined children's choice of conjunctions (Hutson and Shub, 1975); and the transition from the use of conjunctions to the use of conditionals (Taplin, Staudenmayer and Taddonio, 1974). Johnson-Laird (1975) would urge us to consider such developments the very basis of logical thought.

> Indeed, it may be said that reasoning with propositions is simply a matter of grasping the meaning of those lexical items that happen to be connectives. This view is certainly suggested by considering the question of how patterns of inferences are acquired in the first place. Where, indeed, do they come from? And how are they fitted together into a coherent system? One plausible conjecture is that the basis of the whole process is the acquisition of the truth conditions of the various connectives. (Johnson-Laird, 1975, p. 23)

The problem, of course, is that such acquisition is itself a result of cognitive growth, not the cause of it; if, indeed, we are to believe Piaget.

(4) SUMMARY

In this section, we have reviewed some of the new research in the field of language usage and development. This research is generated by theoretical principles of action, classification, propositional logic, and growth-by-stages—principles which also characterize cognitive studies of logical behaviour. The appearance of these principles in language has opened up an important parallel avenue of investigation.

V. INFORMATION PROCESSING MODELS OF REASONING

(1) WHAT IS TO BE REPRESENTED AND HOW SHOULD REPRESENTATION BE IMPLEMENTED

Suppose we were to build a robot that could reason logically, what would be put in it? (Assume there were no technological limitations.) First of all, it would have to be able to register the problem, to represent, interpret, or encode some kind of statement. How do people do that? Does the way they do it change with age? Once the problem is represented, aspects of it must be operated on. Something may be compared to something else. Something may be added to or subtracted from something else. The idea of causation may be called up. Where *are* these operations? Are they stored as a list in long-term memory? How does working memory (the part of memory that is actively working on the problem) know which of these operations to call up?

What about working memory itself? Since it can hold only a few ideas or "chunks" at a time, strategies must be developed for manipulating and recalling those chunks economically. How do we do that? How does a child do it? What changes with age—the size of the working memory, or the efficiency of its use?

These are some of the general questions addressed by information processing (IP) model builders. We will see examples of their answers shortly.

To begin with, what level of detail is the model-builder interested in? In Piaget's system, such units as *operations* are large and complex, veritable macrocosms. In some of the models to be examined below, the units are tiny cycles postulated to occur every 50 msec. In other models, such as the stage models of linguistic reasoning, the units are in between these two extremes.

What notational system should be used? Programming language? the p's and q's of propositional logic? Functional notations— $f(x) = y$? Tree diagrams? Nested parentheses? Or plain words? These systems often overlap each other, but the choice of notation is not arbitrary. There are rules governing the notational system which may illuminate and advance the theory, even for the theorist himself. When his ideas are "out there" on the page, he can make discoveries that he could not have made when his ideas were still inside his head. The notational system should facilitate those discoveries.

We present here very abbreviated descriptions of current work on IP models of human reasoning. The articles themselves should be consulted for details. Additional background reading should include Newell and Simon (1971); Newell (1972, 1973); Gregg (1967); Lindsay and Norman (1972); Hunt (1971); and Hunt and Poltrock 1974).

(2) PRODUCTION SYSTEM MODELS

Production system models (computer simulations) have been investigated by Klahr and Wallace (1976). This team has been working for several years towards the construction of a general theory of cognitive development. Some of their previous publications have concerned pieces of this theory: class inclusion (Klahr and Wallace, 1972), serial completion (Klahr and Wallace, 1970a), and other Piagetian tasks (Klahr and Wallace, 1970b). Several papers explain their goals and methodology (Klahr, 1973, 1975). The last one in particular (Klahr, 1975) provides an excellent introduction to the art of simulation and the rationale behind it.

The Klahr-Wallace approach is built on the work of Allen Newell, who has developed a unique simulation language based on the general programming principles of *production systems* (Newell, 1973). A production is simply a conditional action. If such-and-such occurs, then do so-and-so. If it rains, then get your umbrella; if x, then y; if p, then q. Anything can be a condition, and anything can be the action "fired" by the condition.

Production systems are, however, *systems*. They are lists of condition-action pairs. Thus:

> If it rains, go and find your umbrella.
> If you find your umbrella, look for the catch.
> If you find the catch, open it.

Suppose we could type on a magic keyboard, and enter those commands into the head of our robot. Would he behave properly? Not a chance. In the first place, we have not explained to him what *rain* is, or what *go*, *find*, *your*, or *umbrella* are. How will he know them?

The value of that exercise is not that we are learning how to build a robot, but that we are confronting the amount we take for granted in our usual forms of psychological analysis. Our human subjects come equipped with a huge repertoire of skills and concepts. We understand next to nothing about what they are, how they were acquired, or how they are being applied in our experiment. Suppose we are not allowed to take all that for granted, but must try to explain, theoretically, every bit of it? That is what a simulation forces us to do. The fact that the effort may not be wholly successful is to be expected. No other form of theorizing forces us to confront our own ignorance so completely.

The fundamental units of the Klahr-Wallace theory are very small, approaching the neurological level, but they are aggregated into larger units, hierarchically. Some of the larger units are determined by the system architecture. For example, there are visual, auditory, and semantic short-term memory systems. Lists of productions and production rules are specific to each. Other large units come into existence through growth. Productions which are discovered to be redundant are recast as new productions with redundancy eliminated. Still other large units come into existence through the detection of redundancy in the new productions. Thus, a processing economy rule generates a self-developing mental structure. Finding a way to produce such a structure is a major problem, but produce it we must if development is ever to be explained. The child does not have a homunculus sitting in his head (or pineal gland?) saying, "Now then, formal operations is the goal. Let's do this, this, and this in order to get on with it". The child does not have any way of representing mature cognitive development as a beam guiding his growth. What, then, guides it? What principles, if exercised over a sufficient period of time, must inevitably produce mature cognition?

The Klahr-Wallace *processing economy* principle is a good candidate. Eleanor Gibson (1969), among others, has postulated a similar principle. But postulating it is only the first, easy step. The hard part is detailing exactly how such a principle might operate, and how it might operate differently in different people. For it is clear that higher-order structures, economical forms of information-processing, do not develop equally or at the same rate in everyone. The Klahr-Wallace explanation currently includes the following:

1. A set of productions which scan other, ongoing sequences of productions for commonalities.

2. A set of productions which mark the commonalities, when they are detected.

3. A set of productions which specify the degree of resemblance necessary to count as a commonality.

4. A set of productions which adjust that parameter (resemblance) with circumstances.

5. A set of productions which specify a threshold for the construction of a higher-order symbol (token) which will stand for the repeating commonalities (types).

This is, essentially, a model of an abstraction process. Simulating each of those numbered items may require many pages of programming code. This code, then, amounts to a highly detailed theory of the abstraction process. Running the programme provides a dynamic trace of how the theory works.

We have discussed, illustratively, only a fragment of the Klahr-Wallace theory. Their book should be consulted for the whole picture.

Another production system theory has been created by Baylor and Gascon (1974) at the University of Montreal. They are currently working on the simulation of behaviour on a particular task weight seriation, rather than on a general theory of development. In their task, the child is given a pan balance and seven blocks of the same size but of different weights. The child's task is to order the blocks by weight. He is allowed to weigh two of them at a time. In their simulation, Baylor-Gascon represented the initial positioning of the blocks (where the child began), the placement and weight of the blocks on the scale, and where the child put the blocks after weighing them. For any given snapshot, or time-slice of the child's behavioural sequence, those three arrangements could be specified. If one puts together consecutive time-slices, the problem-solving sequence should be discernible. One can then infer what the problem-solving rules are, and how they operate on the materials (blocks, scale). With that information, a computer programme can be written which incorporates those principles, representations, and rules.

When one subject is a pre-operational child, and another subject is an operational child, the principles, representations, and rules are quite different. For example, there are only seven production rules in the model of the pre-operational child :

P1 (Production Rule 1) : When there are some blocks that need to be seriated, set up the goal to find a heavy and a light member of a pair.

P2 : When there are no more blocks to be seriated, stop.

P3, P4 and P5 all refer to the scale : P3 says when there are no blocks on the scale, put some there; P4 says when there is only one block on the scale, put it in the series; and P5 says when there are two blocks on the scale (usually the case) move the heavier one to the end of the line first.

P6 and P7 refer to the pool of unseriated blocks : P6 says if there are two blocks remaining in the pool, put two of them on the scale. (Note : this is not the same as P1, which is to set up the goal that motivates P6.) And P7 says if there is only 1 block, put it on the scale by itself.

These seven rules produce simulated behaviour which resembles the actual behaviour of the pre-operational child. Pairs of blocks are weighed and put down side by side in a line, as "juxtaposed couples". Much more complex rules are necessary to generate simulated behaviour which resembles the actual behaviour of an operational child. These two programmes, then, constitute a detailed theory of the development of weight seriation skills and structures. The trace of the running programme shows exactly how the theory works.

(3) LOGIC MODELS

Like Piaget, a number of theorists have called upon the notational system of formal logic to model theories of child and adult thinking. Three of them are summarized by Falmagne (1975)—those of Staudenmayer (1975), Osherson (1975), and Johnson-Laird (1975). Only one will be described here.

The interesting aspect of Osherson's (1974, 1975) model is that it is a dynamic one, consisting of rewrite rules which resemble production systems in spirit. Osherson has postulated a set of natural rules of inference, where natural means "acceptable... from the subject's point of view" (Osherson, 1975, p. 85). The conditions for the use of these rules are explicit, as are the condition terms of productions. Given a particular logical problem, the subject can presumably move from the initial statement to a test of the conclusion by invoking a series of inferential steps. Of course the subject will not do this formally; the postulated processes are intuitive. If the list of steps is a long one, the subject should take more time to evaluate the conclusion. Experimentally, Osherson found this to be the case. For example, the following problem has the form: "If A or B is true only if C is true, then not-C and not-B is true only if not-A is true."

> All the red jars and all the large jars have tacks. Can you be sure that every jar which does not have tacks, and is not large, is not red?

To answer the above questions, the subject would need to call up rules 2a, 3, and 5b, in Osherson (1975). Other problems require other rules, and other orders. If the list is a long one, the subject will answer more slowly. The size of the units in this formulation are, of course, large and Osherson is not concerned with the representational issue. It will be interesting to see if he can continue to find ways of formalizing complex mental processing within the framework of such a simple set of principles. His concern with the child's short-term memory capacity, and with certain other psychological processes, suggest a broader approach.

(4) GENERAL PROCESS MODELS

We consider now a class of models which are less constrained by notational formalities than those in the foregoing section. General models of cognitive processing may utilize a computer simulation style, or a mathematical modelling style, but concern is primarily with psychological rules and concepts.

Although the model of Revlis (1975a,b) is not a developmental model, it illustrates a formalization technique that could well be applied to developmental issues. Revlis has been studying formal syllogistic reasoning, and has tested two models of this. In one, the subject is hypothesized to carry out the following mental operations: extract the features of polarity and quantity from the premises, form a composite representation of the problem (the rules for the formation

of the composite are strictly specified), extract the features of the conclusion, and compare the composite representation to the conclusion.
In the second model, errors are hypothesized to result primarily from
an incorrect encoding or representation of the basic propositions. This
is called *conversion*, and rules for its occurrence are strictly specified,
as are subsequent stages in the reasoning process. Data collected so
far suggest that the conversion model is the more appropriate one.
Subjects, in other words, represent the syllogism incorrectly to begin
with. Their errors are not a matter of poor reasoning at a later stage
of processing.

Also concerned with the representation issue are Trabasso and his
colleagues (Riley and Trabasso, 1974; Trabasso, Riley and Wilson,
1975). They argue that there are two ways of representing and
holding in working memory syllogistic propositions; each premise may
be stored separately as an ordered pair of terms, or the premises may
be integrated and stored as a linear ordering. If the latter, then
transitivity responses should show a *serial position effect* typical of
learned material that is serially represented.

Children were taught the relative lengths of a set of sticks, pair-by-
pair. When given transitivity tests, both errors and latencies were
higher for questions about sticks which were located in the middle
of the series, even though the children had never seen the series as a
whole. Thus, the hypothesis that the learned information was represented as an integrated series was upheld.

Use of well-established psychological phenomena like the serial
position effect as a modelling device is a very promising approach.
There are many such well-established phenomena—recency *v.* primacy
effects, simple *v.* complex reaction times, pro-active inhibition, and so
forth. These are usually studied as isolated facts. Trabasso's system,
which should prove useful to many psychologists, especially those who
are not technological or mathematical experts, is to construct a
theoretical mosaic of those facts.

(5) EQUATION MODELS

As our final IP topic, we turn to the oldest type of model in
psychology: functions of the form $B = f(x)$, where B stands for
behaviour, and $f(x)$ can stand for almost anything. These models were
first presented by Fechner, and they have continued to be useful
formalization devices. Generally, the mathematics involved consists
only of additive principles.

Details of the theory of Pascual-Leone (1970) and Case (1974a, b)
are contained in Pascual-Leone's unpublished dissertation from the

University of Geneva in 1969, and in Case's updated version of it. The fundamental units of the theory are *schemes*, defined somewhat differently and more precisely than Piaget defines them. There are *figurative schemes*, which are perceptual configurations; *operative schemes*, which are functions that can be applied to figurative schemes; and *executive* schemes, or plans. Schemes can be acquired by modifying or combining other schemes. In solving a problem, the subject is assumed to activate an executive scheme first, which in turn directs figurative and operative schemes in a consecutive fashion. There are rules for resolving conflicts, for knowing when to stop, for assessing individual differences, and for mapping the postulates on to specific tasks. An important aspect of the Pascual-Leone/Case theory is its utilization of a weight for the size of the basic computing space, or capacity, available to a child. This is called *M-power* (M stands for the concept of maximum mental effort). Where cognitive development is normal, M-power is assumed to increase linearly with age. This number is added to a constant which represents the effort necessary to activate an executive scheme.

On the basis of these postulates (which are essentially a task analysis system), predictions can be made about children's performances on Piagetian-type tasks. An extremely detailed paper, available from Pascual-Leone (1972), shows how the predictive functions are computed. Case's work (1972, 1974; Case and Globerson, 1974) is more readily assimilable by empiricists.

In a scaling approach, Hamilton (1972a, b, 1973; Hamilton and Moss, 1974) has devised a Piagetian-type task which systematically varies information processing demands. This is done by subdividing the task as shown on the illustrative cards in Fig. 9.7. Subjects studied each card, and reported whether the amount of solid or liquid remained the same, despite its distribution into new shapes or containers.

In the language of information processing theory we could say that appropriate cues have been attended to and processed through a search-and-scan strategy . . . This has led to the elimination of irrelevant moves and subgoals and to efficient, logical progress along decision trees and pathways. An increase in the number of partitioning operations will increase the number of choice points and paths in the decision tree and thus the number of the steps involved. In this way the total content of a conservation-problem display (always on cards), and the test questions directed at different points of an information chain, could determine the difficulty level of the problem. The most competent subjects will not only produce a correct answer, they will also achieve it by using the minimum rather than the maximum number of steps. (Hamilton and Moss, 1974, p. 738).

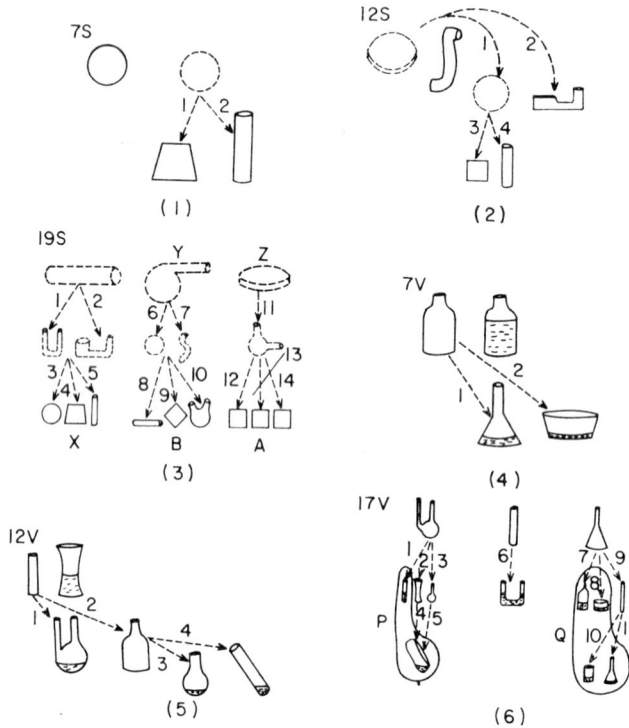

Fig. 9.7 Sample cards showing ways of subdividing the conservation task into a sequence of additional steps. (*After* Hamilton, 1972a, p. 432.)

The predictive equation includes terms for the number of steps, the number of parts, the number of distributions which must be used for solution, and the number of transformations in the problem display. The equation has successfully predicted scaling functions in several experiments. It would be extremely valuable to have data on eye-movements of subjects working on these problems.

(6) SUMMARY

We have now considered a number of basic principles and formats used in the construction of IP models of logical behaviour, and summarized models of four types: computer simulations, models based on propositional logic, general process models, and equation models. Each type of model was illustrated by the work of one or more theorists. All the approaches are concerned with the problem of detailing the process of reasoning. In some cases, a programming language is used; in other cases, the language of mathematical functions;

in still other cases natural language; and, finally, the language of propositional logic. Each of these notational systems incorporates rules of usage which are compatible with the theoretical points of interest. The models do not, as yet, increase the power of theory much beyond the intuitive capacities of theorists. However, formal, predictive power will certainly increase as more work of this type is undertaken.

VI. CONCLUSION

In this chapter, we have reviewed four general approaches to the study of the development of human logical skill: general intelligence testing, Piagetian theory, psycholinguistics, and information processing. Although all four approaches co-exist, one can discern a steady movement toward analytical detail. Werner (1961) has referred to such development as a *differentiation* process. Scientifically, the study of human reasoning is becoming more differentiated with respect to the processes and mechanisms involved.

Intelligence test items are selected from large pools of superficially similar items on the basis of a population pass-rate. The items are not subjected to detailed experimental analysis. Piagetian theory introduced a number of principles upon which such an analysis could be based. Psycholinguistics has provided additional principles, and IP theorists have provided additional processes. We are all now focused on the need for precise, analytical methodology in the study of reasoning. We no longer accept "right answers" as sole evidence of reasoning (although we are still interested in them), but are preoccupied as well with the process of arriving at those answers.

As yet, we can offer no simple list of steps that characterize the growth of logical skill in the mind of a child. The best we can do is learn how growth principles are being formulated and analyzed by current workers in the field. That is, in itself, a formidable exercise in reasoning and logic. But there is no enterprise more important.

REFERENCES

Agranoff, B. W. (1967). Memory and protein synthesis. *Scientific American, 216,* 115–22.

Ahr, P. R. and Youniss, J. (1970). Reasons for failure on the class inclusion problem. *Child Development, 41,* 131–43.

Barondes, S. (1973). Brain and memory storage: effects of drugs on essential enzyme mechanisms. In F. Richardson (Ed.), *Brain and Intelligence: The Ecology of Child Development.* Maryland: National Educational Press.

Baylor, G. W. and Gascon, J. (1974). An information processing theory of aspects of the development of weight seriation in children. *Cognitive Psychology, 6,* 1–40.

Berzonsky, M. D. (1975). Compenent abilities of children's causal reasoning. *Developmental Psychology, 11,* 111.

Bozinov, E. and Goulet, L. R. (1974). Acquisition and transfer of sorting mechanisms in discrimination learning and free recall by nursery school children. *Child Development, 45,* 816–20.

Brainerd, C. J. (1974a). Inducing ordinal and cardinal representations of the first five natural numbers. *Journal of Experimental Child Psychology, 18,* 520–34.

Brainerd, C. J. (1974b). Training and transfer of transitivity, conservation, and class inclusion of length. *Child Development, 45,* 324–34.

Brainerd, C. J. and Kaszor, P. (1974). An analysis of two proposed sources of children's class inclusion errors. *Developmental Psychology, 10,* 633–43.

Bransford, J. D., Barclay, J. R. and Franks, J. J. (1972). Sentence memory: a constructive versus interpretive approach. *Cognitive Psychology, 3,* 193–209.

Bransford, J. D. and Franks, J. J. (1972). The abstraction of linguistic ideas. *Cognitive Psychology, 3,* 193–209.

Bransford, J. D. and Johnson, M. K. (1972). Contextual prerequisites for understanding: some investigations of comprehension and recall. *Journal of Verbal Learning and Verbal Behavior, 11,* 717–26.

Brown, R. (1958). How shall a thing be called? *Psychological Review, 65,* 14–21.

Bryant, P. E. and Trabasso, T. (1971). Transitive inferences and memory in young children. *Nature, 232,* 456–8.

Case, R. (1972). Validation of a neo-Piagetian mental capacity construct. *Journal of Experimental Child Psychology, 14,* 287–302.

Case, R. (1974a). Mental strategies, mental capacity, and instruction: a neo-Piagetian investigation. *Journal of Experimental Child Psychology, 18,* 382–97.

Case, R. (1974b). Structures and strictures: some functional limitation on the course of cognitive growth. *Cognitive Psychology, 6,* 544–73.

Case, R. and Globerson, T. (1974). Field independence and central computing space. *Child Development, 45,* 722–8.

Cattell, R. B. (1971). *Abilities: Their Structure, Growth, and Action.* Boston: Houghton Mifflin.

Clark, E. V. (1971). On the acquisition of the meaning of *before* and *after. Journal of Verbal Learning and Verbal Behavior, 10,* 266–75.

Clark, E. V. (1972). On the child's acquisition of antonyms in two semantic fields. *Journal of Verbal Learning and Verbal Behavior, 11,* 750–8.

Clark, E. V. (1973). What's in a word? On the child's acquisition of semantics in his first language. In T. E. Moore (Ed.), *Cognitive Development and the Acquisition of Language*. New York: Academic Press.

Clark, H. H. (1969). Linguistic processes in deductive reasoning. *Psychological Review, 76*, 387–404.

Clark, H. H. (1970). The primitive nature of children's relational concepts. In J. R. Hayes, (Ed.), *Cognition and the Development of Language*. New York: Wiley.

Clark, H. H. and Lucy, P. (1975). Understanding what is meant from what is said: a study in conversationally conveyed requests. *Journal of Verbal Learning and Verbal Behavior, 14*, 56–72.

Cohen, L. B. (1973). A two process model of infant visual attention. *Merrill-Palmer Quarterly, 19*, 157–80.

Cohen, S. (1974). Developmental differences in infant's attentional responses to face-voice incongruity of mother and stranger. *Child Development, 45*, 1155–8.

Collins, A. M. and Quillian, M. R. (1972a). Experiments on semantic memory and language comprehension. In L. W. Gregg (Ed.), *Cognition in Learning and Memory*. New York: Wiley.

Collins, A. M. and Quillian, M. R. (1972b). How to make a language user. In E. Tulving and W. Donaldson, *Organization of Memory*. New York: Academic Press.

Collis, K. F. (1974). The development of a preference for logical consistency in school mathematics. *Child Development, 45*, 978–83.

Corrigan, R. (1975). A scalogram analysis of the development of the use and comprehension of "Because" in children. *Child Development, 46*, 195–201.

Dahlem, N. (1969). Reconstructive memory in children revisited. *Psychonomic Science, 17*, 101–2.

Damon, W. (1975). Early conceptions of positive justice as related to the development of logical operations. *Child Development, 46*, 301–12.

Denney, N. W. and Acito, M. (1974). Classification training in two and three year-old children. *Journal of Experimental Child Psychology, 17*, 37–48.

Denney, N. W. and Connors, G. J. (1974). Altering the questioning strategies of preschool children. *Child Development, 45*, 1108–12.

DeVries, R. (1974). Relationships among Piagetian, IQ, and achievement assessments. *Child Development, 45*, 746–56.

Donaldson, M. and Balfour, G. (1968). Less is more: a study of language comprehension in children. *British Journal of Psychology, 59*, 461–71.

Donaldson, M. and Wales, R. J. (1970). On the acquisition of some relational terms. In J. R. Hayes (Ed.), *Cognition and the Development of Language*. New York: Wiley.

Eimas, P. D. (1969). A developmental study of hypothesis behavior and focusing in young children and adults. *Journal of Experimental Child Psychology, 8*, 160–72.

Entwisle, D. R. (1966). Form class and children's word association. *Journal of Verbal Learning and Verbal Behavior, 5*, 558–65.

Entwisle, D. R., Forsyth, D. F. and Muuss, R. (1964). The syntactic-paradigmatic shift in children's word associations. *Journal of Verbal Learning and Verbal Behavior, 3*, 19–29.

Eysenck, M. and Baron, D. (1974). Effects of cuing on recall from categorized word lists. *Developmental Psychology, 5*, 665–6.

Falmagne, R. (Ed.), (1975). *Psychological Studies of Logic and its Development*. Hillsdale, N.J.: Lawrence Erlbaum.

Farnham-Diggory, S. and Simon, E. (1975). Eye-hand coordination of 5-year-olds during pattern drawing. Presented to the Biennial Meeting of the Society for Research in Child Development, Denver.

Faulkeneder, P. J., Wright, J. C. and Waldron, A. (1974). Generalized habituation of concept stimuli in toddlers. *Child Development, 45*, 1002–10.

Fillmore, C. J. (1968). The case for case. In E. Back and R. Harms (Eds.), *Universals in Linguistic Theory*. New York: Holt, Rinehart and Winston.

Furth, H. G. Ross, B. and Youniss, J. (1974). Operative understanding in children's immediate and long-term reproductions of drawings. *Child Development, 45*, 63–70.

Gelman, R. (1969). Conservation acquisition: a problem of learning to attend to relevant attributes. *Journal of Experimental Child Psychology, 7*, 167–87.

Gelman, R. (1972a). Logical capacity of very young children. *Child Development, 43*, 75–90.

Gelman, R. (1972b). The nature and development of early number concepts. In H. W. Reese (Ed.), *Advances in Child Development and Behavior*, Vol. 7. New York and London: Academic Press.

Gelman R. and Tucker, M. F. (1975). Further investigations of the young child's conception of number. *Child Development, 46*, 167–75.

Gentner, D. (1975). Towards a psychological theory of the meaning of possession verbs. University of California, San Diego (mimeographed report).

Gholson, B. and McConville, K. (1974). Effects of stimulus differentiation training upon hypotheses, strategies, and stereotypes in discrimination learning among kindergarten children. *Journal of Experimental Child Psychology, 18*, 81–97.

Gibson, E. J. (1969). *Principles of Perceptual Learning and Development*. New York: Appleton-Century-Crofts.

Goldberg, S., Perlmutter, M. and Myers, N. (1974). Recall of related and unrelated lists by 2 year-olds. *Journal of Experimental Child Psychology, 18*, 1–8.

Gregg, L. W. (1967). Internal representation of sequential concepts. In B. Kleinmuntz (Ed.), *Concepts and the Structure of Memory*. New York: Wiley.

Halperin, M. (1974). Developmental changes in the recall and recognition of categorized word lists. *Child Development, 45*, 144–51.

Hamilton, V. (1972a). Continuities and individual differences in conservation. *British Journal of Psychology, 63*, 429–40.

Hamilton, V. (1972a) Maternal rejection and conservation: an analysis of suboptimal cognition. *Journal of Child Psychology and Psychiatry, 13*, 147–66.

Hamilton, V. (1973). An information processing analysis of conservation. *Bulletin of the British Psychological Society, 26*, 149. (Abstract)

Hamilton, V. and Moss, M. (1974). A method of scaling of conservation-of-quantity problems by information content. *Child Development, 45*, 737–45.

Harlow, H. G. (1949). The formation of learning sets. *Psychological Review, 56*, 51–65.

Hasher, L. and Clifton, D. (1974). Developmental study of attribute encoding in free recall. *Journal of Experimental Child Psychology, 17*, 332–46.

Holland, V. M. and Palermo, D. S. (1975). On learning "less": language and cognitive development. *Child Development, 46*, 437–43.

Hughes, G. E. and Cresswell, M. J. (1968). *An Introduction to Modal Logic*. London: Methuen.

Hunt, E. (1971). What kind of computer is man? Cognitive Psychology, 2, 57–98.

Hunt, E. (1974). Quote the Raven? Nevermore! In L. Gregg (Ed.), Knowledge and Cognition. Hillsdale, N.J.: Lawrence Erlbaum.

Hunt, E., Frost, N. and Lunneborg, C. (1973). Individual differences in cognition. In G. Bower (Ed.), Advances in Learning and Motivation, Vol. VII. New York: Academic Press.

Hunt, E., Lunneborg, C. and Lewis, J. (1975). What does it mean to be high verbal? Cognitive Psychology, 7, 194–227.

Hunt, E. and Poltrock, S. (1974). The mechanics of thought. In B. Kantowitz (Ed.), Human Information Processing. Hillsdale, N.J.: Lawrence Erlbaum.

Hutson, B. and Shub, J. (1975). Developmental study of factors involved in choice of conjunctions. Child Development, 46, 46–52.

Inhelder, B. and Piaget, J. (1958). The Growth of Logical Thinking from Childhood to Adolescence. New York: Basic Books.

Inhelder, B. and Piaget, J. (1964). The Early Growth of Logic in the Child New York: Harper and Row.

Jeffrey, W. E. and Cohen, L. B. (1971). Habituation in the human infant. In H. Reese (Ed.), Advances in Child Development and Behavior, Vol. 6. New York: Academic Press.

Johnson-Laird, P. N. (1975). Models of deduction. In R. Falmagne (Ed.), Psychological Studies of Logic and its Development. Hillsdale, N.J.: Lawrence Erlbaum.

Johnson-Laird, P. N. and Wason, P. C. (1970). A theoretical analysis of insight into a reasoning task. Cognitive Psychology, 1, 134–48.

Just, M. A. (1974). Comprehending quantified sentences: the relation between sentence-picture and semantic memory verification. Cognitive Psychology, 6, 216–36.

Just, M. A. and Carpenter, P. A. (1971). Comprehension of negation with quantification. Journal of Verbal Learning and Verbal Behavior, 10, 244–53.

Kalil, K., Youssef, Z. and Lerner, R. M. (1974). Class inclusion failure: Cognitive deficit or misleading preference? Child Development, 45, 1122–8.

Keating, D. P. (1975). Precocious cognitive developments at the level of formal operations. Child Development, 46, 270–5.

Klahr, D. (1973). An information processing approach to the study of cognitive development. In A. Pick (Ed.), Minnesota Symposia on Child Psychology, Vol. 7. Minneapolis: University of Minnesota Press.

Klahr, D. (1975). Steps toward the simulation of intellectual development. In L. B. Resnick (Ed.), The Nature of Intelligence. Hillsdale, N.J.: Lawrence Erlbaum.

Klahr, D. and Wallace, J. G. (1970a). The development of serial completion strategies: an information processing analysis. British Journal of Psychology, 61, 243–57.

Klahr, D. and Wallace, J. G. (1970b). An information processing analysis of some Piagetian experimental tasks. Cognitive Psychology, 1, 358–87.

Klahr, D. and Wallace, J. G. (1972). Class inclusion processes. In S. Farnham-Diggory (Ed.), Information Processing in Children. New York and London: Academic Press.

Klahr, D. and Wallace, J. G. (1973). The role of quantification operators in the development of conservation of quantity. Cognitive Psychology, 4, 301–27.

Klahr, D. and Wallace, J. G. (1976). *Cognitive Development: An Information Processing View.* Hillsdale, N.J.: Lawrence Erlbaum.

Klatzky, R. L., Clark, E. V. and Macken, M. (1973). Asymmetries in the acquisition of polar adjectives: linguistic or conceptual? *Journal of Experimental Child Psychology, 16,* 32–46.

Knifong, J. D. (1974). Logical abilities of young children—two styles of approach. *Child Development, 45,* 78–83.

Kodroff, J. K. and Roberge, J. J. (1975). Developmental analysis of the conditional reasoning abilities of primary-grade children. *Developmental Psychology, 11,* 21–8.

Kohlberg, L. (1963). The development of children's orientations toward a moral order, I: sequence in the development of moral thought. *Vita Humana, 6,* 11–33.

Kohlberg, L., (1969). Stage and sequence: the cognitive-development approach to socialization. In D. Goslin (Ed.), *Handbook of Socialization Theory and Research.* Chicago: Rand McNally.

Kohlberg, L. (1970). Stages of moral development as a basis for moral education. In C. Beck and E. Sullivan (Eds.), *Moral Education.* Toronto: University of Toronto Press.

Kuczaj, S. A. and Maratsos, M. P. (1975). On the acquisition of *front, back,* and *side. Child Development, 46,* 202–10.

Kun, A., Parsons, J. and Ruble, D. (1974). Development of integration processes using ability and effort information to predict outcome. *Developmental Psychology, 5,* 721–32.

Landauer, T. K. and Meyer, D. E. (1972). Category size and semantic-memory retrieval. *Journal of Verbal Learning and Verbal Behavior, 11,* 539–49.

LaPointe, K. and O'Donnell, W. J. (1974). Number conservation in children below age six: its relationship to age, perceptual dimensions, and language comprehension. *Developmental Psychology, 10,* 422–8.

Lasky, R. E. (1974). The ability of six year-olds, eight year-olds, and adults to abstract visual patterns. *Child Development, 45,* 626–32.

Lawson, G., Baron, J. and Siegel, L. (1974). The role of number and length cues in children's quantitative judgments. *Child Development, 45,* 731–6.

Levine, M. (1966). Hypothesis behavior by humans during discrimination learning. *Journal of Experimental Psychology, 71,* 331–8.

Levinson, P. J. and Carpenter, R. L. (1974). An analysis of analogical reasoning in children. *Child Development, 45,* 857–61.

Liben, L. (1975). Evidence for developmental differences in spontaneous seriation and its implications for past research on long term memory improvement. *Developmental Psychology, 11,* 121–5.

Lindsay, P. and Norman, D. A. (1972). *Human Information Processing.* New York: Academic Press.

Loftus, E. F. (1973). Category dominance, instance dominance, and categorization. *Journal of Experimental Psychology, 97,* 70–4.

Loftus, E. F. and Grober, E. H. (1973). Retrieval from semantic memory by young children. *Developmental Psychology, 8,* 310.

Loftus, E. F. and Loftus, G. R. (1974). Changes in memory structure and retrieval over the course of instruction. *Journal of Educational Psychology, 66,* 315–18.

Macnamara. J. (1972). Cognitives basis of language learning in infants. *Psychological Review, 79,* 1–13.

Maratsos, M. P. (1973). Decrease in the understanding of the word "Big" in preschool children. *Child Development, 44*, 747–52.

Matheny, A. P. (1975). Twins: concordance for Piagetian-equivalent items derived from the Bayley mental test. *Developmental Psychology, 11*, 224–7.

Moely, B. and Jeffrey, W. E. (1974). The effect of organization training on children's free recall of category items. *Child Development, 45*, 135–43.

Neimark, E. D. and Chapman, R. H. (1975). Development of the comprehension of logical quantifiers. In R. Falmagne (Ed.), *Psychological Studies of Logic and Its Development*. Hillsdale, N.J.: Lawrence Erlbaum.

Neimark, E. D. and Lewis, N. (1967). The development of logical problem solving strategies. *Child Development, 38*, 107–17.

Nelson, K. (1973). Structure and strategy in learning to talk. *Monographs of the Society for Research in Child Development*, Serial No. 149.

Nelson, K. (1974). Variations in children's concepts by age and category. *Child Development, 45*, 577–85.

Newell, A. (1972). A note on process-structure distinctions in developmental psychology. In S. Farnham-Diggory (Ed.), *Information Processing in Children*. New York and London: Academic Press.

Newell, A. (1973). Production systems: models of control structures. In W. G. Chase (Ed.), *Visual Information Processing*. New York and London: Academic Press.

Newell, A. and Simon, H. A. (1971). *Human Problem Solving*. Englewood Cliffs, N.J.: Prentice Hall.

Offenbach, S. (1974). A developmental study of hypothesis testing and cue selection strategies. *Developmental Psychology, 10*, 484–90.

Osherson, D. N. (1974). *Logical Abilities in Children*, Vol. 1 and Vol. 2. Hillsdale, N.J.: Lawrence Erlbaum.

Osherson, D. N. (1975). Logic and models of logical thinking. In R. Falmagne (Ed.), *Psychological Studies of Logic and its Development*. Hillsdale, N.J.: Lawrence Erlbaum.

Palermo, D. S. (1973). More about less: A study of language comprehension. *Journal of Verbal Learning and Verbal Behavior, 12*, 211–21.

Paris, S. G. and Carter, A. Y. (1973). Semantic and constructive aspects of sentence memory in children. *Developmental Psychology, 9*, 109–13.

Paris, S. G. and Mahoney, G. (1974). Cognitive integration in children's memory for sentences and pictures. *Child Development, 45*, 633–42.

Pascual-Leone, J. (1970). A mathematical model for the transition rule in Piaget's developmental stages. *Acta Psychologica, 32*, 301–45.

Pascual-Leone, J. (1972). A theory of constructive operators, a neo-Piagetian model of conservation, and the problem of horizontal decalages. York University, Toronto (mimeographed report).

Piaget, J. (1928). *Judgment and Reasoning in the Child*. New York: Harcourt, Brace and World.

Piaget, J. (1952). *The Child's Conception of Number*. New York: Norton.

Piaget, J. (1954). *The Construction of Reality in the Child*. New York: Basic Books.

Piaget, J. (1965). *The Moral Judgment of the Child*. New York: Free Press.

Piaget, J. (1971a). The theory of stages in cognitive development. In D. R. Green, M. P. Ford and G. B. Flamer (Eds.), *Measurement and Piaget*. New York: McGraw-Hill.

Piaget, J. (1971b). *The Child's Conception of Movement and Speech*. New York: Ballantine Books.

Piaget, J. and Inhelder, B. (1941). *Le Dévelopment Des Quantités Chez L'énfant*. Neuchatel: Delachaux et Niestlé.

Piaget, J. and Inhelder, B. (1967). *The Child's Conception of Space*. London: Routledge and Kegan Paul.

Piaget, J. and Inhelder, B. (1969). *The Psychology of the Child*. New York: Basic Books.

Piaget, J. and Inhelder, B. (1973). *Memory and Intelligence*. New York: Basic Books.

Piaget, J., Inhelder, B. and Szeminska, A. (1964). *The Child's Conception of Geometry*. New York: Harper and Row.

Pick, A. D. and Frankel, G. (1974). A developmental study of visual selectivity. *Child Development*, 45, 1162–5.

Revlis, R. (1975). Two models of syllogistic reasoning: feature selection and conversion. *Journal of Verbal Learning and Verbal Behavior, 14*, 180–95. (a).

Revlis, R. (1975). Syllogistic reasoning: logical decisions from a complex data base. In R. Falmagne (Ed.), *Psychological Studies of Logic and its Development*. Hillsdale, N.J.: Lawrence Erlbaum. (b).

Riley, C. A. and Trabasso, T. (1974). Comparatives, logical structures, and encoding in a transitive inference task. *Journal of Experimental Child Psychology, 17*, 187–203.

Rips, L. J., Shoben, E. J. and Smith, E. E. (1973). Semantic distance and the verification of semantic relations. *Journal of Verbal Learning and Verbal Behavior, 12*, 1–20.

Rogoff, B., Newcombe, N. and Kagan, J. (1974). Planfulness and recognition memory. *Child Development, 45*, 972–7.

Schaeffer, B. (1974). Skill integration during cognitive development. In B. Kennedy and K. S. Wilkes (Eds.), *Studies in Long Term Memory*. New York: Wiley.

Schaeffer, B., Eggleston, V. H. and Scott, J. L. (1974). Number development in young children. *Cognitive Psychology, 6*, 357–79.

Schaie, K. W. (1965). A general model for the study of developmental problems. *Psychological Bulletin, 64*, 92–107.

Schaie, K. W. (1973). Methodological problems in descriptive developmental research on adulthood and aging. In J. R. Nesselroade and H. W. Reese (Eds.), *Lifespan Developmental Psychology: Methodological Issues*. New York and London: Academic Press.

Sheppard, J. L. (1974a). Concrete operational thought and developmental aspects of solutions to a task based on a mathematical three group. *Developmental Psychology, 10*, 116–23.

Sheppard, J. L. (1974b). Compensation and combinatorial systems in the acquisition and generalization of conservation. *Child Development, 45*, 717–30.

Shultz, T. R. (1974). Development of the appreciation of riddles. *Child Development, 45*, 100–5.

Shultz, T. R. and Horibe, F. (1974). Development of the appreciation of verbal jokes. *Developmental Psychology, 10*, 13–20.

Siegel, L. S. (1974). Development of number concepts: ordering and correspondence operations and the role of length cues. *Developmental Psychology, 10*, 907–12.

Siegler, R. S. (1975a). Utility of interactional strategies in the study of formal operations reasoning. Paper presented to the Society for Research in Child Development, Denver.

Siegler, R. S. (1975b). Defining the locus of developmental differences in children's causal reasoning. *Journal of Experimental Child Psychology*, 20, 512–25.

Siegler, R. S. and Liebert, R. (1974). Effects of contiguity, regularity, and age on children's causal inferences. *Developmental Psychology*, 10, 574–9.

Siegler, R. S., Liebert, D. E. and Liebert, R. M. (1973). Inhelder and Piaget's pendulum problem: teaching preadolescents to act as scientists. *Developmental Psychology*, 9, 97–101.

Siegler, R. S. and Simon, E. (1975). Stages in children's understanding of the balance scale problem. Carnegie-Mellon University (mimeographed report).

Slobin, D. I. (1970). Developmental psycholinguistics: cognitive prerequisites for the development of grammar. In W. W. Dingwall (Ed.), *A Survey of Linguistic Science*. College Park: University of Maryland Linguistics Program.

Slobin, D. I. (1973). Cognitive prerequisities for the development of grammar. In C. A. Ferguson and D. I. Slobin (Eds), *Studies of Child Language Development*. New York: Holt, Rinehart and Winston.

Smither, S., Smiley, S. and Rees, R. (1974). The use of perceptual cues for number judgment by young children. *Child Development*, 45, 693–9.

Spearman, C. and Wynn-Jones, L. (1951). *Human Ability*. London: MacMillan.

Staudenmayer, H. (1975). Understanding conditional reasoning with meaningful propositions. In R. Falmagne (Ed.), *Psychological Studies of Logic and its Development*. Hillsdale, N.J.: Lawrence Erlbaum.

Stenhouse, D. (1973). *The Evolution of Intelligence*. London: Allen and Unwin.

Taplin, J. E., Staudenmayer, H. and Taddonio, J. (1974). Developmental changes in conditional reasoning: linguistic or logical? *Journal of Experimental Child Psychology*, 17, 360–73.

Tatarsky, J. H. (1974). The influence of dimensional manipulations on class-inclusion performance. *Child Development*, 45, 1173–5.

Thorndike, E. L. (1898). Animal intelligence. *Psychological Review Monograph Supplement*, No. 8.

Tomlinson-Keasey, D. and Keasey, C. B. (1974). The mediating role of cognitive development in moral judgment. *Child Development*, 45, 291–8.

Toussaint, N. A. (1974). An analysis of synchrony between concrete-operational tasks in terms of structural and performance demands. *Child Development*, 45, 992–1001.

Trabasso, T. and Riley, C. A. (1973). An information processing analysis of transitive inferences. Presented to the Eastern Psychological Association.

Trabasso, T., Riley, C. A. and Wilson, E. G. (1975). The representation of linear order and spatial strategies in reasoning: a developmental study. In R. Falmagne (Ed.), *Psychological Studies of Logic and its Development*. Hillsdale, N.J.: Lawrence Erlbaum.

Turiel, E. (1974). Conflict and transition in adolescent moral development. *Child Development*, 45, 14–29.

Vandenberg, S. G. (1968). *Progress in Human Behavior Genetics*. Baltimore. Johns Hopkins University Press.

Warden, C. J. (1951). Animal intelligence. *Scientific American*.

Wason, P. C. (1959). The processing of positive and negative information. *Quarterly Journal of Experimental Psychology*, 11, 92–107.

Wason, P. C. and Johnson-Laird, P. N. (1972). *Psychology of Reasoning: Structure and Content*. Cambridge, Mass.: Harvard University Press.

Weinreb, N. and Brainerd, C. J. (1975). A developmental study of Piaget's groupment model of the emergence of speed and time concepts. *Child Development, 46,* 176–85.

Werner, H. (1961). *Comparative Psychology of Mental Development.* New York: Science Editions.

Winer, G. (1974a). Conservation of different quantities among preschool children. *Child Development, 45,* 839–42.

Winer, G. (1974b). An analysis of verbal facilitation of class-inclusion reasoning. *Child Development, 45,* 224–7.

Wohlwill, J. F. (1968). Responses to class-inclusion questions for verbally and pictorially presented items. *Child Development, 39,* 449–65.

Worden, P. E. (1974). The development of the category-recall function under three retrieval conditions. *Child Development, 45,* 1054–9.

Youniss, J. (1975). Inference as a developmental construction. In R. Falmagne (Ed.), *Psychological Studies of Logic and its Development.* Hillsdale, N.J.: Lawrence Erlbaum.

Zimmerman, B. J. (1974). Modification of young children's grouping strategies: the effects of modeling, verbalization, incentives, and age. *Child Development, 45,* 1032–41.

Zimmerman, B. J. and Rosenthal, T. (1974). Conserving and retaining equalities and inequalities through observation and correction. *Developmental Psychology, 10,* 260–8.

CHAPTER 10

Development of Learning Processes

Hayne W. Reese and Stephen W. Porges

I. PHILOSOPHICAL BACKGROUND

Perhaps we should begin with some remarks about our orientation to the philosophy of psychology. We accept the argument that the cognitive and behavioral branches of psychology are derived from different paradigms or world views, specifically the organismic and mechanistic models, respectively, which are fundamentally incompatible and irreconcilable (see Overton and Reese, 1973; Pepper, 1942; Reese and Overton, 1970). The cognitive and behavioural (stimulus-response) approaches to learning are consequently mutually exclusive alternatives, and the adequacy of each must be evaluated within its own ground rules. Adequacy is evaluated in terms of scope—the variety of phenomena covered, and in terms of precision—the ability to generate an explanation of or a fit to the phenomena covered (Pepper, 1942). The scope criterion is consistent with the principle of parsimony, and the precision criterion is consistent with the notion that a theory is scientifically useful to the extent that it is falsifiable (Popper, 1959) or to the extent that it is plausible (see Kaplan, 1964).

The difference in world views reflected in cognitive and behavioral analyses imposes a difference in permissible concepts. In both types of analysis, performance is observed; and in both types of analysis, intervening variables or inferred processes may be postulated to explain that performance. However, in behaviorism the permissible concepts are forces and elements, and the elements are stimuli and responses. Furthermore, the relations among the forces and elements are the same whether the elements are observed to occur or are inferred or postulated to occur covertly. In cognitive psychology, in contrast, there are elements but the structure that comprises them is primary and changes in the structure can change the meanings or functions of the elements.

These functions are dependent upon the present structure (in inter-action with the present environment), and are therefore emergent in the sense of being independent of developmentally prior structures. It follows that there is no rationale for any assertion that overt and covert processes—or behaviours and cognitions—necessarily follow the same laws of operation. (For discussion of other differences between the two types of analysis, see Baltes and Reese, 1976; Overton, 1973, 1976; Overton and Reese, 1973; Reese, 1976c; Reese and Overton, 1970.)

Another relevant consideration is that the different world views cannot be merged or blended; eclecticism is confusing (Kuhn, 1962; Pepper, 1942). Nevertheless, research evidence suggests that neither view by itself is adequate to explain the developmental changes found in learning processes, some of which are more consistent with a be-havioural analysis and some with a cognitive analysis. The evidence that leads to this dilemma, and a possible resolution of the dilemma, are the primary concerns of the present chapter.

II. INFANT LEARNING

(1) INTRODUCTION

Underlying study of the development of learning processes is the assumption that changes in the nervous system parallel stages of the development of learning. These changes have often been attributed to time-related and biologically-inherent concepts such as maturation. In this section of our chapter we present a discussion of the parallel *maturation* of behavioural and biological response systems. By viewing developmental change as an effect which influences the *total organism* as a *complete system* we shall attempt to demonstrate that, regardless of the level of observation (that is to say behavioural or biological), critical developmental changes may be identified which are temporally linked to the ontogeny of learning processes.

Four systems will be briefly introduced as examples exhibiting changes that parallel the development of learning. The first is a shift from primarily reflexive behaviour to more organized and instrumental behaviour. The second is a shift in physiological activity in the autono-mic nervous system from responses characterized primarily by the exitatory influences of the sympathetic nervous system to responses characterized by the inhibitory influences of the parasympathetic ner-vous system. The third is a shift in the putative neurotransmitter systems from catecholaminergic to cholinergic. The fourth is a shift in the morphology of the central nervous system from low brain weight, high cell density, short dendrites, and limited myelination to greater brain weight, lower cell density, longer dendrites, and more complete myelination.

It appears that regardless of the system observed, developmental changes may be identified. Moreover, it can be demonstrated that many of the behaviours associated with learning and information processing have biochemical, physiological and morphological parallels. Given these multiple levels of functioning, the observed changes in the development of learning might be accounted for by a *preparedness* notion of maturation. This type of maturation would result from the collective development of the various systems which would adequately prepare the organism for successful interaction with the environment.

(2) Changes that parallel the development of learning

(i) *Observable behaviour: maturational shifts from reflexive to voluntary behaviour.* In any discussion of the developmental shift from reflexive to voluntary behaviour, an initial assumption is that behaviour can be categorized into two distinct classes, reflexive and voluntary. However, some experimenters reject the further assumption of an essential difference between the two categories and insist that both are products of the same principles and are distinguished only in complexity. Rather than reiterate the arguments of mentalists and behaviourists, we shall simply assert that the two kinds of behaviour exist in relatively non-overlapping realms.

Berlyne (1970) has distinguished between two levels of behaviour. The first is a voluntary type of behaviour and the second is a lower or more autonomic form of behaviour. Zaporozhets (see Berlyne, 1970) used the role of feedback to distinguish between voluntary and involuntary behaviour. Involuntary behaviour, according to Zaporozhets, is guided simply by feedback from the end result. The subject engages in the behaviour and at the completion of the behaviour receives information as to whether the goal has been reached. In contrast, voluntary behaviour is continuously monitored and corrections may be introduced while the action is still in progress. Voluntary behaviour requires a repertoire of active attentive processes and exploratory responses directed towards both key external cues and proprioceptive feedback cues. Both Berlyne and Zaporozhets acknowledged the developmental shift from more primitive reflexive behaviour to behaviour involving more exploratory and instrumental components.

A model of developmental increase in voluntary behaviour is also mapped into Piaget's theory (1970). According to Piaget, as a child becomes older, there is a progressive organization of perceptual and intellectual activities. This increased organization mediates the increase involuntary behaviour. Piaget has asserted that neither the maturation of behaviour associated with unlearned mechanisms nor learning due to experience or social influences, nor even both together, can account for the progressive organization of perceptual and intellectual activities of the child. He believed that there is an additional factor resulting in the development of superior adaptiveness or intelligence in the child. This factor, *equilibration*, is an autonomous tendency of activities to achieve more complete equilibrium. Equilibration is a type of voluntary behaviour, an instrumental form of learning that may be activated by conflict and reinforced by a reduction of conflict.

In all of the models of development outlined above, it is assumed that as a child matures, his behavioural repertoire changes and the constellation of observable behaviour shifts from a predominance of stimulus-determined reflexive activities and unlearned homeostatic mechanisms to behaviours that are more organized and are cognitively mediated.

(ii) *Physiological activity: maturational shifts in the autonomic nervous system.* Many psychologists have attempted to investigate the development of cognition and learning by utilizing physiological responses, particularly when the organism is in preverbal stages of development. Inherent in this technique is a series of assumptions. It is assumed, first, that physiological responses are reliable indicators of psychological processes; second, that the physiological responses identified as reliable indicators of psychological responses in older, verbal individuals reflect the same psychological processes in the young child; and third, that maturation selectively influences only the physiological response components which index or are mediated by developmental changes in cognition.

Violations of these assumptions may not create a serious problem if the investigator is merely looking for indicators of responsiveness to various stimulus situations. For example, a reliable response in *any* direction in the cardiovascular system (that is to say, heart rate deceleration, heart rate acceleration, or change in heart rate variability) can be interpreted to reflect the subject's detection of the stimulus. However, unless the above assumptions are valid, the response is ambiguous as an indicator of affective properties of the stimulus. Furthermore, if the same stimulus array is presented at various stages of maturation, response occurrence would be interpretable as indicating stimulus detection, but no other response characteristic would be interpretable unless the assumptions are valid.

Structurally, the autonomic nervous system can be divided into two antagonistic sub-systems, the parasympathetic and the sympathetic.

Although not totally consistent with the physiology of cardiac innerva-
tion, heart rate responses which have often been used to monitor
cognitive activity may be simplistically mapped into these sub-systems,
heart rate acceleration resulting from the excitatory sympathetic influences and heart rate deceleration resulting from the inhibitory parasympathetic influences (bi-directional responses could actually be the
result of either excitation or inhibition within either the sympathetic
or parasympathetic system). Developmentally, in response to simple
physical stimuli such as auditory signals there is a shift in the primary
direction of the response from acceleration to deceleration (Graham
et al., 1970). This developmental shift has been often interpreted
(Graham and Jackson, 1970) to suggest that very young infants, who
primarily show acceleration, are responding in a protective-defensive
system while older infants, who show deceleration, are attending or
orienting to the stimulus.

This simplistic analysis of the cognitive correlates of heart rate responses becomes complicated when information about differential development of the autonomic subsystems is considered. For example, if
there is a developmental shift in parasympathetic influences on heart
rate responses, then the directionality of the heart rate response may
not reflect the same psychological properties as have been observed in
adults (for instance, acceleration associated with startle or defence
and deceleration associated with orienting or attention). However, if
the shift in the autonomic nervous system actually parallels a psychological shift from defensive to orienting behaviour, then the directionality of the heart rate response can be used as an important indicator
of psychological activity. A test of the assumption of parallel shifts
would be extremely difficult since it would necessitate psychological
indicators in the first place.

Although the directionality of the heart rate response is critical to
theoretical models of orienting and attention (Graham and Clifton,
1966), it is still possible to detect reliable responses without attributing
complex psychological value to the response other than acknowledging
the detection of the stimulus. If concern is limited to detection, then
it may be possible to assess perceptual thresholds or to detect responsiveness to contingent pairings of stimuli, as in the classical conditioning paradigm (Porges, 1974).

(iii) *Neurotransmitter systems: the maturational shift towards cholinergic systems.* It is apparent that there are neurotransmitter systems which
reflect the developmental shift from more primitive reflexive activity to
more organized cognitively mediated behaviour. It has been suggested
that the catecholaminergic systems (the behavioural concomitants of

which are involved in excitation) act antagonistically towards the cholinergic systems (the behavioural concommitants of which are involved in inhibition of ongoing activities). These two neurotransmitter systems have structural parallels in the autonomic nervous system. The catecholaminergic system maps into the excitatory activities of the sympathetic nervous system and the cholinergic system maps into the inhibitory activities of the parasympathetic nervous system.

If these biochemical neurotransmitter systems parallel the same developmental shifts observable in the autonomic nervous system and in overt behaviour, one would expect that, as the organism matures, pharmacological agents that block cholinergic transmission would have a more profound effect on older, more mature organisms which exhibit complex mediated voluntary behaviours. To demonstrate this effect on the two categories of behaviour, reflexive and voluntary, the levels of the neurotransmitters can be manipulated pharmacologically or allowed to change normally as a function of development.

Williams, Hamilton and Carlton (1974) presented evidence that two different processes, reflexive and voluntary, may be pharmacologically extracted from a habituation task. Specifically, they found that the normally observed decrement of the reflexive response to change in stimulation was relatively unaffected by an anticholinergic drug, but the normal decrement in voluntary exploratory behaviour was profoundly attenuated by this drug. These findings suggest that the reflexive components of the habituation process are not affected by cholinergic neurotransmitters while exploratory or voluntary behaviour is.

Given the above data, the next question to be addressed regards time changes in the decrement of reflexive behaviour as a function of age, as compared to the decrement of voluntary behaviour. Underlying the question is the assumption that behavioural changes as a function of age will be influenced by the developmental shift in neurotransmitters. To test this model, Williams, Hamilton and Carlton (1975) assessed the rates of decrement of the two classes of responses (startle reflexes and exploratory behaviour) in rats of two different ages. The rate of response decrement of the startle reflex was unaffected by age. In contrast, there was no evidence of habituation of exploration in the younger animals whereas the older animals uniformly showed profound response decrements.

Campbell, Lytle and Fibiger (1969) investigated the ontogeny of catecholaminergic arousal and cholinergic inhibitory mechanisms in the rat. In studying spontaneous activity, they noted that amphetamine, which stimulates the catecholaminergic system, always increased activity independent of the age of the animal, while scopolamine, which competes with acetylcholine at the receptor sites, had no effect in younger rats. They interpreted this finding to suggest that catecholaminergic excitory areas of the brainstem mature more rapidly than cholinergic inhibitory areas of the forebrain, thus adding more evidence to the convincing model that maturation results in developmental shifts from reflexive excitatory activity to more organized voluntary behaviour characterized by inhibitory controls. Regarding the generalizability of this model from rats to humans, Campbell and Spear (1972) noted that in the child during the first years of life, changes in central nervous system structure and function occur and are comparable to those occurring in the rat during the first months of life.

(iv) *Morphological changes: changes in brain structures.* There are distinct anatomical parallels to the excitatory and inhibitory classes of behaviour. For example, reflexive and excitatory types of behaviour have an anatomical parallel in the brainstem reticular formation, which has a biochemical substrate characterized by catecholaminergic systems. Inhibitory activity, like exploratory behaviour, has an anatomical parallel in the forebrain, in which the biochemical substrate is characterized by cholinergic systems.

Morphologically, the brain develops rostrally, in that the phylogenetically primitive hindbrain or brainstem structures mature earlier than the forebrain systems. This trend would account for the developmental delay in inhibitory behaviour, since the forebrain system, which develops later, modulates and controls the activity of the lower-level reticular formation. The changing myelination in the brain also parallels those behaviours. In rats, although myelin is present in the brainstem at birth, it is not seen in the forebrain until about ten days after birth. Similarly, the number of synaptic junctions in the cortex undergoes massive proliferation between 15 and 25 days of age.

In humans, during the first two years of life, there is roughly a 350 per cent increase in the weight of the brain. By the age of 14 years, the brain has reached its adult weight and no further increase occurs. The increase in brain weight and size reduces the packing density of the neurons in the brain; the number of neurons in the brain does not change drastically as a function of development, but the distance between the cell bodies increases. The increased distance between neurons allows the dendrites to branch. The amount of dendritic branching has been related in rats to experiential factors (see for instance, Greenough, 1975). The grey cell coefficient, the ratio of volume of cortical grey matter to the volume of nerve cells contained in it, reaches asymptote near puberty. The myelinization rate (Folch-Pi, 1952) shows that in the development of white matter there are some components such as cholesterol and cerebrosides that show a relative growth which reaches asymptote during the early teens. Other indicators of the morphological development of the brain are electrophysiological changes. There is a marked increase in alpha frequencies (7–11 Hz) during the first three years of life. Lenneberg (1967) considered the alpha growth curve to be directly relevant to language development. In contrast to the increase in alpha, there is a decrease in the slower frequencies (for instance, 6 Hz).

Virtually every morphological change in the nervous system exhibits a rapid growth period during the first two years and then an asymptote at or around puberty. These morphological shifts may be viewed as prerequisites or limiting factors for cognitive behaviour. The morphological changes in themselves are not specific causes of cognitive behaviour, but in their absence cognitive development is greatly retarded.

(3) Changes in learning

(i) *Preparedness.* The multiple levels of development may be viewed as collectively preparing the organism for more complicated and organized behaviour. According to Seligman (1970), the individual brings certain *equipment* and a *predisposition* which are more or less appropriate to the demands of the situation. Developmentally, we have described the shifts in biological systems which predispose the child to perform adequately. However, the behavioural resultant is not totally a function of developmental changes in the mechanical attributes of the nervous system. There is another form of preparedness that cannot be described in simple mechanistic terms. Rather, this type of preparedness is the subtle ability to link stimulus contingencies. Thus, for successful classical conditioning of young infants, not only must the conditional stimulus be above threshold and the unconditioned stimulus elicit a response, but the conditional stimulus and the unconditioned stimulus must be associable. The organism may be more or less prepared by evolution and by maturation to associate specific stimuli.

The developmental shift in learning potential is obviously a function of both the changing mechanical attributes and functional associability of the organism. This shift from simple reactive response to more cognitively mediated learning will be described in the remaining parts of this section.

(ii) *Orienting reflex and habituation.* The concept of learning necessitates that the subject respond appropriately to stimulus contingencies. The first response the organism makes to any change in stimulation is often called an orienting reflex. The reflex functionally *tunes* the appropriate receptor and insures optimal conditions for reception of the stimulus (Sokolov, 1963). The reflex has several components : somatic (body movement to source of stimulation), autonomic (changes in heart and respiration), electroencephalographic (alpha blocking) and sensory (enhanced receptor sensitivity). According to Lynn (1966), the ontogeny of the orienting reflex follows a maturational shift from strictly reflexive components at birth to exploratory-type behaviour at later ages. Initially at birth and during the neonatal period the orienting reflex is characterized by autonomic responses and gross undirected movements. As the infant matures and motor control improves, the behaviour becomes more exploratory; at approximately 45 days of age, infants start making gross motor movements in the direction of the source of stimulation.

According to Sokolov, when a novel stimulus is introduced into the organism's environment, an orienting reflex is elicited. Upon repeated stimulus presentations, the brain forms a neuronal model that incorporates the salient features of the stimulus. Once the neuronal model is established, the stimulus no longer elicits the orienting reflex, which is then said to have *habituated*. If, however, a mismatch occurs between the neuronal model and the stimulus input, the input disconfirms the organism's expectancy and the orienting reflex is elicited again, or dishabituated. A slight extension of Sokolov's proposal brings us close to studies of attention and memory in infants.

The process of habituation, according to Sokolov, necessitates a form of cortical inhibition. If the cortex is not adequately developed, the stimulus will continue to elicit the orienting reflex until the organism fatigues. In an intriguing study, Brackbill (1971) attempted to habituate motor responses to auditory stimulation in an anencephalic infant, an infant born without a cortex. If the inhibitory processes associated with habituation of the orienting reflex have a locus in the cortex, the response to changes in stimulation would not habituate in the anencephalic infant. In support of this hypothesis, Brackbill found that the infant's motor responses did not habituate to intense auditory stimuli. It is, however, difficult to infer conclusively from these data the role of the cortex in the habituation of the orienting reflex, because the auditory stimulus used was so intense that it may well have elicited a defensive reflex, which is resistant to habituation (Sokolov, 1963).

Another class of response difficult to habituate includes responses to unique stimuli. These responses may be impossible to habituate because of their signal value, which may be either determined via phylogenetic programming or acquired via association. The selective ability of the organism to habituate responses to some stimuli and not to others is obviously behaviourally economical and demonstrates the ability of the organism to learn not to respond to inappropriate stimuli and to continue to respond to stimuli that may be related to survival.

The study of habituation from a developmental point of view might permit assessment of neurological development; the differential ease of habituation of the reflexive responses and the voluntary-exploratory behaviours may generate more specific information regarding the neurophysiological mechanisms of the habituation process.

Williams, Hamilton and Carlton (1975) described a model of habituation in which one process is postulated to be associated with reflexive responses and a different process is postulated to be associated with voluntary-exploratory behaviours. The reflexive responses may habituate regardless of the status of the cortex, while the exploratory-voluntary behaviours may necessitate the level of cortical development postulated by Sokolov, which appears within the first few months following birth.

Another model of habituation, proposed by Thompson and Spencer (1966), deals with nine essential characteristics. First, given that a particular stimulus elicits a response, repeated applications of the stimulus result in a decreased response, that is, habituation. Second, if the stimulus is withheld, the response tends to recover over time, that is, spontaneous recovery occurs. Third, if repeated series of habituation training and spontaneous recovery are given, habituation becomes successively more rapid. Fourth, the more rapid the frequency of stimulation, the more rapid is habituation. Fifth, the weaker the stimulus, the more rapid is habituation. Sixth, strong stimuli may yield no significant habituation. Seventh, the effects of habituation training may proceed beyond a zero asymptotic level. Eighth, habituation of a response to a given stimulus generalizes to other stimuli. Ninth, presentation of another stimulus, especially a strong one, results in recovery of a habituated response, that is, dishabituation.

There is some evidence that the very young infant is capable of habituation. Using a procedure of repeatedly presenting one stimulus and then testing with a novel one, Engen, Lipsitt and Kaye (1963) and Engen and Lipsitt (1965) examined habituation of neonatal activity and respiratory changes to olfactory stimulation. They found response decrement on later trials with the odour, and response increment when either a new odour or a component of the old odour was presented. Both Bridger (1961) and Bartoshuk (1962) have reported that cardiac acceleration in the neonate habituates to repeated presentations of the same tone and reappears when a tone of new frequency is given. Porges, Stamps and Walter (1974) found that newborns with a more labile heart rate tended to exhibit greater plasticity of responding to the offset of a visual stimulus. This plasticity was characterized by the following sequence: initial acceleration, attenuated acceleration, no response, and finally deceleration. The newborns with a more stable heart rate did not respond significantly to the offset of the visual stimulus.

Many developmental psychologists who utilize the habituation procedure have assumed that the rate of habituation reflects efficiency of encoding information (Cohen, 1973; Kagan, 1971; Lewis, 1971). These investigators tend to be concerned with the habituation of visual fixation. The duration of visual fixation within the paradigms of these investigators may be viewed as a component of exploratory behaviour. Consistent with the maturational trend towards more voluntary behaviour, habituation of visual fixation is more prevalent in older infants.

During the first few months, human infants start to exhibit more organized behaviour associated with visual fixation. Salapatek (1975) reported that when a visual stimulus is presented, newborns turn and fixate the first edge while 2-month-old infants scan the stimulus. Cohen (1975) reported that as infants mature, their responses when turning from a stimulus become more consistent. Cohen interpreted this pattern of behaviour to reflect the development of more voluntary, organized behaviour, which is absent or at least less developed in younger infants.

Habituation does not require the occurrence of a new response, hence may predate active learning. Habituation may thus provide an index of early learning unconfounded by age-related problems of behavioural-repertoire. The emerging picture is one of an infant who gives high priority to novel events. If they are significant, or have *intrinsic signal value*, he continues to respond or to attend; if not, he habituates. Operant and classical conditioning and habituation share a common characteristic in that in each case behaviour changes with exposure to a stimulus. They differ in that learning typically consists in the acquisition of a new response or a change in the control of an old response, while habituation consists in the weakening of an unlearned response to stimulation.

(iii) *Operant conditioning*. Elicited and conditioned reflexes, or respondents, represent a relatively small proportion of behaviour of higher organisms; the remaining behaviour is operant. Unlike respondents, which require specific eliciting stimuli, operant behaviour simply occurs. Like habituation, operant conditioning becomes easier as the child

15—CP * *

matures. As the sensory-motor systems mature, the child's ability to respond to and discriminate among stimuli parallels an increase in motor-behavioural control, resulting in greater *stimulus control* (operant conditioning) of more behaviours.

In their 1965 review of infant conditioning, Bijou and Baer concluded that the question of whether operant conditioning can be demonstrated in human neonates was unanswered. Their conclusion was based in part on the lack of available studies of operant conditioning in infants. One reason for this lack was that the established conditioning methods employed with adults and children required well-differentiated response systems that would permit complex manipulative responses. A demonstration of operant conditioning in the new-born would therefore require in the infant's limited repertoire responses that are sufficiently viable and stable for experimental manipulation.

Relatively few studies of operant conditioning with infants were undertaken prior to the early 1960s. However, during the 1960s, techniques were being developed which acknowledged the uniqueness of the newborn in terms of a limited response repertoire and an immature sensory system. Rheingold, Stanley and Cooley (1962) introduced the use of visual and auditory displays as effective reinforcers. Lipsitt, Pederson and DeLucia (1966) added Lindsley's procedure (see Lindsley, Hobika and Etsten, 1961) of "conjugate" reinforcement, through which a visual display is made available and its illumination is proportionate to the infant's rate of response (such as kicking or sucking). The perceptual opportunity is a direct consequence of the infant's activity, and has been found to be a potent reinforcer. Siqueland and DeLucia (1969) developed a modification of this procedure, in which the readily available motor activity of non-nutritive sucking was used as the operant with proportionate visual feedback of sustained illumination of rear-projected coloured slides. This procedure resulted in rapid conditioning in infants as young as 3 weeks of age and as old as 12 months.

Several reviewers (H. E. Fitzgerald and Porges, 1971; Hulsebus, 1973; Siqueland, 1970) have concluded that if the response is carefully selected and the reinforcer is adequate, the newborn can be operantly conditioned. The behaviours most often studied during infancy have been sucking, head-turning, visual fixation, vocalization, and kicking. For example, Kron (1966) utilized nutritive sucking as an operant, and obtained evidence of instrumental conditioning in the human infant as early as the first day post partum. The success of the conditioning procedure is often a function of maturation, in that more organized behaviours necessitate greater neurological development.

(iv) *Classical conditioning.* Within developmental psychology, there has been controversy about whether the newborn infant can be classically conditioned. During the first fifty years of this century the behavioristic approach, with its mechanistic stimulus-response model, supported the notion that the newborn can be conditioned; newborn conditionability was a viable research problem and the data produced by these early studies were readily incorporated in existing theories. Since the 1950s the influence of Piaget's model of cognitive maturation and organization has stressed that conditionability necessitates the development of a type of *memory* which appears later in life as a function of maturation. This model is reflected in Sameroff's (1971, 1972) questioning as to whether the newborn can be conditioned. Sameroff critically discussed the newborn conditioning literature, rejected previous reported successes on methodological grounds, and interpreted the conditioned response within a Piagetian-cognitive context. Taking a maturational view, he explained that as a prerequisite for the classically conditioned response, there must be a differentiation of new schema systems related to both the conditional stimulus and the unconditioned stimulus. This differentiation would allow the infant to co-ordinate his differentiated perceptual response system with the sensori-motor schemas characteristic of his limited behavioural repertoire. Thus, although the infant may respond to a specific stimulus, Sameroff invoked the concept of preparedness and postulated that the infant is not maturationally prepared to associate any one of his limited responses with a specific stimulus. Regardless of the question of newborn conditionability, there is an obvious trend that, as an infant matures, classical conditioning occurs more easily (H. E. Fitzgerald and Brackbill, in press; Stevenson, 1970).

Related to the notion of preparedness is Kasatkin's hypothesis of an immutable developmental sequence of effectiveness of conditional stimuli (see Brackbill and Koltsova, 1967). Kasatkin's first principle was that there is an invariant, ontogenetic sequence in which sensory modalities can contribute effective conditional stimuli for establishing conditioned responses. This hypothesized sequence, from the earliest to the last to gain effectiveness, is : vestibular, auditory, tactile-kinesthetic, olfactory, gustatory, visual. Kasatkin's second principle was that the success or failure of early conditioning depends entirely on the nature of the conditional stimulus.

Kasatkin (1972) later revised his views on infant conditionability. In this revision, he reaffirmed both the invariant sequence of conditional stimulus effectiveness and the importance of the conditional stimulus for conditioning. However, he also proposed an invariant developmental sequence of effectiveness of the unconditioned stimulus (although this sequence was not specified). Moreover, he proposed that the ontogenetic sequences of effectiveness of conditional and unconditioned stimuli are phylogenetically determined. Thus, sensory systems that are phylogenetically older (vestibular, cutaneous, gustatory, and olfactory modalities) are more important initial determinants of conditioning than are the phylogenetically younger systems (auditory and visual). In addition, phylogenetically older response systems, such as the autonomic, can be conditioned earlier than the phylogenetically younger motor responses. Consistent with this last hypothesis, much of the recent successful research on classical conditioning of very young infants has involved autonomic responses (for instance, Clifton, 1974a, b; Forbes and Porges, 1972; Porges, 1974; Stamps and Porges, 1975).

Maturation appears to prepare the organism for and limit the extent of conditioning. The types of behaviours observable as conditioned responses tend to exhibit a maturational shift from reflexive autonomic responses (heart rate changes, etc.) to motor responses. However, regardless of the theoretical orientation, there is little doubt that the infant, even at birth, is capable of responding to specific stimuli, of exhibiting a response decrement to repeated stimulus presentations, and of developing responses that reflect a developing expectancy relationship between stimuli.

III. LEARNING IN CHILDHOOD AND ADULTHOOD

(1) MODEL OF THE DEVELOPMENT OF LEARNING

(i) *The associative and cognitive levels of functioning.* In Section II we noted a developmental trend in learning processes during infancy such that cognitive processes begin to replace reflexive processes. The trend continues in early childhood, and there is considerable evidence that by the age of about 7 years learning is primarily a cognitive process. In the early 1960s several reviews were published indicating a major transition in learning processes between the ages of 5 and 7 years (T. S. Kendler, 1963; Reese, 1962; White, 1965). White (1965) concluded that before the transition behaviour follows the laws of stimulus-response association, and after the transition behaviour can be controlled by cognitive processes. In the latter stage, however, "human behaviour may or may not follow associative laws closely, depending upon eliciting conditions" (p. 216). He suggested, in addition, that factors such as stress may result in regression to an associative level of functioning, but one that has continued to develop during the cognitive stage. "The stressed adult might revert to a more sophisticated, more grown up, better developed version of the associative system which young children also favor" (p. 216).

A theoretical, or perhaps meta-theoretical, problem in such an analysis is to avoid the confusion that arises when paradigms or world views are mixed (Kuhn, 1962; Pepper, 1942; Reese and Overton, 1970). White's analysis includes the mechanistic stimulus-response system and the non-mechanistic cognitive system, but confusion is avoided by White's assumption that the systems are separate and do not function simultaneously. It might be noted that there is a basic contradiction in this analysis, namely the assumption that the organism can be represented simultaneously by mechanistic and non-mechanistic models. This contradiction is resolved if one adopts a dialectical model, and other elements in White's analysis are also consistent with a dialectical model. For example, one could interpret the appearance of the cognitive level of functioning as the negation of the associative level, but this negation is itself negated by the dialectical level which incorporates the cognitive level and the associative level, the latter at a higher plane than that at which it existed previous to the transition. (Parenthetically, White mentioned the "curious and interesting fact that the history of psychology shows an almost continuous reissue of an essentially associative scheme of thought and, in each epoch, strong rejection of that associative scheme by a dissident group" [p. 216]. The dialectical nature of this history seems obvious.)

In a model such as White's it is useful to be able to predict the level of functioning that will characterize behaviour in particular situations. White mentioned stress as a possible variable predicting associative functioning, and suggested that other variables are the "eliciting conditions". Similar models have often been proposed (for instance, by Uznadze, 1966; Woodworth, 1918), in each of which behaviour is assumed to be habitual or mechanical until a problem arises, or conflict occurs, when the organism shifts to a cognitive level of operation. Ongoing behaviour is inhibited—White characterized the process as inhibition of the first-available associative response—and control shifts to cognitive processes. Anecdotally, however, it seems obvious that the two levels can operate simultaneously, as when an adult drives an automobile on a thoroughly familiar route while mentally solving a problem unrelated to the driving.

Later (in Sections III, (2) and (3)), we shall examine the evidence for the developmental shift from an associative stage of functioning to the dialectical stage in which behaviour may be controlled either associatively or cognitively. We shall have little to say about the variables that determine which level will operate in the latter stage, because little relevant research has been done. Before proceeding to the evidence, however, we need to consider the theory in further detail.

(ii) *Operative deficiencies.* In the 1960s, as already noted, reviews of research indicated a transition at about 5 to 7 years of age (T. S. Kendler, 1963; Reese, 1962; White, 1965). These reviews were organized around the theoretical concept of mediation. A mediator, in stimulus-response theory, is a cue-producing response that is aroused by stimulation and that controls further responding through the associative function of the cue produced (for instance, Goss, 1961). Symbolically,

$$S \rightarrow r_m - s_m \rightarrow R$$

where S is the initial stimulus eliciting the mediating response r_m, which produces a cue, s_m, that elicits the terminal response, R. When mediation fails to occur, according to this formulation, the S–R chain must have been broken either because the initial stimulus failed to arouse the mediating response or because the cue produced by the potential mediator failed to arouse the terminal response. (Reese [1970b] noted the additional possibility that the potential mediator may fail to produce a discriminable cue, and although an experimental analogue of this possibility could be constructed, no relevant research has been published.)

The first type of failure has been labelled a "production deficiency" (Flavell, Beach and Chinsky, 1966); the subject fails to produce the potential mediator in response to the initial stimulus. The second type of failure has been labelled a "mediational deficiency" (Flavell *et al.*, 1966) or a control deficiency (T. S. Kendler, 1972); the potential mediator is produced but fails to control further behaviour. These "deficiencies" are not necessarily all-or-none, and might better be labelled "inefficiencies" (Jeffrey, 1965). There may also be production and control *errors* (Reese, 1970b); the subject produces an inappropriate or incorrect mediator, or the mediator arouses inappropriate or incorrect responses. For example, children who fail to exhibit intermediate-size transposition would ordinarily be considered not to be mediating their response. However, Zeiler (1967) reported that some children seemed actually to have made the production error of transposing the mediating response. That is, on the test trial they applied the mediating label ("middle-sized") to the test stimulus that was most similar to absolute size to the middle-sized training stimulus. Given this production error, mediation would produce an "absolute" response.

An example of control error might occur in the paired-associate mediated-association task, A–B, B–C, A–C. In the A–C list, A might correctly elicit B subvocally, but B might elicit a strong pre-experimentally acquired associate instead of the learned associate, C. In this case, the control error would presumably result from proactive interference; the previously acquired associate of B would interfere with retention of the recently learned B–C association.

The concepts of production and control deficiencies, which originated in stimulus-response analyses of elementary mediators such as verbal labels and button-pushing responses, have been extended to refer to the production and utilization of cognitive operations such as mnemonic strategies (for instance, Brown, 1975; Flavell, 1970; Hagen, Jongeward and Kail, 1975; Reese, 1976b). The concepts have, in other words, been taken from the mechanistic domain into the cognitive domain. The motivation for this transformation of the concepts was the observation of developmental trends in various kinds of memory tasks, trends that could readily be interpreted as reflecting cognitive analogues of the production and control, or mediation, deficiencies. "Control" and "mediation" seem misnomers in the cognitive context, however, and it might be better to keep the domains of application of the concepts clearly separate by changing the names of the concepts. Flavell (1971) has suggested "evocation" and "utilization" deficiencies, and although these terms have not been used as often as "production" and "mediation" deficiency in the cognitive domain, they are used in the present chapter.

(iii) *An illustrative case: memory development.* The development of learning processes can be illustrated by an example from the literature on memory. Suppose that a series of objects is presented, and later the subject is required to recall their names in the correct serial order. It is known that naming at the time of presentation enhances later recall (for review, see Hagen *et al.*, 1975). Recall is enhanced even more, however, if the subject rehearses the names serially during the study trial. However, if the objects are presented at a fast pace, or if there are many objects to be remembered, the serial rehearsal strategy does not work well because the subject has no time to rehearse except early in the list when few objects have yet been presented. An effective strategy would be to rehearse subsets of names, breaking the complete list into a series of clusters of objects. Even more effectively, the subject might use a version of the "places and images" memory system (Yates, 1966), imagining an interaction between each object in the serial list and a code-object representing the serial position. In the recall test, the subject would recall the images sequentially by transforming the serial-position numbers into the imagined code-objects, which in turn would redintegrate the imagined interactions, from which the names of the objects presented would be retrieved (see Reese, 1976d).

Consider naming as an aid to memory. If the naming strategy is not evoked—an evocation deficiency—then naming obviously would not occur. However, even if the naming strategy is evoked, naming would fail to occur if the names of the objects presented were not in the subject's vocabulary—a production deficiency. Furthermore, even if the strategy is evoked and names are known, the subject may utilize the strategy inefficiently; he may name some objects and not others, or may change names from trial to trial.

Consider now serial rehearsal. The same kinds of deficiencies could be present, but in addition serial rehearsal cannot occur if there is any deficiency in naming. Consequently, serial rehearsal can be considered to be more complex than naming; serial rehearsal presupposes naming, and consequently is farther along than naming in a chain of strategies, or higher in a hierarchy of strategies. Research has shown that each strategy goes through the same stages of development. First, the strategy does not occur, presumably because it has not yet been acquired. Next, there is a stage of evocation and utilization deficiency, in which the strategy is not used spontaneously but can be evoked by training or instructions. At this stage, the strategy is not utilized efficiently when it is evoked. Next is a stage of evocation deficiency in which the strategy is utilized efficiently, but is not used unless it is evoked by training or instructions. Finally, there is a mature stage in which the strategy is used spontaneously and is utilized efficiently. However, at this stage it may not always be used appropriately. Naming, for example, is more appropriate for free recall than for serial recall, and serial rehearsal is not appropriate if the pacing is fast or the list is long.

In White's model, the transitional period is around 5 to 7 years of age. The specific age at which the transition occurs is of no theoretical significance; it was determined empirically. Therefore, the model is not harmed by research showing that mediation can occur in children younger than 5. In fact, research published after the reviews of the early 1960s has fairly consistently demonstrated mediation in even 3- and 4-year-old children. The evidence from these studies and other considerations (see Reese, 1976b) can be interpreted to reflect a secular trend or cohort change in the rate of cognitive development, which would result in an earlier transition from the associative level to the cognitive level of functioning. However, the point to be emphasized is that White's transition is unique in only one way. It is the same as is found with any strategy, going from deficiency in evocation and utilization through deficiency only in evocation to maturity. Its unique feature is that it refers to perhaps the simplest kind of deliberate learning strategy, analogous to naming or, in the experimental laboratory, often identical to naming.

(2) DISCRIMINATIVE LEARNING AND TRANSFER

The trend towards cognitive influences on learning can be seen in studies of discriminative learning and transfer. In the simplest design, two objects are presented simultaneously, varying at random in left-right positions from trial to trial, and choice of one of the objects is rewarded while choice of the other is not. After this simple discrimination has been learned, transfer can be tested by changing one or both of the objects. Close examination of the pattern of performance, including speed of learning and the nature of errors that precede learning, reveals findings that are anomalous from a behaviouristic position but that are sensible from a cognitive position. The relevant theoretical positions and findings are surveyed in this section.

(i) *Role of attention.* The role of attention in discriminative learning and transfer has been analyzed by several theorists (see Eimas, 1970; Reese, 1968). Among these are Zeaman and House (for instance, 1963), who developed a quantitative formulation. In order to stay within the categorical boundaries of behaviourism, Zeaman and House postulated that attention is a kind of response, subject to the same laws of behaviour as overt responses. Zeaman and House had observed that in discriminative learning both normal and retarded children exhibited two-phase learning curves (see Eimas, 1970). Little evidence of learning was apparent in the first phase, and learning was rapid in the second phase. According to the Zeaman and House theory, the first phase is devoted to learning which stimulus dimension (for instance, colour) is relevant to the discrimination, and the second phase is devoted to learning which particular value (for instance, red) on the relevant dimension is associated with reward.

Of developmental interest, Zeaman and House also found that retarded and normal children differed in the duration of the first phase and did not differ in the second phase, implying that the retarded child's problem in this kind of task, at least, is an attentional deficit rather than a deficit in associative learning. Development, in the Zeaman and House theory, would be reflected by changes in the

probabilities of the various possible attentional responses, or in parameters representing rates of change in these probabilities as a function
of training. Both kinds of developmental change seem reasonable.

Nevertheless, it appears that the analysis is inadequate in scope and
in precision. The version of the Zeaman and House theory that has had
demonstrated success is based on a "one-look" model, in which only
one dimension is attended to at any one time and other dimensions
present are ignored. However, many investigators have concluded that
subjects can attend to more than one dimension at a time, perhaps
with different intensities of attention (see Reese, 1968). This "multiple-
look" capability is not possible in the one-look model, and although
an extension to a multiple-look model has been discussed, it seems to
be mathematically intractable. Furthermore, the Zeaman and House
equations predict chance-level performance in the first phase of acquisition, yet the actual learning curves show steady improvement during
that stage (see Eimas, 1970, Figs 9.4, 9.5, 9.6).

In the cognitive model, attention is not an explanatory concept, but
rather is an effect of the operation of cognitive systems. Thus, attention to a single dimension or simultaneously to more than one dimension reflects assimilation of the stimuli to stimulus schemas, which can
be unidimensional or multidimensional and which may undergo
accommodation during the course of training. Application of these
notions to discriminative learning is difficult because cognitive psychologists have usually been concerned with the cognitive systems reflected by performance rather than in the performance reflected by
cognitive systems. It should be apparent, then, that what this approach
gains in scope is lost in precision if precision is evaluated by the falsi-
fiability criterion. However, precision may not be lost when it is evaluated by the plausibility criterion.

(ii) *Role of verbal processes.* Perhaps the best-developed stimulus-
response analysis of the role of verbal processes in discriminative learning and transfer is that of Spiker and Cantor (1973). The analysis is
articulated with Spiker's (1963, 1970, 1971) generalization theory of
discriminative learning, which is derived from earlier Hull-Spence
analyses (see for instance, Hull, 1943; Spence, 1956, 1960, Chap. 22).
In these analyses, discriminative learning consists of conditioning and
inhibition of approach responses to various stimuli, but the functional
or effective stimuli are not limited to those presented by the experimenter. Subjects may make cue-producing responses, such as emitting
verbal labels for the stimuli presented, and the cues produced by these
responses can function as stimuli influencing further responses. Spiker's
major contributions to the stimulus-response analysis of discriminative

learning have been, first, to quantify the role of generalization among stimulus elements and, second, to formalize the role of response-produced cues. The latter contribution is the more immediately relevant in the present chapter, in that it represents a behaviouristic formalization of a function that in other analyses (for instance, Wozniak, 1972) has been considered to be "cognitive". This function is the regulative role of verbal behaviour, or, in the more specific context being considered here, the regulation of discriminative behaviour by verbal responses.

In Spiker's stimulus-response analysis, the role of verbal processes in discriminative learning is to add additional stimulus components to the compounds of stimuli to be discriminated, thus affecting generalization among the compounds. In another stimulus-response analysis, Kendler and Kendler (for instance, 1962) attributed the effects of verbal processes in discriminative learning to the process of mediation.

The Kendlers dealt explicitly with developmental issues in their theory, by postulating developmental changes in the probability of producing the required mediators and in the probability that the potential mediator will control further responding. Research has confirmed these postulates (T. S. Kendler, 1972). In Spiker and Cantor's generalization theory of the role of verbal responses, development can be represented by appropriate changes in the values of the parameters of the equations. These include a parameter representing the relative discriminability of differences between stimulus elements, a parameter representing the maximum range of generalization and parameters determining speed of habit formation. All these parameters could reasonably be expected to change developmentally.

Nevertheless, like the Zeaman and House theory, these theories now appear to be inadequately precise. For example, in certain situations Spiker's equations can fit either the early portion of learning curves or the later portion, but not both (see Spiker and Cantor, 1973). Similarly, although a large literature supports the Kendlers' contentions about deficiencies in the mediation process in an early stage of development, a substantial literature demonstrates the occurrence of mediated behaviour at that stage (see Eimas, 1970; Flavell, 1970).

These findings are anomalous for stimulus-response analyses, because they imply the intervention of cognitive processes. Other anomalous findings have been reported. For example, Reese (1972) tested children in the kindergarten and in the first and second grades (roughly 5, 6, and 7 years old) in the acquired-equivalence acquired-distinctiveness design, in which names were learned for nonsense designs in a first phase and a successive-discrimination task was given in a test phase. In the test phase, the two stimuli used had been associated with different names in the first phase (acquired-distinctiveness condition) or with the same name (acquired-equivalence condition). The standard "same-different" training was given to another group in the first phase (control condition). An important feature of the test phase was that one of the stimuli was presented on Trials 1 and 2 and the other stimulus was presented on Trial 3. Thus, performance might be expected to be better on Trial 2 than on Trial 1, if the subject remembered on Trial 2 which response was signalled as correct on Trial 1. On Trial 3, acquired distinctiveness should produce a correct response if the subject remembered the Trial 1 and 2 information, and acquired equivalence should produce an error—choice of the same response as was correct on Trials 1 and 2. The control condition should produce about chance-level performance on Trial 3, since the subject would have no way of knowing whether the same or a different response was to be required for the two stimuli.

The results were closely consistent with the expectations. The groups were not significantly different on Trials 1 and 2; performance improved from Trial 1 to Trial 2; and the groups were significantly different in the expected directions on Trial 3. Reese argued, however, that the rapidity with which these effects developed (together with other findings) implied a cognitive basis rather than an associative basis; specifically, short-term memory rather than learning seemed to have been involved.

Other studies have also yielded results that pose problems for a stimulus-response analysis (for review, see Cantor, 1965; Jeffrey, 1970). In one of these studies, J. M. Fitzgerald (1974) used a design essentially the same as Reese's, to determine the causes of the mediation deficiency postulated by the Kendlers. Fitzgerald tested children of $4\frac{1}{2}$ to $5\frac{1}{2}$ years, and found that about 65 per cent of the group performed on the critical trial (Trial 3) in the way expected if mediation occurred and the other 35 per cent as though mediation did not occur. Of the children who apparently used mediators, 70 per cent performed as "classifiers" on a standard Piagetian test of classification ability; and of the children who apparently did not use mediators, only 20 per cent were "classifiers". These findings support the hypothesis that the occurrence of mediation depends on the presence of particular cognitive structures (see also Osler and Madden, 1973).

Even simple discriminative-learning tasks have sometimes yielded evidence that is more readily interpreted cognitively than behaviouristically. For example, Stevenson, Iscoe and McConnell (1955) found that fifth grade children learned a two-stimulus discrimination faster than college students, presumably because the college students were trying out complex solutions that were incorrect but that would have made the task a challenge for college-level subjects, while the children were either trying out simpler, more relevant solutions or were learning in an associative manner. (See also Kendler, Kendler and Learnard, 1962; Rabinowitz and Cantor, 1966; Shirai, 1951.) "Trying out solutions" is at the cognitive level of functioning.

Another example is a report by Zeiler (1964) on the performance of human adults in the intermediate-size transposition problem. After solving the initial discrimination, the subjects were given two test trials without warning *and without reward for any choice.* Zeiler found that some of the subjects transposed on the first test trial and others made an "absolute" choice. Virtually all (96 per cent), however, switched to the other response on the second test trial. Presumably, the subjects were in a quandary on the first test trial as to whether the experimenter wanted them to base their response on the relational property or the absolute property of the stimuli. Whichever basis they chose, they apparently interpreted the non-reward as information that the other basis was correct. Such ratiocinations do not occur in the behaviouristic organism, but of course are expected in the cognitive organism.

It is important to note that other evidence supports White's suggestion that cognitive processes do not completely replace associative learning processes. Spence (1963) reported that cognitive factors can influence the performance of college students in eyeblink conditioning. However, when special care is taken to disguise the purpose of the training, evidence for conditioning is obtained. Thus, it appears that without the subject's awareness—and hence presumably without the intervention of cognitive processes—associative learning can occur in adults.

(3) ACQUISITION OF SETS

(i) *Discrimination learning set.* The phrase "discrimination learning set" has been used to refer to (a) a particular kind of training procedure, (b) the performance that results from that training, and (c) the theoretical mechanism that produces this performance. As a procedural term, it refers to training on a series of discriminative-learning problems, all with different stimuli and generally with a small, fixed number of trials in each problem. As a performance term, it refers in its most strict sense to perfect performance on Trial 2 of new discriminative learning problems ("one-trial solution") following training on the series of problems. (It has been used loosely to refer to any magnitude of improvement between problems, but it seems preferable to use "discrimination learning set" in its strict sense and to use' "inter-problem improvement" or "learning to learn" in the loose sense [see Reese, 1970b].) As a theoretical term, it refers to a mechanism, variously identified as set, hypothesis, strategy, or factor, that produces the one-trial solution of new problems (see Levinson and Reese, 1967; Reese, 1963a, 1965, 1970b).

In the section on discriminative learning and transfer, it was noted that Zeaman and House had observed two-phase curves of discriminative learning, and had found that retarded and normal children differed in the duration of the first phase, presumably devoted to attentional learning, but did not differ in the second phase, presumably devoted to associate learning. These results are closely similar to results obtained by Levinson and Reese (1967) in a life-span study of discrimination learning set. Levinson and Reese tested pre-school children (mean age about 4 years), fifth grade children (mean age roughly 10 years), college freshmen, and several groups of old persons (age range 60 to 97 years). Two-phase acquisition curves were evident at every age level, and the age groups differed primarily in the duration of the first phase, which was most rapid in the college students, next in the fifth grade children, then in the pre-school children, and slowest in the elderly subjects. Furthermore, within each age group, *post hoc* sub-groups were formed on the basis of speed of attaining the learning-set criterion, and these sub-groups were also found to differ primarily in the duration of the first phase of acquisition.

Noting that the acquisition curves consistently had the same general form as the curves for simple discriminative learning reported by Zeaman and House, one might infer that attention is also involved in the acquisition of a discrimination learning set. However, Levinson and Reese analysed patterns of errors and found that the group and sub-group differences could be attributed to the variety and duration of error patterns exhibited. Theoretically, error patterns result from "hypotheses" or "strategies" (see for instance, Bowman, 1963; Levine, 1959, 1963), which are more readily interpreted as cognitive factors than as associative factors. For example, "stimulus alternation" refers descriptively to alternating choice between the stimuli presented, and refers theoretically to the hypothesis or strategy that produces this pattern of choices. It ocurs in children (Levinson and Reese, 1967) but is relatively rare in monkeys (see Reese, 1976a). Stimulus alternation poses no special problem for a cognitive analysis, but is diffcult to explain in a stimulus-response analysis; Hull's (1943) concept of reactive inhibition can explain it, but only with the additional assumption that the correct and incorrect stimuli have essentially equal habit strength.

In monkeys, acquisition in the discrimination learning-set task is influenced by the same variables that influence acquisition in the simple discriminative-learning task. For example, acquisition in both kinds of task is enhanced by (a) using three-dimensional objects instead of printed patterns, (b) reducing separation between the locus of the stimuli and the locus of responding, and (c) increasing the size of the stimuli relative to the background (see Reese, 1964). Thus, it seems reasonable to suppose that in monkeys discriminative learning and discrimination learning set are attributable to the same underlying variables. Although a "cognitive" type of explanation has been suggested (Restle, 1958, 1960, 1962), (Reese 1964) showed that a simple extension of Hull-Spence stimulus-response theory adequately explains the data.

In children, the major similarity between discriminative learning and discrimination learning set is in the nature of the acquisition curves. There are some similarities in the variables that influence both kinds of acquisition, but there are also differences (see Reese, 1963a). For example, the use of three-dimensional objects, as opposed to flat stimuli or patterns, enhances discriminative learning but not discrimination learning-set accquisition. It is possible, therefore, that the basis of acquisition by children is not the same in the two kinds of task. If so, then the similarity in acquisition curves is fortuitous. However, it is possible that the discrimination learning-set task is "solved" on a cognitive basis, and that the basis for discriminative learning can be associative or cognitive or a sequential combination of both. Young children generally do not solve a discriminative-learning problem in a single trial; but solving a single discriminative-learning problem can yield a discrimination learning set (Reese, 1965). In contrast, the acquisition of a discrimination learning set is retarded in monkeys if more than fifty trials are given on each training problem (see Reese, 1964). If the discrimination learning set reflects a cognitive process in children, then presumably that process can be acquired or activated during the course of solving a single discriminative-learning problem. The discrepancies between variables affecting the two kinds of acquisition could be interpreted to mean that the young child initially performs at the associative level in the discriminative-learning problem and shifts to the cognitive level to solve the problem.

In a single discriminative-learning problem subjects typically start with responses to the absolute properties of the stimuli, and subsequently shift to the relational properties. This generalization holds for animals (the sea lion, bottlenose porpoise, dancing mouse, rat, and monkey) as well as children (see Reese, 1968). One might interpret the shift as reflecting a shift from associative to cognitive responding, but there is a strong argument against this interpretation. Following attainment of the learning criterion, both animals and children shift back to the absolute properties. One could add a cognitive assumption that would explain this latter shift, but stimulus-response theory (Spence, 1960, Chap. 22) already explains not only the initial increase in the behaviour that is taken to imply relational responding ("comparison behaviour," or "vicarious trial and error"), but also the later decrease, and furthermore the explanation assumes that the subject responds throughout to the absolute properties of the stimuli. Thus, the stimulus-response explanation is more parsimonious than a cognitive explanation presumably would be, and although nature is notoriously unparsimonious, Occam's razor demands that scientists accept the most parsimonious adequate explanation (but only when adequacy is evaluated by the dual criteria of scope and precision—Pepper, 1942).

This evidence, then, provides no support for the contention that the basis of responding shifts from associative to cognitive as the child progresses through a discriminative-learning problem. In fact, other evidence (from the studies reviewed in Section III, (2) (ii)) implies that the child responds cognitively from the beginning of the problem. Hence, we are left with the slightly uncomfortable conclusion that the discrepancy in the way acquisition is affected by manipulated variables results from differences in the way the tasks are programmed : training to criterion on a single problem for discriminative learning versus sub-criterion training on each of a series of problems for discrimination learning set. The conclusion is uncomfortable because this procedural difference does not cause a discrepancy in the relevant variables for monkeys in the two kinds of task, both of which the monkey seems to solve on an associative level.

(ii) *Other sets.* Other kinds of learning set have been identified and studied, though not as extensively as discrimination learning set. However, "cognitive set" has been studied extensively in children and adults, and the training procedures are analogous to the procedure used in discrimination learning set. In one kind of procedure for training cognitive set, the subject is given a series of problems, all of which have the same conceptual solution. For example, all of the Luchins jars problems in the training series are solved with the same equation.

For another kind of cognitive set, sometimes called "functional fixedness" or "rigidity", a single problem is presented together with objects that can be used in a novel way to solve the problem. This kind of set is exhibited when the subject is unable to use the objects in the novel way. Although the task itself is not at first sight analogous to the discrimination learning-set task, upon theoretical analysis it turns out to be analogous in that use of the objects in novel ways is prevented by the subject's pre-experimental training in the use of the objects. In the classic example, having learned that pliers are used for grasping, the subject is inhibited from using them as a pendulum (Maier, 1931). Here, the analogue is having training on series of different kinds of problems, analogous to having training on different kinds of learning set, which then converge on a single new problem.

One could include under "cognitive set" the phenomena sometimes identified as "perceptual set", an appealingly parsimonious move. As in cognitive set studies, two different procedures have been used in perceptual-set studies. One procedure is closely analogous to the discrimination learning-set procedure : the subject is shown a series of exemplars of some conceptual category, such as a series of different animals, and then is shown an ambiguous figure that can be seen as an animal or as some nonanimal form. An example is the rat-man figure (illustrated in Bugelski, 1960, Fig. 3, p. 129; Bugelski and Alampay, 1961, Fig. 1, p. 206; Reese, 1963b, Fig. 1, p. 152; Reese, 1976a, Fig. 7.4, p. 152; Reese 1970b, Fig. 8.1, p. 265). A perceptual set is exhibited when the subject reports that the ambiguous figure is a rat, following exposure to a series of unambiguous animal figures, or reports that it is a man, following exposure to a series of human faces. As in discrimination learning-set training, the subject is given a series of "problems", all with the same "solution". In perceptual-set training, the "problems" are figures to be named, and the "solution" is to name the animal and think of the name of the category ("animal"). The test problem—responding to the ambiguous figure—is solved at once ("animal, therefore rat").

In another kind of perceptual set, the perception of figures or settings is influenced by previous experience that is experimentally unrelated to the figures or settings. In the classic example, playing the game of Murder resulted in rating neutral human faces as sinister (Murray, 1933; see also Solley, 1966, and the brief review by Wohlwill, 1970). Here, the analogue to the discrimination learning-set task breaks down, or at least becomes implausible.

Another phenomenon that resembles discrimination learning set is the development of imitation. Children who do not imitate can be trained to imitate by being given a series of tasks in each of which imitation is rewarded (Sherman, 1971). That is, in each training problem imitation of a different behaviour is shaped, and after a series of problems new behaviours of the same kind are imitated at once.

Each kind of set can be conceptualized as involving the learning of a rule : for discrimination learning set and reversal learning set, "continue to choose rewarded object, shift from non-rewarded object"; for oddity learning set, "choose odd object"; for cognitive sets of the Luchins jars type, "use the same equation (or other principle)"; for cognitive sets of the functional fixedness type, "use the objects in the usual way"; for the ambiguous-figure type of perceptual set, "the next item will be from the same conceptual category as the previous items"; for perceptual sets of the "Murder" type, "things are frightening"; and for imitation, "do what the model does".

In short, all these kinds of set can be interpreted to reflect rule-learning, and although the training procedures are analogous for most of them, the analogy does not hold for at least one (the "Murder" type of perceptual set). It seems reasonable to conclude that they all involve the same basis, cognitive-level functioning.

As already mentioned, an associative-level interpretation of discrimination learning set adequately accounts for acquisition by monkeys, but at best is less reasonable than a cognitive account of acquisition by children and human adults. Similarly, the ambiguous-figure type of perceptual set can be explained associatively (e.g., Reese, 1963b, 1970b), but the Luchins jars type of cognitive set, the "Murder" type of perceptual set, and imitation seem to be more reasonably explained cognitively (see Reese, 1976a; Wohlwill, 1970). Therefore, the more consistently reasonable explanation is cognitive, and the principle of parsimony argues for that one explanation. The alternative is to assume that the ambiguous-figure type of perceptual set and perhaps discrimination learning set are acquired at an associative level, while the others are cognitively based. This alternative would be consistent with White's analysis, implying a dialectical model in which both levels exist, but if this alternative is adopted then additional assumptions are required to explain why analogous procedures are effective for the different kinds of set. Again, parsimony argues for the cognitive explanation.

IV. CONCLUSIONS

The trend is towards more and more complex cognitive operations or strategies intervening to determine responses to stimulation. Learning becomes more and more a matter of cognitive processes. Furthermore, the processes are predominantly voluntary, as opposed to such involuntary processes as the orienting reflex, a "primitive" reflexive attentional process. Like attention, the voluntary cognitive processes transform the stimulus situation. Thus, the trend in infancy from involuntary to voluntary attentional processes continues in childhood with the development of more complex voluntary processes.

Furthermore, the trend in infancy beginning with reflexive excitatory processes and continuing to the development of inhibitory processes also continues in childhood, with the development of more sophisticated inhibitory processes. As White noted, one function of cognitive processes is to inhibit the first-available associative responses, allowing time for the higher level of problem-solving to operate.

Trends in the development of learning processes are therefore seen to be largely attributable to the development of cognitive processes. It appears, however, that an associative level remains operative and can serve as the basis for learning even in adulthood. Given these conclusions, what is needed now is research to identify the conditions that determine which level or type of process will be used. It might help to have a well-developed cognitive theory of learning, covering conditioning, discriminative learning and transfer, set, and other simple kinds of learning tasks; but as yet the cognitive theorists have provided only the outlines of the necessary analysis. Perhaps, however, the current theoretical level reflects the current empirical level : we believe that the behaviouristic account is incomplete and that a cognitive account is needed to supplement it (at least), but the evidence we have available is incomplete and missing in details, especially details relevant to a cognitive account.

REFERENCES

Baltes, M. M. and Reese, H. W. (1976). Operant research and operant paradigm: contradictions are apparent but not real. In J. M. LeBlanc, D. M. Baer and B. C. Etzel (Eds.), *New Developments in Behavioral Research*. Hillsdale, N.J.: Lawrence Erlbaum.

Bartoshuk, A. K. (1962). Human neonatal cardiac acceleration to sound: habituation and dishabituation. *Perceptual and Motor Skills, 15*, 15–27.

Berlyne, D. E. (1970). Children's reasoning and thinking. In P. H. Mussen (Ed.), *Carmichael's Manual of Child Psychology*, Vol. 1. New York: Wiley.

Bijou, S. W. and Baer, D. M. (1965). *Child Development II: Universal Stage of Infancy*. New York: Appleton-Century-Crofts.

Bowman, R. E. (1963). Discrimination learning-set performance under intermittent and secondary reinforcement. *Journal of Comparative and Physiological Psychology, 56*, 492–34.

Brackbill, Y. (1971). The role of the cortex in orienting: orienting reflex in an anencephalic human infant. *Developmental Psychology, 5*, 195–201.

Brackbill, Y. and Koltsova, M. M. (1967). Conditioning and learning. In Y. Brackbill (Ed.), *Infancy and Early Childhood*. New York: Free Press.

Bridger, W. H. (1961). Sensory habituation and discrimination in the human neonate. *American Journal of Psychiatry, 117*, 991–6.

Brown, A. L. (1975). The development of memory: knowing, knowing about knowing, and knowing how to know. In H. W. Reese (Ed.), *Advances in Child Development and Behavior*, Vol. 10. New York and London: Academic Press.

Bugelski, B. R. (1960). *An Introduction to the Principles of Psychology*. New York: Holt, Rinehart and Winston.

Bugelski, B. R. and Alampay, D. A. (1961). The role of frequency in developing perceptual sets. *Canadian Journal of Psychology, 15*, 205–11.

Campbell, B. A., Lytle, L. D. and Fibiger, H. C. (1969). Ontogeny of adrenergic arousal and cholinergic inhibitory mechanisms in the rat. *Science, 166*, 635–7.

Campbell, B. A. and Spear, N. E. (1972). Ontogeny of Memory. *Psychological Review, 79*, 215–36.

Cantor, J. H. (1965). Transfer of stimulus pretraining in motor paired-associate and discrimination learning tasks. In L. P. Lipsitt and C. C. Spiker (Eds.), *Advances in Child Development and Behavior*, Vol. 2. New York and London: Academic Press.

Clifton, R. K. (1974a). Cardiac conditioning and orienting in the infant. In P. O. Obrist, A. H. Black, J. Brener and L. V. Dicara (Eds.), *Cardiovascular Psychophysiology*. Chicago: Aldine.

Clifton, R. K. (1974b). Heart rate conditioning in the newborn infant. *Journal of Experimental Child Psychology, 18*, 9–21.

Cohen, L. B. (1973). A two-process model of infant visual attention. *Merrill-Palmer Quarterly, 19*, 157–80.

Cohen, L. B. (1975). *Infant Perception: From Sensation to Cognition*, Vol. 1. New York: Academic Press.

Eimas, P. D. (1970). Attentional processes. (With editorial additions.) In H. W. Reese and L. P. Lipsitt (Eds.), *Experimental Child Psychology*. New York and London: Academic Press.

Engen, T. and Lipsitt, L. P. (1965). Decrement and recovery of responses to olfactory stimuli in the human neonate. *Journal of Comparative and Physiological Psychology, 59,* 312–16.

Engen, T., Lipsitt, L. P. and Kaye, H. (1963). Olfactory responses and adaptation in the human neonate. *Journal of Comparative and Physiological Psychology, 56,* 73–7.

Fitzgerald, H. E. and Brackbill, Y. Classical conditioning in infancy: Development and constraints. *Psychological Bulletin* (in press).

Fitzgerald, H. E. and Porges, S. W. (1971). A decade of infant conditioning and learning research. *Merrill-Palmer Quarterly, 17,* 79–117.

Fitzgerald, J. M. (1974). Verbaliation effects in young children: When and how a label becomes a label. West Virginia University (unpublished Doctoral Dissertation).

Flavell, J. H. (1970). Developmental studies of mediated memory. In H. W. Reese and L. P. Lipsitt (Eds.), *Advances in Child Development and Behavior,* Vol. 5. New York and London: Academic Press.

Flavell, J. H. (1971). Stage-related properties of cognitive development. *Cognitive Psychology, 2,* 421–53.

Flavell, J. H., Beach, D. R. and Chinsky, J. M. (1966). Spontaneous verbal rehearsal in a memory task as a function of age. *Child Development, 37,* 283–99.

Folch-Pi, J. (1952). Chemical constituents of brain during development and in maturity. In *The Biology of Mental Health and Disease. The 27th Annual Conference of the Milbank Memorial Fund.* New York: Hoeber.

Forbes, E. J. and Porges, S. W. (1972). Heart rate classical conditioning with a noxious auditory stimulus in human newborns. Paper presented at the meeting of the Society for Psychophysiological Research, Boston.

Goss, A. E. (1961). Verbal mediating responses and concept formation. *Psychological Review, 68,* 248–74.

Graham, F. K., Berg, K. M., Berg, W. K., Jackson, J. C., Hatton, H. M. and Kantowitz, S. R. (1970). Cardiac orienting response as a function of age. *Psychonomic Science, 19,* 363–5.

Graham, F. K. and Clifton, R. K. (1966). Heart rate change as a component of the orienting response. *Psychological Bulletin, 65,* 305–20.

Graham, F. K. and Jackson, J. C. (1970). Arousal systems and infant heart rate. In L. P. Lipsitt and H. W. Reese (Eds.), *Advances in Child Development and Behavior,* Vol. 5. New York and London: Academic Press.

Greenough, W. T. (1975). Experimental modification of the developing brain. *American Scientist, 63,* 37–46.

Hagen, J. W., Jongeward, R. H., Jr. and Kail, R. V., Jr. (1975). Cognitive perspectives on the development of memory. In H. W. Reese (Ed.), *Advances in Child Development and Behavior,* Vol. 10. New York and London: Academic Press.

Hull, C. L. (1943). *Principles of Behavior.* New York: Appleton-Century-Crofts.

Hulsebus, R. C. (1973). Operant conditioning in infant behavior: a review. In H. W. Reese (Ed.), *Advances in Child Development and Behavior,* Vol. 8. New York and London: Academic Press.

Jeffrey, W. E. (1965). Variables affecting reversal-shifts in young children. *American Journal of Psychology, 78,* 589–95.

Jeffrey, W. E. (1970). Transfer. (With editorial additions.) In H. W. Reese and L. P. Lipsitt (Eds.), *Experimental Child Psychology.* New York and London: Academic Press.

Kagan, J. (1971). *Change and Continuity in Infancy.* New York: Wiley.
Kaplan, A. (1964). *The Conduct of Inquiry.* San Francisco: Chandler.
Kasatkin, N. I. (1972). First conditioned responses and the beginnings of the learning process in the human infant. In G. Newton and A. H. Riesen (Eds.), *Advances in Psychobiology,* Vol. 1. New York: Wiley.
Kendler, H. H. and Kendler, T. S. (1962). Vertical and horizontal processes in problem solving. *Psychological Review, 69,* 1–16.
Kendler, T. S. (1963). Development of mediating responses in children. In J. C. Wright and J. Kagan (Eds.), Basic cognitive processes in children. *Monographs of the Society for Research in Child Development, 28,* (Whole No. 86), 33–48.
Kendler, T. S. (1972). An ontogeny of mediational deficiency. *Child Development, 43,* 1–17.
Kendler, T. S., Kendler, H. H. and Learnard, B. (1962). Mediated responses to size and brightness as a function of age. *American Journal of Psychology, 75,* 571–86.
Kron, R. E. (1966). Instrumental conditioning of nutritive sucking behavior in the newborn. *Recent Advances in Biological Psychiatry, 9,* 295–300.
Kuhn, T. S. (1962). *The Structure of Scientific Revolutions.* Chicago: University of Chicago Press.
Lenneberg, E. H. (1967). *Biological Foundations of Language.* New York: Wiley.
Levine, M. (1959). A model of hypothesis behavior in discrimination learning set. *Psychological Review, 66,* 353–66.
Levine, M. (1963). Mediating processes in humans at the outset of discrimination learning. *Psychological Review, 70,* 254–76.
Levinson, B. and Reese, H. W. (1967). Patterns of discrimination learning set in preschool children, fifth-graders, college freshmen, and the aged. *Monographs of the Society for Research in Child Development, 32* (Whole No. 115).
Lewis, M. (1971). Individual differences in the measurement of early cognitive growth. In J. Hellmuth (Ed.), *Exceptional Infant,* Vol. 2. Bainbridge Island, Washington: Brunner/Mazel.
Lindsley, O. R., Hobika, J. Y. and Etsten, B. E. (1961). Operant behavior during anesthesia recovery: a continuous and objective method. *Anesthesiology, 22,* 937–46.
Lipsitt, L. P., Pederson, L. J. and DeLucia, C. A. (1966). Conjugate reinforcement of operant responding in infants. *Psychonomic Science, 4,* 67–8.
Lynn, R. (1966). *Attention, Arousal and the Orientation Reaction.* New York: Pergamon.
Maier, N. R. F. (1931). Reasoning in humans. II. The solution of a problem and its appearance in consciousness. *Journal of Comparative Psychology, 12,* 181–94.
Murray, H. A. (1933). The effect of fear upon estimates of the maliciousness of other personalities. *Journal of Social Psychology, 4,* 310–29.
Osler, S. F. and Madden, J. (1973). The verbal label: mediator or classifier? *Journal of Experimental Child Psychology, 16,* 303–17.
Overton, W. F. (1973). On the assumptive base of the nature-nurture controversy: additive versus interactive conceptions. *Human Development, 16,* 74–89.
Overton, W. F. (1976). The active organism in structuralism. In H. W. Reese

(Ed.), Symposium: Conceptions of the "active organism". *Human Development* (in press).

Overton, W. F. and Reese, H. W. (1973). Models of development: methodological implications. In J. R. Nesselroade and H. W. Reese (Eds.), *Life-span Developmental Psychology: Methodological Issues*. New York and London: Academic Press.

Pepper, S. C. (1942). *World Hypotheses*. Berkeley, California: University of California Press.

Piaget, J. (1970). Piaget's theory. In P. H. Mussen (Ed.), *Carmichael's Manual of Child Psychology*. New York: Wiley.

Popper, K. R. (1959). *The Logic of Scientific Discovery*. New York: Basic Books.

Porges, S. W. (1974). Heart rate indices of newborn attentional responsivity. *Merrill-Palmer Quarterly*, *20*, 231–54.

Porges, S. W., Stamps, L. E. and Walter, G. F. (1974). Heart rate variability and newborn heart rate response to illumination change. *Developmental Psychology*, *10*, 507–13.

Rabinowitz, F. M. and Cantor, G. N. (1966). Children's stimulus alternation, response repetition, and circular behavior as a function of age and stimulus conditions. Paper presented at the meeting of the American Psychological Association, New York.

Reese, H. W. (1962). Verbal mediation as a function of age level. *Psychological Bulletin*, *59*, 502–9.

Reese, H. W. (1963a). Discrimination learning set in children. In L. P. Lipsitt and C. C. Spiker (Eds.), *Advances in Child Development and Behavior*, Vol. 1. New York and London: Academic Press.

Reese, H. W. (1963b). "Perceptual set" in young children *Child Development*, *34*, 151–9.

Reese, H. W. (1964). Discrimination learning set in rhesus monkeys. *Psychological Bulletin*, *61*, 321–40.

Reese, H. W. (1965). Discrimination learning set and perceptual set in young children. *Child Development*, *36*, 153–61.

Reese, H. W. (1968). *The Perception of Stimulus Relations: Discrimination Learning and Transposition*. New York and London: Academic Press.

Reese, H. W. (1970a). Age trend in efficiency of mediation. In H. W. Reese and L. P. Lipsitt (Eds.), *Experimental Child Psychology*. New York and London: Academic Press.

Reese, H. W. (1970b). Set. In H. W. Reese and L. P. Lipsitt (Eds.), *Experimental Child Psychology*. New York and London: Academic Press.

Reese, H. W. (1972). Acquired distinctiveness and equivalence of cues in young children. *Journal of Experimental Child Psychology*, *13*, 171–82.

Reese, H. W. (1976a). *Basic Learning Processes in Childhood*. New York: Holt, Rinehart and Winston.

Reese, H. W. (1976b). The development of memory: life-span perspectives. In P. B. Baltes (Chm.), Implications of life-span developmental psychology for child psychology. In H. W. Reese (Ed.), *Advances in Child Development and Behavior*, Vol. 11. New York and London: Academic Press.

Reese, H. W. (1976c). Discussion. In H. W. Reese (Ed.), Symposium: Conceptions of the active organism". *Human Development*. (in press).

Reese, H. W. (1976d). Imagery in associative memory. In R. V. Kail, Jnr. and J. W. Hagen (Eds.), *Perspectives on the Development of Memory and Cognition*. Hillsdale, N.J.: Lawrence Erlbaum.

Reese, H. W. and Overton, W. F. (1970). Models of development and theories of development. In L. R. Goudet and P. B. Baltes (Eds.), *Life-span Developmental Psychology: Research and Theory.* New York and London: Academic Press.

Restle, F. (1958). Toward a quantitative description of learning set data. *Psychological Review, 65,* 77–91.

Restle, F. (1960). Note on the "hypothesis" theory of discrimination learning. *Psychological Reports, 7,* 194.

Restle, F. (1962). The selection of strategies in cue learning. *Psychological Review, 69,* 329–43.

Rheingold, H. L., Stanley, W. C. and Coloey, J. A. (1962). Method for studying exploratory behavior in infants. *Science, 136,* 1054–5.

Salapatek, P. (1975). Pattern perception in early infant. In L. B. Cohen and P. Salapatek (Eds.), *Infant Perception: From Sensation to Cognition,* Vol. 1. New York and London: Academic Press.

Sameroff, A. J. (1971). Can conditioned responses be established in the new-born infants? *Developmental Psychology, 5,* 1–12.

Sameroff, A. J. (1972). earning and adaptation in infancy: a comparison of models. In H. W. Reese (Ed.), *Advances in Child Development and Behavior,* Vol. 7. New York and London: Academic Press.

Seligman, M. E. P. (1970). On the generality of the laws of learning. *Psychological Review, 77,* 406–18.

Sherman, J. A. (1971). Imitation and language development. In H. W. Reese (Ed.), *Advances in Child Development and Behavior,* Vol. 6. New York and London: Academic Press.

Shirai, T. (1951). Developmental variation in the visual discrimination of cube size by children 2 to 13 years of age. University of Toronto (unpublished Master's thesis).

Siqueland, E. R. (1970). Instrumental conditioning in infants. In H. W. Reese and L. P. Lipsitt (Eds.), *Experimental Child Psychology.* New York and London: Academic Press.

Siqueland, E. R. and DeLucia, C. A. (1969). Visual reinforcement of non-nutritive sucking in human infants. *Science, 165,* 1144–6.

Sokolov, E. N. (1963). *Perception and the Conditioned Reflex.* New York: Pergamon.

Solley, C. M. (1966). Affective processes in perceptual development. In A. H. Kidd and J. L. Rivoire (Eds.), *Perceptual Development in Children.* New York: International Universities Press.

Spence, K. W. (1956). *Behavior Theory and Conditioning.* New Haven, Conn.: Yale University Press.

Spence, K. W. (1960). *Behavior Theory and Learning: Selected papers.* Englewood Cliffs, N.J.: Prentice-Hall.

Spence, K. W. (1963). Cognitive factors in the extinction of the conditioned eyelid response in humans. *Science, 140,* 1224–5.

Spiker, C. C. (1963). The hypothesis of stimulus interaction and an explanation of stimulus compounding. In L. P. Lipsitt and C. C. Spiker (Eds.), *Advances in Child Development and Behavior,* Vol. 1. New York and London: Academic Press.

Spiker, C. C. (1970). An extension of Hull-Spence discrimination learning theory. *Psychological Review, 77,* 496–515.

Spiker, C. C. (1971). Application of Hull-Spence theory to the discrimination learning of children. In H. W. Reese (Ed.), *Advances in Child Development and Behavior*, Vol. 6. New York and London: Academic Press.

Spiker, C. C. and Cantor, J. H. (1973). Applications of Hull-Spence theory to the transfer of discrimination learning in children. In H. W. Reese (Ed.), *Advances in Child Development and Behavior*, Vol. 8. New York and London: Academic Press.

Stamps, L. E. and Porges, S. W. (1975). Heart rate conditioning in newborn infants: relationships among conditionability, heart rate variability and sex. *Developmental Psychology, 11*, 424–31.

Stevenson, H. W. (1970). Learning in children. In P. H. Mussen (Ed.), *Carmichael's Manual of Child Psychology*. New York, Wiley.

Stevenson, H. W., Iscoe, I, and McConnell, C. (1955). A developmental study of transposition. *Journal of Experimental Psychology, 49*, 278–80.

Thompson, R. F. and Spencer, W. A. (1966). Habituation: a model phenomenon for the study of neuronal substrates of behavior. *Psychological Review, 73*, 16–43.

Uznadze, D. N. (1966). *The Psychology of Set.* (Translated by B. Haigh.) New York: Consultants Bureau.

White, S. H. (1965). Evidence for a hierarchical arrangement of learning processes. In L. P. Lipsitt and C. C. Spiker (Eds.), *Advances in Child Development and Behavior*, Vol. 2. New York and London: Academic Press.

Williams, J. M., Hamilton, L. W. and Carlton, P. L. (1974). Pharmacological and anatomical dissociation of two types of habituation. *Journal of Comparative and Physiological Psychology, 87*, 724–32.

Williams, J. M., Hamilton, L. W. and Carlton, P. L. (1975). Ontogenetic dis-association of two classes of habituation. *Journal of Comparative and Physiological Psychology, 89*, 733–7.

Wohlwill, J. F. (1970). Perceptual development. (With editorial additions.) In H. W. Reese and L. P. Lipsitt (Eds.), *Experimental Child Psychology*. New York and London: Academic Press.

Woodworth, R. S. (1918). *Dynamic Psychology*. New York: Columbia University Press.

Wozniak, R. H. (1972). Verbal regulation of motor behavior—Soviet research and non-Soviet replications. *Human Development, 15*, 13–57.

Yates, F. A. (1966). *The Art of Memory*. Chicago: University of Chicago Press.

Zaporozhets, A. V. (1961). The origin and development of the conscious control of movements in man. In N. O'Connor (Ed.), *Recent Soviet Psychology*, New York: Liveright.

Zeaman, D. and House, B. J. (1963). The role of attention in retardate discrimination learning. In N. R. Ellis (Ed.), *Handbook of Mental Deficiency*. New York: McGraw-Hill.

Zeiler, M. D. (1964). Transposition in adults with simultaneous and successive stimulus presentation. *Journal of Experimental Psychology, 68*, 103–7.

Zeiler, M. D. (1967). Stimulus definition and choice. In L. P. Lipsitt and C. C. Spiker (Eds.), *Advances in Child Development and Behavior*, Vol. 3. New York and London: Academic Press.

PART III

CHAPTER 11

Motivation and Personality in Cognitive Development

Vernon Hamilton

I. INTRODUCTION

This chapter deals with the interrelationship of three aspects of human functioning which, if interpreted generously, probably encompass the determinants of the major proportion of human behaviour. Any instance of adaptive behaviour is selected at some central stage of human information processing from a number of alternative responses which may be functionally similar. The selected response can only occur because the individual is able and willing to channel executive energy into this particular area of behaviour, and in many instances the observed response is consistent with, or could be predicted on the basis of, previously demonstrated regularities in the responsiveness of this particular individual. In other words, every adult human response is based on cognitive representations of the behavioural environment and its adaptive requirements; every experience requires motivational activation and direction; and the characteristic type, intensity and persistence of the response is a reflection of dominant and hierarchically organized patterns of activities which are said to be representative of an individual personality.

Our conception of the complexities of human response selection is directly related to three known facts: (a) all stimulation, especially from a social source and in a social context, is potentially and increasingly multivariate; (b) response selection is *guided* by an individual history of stimulus exposure and the effects on that person of previous responses, so that (c) response to identical stimulation yields evidence of between-individual variations. *Some* stimulation from *some* social sources and *some* contexts comes to be evaluated as more important, more pleasant or more potentially rewarding than differently evaluated stimuli. Some goals occupy a higher position in a hierarchy of individually learnt goals, and will produce a structure of differential thresholds, intensities, memory processes, preferences and priorities, which will serve the most desired goal.

Psychological science has not yet acquired the skills needed for an orderly analysis of the integration of a complex set of determinants in response selection. This may be because comparative, laboratory and computer analogues of human behaviour are insufficiently complex, or are misleading or false, or because the application of the methodology of mechanistic physics, which no longer even represents the concepts of modern physics, is basically ill-conceived (Brandt, 1973). These doubts cannot be answered at present. It may be pertinent, however, to take issue with an approach which effectively states that the elucidation of regularities and laws pertaining to brain processes necessarily must be demonstrated before any attempt is made to investigate the role of so-called individual differences in the operation of these processes. The same brain and the same processing stages are involved in the transmission, coding and integration of stimuli whether they are emotively or motivationally "neutral" or whether or not they possess socio-emotional relevance. That part of a central processing system which decides that stimulation is "neutral" must also decide instances when it is not. What is "neutral" and what has high personal relevance is a function of history of personal experience, and of the weight which a person has learnt to give to the importance of *deciding this question first*, when exposed to stimulation. Thus the acquisition of differential individual strategies for the analysis of stimulation relevant to motivational and personality factors appears to be sufficient grounds for demoting the so-called "classical" experimental paradigm of single pairs of independent-dependent variables, however well-defined objectively or operationally.

A decision to stress the importance of complex factors in the analysis of human cognition inevitably requires the consideration of interaction processes arising in motivation and in personality. Until fairly recently it would have been sufficient to refer to the effects of *non-cognitive* variables in cognitive performance, and to emotional, physiological and electro-chemical events in the interpretation of motivation and personality. Since then, a number of researchers and theorists has begun a cognitive analysis of these influences on behaviour. The new conceptual developments appear to have important implications for any general theories of child development, for maturationally conceived approaches to the development of cognitive skills, and for existing findings over the last quarter century bearing on motivational and personality influences in cognitive behaviour. An attempt to expand the cognitive approach will be offered in the last section of this chapter. We shall begin with a résumé of present conceptions of motivation and personality. The discussion will then recapitulate the position of cognitive control theories. This will be followed by considerations of the effect of socialization experiences on personality, motivation and cognitive development.

II. CONCEPTS OF MOTIVATION

The study of human motivation appears to have two general aims : to account for human ability to produce almost inexhaustible amounts of energy in the pursuit of a great variety of goals, and to explain the reasons why people differ in the number and the type of goals they are seeking, and the intensity of their seeking. In the comments which follow, no attempt will be made to present a review of the results of experimental and theoretical developments in this area because there is no lack of comprehensive expositions (for instance, Cofer and Appley, 1964; Haber, 1966; Bindra and Stewart, 1966; Vernon, 1969; Weiner, 1972; McClelland and Steele, 1973; Korman, 1974). References to "goals" conveys, however, the general consensus that physiological need states, drives or internal cues of biochemical imbalance or deficiencies, provide insufficient explanations of observed behaviour. The behavioural goal may well be a reduction of these insufficiencies, but this may be incidental if we find that eating occurs in the absence of hunger, that children continue to draw pictures or do sums after they have already completed their assignments, that people continue to amass wealth beyond the point where they are able to spend it, or that environmental situations are being avoided with evidence of discomfort and tension in the absence of any objective signs of threat or danger to the individual.

Elements of subjective and individualized satisfaction or goal-seeking may be perceived in the variety of defining criteria offered by different theorists for motivational behaviour. Many of these are implicitly or explicitly multivariate, and may concurrently refer to operational levels of different generality (for instance, Hebb, 1955; Spence, 1956; Atkinson, 1958; Young, 1961). The differences in theoretical emphasis primarily reflect our problems of matching the organic requirements of a bio-physiological system with the evidence of behavioural differentiation and elaboration in environments containing differently constituted stimulus and reward values, in the context of co-operation and competition with other people requiring similar or different goals at the same point in time.

Efforts to list and classify motivation do not appear to have added substantially to our ability to identify and weigh statistically the components of any activity which appears to be sustained in a particular direction, and is followed by evidence of quiescence or subjective satisfaction. Comparison, however, of the number of motives listed under a primary/innate/biological/physiological heading with the much longer list of identified secondary/acquired/social/psychogenic motives, should continue to cast doubt on the utility of extrapolating from mammalian animal studies to human behaviour. More relevant, perhaps, is an analysis of stimuli and rewards available in human *developmental experience* which are clearly associated with motivational diversification, and the capacity of the human brain to make fine-grain discriminations between wants, goals and the means to achieve them, possibly with a minimum of wasted effort and aversive experience, and a maximum of gratification. The role of cognitive components in goal-directed behaviour is only gradually achieving credibility, although it was implicit already in Tolman's (1932) concept of cognitive maps.

The rephrasing of motivation as drive and habit in the attempt to achieve scientific respectability for the analysis of behaviour does not appear to have achieved its hoped-for aim. Components of motivation continue to be inferred (for instance, K in Hull's later theory), and it does not seem to matter whether drive and incentive are considered as additive or multiplicative if the value of an incentive term cannot be measured directly. Moreover, a complex cognitive processing system is capable of generating alternative directions in goal-seeking as well as substitute or temporary goals, so that stimulus-response bonds may be less critical for motivated behaviour than the capacity to *know* about, to anticipate through cognitive representation, the outcomes of a range of possible responses.

Developmentally of great importance is the evidence that the waking brain is always active. It seeks for information as if motivated to do so without any apparent reward (for instance, Harlow *et al.*, 1950; Berlyne, 1960). If experimentally deprived of information, it will either seek alternatives to sensory input (Bexton, Heron and Scott, 1954), or if given opportunity will show self-regulating processes for reducing informational deficit (Jones, 1966). If restrictions in memory input, and boredom resulting from undifferentiated stimulation, elevate cortical arousal levels, a fully rational basis becomes available to the advocates of a rich and varied stimulus environment for optimum child development.

From an early age onwards, human motivation seeks more than one goal at the same time. An infant will cry not only because he is hungry but also because of the discomforts arising from the effort of crying, and because a threshold value for attachment need has been reached. An achievement-oriented child will usually plan to reach his goals without upsetting his relationship with his family, friends and peers, which would raise his level of conflict, anxiety, guilt and stress. He will have to be able to integrate his concurrent motives, so that they become consistent with one another, if none of them are to suffer. In the process, levels of frustration, capacity for delaying gratification, and externally or internally directed aggressive responses, require additional control. Motivated behaviour may thus express compromise solutions on the model offered by field theorists (for instance, Lewin, 1951; Weiner, 1972). Alternatively, where a unidimensional motive appears to be operating in a situation apparently requiring multi-dimensional motivational orientation, cognitive inconsistencies and complex stimulus situations may have been restructured into simple cognitions (Bieri, 1955), or conflict and anxiety inducing cognitive ambiguities may have been defensively avoided (Hamilton, 1957; 1960).

The concepts of behavioural differentiation (for instance, Werner, 1948; Wilkin et al., 1962) and of multivariate patterns of motivation imply that individual differences in the elaboration and organization of motives are acquired during important developmental periods. They further imply that there are many possible outcomes for individual motivation resulting from early learning. At the same time there appear to be considerable degrees of developmental consistency, so that distinctive and characteristic patterns of motives show some continuity from childhood to adulthood (Kagan and Moss, 1962).

III.   CONCEPTS OF PERSONALITY

The study of personality has been guided by a number of historically determined aims. Each of these was concerned with achieving methods of description of individuals which would reflect that which could be termed characteristic, internally consistent, dominant and predictive. Whether the approach was holistic in terms of a broad generalization about response dispositions, or segmentally oriented in terms of more narrowly defined single dominant traits, or a limited conjunction of traits defining a type, the underlying scientific conceptualization considered this area of human behaviour a separate deterministic source. It represented the influence of a relatively unmodifiable bio-physical response system, common to the species, an acquired habit response system which developed in interaction with significant other people at significant points of a developmental sequence, and the application of

16—CP * *

these systems in most actions and tasks which had adaptive significance for the person. Personality psychology was, and still is, concerned with those aspects of behaviour which define the manner and aim of individual adaptation rather than with the cognitive capacity and operations exhibited in the process of adaptation.

The manner and aim of adaptation has been described by its own vocabulary which has hardly been distinguished by its objectivity, specificity or testability. At the same time, the methodology of personality assessment or testing frequently has not progressed beyond the techniques of projective probes, except in instances where criterion measures of isolated traits of, say, achievement orientation (for instance, Helmstatter and Ellis, 1962; Feather, 1967), or types of anxiety (for instance, Endler and Hunt, 1966; Gaudry and Spielberger, 1971), or of defensiveness (for instance, Sarason, 1961) were experimental requirements. Since it was realized, however, that individuals may differ complexly in, for example, their motivation to achieve, to respond with anxiety to non-achievement, and to defend themselves differentially against the aversive effects of anxiety and non-achievement, multiple personality criteria have begun to be used to reflect better these complexities of individual differences in adaptive manner and aims (for instance, Heckhausen and Weiner, 1972; Heilbrun, 1973). There is nevertheless continuing doubt whether the term personality characteristics describes sets of functions which can be independently defined outside the field of study of general experimental psychology (Sanford, 1970), whether the relative absence of theoretical advances is the result of relying excessively on a conventional vocabulary of words which primarily convey non-specialist and unsophisticated meaning (Fiske, 1974), or whether the real problem has been the search for rigorous yet generalized models which match holistic concepts of personality.

Dimensional studies of characteristic, consistent and predictable behaviour dispositions, have had the primary aims of (1) identifying structural and organizational factors of personality, and (2) demonstrating that these factors influence perception, memory, attention and thinking through processes which are not explicit in the stimulus and demand characteristics of an external task or situational setting. Once assumptions are held about the influence of behaviour variables additional to those required for the analysis of sensory inputs, even at the point at which individual decisions about the distribution of attention are first made, it follows that stimuli are complexly defined for the responder, and that some aspects of this complexity stimulate individually differing response strategies which serve more general and more long-term personal goals. The generality, intensity and persistence of these goals appear to reflect individually acquired hierarchies of motives, and their associated emotional components.

Complexly motivated, adaptive behaviour requires dynamically variable response priorities including an inhibitory, non-responding strategy. Arousal and drive states supply the energizing components (for instance, Atkinson and Raynor, 1974; Eysenck, 1967) which play a contributory role in whether a response is spontaneous and impulsive, and thereby possibly maladaptive, or whether an individual has the capacity to inhibit and delay an immediate response (for instance, Mischel et al., 1972). The capacity to reflect upon and delay a response increases with age, but may be indicative of individual differences in dispositions to discharge pre-response tension either in expressive motor behaviour or in thought, or it may reflect constellations of so-called introvert or extravert traits. Developmentally early and later learning may have established a general disposition to examine each stimulus field initially for the rewards which it may offer, or for its capacity to expose the individual to danger, to attack, to isolation or rejection. In addition, the sources of rewards and punishment, of desirable or aversive experience may be seen as being under the control of external agents, or they may be attributed to the person's own behaviour, engendering a belief in internal control (Rotter, 1966).

The components of personality may be either within the range of self-report of the individual, or consciousness may be confined to only limited aspects of the behavioural determinants. Thus, self-knowledge of the traits of urgency, perseverance and dutifulness, may not imply a parallel awareness of a more general disposition to overcome self-concepts of inadequacy, inferiority, insecurity or self-importance. Since overtly identical behaviour may be determined by quite different motives, causal explanations may be of low validity unless a sufficiently wide range of possible determinants is sampled, and as long as the use of metaphor prevails (Mehrabian, 1968).

A beginning has been made with the introduction of cognitive concepts among the defining criteria of personality. Feffer (1970) has applied the Piagetian processes of assimilation, accommodation and those affecting the conservation skill to social group interaction. He pointed out that successful co-operation may depend on the ability to perceive the role expectations of other group members, and thus require the processes of cognitive de-centration from the self and centration on the other group members. A more direct cognitive contribution may be the new emphasis on situational factors which both support and detract from the consistency component in personality. Mischel (1973), elaborating a social learning view of personality, suggests that differential responses to situations require the cognitive competence to construct situation-appropriate behaviour, the encoding and categorization of present events, analyses of expectancies and values of outcome of behaviour, in the context of long-term self-regulatory systems and plans. Not only are all these processes determined by past learning experience in social contexts, but they are also sufficiently flexible, again through past learning, to take into account situational differences in adaptive requirements. Since situations do not only differ objectively, the cognitive processes operating in adaptation will also reflect more long-term self-regulatory expectancies and values of the person. Thus, individual differences can be parsimoniously perceived as differences in cognitive operations adapting to sometimes minimally differing situations. Apparent inconsistencies of behaviour are then situationally determined. They may themselves reflect traits of flexibility, resourcefulness, or in Mischel's case, children's capacity to tolerate considerable delays in gratification. In other cases, however, they may be indicative of cognitive operations aimed not at the objective performance required from the individual, but at more long-term goals or needs. In this event, the degrees of cognitive categorization, coding and integrating operations will be unevenly distributed between objective and subjective goals, and performance may be said primarily to be personality-determined. Where performance fails to reach some objective and achievable standard of competence, it may be appropriate to suggest that the cognitive processing capacity of the person has been over-extended by the simultaneous presence of objective as well as subjective goals (Hamilton, 1975b).

IV.   COGNITIVE CONSISTENCY AND COGNITIVE CONTROLS

(1) INTRODUCTION

It is often assumed that theories of cognitive consistency and controls derive primarily from psycho-analytic assumptions about the interaction and integration of motivational and personality variables with sensory and cognitive data. Such statements are only partially valid if one considers the much older perceptual and mnemonic theories of Thurstone and Bartlett, or even Galton's notions of dominant styles of imagery. Thurstone's (1944) monograph provided evidence of individual consistencies in a large number of perceptual test situations, and Bartlett's (1932) demonstrations of a dynamic and organized "effort after meaning" in the constructive operation of recall, refer to dynamic integrative processes which attempt to fill the gaps in a manner consistent with past experience, interest and social attitudes.

The first approach to the question of persisting functional relationships between modes of cognitive operations and characteristic ways of expressing need, motive and aims of adaptation, came from the contributors to the concept of perceptual defence. This concept, although never formally embodied in one particular theory, was concerned with a description of the effects of internal events on the perception of external stimuli. The stimuli used in many of the supportive studies were assumed to generate resistances to veridical perception or delays in response times, because an internal scanning mechanism interpreted them as dangerous, or harmful to the person (for instance, Bruner and Postman, 1947; McGinnies, 1949; Eriksen, 1951; Howie, 1952). Many methodological criticisms were levelled against the conclusions drawn from the experiments (see Erdelyi, 1974, for a recent summary), particularly against the dual manner in which defensive vigilance was said to be demonstrated. Some of these problems appeared to receive a satisfactory explanation by the labelling of subjects as repressors and sensitizers (Byrne, 1964), and by conceptualizing cognitive control operations outside the range of awareness as the result of idiosyncratic selective attention and multi-stage scanning and processing (Bruner, 1957).

Abandonment of perceptual defence research was probably premature since examples of motivated sharpening or levelling of external information, differentiated in its effects from selective response bias, can be demonstrated to occur in most people's ordinary lives. They reflect temporal hierarchies of needs and intentions and the ability to handle the conjunction of internal and external messages or information, the processing of which is energized by given amounts of emotional arousal or activation. Recent information processing models appear to be capable of casting a new light on perceptual defence, and will be discussed at a later stage.

The regulative aspects of response consistency are not confined to handling the demands of motivational and other personal characteristics. Because most stimuli are complex in informational content, rules and strategies must develop to deal with them efficiently so as to yield an integrated sequence of actions. To the extent that rules and strategies describe a repertoire of preferred modes of acting upon informational demands, it is plausible to seek in them the origins of intra-individual consistency. A consistent style of cognitive organization and processing implies the presence of control processes through which the dispositions to handle information according to a particular set of rules and strategies can express themselves. In computer language, the controls may be conceptualized as sets of basic instructions. This is surprisingly close to one of the original statements (Gardner *et al.*, 1959) that controls supply ". . . the means of programming the properties, relations and constraints of events and objects in such a way so as to provide an adaptively adequate resolution of the intentions which brought the person into an encounter with reality". The body of theory and experiments derived in the first instance from adults. The decision to review this work, in addition to that from children, reflects the orientation of the writer towards a greater understanding of the *development* of complex processes in adults.

(2) DIMENSIONS OF COGNITIVE CONTROL

Gardner *et al.* (1959) defined cognitive controls as slow-changing, developmentally stabilized structures which are relatively invariant over a given class of situations and intentions, where they operate despite shifts in situational and behavioural contexts. The term controls refers to levels of behaviour organization which are more general than the structural components underlying perception, recall and judgment. The term cognitive style was applied by the same authors, and by Smith and Klein (1953), to the characteristic behaviour which may appear as the result of a regulative interaction between cognitive control systems. This distinction has never appeared very clear because elsewhere (Gardner, 1953) a control system of broad versus narrow categorizing behaviour seems to define a style of equivalence-range preference which in the 1959 reference is termed a control principle. A similar lack of precision seems to affect the use of style *versus* control by Witkin and his collaborators. Field dependence–independence as a dimension of psychological differentiation (Witkin *et al.*, 1954; Witkin *et al.*, 1962) may be seen as either a style or a control principle, yet the terms cognitive style is applied to a global-articulated strategy (Witkin, 1965). It is likely that these difficulties have arisen because two terms are employed to described three variables (1) a generalized principle which reflects the overall aims of an organized system of goals; (2) a set of cognitive mediating structures and processes which are ultimately in the service of motives and characteristic methods of achieving them; and (3) the operational descriptive applied to observed behaviour, e.g. scanning, or field independence. Because of these defining difficulties the term style will not be used here.

The number of control dimensions postulated has increased since Klein, Schlesinger, Holzman, Gardner and Witkin *et al.*, first presented their findings. The best-known are: levelling–sharpening; form boundedness–form lability or intolerance of instability–tolerance of instability; interference proneness–resistance to interference, also referred to as constricted–flexible; narrow equivalence range–broad equivalence range, also referred to as narrow classification–broad classification. The *levelling–sharpening* dichotomy owes its terminology to the assimilation processes shown by other investigators in changes in the memory trace, but in this context refers to the effect of individual items in a series of displays, on an item that follows it. In the "schematizing" test, series of squares are presented in ascending or descending order for size estimation. The critical variable is the relationship between actual and subjective changes in size. Other measures of this dimension have been a kinaesthetic time error test, or the Gottschaldt Hidden Figures test which subsequently were found to be relatively unrepresentative, or by factorial analysis could be demonstrated to describe another virtually independent factor (e.g. Smith and Klein, 1953; Gardner *et al.*, 1959). Gardner and Moriarty's (1968) study on pre-adolescent children, however, did not yield a levelling–sharpening factor. Performance on the "schematizing" test seemed to be better described by the operation of field dependence–independence, or field articulation.

The handling of stimulus instability was also referred to as *tolerance or intolerance of unrealistic or reality-defying experience*. While movement responses to Rorschach plates and adaptation to aniseikonic lenses were occasionally used, the key measure appears to have been apparent movement (Klein *et al.*, 1962). The best known measure of the *constricted–flexible* control dimension has been the Stroop Colour-Word test, alternatively defined as a measure of resistance to cognitive interference. Smith and Klein (1953) found that criterion groups on this dimension differed significantly in speed of finding the Gottschaldt Embedded Figures, and in the levelling–sharpening dimension as represented by size estimation of the square series. Colour–object interference has also been tested in children, where the critical element was the inappropriate colour of a fruit (Santostephano and Paley, 1964). Although the intrusive effect was strongest in younger children, it is not yet clear whether the finding has primarily maturational implications. The Gardner and Moriarty study also failed to identify a substantial constricted–flexible control factor. Broverman (1964) described *two* related control dimensions from different indices of performance on the Stroop test. He termed them conceptual–perceptual motor dominance and strong–weak automatization. The relationship between this and the other controls, however, has not been investigated adequately. Some doubt must remain, therefore, of the importance of this dimension, and there is every possibility that, particularly for children, there may be a strong interaction with an impulsivity–reflectivity response principle (for instance, Kagan, 1966).

Measures of the *width of an equivalence range* are usually expressed by the number of categories into which a number of heterogeneous objects is sorted, and/or by the size, in terms of included items, of the constructed categories. An early study by Gardner (1953) indicated that broad versus narrow categorizers are characterized by predictable difference in what they will accept as similar or identical in constancy and brightness judgments. In the later factorial study, however (Gardner et al., 1959), this dimension produced a sizeable factor loading only for women, while in the Gardner and Moriarty study with children the classification factor, re-named conceptual differentiation, was the second largest of six factors, and was primarily identified by the number of classificatory groups. Substantial improvements have been achieved in the definition of individual differences in classification by objective definitions of category band-width (Pettigrew, 1958) or target patterns (Bruner and Tajfel, 1961; Tajfel et al., 1964). Using a wide range of test situations requiring classifying responses, Hamilton (1957, 1960) demonstrated a considerable degree of consistency for ambiguous perceptual situations ranging from psycho-physical comparisons to apparent movement. These results were particularly marked in subjects who had been predicted to show extreme classifying controls (see below), and three major factors accounted for almost 50 per cent of the subject variance.

The factorial impurities of the Gardner et al. (1959) study led this group of investigators to give prominence to only two major cognitive control dimensions: scanning and field articulation. *Scanning* defines the type and amount of perceptual sampling of situations, and has been demonstrated either directly by recording eye-movements, or by inferring it from size estimation tasks, from susceptibility to visual illusions or from speed of performance on the Stroop test (Schlesinger, 1954; Gardner, 1961; Gardner and Long, 1962a; Gardner and Long, 1962b). *Field-articulation* is Gardner's term (1961) to describe characteristic ways in which scanning strategies may be used in the elaboration or manipulation of a perceptual display. While in the original work goodness of form in Rorschach responses was used to identify this dimension, this control principle is now primarily linked to performance on tests describing Witkin's field dependence–independence dimension and to the size of error in the Müller-Lyer illusion.

Field dependence–independence describes degrees of individual consistency in susceptibility to misleading postural and visual frames of reference. In a number of studies these are shown to be covariant with the ability to isolate an individual item from a more complex context as in the Gottschaldt test (Witkin et al., 1954; Witkin et al., 1962). Like the dimensions discussed above, it is related to other control dimensions. It is influenced by level of intelligence (Goodenough and

Karp, 1961), and while it differs from a dimension describing inter-
ference- or distraction-proneness, it is nevertheless related to it (Karp,
1963). Because the criterion measures range from cerebellar to cognitive
process functions they have been described, rather unkindly perhaps, as
"measures in search of a theory" (Zigler, 1963).

While Witkin et al. (1954), and Gardner et al. (1959) reported quite
high correlations between, e.g., the Rod-and-Frame test and the Witkin
version of the Embedded Figures test, other investigators were unable
to confirm these (for instance, Elliott, 1961). It seems clear, however,
that individual differences in field independence–dependence occur,
that extreme scoring individuals defining the dimension may be
isolated, that females are consistently more field dependent, and perhaps most importantly, that individual differences possess developmental consistency over and above the tendency for a positive
correlation between age and field independence (Witkin et al., 1967).
Table 11.1 and Fig. 11.1 demonstrate these results. It is unlikely,

TABLE 11.1

Coefficients of Stability for RFT for two longitudinal groups

Age	Sex	13 r	13 N	14 r	14 N	17 r	17 N	24 r	24 N
8	M	0.76[ac]	26						
	F	0.48[b]	21						
10	M			0.71[c]	27	0.72[c]	27	0.66[c]	27
	F			0.81[c]	24	0.62[c]	24	—	—
						0.92[c]	27	0.84[c]	27
14	M					0.76[c]	24	—	—
	F							0.90[c]	27
								—	—
17	M								
	F								

[a] One-tailed test used
[b] p < 0.05
[c] p < 0.01
(*After* Witkin et al., 1967, p. 295)

therefore, that covariance with intelligence provides a full explanation
of the findings. It is probable, though not established, that the dimension demonstrated by the Witkin group is affected by early developing
individual differences in attention deployment, by the range of cues
which a person is able to sample (Easterbrook, 1959), and by the distribution of articulating attentional processes between task-relevant and

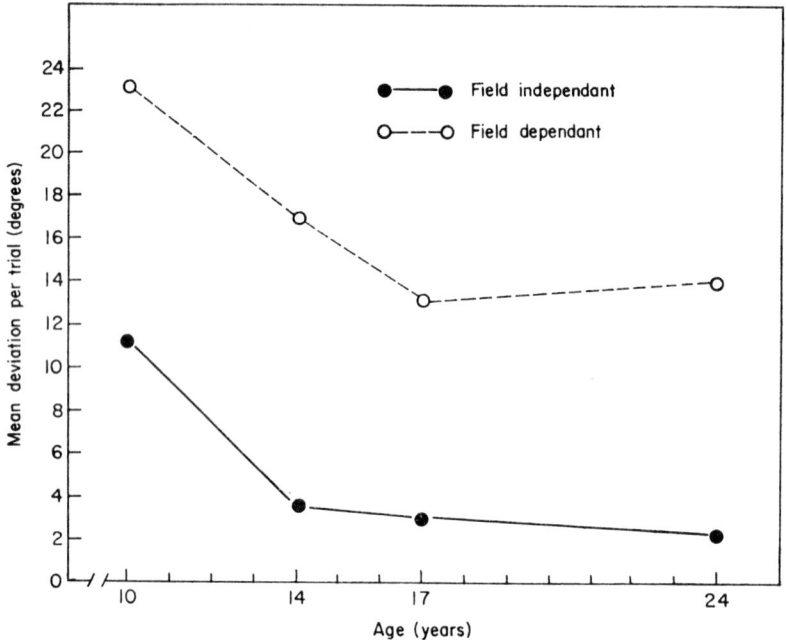

Fig. 11.1. Differences between field independents and field dependents. (*After* Witkin *et al.*, 1967, p. 296.)

irrelevant aspects of a stimulus display (Gardner, 1961). These considerations seem to be supported by Gardner and Moriarty (1968) who found a major field articulation factor in their study on pre-adolescent children.

An abstract–concrete dimension was not originally conceived in terms of cognitive control (Goldstein, 1939). More recently, however, it has been re-interpreted as a dimension of cognitive adaptation in response to different developmental antecedents. Harvey, Hunt and Schroder (1961) postulated that systems of conceptual functioning, or "belief systems", represent predispositions to construe, interpret or filter ego-involving stimuli consistently. Some evidence for the developmental antecedents is now available (Harvey and Felknor, 1970) and is discussed below.

A thoroughly studied control dimension in children is *impulsivity–reflectivity* (Kagan *et al.*, 1964; Kagan, 1965; Kagan *et al.*, 1966). Its basic premise is that there are individual differences and consistencies in the amount of time that is given to the evaluation of problems, and that this may provide a substantive explanation of the usually significant correlation between errors and time taken on a task. Working with a criterion test of Matching Familiar Figures, impulsivity–reflectivity was shown to be related to, *inter alia*, tachistocopic recognition time, inductive reasoning, serial recall and reading ability. Reflective children have been shown to prefer form to colour, to be good at discriminating form (Katz, 1972), to be better at sustained attention, as shown by scanning and search strategies, and at concept identification (Nuessle, 1972). Nuessle's additional finding that reflective children have a longer latency between feedback of an error and the next response, appears in some respects to fit equally well into Broverman's (1964) control dimensions of conceptual–perceptual/motor dominance and strong versus weak automatization. Impulsivity might well express strong automatization and preference for rapid motor discharge in cognitive tasks. Kagan's dimension has also been plausibly related to caution, competence or risk-taking, but outside the frame of reference of test anxiety studies there is rather little evidence so far of genotypic determinants.

Alternative interpretations of the dimension and its determinants have been offered by Block *et al.* (1974). Evaluating the separate contributions of latency and accuracy to performance, the authors conclude that latency is inconsequential, but that fast/inaccurate children were anxious, hypersensitive, vulnerable and structure-seeking. They could not be described as impulsive or minimally concerned.

(3) Determinants of control dimensions

In a number of important respects the determinants of cognitive controls may be conceptualized as hierarchical structures of subordinate and super-ordinate processes. Looking at the system employed by the researchers from the Menninger Foundation first, we see that psycho-analytic defence concepts were most influential in their thinking. Thus, gratification of motives and biological needs, appraisal of reality factors, and reality-appropriate modifications of goal-directed behaviour, supply a super-ordinate set of primary instructions to a central integrating processing system. Control, we may now say, is facilitated by what Neisser (1967) called an "executive"—an evaluative integrating process—which receives information from a number of memory buffer stores (Sternberg, 1975), from which, depending on the capacity resources of the system (Norman and Bobrow, 1975), the individually most acceptable response is generated. The concepts used by these theorists were not available to the earlier investigators. They appear to supply now a plausible set of mechanisms and processes which would mediate the influence of motivational and ego-supportive schemata in "conflict-free" cognitive tasks.

Constellations of super-ordinate self-regulating systems define a systematic conception of personality (Gardner *et al.*, 1959). Subordinate processes contain their own coherence and, therefore, a certain degree of autonomy, except when a super-ordinate process is stimulated by events or signals which are interpreted as a possible threat to the integrity of the whole system or any part of it. By definition, super-ordinate systems are not only exceedingly complex, but because of their functional distance from behaviour, are only indirectly testable. The majority of studies of the control determinants has been aimed, therefore, at levels of behaviour organization of which people have relatively little self-awareness and where constituent processes are difficult to isolate. This problem was probably overcome, however, by Klein (1954) in an experimental manipulation of thirst. When thirsty adult subjects were tachistoscopically shown thirst-related displays, they gave more thirst-relevant responses, consistent with the earlier studies of McClelland and Atkinson (1948). At the same time, however, subjects were also allocated to cognitive criterion groups which were inter-ference-prone and interference-resistant, respectively, on the Stroop test, reflecting constricted–flexible controls. Interference-prone, constricted subjects gave more thirst-related responses, and, therefore, showed a greater super-ordinate influence from motivational components, and thus a greater motivation-cognition interaction.

In the comprehensive study by Gardner *et al.* (1959) the super-ordinate factors were investigated by Rorschach protocol analysis and a Personal Inventory of some 200 items, methods which are today no longer considered either fully reliable or valid to yield measures of repression and isolation. Repression was defined by: constriction of ideation, absence of intellectualizing, unreflectiveness, naivety and relatively unmodulated affect. Isolation was defined by: intellectualization, expression of doubt and qualification, and unusual specificity of responses. With rather a small number of subjects identifiable as "repressors", an association between repressive super-ordinate systems and a levelling control principle was established at a low level of statistical significance. The small number of subjects identified as "isolators" showed a significant relationship with extreme scanning for men, and a tentative relationship in the same direction, as well as constricted control, for women. The investigators concluded that ego-control processes requiring the separation of thought and affect would result in extreme forms of scanning and control in order to be prepared for the defensive isolation of aversive affective material.

In their study on pre-adolescent children, Gardner and Moriarty (1968) report a replication study of the consistency as well as the defensive hypothesis in respect of control dimensions. The major factors extracted were : scanning, conceptual differentiation (classifying), field–articulation and constricted–flexible control. The factors and factor loadings supplied a gratifying degree of similarity with the earlier adult studies. The general defensive hypothesis, however, received at the most only weak support, with only a tendency for repression scores and field dependence to be related. Although the material presented by the authors contains a great deal that is of clinical interest, the study must lead to the conclusion that the super-ordinate organizing processes are too complex to be elucidated by the rather restricted research tools employed in the investigation. Furthermore, it is perhaps inappropriate to expect fully integrated cognition/motivation/personality interactions in children.

Extreme examples of repression and isolation are to be found perhaps only in clinically and behaviourally identified neurotics, if psycho-analytic theories of neurosis and mechanisms of defence have any validity at all. On this assumption it was possible to demontrate that clinical sub-groups of conversion hysterics and obsessionals were extreme classifiers in a substantial number of test situations reflecting the tolerance–intolerance of ambiguity dimensions (Hamilton, 1957, 1960). The results of these studies were a confirmation and amplification of Frenkel-Brunswik's earlier statements (1948, 1949, 1951) that intolerance of cognitive ambiguity as a cognitive control process in children and adults reflects a need for unqualified certainty in the service of anxiety control.

The real origins of the field dependence–independence dimension reside in the theories of Werner (1948) and Lewin (1951), who regarded behavioural *differentiation* as one of the most important aspects of human development. Differentiation leads not only to the establishment of a progressively larger number of functional units by which adaptive behaviour may be mediated. The units themselves become progressively more complex on the basis of an accumulation of complex experience, as well as becoming progressively more independent of one another and more specialized. These developments apply to purely cognitive as well as to social and affective functions and response dispositions. Field dependence assumes a global and undifferentiated response, in that people find it difficult to isolate and subsequently re-integrate the separate parts of a stimulus field. In field independence separation between distinct stimuli can be achieved by regarding them at first analytically as separate, and after independent articulation actively construct an adaptive response.

Witkin (1965) appears to prefer to define field dependence–independence as a control strategy in the service of an articulated *v.* global super-ordinate organizing dimension. An articulating disposition can overcome the constraints of context, whereas a global disposition is more bound by the synthetic Gestalt of a perceptual as well as a social stimulus field. In the original studies (Witkin *et al.*, 1954; Witkin *et al.*, 1962), the influence of motivational and ego-expressive super-ordinate structures was assessed, just as it was in Menninger Foundation studies, by responses to projective techniques. Field dependence was shown to be related to a passive and dependent personality, character-ized by submissiveness, low self-esteem and self-reliance, relatively little insight, and more unquestioning acceptance of social norms and standards. Field independent subjects showed a significantly greater capacity for mastering their own feelings and shortcomings, they were more dominant personalities and had greater reserves of behavioural autonomy. Their defensive and adaptive energies appeared to be more selectively available, and they possessed a more sophisticated and better integrated body schema (Witkin, 1965). Data supporting this theory have been reported with reference to poor memory for dreams, and to superior recall for social stimuli by field dependent subjects. One of the statistically strongest supports remains one of the original findings on children : a correlation of 0.61 between blindly scored defensive indices on the Rorschach, T.A.T. and Figure Drawing test, and the perceptual index of dependence/independence. Cross-cultural data (Witkin *et al.*, 1974) have supported the basic hypothesis : the more conformity-oriented the socialization strategies of a community, the lower the development of differentiation (see also Chap. 13 by Price-Williams).

The conceptualization of the global-differentiated dimension is intellectually exciting and challenging, and of real importance in the study of early attentional processes and exploration. The non-cognitive data are much poorer, however, than the evidence of consistencies in responding to perceptual embeddedness, and the motivation/person-ality/cognition links so far demonstrated are weak. This does not mean the postulated relationships are either implausible or absent (for instance, Vernon, 1969).

Similar conceptualizations of degrees of functional cognitive/affective differentiation have been proposed by Harvey, Hunt and Schroder (1961) and Schroder, Driver and Streufert (1967). The latter distinguish between high and low integrative capacity, defined by an index of conceptual connections, in relational thinking, and proposed a gradient of development which defines age changes as well as individually consistent strategies. Figure 11.2 illustrates this approach which is based on general concept differentiation and integration theory, and employs a so-called Paragraph Completion test. This presents words like "Rules . . ." or "Parents . . ." to subjects who are

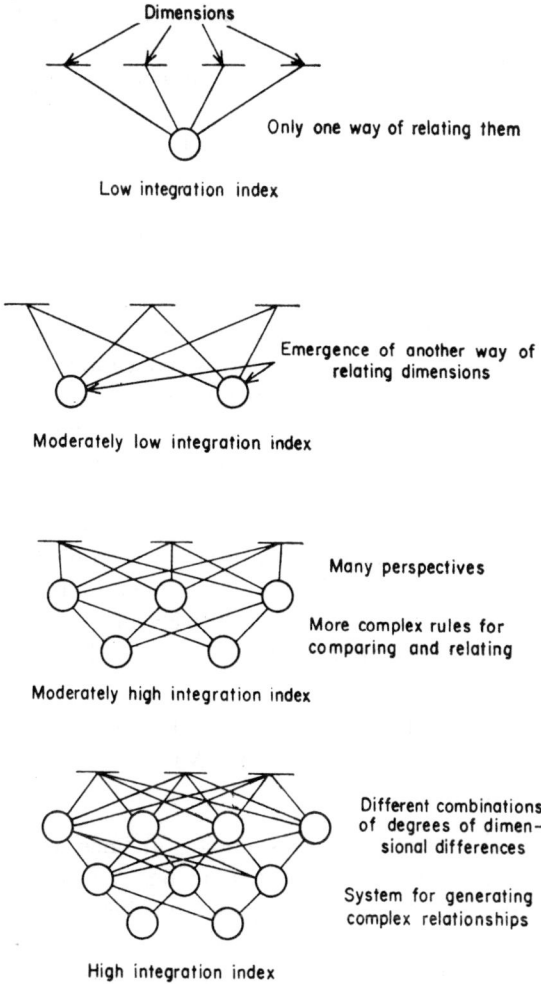

Fig. 11.2. Diagrams of the degree of cognitive development. (*After* Schroder, Driver and Streufert, 1967, pp. 15–22.)

asked to write a paragraph completing the thought introduced by the word. The complexity and connectiveness of the written passage reflect the cognitive strategy and conceptual level of the individual. Harvey *et al.* addressed themselves to a more limited set of conceptual functions systems, and their "concrete" type has more than superficial similarity with field dependence. It was defined by them as cognitively poorly structured and unintegrated, as distraction-prone from salient cues even if these were false, proneness to snap judgments and dichotomous evaluations, rigidity and stereotyping in problem solving, insensitivity and resistance to stimulus data which do not fit an existing cognitive organization. These and other cognitive characteristics were found in children and adults who were concurrently described as characterized by dependence on external, institutionalized authority, ritualistic acceptance of rules, conventional norm conformity, and dogmatic and dichotomizing social attitudes. The cognitive and motivational components are assumed to share a common basis in the internalized structures of socialization experiences. In a retrospective study of the concrete-abstract belief system, Harvey and Felknor (1970) found that the antecedent parental attitudes and strategies of concretely organized students included many restrictive injunctions, dogmatic demands for obedience, and narrow conceptions of child needs and of normative social class requirements.

Objectively speaking, the evidence for super-ordinate cognitive consistency and control has remained weak. The major difficulty appears to have been the lack of theoretical costructs permitting more tightly controlled testing of the interaction of motivation, personality and cognitive characteristics. Equally decisive were probably the inadequacies of projective probes for the construction of clearly defined criterion groups of subjects, and the relatively unsystematic variations in the cognitive tasks employed in testing a general theory.

V. PARENT-CHILD INTERACTION IN COGNITIVE DEVELOPMENT

(1) INTRODUCTION

The preceding discussion of the postulated influence of super-ordinate control strategies on cognitive behaviour has stressed not only the role of an individual's fundamental goals and his preferred and relatively consistent way of achieving them, but also the necessary developmental antecedents of the observed strategies. Consideration must now focus on the evidence for particular types of outcome of the socialization interaction for child motivation and personality, and thus for the development of cognitive processes.

It is apparent that this attempt has to be made with only sketchy evidence of some of the major developmental events or cognitive structures. Two of these are the nature of stimulus evaluation in early experience, and the type or types of long-term memory stores from which originate a variety of mediating processes and interactions at different levels of an information processing and response-generating system.

At one level we are dealing with the effects of parental characteristics on children's motives and personality characteristics, which are discussed in Section 2, and at a further level of interaction we have to consider the influence of these mediators combined on the analysis of an objective, external environment composed initially of low grade and subsequently complex information. These cognitive aspects will be considered in Section 3.

Since Sears *et al.* (1957) published their influential monograph there has been a shift of emphasis in discussions of the supposed effect of parental child-rearing attitudes and strategies on child motivation and personality. Instead of looking for a simple stimulus-response type of determination of child behaviour, the *reciprocal* nature of the relationship has been more clearly identified. There is some evidence, however, that the critical re-assessment of earlier approaches may have been excessive, by statements suggesting that all previous formulations and findings are suspect (Bell, 1971; Schaffer, 1974), because they omit reference to reciprocity. This criticism appears to be largely unjustified, if cross-sectional or longitudinal covariance data are sought. In that context it matters little whether the dominant maternal attitudes are influenced by the responding child, and thus affect significant aspects of his development. It is a separate issue, referring primarily to modifiable and dynamic aspects of maternal behaviour and the true complexity of socialization variables. Furthermore, there appears to be a related fashionable, but rash, tendency to re-name complex variables on the basis of simplified, concrete and observable criteria, and then to forget that operationalism may have deprived a concept of its full meaning. There is some evidence that this procedure has been applied to motivational and personality development by the study of "social interaction"; to the development of feelings of security, independence and personal acceptability by the study of "attachment"; and to the development of dependence by equating it with "attachment needs". Objective measurement of type and degree of social interaction and attachment is desirable and necessary, as long as it is realized that a premature change of terminology towards fully behavioural criteria may simply side-step the complex variables resulting from the human capacity for multivariate experience and experience encoding.

(2) MOTIVATIONAL AND PERSONALITY DEVELOPMENT

(i) *Maternal stimulation, infant activation and attachment.* Because of the general lack of studies involving the role of paternal influences on child development, our discussion will be almost entirely devoted to the established effects of maternal child-rearing attitudes and strategies.

The maternal role may be described by three major functions: protection, stimulation and socializing. These functions are supplied by mothers who themselves project large amounts of individual differences in personal, social and marital needs, who differ in capacities for accepting interruption, in patience, in capacity to offer love and warmth, in group conformity, in self-esteem, and in preferred methods of achieving goals and aims. Since infants vary fundamentally on a biological activity–inactivity dimension, optimum maternal attitudes and strategies should attempt to adapt to an infant's dominant characteristics. Thus, the relatively inactive infant may require stronger maternal stimulation and interaction than the more active infant to achieve an optimum level of animation, and maturational progression. In most instances, relatively high levels of infant activities increase developmental status and pleasure in functioning, but they need to be obtained by variations in the intensity, rhythm and type of activation supplied by the mother (Escalona, 1968). It would seem that Escalona's careful observations are relevant to motivational and personality development as much as to cognitive development where their importance is easier to perceive. For example, infants who are prevented by over-protective maternal action from experiencing strong hunger, discomfort or delay in gratification, may not easily learn in later stages how to cope with or overcome frustration and obstacles to need satisfaction. Conversely, where strong needs remain unsatisfied for long periods, at a time when the capacity for self-help is undeveloped, the caretaker may be experienced as frustrating and rejecting, and thereby become an ambivalent source for meeting attachment needs. One illustration of the relationship between maternal behaviour and infant attachment at 9–18 months is shown in Fig. 11.3. In this study (Clarke-Stewart, 1973), maternal attitude and behaviour was assessed on thirty-three variables, and attachment on thirty-two variables. It is apparent that secure attachment requires not only stimulation and responsiveness to attention- and support-seeking signals, but a predominant capacity to express warmth, affection and empathy. Since specific attachments do not develop much before the second half of the first year, the earlier development of reciprocal mother-infant responsiveness must play a role in the child's evaluation of maternal behaviour. Usually very high degrees of covariance are found between high maternal stimulation and strong infant responsiveness (e.g., Brody and Axelrad, 1971). It should be noted, however, that in studies of this kind one is dealing with rather over-simplified data from children whose behaviour repertoire is still small. They cannot amplify their attachment to the mother by self-report, and their emotional experience and possible ambivalence need not appear in a behaviour check list. It is unlikely, therefore, that cross-sectional data on even secure attachment is necessarily capable of being interpreted as evidence of a close, warm and continuous

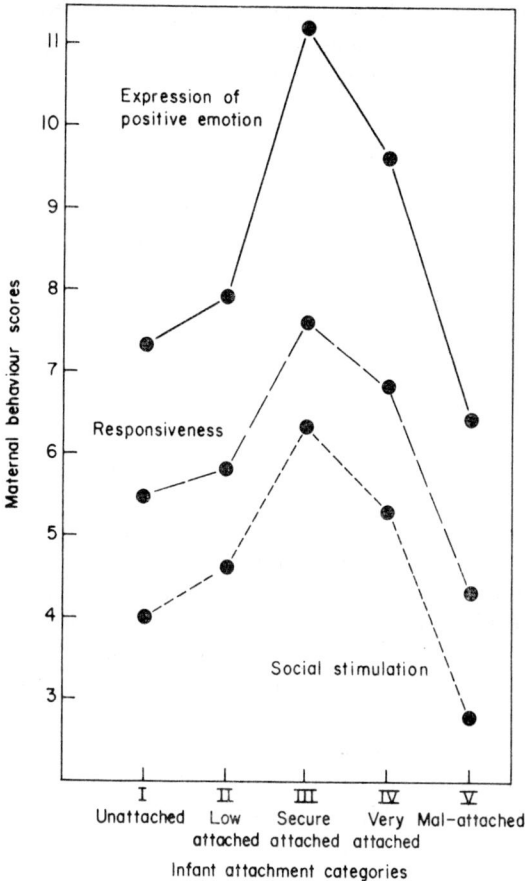

Fig. 11.3. Relations between maternal behaviours and categories of infant attachment. (*After* Clarke-Stewart, 1973, p. 78.)

relationship (Bowlby, 1951) which will develop into the adult capacity of making social object relationships, or as evidence for the development of trust which will develop into a capacity to give to others, and the motivation of hope (Erikson, 1963). This conclusion seems to be echoed by Ainsworth, Bell and Stayton (1972). They note that there appears to be no single criterion of attachment in studying following behaviour or active contact-seeking, so that a valid basis is not yet available for assessing the strength of attachment. While these authors are able to present a significant correlation of $+0.47$ between the number of times mothers picked up their infants non-routinely in the first quarter of the first year, and the infants' positive response to being held in the fourth quarter of the first year, the quality of the maternal action seems equally important. Thus, abrupt picking-up correlated – 0.43 with response to being held. It is appropriate, therefore, that attention should focus also on maternal needs and attitudes, and not exclusively on operationally defined maternal acts. For this reason (and others) it may be unsafe to infer from improvements in the social responsiveness of institutionalized young children following close personal attention from a single female mother-substitute (Rheingold, 1955) that successful replacement of a natural, affectionate and continuous mother-care had been achieved. The substitution hypothesis also tends to ignore the long-term effect of early separation or deprivation experience. Apart from the possibly clearer registration of early emotional distress in a relatively undifferentiated cognitive system (Thompson and Grusec, 1970), the "reinstatement" theory (Campbell and Jaynes, 1966) suggests that the long-term retention of early experience can occur if it is only minimally revived at intervals.

Neither long-term retention of aversive early experience nor high levels of stimulation are necessarily desirable goals for the individual since both may disturb or interrupt a more desirable state of quiescence. While it is usual to consider development in the context of stimulus- or information-seeking (e.g., Hutt, 1970; Jones, 1966), or in achieving adaptive effectance or mastery of self in relation to the environment (White, 1959), a contrary position can be adopted which holds that stimulation is unpleasant, but that the experience of unpleasant disruption and "intention" is necessary for fostering development (Zern, 1974). The importance of the maternal role may lie in the creation of disequilibrium for the child, and as a model and teacher in helping him to learn to cope successfully with stimulus intrusion. These propositions are consistent with the findings of animal experiments which suggest that stress in infancy may produce stress-resistant, and thus more adaptive, adults (for instance, Levine, 1971), and with a generalization of the psycho-analytic theory of mechanisms of defence.

(ii) *Socialization strategies and maternal attitudes.* The dimensions of maternal behaviour which have been used in the majority of more recent studies are derived either from Sears *et al.* (1957) or Schaefer (1965). They are, respectively, "permissiveness–strictness", "warmth–coldness"; "acceptance–rejection", "autonomy–control" and "firm control–lax control", all of which have emerged from factor-analytic treatment of interview ratings or questionnaire data. An "anxious involvement–calm detachment" dimension was additionally suggested by Becker (1964), but this appears to have been employed less frequently. The maternal characteristics which were related to child characteristics in the Berkeley Growth Studies were more multivariate

(Jones *et al.*, 1971). For example, Bayley and Schaefer (1960) employed eighteen variables to assess maternal effects on four child characteristics.

A methodologically and statistically well-designed study was carried out by Baumrind (1967). Here the parent-child data were obtained by home visits, structured observation and focused interviewing, and five specific propositions were tested : (1) non-permissive, nurturant parents are more effective reinforcing agents than non-permissive, non-nurturant parents or permissive, nurturant parents; (2) non-permissive, nurturant parents will effectively model self-assertive and affiliative behaviour; (3) low demands for maturity from a nurturant parent will result in low self-reliance; (4) high maturity demands from nurturant parents will result in higher aspirations, greater self-reliance and a more buoyant attitude; and (5) clarity of communication with high parental control will promote the development of conformity without the loss of self-assertiveness.

These propositions were tested by relating four composite parental dimension scores to the characteristics of three criterion groups of 3–4-year-old children. Pattern I children were described as self-reliant, self-controlled, approach-oriented and buoyant. Pattern II children were described as "dysphoric" (either anxious or unhappy or angry and obstructive), and having poor peer group relationships. Pattern III children were dependent and immature. A summary of the results is shown in Fig. 11.4. Whatever the effect of the children's behaviour on the attitudes and strategies of both parents, the results are fairly unambiguous. The parents of Pattern I children were firm, loving, demanding and understanding; those of Pattern II children were firm, punitive and unaffectionate; and mothers of Pattern III children lacked control and were moderately loving, but the fathers were ambivalent and lax. The latter finding appears to provide a clearer notion of what we mean by over-protection. It also indicates the need for multivariate assessment of parental characteristics to avoid confusion between groups selected only on the basis of acceptance–rejection, or high or low nurturance.

A similar multivariate conception of parental behaviour guided a study specifically directed at the development of obedience in infants throughout the first year of life (Stayton, Hogan and Ainsworth, 1971). These authors predicted that an infant whose mother is accepting, co-operative and sensitive to signals will tend to obey her verbal commands and prohibitions more consistently than the offspring of mothers who are rejecting, interfering and insensitive. Observed maternal characteristics were assessed by rating scales aimed at the

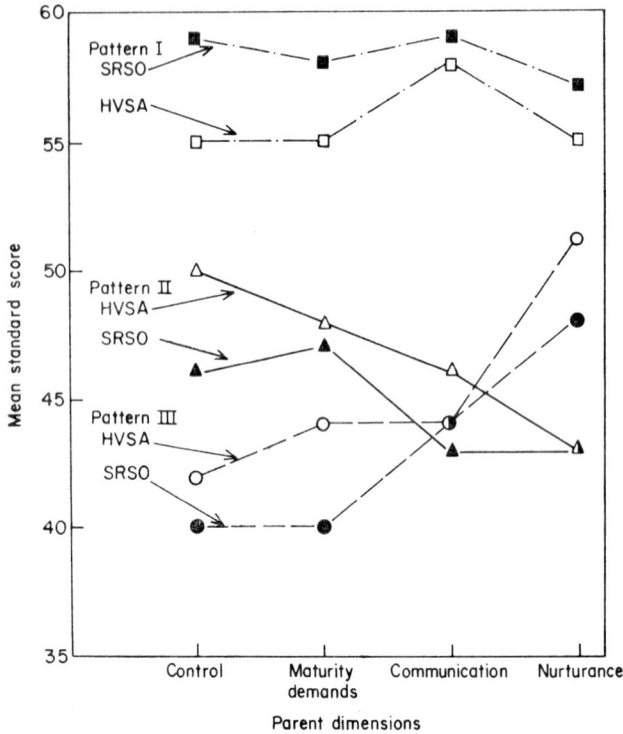

FIG. 11.4. Profile of composited parent dimension scores from the summary ratings for the structured observation (SRSO) and the home visit sequence analysis (HVSA) for each pattern. (*After* Baumrind, 1967, p. 73.)

sensitivity–insensitivity, acceptance–rejection, and co-operation–inter-ference dimensions, with a high degree of reliability. In addition, mothers were scored on frequency of verbal commands, and of physical intervention, and the "extent of floor freedom" permitted to the child. The infant variables were sex, scores on the Griffith Scale of Mental Development, compliance to commands and internalized controls, i.e. self-inhibiting or self-controlling behaviour. Highly signifi-cant correlations were obtained between obedience and the maternal attitude dimension, particularly acceptance–rejection. Although there were significant relationships between the maternal variables and infant intelligence and internalized control, a step-wise multiple regression analysis indicated that the predictive power of this single dimension could not be improved substantially by entering other variables into the equation.

A more comprehensively conceived study of the relationship between observed maternal needs and behaviour and infant development at one year was reported by Stern *et al.* (1969). These investigators employed fifty rating scales for the identification of maternal characteristics, and thirty-seven scales for the assessment of infant needs, behaviour and feeling. The correlations were treated by "interactive principal axis factor analysis followed by equimax rotation and blind approximation to orthogonal simple structure". Nine factors accounted for nearly 70 per cent of the total variance. A summary of the findings is given in Table 11.2. Apart from the replication value of these findings, the authors conclude that the nine factors appear to describe a continuum from child-centred to mother-centred maternal behaviour, and that disturbances in the development of infant behaviour increase with the degree of self-centredness in the mother.

Although none of the studies reviewed has been controlled for genetic determinants or for heritance/experience interaction, enough evidence appears to be available to support a social learning explanation for this consistent body of findings. Even if concordant constitutional factors were interacting in the mother-child dyad this would not detract from an experience-based interpretation of the demonstrated behavioural relationships. Four reasons are offered for this contention: (i) the multivariate nature of maternal and child behaviour favours situational explanations; (ii) genetic explanations would have to operate at a more general behaviour-determining level than the situational levels considered here; (iii) the evidence for a systematic relationship between innate response type and motivational and trait differentiation is unconvincing (see for instance, Hamilton, 1959; Eysenck, 1967; Gray, 1970); and (iv) genetic explanations must ignore the essential cognitive elements which operate in response generation and selection to which motivational and personality notations are applied.

(iii) *Stability of motivational and personality development.* A social habit-learning and cognitive-informational approach appears to provide a useful basis to account for the evidence of the stability of child characteristics arising in parental interaction. Stability interpreted in a narrow sense is the continuity from early to later behaviour of characteristics designated by the same term. An equally valid interpretation defines stability in terms of functional equivalence and functional continuity, but has found greater difficulty in general acceptance outside psycho-analytic theory and the field of behavioural abnormality. Interesting data are available, however, and must be explained. Murphy *et al.* (1962) presented a substantial number of significant correlations between infant experience and pre-school motivational and personality characteristics. These relationships were particularly

TABLE 11.2

Mother-infant

	FACTOR			
	2	1	3	8
Mother's needs	Emotional, involvement	Warm, supportive, organized, dependent, anxious	Achievement oriented, high drive, good-humoured, extroverted, friendly	Exhibitionistic, involved
Mother's behaviour	Loving, emotionally involved, high vocal and visual contact, skilful care	Involved, high visual contact, high play, exhibitionistic with baby	Exhibitionistic with baby	V igilant, warm physical contact, overtly maternal
Baby's needs and behaviour	Accelerated development	Lovingness and involvement with mother	Achievement oriented, energetic attempts to dominate mother	Environmentally responsive, sensual
Composite factor description	Involved mothers with accelerated infants	Symbiotic mother-child affective rapport	Parallel active and social achievement orientation	Maternal display behaviour with infant sensuality

(*After* Stern *et al.*, 1969, p. 178)

interaction factor summary

		FACTOR		
7	6	9	4	5
Anxious	Avoidance of physical contact or stimulation	Self-centred, disorganized, low frustration tolerance	Dis-organized, low frustration tolerance, abasive	Permissive, warm, supportive, good-humoured, abasive
Solicitous, emotionally involved, high rate of response and physical contact	Vigilant, enjoys baby	High play, indifferent to baby's health, overconfident	...	Solicitous exhibitionism
Responsive to comforting, comfortable, attractive, active, low mental age	Good-humoured, advanced development, achievement oriented, high drive, fearless, avoidance of physical contact	Impulsive, changeable	Hostile to mother, excitable, self-centred	Good-humoured and nurturant toward mother
Slow infants with solicitous and concerned mothers	Mutual maintenance of distance with accelerated infant development and drive	Unwarranted maternal satisfaction with disorganized interaction	Maternal, self-criticism reinforced by demanding and hostile infant behaviour	Exhibitionistic indulgence with happy child response

strong for boys. For example, satisfaction experienced in feeding correlates with a positive evaluation of other people and self, perceptual clarity under stress, strength of interests, ability to control the environment and energy level, to mention only the most significant results. Satisfactory solutions of mother-infant conflict during feeding correlate with: ability to forestall danger, knowing where to stop, impulse control, persistence, development of self-concept and a number of cognitive capacity variables. Being given autonomy at infancy related at the pre-school stage to: capacity in maintaining internal integration, control of excessive stimulation, energy to meet challenge or stress, self-esteem, sex-role concepts and resistance to discouragement. This evidence is consistent with Winterbottom's findings (1953) on the facilitating influence of self-reliance training on achievement orientation in children, and, despite the wide conceptual gap, with McClelland's challenging data (1961, 1962) on the relationship between independence training and the economic growth of societies.

The most frequently cited evidence on personality consistency and change comes from the Berkeley Growth Study and the Fels Research Institute findings (for instance, Schaefer and Bayley, 1960, 1963; Kagan and Moss, 1962). They are well known and do not require extensive restatement. While it is generally accepted that the methodology and the tests used inevitably reflect early deficiencies in research strategy, it may be equally true that the demonstrated relationships must be very robust if they can be shown repeatedly by inadequate techniques. The strongest relationships shown in the Fels studies were that childhood aggression predicted adult anger (males only), and that early passive-dependent behaviour predicted adult dependence (females only). Significant stability for both sexes was found for a number of achievement indices. The role of maternal influences was strongest for maternal attitudes operating under 3 years of age. These relationships, although containing large error variances, and thus deficiencies in reliability as well as validity, are nevertheless substantiated by other reports, at least one of them covering a predictive period of thirty years (Block, 1971). Bayley and Schaefer (1960) have thrown an interesting additional light on the interaction between socio-economic status and maternal characteristics. The more educated, higher socio-economic status American mother tended to score higher on giving autonomy, and on being co-operative and egalitarian, whereas lower status mothers were more often controlling, punitive and unwilling to interact with their children. As with other investigations, there were considerable and important sex differences in which cultural rather than socio-economic status factors may play the chief role, and subsequent social and cultural changes probably diminish the degree of validity for some of the results.

An investigation of the long-term effects of maternal behaviour on child personality by Yarrow *et al.* (1974) was aimed at the development of the capacity for making meaningful social relationships which are close and of some depth, and at social effectiveness and social dominance. As in the Murphy *et al.* study, significant data were mainly confined to the mother–boy pair. Maternal responsiveness to child communication, the appropriateness and warmth of maternal responses, and the capacity to treat the child as an individual, all at infancy, were consistently and positively related to depth of social relationships, social effectiveness and social dominance at age 10.

Our conclusions from the results of most of the studies on the relationship between parental child-rearing attitudes and strategies and the development of particular types of motivational and personality structures in the children, are fairly unambiguous. While the majority of correlations are low, and while cause-and-effect conclusions require a non-correlational methodology, it is clear that a warm, tolerant, stimulating, accepting mother is more likely to encourage the development of subjectively, socially and cognitively valuable child characteristics. The optimal mother who is child-centred appears to have the ability to be sensitive to the quality and strength of infant needs, to communicate her affection and attitudes clearly, at appropriate intervals and without personal strain, and to encourage a full interaction between the child and the environment, while yet employing fairly strict controls and restrictions which are relevant for the child's safety and for family cohesion. The major effects of an optimum mother-child relationship may well be found in unaggressive but competent achievement-orientation, and perhaps more strongly, in a relatively greater freedom from anxiety in the child. In turning to the discussion of cognitive development in the context of motivational and personality differences, it will be necessary to be aware that the effects of parental attitudes, as the child structures them for himself, operate as mediating processes in cognitive operations. It is thus not only the quantity of stimulation or exploration instigated by the adult which effects optimum cognitive capacity, but particularly, perhaps, the *quality* of maternal stimulation which the child *registers*.

(3) COGNITIVE DEVELOPMENT

(i) *Intelligence.* Until relatively recently the term cognitive development referred to the development of intelligence. Intelligence itself has rarely been conceived as a univariate function, and doubt is now being cast on the continuing usefulness of the concept (see Chap. 12). Preceding chapters in the present volume provide considerable evidence that the cognitive capacities which emerge and reach full competence in perception, in the formation and use of conceptual structures, in linguistic skills, and in the conditions and processes of learning and attention deployment, are the essential raw material of intelligence. Intelligence is, therefore, perceived more usefully as an "effect" rather than as a "cause".

Socialization experiences, and the mediating effects of parental attitudes with their resulting effects on child motivation and personality, influence intelligence-relevant processes. They modulate the need for and the utilization of stimulation and exploration, they guide attention, determine the extent of imitative learning, affect the ability and willingness to participate in verbal interaction and communication, and through them influence simple and complex conceptual development. Conceptualizations of the important and lasting effects of the child's early environment were initially, and inevitably, concerned with gross interactions in mother-child separation (Bowlby, 1951), and with the unfavourable effects of institutionalization on cognitive development (for instance, Goldfarb, 1945; Skodak and Skeels, 1949). When the results of the Berkeley Growth Study (for instance, Bayley, 1965; Honzik, 1967) began to appear, finer-grain data became available on the covariance of maternal behaviour and the development of intelligence, including the role of the sex of the child in the interaction. For example, substantial correlations were found between a "happiness" rating of children and intelligence test score. These are shown in Fig. 11.5. The data are complemented by more analytic data of the maternal characteristics involved in the relationship with intelligence, and presumably also some of the *reasons* for the children's happiness, or otherwise. The most significant findings for girls seem to contain culturally loaded differential attitudes involving maternal identification, showing itself as reinforcement of dependence, behavioural restriction and intrusiveness. A similar relationship was also found by Hurley (1965). Substantial correlations between the quality of the early environment and WISC IQ of boys aged 10 years emerged from a long-term study carried out by Yarrow (Yarrow *et al.*, 1974). Here the optimal maternal variables were : physical contact, acceptance, positive emotional expression, emotional involvement, communication, individualization, appropriateness of stimulation and achievement stimulation. Appropriateness of stimulation was defined by Yarrow in another publication (Yarrow *et al.*, 1972) by amount and intensity, variety, positive affect and contingent responses to vocalization and distress. The relationships of these maternal variables to infant behaviour measured by the Bayley Mental Development Scales were almost wholly significant, though of moderate size.

Bayley and Schaefer's (1960) and Baumrind's (1967) studies (see Section V (1)) provide a broad basis for considering the facilitating and inhibitory effects of motivational and personality dimensions on intelligence test performance. In the absence of stressful instructions and

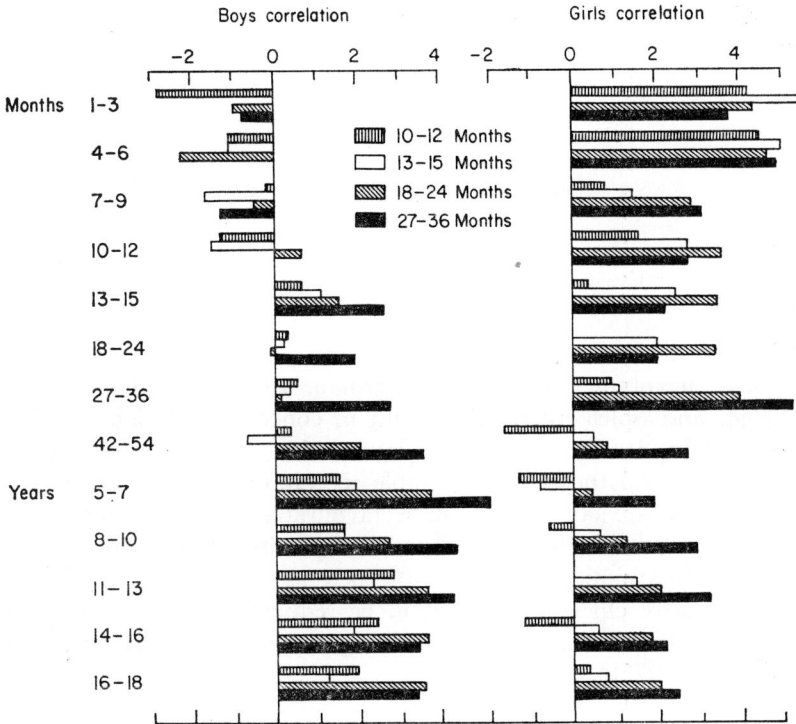

FIG. 11.5. Correlations between child's happiness at four age levels and intelligence. (*After* Bayley and Schaefer, 1960.

task settings, children's performance is better than in anxiety-inducing conditions. Furthermore, test conditions interact with questionnaire measures of anxiety. An example of the kind of relationships found between concurrent assessments of anxiety and intelligence over a number of school years, is given in composite form in Fig. 11.6. The data are adapted from Sarason, Hill and Zimbardo (1964) and Hill and Sarason (1966), and all the correlation coefficients are significant. Other studies have found anxiety-related cognitive decrements in solving anagrams (Sarason, 1961; Russell and Sarason, 1965), in

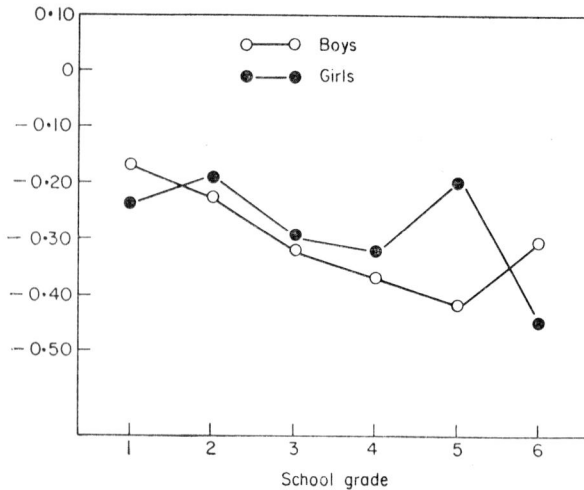

FIG. 11.6. Correlations between TASC scores and intelligence. (*Adapted from* Sarason, Hill and Zimbardo, 1964 and Hill and Sarason, 1966.)

response stereotypy (Weiss and Silverman, 1966), in serial learning (Hodges and Spielberger, 1969), and in concept formation (Denny, 1966; Dunn, 1968). None of the latter evidence was obtained from children, but all the studies are able to confirm that the energizing capacities of anxiety operate in a favourable direction only when intelligence is relatively high and task complexity relatively low. Thus, when the information load from the task as well as from anxiety is high, cognitive efficiency is likely to be reduced, suggesting that the limits of optimal information processing capacity have been reached (Hamilton, 1975b).

(ii) *Stimulation and attention.* If we were required to name the most important single set of influences on the development of cognitive skill and capacity, we might have to refer to the *pattern of optimal reciprocal stimulation* to which reference has been made earlier in connection with Escalona's and Murphy's observations (see Section V (2)). Stimulation that is experienced as fulfilling early social needs will influence and reinforce attentional processes and exploratory activities without which the formation of perceptual and conceptual schemata would be adversely affected. Sensory input is not only necessary for the development of the knowledge of objects, people, and their spatial arrangements from which children initially acquire the concept of their separate identity, but for the development of discrimination : a central operation in the production of adaptive responses. In other words, perceptual learning must precede the development of appropriate response selection mechanisms (Schaffer, 1971).

Optimal animation and stimulation must always be defined in relation to the observed requirements of infant and child. We must be clear, therefore, that there is no necessary monotonic relationship between amount of stimulation and either rates or levels of cognitive development. Beneficial developmental consequences may be absent if stimulation is defined by high noise levels in infants' homes from radio, TV, by frequent visits to and from neighbours, and by frequent maternal communication and contact not initiated by the child (Wachs, Uzgiris and Hunt, 1971; Tulkin and Kagan, 1972). The effects of exposure to background auditory stimulation on 7–10 year old children were also studied by Cohen, Glass and Singer (1973). The children were living in apartments above a busy motorway. The effects of noise were investigated by comparing the auditory discrimination and reading ability of children living at variable distances from the noise source, i.e. on different floors. Only auditory discrimination was significantly related to floor level of the child's home, and length of residence above 6 years. Similar effects were found by Wohlwill and Heft (1975) in a more recent experimental study in which they related environmental noise to distraction proneness and selective attention.

Optimal patterns of stimulation, and the maternal skill, capacity and motivation supplying it, seem to be additionally related to socioeconomic group characteristics which have been well described for older children by Hess and Shipman (1965), and for younger children by Kohn and Rosman (1973) and Pytkowicz Streissguth and Bee (1972). Birth order and family size must be considered further variables affecting the degree and pattern of maternal stimulation.

A considerable amount of work is now available from studies of the development of attentional processes. Much of this has not been concerned, however, with the identification of maternal attitude variables, or the equally relevant continuities or variabilities in infants' or older children's motivational systems. For example, the careful studies of the development of object perception by Bower and Paterson (1972) and of visual tracking by Bower et al. (1971) implicitly assume that the demonstrated processes, and the stages at which these occur, depend primarily on an interaction between maturing neuro-physiological structures and stimulation per se. It may be correct to hold, as others do, that the critical process in cognitive development is perceptual (or is it conceptual?) conflict triggering Piagetian equilibration processes (Bower, 1974). It may be equally correct to hold that self-induced activities, including play, provide at least one source of incongruity or falsified expectancy. What may be easily forgotten, however, is that object perception may start with the scanning and articulation of a human face and body, and that subsequent attentional styles and strategies may be affected by differential experiences of early reinforcement from maternal contact, handling and vocalization. Thus, preference of linear over circular arrangements of line segments by institution-reared infants in the first 24 weeks suggest that non-maturational factors may not be ignored (Fantz and Nevis, 1967). Similarly, White (1969) was able to demonstrate that supra-optimal handling of infants aged 6–36 days increases fixation time at 3–6 months.

Of equal importance appears to be the ability to habituate attention, and to shift to a novel focus. Evidence of attentional decrement has been found in association with low maternal responsiveness. It suggests that optimal attentional behaviour may require rewards (Lewis and Goldberg, 1969), and that it reflects an expectancy that the activity may have consequences for the manipulation of the environment. One of these rewards may be uncertainty reduction (Feldstein, 1973).

The more complex the environment becomes for the older child, the greater the requirements for selective attention and for inhibition of responses to irrelevant cues or foci. Here the restless or anxious child may be less able to exercise the necessary degree of control. Anxiety, as in fear of strangers or strange environments, may inhibit attention to novelty, with unfavourable results for manipulative play, exploration and cognitive development. While it has been more fashionable to consider interference with cognitive processes by anxiety as the result of excess arousal (for instance, Easterbrook, 1959; Broadbent, 1971) or activation (for instance, Lindsley, 1957; Eysenck, 1967), at least one recent study casts doubt on this assumption : the arousing effects of white noise do not reliably summate with tested manifest anxiety in its effect on attentional processes (Basow, 1974). This disconfirmation may have resulted from controlling the basic levels of arousal, which is rarely done. It is highly likely that the functionally most sensitive areas of cognitive processing are in attentional selection and inhibition. Central or primary task performance may be impaired by irrelevant processes concerned with self-evaluation (Wine, 1971), or by investing secondary or non-emphasized stimuli with motivational importance, as when failure to respond would be followed by unpleasant consequences such as electric shock (Cornsweet, 1969). Since the capacity to control distraction covaries with age (Doyle, 1973), particularly with auditory distraction (Turnure, 1970), anxiety-distraction in early life is likely to be related to over-simplifying cognitive processes in which less external information is adaptively sampled and integrated for response selection.

One possible re-statement of the origin of super-ordinate cognitive controls may be phrased along these lines.

(iii) *Exploration and curiosity.* Stimulation and attention are the pre-requisites of play and exploration, and all of these must be assumed to be affected by the same or very similar early reinforcement factors. While longitudinal studies have not been carried out, considerable evidence is available that maternal characteristics are associated with differential infant responsiveness to opportunities for exploration in the presence of a stranger and in a strange environment (Ainsworth, Bell and Stayton, 1971). Infants at 51 weeks of the more sensitive, accept-ing, co-operative and accessible mothers, explore more, and seek sup-port from a secure-base mother less frequently as the strangeness of the test situation increases, and show less distress when this occurs. This study was rather complex and numbers small, and it is unlikely that the relationship between infant avoidance of strange or novel situations and type of mothering is univocal. Bronson (1971), for example, finds significant correlations between maternal care and age of onset of fear of the unfamiliar for 4–12 months males only, and Rubinstein (1967) with infants 4–5 months old, and others, have referred to results which indicate that exploration may be confined to particular objects or situa-tions. This may be due partly to a balancing preference for the familiar, or it may be a function of two dimensions which can describe a strange object : novelty and complexity (Hutt, 1970). While novelty is in some instances defined by complexity, both arouse greater exploratory be-haviour in absolutely older children (Hutt, 1969; Kail, 1974), or relatively older children (Switzky *et al.*, 1974), whenever two or more age groups were compared. Complex stimulation is also more arousing, as shown by amount of EEG desynchronization in young adults (Berlyne and McDonnell, 1965), and where there is parallel evidence of stimulation avoidance, it may be suggested that complex stimuli receive *defensively* less exploratory attention and manipulation. Appropriate studies have not been carried out, but the conclusions seem to fit the behaviour of one type of anxious and inhibited child. A less defensive but equally anxious child may be disturbed by a *lack* of information which only "specific" exploration can provide (Berlyne, 1970). On the basis of studies with adults it could be said that this child may have an overriding need to control for lack of certainty and knowledge which will enable him to avoid perceptual ambiguities (Hamilton, 1957), which may be causally, but probably complexly, related to his early exposure to maternal nurturance and control (Heilbrun, 1973). In the light of evidence that stimulus or information need may be a primary motive like hunger or thirst (Jones, 1966), it may be postulated that

17—CP * *

exploration receives support from a biological source of individual differences.

"Specific" as well as "diversive" exploration (Hutt, 1970) may be defined as forms of play with their own essential contribution to schema and concept formation. Apart from the opportunity of gaining in effective control over their environment (Erikson, 1963), the imaginative element in free play provides children with opportunity for testing more narrowly defined cause-and-effect hypotheses, as well as for actively manipulating cognitive-affective identification, anxiety, aggression, dependence and control. Since intrusive and restrictive parental control will provide less opportunity for the child to express himself freely, it is plausible to predict that the direction of cognitive development through imaginative behaviour is substantially influenced by parent-child interaction. Evidence suggests that children scoring high on fantasy—definable as internally generated cognitive processes —have significantly more contact with parents, frequently show identification with and preference for one parent, have superior ability for tolerating delay in gratification, and exhibit higher levels of creativity and achievement orientation (Singer, 1973). Unfortunately, the evidence is not clear on what constitutes a cut-off point dividing constructive and adaptive fantasy at play from maladaptive withdrawal from reality.

Brief mention should be made of exploratory behaviour less frequently studied under this heading by researchers: verbal exploration as defined by children's questions, as well as by parents' answers. The role of language in the development of optimal cognitive processes has been adequately discussed in earlier chapters. Children's questions may be either purely playful without indicating a wish for real knowledge, or they may form part of an attention—or attachment—seeking strategy. If they reflect cognitive curiosity, however, suboptimal maternal replies may play a considerable role in the retardation of linguistic and conceptual differentiation, quite apart from those elements of maternal speech which may convey rejection and disinterest. For example, a recent study on language-delayed children (Wulbert et al., 1975) found that the mothers of these children scored relatively low on emotional and verbal responsiveness, on involvement with the child, and on provision of play material. The children were of average non-verbal intelligence. The North American findings of Hess and Shipman appear to have been replicated by English studies in the evidence of social class factors which characterize maternal answers to children's questions (Robinson, 1972; Robinson and Rackstraw, 1972). The affective slant of the answers may additionally determine for the child the long-term defining criteria of objects and people by the nature of the answers which he has habitually received (Newson and Newson, 1970). Recent studies on the development of imitation or modelling have been able to demonstrate the importance of verbalization by the model. Verbalized approval by an adult model appears to be more effective than passive observation (Hartup and Coates, 1970; Geshuri, 1972; Jeffrey et al., 1972; Zimmerman and Pike, 1972; Denney et al., 1973).

(iv) *Conservation and information processing capacity.* Probably one of the most frequently studied and fundamental cognitive operations is conservation—the development of notions of equivalence or invariance despite misleading perceptual cues. A number of studies have been completed on the interaction between affective, motivational variables and conserving capacity. Modgil and Lunzer (1971) found that combinations of parental dominance, possessiveness and ignoring the child were associated with depressed scores on Piagetian tests of conservation, as well as on tests of classification and spatial operativity. Goldschmid (1969) showed that children scoring high on conservation tend to be more objective in their self-evaluation, are described in more favourable terms by their teachers and their peers, and are less dominated by their mothers, compared with children scoring low on conservation. Neither study, however, was able to generate theoretical concepts to account for these interactions. An attempt in this direction has been made recently by Hamilton (1975b), by suggesting that mediating processes of socialization anxiety and of the child's self-concepts coded as long-term memories need to be interpreted as cognitive data. Studies of self-esteem (Coopersmith, 1967), of the interfering function of anxiety in cognitive operations, in addition to the findings already reviewed, led to the proposition that the cognitive operations of suboptimally reared children are adversely affected by the intrusion of task-irrelevant, internally generated aversive information. It was proposed that the suboptimally reared child was more prone than an optimally reared child to the emergence of cognitive structures containing anxiety information when confronted in a social test situation. Since the conserving capacity develops at a time when socialization pressures in the home are stepped up, crucial cognitive learning may be affected by motivationally more important attempts by the child to be found acceptable, and the development of the conserving skill might be retarded as the result of this interference from a simultaneous task, that is to say, to appear acceptable, and thus avoid anxiety. Since these propositions involved quantitative concepts of information processing capacity, it was necessary to obtain fine-grain differences for maternal attitudes on an optimal–suboptimal dimension, and to quantify in informational terms the cognitive load of conservation test problems. The prediction of a relationship between maternal acceptance–rejection, permissiveness–strictness, warmth–coldness, stimulation–non-stimulation and conservation of quantity was confirmed in two separate studies (Hamilton, 1972; 1975a). Figure 11.7 gives the results of the latter study showing not only the basic differences between the children of criterion groups of mothers, but also the effect of maternal participation in a re-test (Session 2) with a parallel version of the test of conservation. The construction of this test is discussed in detail

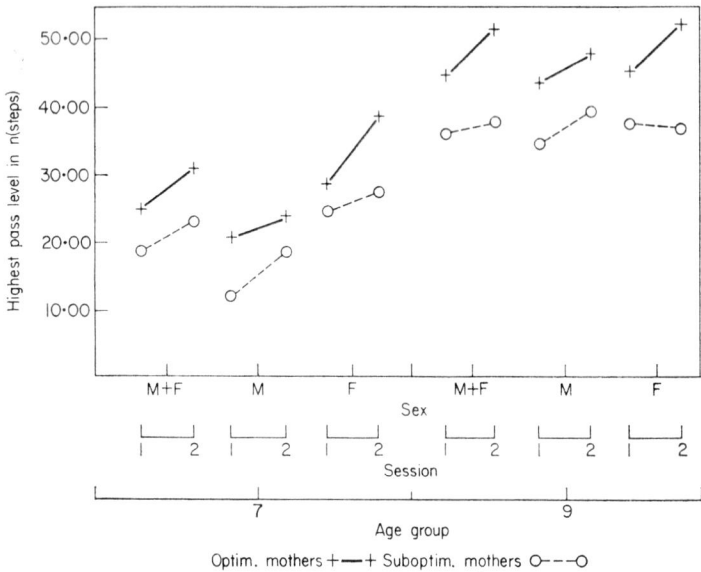

Fig. 11.7. Effect of maternal participation on conservation. (*After* Hamilton, 1975a, p. 64.)

elsewhere (Hamilton and Moss, 1974). The same children were re-tested several months later with the Test Anxiety Scale for children (Sarason *et al.*, 1960), to verify in a more orthodox fashion the postulated relationship between socialization anxiety and information processing capacity.* On the supposition that anxiety is basically internally generated information which would reduce the processing capacity for task-relevant information, it was predicted that high anxiety children compared with low anxiety children would show significantly higher reaction times to a visual signal if they were simultaneously required to rehearse a series of digits for subsequent recall. The results are shown in Fig. 11.8.

* This study forms part of a doctoral research project by G. Launay.

These studies appear to provide a useful link with the findings on the adverse effects of anxiety on cognitive performance discussed above.

(v) *Achievement orientation.* Previous discussion has referred briefly to the relationship between child rearing strategies and achievement motivation. The latter may be reduced by an over-protective early environment, or one in which encouragement for exploration and

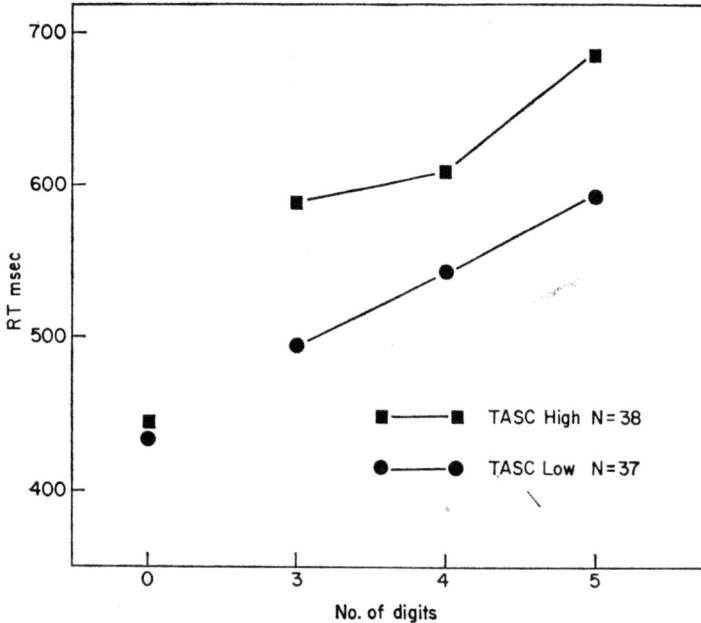

FIG. 11.8. Effect of anxiety on RT in single and simultaneous task conditions.

independence is relatively low. Where achievement orientation forms part of the pattern of socializing strategies, however, two types of goals are possible : to achieve or approach success, or to avoid failure. It is likely, but not established, that success-seeking further involves a need for praise, while failure-avoidance may be primarily an avoidance of criticism (Hill, 1972). In addition to early independence training, orientation towards the achievement of success was found in children who were rewarded for the display of physical affection, and were subjected to fewer maternal restrictions which were imposed earlier (Winterbottom, 1953). Coopersmith (1967) found self-esteem in 10–12-year-old boys significantly related to goal setting in level of aspiration tasks. In this group of studies, high self-esteem was positively related to a close relationship between boys and parents. This was characterized by parental interest in the boy's welfare, concern about his companions, being available for discussions of his problems and as a participant in his play activities. The high-esteem boy was regarded as a significant person, worthy of parental interest. Moreover, parents' positive attitude did not necessarily extend to an overt show of affection, or extending unlimited time, or permissiveness. Standards were set high for this group, and praise and reward were the favoured methods of discipline, so that social anxiety was low. Positive self-evaluation is probably one of the main reasons for the consistent, though relatively low correlations between achievement orientation, level of aspiration, school performance and intelligence (Rosen, 1961). The relationship is complex, however, and social class factors which have been referred to before appear to operate as moderator variables (Veroff et al., 1960).

Fear of failure appears to be an expression of generalized socialization anxiety. With a variety of measures of anxiety, the usual findings are not only that high achievement orientation and low anxiety yield the best performance scores, but that high anxiety subjects tend to set their goal often either too low or too high (Atkinson and Litwin, 1960). Moreover, high achievement orientation coupled with a high need for social approval and *anticipated public feedback of performance* impairs performance (Atkinson, 1974). The fear of criticism in highly anxious boys is clearly brought out in a study by Cox (1968), in which the presence of a teacher or the boys' father during a repetitive motor task significantly and adversely affected performance, compared with absence of authority figures, and compared with low anxious boys. Since a greater tendency to stimulus generalization is positively related to anxiety in adults (for instance, Mednick and Freedman, 1960), as well as in children (Nicholson and Gray, 1972), a basis would appear to exist for the development of individual consistency in the types of cognitive controls used to mediate between subjective self-evaluation and a positive or negative interpretation of problem situations. A theoretical model to account for these interactional processes is not yet available, but some tentative suggestions as to its general requirements are offered next.

VI. TOWARDS A COGNITIVE MODEL OF MOTIVATION AND PERSONALITY

This review of the role of parental influences on the development of children's motivation, personality and cognitive processes has provided some evidence of the origin of the cognitive structures and operations which subserve them. Mediating processes appear to be operating at several levels of stimulus encoding and response selection, so that no maternal stimulus is univocal and no response univariate, and a multi-channel model of attention deployment and response generation appears to be required to describe an optimally adaptive child. For example, satisfaction from exploratory behaviour may be ultimately reduced and impaired if maternal conflict of motives—as in supplying stimulation while worrying about the safety of other children in the house—remain unperceived by the child, so that he cannot modulate his egocentric goal-seeking. The maternal cues may be more complex than this since they may also convey threats of control, of deprivation, or of punitive rejection. From the point of view of competence in action, the registration and integration of such aversive cues is task-irrelevant, and succeeds only in making additional and irrelevant demands on storage and processing resources.

In the light of the evidence that maternal behaviour substantially affects child motivation and personality as well as cognitive competence, and in view of the demonstrations of covariance between cognitive controls and consistencies and at least some motivational and personality variables, we must search for a system with plausible structures and processes which facilitate these interactions. Such a system must embody and employ major interfaces for the expression in a response-generating process of (1) *characteristic paths and patterns of seeking adaptation or goals* (i.e. personality), (2) *types and intensities of goal-seeking* (i.e. motivation), and (3) *goal-achieving and "problem" solving capacity* (i.e. cognition). Formulating the interaction situation in this way, however, requires a re-statement of motivational and personality concepts in cognitive, informational terms.

A number of propositions are offered to confer at least face validity on this attempt. (1) Types and intensities of goal-seeking, and the consistent, characteristic way in which it is expressed reflect response-selection strategies based on schematized information retrieved from one or several long-term memory stores. (2) Reinforcement contingencies present information concerning behaviour and outcome to the central integrating parts of a processing system, and attach identifying codes to the information before channelling it to a long-term store. (3) Information from habit-outcome contains adequate data from which on a subsequent occasion probabilistic expectancies of stimulated behaviour can be inferred. (4) Adaptation is defined either as a sequence of approximating internal matches with negative feedback characteristics (Miller, Galanter and Pribram, 1960), or as a sequence of search-match-and-scan operations along decision trees and pathways (Newell and Simon, 1972). Both models define individual methods and characteristics of goal-seeking, though with different degrees of specificity. Habit development and need-reducing expectancies will emerge if the analysis of the cognitive data by a central comparator yields a match with previously learnt, and initially biogenic, codes of pleasure and satisfaction. Individual differences in characteristic dispositions towards action arise because of multiple interactions between subject and situational variables, because of inevitably idiosyncratic cognitive coding and integrating processes, and because the experience of what gives pleasure and satisfaction is, by definition, subjective.

In concrete terms, what is here proposed is that the development of characteristic ways and patterns of seeking adaptation or goals (i.e. personality), as in being dependent, aggressive, introverted or competence-oriented, reflect cognitive schemata in which reside the outcomes of previously evaluated response strategies, the anticipated results of potential response tendencies, the concepts of self and others as they are relevant to a temporal hierarchy of goals, and the cognitive data deposited by previous experiences of pleasure and satisfaction.

The types and intensities of goal-seeking (i.e. motivation) are similarly defined, and, as will have been observed, are considered here as logically inseparable from an analysis of personality—the characteristic and often predictable strategies which describe the behaviour. The *dispositions* to action obtain guidance from the cognitive data of an internal representation of the goal, and will be determined by previously evaluated expectancies. Along the path to the goal, negative feedback will correct deviations from optimal directions by integrating the information from gradients of environmental data. The utilization of feedback processes defines *competence* in action. Thus, detours, delay of gratification, or goal substitution reflect on-going cognitive operations. These are complex and may involve all the individual's resources: attention and consciousness, concepts, skills, beliefs, inferences, attitudes, and handling of interference from e.g., signals of somatic events or conflicting goals, and the required storage space for memory and processing time for an information-integrating system (Kiss, 1973). Pleas for a cognitive mediator theory of motivation have also been voiced by Weiner (1972), who finds it implicit in the requirements of achievement and attribution theories. *Generalized notions of drive and arousal appear to lack the essential cognitive components which form the foundation of response choice and selection, and provide internal representational data from which to anticipate the outcome of behaviour.*

An analysis of motivation and personality in cognitive, informational terms requires the conception of a processing system which needs to deal with only *one signal language*, in which cognitive data differ only in the *content or connotation* of signal patterns, in the *size and density of patterns,* and in the degree to which the processing operations are *available for subjective report* and *conscious control.* It is proposed that awareness of and full control over adaptive response-integrating processes is possible only if (1) the relevant data are re-channelled through short term or temporary memory stores, (2) the cognitive data do not also contain non-processing instructions, and (3) the amount and type of information do not also generate inhibitory processes such as cognitive masking and decay in buffer stores (for instance, Sternberg, 1975), or lateral inhibition (Walley and Weiden, 1973). If the informational content of signal patterns is decoded as strongly aversive, and contains non-processing instructions, alternative data- and response-selection processes may be generated. These would find an outlet through habits lying on a generalization gradient (Broen and Storms, 1961), and could supply a necessary as well as sufficient re-conceptualization of the defence mechanisms postulated by psycho-dynamic theorists.

We may now consider the implications of our analysis for the concepts of cognitive consistency and controls. As anticipated earlier (Section IV (1)), Erdelyi (1974) has already argued for a re-formulation of the perceptual defence concept as a special instance of selectivity in cognitive processing under regulating control at multiple loci of an information processing sequence. His model shows cognitive control processes organized in a long-term memory store exercising selective strategies at the peripheral receptor point and on an output generator, as well as at other points of a storage, encoding, comparing, rehearsing and consolidating system. It is now possible to argue that cognitive consistency is supplied by low threshold, high priority response strategies or habits which, by definition, have been frequently associated with similarly coded experiences of satisfaction. We may now also argue that control is exercised by sets of generalized super-ordinate schemata which scan information input for either rewarding or aversive information, and that controlling processes of over-structuring, of simplification or constriction of information, serve anxiety-avoidance functions. Without these, the resources of a processing system might be inadequate (Norman and Bobrow, 1975), or the allocation of adequate energy for simultaneous goals (Kahneman, 1973) would generate unacceptable stress. Evidence has been presented elsewhere in support of the proposition that anxiety is fundamentally information which may compete for space and time with task-relevant information, and thus account for the established unfavourable interaction between anxiety and, for instance, learning or problem solving (see Hamilton, 1975b, and Chap. 12).

The choice of goals and characteristic ways of achieving them depends on a reinforcement history occurring in the context of constitutional factors supplying base lines for activation, animation, arousal and de-arousal. The more complementary the parent-child interaction with obvious signs of satisfaction in the child, the greater the possibility that *objective* external information will guide response selection, and the smaller the chance that idiosyncratic defensive structures of schemata will develop. The more optimal the informational structure of an environment in the absence of aversively experienced additional information, the greater the capacity for objective, relational operations. The lower the level of anxiety-related signals, the greater the possibility that the storage, comparison, selection and integrating capacity of a processing system may be optimal in relation to the limits imposed by the biogenetically determined structures. A central processing system must be limited in capacity by virtue of these structures, not necessarily because it needs to be conceived as a single, limited capacity channel (Broadbent, 1958, 1971), but because multi-channel activity can quickly exceed the functional capacity of its components.

REFERENCES

Ainsworth, M. D. S., Bell, S. M. V. and Stayton, D. J. (1971). Individual differences in strange-situation behaviour of one-year-olds. In H. R. Schaffer (Ed.), *The Origins of Human Social Relations*, pp. 17–52. London and New York: Academic Press.

Ainsworth, M. D. S., Bell, S. M. V. and Stayton, D. J. (1972). Individual differences in the development of some attachment behaviours. *Merrill-Palmer Quarterly, 18,* 123–43.

Atkinson, J. W. (Ed.) (1958). *Motives in Fantasy, Action and Society.* Princeton: Van Nostrand.

Atkinson, J. W. (1974). Strength of motivation and efficiency of performance. In J. W. Atkinson and J. O. Raynor (Eds.), *Motivation and Achievement,* pp. 193–236. New York: Wiley.

Atkinson, J. W. and Litwin, G. H. (1960). Achievement motive and test anxiety conceived as motive to approach success and motive to avoid failure. *Journal of Abnormal and Social Psychology, 60,* 52–63.

Atkinson, J. W. and Raynor, J. O. (Eds.) (1974). *Motivation and Achievement.* New York: Wiley.

Bartlett, F. C. (1932). *Remembering.* Cambridge University Press.

Basow, S. A. (1974). Effect of white noise on attention as a function of manifest anxiety. *Perceptual and Motor Skills, 39,* 655–62.

Baumrind, D. (1967). Child care practices anteceding three patterns of preschool behavior. *Genetic Psychology Monographs, 75,* 43–88.

Bayley, N. (1965). Research in child development: a longitudinal perspective. *Merrill-Palmer Quarterly, 11,* 183–208.

Bayley, N. and Schaefer, E. S. (1960). Maternal behavior and personality development: data from the Berkeley Growth Study. *Child Development Research Reports of the American Psychiatric Association, 13,* 155–73.

Becker, W. C. (1964). Consequences of different kinds of parental discipline. In M. L. Hoffman and L. W. Hoffman (Eds.), *Review of Child Development and Research* I, pp. 169–208. New York: Russell Sage Foundation.

Bell, R. Q. (1971). Stimulus control of parent or caretaker behavior by offspring. *Developmental Psychology, 4,* 63–72.

Berlyne, D. E. (1960). *Conflict, Arousal and Curiosity.* New York: McGraw-Hill.

Berlyne, D. E. (1970). Children's reasoning and thinking. In P. H. Mussen (Ed.), *Carmichael's Manual of Child Psychology,* 3rd Ed., pp. 939–81. New York: Wiley.

Berlyne, D. E. and McDonnell, P. (1965). Effect of stimulus complexity and incongruity on duration of E.E.G. desynchronization. *Electroencephalography and Clinical Neurophysiology, 18,* 156–61.

Bexton, W. H., Heron, W. and Scott, T. H. (1954). Effects of decreased variation in the sensory environment. *Canadian Journal of Psychology, 8,* 70–6.

Bieri, J. (1955). Cognitive complexity—simplicity and predictive behavior. *Journal of Abnormal and Social Psychology, 51,* 263–8.

Bindra, D. and Stewart, J. (Ed.) (1966). *Motivation: Selected Readings.* Harmondsworth: Penguin Books.

Block, J. (1971). *Lives through Time.* Berkeley, Calif.: Bancroft.

Block, J., Block, J. H. and Harrington, D. M. (1974). Some misgivings about the matching familiar figures test as a measure of reflection–impusivity. *Developmental Psychology, 10,* 611–32.

Bower, T. G. R. (1974). *Development in Infancy.* San Francisco: Freeman.

Bower, T. G. R., Broughton, J. M. and Moore, M. K. (1971). Development of the object concept as manifested in changes in the tracking behaviour of infants between 7 and 20 weeks of age. *Journal of Experimental Child Psychology, 11,* 183–93.

Bower, T. G. R. and Paterson, J. G. (1972). Stages in the development of the object concept. *Cognition, 11,* 47–55.

Bowlby, J. (1951). *Maternal Care and Mental Health.* Geneva: World Health Organization, Monograph Series, No. 2.

Brandt, L. W. (1973). The physics of the physicist and the physics of the psychologist. *International Journal of Psychology, 8,* 61–72.

Broadbent, D. E. (1958). *Perception and Communication.* London: Pergamon.

Broadbent, D. E. (1971). *Decision and Stress.* London: Academic Press.

Brody, S. and Axelrad, S. (1971). Maternal stimulation and social responsiveness in infants. In H. R. Schaffer (Ed.), *The Origins of Human Social Relations,* pp. 195–209. London and New York: Academic Press.

Broen, W. E. and Storms, L. H. (1961). A reaction potential ceiling and response decrements in complex situations. *Psychological Review, 68,* 405–15.

Bronson, G. W. (1971). Fear of the unfamiliar in human infants. In H. R. Schaffer (Ed.), *The Origins of Human Social Relations,* pp. 59–64. London and New York: Academic Press.

Broverman, D. M. (1964). Generalities and behavioural correlates of cognitive styles. *Journal of Consulting Psychology, 28,* 487–500.

Bruner, J. S. (1957). On perceptual readiness. *Psychological Review, 64,* 123–52.

Bruner, J. S. and Postman, L. (1947). Emotional selectivity in perception and reaction. *Journal of Personality, 16,* 69–77.

Bruner, J. S. and Tajfel, H. (1961). Cognitive risk and environmental change. *Journal of Abnormal and Social Psychology, 62,* 231–41.

Byrne, D. (1964). Repression–sensitization as a dimension of personality. In B. A. Maher (Ed.), *Progress in Experimental Personality Research* I, pp. 169–220. New York and London: Academic Press.

Campbell, B. A. and Jaynes, J. (1966). Reinstatement. *Psychological Review, 73,* 478–80.

Clarke-Stewart, K. A. (1973). Interactions between mothers and their young children: characteristics and consequences. *Monographs of the Society for Research in Child Development, 38,* Serial No. 153.

Cofer, C. N. and Appley, M. H. (1964). *Motivation: Theory and Research.* New York: Wiley.

Cohen, S., Glass, D. C. and Singer, J. E. (1973). Apartment noise, auditory discrimination and reading ability in children. *Journal of Experimental Social Psychology, 9,* 407–22.

Coopersmith, S. (1967). *The Antecedents of Self-Esteem.* San Francisco: Freeman.

Cornsweet, D. M. (1969). Use of cues in the visual periphery under conditions of arousal. *Journal of Experimental Psychology, 80,* 14–18.

Cox, F. N. (1968). Some relationships between test anxiety, presence or absence of male persons, and boys' performance on a repetitive motor task. *Journal of Experimental Child Psychology, 6,* 1–12.

Denney, D. R., Denney, N. W. and Ziobrowski, M. J. (1973). Alterations in the information processing strategies of young children following observation of adult models. *Developmental Psychology, 8,* 202–8.

Denny, J. P. (1966). Effects of anxiety and intelligence on concept formation. *Journal of Experimental Psychology, 72,* 596–602.

Doyle, A. B. (1973). Listening to distraction: A developmental study of selective attention. *Journal of Experimental Child Psychology, 15,* 100–15.

Dunn, R. F. (1968). Anxiety and verbal concept learning. *Journal of Experimental Psychology, 76,* 286–90.

Easterbrook, J. A. (1959). The effect of emotion on cue-utilization and the organization of behavior. *Psychological Review, 66,* 183–201.

Elliott, R. (1961). Inter-relationship between measures of field-dependence, ability and personality traits. *Journal of Abnormal and Social Psychology, 63,* 27–36.

Endler, N. S. and Hunt, J. McV. (1966). Sources of behavioral variance as measured by the S-R Inventory of Anxiousness. *Psychological Bulletin, 65,* 336-46.

Erdelyi, M. H. (1974). A new look at the new look: perceptual defense and vigilance. *Psychological Review, 81,* 1–25.

Eriksen, C. W. (1951). Perceptual defense as a function of unacceptable needs. *Journal of Abnormal and Social Psychology, 46,* 551–64.

Erikson, E. H. (1963). *Childhood and Society.* New York: Norton.

Escalona, S. K. (1968). *The Roots of Individuality: Normal Patterns of Development in Infancy.* Chicago: Aldine Publishing Co.

Eysenck, H. J. (1967). *The Biological Basis of Personality.* New York: C. C. Thomas.

Fantz, R. L. and Nevis, S. (1967). Pattern preferences and perceptual–cognitive development in early infancy. *Merrill-Palmer Quarterly, 13,* 77–108.

Feather, N. T. (1967). Level of aspiration and performance variability. *Journal of Personality and Social Psychology, 6,* 37–46.

Feffer, M. (1970). Developmental analysis of interpersonal behaviour. *Psychological Review, 77,* 197–214.

Feldstein, J. H. (1973). Effects of uncertainty reduction, maternal rewards, and variety of rewards on children's choice behaviour. *Journal of Experimental Child Psychology, 15,* 125–36.

Fiske, D. W. (1974). The limits for the conventional science of personality. *Journal of Personality, 42,* 1–11.

Frenkel-Brunswik, E. (1948). Dynamic and cognitive categorization of qualitative material: II. Interviews of the ethnically prejudiced. *Journal of Psychology, 25,* 261–77.

Frenkel-Brunswik, E. (1949). Intolerance of ambiguity as an emotional and perceptual personality variable. *Journal of Personality, 18,* 108–43.

Frenkel-Brunswik, E. (1951). Personality theory and perception. In R. R. Blake and G. V. Ramsay (Eds.), *Perception—An Approach to Personality,* pp. 356–419. New York: Ronald Press.

Gardner, R. W. (1953). Cognitive styles in categorizing behavior. *Journal of Personality, 22,* 214–33.

Gardner, R. W. (1961). Cognitive controls of attention deployment as determinants of visual illusions. *Journal of Abnormal and Social Psychology, 62,* 120–7.

Gardner, R. W., Holzman, P. S., Klein, G. S., Linton, H. B. and Spence, D. P. (1959). Cognitive control: a study of individual consistencies in cognitive behavior. *Psychological Issues, 1,* Monograph 4.

Gardner, R. W. and Long, R. I. (1962a). Control, defense and centration effect: a study of scanning behavior. *British Journal of Psychology, 53*, 129–40.

Gardner, R. W. and Long, R. I. (1962b). Cognitive controls of attention and inhibition: a study of individual consistencies. *British Journal of Psychology, 53*, 381–8.

Gardner, R. W. and Moriarty, A. (1968). *Personality Development At Pre-Adolescence: Exploration of Structure Formation.* Seattle: University of Washington Press.

Gaudry, E. and Spielberger, C. D. (1971). *Anxiety and Educational Achievement* Sydney: Wiley.

Geshuri, Y. (1972). Observational learning: effects of observed reward and response patterns. *Journal of Educational Psychology, 63*, 374–80.

Goldfarb, W. (1945). Psychological deprivation in infancy. *American Journal of Psychiatry, 102*, 19–33.

Goldschmid, M. L. (1969). The relation of conservation to emotional and environmental aspects of development. *Child Development, 39*, 579–89.

Goldstein, K. (1939). *The Organism.* New York: American Book Co.

Goodenough, D. R. and Karp, S. A. (1961). Field dependence and intellectual functioning. *Journal of Abnormal and Social Psychology, 63*, 241–6.

Gray, J. A. (1970). The psychophysiological basis of introversion-extraversion. *Behaviour Research and Therapy, 8*, 249–66.

Haber, R. N. (Ed.) (1966). *Current Research in Motivation.* New York: Holt, Rinehart and Winston.

Hamilton, V. (1957). Perceptual and personality dynamics in reactions to ambiguity. *British Journal of Psychology, 48*, 200–15.

Hamilton, V. (1959). Eysenck's theory of anxiety and hysteria: a methodological critique. *British Journal of Psychology, 50*, 48–63.

Hamilton, V. (1960). Imperception of phi: some further determinants. *British Journal of Psychology, 51*, 257–66.

Hamilton, V. (1972). Maternal rejection and conservation: an analysis of suboptimal cognition. *Journal of Child Psychology and Psychiatry, 13*, 147–66.

Hamilton, V. (1975a). *The Effect of Maternal Attitude on the Development of Children's Thinking.* Final Report on S.S.R.C. Grant No. HR1556.

Hamilton, V. (1975b). Socialization anxiety and information processing: a capacity model of anxiety induced performance deficits. In I. G. Sarason and C. D. Spielberger (Eds.), *Stress and Anxiety* II, pp. 45–68. Washington D.C.: Hemisphere Publishing.

Hamilton, V. and Moss, M .(1974). A method of scaling conservation of quantity problems by information content. *Child Development, 45*, 737–45.

Harlow, H. F,. Harlow, M. K. and Meyer, D. R. (1950). Learning motivated by a manipulation drive. *Journal of Experimental Psychology, 40*, 228–34.

Hartup, W. W. and Coates, B. (1970). The role of imitation in childhood socialization. In R. A. Hoppe, G. A. Milton and E. C. Simmel (Eds.), *Early Experiences and the Processes of Socialization*, pp. 109–42. New York and London: Academic Press.

Harvey, O. J., Hunt, D. E. and Schroder, H. M. (1961). *Conceptual Systems and Personality Organization.* New York: Wiley.

Harvey, O. J. and Felknor, C. (1970). Parent-child relations as an antecedent to conceptual functioning. In R. A. Hoppe, G. A. Milton and E. C. Simmel

(Eds.), *Early Experiences and the Processes of Socialization.* New York and London: Academic Press.

Hebb, D. O. (1955). Drives and the conceptual nervous system. *Psychological Review, 62,* 243–54.

Heckhausen, H. and Weiner, B. (1972). The emergence of a cognitive psychology of motivation. In P. C. Dodwell (Ed.), *New Horizons in Psychology,* 2, pp. 126–47. Harmondsworth: Penguin Books.

Heilbrun, A. B. Jnr. (1973). *Aversive Maternal Control: A Theory of Schizophrenic Development.* New York: Wiley.

Helmstatter, G. C. and Ellis, D. S. (1952) Rate of manipulative learning as a function of goal-setting activity. *Journal of Experimental Psychology, 43,* 125–9.

Hess, R. D. and Shipman, V. C. (1965). Early experience and the socialization of cognitive modes in children. *Child Development, 36,* 869–86.

Hill, K. T. (1972). Anxiety in the evaluative context. In W. W. Hartup (Ed.), *The Young Child: Reviews of Research,* 2, pp. 225–63. Washington, D.C.: National Association for the Education of Young Children.

Hill, K. T. and Sarason, S. B. (1966). The relationship of test anxiety and defensiveness to test and school performance over the elementary school years: a further longitudinal study. *Monographs of the Society for Research in Child Development, 31,* Serial No. 104.

Hodges, W. F. and Spielberger, C. D. (1969). Digit span: an indicant of trait or state anxiety? *Journal of Consulting and Clinical Psychology, 33,* 430–4.

Honzik, M. P. (1967). Environmental correlates of mental growth: prediction from the family setting at twenty-one months. *Child Development, 38,* 337–64.

Howie, D. (1952). Perceptual defense. *Psychological Review, 59,* 308–15.

Hurley, J. R. (1965). Parental acceptance—rejection and children's intelligence. *Merrill-Palmer Quarterly, 11,* 19–31.

Hutt, C. (1969). Do children really prefer visual complexity? *Psychonomic Science, 17,* 113–14.

Hutt, C. (1970). Specific and diversive exploration. In H. W. Reese and L.P. Lipsitt (Eds.), *Child Development and Behaviour,* Vol V, pp. 120–80. New York and London: Academic Press.

Jeffrey, D. B., Hartman, D. P. and Gelfand, D. M. (1972). A comparison of the effects of contingent reinforcement, nurturance and non-reinforcement on imitative learning. *Child Development, 43,* 1053–9.

Jones, A. (1966). In B. A. Maher (Ed.), *Progress in Experimental Personality Research,* III, pp. 241–307. New York and London: Academic Press.

Jones, M. C., Bayley, N., Macfarlane, J. W. and Honzik, M. P. (1971). *The Course of Human Development.* Waltham: Xerox College Publishing.

Kagan, J. (1965). Reflection–impulsivity and reading ability in primary grade children. *Child Development, 36,* 609–28.

Kagan, J. (1966). Reflection–impulsivity: the generality and dynamics of conceptual tempo. *Journal of Abnormal Psychology, 71,* 17–24.

Kagan, J. and Moss, H. A. (1962). *Birth to Maturity.* New York: Wiley.

Kagan, J., Pearson, L. and Welch, L. (1966). Conceptual impulsivity and inductive reasoning. *Child Development, 37,* 583–94.

Kagan, J., Rosman, B. L., Day, D., Albert, J. and Phillips, W. (1964). Information processing in the child: significance of analytic and reflective attitudes. *Psychological Monographs, 78,* No. 1, Whole No. 578.

Kahneman, D. (1973). *Attention and Effort*. New Jersey: Prentice-Hall.

Kail, R. V. (1974). Familiarity and attraction to stimuli: developmental change or methodological artifact. *Journal of Experimental Child Psychology, 18*, 504–11.

Karp, S. A. (1963). Field dependence and overcoming embeddedness. *Journal of Consulting Psychology, 27*, 294–302.

Katz, J. M. (1972). Cognitive tempo and discrimination skill on color-form sorting tasks. *Perceptual and Motor Skills, 35*, 359–62.

Kiss, G. (1973). Outlines of a computer model of motivation. Proceedings of the 3rd International Conference on Artificial Intelligence, Stanford.

Klein, G. S. (1954). Need and regulation. In M. R. Jones (Ed.), *Nebraska Symposium on Motivation*, pp. 244–74. Lincoln: University of Nebraska Press.

Klein, G. S., Gardner, R. W. and Schlesinger, H. J. (1962). Tolerance for unrealistic experiences: a study of the generality of a cognitive control. *British Journal of Psychology, 53*, 41–55.

Kohn, M. and Rosman, B. L. (1973). Cognitive functioning in five-year old boys as related to socio-emotional and background demographic variables. *Developmental Psychology, 8*, 277–94.

Korman, A. K. (1974). *The Psychology of Motivation*. Englewood Cliffs: Prentice-Hall.

Levine, S. A. (1971). Stress and behaviour. *Scientific American, 224*, 26–31.

Lewin, K. (1951). *Field Theory in Social Science*. New York: Harper and Row.

Lewis, M. and Goldberg, S. (1969). Perceptual-cognitive development in infancy: a generalized expectancy model as a function of the mother-infant interaction. *Merrill-Palmer Quarterly, 15*, 81–100.

Lindsley, D. B. (1957). Psychophysiology and motivation. In M. R. Jones (Ed.), *Nebraska Symposium on Motivation*, pp. 44–105. Lincoln: University of Nebraska Press.

McClelland, D. C. (1961). *The Achieving Society*. Princeton: Van Nostrand.

McClelland, D. C. (1962). Business drive and national achievement. *Harvard Business Review, 40*, 99–112.

McClelland, D. C. and Atkinson, J. W. (1948). The projective expression of needs, I: The effect of different intensities of hunger drive on perception. *Journal of Psychology, 25*, 205–32.

McClelland, D. C. and Steele, R. S. (Eds.) (1973). *Human Motivation: A Book of Readings*. Morristown: General Learning Press.

McGinnies, E. (1949). Emotionality and perceptual defense. *Psychological Review, 56*, 244–51.

Mednick, S. and Freedman, J. (1960). Stimulus generalization. *Psychological Bulletin, 57*, 169–200.

Mehrabian, A. (1968). *An Analysis of Personality Theories*. Englewood Cliffs: Prentice-Hall.

Miller, G. A., Galanter, E. and Pribram, K. H. (1960). *Plans and the Structure of Behavior*. New York: Rinehart and Winston.

Mischel, W. (1973). Toward a cognitive social learning reconceptualization of personality. *Psychological Review, 80*, 252–83.

Mischel, W., Ebbesen, E. B. and Zeiss, A. R. (1972). Cognitive and attentional mechanisms in delay of gratification. *Journal of Personality and Social Psychology, 21*, 204–18.

Modgil, S. and Lunzer, E. A. (1971). The patterning of educational performance in relation to parental attitudes. *Bulletin of the British Psychological Society, 24* (No. 84), 232 (Abstract).

Murphy, L. B. and Associates (1962). *The Widening World of Childhood: Paths Towards Mastery.* New York: Basic Books.

Neisser, U. (1967). *Cognitive Psychology.* New York: Appleton-Century-Crofts.

Newell, A. and Simon, H. A. (1972). *Human Problem Solving.* New Jersey: Prentice-Hall.

Newson, J. and Newson, E. (1970). *Four Years Old in an Urban Community.* Harmondsworth: Penguin Books.

Nicholson, J. and Gray, J. A. (1972). Peak shift, behavioural contrast and stimulus generalization as related to personality and development in children. *British Journal of Psychology, 63,* 47–62.

Norman, D. A. and Bobrow, D. G. (1975). On data-limited and resource-limited processes. *Cognitive Psychology, 7,* 44–64.

Nuessle, W. (1972). Reflectivity as an influence on focusing behavior. *Journal of Experimental Child Psychology, 14,* 265–76.

Pettigrew, T. F. (1958). The measurement and correlates of category width as a cognitive variable. *Journal of Personality, 26,* 532–44.

Pytkowicz Streissguth, A. and Bee, H. L. (1972). In W. W. Hartup (Ed.), *The Young Child: Reviews of Research,* 2, pp. 158–83. Washington, D.C.: National Association for the Education of Young Children.

Rheingold, H. L. (1955). The modification of social responsiveness in institutional babies. *Monographs of the Society for Research in Child Development, 21,* Serial No. 23.

Robinson, W. P. (1972). *Language and Social Behaviour.* Harmondsworth: Penguin Books.

Robinson, W. P. and Rackstraw, S. J. (1972). *A Question of Answers.* London: Routledge and Kegan Paul.

Rosen, B. C. (1961). Family structure and achievement motivation. *American Sociological Review, 27,* 612–24.

Rotter, J. B. (1966). Generalized expectancies for internal versus external control of reinforcement. *Psychological Monographs: General and Applied, 80,* Whole No. 609.

Rubinstein, J. (1967). Maternal attentiveness and subsequent exploratory behavior in the infant. *Child Development, 38,* 1089–100

Russell, D. G. and Sarason, I. G. (1965). Test anxiety, sex, and experimental conditions in relation to anagram solution. *Journal of Personality and Social Psychology, 1,* 493–6.

Sanford, N. (1970). *Issues in Personality Theory.* San Francisco: Jossey-Bass.

Santostephano, S. G. and Paley, E. (1964). Development of cognitive controls in children. *Child Development, 35,* 939–49.

Sarason, I. G. (1961). The effects of anxiety and threat on the solution of a difficult task. *Journal of Abnormal and Social Psychology, 62,* 165–8.

Sarason, S. B., Davidson, K. S., Lighthall, F. F., Waite, R. R. and Ruebush, B. K. (1960). *Anxiety in Elementary School Children: A Report of Research.* New York: Wiley.

Sarason, S. B., Hill, K. T. and Zimbardo, P. G. (1964). A longitudinal study of the relation of test anxiety to performance on intelligence and achievement tests. *Monographs of the Society for Research in Child Development, 29,* Serial No. 98.

Schaefer, E. S. (1965). A configurational analysis of children's reports of parent behavior. *Journal of Consulting Psychology, 29*, 552–7.

Schaefer, E. S. and Bayley, N. (1960). Consistency of maternal behavior from infancy to preadolescence. *Journal of Abnormal and Social Psychology, 1*, 1–6.

Schaefer, E. S. and Bayley, N. (1963). Maternal behavior, child behavior, and their intercorrelations from infancy through adolescence. *Monographs of the Society for Research in Child Development, 28*, Serial No. 87.

Schaffer, H. R. (1971). Cognitive structure and early social behaviour. In H. R. Schaffer (Ed.), *The Origins of Human Social Relations*, pp. 247–62. London: Academic Press.

Schaffer, H. R. (1974). Early social behaviour and the study of reciprocity. *Bulletin of the British Psychological Society, 27*, 209–16.

Schlesinger, H. J. (1954). Cognitive attitudes in relation to susceptibility to interference. *Journal of Personality, 22*, 354–74.

Schroder, H. M., Driver, M. J. and Streufert, S. (1967). *Human Information Processing*. New York: Holt, Rinehart and Winston.

Sears, R. R., Maccoby, E. E. and Levin, H. (1957). *Patterns of Child Rearing*. Evanston: Row, Peterson.

Singer, J. L. (1973). *The Child's World of Make-Believe*. New York: Academic Press.

Skodak, M. and Skeels, H. M. (1949). A final follow-up study of one hundred adopted children. *Journal of Genetic Psychology, 75*, 85–125.

Smith, G. J. W. and Klein, G. S. (1953). Cognitive controls in serial behavior patterns. *Journal of Personality, 22*, 188–213.

Spence, K. W. (1956). *Behavior Theory and Conditioning*. New Haven: Yale University Press.

Stayton, D. J., Hogan, R. and Ainsworth, M. D. S. (1971). Infant obedience and maternal behavior: the origins of socialization reconsidered. *Child Development, 42*, 1057–69.

Stern, G. G., Caldwell, B. M., Hersher, L., Lipton, E. L. and Richmond, J. B. (1969). A factor analytic study of the mother-infant dyad. *Child Development, 40*, 163–81.

Sternberg, S. (1975). Memory scanning: new findings and current controversies. *Quarterly Journal of Experimental Psychology, 27*, 1–32.

Switzky, H. N., Haywood, H. C. and Isett, R. (1974). Exploration, curiosity and play in young children: effects of stimulus complexity. *Developmental Psychology, 10*, 321–9.

Tajfel, H., Richardson, A. and Everstine, L. (1964). Individual consistencies in categorizing: a study of judgmental behaviour. *Journal of Personality, 32*, 90–108.

Thompson, W. R. and Grusec, J. (1970). Studies of early experience. In P. H. Mussen (Ed.), *Carmichael's Manual of Child Development*, 3rd Ed., pp. 565–654. New York: Wiley.

Thurstone, L. L. (1944). *A Factorial Study of Perception*. University of Chicago Press.

Tolman, E. C. (1932). *Purposive Behavior in Animals and Man*. New York: Appleton-Century.

Tulkin, S. R. and Kagan, J. (1972). Mother-child interaction in the first year of life. *Child Development, 43*, 31–41.

Turnure, J. E. (1970). Children's reactions to distractors in a learning situation. *Developmental Psychology, 2,* 115–22.

Vernon, M. D. (1969). *Human Motivation.* Cambridge University Press.

Veroff, J., Atkinson, J. W., Feld, S. J. and Gurin, G. (1960). The use of thematic apperception to assess motivation in a nationwide interview study. *Psychological Monographs, 74,* No. 12, Whole No. 499.

Wachs, T. D., Uzgiris, I. C. and Hunt, J. McV. (1971). Cognitive development in infants of different age levels and from different environmental backgrounds: an explanatory investigation. *Merrill-Palmer Quarterly, 17,* 283–317.

Walley, R. E. and Weiden, T. D. (1973). Lateral inhibition and cognitive masking: a neuropsychological theory of attention. *Psychological Review, 80,* 284–302.

Weiner, B. (1972). *Theories of Motivation: From Mechanism to Cognition.* Chicago: Markham Publishing Co.

Weiss, R. L. and Silverman, J. (1966). Anxiety and response stereotyping: an experimental critique. *Perceptual and Motor Skills, 22,* 95–104.

Werner, H. (1948). *Comparative Psychology of Mental Development.* Chicago: Follett.

White, B. L. (1969). Child development research: an edifice without a foundation. *Merrill-Palmer Quarterly, 15,* 49–79.

White, R. W. (1959). Motivation reconsidered: the concept of competence. *Psychological Review, 66,* 297–323.

Wine, J. (1971). Test anxiety and direction of attention. *Psychological Bulletin, 76,* 92–104.

Winterbottom, M. (1953). The relation of childhood training in independence to achievement motivation. In J. W. Atkinson (Ed.), *Motives in Fantasy, Action and Society,* pp 453–78. Princeton: Van Nostrand.

Witkin, H. A. (1965). Psychological differentiation and forms of pathology. *Journal of Abnormal Psychology, 70,* 317–36.

Witkin, H. A., Dyk, R. B., Faterson, H. F., Goodenough, D. R. and Karp, S. A. (1962). *Psychological Differentiation: Studies of Development.* New York: Wiley.

Witkin, H. A., Goodenough, D. R. and Karp, S. A. (1967). Stability of cognitive style from childhood to young adulthood. *Journal of Personality and Social Psychology, 7,* 291–300.

Witkin, H. A., Lewis, H. B., Hertzman, M., Machover, K., Meissner P. B. and Wapner S. (1954). *Personality through Perception.* New York: Harper.

Witkin H. A., Price-Williams, D., Bertini, M., Christiansen, B., Oltman, P. K., Ranvirez, M. and Meel, J. V. (1974). Social conformity and psychological differentiation. *International Journal of Psychology, 9,* 11–29.

Wohlwill, J. F. and Heft, H. (1975). Environments fit for the developing child. Paper presented at the 3rd Biennial Conference of the International Society for the Study of Behavioural Development, Guildford, England.

Wulbert, M., Inglis, S., Kriegsmann, E. and Mills, B. (1975). Language delay and associated mother-child interactions. *Developmental Psychology, 11,* 61–70.

Yarrow, L. J., Goodwin, M. S., Manheimer, H. and Milowe, I. D. (1974). Infant experiences and cognitive personality development at ten years. In L. J. Stone, H. T. Smith and L. B. Murphy (Eds.), *The Competent Infant,* pp. 1274–81. London: Tavistock Publications.

Yarrow, L. J., Rubinstein, J. L., Pedersen, F. A. and Jankowski, J. J. (1972). Dimensions of early stimulation and their differential effects on infant development. *Merrill-Palmer Quarterly, 18,* 205–18.

Young, P. T. (1961). *Motivation and Emotion.* New York: Wiley.

Zern, D. S. (1974). An interpretation of the effects of stimulation on development: its role as a resolvable disequilibrator. *Genetic Psychology Monographs, 90,* 325–47.

Zigler, E. (1963). A measure in search of a theory. *Contemporary Psychology, 8,* 133–5.

Zimmerman, B. J. and Pike, E. O. (1972). Effects of modeling and reinforcement on the acquisition and generalization of question-asking behavior. *Child Development, 43,* 892–**907.**

CHAPTER 12

Development of Intelligence

Philip E. Vernon

I. THE CONCEPT OF INTELLIGENCE

The very phrase "Development of Intelligence" suggests that intelligence is an attribute which can be recognized and measured among persons of any age or background; that it is a homogeneous entity or mental power which, like height or weight, can vary in amount or in rate of growth or decline, but is essentially stable in its nature throughout life. Very widely, too, it has been regarded as the basic innate potentiality of the species, (e.g., apes are more intelligent than hens), and of individuals within the species, so that a child who is superior in intelligence in his early years would grow up to be superior as an adult. Unfortunately none of these statements has stood up to research that has been carried out by mental testers and psychometrists since the early years of this century; or in so far as they are acceptable they require considerable qualification. Indeed in recent years they have been strongly attacked. Thus it is necessary to preface this chapter with a rather lengthy discussion of what *is* intelligence, in lower animals, in human infants, older children and adults, and we must discover what intelligence tests measure.

Francis Galton (1869) was the first to suggest the scaling of human ability or general intelligence, distinguishing fourteen grades from the most illustrious and eminent at the top to imbeciles and idiots at the bottom. He sought to show that such ability was, in the main, hereditarily determined, though not unaware that most eminent individuals were reared in intellectually stimulating environments, and willing to admit that outstanding ability or genius depended considerably on strength of character as well as on intellect. Early views on the nature of intelligence also owed much to the accumulating knowledge of the evolution of species from the simplest organisms and insects, whose behaviour was governed almost wholly by innate reflexes, tropisms and instincts, through the mammalian species which showed greater adaptability and learning capacity, up to humans whose behaviour was attributed more to reasoning and intelligence. This fitted in with the progressive growth and complexity of the nervous system and the vast development of the neopallium or cortical structures at the human level. It was natural to identify the growth of mental powers in children with physiological maturing of the neurones and brain centres. J. McV. Hunt's book, *Intelligence and Experience* (1961), gives a good description of the early emphasis on maturation, as contrasted with learning, exemplified particularly in Gesell's studies of infants; and shows how it yielded in the 1940s onwards to a more interactionist viewpoint, largely as the result of the work of Hebb and Piaget. The genes, we now realize, do not completely determine any animal or human attributes, physical or mental. Though they provide a kind of blueprint or model of development, there is considerable latitude in most attributes, and the phenotype, that is the observable characteristics of the organism, always depends on the interaction of the genotype with environmental conditions, whether internal (e.g. nutrition) or external (e.g. physical or sociocultural).

II. PSYCHOLOGICAL APPROACHES

During the early decades of this century, psychological analyses of intelligence consisted mainly of rather fruitless attempts to reach a definition of the essential faculty or quality of mind that it involved. Abstract thinking, problem solving, planning capacity, attention, adaptation, educability or learning capacity, insight, and grasping relations, were variously stressed. Binet considered it as a number of qualities in which older children generally surpass younger ones, but chiefly emphasized the faculty of judgment. However there was a fair consensus that intelligence refers only to the cognitive realm, and mainly to the higher thinking capacities rather than to sensorimotor and perceptual processes, though it was realized that actual achievement in any situation always depends on affective and motivational, not only intellectual, components.

Spearman's conception of general mental energy was unpopular, though his "eduction of relations and correlates", and his study of different kinds of cognitive relations (1923), had some influence. More important, he was the first operationist, since he realized that by measuring and comparing intellectual operations, i.e. test performances, a better answer would be achieved than through armchair theorizing. Several contributors to the famous 1921 symposium (Thorndike *et al.*) likewise took the view that intelligence is what intelligence tests measure; though this obviously begged the question— what were the authors of the tests aiming to measure? Much later Gilbert Ryle (1949) pointed out the fallacy of the "ghost in the machine", implying that intelligence is not a thing, but just a label which we apply to actions or words which seem to us clever, efficient, complex or difficult. Nevertheless it can be a useful construct if defined in terms of observable competences or skills.

An early attempt to formulate a theory was Thorndike's (1927) view that intelligence represents the total quantity of associations or connections in mind, or, as Godfrey Thomson put it (1939)—bonds, which could be either innate or acquired. However experimental and theoretical psychology were adding immensely to our knowledge of learning, perceptual processes, concept formation and thinking, even though, owing to the gulf between the "pure" and the "applied" psychologists, little attention was paid to individual differences. It became clear to any but ardent Watsonians that S-R bonds were inadequate to account for the observed phenomena, particularly when linked to the telephone-switchboard conception of neurological functioning. In addition to the findings of Gestalt psychologists, we had Tolman's postulation of "cognitive maps" and "hypotheses" in rats.

Head and Bartlett's (1932) notion of the schema suggested a more apt basic unit, that is a flexible mental structure or template which brings to bear the totality of relevant experience on any percept or concept. For example a schema enables us to recognize a white plate as a white plate, regardless of the distance and angle of viewing, or lighting conditions. Similarly Piaget's schemata are built up by assimilating incoming experience to existing structures, and accommodation or modification of structures by new experience. Piaget (1950) rejected both the psychometric conception of intelligence and S-R associationism, seeing development not as an additive process but rather as a series of qualitatively different stages, in the course of which earlier structures are reorganized. Intelligence, then, is identified with the formation of a hierarchy of more inclusive and more effective schemata. However it is not any distinct faculty; it is present in the simplest adaptation of subhuman organisms and becomes more marked in the sensorimotor learning of the infant, culminating in the formal stage of logical reasoning.

Whereas Piaget was primarily an epistemologist and developmental psychologist, Hebb (1948) was a Behaviourist and neurologist, who was concerned to describe the brain mechanisms—the phase sequences and cell assemblies—which might underly the development of object perception and higher conceptual functions. Nevertheless their conclusions were remarkably concordant, both seeing intelligence as increasingly involved the more complex the mediating processes or autonomous cerebral activity between stimulus input and behavioural output. To Hebb we are particularly indebted for pointing out that much of the confusion and controversy over intelligence is semantic, since we commonly used the term in two quite different senses. He proposed to clarify the matter by distinguishing Intelligence A and Intelligence B. Intelligence A is the genetically determined potentiality of the brain, its capacity for any kind of learning and development; whereas Intelligence B is the current level and complexity of mental functioning, which depends also on the stimulation provided by the environment. Just as animals are born with the potentiality to see, but do not develop visual capacities if reared in the dark, so Hebb and his colleagues showed that rats or dogs brought up in the restricted environment of a cage do not develop as effective learning and problem solving capacities as those given the freedom of a rich and varied environment. Intelligence A, the genotype, is not directly observable nor measurable with our present techniques; it is Intelligence B which is expressed in, or inferred from, a child's or adult's clever or stupid behaviour, and which is sampled fairly effectively by our tests. Note that it follows that measurable intelligence is always culture-bound; it is based on acquiring and using the concepts and skills which are current in, and valued by, the particular society in which the child is reared (cf. Vernon, 1969). Nevertheless the rate of acquisition and its overall effectiveness are largely determined, or limited, by the basic Intelligence A. Thus it used to be said that intelligence tests represented innate intelligence, provided children had had equal opportunities to learn. But interactionist theory recognizes that no two children do have equal opportunities, and that what is measured is the product of Intelligence A and environment.

An alternative formulation, which has stimulated theory and research, is R. B. Cattell's (1963, 1971) distinction between fluid and crystallized intelligence, G_f and G_c. G_f is "the total associational or combining mass" of the brain, that is the biologically determined aspect of intellectual functioning which enables us to solve new problems, or grasp relations. Whereas G_c represents the concepts, skills and strategies which we have acquired under the influence of the cultural environment and education. Normally both are involved in any intellectual operation, hence the difficulty of distinguishing their contributions. But Cattell claims that his non-verbal, culture-fair, tests mainly measure G_f, whereas conventional verbal individual or group tests are much more dependent on G_c. Clearly, however, this is not the same distinction as Hebb's A and B, and most psychologists would probably regard performance on non-verbal tests such as Progressive Matrices, or Cattell's own battery, as depending at least as much on the relevant experience and stimulation provided by the culture as do verbal or pictorial tests.

Another theory which aroused considerable interest was that of G. A. Ferguson (1954) who considered intelligence as the more generalized techniques of learning, comprehending, problem solving and thinking, and the all-round conceptual level, which have crystallized out of the child's or adult's cognitive experiences during his home and school upbringing. These habits and strategies have broad transfer value to a variety of problems or to new learning; they become over-learned and thus achieve considerable consistency and stability. However this sounds much like Cattell's G_c, and would not readily account for the intelligent person's capacity to reach new principles and original solutions.

Bruner (1965), besides exploring "strategies" used in problem solving, talks of techniques or amplification systems which man has developed for extending the range and effectiveness of his abilities, for example tools, and above all language and symbolic thinking. Though differing in several respects from Piaget, he likewise recognizes developmental stages in the schemata and modes of processing adopted by children at different ages: the enactive or sensorimotor, the iconic which is dominated by perception and concrete images, and the symbolic or abstract. Finally, reference should be made to Miller, Galanter and Pribram's (1960) discussion of "plans" as the underlying mechanisms of human responses and thought. Reflexes and instincts are simple, inherited plans, which permit more adaptive and flexible behaviour than could the S-R bond. They operate more like hypotheses which the organism tries out, and tests against the outcome. These are referred to as TOTES or feedback loops. In the course of development, more and more complex plans are learned or built up, and organized hierarchically, often being verbalized to facilitate manipulation. This theory obviously relates to those of Tolman, Bartlett, Piaget and Bruner, but in addition it derives from information theory and computer programming; since a higher order plan is quite comparable to a heuristic programme.

Information theory represents an attempt to map out the coding, storage, retrieval and decoding of information, i.e. the processing or mental manipulation which underlies what we call intelligence. However it has had less impact on the theory and practice of intelligence testing than might have been anticipated, since intelligence seems to be

involved at every stage. It is necessary in the initial filtering and immediate memory storage, since the familiar Digit Memory test correlates
well with other intelligence tests although it does not depend on
chunking or coding. However Digits Backward, which does require
more mental manipulation, has a higher "g" loading. The chunking,
coding, and relating to past structures before entering long-term storage
obviously correspond to Spearman's eduction of relations. Successful
reasoning, or solution of intelligence test problems, must depend on
efficient organization of previous relevant information in the LTS and
ability to retrieve when required. Biggs (1968) points out also that level
of arousal or attention, and rate of processing, play a part. He is one
of a number of psychologists (cf. Estes, 1974) who currently argue that
intelligence is an outdated construct. Indeed it has been misleading in
giving far too static and simplistic a notion of children's learning
potentialities. Instead of merely measuring the overall efficiency or
products of cognitive functioning, we should be studying the underlying processes. Glaser's (1972) emphasis on behaviourally-defined
objectives and criterion-referenced testing is similar; and Stott (1971)
argues that scholastic backwardness arises because children have
acquired inefficient cognitive strategies and maladaptive behaviour
patterns, rather than because they are lacking in general intelligence.
Such children are often quite bright in non-scholastic situations, and
Stott believes that it is possible nowadays to remedy these conditions
by appropriate behaviour modification procedures, and to train
children in more effective learning skills.

In the present writer's view, these contradictory approaches are
complementary rather than antithetical. Developmental psychologists
and teachers would benefit from fuller knowledge of cognitive processing, and this might lead to diagnostic tests which would usefully supplement our tests of "g" or other psychometric factors. But it would be
unwise to ignore the influence of genetic, or of deeply entrenched,
differences between children in their overall learning capacities. True,
one could cite examples of successful training of transferable skills,
including Harlow's classical work with rats "learning how to learn"
(cf. Clarke et al., 1967). But there are also many instances of
failure, e.g., in attempting to accelerate Piagetian stages, and, as
described below, in the Head Start project.

III. INTELLIGENCE: UNITARY OR MULTIPLE?

From the earliest days of mental testing, a major issue has been the
unitariness v. the diversity of mental abilities. People obviously differ
in their abilities at different kinds of task, and yet show some con-

sistency both in their overall level and specialized types of ability. Spearman in 1904, and innumerable subsequent factor analysts, believed that mathematical analysis of the intercorrelations of batteries of tests would provide objective evidence regarding the major underlying dimensions or factors; in other words, it would map out the chief components of intelligence. Unfortunately it has not turned out this way; different factorists have adopted different models of mental structure, and different techniques. And since the results vary also with the age level and other characteristics of the groups that are tested, and with the particular tests used, we seem to be no nearer a final, agreed, solution than were Spearman and his critics sixty to seventy years ago.

Spearman was justified in postulating a prominent general or "g" factor running through all cognitive tests to a greater or lesser extent, which could be identified with what we call general intelligence. But he played down the existence of additional, more specialized, types of ability (verbal, number, spatial, fluency, etc.), or group factors, as Burt called them. Burt (1949) and Vernon (1950) therefore advocated an hierarchical model with g at the top, branching into major subtypes (e.g., verbal-educational v. spatial-mechanical), minor group factors and specifics. In the 1930s, Thurstone (1938) broke away and postulated a series of some seven distinct primary factors or components—a multiple factor model. Though Thurstone's primaries tend to recur in many subsequent investigations, there has been a tremendous proliferation of additional ability factors. The most comprehensive attempt at systematic classification is Guilford's (1967) model or structure of intellect. He recognizes three principles of classification :

1. By materials—verbal, figural, symbolic, behavioural.

2. By operations—cognition, memory, divergent and convergent thinking, evaluation.

3. By products—units, classes, relations, systems, transformations, implications.

This implies the existence of $4 \times 5 \times 6 = 120$ different intellectual factors, and his numerous large-scale investigations have confirmed some two-thirds of these. Guilford rejects the notion of any general factor, partly because low or zero correlations occur quite frequently between different factor tests; and partly because there is evidence to suggest that different factors show different curves of growth and decline, and are differently affected by pathological or environmental conditions. Doubtless he is justified in arguing that intelligence is too rich and variegated, especially at higher levels, to be adequately covered by a single g score or IQ. But his system is too elaborate to have won many followers, and there is rather little evidence to prove that his ingenious batteries of tests measure recognizably distinct abilities in daily life. They are test factors rather than dimensions of everyday cognitive and thinking processes.

However one of his distinctions, that between convergent and divergent thinking, has been taken up widely, and many studies of so-called "creativity" tests do indicate certain differences between high divergers and convergers (cf. Getzels and Jackson, 1962; Wallach and Kogan, 1965). Most ability tests devised by psychologists, and most scholastic achievement tests, are in multiple-choice form; each item calls for one right answer, and the student's thinking has to converge on this predetermined solution. However there are other types of test which permit a wide variety of responses, and subjects are scored for the number (fluency) and originality or unusualness of responses. Here again the problems of distinctiveness and validity intrude. Many psychologists, usually when working with high-grade groups, have found little correlation between divergent and convergent scores. But in heterogeneous groups, the correlations can be quite high. There is some evidence of non-linear regression; i.e. above an IQ of about 115, divergent scores become increasingly independent of convergent performance. The implication of work in this area is that intelligence and achievement tests, and indeed education generally, ignore or discriminate against creative and imaginative students. However there is little evidence to justify identifying divergent thinking with present, let alone future, creativity. Divergent tests do measure something rather different from conventional convergent ones, but should not be regarded as valid for picking out budding geniuses.

Both Eysenck (1967) and Cattell (1971) criticize Guilford's refusal to recognize hierarchy, or obliquity among his vast list of factors, and they put forward their own schemes. Eysenck largely accepts classification by materials and by mental functions; but his third principle contrasts tests mainly dependent on speed with those more dependent on power and persistence. This enables him to link up ability factors with information theory and with personality differences.

Cattell has greatly elaborated his initial theory of fluid and crystallized intelligence, and recognizes several additional general factors: spatial retrieval or fluency, cognitive speed, possibly carefulness, and memorizing; also, lower in the hierarchy, a series of "powers" and "agencies", more akin to Thurstone's primaries. While Cattell presents many stimulating ideas on the complexity of intelligence, it is not yet clear how these numerous factors can be measured in practice.

We can see then that factor analysis does not yield any unique or invariant solution to the problem of the dimensionality of intelligence.

For some purposes, and with some populations, a hierarchical model of g plus specialized group factors seems most appropriate; in other circumstances, multiple primary factors, showing little or no obliquity, are more effective. There is no necessary contradiction between these, as can be seen by drawing an analogy with school marks. School pupils can be classified in terms of all-round or average achievement, or else in terms of their marks in each of the main subjects—English, mathematics, French, science, etc. Many may show considerable unevenness in these various achievements. Further we can readily break down to still more specialized skills, e.g., spelling, grammar, quality of composition, knowledge of literature, etc. in the major dimension of English.

What then are the most generally useful factors of intelligence, i.e. those which cover the greatest amount of variance in cognitive skills? Over most of the age range, say from 5 to 25 years, V, or verbal comprehension, would certainly come first, and this is well measured by the verbal scale of the Wechsler tests (WPPSI, WISC and WAIS), or, from about 10 years on, by a group test consisting of a variety of verbal items. Non-verbal reasoning which, following Thurstone, might be termed R, or I (Induction), is to some extent distinct from V, and can be measured by tests based on figural or symbolic materials (letters, numbers, shapes). But group tests based on pictures, and most performance tests, are generally lower in reliability and show little predictive value. V and I combined probably give the best measure of g, and many group tests for older children and adults do contain verbal and non-verbal sections. The Binet, or Terman-Merrill, though very widely used in developmental research, is somewhat unsatisfactory in that its single MA or IQ is based on rather haphazard choices of items at different ages, and on the whole it has a strong verbal bias. Several factorial studies (for instance, Cohen, 1959) of the WISC and WAIS suggest that, in addition to verbal and visuo-spatial factors, a third component can be distinguished. This is sometimes identified as nondistractibility, sometimes as number ability; it enters into the Digits, Coding and Arithmetic subtests. Other frequently appearing factors would be S (the spatial or visualization factor), F (ideational fluency or divergent thinking), and possibly N (number or arithmetic ability), though the simple number operations that Thurstone used have little predictive value for secondary school mathematics. Rote memory (Thurstone's M) tends to be too specific to the particular type of test to have much predictive use; and the familiar Digit Memory test in Binet or Wechler scales correlates better with verbal tests than with paired associate or other forms of memorizing. Many factorists might, of course, add considerably to this list, but further factors tend to be more specific (less generalizable); and the more one adds, the less practicable is it to measure them reliably in restricted time.

IV. DEVELOPMENTAL CHANGES IN THE STRUCTURE OF INTELLIGENCE

For the reasons given above, factor analysis is unlikely to be of much help in developmental studies. Not only may the populations available for testing differ at different ages (e.g., senior secondary classes are less heterogeneous because many of the duller pupils have dropped out), but also we can never be sure how far our tests are measuring the same skills at different ages, or with equal reliability. Even in a vocabulary test, for example, the child's response to "regard" or "tolerate" is surely qualitatively different from his response to "orange" and "puddle", not merely quantitatively superior. However one theory, which has considerable plausibility, has been advocated by H. E. Garrett (1946) and Burt (1949), namely that abilities tend to differentiate with increasing age. This was held to account for the orthogonality of Thurstone's factors from college students, and the obliquity and lesser distinctiveness among children (Thurstone, 1941). Many studies have been reported in which the same tests (at different difficulty levels) have been applied to several age groups. Among the most extensive were those of Very (1967) and Dye (1968), where three tests designed to measure each of nine factors were given to samples ranging from 4th Grade to college level. Although there were no very clearcut trends, and results differed between the sexes, there certainly were changes in factorial structure with age, and a greater number of distinguishable factors at later ages. For example, Number and Perceptual Speed constituted a single factor up to 9th Grade, but then separated out. Several other investigations, however, have failed to demonstrate any such effect, particularly when designed to show what proportion of variance is general at different ages. Thus Vernon (1950) found at least as large a general factor in a varied battery of tests given to a heterogeneous adult population, namely army recruits, as commonly occurs among primary school children taking equally varied tests. His findings suggested also that while certain factors become clarified or more distinctive with increased age or practice, others may tend to fuse. For example Number and Space may be relatively distinct around 9–11 years, but then seem to coalesce to yield scientific or technical ability during adolescence. It may still be true that development during infancy is characterized by differentiation from global to more focused, analytic, responses; but in older children and adults, any reduction in generality is certainly affected by, and maybe wholly explicable by, the reduction in heterogeneity among the groups available for testing.

An important investigation in this area is that of Hofstaetter (1954), who analyzed the IQs of children included in the Berkeley Growth Study from 2 months to 13 years. Three major factors appeared: the first, which was most prominent in the tests given in infancy, was identified as sensorimotor alertness. The second, called persistence or rigidity, loaded the tests given from 20 to 40 months; while the third, appearing in tests from 4 years onwards, represented the conventional g and V. Actually these conclusions could have been reached without factor analysis from observing the content of developmental tests given from 0 to 5, and the low correlations between early and later developmental or intelligence quotients. But it neatly confirms Piaget's sensorimotor, preoperational and operational stages, each stage representing a new reorganization of the child's schemata. To quote Bayley: "There was no evidence of a general factor of intelligence during the first three years, but the findings indicated, instead, a series of developing functions or groups of functions, each growing out of, but not necessarily correlated with, previously matured behavior patterns" (Jones et al., 1971). The child concentrates, as it were, on the development of particular sets of skills at certain ages, and then moves on to largely new ones.

V. VARIABILITY IN GROWTH OF INTELLIGENCE

In view of such findings it is not surprising that earlier beliefs in the constancy of the IQ have had to be modified. When the Stanford-Binet test was given twice to children a few weeks or months apart, the reliability coefficients were indeed very high, about 0.90. But by 1933, R. L. Thorndike surveyed a number of retest studies and showed that correlations fell regularly over longer time intervals, till they averaged only 0.70 at a five-year gap. Moreover the instability is considerably greater when children are tested in the pre-school years than in later childhood. Table 12.1, adapted by Cronbach (1970) from Bayley's (1949) data, illustrates the findings. Note, for example, that tests around 2 to 3 years correlate 0.6 to 0.7 with Stanford-Binet one year later, but only 0.3 to 0.4 with the same test at age 14–15.

In the California Growth Studies,* there was not only negligible, but even slightly negative, correlation between early development on infant tests given in the first year of life, and later IQ. Such tests would of course be based mainly on psychomotor characteristics, i.e.

* Rather than listing all the original articles published by the Berkeley group, the reader may be referred to Jones et al. (1971).

TABLE 12.1

Correlations Between Developmental and Intelligence Quotients at Differing Ages

Age at first test	Name of test	Years until retest			
		1	3	6	12 yrs
3 mths	CFY	0.10 (CFY)	0.05 (CPS)	−0.13 (SB)	0.02 (SB)
1 yr	CFY	0.47 (CPS)	0.23 (SB)	0.13 (SB)	0.00 (SB)
2 yrs	CPS	0.74 (CPS)	0.55 (SB)	0.50 (SB)	0.42 (SB)
3 yrs	CPS	0.64 (SB)	—	0.55 (SB)	0.33 (SB)
4 yrs	SB	—	0.71 (SB)	0.73 (SB)	0.70 (SB)
6 yrs	SB	0.86 (SB)	0.84 (SB)	0.81 (SB)	0.77 (W)
7 yrs	SB	0.88 (SB)	0.87 (SB)	0.73 (SB)	0.80 (W)
9 yrs	SB	0.88 (SB)	0.82 (SB)	0.87 (SB)	—
11 yrs	SB	0.93 (SB)	0.93 (SB)	0.92 (SB)	—

CFY = California First-Year Scale   CPS = California Pre-school Scale   SB = Stanford-Binet   W = Wechsler-Bellevue
The name of the test used for retesting is given in brackets after the correlation coefficient. (*After* Cronbach, 1970.)

Hofstaetter's first factor. But, taking Stanford-Binet IQ at 17 as a criterion, the correlation at 2 years had already risen to 0.41, by 4 years to 0.71, and by 11 years to 0.92.

Bloom (1964) has surveyed the main published growth studies and shows that they yield substantially similar results. However, obtained figures are affected by a number of conditions and therefore very difficult to interpret. In the first place, infants are highly variable in performance, distractibility, etc. from day to day, and much depends on the social reactions of the infant to the tester. Hence reliabilities are low at this age even apart from changes in test content or function. Thus Bayley noted a correlation of 0.57 between infant tests at three-month intervals, whereas for the same group in the elementary school, the correlation was 0.92 at three-year intervals. Also, when ten-, eleven- and twelve-month test results were combined, they already gave a substantial positive correlation with 17-year IQ, although performance at a single testing had virtually no predictive value.

Some test items are naturally more predictive of later intelligence than others, though there seems to be no consensus regarding which, or why. Bayley found vocalization items in the first year correlating about 0.40 with IQ from 12 to 21 among girls, though not with boys.

Another approach to the stability issue is to chart the IQs of individual children who are tested repeatedly over several years. This was done by Honzik in the Californian studies, Dearborn and Rothney (1941) in the Harvard Growth Study of later childhood and adolescence, and others. Typically such charts show three or more children with identical IQs at an early age, whose subsequent records criss-cross and deviate as much as 30 to 50 IQ points later on. Alternately, a few children identical at a late age, whose previous records are traced back, again show astonishing variations. Thus Honzik et al. (1948), in a much quoted study, concluded that over the years of schooling only 15 per cent of children vary in their IQs less than 10 points; 58 per cent vary more than 15 points up or down, and changes of 30 points and over often occur in 9 per cent. She describes a few cases who fluctuated over as much as 4σ, i.e. roughly 60 IQ points. However, as Vernon argued in 1957(a), these and other such figures are likely to be exaggerated for a number of reasons including.

(a) Changes in test content, particularly when a number of different individual or group tests are used.

(b) Uneven standardization; one test may give higher IQs all round than another.

(c) Differences in variance; one test may yield far more very high and very low IQs than another. In tests that employ classical, or ratio, IQs, rather than deviation quotients, there are variations from one age level to another.

(*d*) The short-term reliability and internal consistency of the tests may be low. This includes variations attributable to conditions of testing and motivation of testees.

(*e*) Practice effects, if the same or similar tests are given frequently, can be quite considerable (cf. Vernon, 1960).

(*f*) The level of ability of the group. Terman and Merrill's results showed greater variations around IQ 120 than at IQ 80; and most follow-up groups have been of superior ability.

(*g*) When several tests are given, maximum differences are naturally larger than the median difference between any two testings— typically about $1\frac{1}{2}$ times larger.

(*h*) Only when these factors are allowed for should we interpret alterations as attributable to developmental changes, environmental circumstances, personality adjustments, etc. Both Honzik's and other published studies indicate the correlation over, say, 6 to 10 years or 10–17, to be approximately 0.70, and this figure implies that only 17 per cent of children vary 15 IQ points or more for single retests, while 63 per cent stay within ±10 points of the first IQ. However, with repeated retestings, 33 per cent can vary 15 points or more, and 48 per cent stay relatively stable.

Bloom (1964) likewise attempted to correct for distortions and arrived at distinctly high correlations between child and 17-year IQs. He shows that the results can well be accounted for by Anderson's (1939) Overlap Hypothesis. If a child's Mental Age or test scores are a_1 and a_2 at different ages, say one year apart, then there is no correlation between a_1 and the gain (a_2-a_1). Nevertheless a_1 correlates highly with a_2, simply because a_1 constitutes a considerable proportion of a_2. To quote Bloom : "In other words, Anderson was hypothesizing that the correlations in longitudinal data are a direct function of the per- cent of the development at one age which has been attained at an earlier age." At first sight, we would surely expect a child with high IQ, say at age 9, to increase more in M.A. by 10 years than one of low IQ over the same period. However the evidence shows that corre- lations are low or zero, which suggests that miscellaneous circumstances (rather than maturation) greatly affect growth over any limited period.

On the basis of the Overlap Hypothesis, Bloom was able to estimate what proportion of 17-year intelligence is already developed by certain ages, namely : 1 year—20 per cent, 4 years—50 per cent, 8 years—

80 per cent and 13 years—92 per cent. These figures imply that intellectual growth is so rapid in the early years that half of the adult intellectual capacity has either matured genetically, or been acquired through environmental stimulation, by 4 years; and that the possibilities of change after, say, 13 years are quite small (other than what could be produced by the factors (a) to (g), listed above). While his analysis certainly carries conviction, it appears to the present writer to overestimate stability, especially during the adolescent years, for two main reasons. First his correlations were corrected for attenuation, which boosts them above the level actually obtainable in practice. Secondly, we will cite definite evidence below that environmental factors can make substantial differences in intellectual growth after 11 years. Thus Bloom's estimates indicate the variations in IQ attributable to chance environmental or other influences, some good, some bad. They do not show what changes can be brought about by systematic influences which tend to raise the ability of a certain group, or to depress the growth of another group.

V. DIFFICULTIES IN LONGITUDINAL STUDIES

The data surveyed so far are based purely on the extent to which a group of children retain, or do not retain, the same rank order of ability as they grow from birth to maturity. It is much more difficult to delineate the actual gains made by one child, or a group, than it is in the case of height, because our units for psychological measurements are not on a ratio scale. Since there is no zero point, we can only assess a child as high or low in relation to the mean and variance for his age-peers. While we are generally entitled to assume that test scores give us an interval scale, this is certainly not true of Mental Ages where the growth from say 2 to 3 is likely to be much greater than that from 12 to 13. The units are far from equal.

Another major difficulty is that it is never possible to obtain a representative sample over a long period. In addition to attrition due to death, which mainly affects the initially least healthy, families move away and it becomes more and more costly to keep in touch with them. On the whole the poorer socioeconomic strata are more likely to become untraceable, or to drop out through lack of interest. Thus in Terman and Oden's (1959) follow-up of highly gifted children, mostly from superior families, over 90 per cent of cases were retained from middle childhood till over 30 years later. Whereas in Douglas, Ross and Simpson's (1968) follow-up from birth of 5362 children in the National Survey of Health and Development, full data up to $16\frac{1}{2}$ years were obtained only on 68 per cent. In consequence a good deal of our developmental information is collected on different groups at different ages, whose comparability may be dubious. This applies not only to groups used for test standardization, such as the 10 to 60-year subjects for the Wechsler-Bellevue scale, but also to all of Piaget's school-age samples.

Various attempts have been made to arrive at "absolute" scales of intelligence, with a true zero and equal intervals. Thurstone (1928) postulated a linear relationship between score (for instance, M.A.) and variations around the mean, and this enabled him to extrapolate to a hypothetical zero point at birth or shortly before. At one time Heinis's (1926) "Personal Constant", based on a logarithmic curve for mental growth, offered promise, but seems now to have dropped out. G. Rasch (1960) claims to have devised a technique for absolute scaling of test difficulty; however this does not appear to have been adopted by psychometrists.

Such attempts usually yield a negatively accelerated, or slightly S-shaped, curve for the growth of intelligence in childhood. Since the increments are greatest in the early years, they tend to show the mid-point of total growth is reached around 3 to 4 years (as Bloom claimed). However such curves are not very meaningful, both because they refer to different psychological functions at different ages, and because they hold only for groups. Any one child's curve is liable to fluctuate quite widely, and to be characterized by spurts, plateaus, etc. Little can be said regarding the causes of rapid, or slow, growth, though we will quote some data on associated personality and environmental factors below.

One might have hoped to obtain a clearer picture from comparing growth on different mental factors instead of just on the general component of successive individual scales or group tests. But here too the lack of absolute units creates difficulties. Thurstone (1955) analysed cross-sectional (not longitudinal) data on his Primary Mental Abilities tests, plotting the percentage of adult performance reached at different ages. Apparently P, Perceptual Speed, was the fastest growing of his factors, reaching 80 per cent of adult level by 12 years. Space and Reasoning came next, then Number, Rote Memory and Verbal, which reached 80 per cent level by 16 to 18 years, and Word Fluency was slower still. However other approaches seem to yield quite inconsistent results. Thus it is known that non-verbal IQs tend to have larger standard deviations than verbal (Cattell, 1963), and this must mean that performance on the former tests increases more slowly with age than on the latter. This difference is plausibly explained by Cattell's G_f and G_c theory, since social and educational pressures would have a greater effect on verbal abilities.

VI. AGE OF MAXIMAL GROWTH OF ABILITY

This again is a controversial and difficult issue. American army recruits in 1918 obtained average Army Alpha scores equivalent to those of 13-year children. Thus when the Stanford-Binet was applied to subjects of 14 and over, it became customary to divide their Mental Ages by 14 to get their IQs, rather than by their Chronological Ages. Some psychologists regarded 15 or 16 as the appropriate average Mental Age for adults. Obviously, however, mental growth was not linear with age up to 14, 15 or 16, and thereafter stationary. Thus the Terman-Merrill scale (1937) introduced a gradual tailing off from 13 in its IQ tables. As more evidence accumulated it became apparent that mean performance on group tests went on increasing up to 20 years or beyond. Nevertheless several investigations indicated decreasing scores beyond that age. For example Vincent (1952) standardized a general verbal group test on 7000 civil servants, and obtained an almost linear decrease with age from the 20–25 year to the 55–60 group, amounting to 0.3 of a standard deviation per decade (i.e. 9 IQ points per twenty years). When Wechsler (1939) standardized the Bellevue scale, maximal scores occurred in the 20–24-year group. Thereafter there was fairly rapid decline on some subjects, e.g., Kohs Blocks, Similarities, Digit Memory, whereas tests such as Information and Vocabulary held up considerably longer. Similarly Foulds and Raven (1948) gave the Progressive Matrices and Mill Hill Vocabulary to comparable groups of employees in the same company covering a wide age range. Performance in the former test reached its maximum at approximately 18 years, on the latter not till 37 (even 50 years among the most intelligent). These and other studies indicate earlier decline in reasoning (especially non-verbal) and spatial tests, also in tests markedly dependent on speed; and by contrasting these with vocabulary, measures of so-called mental deterioration were obtained.

However, following on Hebb's theory of Intelligence B, it was realized that continued mental growth would depend largely on continuing educational and other environmental stimulation. The astonishingly low figure of 13 years was found in 1918 because at that time the majority of the population probably left school around that age. In 1949, Vernon and Parry published the scores on the Progressive Matrices test of 90,000 naval recruits of different ages and occupational backgrounds. These showed a tendency to decline even as early as 18 years among men who came from unskilled and labouring jobs, which presumably made little call on their "brains"; whereas in skilled tradesmen and clerical workers, scores went on increasing till a later age, and declined much more slowly thereafter.

Research in the 1960s began to show that the above cross-sectional studies of successive age groups could be seriously misleading. When the same individuals were tested in early and later adulthood, scores on verbal tests tended to increase up to 50–60 years, and even on spatial and reasoning tests up to 40 and beyond. Why these two different approaches yielded such different results has not been satisfactorily explained, though probably part of the reason is that people who are now aged 50 to 70 would mostly have had a shorter and perhaps less stimulating education than do present-day adolescents and young adults. Possibly also leisure conditions nowadays help more people to keep their intelligence "alive" than in the 1930s and earlier, e.g., television, easier access to books and periodicals, better medical care, etc. Mention should be made of the ingenious strategy devised by Schaie and Strother (1968). They collected samples aged 25, 30, 35, ... 70, and then retested each of these five years later. Hence they were able to calculate the rise or fall over each five-year period without having to compare one sample with another, nor having to keep in touch with the same group over a very long period.

From the psychological angle, then, it would appear that the basic coding and integrative powers of the brain do reach a limit in early or middle adulthood, depending considerably on education and active exercise of the mental "faculties". However, for a much longer period adults can continue to acquire concepts and build up further skills appropriate to their occupation and avocations, which survive the onset of the decline that comes with neurological decay.

VII. ENVIRONMENTAL FACTORS

(1) FAMILY CHARACTERISTICS

So many factors in the home, the school, and general social environment correlate with child intelligence that it is extremly difficult to sort out which of these are causal, or to rule out possible genetic differences. For example, numbers of books and periodicals in the home generally give a substantial correlation with child IQ. But we cannot infer that they provide an independent stimulus to intellectual growth, since it may be merely that the possession of reading matter is more common among well educated parents, and such parents are more likely to stimulate their children's growth in many ways. Alternatively such parents are probably superior in intelligence and pass on better genes to their offspring. Again, parental socio-economic class (SES) always correlates around 0.30 with child IQ (Neff, 1938). In many studies the mean IQ of children of the top professional-executive groups of families approximates 1σ above 100, while the mean IQ of the children of the lowest labouring and unskilled group is about $\frac{1}{2}\sigma$ below 100 (cf. Terman and Merrill, 1937). Now it is usually taken for granted by most American writers that the superior environment of upper and middle class children is responsible. Nevertheless, as shown below, there is strong evidence of genetic differences between social class groups; hence this finding is uninterpretable.

Hoffman and Lippitt (1960) point out that we sadly lack an agreed taxonomy of the major family parameters which have most influence on child ability and personality. However, some progress has been made : thus parental education always gives higher correlations with child intelligence than does job status, wealth and material aspects of SES. According to Jones and Bayley, parental education correlates negatively with children's scores below 6 months, zero at 1 year, +0.40 and over by 3 years, rising to 0.60 and over by 6 years. Thus parental education is actually a better indication of later childhood IQ than are test results of children themselves in the first 3 years. This result too could be explained either by rate of maturation of children with differing genetic potentialities, or by the cumulative effects of home upbringing—the latter perhaps being less likely in so far as there is little increase in correlation after 6 years.

Several studies have obtained multiple measures of home variables. Thus Van Alstyne (1929) obtained the following correlations with child's M.A. at 3 years :

Mother's education	0.60	No of playmates in the	
Father's education	0.51	home	0.16
Opportunities for use of		Father reading to the	
constructive play mater-		child	0.06
ials	0.50	Nutritional index	−0.03
Hours spent by adults			
with child daily	0.32		

Wolf (cf. Bloom, 1964) obtained a multiple correlation as high as 0.76 when thirteen variables assessed in the homes were compared with group test IQs of 5th Grade children. These variables chiefly emphasized parental intellectual aspirations, provision of linguistic stimulation, and of learning opportunities and materials. Likewise E. Fraser (1959) obtained a multiple correlation of 0.69 among over 400 12-year-olds in Aberdeen with similar home variables, the major contribution being made by parental encouragement, parental education, small family size, and general family atmosphere of emotional security.

Other socio-economic indices such as rooms per family member likewise correlate with child ability (Scottish Council for Research in Education, 1953). But Wiseman (1964) found less influence nowadays than Burt did in his studies in the 1920s by sociological factors such as bad housing area, overcrowding, infant mortality, etc. More important than these economic conditions seemed to be the morale v. social disorganization of the neighbourhood, standards of maternal care, and quality of schooling. J. W. B. Douglas and his colleagues (1964, 1968) have published exhaustive follow-up studies of the abovementioned British sample, which indicate the cumulative effects of environmental and educational handicap, not merely in early childhood, but from 8 to 11, and 11 to 15 years. The achievement and intelligence scores of upper and lower SES groups tend to diverge further during these periods.

Now other writers such as Klineberg (1935) and M. Deutsch (1967) have claimed that deprived children, e.g., Negroes, fall more and more behind because early inferiority generates more frustration, bewilderment, poor motivation, and therefore greater inferiority. However Jensen (1974c) has thoroughly surveyed work on "cumulative deficit" or "progressive decrement", and found that the available evidence is technically defective, or inconclusive. Differences between whites and Negroes in raw test scores or school grades do increase with age, but not usually when expressed in terms of standard scores. Using comparisons of siblings to control for various sources of error, he showed that a small, just significant decrement occurred on Lorge-Thorndike Verbal IQ in older Negro boys, but it was not significant in girls, nor on Non-verbal IQ.

The small but consistent negative correlation of 0.2 to 0.3 found between child intelligence and size of family caused a good deal of concern in the 1930s, when Burt (1946) and others argued that the greater fertility of the less intelligent families would produce a progressive decline in national intelligence. In a survey of army recruits by Vernon (1951), the mean IQ of men from one- to two-child families was 106; whereas among those from families of 13 and over, it was 87. Also the differential was as marked on measures of g as on verbally loaded tests. However the Scottish Council for Research in Education carried out two surveys of the whole 11-year population of Scotland (1933, 1949), but found no decline in mean IQ over a 15-year period. The reasons for this negative finding are complex: the relatively low fertility of very low IQ individuals may have compensated, or improvements in child health and education over the period might mask any small genetic decline. Alternatively the correlation may merely reflect the likely possibility that children in larger families receive less parental attention and stimulation. Or it may be simply that children in general had become more accustomed to, and sophisticated at, tests at the later date.

The importance of education and of sophistication was indicated by Tuddenham's (1948) investigation of American army intelligence in World Wars I and II. A rise equivalent to over 10 points of IQ was found in the average recruit. Much the same increase was reported by Wheeler (1942) among East Tennessee children between 1930 and 1940, during which period there had been great improvements in cultural and educational conditions; though again the familiarization factor might be involved.

Birth order makes no consistent difference, except that first-born tend to get IQs $1\frac{1}{2}$ to 3 points higher than later born (cf. Record, McKeown and Edwards, 1969). There is also considerable evidence that they yield more high achievers than later born. This might be partly due to the fact that a greater percentage of first-born are naturally more frequent in small than large families; but it seems very plausible that such children get more talking to, and stimulation, from adults, and that parental aspirations regarding the child's education and career would be stronger. Thus an environmental influence is certainly indicated.

(2) LINGUISTIC FACTORS

Great interest has been taken in recent years in the linguistic stimulation that families of different SES provide, and in the nature of mother-child interactions. Bernstein (1961) has described contrasted language "codes"—the "formal" and the "public". The former is more impersonal and analytic, making possible precise description of experiences and their relationship; while the latter to a greater extent expresses emotions and personal relations through ungrammatical phrases and gestures. Middle class children can understand both codes, but their parents use the formal language for explaining concepts, giving information and reasoning, whereas lower class children are handicapped in intellectual and educational development because they are accustomed only to the public mode of discourse. The middle class child is encouraged to plan and organize rationally; but the lower class live more in the present and are subjected to arbitrary and inconsistent rewards and punishments. That is, the liguistic differences tend to reflect very different values which may well affect the building up of concepts and thinking skills. Bernstein and Young (1966) also noted contrasted attitudes among middle and working class mothers to children's toys. The former emphasize that they help children to find out about things, whereas the latter see them more as means of keeping children occupied while they (the mothers) get on with other chores.

Hess and Shipman (1965) similarly draw attention to the relative poverty of mother-child interactions in lower class families; and they contrast the cognitive environment of the middle class child, which focuses on the intrinsic demands of the task, with that of the deprived child, whose behaviour is controlled more by imperatives. Again Deutsch (1965) points out the lack of reinforcement of cognitive and linguistic achievement among the disadvantaged, adding that they learn to be inattentive in a noisy and disorganized environment. However Bernstein's work has been attacked, partly because he exaggerates by describing contrasted types, rather than recognizing formal linguistic stimulation as a matter of degree. Also such writers as Labov (1970) and Ginsburg (1972) refuse to accept that lower class, or—in the US —Negro, language is less competent than that of middle class children. It is different; yet in familiar social contexts it is as grammatical and fluent as standard English. Nevertheless the notion that intellectual development depends largely on child modelling and parental exemplification and reinforcement of perceptual and conceptual skills has become widely accepted.

It is relevant to mention R. L. Thorndike's interesting finding in renorming the Terman-Merrill test in 1973. He showed scores over 2–5 years had increased markedly since 1937, up to an equivalent of 10 IQ points. The average IQ on 1937 norms dropped back to 101 by age 10, and then rose again to 107 by 18 years. He suggests, plausibly, that a major factor in early acceleration is the impact of television, whereas the rise in adolescence could be accounted for by larger proportions of children staying on longer at school. Note that he is not claiming any overall rise among American youth in intelligence (as measured by Terman-Merrill), only an acceleration at certain stages of development. How far these rises generalize or transfer to everyday life intellectual functioning cannot, of course, be answered.

(3) PERCEPTUAL STIMULATION

Another popular environmental hypothesis is that perceptual deprivation, i.e. the lack of a variety of stimulating visual experience, toys, and opportunities to explore and experiment, retards the development of intelligence. This gains plausibility from Hebb's experiments on dogs and rats, and from the severe emotional and perceptual disturbances in human adults resulting from prolonged sensory deprivation. Elsewhere the present writer has queried this claim; for though lower working class and Negro homes are doubtless more meagre than middle class, children in the early stages of building up object constancy and other perceptual skills get plenty of visual experience, and are likely to create their own toys when bought ones are not available. A stronger case may be made, on the basis of cross-cultural evidence (cf. Vernon, 1969), for the effects of such deprivation on visuo-spatial abilities.

Recently Kagan and Klein (1973) have described child development in remote Guatemalan villages, where the young children up to about 8 get little attention or stimulation and appear to be passive, apathetic, and seriously retarded in any kind of problem solving. Yet by 11 years they are typically active, gay, and intellectually competent. Such evidence, they argue, runs counter to the conventional American view that cognitive development is wholly moulded by environment, and that early stimulation is particularly crucial. They suggest that the mind has its own "blueprint" for growth, which may be delayed, but not irremediably, by unfavourable circumstances.

(4) HEALTH AND NUTRITIONAL FACTORS

There are marked social class differences in prenatal care, nutrition, birth complications, infant mortality, liability to disease or physical and sensory defects, and mental retardation. The incidence of such conditions is greater in Negroes than whites, and greater still in underdeveloped countries. Naturally though, it is extremely difficult to disentangle cause and effect in such a complex syndrome, and much of the evidence from western countries is contradictory (cf. Jensen, 1973). It seems that nutrition in the prenatal and early postnatal months does not have significant effects on neurological and mental growth among whites. Thus Stein et al. (1972) tested some 20,000 Dutch recruits at age 19, many of whom had been subjected to severe undernourishment during the German occupation in 1944–5. There was a slight suggestion of increased incidence of low grade defect, but the Progressive Matrices scores showed no general and lasting retardation. On the other hand Harrell, Woodyard and Gates (1955) studied Negro or very low income white families, and gave some of the mothers vitamins or polynutrient dietary supplements before the birth of their children. At age 3–4 the children of these mothers averaged some 5 points higher in IQ than children whose mothers had received placebos. There is also no doubt that severe nutritional deficiencies associated with kwashiorkor in Africa are responsible for poorer brain development.

Stott (1960) has surveyed some fairly extensive evidence that maternal stress or anxiety, malnutrition, and certain diseases during pregnancy have harmful effects on the health, abilities and adjustment of the offspring (cf. also Lilienfeld and Pasamanick, 1956).

(5) CHILD UPBRINGING

Turning to affective factors, a great deal of information has been collected on the relations of parental handling and attitudes to the personality and abilities of children, through the long-term studies at Berkeley and at the Fels Institute. The results are complex and, with the rather small numbers, variable; also they tend to differ considerably for boys and girls, and at different ages. (It is an unsatisfactory research strategy to pick out the most favourable from among hundreds of correlations.) However it seems that mother characteristics related to Schaefer and Bayley's (1963) two dimensions Warmth v. Rejecting and Autonomy v. Control, when rated between 0 to 3 years, are associated with child ability. In boys, for example, mother Irritability, Punitiveness, Ignoring give negative correlations around 0.4 with intelligence from 5 to 18; whereas Egalitarianism, Positive Evaluation and Achievement Demand give positive coefficients. In girls, however, mother's Intrusiveness gives the highest (negative) correlation. On the whole, a warm-supportive emotional climate, but one which stresses independence and demands for achievement, seems most favourable (Bayley, 1965). Moss and Kagan (1961) and Sonntag, Baker and Nelson (1958) studied factors which correlate with IQ rise during childhood. The former authors report correlations of 0.49 for boys, 0.42 for girls, between Mother's Concern for Cognitive-Motor Development and gains between 6 and 10. Sonntag et al. find that children who are aggressive, competitive, non-conforming, and actively exploring, tend to show most IQ rises. Likewise Witkin et al. (1962) claim that the sons of mothers who encourage autonomy rather than social dependence and conformity, score more highly on field independence tests, which appear to measure a combination of g and spatial ability. An earlier study by Baldwin, Kalhorn and Breese (1945) had indicated that young children developed more intellectually in "democratic" climates than in families where the parents were over-authoritarian and rejecting, or over-protective and indulgent. Kent and Davis's (1957) cross-sectional rather than longitudinal study of 8-year-olds gives interesting confirmation. The mothers were classified, on the basis of interviews, as "Normal", "Demanding", "Over-anxious" or "Unconcerned". The highest mean child IQs, especially on verbal tests, were found in the "Demanding" group; the "Over-anxious" were near average on verbal but lower on performance tests, while the "Unconcerned" were low on both, particularly on verbal. It is of course possible that there were genetic differences between the contrasted groups.

A sidelight on family influence is provided by Conrad's and Jones's (1940) finding of practically the same parent-child IQ correlations, regardless of sex, when they tested almost all adults and children in several New England villages. One might have expected some reflection of intrafamilial relations, e.g., mother-child correlation greater than father-child; or mother-daughter and father-son greater than cross-sex pairs; and greater resemblance between same-sex siblings than between brothers and sisters.

Jones et al. (1971) reiterate the variability of IQs from childhood to adulthood, and go on to ask why many children of about average intelligence, with undistinguished school careers, end up as successful adults in creative professions and business; whereas others with good abilities and home support become "brittle, discontented and puzzled adults whose potentialities have not been actualized". Their evidence is impressionistic rather than statistical, but they point out various reasons why people are non-predictable. Many children react unexpectedly to family and environmental pressures because of differences in temperament or in level of maturity. During their early, and particularly their adolescent, growth they meet many frustrations and traumatic problems, and learn to cope more or less successfully, and thus build up well-adjusted personalities, or the opposite. Throughout this process, their cognitive skills may be enhanced or depressed, and although we can sometimes observe this happening and find plausible explanations in the individual case, we do not know enough about the interplay of individual dynamics with life experiences to be able to control or predict cognitive development, apart from a few rather vague generalizations such as those listed above.

(6) EFFECTS OF SEVERE DEPRIVATION

Spitz (1946) has described the appalling effects of early upbringing in a hospital with a minimum of adult care—apathy, failure in psychomotor maturation, even resulting in death. W. Dennis and Narjarian's (1957) observations in a Lebanese children's hospital were similar. In the absence of any control group we do not know, of course, whether some of these children were not constitutionally low-grade defectives. However Skeels's (1966) long-term follow-up of twenty-four orphan children did meet this objection. They were first tested at around $1\frac{1}{2}$ years when living in a highly unstimulating institution. Thirteen of them were transferred to another home, where they were cared for and much played with by older mentally defective girls; subsequently most of them were adopted into good foster homes. When traced twenty-five years later, the thirteen transferred cases were normal, self-supporting adults, holding a wide range of employments. Whereas the eleven who had been left in the original hospital were all still institutionalized, or in very low-grade jobs. Actual test scores are available only in childhood, and thus rather untrustworthy; but the later adjustment data bear out Skeels's claim of an average rise in the transferred group of 30 IQ points or more.

Equally striking is an account by Koluchova (1972) of two twin boys who, up to the age of 7, were brought up almost as animals with scarcely any human contacts. When first rescued they were severely sub-normal, with IQs—in so far as testable—of about 40. But after four years of normal upbringing they tested at 94 and 95, suggesting a rise of over 50 points. Stone (1954) comments on two other similar cases, one of whom did, the other did not, recover from the effects of extreme isolation. He points out that the first one lived with a deaf mute mother; hence although she developed no speech till removed from this environment, she had experienced social interaction. Possibly the Koluchova twins were remediable since at least they experienced one another's company.

According to John Bowlby, prolonged separation from the mother, e.g., through hospitalization of mother or child, produces intellectual impairment as well as abnormal emotional development. However his own follow-up study (1956) of such cases failed to support this, presumably because the children still had social contacts and adult care from mother substitutes. Goldfarb's (1947) study of adolescents who had been institutionalized during their first three years, and others who were placed in foster homes, did reveal considerably lower intelligence, language and conceptual development, as well as more emotional disturbance in the former group.

Another investigation which is much quoted is that of Heber in Milwaukee; however, few details have been published, so that evaluation of its findings is difficult (cf. Clarke and Clarke, 1974). This involved an all-out effort to improve the child care, cognitive and linguistic stimulation from birth onwards of twenty children of mentally retarded mothers. Under normal conditions of slum upbringing they would be expected to achieve a mean IQ of about 80. However, from 3 months they attended a centre where a specially stimulating environment was provided for seven hours a day, five days a week. Simultaneously their mothers were given an educational programme including home-making and child-rearing. Compared with a control group of twenty similar children who received no special treatment, their scores on the Gesell scale up to 14 months were the same; but on preschool intelligence scales between 2 and $4\frac{1}{2}$ years, Heber claims mean IQs of 122.6 in the experimental, 95.2 in the controls, a difference of 27.4 points. Further testing at 6–7 placed them at IQ 111, though still much superior to the controls. Heber agrees that the programme will have to continue if the gain is to be maintained. Thus we cannot tell as yet how far genetic lack has been overcome by extra stimulation. One might comment, also, that it would be quite impracticable to supply similar treatment to all deprived children.

In summary, then, severe social and linguistic deprivation, particularly in the early years, do markedly affect the development of Intelligence B, though at the same time children are remarkably resilient. They can survive when the conditions are not too extreme, and may very largely catch up if removed to more normal surroundings, even after several years. The evidence does not support the notion of critical periods for the acquisition of intellectual skills, comparable to those that Hebb and others have demonstrated in the growth of sensorimotor and perceptual skills.

(7) FOSTER HOME STUDIES

The evidence from such studies is very difficult to interpret, and little advance has been made since the work of Burks, Leahy and the Iowa group in the 1920s–40s, which is well summarized by Jones (1954). It is almost impossible to avoid distortion by selective adoption (e.g., more educated foster parents looking for good heredity, health and early development before adoption). Also any tests applied much before 5 years are too unreliable and invalid to provide good control data.

However it is generally found that children transferred to foster homes tend to gain in intelligence by about 10 IQ points, or even up to 20. Yet it is not true that they come to resemble the foster parents in intelligence level, since the correlation between their scores and foster parent ability is lower than that with the ability of their true parents who have not brought them up. Skodak and Skeels (1949) obtained a coefficient of 0.38 for foster child with true mother's IQ, and Lawrence (1931) likewise found a correlation with true father's occupational level. According to Erlenmeyer-Kimling and Jarvik (1963), the median child-parent correlation for children reared in their own homes is 0.50, and for children with foster parents only 0.20. Again the correlation between unrelated children brought up in the same home averages 0.23, and even this may be an overestimate on account of selective adoption. Thus the evidence supports limited environmental effects of the kind of home, but also suggests stronger genetic determination.

(8) THE INFLUENCE OF EDUCATION

One would anticipate that the mental stimulation most children get at school would be as important an influence in the development of their intelligence from 5 years on as the home, or more so. But this is not necessarily so, since schooling that is highly formal and mechanical might train children in rote learning skills, and the home or leisure activities provide more opportunity for the kind of discovery learning that Piaget emphasizes. Nevertheless cross-cultural studies such as those of Bruner *et al.* (1966) frequently indicate better performance (often on Piaget-type tasks) among children in developing countries who get even poor quality schooling as against those who get none. Vernon (1969) quotes a well-controlled study by C. Ramphal of Indian children in South Africa, which indicated that absence of schooling during years 7 to 9 brought about a retardation in intellectual growth equivalent to 5 IQ points a year. Much earlier, Gordon's (1923) investigation of canal boat and gipsy children pointed in the same direction These children developed normally in intelligence up to about age 6, but thereafter, when they failed to get any schooling, they progressed more slowly so that their IQs dropped.

Lorge (1955) and Husén (1951) have shown, in the US and Sweden respectively, that children of initially the same IQ continue to grow intellectually so long as their secondary or tertiary schooling continues. Husén found that, compared with 10-year level, recruits tested at 20 years were 12 IQ points higher if they had completed secondary school and matriculation, than those with no secondary schooling. We have already mentioned the effects of schooling on the age to which growth continues. Vernon (1957b) likewise found that quality of schooling made a difference by comparing boys tested at 11 and at 14 years. Those going to the more stimulating grammar schools in the area averaged 7 IQ points higher than those attending poorer secondary modern schools, after allowing for initial differences; indeed there was a 12-point difference between the best and worst school. However the school quality factor would be confounded here with the greater pressures and encouragement in the home from which the grammar school pupils came.

Several studies were carried out in the 1920s-30s into alleged effects of nursery school attendance (cf. Stoddard, 1940; Goodenough, 1940). The results were inconsistent, and though the Iowa group claimed striking improvements these might be largely, if not wholly, explained by the greater sophistication and co-operation of nursery school children in taking tests, or by the training effect of nursery school activities on materials very similar to those included in the tests. Selective differences between attenders and non-attenders are also extremely difficult to control.

A massive attempt at compensatory education for deprived children was instituted in the USA in the 1960s, under the label Head Start. It was hoped to counteract retardation due to poor environment by giving children a few weeks or months of stimulating preschool training. The programmes in different parts of the country were very various, and many yielded no worthwhile follow-up data. But among those that did compare the experimental group with controls, several showed no difference in later ability or achievement, or there was a temporary improvement of 5 to 10 IQ points, which disappeared by a year later. A few schemes such as Bereiter and Engelmann's (1966), which concentrated on intensive training of certain scholastic skills rather than on improving all-round intelligence, appeared more promising. The failure of the operation was often attributed to the schooling being "too little and too late" to compensate for five years of upbringing in a deprived environment. Nevertheless psychologists who supported the project had clearly expected, in view of our knowledge of environmental factors and of Piaget's theories, that it would work (cf. Hunt, 1968). On the other hand Jensen (1969) attributed the results to disregard of the strength of genetic determination of ability.

Since the publication of Rosenthal and Jacobson's investigation (1968), and the unwarranted publicity that it received, intelligence tests have been widely criticized on the grounds that children's IQs will rise if teachers believe them to be bright and treat them accordingly. K. B. Clark (1963) argues that teachers' beliefs that disadvantaged children are inferior makes them more so. In other words the predictive value of the tests is a self-fulfilling prophecy. Unfortunately the press did not publicize the criticisms by psychologists of technical faults in Rosenthal's study, and the complete failure of subsequent, better controlled, replications to support it (cf. Claiborn, 1969). It seems highly probable that teachers' expectations of good school achievement may fulfil themselves partly because they provide greater reinforcement and stimulus to apparently promising pupils. General intellectual growth and test scores might be similarly influenced, but there is no evidence as yet to support this, other than the correlations, noted above, with high parental aspirations and encouragement.

(9) CHILDREN'S CREATION OF THEIR OWN ENVIRONMENT

Probably a more important factor, which is habitually ignored by supporters of environmental views, is that to a large extent children fashion their own environments. Those with favourable genes and early development are more likely to explore and experiment, and to seek stimulation by questioning adults, or from toys, books, etc. Whereas the initially dull child is more often passive and restricted in his interests. Again the parents of the former, who realize his potentiality, are more likely to provide opportunities, together with more extended and higher quality education. Thus it is not only true that education stimulates ability, but also that ability provokes better education.

(10) URBAN–RURAL AND ETHNIC GROUP DIFFERENCES

This area is so complex and controversial that we can attempt only a brief outline. Children in rural areas generally score lower than urban dwellers. For example in standardizing the 1937 Terman-Merrill, there was a 10-point IQ difference at ages 6–14 (McNemar, 1942). This is commonly attributed to lower stimulation, less need for rapidity of thought, often poorer education, which might affect mental growth. But it might also arise because the more progressive and intelligent families tend to migrate to towns, or because of genetic class differences in so far as farm labour is relatively unskilled, and the proportion of professionals and executives is small (except within commuting distances of urban centres). In fact, though, results vary considerably in different parts of the world. For example in Scotland, children in rural areas score slightly higher than those in large cities or in the industrial belt (Scottish Council for Research in Education, 1949). Probably this is due to the bad slum conditions, and the inclusion of considerable proportions of families of Irish peasant ancestry, in the industrial areas.

Racial and ethnic comparisons fell into disrepute when it was realized that tests devised for children in western cultures would be grossly unfair to children in other societies whose life experiences, values, perceptual and conceptual skills might be very different (cf. Vernon, 1969). The list of average scores on the Army Alpha test obtained from recruits of different ethnic origin was severely criticized, since it was obvious that the groups which headed the list, such as English, German and French, had far greater economic and educational advantage than those at the bottom such as south-east European and American Negro. Investigations by Klineberg (1935) and Lee (1951) showed that Negro children whose families had migrated from the southern states to New York or Philadelphia obtained higher IQs according to length of residence in the northern cities, where economic and educational conditions were better. However the maximum gain was some 6–8 IQ points, so that they did not make up the full 15–20 points which usually differentiate white and black means.

More puzzling are reports from Lieblich *et al.* (1972) in Israel, and Barron and Young (1970) concerning Italian immigrants to the US. Both indicated that the descendants of quite backward peasant immigrant parents catch up with local intelligence norms in a generation or two. Interpretation is difficult since there are no adequate controls, and regression effects alone would tend to produce some rises in the second and later generations. But the findings certainly seem to contradict the notion that certain ethnic subgroups carry poor genes and that their descendants retain this inferiority in a new, more stimulating environment.

In 1951, a group of expert consultants to UNESCO issued a declaration which concluded : "there is no proof that the groups of mankind differ in their innate mental characteristics, whether in respect of intelligence or temperament". But they failed to add that there is also no proof that such differences do not exist, and common observation would suggest that, just as groups differ in height and other physical attributes, so also some have exploited their environments more effectively or intelligently than others.

(11) NEGRO–WHITE DIFFERENCES

By far the greatest number of cross-cultural comparisons have been made between American whites and blacks. Shuey (1958) published a comprehensive survey, bringing out the consistency of differences in intelligence and achievement at all ages except preschool, together with the very considerable overlap of distributions. As we saw earlier, tests for very young children measure a psychomotor rather than an intellectual *g*, and blacks are accelerated over whites in several aspects of psychomotor development. In general Shuey favours a genetic interpretation of the findings. However Dreger and Miller (1960) pointed out the complexity of conditions that might affect test performance, and indicated that no definite conclusions regarding heredity and environment were warranted.

Hence the outcry when Arthur Jensen (1969) claimed, on the basis of twin studies and other evidence, that genetic factors contribute four times as much to variance in intelligence among whites as do environmental factors; and went on to state as "a reasonable hypothesis that genetic factors are strongly implicated" in the mean black–white difference. There is no need to comment here on the violence of the controversy that ensued, or the attempts to suppress free discussion and further scientific investigation of genetic influences. Much of the evidence that we have outlined above is soundly established, and this had persuaded many, even a majority, of American and British psychologists and sociologists to take it for granted that Negro–white, or social class, differences were wholly environmental in origin. On the other hand, many environmentalist claims, and interpretations of the available data, are logically weak, or virtually untestable. We have pointed out already that the existence of a correlation between certain environmental conditions and IQ does not prove causation. But when such explanations are disproved, the environmentalist is apt to shift his ground and think up some other possible influence. Such indefinitely extensible theories and *ad hoc* patching are scientifically valueless (cf. Urbach, 1974).

For example, Jensen (1973) showed that poor economic conditions as such could not satisfactorily account for the Negro-white difference, since Indian and Mexican Americans, who in fact live under even worse conditions than blacks, yet score more highly than blacks on non-verbal intelligence tests. Thus the emphasis has now shifted to the inferiority feelings of blacks, brought about by generations of discrimination against them by the white majority. In fact, on tests of positive *v.* negative self-concept, blacks tend to score higher than whites. Moreover, notwithstanding some claims that Negroes feel threatened when tested by a white tester (cf. Katz, 1963), the better planned investigations on the whole disconfirm any such effect of race of tester, or of poorer motivation to succeed among black children (cf. Sattler, 1970; Jensen, 1974a).

Another important point made by Jensen (1973) is that so many factors in upbringing and environment appear to relate to intellectual growth, that it is tempting to conclude that, in combination, they would account for the whole of the differences. In fact, however, such factors and conditions tend to be quite highly intercorrelated. Thus the situation is the same as in a multiple regression equation, where a few variables give as good a prediction as possible, and additional variables do little or nothing to raise the multiple correlation coefficient.

VIII. SUMMARY OF EVIDENCE FOR GENETIC FACTORS

What then are the main lines of evidence for genetic factors which environmentalist psychologists tend to ignore or deny?

Studies of identical twins reared apart are less convincing than Burt and Jensen imply, since it is impossible to control selective placement (i.e. the homes in which the separated twins are reared tend to be similar, not random). Also such twins have been subjected to the same prenatal environment and are often not separated till some weeks after birth. Results for only 122 cases have been published, and doubts have been cast on the adequacy of Burt's data (cf. Jensen, 1974b). For the other sixty-nine cases, the mean correlation is still 0.74, and if this is compared with the figure of 0.23 for unrelated children reared together (which also tends to be boosted by selective placement), it seems clear that genetic similarity is far more powerful than environmental. On the other hand the difference between 0.74 and the mean figure for identicals reared together of 0.87 certainly shows that common environment is influential, which Jensen himself admits. Jinks and Eaves (1974) have recently published a sophisticated statistical analysis of data for all degrees of kinship (not just separated identical twins), and arrive at a heritability estimate of 0.68—that is a 2 to 1, rather than Burt and Jensen's 4 to 1, ratio. A well-reasoned exposition of the arguments against Jensen's conclusions is given by Block and Dworkin (1974).

An entirely different line of argument may be based on the resemblances and differences between siblings, and between children and parents. The conventional correlation of 0.50 can, of course, be attributed to common heredity, or common environment, or both. But the discrepancies are often quite large, and it seems highly improbable that upbringing could be so dissimilar for different children in the same family. But variations between offspring would be expected on genetic theory, just as they occur in plants or sub-human mammals.

Still more convincing is the evidence, already cited above, that the IQs of foster children continue to correlate more highly with the ability of the true parents than with that of the foster parents, although the figure is naturally lower than that for children brought up by their own parents.

An important consideration, even if inconclusive, is that physical attributes such as height are certainly mainly genetic, though subject to some modification by healthy or unhealthy upbringing; thus there seems no reason to suppose that neurological attributes, which must underlie intellectual growth, follow different biological principles. Moreover rats and dogs can be bred to ennance such abilities as maze-running, retrieving, etc., so why not humans?

Several other contributory lines of evidence are cited by Jensen, for example the demonstration, in a well-controlled study by Schull and Neel (1965) of a 7-point deficit in mean IQ of the children of first-cousin marriages, which could only be explained by the genetically harmful effects of inbreeding. In respect of Negro-white differences, the finding most difficult to account for environmentally is that the siblings or the offspring of highly intelligent Negroes tend to regress—not to the white mean IQ of 100, but to the Negro population mean of about 85. Hence, for example, children of upper middle class Negro parents actually score slightly lower than children of lower class whites, though surely the environmental circumstances of the former must be far superior to those of the latter.

IX. DISCUSSION

These many types of evidence demonstrate beyond reasonable doubt the importance of genetic factors in intelligence, at least within a single culture such as whites, though they should not be taken to substantiate any one very high figure, such as 80 per cent, for the variance fixed by heredity. Jensen himself appears willing to accept a somewhat lower figure.

He has also frequently pointed out, as have his critics, that there is no one universal figure for heritability; any result so far obtained applies only to the particular population studied and the particular tests. The range of environments within which the population lives is a crucial consideration. Despite the obvious differences between white families at different socio-economic levels, and variations in patterns of upbringing, the American and British white environment is rather homogeneous, in that almost all children see similar objects and people, hear a common language, and receive a fairly standardized education. But if heritability could be calculated for the whole range of mankind, from Caucasian upper class to Australian aboriginal, the environmental percentage would be far larger. Put another way, we cannot legitimately extrapolate from heritability within an homogeneous group to differences between it and another group reared in a markedly different environment. Jensen argues that it is unlikely that the white–black environmental variance is so large as to negate the likelihood of any genetic differences. But the issue must remain in doubt, and extremist statements in either direction are unwarranted.

A further commonly stated objection to Jensen's heritability estimate is that heredity and environment are not independent factors contributing to growth; there is a complex interaction between them from conception onwards. Biologically, this is true, and Jensen accepts as obvious that the phenotype is a product of their interplay. (He actually states that there is little or no "interaction", but is here using it in the statistical sense, i.e. no irregularity in the effects of environment at different genotypic levels.) Other geneticists, however, prefer different models which yield somewhat different results (cf. Jencks et al. 1972; Jinks and Eaves, 1974). In particular Jensen did not separate off the covariance or joint effects of genotype and environment, which is probably substantial, since parents who pass on better genes usually provide a better environment. In a later paper (1975), he did estimate it from mono- and dizygotic twin comparisons, but arrived at a rather low figure of 7 per cent for covariance, 65 per cent for genotype and 28 per cent for environment. Thus there is reasonable doubt regarding the applicability of an additive analysis of variance model to so complex a construct as human intelligence.

Nevertheless it still seems meaningful to investigate how far such variations in environment as we have at our command account for variations in the phenotype—the IQ; and how far genetic differences affect it. If we conclude that the latter is more influential than the former (within any one environmentally-homogeneous group), this by no means rules out the possibility that future improvements in social and educational conditions could substantially increase the average intellectual level of the population (much as putting orphan children in foster homes tends to raise their average level). But as the genetically well-endowed would probably benefit as much as, or more than, the less endowed, the genetic variance might remain the same or, as Herrnstein (1974) points out, even increase.

Finally we would urge that the evidence supporting genetic, and that supporting environmental, interpretations are much less irreconcilable than might appear. Jensen claims that the 20 per cent he allows for environmental variance will cover such observed environmental differences as those noted by Newman et al. (1937) between separated twins, the data on effects of foster homes or of schooling, and even Skeel's follow-up. If we allow a 2 to 1 rather than 4 to 1 ratio, the Standard Deviation of environmental components of the IQ would reach 8.67, which implies that very good and very poor environments, which might be 5σ apart on a scale of stimulatingness, would produce a mean of 43 IQ points. Further it is often forgotten that all genetic studies show lower heritability for scholastic achievement, and for personality measures, than for IQ. So that while genetic differences are still of considerable importance in a person's educational, occupational and life career, factors of upbringing and environment are likely to play an even more important part.

REFERENCES

Anderson, J. E. (1939). The limitations of infant and preschool tests in the measurement of intelligence. *Journal of Psychology, 8,* 351–79.

Baldwin, A. L., Kalhorn, J. and Breese, F. H. (1945). Patterns of parent behavior. *Psychological Monographs, 58,* No. 268.

Barron, F. and Young, H. B. (1970). Rome and Boston: a tale of two cities. *Journal of Cross-Cultural Psychology, 1,* 91–114.

Bartlett, F. C. (1932). *Remembering.* Cambridge: Cambridge University Press.

Bayley, N. (1949). Consistency and variability in the growth of intelligence from birth to eighteen. *Journal of General Psychology, 75,* 165–96.

Bayley, N. (1955). On the growth of intelligence. *American Psychologist, 10,* 805–18.

Bayley, N. (1965). Research in child development: a longitudinal perspective. *Merrill-Palmer Quarterly, 11,* 183–208.

Bereiter, C. and Engelmann, S. (1966). *Teaching Disadvantaged Children in the Preschool.* Englewood Cliffs, N.J.: Prentice-Hall.

Bernstein, B. B. (1961). Social class and linguistic development: a theory of social learning. In A. H. Halsey (Ed.), *Education, Economy and Society,* pp. 288–314. Glencoe: Free Press.

Bernstein, B. B. and Young, D. (1966). Some aspects of the relationship between communication and performance in tests. In J. E. Meade and A. S. Parkes (Eds.), *Genetic and Environmental Factors in Human Ability,* pp. 15–23. Edinburgh: Oliver and Boyd.

Biggs, J. B. (1968). *Information and Human Learning.* Australia: Cassell.

Block, N. J. and Dworkin, G. (1974). IQ: heritability and inequality. *Philosophy and Public Affairs, 3,* 331–407; *4,* 40–99.

Bloom, B. S. (1964). *Stability and Change in Human Characteristics.* New York: Wiley.

Bowlby, J. *et al.* (1956). The effects of mother-child separation: a follow-up study. *British Journal of Medical Psychology, 29,* 211–47.

Bruner, J. S. (1965). The growth of the mind. *American Psychologist, 20,* 1007–17.

Bruner, J. S. *et al.* (1966). *Studies in Cognitive Growth.* New York: Wiley.

Burt, C. L. (1946). *Intelligence and Fertility.* London: Eugenics Society.

Burt, C. L. (1949). The structure of the mind: a review of the results of factor analysis. *British Journal of Educational Psychology, 19,* 100–11, 176–99.

Cattell, R. B. (1963) Theory of fluid and crystallized intelligence: a critical experiment. *Journal of Educational Psychology, 54,* 1–22.

Cattell, R. B. (1971). *Abilities: Their Structure, Growth and Action.* Boston: Houghton Mifflin.

Claiborn, W. L. (1969). Expectancy effects in the classroom: a faliure to replicate. *Journal of Educational Psychology, 60,* 377–83.

Clark, K. B. (1963). Educational stimulation of racially disadvantaged children. In A. H. Passow (Ed.), *Education in Depressed Areas,* pp. 142–62. New York: Teachers College Columbia.

Clarke, A. D. B. and Clarke, A. M. (1974). Mental retardation and behavioural change. *British Medical Bulletin, 30,* No. 2, 179–85.

Clarke, A. M., Cooper, G. M. and Clarke, A. D. B. (1967). Task complexity and transfer in the development of cognitive structures. *Journal of Experimental Child Psychology, 5,* 562–76.

Cohen, J. (1959) The factorial study of the WISC at ages 7–6, 10–6 and 13–6 *J. Consulting Psychology, 23,* 285–99.

Conrad, H. S. and Jones, H. E. (1940). A second study of familial resemblances in intelligence. *Thirty-ninth Yearbook, National Society for the Study of Education,* Part II, pp. 97–141.

Cronbach, L. J. (1970). *Essentials of Psychological Testing* (3rd ed.). New York: Harper and Row.

Dearborn, W. F. and Rothney, J. W. M. (1941). *Predicting the Child's Development.* Cambridge, Mass.: SciArt.

Dennis, W. and Narjarian, P. (1957). Infant development under environmental handicap. *Psychological Monographs, 71,* No. 436.

Deutsch, M. (1965). The role of social class in language development and cognition. *American Journal of Orthopsychiatry, 35,* 78–88.

Deutsch, M. (1967). *The Disadvantaged Child.* New York: Basic Books.

Douglas, J. W. B. (1964). *The Home and the School.* London: McGibbon and Kee.

Douglas, J. W. B., Ross, J. M. and Simpson, H. R. (1968). *All Our Future.* London: Davies.

Dreger, R. M. and Miller, K. S. (1960). Comparative psychological studies of negroes and whites in the United States. *Psychological Bulletin, 57,* 361–402.

Dye, N. W. and Very, P. S. (1968). Growth change in factorial structure by age and sex. *Genetic Psychology Monographs, 78,* 55–88.

Erlenmeyer-Kimling, L. and Jarvik, L. F. (1963). Genetics and intelligence: a review, *Science, 142,* 1477–9.

Estes, W. K. (1974). Learning theory and intelligence. *American Psychologist, 29,* 740–9.

Eysenck, H. J. (1967). Intelligence: a theoretical and experimental approach. *British Journal of Educational Psychology, 37,* 81–98.

Ferguson, G. A. (1954). On learning and human ability. *Canadian Journal of Psychology, 8,* 95–112.

Foulds, G. A. and Raven, J. C. (1948). Normal changes in the mental abilities of adults as age advances. *Journal of Mental Science, 94,* 133–42.

Fraser, E. (1959). *Home Environment and the School.* London: University of London Press.

Galton, F. (1869). *Hereditary Genius.* London: Macmillan.

Garrett, H. E. (1946). A developmental theory of intelligence. *American Psychologist, 1,* 372–8.

Getzels, J. W. and Jackson, P. W. (1962). *Creativity and Intelligence.* New York: Wiley.

Ginsburg, H. (1972). *The Myth of the Deprived Child.* Englewood Cliffs, N.J.: Prentice-Hall.

Glaser, R. (1972). Individuals and learning: the new aptitudes. *Educational Researcher, 1,* 5–12.

Goldfarb, W. (1947). Variations in adolescent adjustment of institutionally reared children. *American Journal of Orthopsychiatry, 17,* 449–57.

Goodenough, F. L. (1940). Some special problems of nature-nurture research. *Thirty-ninth Yearbook, National Society for the Study of Education,* Part I, pp. 367–84.

Gordon, H. (1923). Mental and scholastic tests among retarded children. *Board of Education Pamphlet,* No. 44. London: HMSO.

Guilford, J. P. (1967). *The Nature of Human Intelligence.* New York: McGraw-Hill.

Harrell, R. F., Woodyard, E. and Gates, A. I. (1955). *The Effect of Mothers' Diet on the Intelligence of Offspring.* New York: Teachers College, Columbia.

Hebb, D. O. (1948). *The Organization of Behavior.* New York: Wiley.

Heinis, H. (1926). A personal constant. *Journal of Educational Psychology, 17,* 163–86.

Herrnstein, R. J. (1973). *IQ in the Meritocracy.* London: Allen Lane.

Hess, R. D. and Shipman, V. C. (1965). Early experience and the socialization of cognitive modes in children. *Child Development, 36,* 869–86.

Hoffman, L. W. and Lippitt, R. (1960). The measurement of family life variables. In P. H. Mussen (Ed.), *Handbook of Research Methods in Child Development,* pp. 945–1013. New York: Wiley.

Hofstaetter, P. R. (1954). The changing composition of "intelligence": a study in T-technique. *Journal of Genetic Psychology, 85,* 159–62.

Honzik, M. P., Macfarlane, J. W. and Allen, L. (1948). The stability of mental test performances between two and eighteen years. *Journal of Experimental Education, 17,* 309–24.

Hunt, J. McV. (1961). *Intelligence and Experience.* New York: Ronald Press.

Hunt, J. McV.(1968). Environment, development and scholastic achievement. In M. Deutsch, I. Katz and A. R. Jensen (Eds.), *Social Class, Race and Psychological Development,* pp. 293–330. New York: Holt, Rinehart and Winston.

Husén, T. (1951). The influence of schooling upon IQ. *Theoria, 17,* 61–88.

Jencks, C. et al. (1972) *Inequality: A Reassessment of the Effects of Family and Schooling in America.* New York: Basic Books.

Jensen, A. R. (1969). How much can we boost IQ and scholastic achievement? *Harvard Educational Review, 39,* 1–123.

Jensen, A. R. (1973). *Educability and Group Differences.* New York: Harper and Row.

Jensen, A. R. (1974a). The effect of race of examiner in mental test scores of white and black pupils. *Journal of Educational Measurement, 11,* 1–14.

Jensen, A. R. (1974b). Kinship correlations reported by Sir Cyril Burt. *Behavior Genetics, 4,* 1–28.

Jensen, A. R. (1974c). Cumulative deficit: a testable hypothesis. *Developmental Psychology, 10,* 996–1019.

Jensen, A. R. (1975). The problem of genotype-environment correlation in the estimation of heritability from monozygotic and dizygotic twins. *Acta Geneticae Medicae et Gemellologiae.*

Jinks, J. L. and Eaves, L. J. (1974). IQ and inequality. *Nature, 248,* 287–9.

Jones, H. E. (1954). The environment and mental development. In L. Carmichael (Ed.), *Manual of Child Psychology* (2nd. ed.), pp. 631–96. New York: Wiley.

Jones, M. C., Bayley, N., Macfarlane, J. W. and Honzik, M. P. (1971). *The Course of Human Development.* Waltham, Mass.: Xerox Publishing.

Kagan, J. and Klein, R. E. (1973). Cross-cultural perspectives on early development. *American Psychologist, 28,* 947–61.

Katz, I. and Greenbaum, C. (1963). Effects of anxiety, threat, and racial environment on task performance of negro college students. *Journal of Abnormal and Social Psychology, 66,* 562–7.

Kent, N. and Davis, D. R. (1957). Discipline in the home and intellectual development. *British Journal of Medical Psychology, 30,* 27–33.

Klineberg, O. (1935). *Negro Intelligence and Selective Migration.* New York: Columbia University Press.

Koluchova, J. (1972). Severe deprivation in twins: a case study. *Journal of Child Psychology and Psychiatry, 13,* 107–14.

Labov, W. (1970). The logic of nonstandard English. In F. Williams (Ed.), *Language and Poverty,* pp. 153–89. Chicago: Markham Publishing.

Lawrence, E. M. (1931). An investigation into the relation between intelligence and inheritance. *British Journal of Psychology Monograph Supplement,* No. 16.

Lee, E. S. (1951). Negro intelligence and selective migration: a Philadelphia test of the Klineberg hypothesis. *American Sociological Review, 16,* 227–33.

Lieblich, A., Ninio, A. and Kugelmass, S. (1972). Effects of ethnic origin and parental SES on WPPSI performance of preschool children in Israel. *Journal of Cross-Cultural Psychology, 3,* 159–68.

Lilienfeld, A. M. and Pasamanick, B. (1956). The association of maternal and fetal factors with the development of mental deficiency. II. *American Journal of Mental Deficiency, 60,* 557–69.

Lorge, I. (1955). Schooling makes a difference. *Teachers College Record, 46,* 483–92.

McNemar, Q. (1942). *The Revision of the Stanford-Binet Scale.* Boston: Houghton Mifflin.

Miller, G. A., Galanter, E. and Pribram, K. H. (1960). *Plans and the Structure of Behavior.* New York: Holt.

Moss, H. A. and Kagan, J. (1961). Stability of achievement and recognition seeking behavior from early childhood through adulthood. *Journal of Abnormal and Social Psychology, 68,* 504–13.

Neff, W. S. (1938). Socio-economic status and intelligence: a critical survey. *Psychological Bulletin, 35,* 727–57.

Newman, H. H., Freeman, F. N. and Holzinger, K. J. (1937). *Twins: A Study of Heredity and Environment.* Chicago: University of Chicago Press.

Piaget, J. (1950). *The Psychology of Intelligence.* London: Routledge and Kegan Paul.

Rasch, G. (1960). *Probabilistic Models for some Intelligence and Attainment Tests.* Copenhagen: Danish Institute for Educational Research.

Record, R. G., McKeown, T. and Edwards, J. H. (1969). The relation of measured intelligence to birth order and maternal age. *Annals of Human Genetics, 33,* 61–9.

Rosenthal, R. and Jacobson, L. (1968). *Pygmalion in the Classroom.* New York: Holt, Rinehart and Winston.

Ryle, G. (1949). *The Concept of Mind.* London: Hutchinson.

Sattler, J. (1970). Racial "experimenter" effects in experimentation, testing, interviewing and psychotherapy. *Psychological Bulletin, 73,* 137–60.

Schaefer, E. S. and Bayley, N. (1963). Maternal behavior, child behavior, and their intercorrelations from infancy through adolescence. *Monographs of Society for Research in Child Development, 22,* No. 87.

Schaie, K. W. and Strother, C. R. (1968). A cross-sequential study of age changes in cognitive behavior. *Psychological Bulletin, 70,* 671–80.

Schull, W. J. and Neel, J. V. (1965). *The Effects of Inbreeding on Japanese Children.* New York: Harper and Row.

Scottish Council for Research in Education (1933). *The Intelligence of Scottish Children*. London: University of London Press.

Scottish Council for Research in Education (1949). *The Trend of Scottish Intelligence*. London: University of London Press.

Scottish Council for Research in Education (1953). *Social Implications of the 1947 Scottish Mental Survey*. London: University of London Press.

Shuey, A. M. (1958). *The Testing of Negro Intelligence*. Virginia: Bell, Lynchburg.

Skeels, H. M. (1966). Adult status of children with contrasting early life experiences: a follow-up study, *Monographs of Society for Research in Child Development, 31*, No. 105.

Skodak, M. and Skeels, H. M. (1949). A final follow-up study of one hundred adopted children. *Journal of Genetic Psychology, 75*, 85–125.

Sontag, L. W., Baker, C. T. and Nelson, V. L. (1958). Mental growth and personality development: a longitudinal study. *Monographs of Society for Research in Child Development, 23*, No. 68.

Spearman, C. (1904). "General intelligence", objectively determined and measured. *American Journal of Psychology, 15,* 201–93.

Spearman, C. (1923). *The Nature of "Intelligence" and the Principles of Cognition*. London: Macmillan.

Spearman, C. (1927). *The Abilities of Man*. London: Macmillan.

Spitz, R. A. (1946). Anaclitic depression: an inquiry into the gensis of psychiatric conditions in early childhood. In A. Freud (Ed.), *The Psychoanalytic Study of the Child*. New York: International Universities Press.

Stein, Z., Susser, M., Saenger, G. and Marolla, F. (1972). Nutrition and mental performance. *Science, 178*, 708–13.

Stoddard, G. D. and Wellman, B. L. (1940) Environmental and the IQ. *Thirty-ninth Yearbook, National Society for the Study of Education,* Part I, pp. 405–42.

Stone, L. J. (1954). A critique of studies of infant isolation. *Child Development, 25*, 9–20.

Stott, D. H. (1960). Interaction of heredity and environment in regard to "Measured Intelligence". *British Journal of Educational Psychology, 30*, 95–102.

Stott, D. H. (1971). Behavioral aspects of learning disabilities: *assessment and remediation. Experimental Publications System, 11*, No. 400–36.

Terman, L. M. and Merrill, M. A. (1937). *Measuring Intelligence*. Boston: Houghton Mifflin.

Terman, L. M. and Oden, M. (1959). *The Gifted Group at Mid-Life*. Stanford, California: Stanford University Press.

Thomson, G. H. (1939). *The Factorial Analysis of Human Ability*. London: University of London Press.

Thorndike, E. L. (1927). *The Measurement of Intelligence*. Columbia, New York: Teachers College.

Thorndike, E. L. *et al.* (1921). Intelligence and its measurement. *Journal of Educational Psychology, 12,* 124–7.

Thorndike, R. L. (1933). The effect of the interval between test and retest on the constancy of the IQ. *Journal of Educational Psychology, 24*, 543–9.

Thorndike, R. L. (1973). *Stanford-Binet Intelligence Scale: 1972 Norms Table*. Boston: Houghton Mifflin.

Thurstone, L. L. (1928). The absolute zero in intelligence measurement. *Psychological Review*, *35*, 175–97.

Thurstone, L. L. (1938). Primary mental abilities. *Psychometric Monographs*, No. 1.

Thurstone, L. L. (1955). The differential growth of mental abilities. *Psychometric Monographs*, No. 14.

Thurstone, L. L. and Thurstone, T. G. (1941). Factorial studies of intelligence. *Psychometric Monographs*, No. 2.

Tuddenham, R. D. (1948). Soldier intelligence in World Wars I and II. *American Psychologist*, *3*, 54–6.

Urbach, P. (1974). Progress and degeneration in the IQ debate. *British Journal of the Philosophy of Science*, *25*, 99–135, 235–9.

Van Alstyne, D. (1929). The environment of three-year-old children: factors related to intelligence and vocabulary tests. *Teachers College Contributions to Education*, No. 366.

Vernon, P. E. (1950). *The Structure of Human Abilities*. London: Methuen.

Vernon, P. E. (1951). Recent investigations of intelligence and its measurement. *Eugenics Review*, *43*, 125–37.

Vernon, P. E. (Ed.). (1957a). *Secondary School Selection*. London: Methuen.

Vernon, P. E. (1957b). Intelligence and intellectual stimulation during adolescence *Indian Psychological Bulletin*, *2*, 1–6.

Vernon, P. E. (1960). *Intelligence and Attainment Tests*. London: University of London Press.

Vernon, P. E. (1969). *Intelligence and Cultural Environment*. London: Methuen.

Vernon, P. E. and Parry, J. B. (1949). *Personnel Selection in the British Forces*. London: University of London Press.

Very, P. S. (1967). Differential factor structure in mathematics. *Genetic Psychology Monographs*, *75*, 169–207.

Vincent, D. F. (1952). The linear relationship between age and score of adults in intelligence tests. *Occupational Psychology*, *26*, 243–9.

Wallach, M. A. and Kogan, N. (1965). *Modes of Thinking in Young Children: A Study of the Creativity-Intelligence Distinction*. New York: Holt, Rinehart and Winston.

Wechsler, D. (1939). *The Measurement of Adult Intelligence*. Baltimore: Williams and Wilkins.

Wheeler, L. R. (1942). A comparative study of the intelligence of East Tennessee mountain children. *Journal of Educational Psychology*, *33*, 321–34.

Wiseman, S. (1964). *Education and Environment*. Manchester: Manchester University Press.

Witkin, H. A., Dyk, R. B. *et al.* (1962). *Psychological Differentiation: Studies of Development*. New York: Wiley.

CHAPTER 13

Cross-cultural Differences in Cognitive Development

*Douglass R. Price-Williams**

I. BOUNDARIES AND APPROACHES

(1) INTRODUCTION

There is a number of difficulties which prevent an easy presentation of cross-cultural differences in cognitive development. First, there is the problem of the boundaries of the topic. The key term "culture" has an extremely wide range of reference. One way of dealing with this is to indicate what topics have been thought of as being relevant by previous writers. Second there is the problem of comparison. This has two aspects. The primary aspect concerns the nature of the samples being compared. The term "cross-cultural" has generally been referred to samples that include people from developing countries, some of which are at a preliterate stage, who are then compared to samples from developed countries, either explicitly by actually utilizing the latter in studies, or implicitly by using norms from developed countries. But the term can also refer to studies comparing samples of two or more developing countries with one another. Then there is the term "cross-national" which generally refers to studies involving samples only from developed nations. The content of these investigations is sometimes collected under the wider term of "cross-cultural". Further boundary problems are reflected by the fact that studies of minority groups within the same country are also enmeshed under the same rubric. And finally we need to consider those studies which focus on just one group, as the results of such investigations become pooled into the total picture.

*The author wishes to acknowledge support from the University of California, and grant No. HD–04612, Mental Retardation Research Center, University of California, Los Angeles.

The secondary aspect of comparison involves the applicability of tasks and tests to different populations. We shall pay attention to this important point later in this section. A third problem concerns the state of the field. This is, of course, a matter of judgment, but in this reviewer's opinion it is doubtful whether flat generalizations about relative development of cognitive processes in diverse peoples can at present be made. There are at least two reasons for stating this. The first reason is that researchers in the field are still groping with the difficulty of finding appropriate methodologies. The second reason is that there are just not sufficient studies on which to base generalizations, outside a very few types of cognitive process that have been given plenty of attention. It would be hazardous then, to generate comprehensive generalizations, let alone position purely cultural factors against biological and genetic factors, for which we have even fewer studies on a global scale. The present state of the art is composed of a search for significant variables, and it is to the aim of discussing such variables that the present chapter is devoted.

(2) Previous approaches

The reviews listed below constitute previous approaches to the topic of this chapter. They do not always discuss development *per se*, but when they do they encompass more than cognitive development, to include the entire range of cross-cultural studies. We will now note how each of these survey articles or sections have divided up the field, thereby both introducing the reader to the relevant background literature, and also indicating the way in which prominent people in the field have conceptualized it.

Triandis (1964) was probably the first to survey the sub-discipline of cognitive processes. His division of labour focused on cultural influences within the following areas: perception, categorization, organization of categories, judgments and evaluation, and behavioural intentions. At this time (early 1960s) there were not many studies to review. Triandis kept strictly to a comparison of two or more societies, and his review included what has been thought of as "cross-national" studies as well as "cross-cultural", taking in research from developed as well as undeveloped countries. A later and fuller review on cross-cultural psychology (Triandis, Malpass and Davidson, 1971) followed much the same headings in that part of the review which paid attention to cognitive processes.

Tajfel (1969), in a chapter for the second edition of Lindzey and Aronson's *Handbook of Social Psychology*, mixed material on social perception with material from the cross-cultural literature. He followed in fact the path that we have selected here, namely focus on variables. In doing so he made a remark that is highly appropriate to cite here :

> But concepts such as "society" or "culture" cannot be very useful in the establishment of hypotheses predicting various kinds of perceptual responses. All such predictions must originate from defined sets of conditions either created by a society or in which a society lives and develops. These hypotheses must then formulate the links between these conditions and the perceptual responses which are expected to occur (Tajfel, 1969, p. 320).

In paying attention to those variables thought to be relevant to cognitive development, we shall in fact introduce the links specified by Tajfel.

In another chapter from the Lindzey and Aronson Handbook, De Vos and Hippler (1969) wrote a substantial section on the issue we are discussing. Their headings included what they called "Primary perception and cognition" which meant research dealing with illusions and memory, plus perceptual responses to the Rorschach test. De Vos and Hippler then paid attention to the influence of language on thought, and particularly to an approach to cognition then taken by anthropologists, namely the employment of the componential analysis technique. In his 1964 article Triandis had also noted this technique and its possible applicability to the interests of psychologists. De Vos and Hippler subsequently delved into the complex thought processes and devoted a part of their chapter to the Piaget method that had by that point in time (late 1960s) been used fairly frequently in the cross-cultural field. Lastly these authors discussed intelligence tests applied in different parts of the world.

In an earlier review Price-Williams (1968) had also discussed intelligence tests but in connection with the problem of equivalence across cultures. This review also took in the subjects of illusions, depth perception, and some of the thinking studies on classification, conservation and object-sorting.

Greenfield and Bruner (1969), while in the course of their chapter they had reviewed previous studies, were really advancing a thesis. Their concern was why some cultures pushed cognitive growth earlier, better and longer than others. They basically saw three factors operating. The first was a value system which they characterized either as having a collective orientation or an individualist orientation. We will return to this distinction later, as it represents one of the variables that we will need to discuss extensively. The second factor was language,

19—CP * *

and the third factor was schooling or training. Greenfield and Bruner were some of the first to divide up the field in terms of explanatory factors rather than in substantive sections.

The last two "reviews of the literature" articles show deliberate focus on development as such. The first is that of LeVine (1970) who was contributing a chapter for Mussen's edition of *Carmichael's Manual of Child Psychology*. LeVine ran over the entire gamut of topics including illusions, pictorial depth percepiton, spatial perception, conservation, learning and intelligence. He makes a point which is useful for us to remember: namely that not much of the literature on cross-cultural differences in perception has actually involved children, but the studies have been addressed to developmental problems. We will be forced to include this point in our own survey.

R. and R. L. Munroe (1975) are probably the first to write an entire book on cross-cultural human development. One of their sections includes cognition. Their division is by age—actually two age periods, birth to two years, and from childhood to adulthood. The second age range takes in studies covered by other reviews, such as conservation tasks, classificatory problems, spatial perception.

This completes the short over-view of previous treatments of the subject. Other publications do bear on the subject. We might mention Price-Williams's readings, *Cross-Cultural Studies* (1969), a whole half of which was devoted to intelligence, perception and field dependence and conservation studies. Vernon's book *Intelligence and Cultural Environment* (1969) is probably the best coverage for intelligence testing across cultures. Goodnow (1975) further analyses some of the problems of assessing intelligence across cultures. She also considers how performances which go together in our own culture fail to go together in other cultures, which is a useful strategy in evaluating cross-cultural results. Berry and Dasen (1974) produced an entire book of readings entitled *Culture and Cognition*. Barbara Lloyd (1972) wrote an introductory book on the subject; and finally Cole and Scribner (1974) have covered the entire spectrum with their book *Culture and Thought*.

(3) COMPARABILITY AND VARIABLES

The problem surrounding the implementation of comparability has been admirably expressed by Robert LeVine in his contribution to Mussen's *Manual of Child Psychology* (LeVine, 1970, p. 566):

> ...even if an instrument is regarded as valid and reliable for intra-cultural comparison, its use in a culturally differing population raises serious doubts concerning whether it is measuring the same disposition

in the context of a different language and system of conventionalized meanings, and there are no generally accepted or followed rules for allaying these doubts. The consequence is that we do not have comparable developmental data for children the world over or even for a diverse sample of societies, and much of the cross-cultural data we do have are of dubious quality because of questions concerning the validity and/or comparability of the data collection procedures.

While LeVine was addressing himself to cross-cultural child psychology at large, we will be similarly forced to admit that his caveat applies also to cross-cultural cognitive development. The available material is not sufficient nor, because of the comparability difficulty, valid enough to allow for a discussion in simple terms of age progression. We do not have the unimpeachable evidence to specify, for example, the perceptual and conceptual development of a Thai peasant child to put alongside that found from children in Zambia, and then to compare both cultures with norms from Western children. There are some instances where, perhaps, there is sufficient material available (for example, studies on the conservation process, to be discussed later). While there may be sufficient material in rare instances, even then we are not confident that a similar methodology was used in all cases.

In many cases the comparison problem is compounded by the fact that investigators have been forced to modify or alter tasks and tests in order to communicate the problem to subjects in the first place. Ord (1968) for example has constructed a set of intelligence tests for the very specific population of the Pacific area. LeVine and Price-Williams (1974), in an investigation of how Hausa children formed concepts of kinship, were forced to reformulate Piaget's questions that had been constructed for European children. A growing number of scholars are questioning the validity of applying the standardized tests that have been used in psychological laboratories to other than Western cultures (for instance, Irvine, 1970). This movement has veered towards a perspective of cultural relativism (Berry, 1974). The consequence of this perspective disallows a strict literal equivalence between results of tests and tasks in different cultural groups. What has been employed has been a functional equivalence (Berry, 1969), that is to say the problem of comparability between two populations has focused on similar functional characteristics of the variable employed, and not on the formal aspects of the test.

Leaving the comparability problem, we recognize that the majority of cross-cultural studies on cognition has embodied a search for significant variables that are thought to influence distinct cognitive processes. Some of this material happens to be on children, and thus qualifies for inclusion in this chapter. Yet the emphasis in many studies is not always on the developmental aspect directly. The reader is given a cross-section of children (within a certain age range) in a certain culture. The real point of the study focuses on the nature of the independent variable. For example, there has been a considerable number of studies on cultural selectivity in perception of the geometric illusions, which followed the initial pioneering study by Segall, Campbell and Herskovits (1966). A number of these later studies used children as their subjects. Although an analysis of such studies tells us something about the developmental aspect, the thrust of the studies has regularly been that of testing rival theories : for example, whether physical ecology is or is not a factor in the judgment of such illusions. As this constitutes the major part of the literature, we shall need to focus on these variables, although the strict relationship of such variables to specific ages may not be always available. Conversely, we need to inspect those investigations which, while not dealing at all with children, have implications for developmental cognition.

We propose to group cultural factors into three divisions. These are : (1) Variables that relate to interaction with the physical environment. This would include physical ecology, the material culture and perceptual-motor skills. (2) Variables that might be termed simply "Psychocultural orientation". This would cover psychological orientations of familiarity and salience; it would also include Greenfield's and Bruner's collectivist versus individualist orientation, and mental sets influenced by formal training, schooling and exposure to Westernization. (3) Variables that are grouped under the rubric of extrinsic social factors, which means specifically certain economic factors, child rearing techniques and aspects relating to social conformity.

This attempt at structuring the field is aimed at finding classifications for the generic term "cultural factors". Like all classifications it is quite arbitrary and selective. The emphasis will be on the independent and not the dependent variable. Although our domain involves cognitive development, we will not concern ourselves with classifications of substantive areas. This unconcern will especially be noted with respect to language. As we have seen many previous reviews have devoted a substantial section to linguistic factors in cross-cultural studies. While we may include linguistic factors in our classificatory scheme, we have decided not to focus on language *per se*. The reason is simple; recent proliferation of both the fields of ethno- and socio-linguistics, together with the recent advances of the field of transformational linguistics, have resulted in a substantial area of study in its own right. One can no longer do justice to this area by including it within another range of studies. The intricacies of the role of language in communication and in thought processes needs to be considered as a separate but obviously closely related field.

II. INTERACTION WITH THE PHYSICAL ENVIRONMENT

(1) ECOLOGY

In cross-cultural psychology the concern with ecology has been associated with visual inference habits, with adaptations to the physical environment. Thus the psychological investigator has been interested as to whether subjects live in enclosed or open terrains, whether a type of subsistence living—such as hunting—demands a perceptual acuity, and so on. The term "ecology" has been handled somewhat loosely throughout different sub-disciplines of the social sciences, including psychology. Berry (1975) has recently analyzed the various meanings given to the term. As the term "ecology" has been associated with visual inference habits in cross-cultural psychology, we intend to include in this section research on perceptual inferences associated with man-made, constructed artefacts, such as buildings, huts, towers and the like, sponsored by the hypothesis of a carpentered world, although the two hypotheses need to be distinguished in explanations. The ecological hypothesis has been invoked predominantly in two branches of psychological studies : that dealing with the study of illusions, and that dealing with the study of differentiation. We will deal with these separately.

(i) *Cross-cultural study of illusions.* Although early work had been done on this subject by Rivers (1901, 1905), the first large-scale research with explicit hypotheses was the research reported by Segall, Campbell and Herskovits (1966). They postulated three hypotheses. The first was this so-called carpentered-world hypothesis. This means that the visual world in which the average Westerner lives is composed of right-angles, carpentered by a slide-rule as it were, which is in marked contrast to many an undeveloped area in which straight lines are disfavoured in place of curves or wavy lines, and in which circularity is preferred to angularity. The second hypothesis was the direct ecological one. People who live in deserts, say, with an unbounded frontal view would have different inference habits from those people who were surrounded by jungle vines, in which case perpendicular lines of orientation would be especially perceived. The third hypothesis was the ability of some groups to retrieve three-dimensional models from two-dimensional representations as is seen in photographs and drawings, a cultural peculiarity first brought to attention by Hudson (1960). The logic of Segall, Campbell and Herskovit's study can be illustrated with respect to two of the four types of illusions used (five forms actually, as there were two forms of the horizontal-vertical illusion). These two are the Müller-Lyer illusion and the horizontal-vertical. The Müller-Lyer illusion is that of two equal distance lines, one line being bounded by obtuse or out-turned arrows. Among Western groups the general tendency is for the line with the out-turned arrows to be judged as longer. The reasoning that Segall *et al.* applied was that for Western people living in a highly carpentered visual environment, the tendency would be for them to rectangularize the junctions of where the arrows meet the straight lines, and to perceive the figures in perspective. Used to two-dimensional representation of three-dimensional entities, they would tend to see the line within the turned-in arrows as if it were the front of a three-dimensional box, seen towards the observer. With the line with the arrows turned the other way, the tendency would be for the Western observer to interpret the line as the back of a box, and thus farther away. The resultant judgment is for the observer to perceive this latter line as longer than the other. People who do not live in a rectangularized environment and who are not used to two-dimensional representations of the real visual world presumably would not make these inferences and therefore would not report the illusion. The reasoning underlying the horizontal-vertical illusion is different. Here the illusion is to report a vertical line, which either bisects or meets one end of a horizontal line, as longer, although in fact both lines are of the same length. The reasoning is that lines extended into the distance away from an observer are less likely to be foreshortened than lines on either side of an observer. This would be particularly increased for people living in an unobstructed visual world, so that people living in deserts, or in vast unlimited fields of snow, or amid the open sea, are more likely to report this illusion than people living in close, urban environments, or in rain forests, or surrounded by mountains.

While the outright carpentered-world hypothesis was strongly supported by the findings of Segall *et al.*, there was less evidence for the hypothesis of ecological validity. Since 1966, when Segall *et al.* published their book, there has been considerable work on this question. The evidence has been somewhat equivocal, and methodological problems have intruded into the assessment. One methodological difficulty has been in comparing the effects of varying instruments to test the illusions. Segall *et al.* had utilized cards upon which the various illusions had been drawn in red and black. Some other investigators have used a form board apparatus by means of which the illusions are manipulated (for instance, Bonte, 1962; Jahoda, 1966). Investigators who favoured a nativistic interpretation of the illusions have used tachistoscopic presentation, which contrasts with the normal observational conditions employed by the ecological validity theorists, as Jahoda pointed out. The overall position, as Stewart (1973) recognizes, is that when comparisons have been made between Western and non-Western samples, significant differences have been found which lean towards the carpentered-world theory. However, when different types of conditions of carpenteredness or ecological milieu have been tested in non-Western groups, the results have not favoured the ecological theory.

We come then to the question of chronological development. The entire thrust of the ecological argument is that homogenous experience is cumulative. But what we find among Western samples is a decrease in susceptibility to the Müller-Lyer illusion—a feature also noted in the Segall *et al.* study (see Stewart, 1973 for full coverage of this point). Stewart herself points out that all the necessary experience for susceptibility towards these illusions may be reached by a very early age, below which it is difficult to test. But the age factor becomes significant in the light of a physiological theory advanced to account for the cross-cultural illusion results (Pollack, 1963; Silvar and Pollack, 1967; Pollack and Silvar, 1967). The argument goes like this: there is a relationship between a higher contour detection threshold and the density of macular pigmentation of the eye. A higher contour detection ability would make one more able to analyse illusions of the Müller-Lyer type and thus there would be a negative correlation between the two. In turn, density of macular pigmentation in the eye is correlated with skin pigmentation, which would mean that darker-skinned individuals would have a higher density of macular pigmentation in the eye, and hence a higher detection threshold for contours, which means less susceptibility to the Müller-Lyer illusion. As those subjects representing the low carpentered group were in fact non-white in the Segall study, this physiological explanation might be thought to have some weight. It becomes necessary to separate out racial factors from environmental factors, a strategy followed by Stewart (1973) in a study incorporating subjects both in the United States and in Zambia.

Stewart held environment constant while testing in the United States, and held race constant while testing in Zambia. In the United States, she tested children within an age range of 6–17, all of whom lived in the same town. However half the subjects were whites and the other half Negroes. In the Zambian samples, the variable manipulated was environment, or degrees of carpenteredness. There were an unschooled and a schooled group that lived in the valley, an intermediate group that lived on a plateau, and two groups that lived in the city (Lusaka): the range indicating an increase in carpenteredness.

Stewart used the Müller-Lyer and the Sanders-Parallelogram illusions, in the form originally used in the Segall studies. If the ecological argument was correct, one would expect to find no significant differences in the urban American sample; and indeed this is what Stewart did find, for both illusions. On the other hand, her Zambian samples showed a neat progression in susceptibility towards the two illusions, with the least-carpentered group (the valley unschooled group) displaying least susceptibility and the hypothetical most-carpentered group (the Lusaka middle class group) displaying the greatest susceptibility.

With respect to the age factor: while Stewart indeed found that her American sample decreased consistently with age in susceptibility to the illusions, and that an analysis of variance indicated a significant age effect in the Zambia sample, she herself considered that the age question was still in debate:

> ... the age trends in the data are clearly explained more parsimoni-ously by Pollack's age-related increase in retinal pigmentation than by Segall *et al.*'s "sophistication effect", which requires the effect of age-increased analytic ability work in one direction and age-increased exposure to carpenteredness in the opposite ... the age findings which are so consistent in the literature may simply have to be accepted as such, with their ultimate relationship to the nativist-empiricist controversy highly uncertain (Stewart, 1973, p. 92)

A study that deals directly with the developmental factor in the illusions is that of Dawson, Young and Choi (1973), in an article which helpfully provides the reader with the literature on age factors for a number of illusions. Dawson, whose subjects were Chinese living in Hong Kong and whose age range was extensive—3 to 21—was in a position to test out theories of developmental trends from European populations. This aspect of his study did not invoke any ecological reasoning to predict similarities or differences; he merely compared findings obtained from European children with those from his Chinese children. This part of his investigation utilized two alternative forms of the horizontal-vertical illusion. The first form is such that the vertical line intersects the horizontal; the second form is that the two lines meet in a corner or non-contiguous shape. Previous work had shown (Walter, 1942; Wursten, 1947) that whereas with the intersection type of the horizontal-vertical illusion the effect decreased with age, with the non-contiguous type there was an increase from age 6 to 10, after which age it declined into adulthood. Other investigators had interpreted these findings in this way, as summarized by Dawson *et al.*:

Piaget and Morf (1956) have thus interpreted Wursten's (1947) findings as reflecting the gradual development of a stable system of spatial coordinates in the age range six to ten, where lines compared are not spatially contiguous, so that their spatial relationships are not clearly defined for the S. However, if the lines intersect as in the inverted T (⊥), they provide their own spatial framework allowing for a more immediate operation of the illusion, and thus Fraisse and Vautrey (1956) confirm that the illusion is considerably stronger in this case (Dawson *et al.*, 1973, p. 52–3)

With the intersection form, the Chinese results showed a significant decrease in susceptibility up to the age of 11. After that there was a slight increase up to the ages of 15 to 17, followed again by a gradual decrease for men, and a downward and then upward curve for women. With the non-contiguous type of the horizontal-vertical illusion, there was indeed an increase in susceptibility from the age of $6\frac{3}{4}$ up to at least age 12, as already noted in Western samples. Taken together, these developmental findings of Dawson *et al.* endorse the theory of Piaget and Morf, and provide developmental agreements across quite different cultures. However these particular applications of the horizontal-vertical illusion say nothing about the ecological and carpentered hypotheses. To throw light on these points, Dawson compared his findings for Hong Kong Chinese with Segall *et al*'s. Evanston, Illinois, sample, and also with some data taken from the Arunta, a group living in the Australian desert. The Evanston data, stretching from the age of 12 up to 21, allow for a strict longitudinal comparison with the Hong Kong Chinese, but with the Arunta all that we have is a cross-section at the very upper limit of the age range.

Dawson *et al.* considered that the Hong Kong group lived in a less carpentered environment than the Evanston samples, but in a more carpentered environment than the Arunta aborigines. Therefore it would be anticipated that the Hong Kong group was less susceptible to the Müller-Lyer and Sander-Parallelogram illusions than the Evanston group, but more susceptible than the Arunta. This proved to be the case in both examples. However when the Chinese data are compared with the American data over the age range which they had in common (12 to 21), it can be seen from Dawson's graphs that whereas in the American samples there is a slight decrease in suscepti-bility for both illusions, with the Chinese sample there is first a similar down trend, then a rise around the age of 17. With the horizontal-vertical illusion, the anticipated ranking would be the very opposite; we would expect the Arunta to be most susceptible and the Evanston group least. We find this for the non-contiguous form of the illusion, the inverted L form (˥), but not for the intersectional form (⊥), in which case the Hong Kong groups are considerably less susceptible than the Evanston group, which in turn are considerably less suscept- ible than the Arunta. With respect to the age range comparisons, it can be seen that whereas in the Evanston samples there is a slight increase in susceptibility for the intersection type over the ages 12 to 21, the Chinese group either remain much the same (for women), or actually decline (for men). In the non-contiguous type, the Evanston groups are fairly stable for the same age range, whereas the Chinese tend first to decline up to age 17, then increase steadily from that age to 21. It is not immediately clear from Dawson's data how to reconcile the age fluctuations of the Chinese data with either nativistic or ecological types of explanation. Possibly, as he points out himself, there is a methodological difficulty involved in the fact that younger age groups in this type of society have been exposed to a more stimu- lating educational environment in contrast to the older age groups. At any rate Dawson's study is one of the few that have handled the developmental sequence head-on.

(ii) *Cross-cultural study of differentiation.* The employment of ecology as a variable has been used in connection with Witkin's concept of psychological differentiation (Witkin *et al.*, 1954, 1962; Witkin, 1967; Witkin and Berry, 1975). The term "psychological differentiation" has been invoked by Witkin as a superordinate term to cover four separate tests which are correlated in varying ratios. The first test, the rod and frame test, has been employed for testing field dependence and in- dependence. The essential task is to perceive the upright position when all visual cues to perpendicularity are absent or distorted. It turns out that some people cannot do this as their judgment is strongly influenced by the surrounding visual field—the so-called field dependent subjects. A second test makes use of embedded figures material : the task here is to select a certain figure embedded in a complex pattern. Again some people find it easier to disembed a figure than others. The third test is either that of Koh's blocks or some other kind of spatial ability test, the task being that of forming shape patterns. Then finally there is the articulation task, analysed from drawing figures of persons (Draw a Person test). What one is looking for here is the ability of the subject to differentiate or articulate various parts of the body. In various cross-cultural applications of the differentiation concept, it is rare that all four components are tested. Mostly, the embedded figures test and Koh's blocks or block design tests have been used. As the rod and frame test has generally correlated highly with the embedded figures test, the latter has been invoked as a measure for field dependence. A practical reason why the rod and frame test was rarely used in early cross-cultural work was the difficulty of local conditions for establishing the required completely dark room with luminous stimuli. With the construction of a portable rod and frame apparatus (Oltman, 1968) this task was made easier. In one of the few cross-cultural studies with the rod and frame technique before the portable version was available, there was found a lack of correlation between this test and the embedded figures (Wober, 1967). The author attributed this lack of correlation to the sensitivity of the Nigerians in the study to the proprioceptive element which is important for success in the rod and frame test, as opposed to the visual analytic skills necessary for success in the embedded figures test. Wober's work has subsequently been criticized on methodological grounds (Witkin and Berry, 1975). Be that as it may, other cross-cultural investigators have tended in the past to use the embedded figures test as a measure for field dependence.

The rationale of postulating ecology as a significant variable in differentiation turns on the visual ability for coping that the physical environment demands. A well-known instance of this was Berry's (1966) work with the Eskimo in which he contrasted their homogenous snow-field environment with that of the Temne of West Africa, who live in a well-defined variegated visual world of bush and shrub. The ecological argument is that a predominantly hunting and/ or fishing community such as the Eskimo would require analytic perceptual skills to maintain their livelihood, and thus would more easily pick out figures from a complex field when this task was given to them in a test such as the embedded figures. In comparison to the sedentary Temne, this proved to be the case; the Eskimo groups performed better than the Temne both on the embedded figures test and with Koh's blocks. Dawson (1969, 1971) pursued the same line of inquiry with two Chinese groups in the Hong Kong area. One was a fishing group, the other was a farming group. The fishing group, the so-called "Boat people", had as their constant environment the uniform expanse of the sea. The reasoning again is that local water patterns require to be delineated from the total field of sea in order for the fishing to be successful. When compared with the agricultural Chinese —the Hakka people—the fishing group was more successful on the various differentiation tasks.

Ecology, however, means more than just a physical stimulus for visual adaptation. As a variable in the groups mentioned, it is contaminated with distinct socialization patterns which we will discuss later under that heading. More recently Berry (1971) and Berry and Annis (1974) have explored the full range of ecology, and established a model with food accumulation as the overriding variable, as well as extending the notion of differentiation itself into other than strictly visual concerns. We will also discuss his model later.

(2) Skills

Consideration of hunting, fishing and farming already includes the factor of skill, but the studies to be mentioned here have concentrated more acutely on the various perceptual and motor components of the behaviour in question, and, moreover, attached the skill more closely to the variable tested in the experimental situation. As it happens most of the studies in this respect have to do with conservation tasks familiar in the Piagetian model. The paradigm for this kind of approach is seen in a study of pottery-making children in Mexico (Price-Williams, Gordon and Ramirez, 1969). The tasks given to the children of this study were the familiar ones initiated by Piaget for the testing of conservation ability, and consisted of the sub-tests for number, liquid, weight, volume and substance. As the task for the conservation of substance is the salient one here, the procedure will be described in detail. The initial condition is that the child is faced with two balls of clay which he judges to be equal in size. Then, while one ball is kept as it was initially, the other is transformed into a variety of shapes— a sausage shape, a cross or perhaps split up into little separate bits. The task for the child is to pronounce whether the experimental ball of clay has the same amount of clay as the untransformed ball kept as a standard. Now, with these Mexican children, from 6 to 9 years, there was one group that grew up in the families of potters, and had either observed or had actually been involved in this skill of pottery. The authors reasoned that this experience was the very essence of conservation ability and that if such children were compared with a group matched in age, education and socio-economic class, but who were not trained in this trade, the pottery-making children should perform better on conservation tasks to do with substance, as clay or plasticine is the essential medium in both cases. When tried first in a suburb of a large Mexican town, the reasoning proved to be correct. With this sample, the only difference between the two groups was the superiority of the pottery children with the one task of conservation of substance. There was no difference in the other conservation tests. However with a second and more rural Mexican sample, the effect appeared to transfer to all the other conservation types.

The same reasoning was adopted with a study of Australian Aborigines by Dasen (1974). Drawing on predominantly ecological considerations, Dasen made the inference that with a hunting economy the concept of space should be more exercised than other cognitive areas. He pointed out that the Australian Aborigine had to travel long distances in a somewhat barren environment, that they had to know where water holes existed as water is a rare commodity, and in general had to have a detailed cognitive map of the area which they traversed. On the other hand, Dasen pointed out, concepts of number and measurement are lacking in Aboriginal culture. Superiority on certain types of experimental tasks, e.g. spatial, such as rotation and horizontality—and inferiority on other types of experimental tasks, e.g., logico-mathematical tasks such as seriation and the conservation of quantity, weight and volume—would be predicted then from consideration of their natural skills. When compared with a European sample, the difference in the two sets of skills is strikingly different. As Dasen put it :

> ... the Aborigines in our samples, on the average, acquire the particular set of spatial operations we are testing before they acquire the particular set of logico-mathematical operations, whereas the Europeans in our sample find the logico-mathematical tests relatively easier (Dasen, 1974, p. 406)

However it is necessary to point out at once that when the less acculturated Aborigines were compared with the more acculturated, the former were not superior to the latter as might be anticipated from ecological reasoning. Dasen correctly noted that this was identical with a finding of Berry (1966), who compared acculturated and non-acculturated Eskimo groups. Dasen makes the point that the kind of spatial tests employed are only partly equivalent to those needed for survival in both Aborigines and Eskimos, and makes the interesting suggestion that tests should be constructed more in keeping with the spatial skills and concepts actually practiced by nomadic people.

Further evidence on the role of experience and skills comes from Bovet's study with children and adults in Algeria (1974), which at first prevented the proper understanding of conservation. It occurred when the conservation of weight task was conducted, and the experimental clay ball had been broken up into small pieces. Several of the women, when asked to judge whether these pieces weighed the same, more or less than the standard ball, exclaimed that it was impossible for them to do so unless they first weighed the clay in their hands. Bovet relates this to the proprioceptive and intuitive method of weight judgment used by these Algerian women in their daily activities. The women alone in this study made an initial conservation judgment on this task, followed by a regression when it was pointed out to them that the experimental balls of clay were different in shape from the standard ball. But only one demonstration on scales was needed for these women to provide a logical justification of the equality of weight.

The skill factor needs to be carefully assessed. In some cases it would seem to enhance some of the tasks of different cultural groups. In other cases, like Bovet's perhaps, the skill might impede the understanding of certain tasks. In other cases again the skill variable might be embedded in a more significant set of factors, as can be seen in Greenfield and Childs' study with Zinacanteco children of Chiapas, Mexico (1975). They took a group of adolescent girl weavers as their subjects. The essence of the experiment was to see whether weaving inculcated a facility for pattern representation, as determined by a task of placing wooden sticks of differing colours and widths into a frame, so as to make patterns. However, when compared to a group of adolescent boys on the same task, the girl weavers were actually less proficient in the pattern task. Greenfield and Childs noted that Zinacanteco culture develops general problem-solving skills more in boys than in girls, especially in economic transactions. The authors further noted that the sex of the children in the Price-Williams, Gordon and Ramirez (1969) study had been male, and that the rural sample who had generalized conservation tasks more than the urban sample were more involved in the entire trade of pottery. This observation has the implication that we need to look beyond the mere manipulative skills, into techniques of trading and selling. On the other hand it also needs to be noted that the age range of the children in the weaving study was far older than that of the children in the pottery study. Other possibilities exist. Cole (1975) noted that in Zinacantan culture only a few weaving patterns were practised. He considered that it would take the practising of a considerable number of different weaving patterns before true generalization would occur.

The above examples are those of indigenous skills that were thought to relate to the type of problem that we encounter in experimental psychology. As Dasen had said in a passage already quoted, what we need is first to analyze what kind of skills traditional peoples employ and then to adapt tests or make new tests given this information. There are in the cross-cultural literature other examples of indigenous skills. Gay and Cole (1967) have provided the most comprehensive series of these with the Kpelle of central Liberia. Their starting-point was observation of routine skills, such as measuring cups of rice from a large bowl, estimating the number of stones in a pile (Kpelle use stones as markers for a variety of tasks), estimation of intermediate distances by arm-spans. These and many more everyday skills were then translated into experiments with both children and adults, using a comparative American population. A thorough in-depth analysis of a single skill was carried out by Gladwin (1970). His population consisted of seafarers of Puluwat Atoll in the Pacific, and the skill was navigation. Gladwin relates the cognitive capacities underlying the skill of navigation to the set of concepts that we use in cognitive psychology. Here there are no experiments as we usually understand the term, only an exhaustive analysis of a single skill.

III. PSYCHO-CULTURAL ORIENTATION

By the somewhat uncouth title of "psycho-cultural orientation" we refer to sets and dispositions that pervade various cultural groups and which are thought to influence responses to tests and experiments.

(1) FAMILIARITY AND SALIENCE

In his previous review of social and cultural differences in perception Tajfel (1969) distinguished between familiarity and salience. Familiarity simply refers to the fact that living in a culture means that an individual is exposed to a set of objects that would be unfamiliar for another person not living in that culture. Salience refers to the fact that certain properties of the environment are functionally more important for some cultures than for others. For example both Europeans and Australian Aborigines are exposed to water, but obviously because of its rarity in the latter group, the discrimination of water becomes more salient for the Aborigines. Tajfel lists various studies in the cross-cultural literature that come under these two headings, and we will not repeat them. Rather we will focus on research investigations that are aimed precisely at the question whether familiarity makes a difference in experimental tasks.

Following studies by Price-Williams (1962) and Kellaghan (1968), who used objects familiar to their respective Tiv and Yoruba subjects in Nigeria, Okonji (1971) set up an experiment deliberately aimed at finding out whether the factor of familiarity with test objects had any effect in classificatory behaviour. Okonji's comparison groups were school children from Glasgow and Ibusa (mid-western Nigeria), aged approximately from 6 to 12 years. He used plastic models of animals, and a collection of objects. The animal models were considered to be equally familiar to both Scottish and African children. The objects, though, were likely to be more familiar to the Ibusa children, consisting of such artefacts as a gourd flute, a cooking pot, a metal gong and a pestle, for instance. The task consisted of choosing a key object and asking the subjects to collect all other objects that were like it in some way or that "went together" with it. Okonji found no significant differences between the two groups, except for the oldest age group, 11–12, in which the African children reached higher levels of abstraction than the Scottish children. While admitting that these results provided only moderate support for the hypothesis that the African children should reach higher conceptual levels for this object task because of their familiarity with the objects, Okonji still thought that the familiarity thesis was viable. He reasoned thus :

> If, however, we take into account the fact that the degree of unfamiliarity of the task to the Glasgow group was not high the importance of the result increases. It seems, therefore, that the obtained level of significance constitutes quite a weighty evidence in support of the view that familiarity with objects to be classified does affect a child's efficiency in classification. The only statistical significant difference (in the 11–12 year age group) may be explained, in part at least, in terms of the probability that it is at these ages that the influence of schooling begins to make a real impact on the Ibusa sample, while the start given the Glasgow sample by longer nursery or home rearing and school experience begins to be closed. At the earlier ages the differential must have been so large that sheer moderate advantage in familiarity could not offset it (Okonji, 1971, p. 45)

What Okonji seems to be stating here is that while familiarity with task items gives an advantage in classificatory behaviour, it is not enough by itself to offset the advantages of formal training in such a task that one gets in school. By the same token, of course, it follows that when a relatively unschooled group is given test objects to be manipulated that are grossly unfamiliar, a severe handicap results.

The familiarity factor, however, appears to vary from one kind of material to another, and with the tasks required of subjects. It operates strongly in the following experiment which opposes photographic reproductions of objects to the real objects. Deregowski and Serpell (1971) used real toy objects of vehicles and animals for a sorting task with Aberdeen and Lusaka, Zambia, third grade children. The experimenters also employed photographs of these same objects, one set coloured and the other set in black and white. Whereas the Scottish children performed vastly better than the Africans in their sorting ability with pictures, the two groups showed no difference when it came to sorting the two models. On the other hand in another experiment with Zambian children performed by Serpell (1971) there was only limited support for the familiarity theory in the orientation of abstract shapes.

The factor of functional salience, added to the factor of familiarity, appears in a study with the Mano tribe, a subsistence rice farming group living in north-east Liberia (Irwin and McLaughlin, 1970). The starting point of this study is the observation that the developmental trend of attention to colour, then to form and then to function, commonly observed in Western children, has been reported conspicuously absent in unschooled African children. The question for these investigators, then, was to find out whether this was because of preference for colour, or an inability to group by form or function. Irwin and McLaughlin's Mano subjects were given two types of stimulus materials. One type were cards on which were triangles or squares, in two different colours and in two alternative number configurations. The other type of stimulus material was a group of rice bowls, which differed in size, type of rice (swamp rice, which is shorter, thinner and yellower than dry land grown rice), and cleanliness of grain. The functional aspects of rice were highly relevant to the experiment. The authors point out that swamp rice and land grown rice are never eaten mixed together. The cleanliness of the rice is equally salient. Rice is always clean before it is cooked; the clean rice in this study had been polished in a mortar after hulling, whereas the dirty rice had been hulled but not polished. In both groups of materials there was a set of eight possible combinations; the task was to divide the eight cards or rice bowls into two groups of four each so that all items in a group were alike in some dimension. The subjects consisted of a large number of elementary school students for one group and a larger number of illiterate men for another group. The results of this experiment showed that while both groups of subjects preferred colour to form as a basis for grouping, and although this was attributed to a genuine lack of ability for making form groupings, the authors did not consider that the lack of equivalence grouping by form of these Africans reflected an arrest of the development of abstraction abilities. They observed that their illiterate farming adult group was far better than the students in the sorting experiment with the rice bowls, and pointed out that when motivation or interest was involved, classification by function would take place.

A later publication (Irwin, Schafer and Feiden, 1974) extended this original Liberian study to include a sample of men from the United States. In this study illiterate Mano men were pitted against American undergraduates on the geometric shapes test and the rice test (as described previously). The expectation was, of course, that the American undergraduates would do better on the geometric shapes test, and that the Liberian farmers would do better at sorting out the characteristics involved in the bowls of rice. Sorting behaviour was measured in the mean number of sorts for each type of material. As predicted the US undergraduates had a higher number of sorts than the Mano group for the geometric shapes, and the Mano farmers a higher number of sorts for the rice task than the American undergraduates. The American sample did take less time for both tasks, and they were able to verbalize the basis for their grouping better than the Mano. Although a disparity was anticipated for each group of subjects between the number of sorts for the familiar task and the unfamiliar task, it was a surprise for the authors to find that the American sample had the greater disparity:

> Though the higher level of emic performance of U.S. sorters no doubt contributed to their greater emic versus unfamiliar difference, the percentage decrement was also greater among U.S. than among Mano subjects (38% versus 32%). Thus, our data do not support the hypothesis that formal education increases the ability to generalize cognitive operations to unfamiliar situations (Irwin *et al.*, 1974, p. 418)

As we pointed out above, the factor of familiarity tends to vary from one kind of task to another. Greenfield (1974) has contributed to the discussion by listing at least four types of familiarity. First there is the *actual object* used in an experiment that may be familiar or alien to a culture. Then *features* can be culturally familiar if their labels follow linguistic usage. The third kind of familiarity refers to *dimensions*. And fourth, an *object-dimension relationship* is culturally relevant if, as Greenfield puts it: "the dimension actually functions to categorize these particular objects in that particular culture" (1974, p. 159). Greenfield complained that in the Irwin and McLaughlin experiment there was a failure to hold the familiarity of features and dimensions constant, while varying the familiarity of the object. In her study with Zinacanteco subjects, two types of object were used for testing sorting ability: flowers and rods. As the children in this Mexican culture tended to arrange flowers in bunches, tie them up and sell them on the highway, the class of flowers was regarded as the familiar set. There were three varying attributes for each class: colour, species and length for the flowers; colour, circumference and length for the rods. The task consisted in sorting and re-sorting the groups of flowers and rods, with the children compared as to age, sex and schooling, and also whether or not they sold flowers. Greenfield reported that familiarity with the type of materials definitely made no difference in these conceptual tasks. The flower sellers did not sort flowers better than the other subjects; grouping and re-grouping by colour for the flowers was often done worse than sorting of rods by colour for the younger age groups; and sorting by the species attribute developed last, although species is the primary basis of organization for flowers in this culture. Greenfield noted that colour is not the relevant dimension for the gathering of flower bouquets in Zinacanteco culture, and she indicated that the species dimension has multidimensional properties. It should further be noted that the samples in this experiment were very small for each group composed by age and schooling or unschooling : N = 12, 12, 12, and 6, as the sequence progresses from the 4- to 5-year-olds to the 18-year-olds. Also as these samples were further subdivided into whether or not the subjects had experience with flower selling, the operative sub-sample had very small numbers. Actually there were sixteen flower sellers versus fourteen non-flower sellers in the whole array, since this occupation did not relate to the youngest age groups. In contrast, Irwin and McLaughlin (1970) had comparable samples of sixty-five school students versus eighty illiterates in their Liberian rice experiment, and 100 American undergraduates versus eighty Liberian farmers in the later study by Irwin et al. (1974). Greenfield, however, makes a valid point when she stresses the necessity of specifying precisely the kind of familiarity that is the operative factor. Recently Price-Williams (1975) has indicated that the factor of familiarity needs to be extended to the nature of the task required of subjects (not just the type of materials used) and also to the context in which the task is embedded.

(2) COLLECTIVE VERSUS INDIVIDUALISTIC ORIENTATION

This value orientation is one put forward by Greenfield and Bruner (1969), who have made it a basis for certain distinctions seen in cognitive work in various cultures. Beginning from their own previous work (Bruner, Olver and Greenfield 1966), Greenfield and Bruner in this later publication noted that some cultures distinguish severely thought from the object of thought, while others do not. Where there is a collectively-oriented society, explaining a statement about an external event is meaningless; what is meaningful is to explain the event. Thus Greenfield and Bruner found with their unschooled Wolof children that when a question was formulated in the following way : "Why do you say (or think) that such and such is true?", it met with incomprehension. When the question was formulated to state : "Why is such and such true?", it could be better answered. Greenfield and Bruner considered that in cultures where individualism was not the prevailing ethos, the usual progression of cognitive development noted in Europe and America from stages of egocentrism through a

distinction of inner and outer events to a final stage where the rela-
tivity of the observer is taken into account, does not take place. The
child remains on an uncompromising realistic basis:

> The argument would be that the child is not cognizant of his own
> psychological properties, does not differentiate these from properties of
> the physical world, and is therefore not cognizant of any psychological
> properties—far be it for him to attribute such properties to inanimate
> objects (Greenfield and Bruner, 1969, p. 637–8)

Rejecting therefore the hypothesis that animism would develop in
those societies where there is no support for an individualistic orientation (a thesis which could presumably be tested through application
of the Human Relation Area Files), these authors go on to suggest
that the egocentric stage does not develop in collectivist oriented
societies, and that this tendency is seen in performance on cognitive
tasks. Thus for example with Eskimo children (Reich, 1966) who performed equivalence tasks with picture material, statements of personal
interaction with things were never found, as with American children
living in the same area.

The collective versus individualistic thesis is further introduced to
explain cultural differences in performance of conservation tasks.
Greenfield and Bruner reasoned that if members of a collective
culture were requested to perform a task on their own initiative, the
action would be reflected in an experimental task. Accordingly they
required an unschooled Wolof sample of children to carry out
individually the Piagetian task of pouring water from one beaker to
another. It was thought that such a self-initiated action would
promote the understanding of conservation. In other words the
realism would disappear, as the child would be forced to make a
distinction between his own actions and the events taking place out
there in the real world. When the "do-it-yourself" experiment was
carried out with these Wolof children, the results were startling. With
both younger and older children, those that did the pouring themselves
achieved conservation more successfully than those children who had
simply watched the experimenter do the pouring. This self-initiation
was thought by Greenfield and Bruner to be the key for the observed
disparity of Tiv children (Price-Williams, 1961) and Wolof children
(Greenfield, 1966) in age of achieving conservation of quantities. The
Tiv children had achieved this by age eight whereas only 50 per cent
of the Wolof children had achieved it at a much later age. Price-
Williams had noted that the successful Tiv children had spontaneously
performed the action of pouring from one container to another, an

action that was never observed among the more passive Wolof children. In commenting on these conservation findings R. and R. L. Munroe (1975) make a point that might well be included in our later section on conformity, but which is more appropriate at this point. It is that in cross-cultural ratings of compliance versus assertiveness, Tiv are lower for compliance in socialization than any other African society. The Munroes consider that those attributes of Tiv of an unusual independence and assertiveness are reflected in the cognitive sphere.

(3) SCHOOLING

It has become clear from the previous discussions that the effect of formal schooling in developing countries is an issue in its own right. Experiments with the performance of literates versus illiterates have developed. The question has arisen as to what kind of psychological processes are facilitated by schooling, and what are not. Although this paradigm has been widely used in cross-cultural psychology, far less is known about the type of schools that are involved in the experiments, nor any assessments given of the relative quality of schools. Then there is the further difficulty of contamination of variables. In many cases with developing countries, attending school has brought with it exposure to European contact and Western cognitive values. Also there is the related problem of bilingualism associated with the teaching of French or English in the school.

Notwithstanding these methodological problems, the employment of schooling as a variable has persisted. Unfortunately the data are not easy to evaluate. Dasen (1972) assembled the available evidence up to 1971 for the effect of schooling on the Piagetian stage of operational development. The evidence was contradictory : six studies indicated that the influence of Western-type schooling had no effect on the development of concrete operations, and four did. Dasen considered that it was contact with European values and its concomitants that were more relevant. The data on concrete operations therefore seems to be in doubt. Another line of reasoning by Goodnow and Bethon (1966) contrasted conservation tasks with combinatorial tasks and found that whereas schooling made no impact on conservation of weight, volume and surface, it did on the task of combining pairs of colours from a larger set. The population in this study came from Chinese living in Hong Kong, who were compared with American children. On the other hand it seems quite clear from both conservation and combinatorial experiments with the Wolof that schooling made a very strong impact (Bruner, Olver and Greenfield, 1966,

p. 316). Children who attended either city or bush schools improved
in colour classification as the grade increased, and form and function
preferences also increased. The non-schooled Wolof, on the other
hand, never did show progression. The effect of education on this
type of task was replicated by Sharp and Cole in rural Yucatan
(reported in Cole and Scribner, 1974, p. 106–8), who found that
education *per se* rather than chronological age was the key. Evans and
Segall (1969) obtained very similar findings with Baganda children,
where educational level was likewise a better predictor for learning
functional criteria in sorting and learning tasks than age in years.

The conservation tasks, however, continue to be paradoxical with
respect to educational criteria. It is not just the matter of comparing
literates with illiterates where the evidence disagrees. There is in addition the kind of finding made by Heron, first with Zambian children
and later in Papuan children (Heron, 1971; Heron and Dowel, 1973)
that weight conservation failed to correlate with psychometric
measures of reasoning ability. One is left with a puzzle as to whether
the failure of correlation is due to specific cultural variations in these
areas, to specific educational factors, or possibly to incorrect assumptions of basic theory. One will just have to agree with Lloyd (1972,
p. 132) that the extent of the influence of schooling on Piagetian tasks
is debatable.

Perhaps a more fruitful way of looking at the role of schools is to
see it in relation to cognition in terms of continuity and discontinuity
with the encompassing society. Scribner and Cole (1973) in particular
have been led to the viewpoint that cultural discontinuities introduced
by formal education entail cognitive discontinuities in the organization
of basic cognitive capacities (see also Cole, 1973). This view has
related mainly to minority populations in culturally heterogeneous
societies, and also with respect to socio-economic differences. The
effect of the home environment in offsetting the input of schooling
has been emphasized for children both in the United Kingdom (see
Morrison and McIntyre, 1971, Chap. 1) and in the United States
(e.g., Coleman *et al.*, 1966). The term "home environment" has
covered a number of variables, of a familial, economic and attitudinal
nature. We shall discuss some of these social variables in the next
section. We notice now that the discontinuity of school and home
environment can be interpreted in two ways. One way is that the
child is seen as having a deficient background; the other interpretation is simply that the child has had a different background (see Cole
and Bruner, 1971, for basic definition of the deficit versus difference
viewpoints).

The dependent variable in this controversy has usually been the intelligence test score. People who have tended to support the "difference" model are inclined to reject the intelligence test as being culturally inappropriate for minority and poverty groups, and reject so-called intervention tactics on the home environment (for instance, Baratz and Baratz, 1970). Some writers have extended the argument to insist that for culturally (or sub-culturally) different populations there are distinct conceptual styles operating. Cohen (1969) has argued that certain types of social organization, which are dominant for poverty groups within the United States, are more attuned to what she calls "relational" intelligence, a term which is opposed to a more analytic and abstract mentation. Recently Castaneda and Ramirez (1975) have indicated that the Chicano has a distinct learning style different from the mainstream Anglo learning style in the United States, and that this has important consequences for educational procedures.

The integration or congruence of school and home environment has now become a major theme for psychologists, sociologists, linguists and anthropologists. We can do no more here than indicate the nature of the problem. For a focus on how the different value factors of school and home interact in a particular cultural population—in this case Hawaiian—we might suggest the recent contribution of Gallimore and his colleagues (Gallimore, Boggs and Jordan, 1974). It is clear from this case, as it is from other parts of the world, that the differing inputs of deficit training in the home and the differing values of the school system introduce a complicated amalgam that cannot simply be answered by rejecting one interpretation and accepting the other. Furthermore, as Ciborowski (1974) has so ably argued there is

> no single unit of cognitive functioning and no simple cultural feature that can be clearly identified as "THE CAUSE" of the differences in performance shown by diverse groups exposed to formalized educational experiences (Ciborowski's italics and capitals)

IV. EXTRINSIC SOCIAL FACTORS

(1) BACKGROUND ECONOMIC CONDITIONS

(i) *The culture of poverty.* As far as the effect on cognitive processes is concerned this phrase of Oscar Lewis' includes such factors as inadequate nutrition, impoverished perinatal care, educational inadequacies so gross as to render a poverty population far behind in intellectual development. Werner (1972) for example in a review of studies concerning infant psychomotor development across the world, has this to say :

> Beginning in the second half of the first year of life, when volume of breast milk was no longer adequate if taken alone, or when supplementary food was low in animal protein or contaminated by a high dose of bacteria, there was a steady downward trend in the psychomotor scores of infants reared in traditional rural communities of Africa, Asia and Latin America.... After age two, mean scores of infants from traditionally reared samples in the developing countries were significantly lower than those of Western children in gross and fine motor development, with the lowest scores in adaptive and language development (Werner, 1972, p. 129)

While studies of infancy can be easier related to impoverished economic and nutritional conditions, it is more difficult to connect these conditions directly to later intellectual development. As Vernon (1969, Chap. VI) has indicated, there is a whole syndrome of factors operating, which include not only poor nutrition and health, but extend to attitudinal factors such as lack of parental interest in education. Nonetheless in a review of socio-cultural factors influencing cognitive processes we cannot afford to omit this class of variables for failure to disentangle the class into its specific elements. The doyen of the study of mental retardation in the United States, George Tarjan, considers (1970) that impoverishment or poverty is the most important cause of socio-cultural retardation. The essential question to resolve for investigators is to what extent are undoubted early deficits, due to impoverished economic and/or educationally unstimulating conditions, irreversible? Studies in the industrialized countries would seem to suggest that these conditions are irreversible (Hess and Shipman, 1965). However there are a few indications from work in developing countries that this may not always be the case. In Nigeria, Abiola (1965) compared children from traditional Yoruba homes with a highly educated elite group of Yoruba children. While the effect of the socio-economic advantages was greatest at age three, Abiola noted that the influences had diminished by age 5. Abiola's findings have been criticized by Lloyd (1971), but a similar observation has been made in a different part of the world : Guatemala. Here, Kagan and Klein (1973), basing their comments on the study of rural children living in an isolated and cognitively restricted environment, concluded that "absolute retardation in the attainment of specific cognitive competences during infancy has no predictive validity with respect to level of competence on a selected set of natural cognitive skills at age 11" (Kagan and Klein, 1973, p. 949). The authors were quick to point out that one should not generalize these findings to refer to the data on American infants. Nevertheless the findings suggest caution in applying unchecked the model of deprivation originating from work in the more industrialized and technological countries to the more undeveloped cultures.

(ii) *Acculturation and Westernization.* It has already been noted that in two cases, that of schooling and socio-economic deficiency, there is difficulty in weeding out the variables concerned. We note it again with the somewhat vague meaning given to Westernization and acculturation into Western type values. There is associated with these terms better socio-economic conditions, urbanization with its wider stimulating conditions, and acceptance of Western values of individualism and competition. Despite the ambiguity of meaning, where Westernization and acculturation have been employed as variables in experimental paradigms with cognitive processes, they have been found to be significant. Considering schools, urbanization and Westernization to be a combined matrix, Furby (1971) thought that the combination could account for better performance on conservation tasks. De Lacey (1970) worked with a low contact (with European populations) and a high contact group of Australian Aboriginal children, on tasks demanding classificatory ability. One task required an understanding of appropriate uses of the terms "some" and "all" with respect to the relationship between a part and its whole in an experiment with coloured shapes. The other task was with a basket of different kinds of fruit that required of the subjects a proper use of hierarchical classification, and a distinction between the class term "fruit" and a member of it, e.g., orange. De Lacey's results showed that the environmental differences of contact with Europeans were decisive for the Aboriginal children; so much so in fact that he believed (1970, p. 303) that the interests of the Aboriginal population could be best served, as far as their cognitive development was concerned, if such groups could be reared near, or integrated into, European settlements. Returning to conservation tasks, Dasen (1972) concluded that even if the contaminating variables of schooling, urbanization and social class are held constant, as it was in his own work with Aboriginal children (Dasen, 1970), high contact with European populations still makes a difference.

When acculturation is considered in the framework of a transition from a rural and agricultural to an urban and industrial life style, its impact has been observed in populations as far apart as Mexico and Hausa Nigeria. Maccoby and Modiano (1969), testing Mexican children in the 12–13 age range, found that urban children were less stimulus bound, differentiated perceptual attributes easier, and were more inclined to use abstract criteria than rural children, when asked to classify a series of objects. In Nigeria the task was attainment of scientific concepts, consisting of a series of items including prediction of spatial relationships, conservation and understanding of mechanical principles. Animism was also tested (Poole, 1968). Poole's sample ranged from rural Hausa, through an intermediate group, to urban Hausa, and he found that the last group mastered the scientific problems better than the other two groups. He saw this progression as a direct response to acculturation, the urban environment making innovational demands of the Hausa children.

(iii) *The food accumulation model.* This is a very precise economic model and emerges from ecological considerations. It has been ably argued in recent publications by Berry (Berry, 1975; Berry and Annis, 1974). It has reference mainly to the cross-cultural differentiation literature (see Witkin and Berry, 1975, for a definitive survey of this literature), although Berry has extended the argument to acculturative stress. The model actually relates economic conditions to cognitive inferences through the medium of socialization, so it is a complex pattern of conditions that is put forward. The economic part of the pattern focuses upon whether a society has high or low food accumulation tendencies. A high food accumulation society is characterized by being sedentary, having a relatively high density of population, being engaged in agriculture and/or animal husbandry. A low food accumulation society is nomadic or semi-nomadic, tends to be migratory, has a relatively low density of population, and is a hunting and gathering group. Co-varying with these social and economic indices are particular types of child-rearing. The original basis for this assertion goes back to the cross-societal study of Barry, Child and Bacon (1959) whose data were based on over 100 non-Western societies. They showed that low food accumulation societies emphasize attention during child-rearing on achievement, self-reliance and independence training. High food accumulation societies, on the contrary, give relatively little attention to these traits and promote obedience and conformity in their children. In turn the socialization patterns are associated with perceptual habits. Previously, when we discussed the role of ecology in perception, we focused on the link between certain kinds of occupations and visual strategies. Omitted in that account had been the role of socialization. Both Berry (1966) and Dawson (1967) in their comparative studies of the Eskimo, and the Temne and Mende of West Africa, had pointed out that perceptual differentiation was associated with child rearing variables. We will return to this point below where further research will be cited. Later work by Berry has now amplified these early findings into a coherent model, integrating economic strategies, socialization training and perceptual modes. Specifically the expectation is that low food accumulation groups will be characterized by high perceptual differentiation and that the reverse will be anticipated for high food accumulation societies. The study of three Amerindian samples, differing on this food accumulation variable, reported in Berry and Annis (1974), is probably the most comprehensive. The dependent variable representing the perceptual differentiation factor was response to Kohs' blocks. There were three Amerindian groups—the Cree, the Carrier and the Tsimishian—which represent respectively: low, medium and high food accumulating societies. Within each sample, there was a relatively traditional and a relatively acculturated group. Results on Kohs' blocks test showed that the eco-cultural setting was significant. Moreover when the samples are inspected from the traditional versus acculturation perspective, the ecological thesis is reinforced. The acculturated group of the high food accumulating Tsimshian society has a lower score on the test than the traditional group of the low food accumulating Cree.

(2) SOCIALIZATION

Although for the sake of exposition we have singled out economic conditions from socialization factors, as we have seen the two are very closely related. However, the connection is only obvious in relatively undeveloped communities in which subsistence economics can be sharply distinguished. A good deal of research has been done in societies in which the economic factor is not so distinguished, and here the emphasis has been on socialization factors alone. Again the differentiation factor has been the chief target of investigation. We can return now to the initial studies by Berry and Dawson, already discussed from the point of view of ecology. In their work socialization emerges as a mediating variable between ecology and psychological differentiation, along the line indicated by the analysis of Barry, Child and Bacon (1959). Dawson's work with the Temne and Mende of Sierra Leone can serve as an illustration (Dawson, 1967). The Temne people have severe socialization practices, discipline in the home is very strict, the Temne mother is very dominating, and individual competitiveness is punishable by social sanctions. This type of personality syndrome had already been associated in the West by Witkin et al. (1962) with perceptual field dependence. In contrast, the Mende encourage individual initiative, have far less severe socialization practices, and the Mende mother is not as dominating as the Temne mother. Dawson now matched male subjects from each trible for all relevant variables and tested them on at least three of the tests relevant to the differentiation theory (Embedded Figures Test, Kohs' Blocks and the Draw a Person Test). As expected the Temne males were significantly more field-dependent than the Mende males for two of the tests—Kohs' blocks being the exception where no significant differences were found. Further analysis of his data indicated to Dawson the role of socialization procedures in terms of the strictness of the mother. First, by relating three degrees of strictness to the whole sample, it could be seen that significantly far more Temne mothers were rated as being very strict, and far more Mende mothers were rated as being not so strict. Then, when these ratings of strictness were correlated with performance on the specific tests, the disciplinary factor was emphasized. Temne mothers in the very strict category (indicating more field dependence) had lower scores for Kohs and the Embedded Figures Test as against the other two categories. The Mende mother scores followed the same pattern but the means for these in the very strict category were not nearly as low as they were for the Temne mother (thus indicating more field independence for the Mende mother).

Subsequent research on socialization and psychological differentiation has tended on the whole to support the initial findings. There have been numerous studies on this point all over the world, in both developing and developed countries. The evidence has been recently presented in the comprehensive review by Witkin and Berry (1975), and we had best quote from that publication :

> The evidence from these studies together suggests that a relatively field-dependent cognitive style, and other characteristics of limited differentiation, are likely to be prevalent in social settings characterized by insistence on adherence to authority both in society and in the family, by the use of strict or even harsh socialization practices to enforce this conformance, and by tight social organization. In contrast, a relatively field-independent cognitive style and greater differentiation are likely to be prevalent in social settings which are more encouraging of autonomous functioning, which are more lenient in their child-rearing practices, and which are loose in their social organization (Witkin and Berry, 1975, p. 46)

What we have now is a set of factors somewhat wider than what is usually merely thought of as child-rearing factors, which together constitute a social ethos. Witkin, Price-Williams et al. (1974) suggested the term "social conformity" for this pattern. The recommendation for this term emerged from an internationally combined study with representatives from Holland, Italy and Mexico. The design in this study was not cross-cultural or cross-national. The performance by the subjects from the various nations was not compared to one another. Rather the design was to select from *within* each country (Holland, Italy and Mexico) two villages which differed in social conformity. The first kind of village was a traditional type, characterized by an extended family, with strong adherence to social, political and religious authority, as well as familial authority often wielded by grand-parents. In the transitional type of village, the mother had a less dominating role, there was less evidence of an extended family structure, individualism was encouraged, and in contrast to the "more conformity" villages, the father had a greater role in child-rearing. This two-village comparison study in four different countries was marked by the fact that the test battery included all four aspects of psychological differentiation, including the rod and frame technique, now applied through the use of the portable instrument. Results indicated overwhelmingly that the social conformity hypothesis was supported, for both sets of children, approximately 10 and 13 years respectively. Without exception for all sub-tests, the mean for the "less conformity" village showed greater differentiation than for the "more conformity" village.

We might add an interesting observation made from the entire spectrum of differentiation studies. It appears that a U-shaped curve can be drawn from the range of societies characterized at one extreme by the nomadic attributes of hunting and gathering, through pastoral and sedentary societies, to the other extreme of industrial and complex communities. Whereas the populations from the first and last are characterized by greater differentiation, it is the societies recognized as sedentary, rural and predominantly agricultural that imbue in their members the perceptual attributes of lesser differentiation or field dependence.

The difficulty which still pursues the linkage between socialization indices and cognitive processes is the lack of specificity. Nerlove and her colleagues (Nerlove *et al.*, 1974) attempted to remedy this by specifying quite specific cognitive processes that are associated with equally specific socializing agents. Nerlove *et al.* were concerned with cognitive development in two villages in Guatemala, in an age range of 5 to 8 years. The socialization agents were classified in two groups: what they called "self-managed sequences" and "voluntary social activities". Observations of these Guatemalan children were carried out in work and play. By "self-managed sequences" is meant behaviour which is either not easily supervised or, even if it is easily supervised, is performed in the absence of an adult or an older sibling. Washing or mending clothes would be an example of the first category; going out of the community and locating a place (indicating some type of cognitive map) is an example of the second category. Such self-managed sequences were directly related to analytic ability exemplified in the Embedded Figures Test and a further test which requires matching of a standard familiar object such as a tree with four alternatives, only one of which is an exact replica of the standard object. As Nerlove *et al.* say: "Tasks such as embedded figures and matching familiar figures require a scanning of the model and mapping of that model onto alternatives, remembering what one had already tried and how well it fits" (Nerlove *et al.*, 1974, p. 287).

Nerlove and her team included in the term "voluntary social activities" all children's behaviour that was not commanded by others (such as being sent on errands in the community) or that required apparent planning or organization by the child himself. What was counted as being voluntary was behaviour that the child clearly wanted to do rather than being told. This kind of behaviour was specifically related to language facility, with learning to name and recognize objects and with relating functions or attributes or objects verbally. The tests involved were a version of the Peabody Picture Vocabulary Test and a Verbal Analogies Test. The association between analytic ability and self-managed sequences was found to be strong in both villages and for both sexes. With respect to the other hypothetical association—language facility and voluntary social activity—the connection was weaker. It appeared to be stronger for boys than for girls, and for the boys in one village rather than the other. However, the combined outcome of both sets of tests indicates the importance of autonomy and is congruent with other work on socialization which is focused more on the determinants of autonomy.

V. CONCLUSIONS

In the preceding review of work, we have attempted to structure the findings by reference to different kinds of variables. It has then become clear that we are faced with the different *levels* of variables. It appears that some variables, thought to be important in the cross-cultural literature, are embedded in another set of variables. For example, it can be seen that a social psychological index like "assertion" or "non-compliance" can contain within its range of reference terms like "curiosity" or "active discrimination", that have direct relevance to cognition. Cross-cultural research is working at different levels at once, but the links in the chain of reasoning between the relatively "molar" level of society and the relatively "molecular" level of individual cognitive behaviour, are not always apparent or even sought. The question then arises as to what kind of theory is necessary for relating the levels. At least two theories have emerged in the literature. One is the systematic model that Berry (1975) has proposed. This model suggests the necessary links between the main segments of ecological, cultural and behavioural components, and connects socialization variables with perceptual variables. The model is largely if not exclusively based on differentiation as the key element, and has not yet been applied to other kinds of cognitive factors. The other theory, introduced into the cross-cultural domain by Cole and Scribner (1974, p.192–7) incorporates the cognitive notions of Vygotsky and Luria of "complex, organized functional systems". The relevance of this viewpoint lies in the assertion that while there may be the same basic processes underlying cognitive behaviour in all cultures, the same process can play different roles in individual cultures. As Cole and Scribner have put it : "We are conceiving of functional systems, then, as flexible and variable organizations of cognitive processes directed towards some fixed end" (Cole and Scribner 1974, p. 193).

The problem for the cross-cultural methodologist lies in the difficulty of detaching the cognitive process from its embedded functional system. There is a growing realization in cross-cultural researchers that the very tools that are relied on to tap psychological processes in people of our own culture are themselves wedded to a specific functional system. It is like the fish in its medium of water which does not realize that the encompassing liquid constitutes a meaningful variable. When attention is given to other cultures, this encompassing medium becomes obvious to the researcher. The techniques that have been so useful and which have real validity in one environment, then, are no longer so readily applicable in others. In the development of cross-cultural research the search for "culture-free" tasks has given way to finding culturally appropriate tasks, as Strodtbeck recognized (1964). A prerequisite of finding a culturally appropriate task is to have some considerable knowledge of the culture in general; a partial ethnography of the culture appears mandatory. This means going beyond the practice of merely performing an experiment in a culture or pair of cultures towards an extended observation that prefaces the experiment. Cole (1975) has recently itemized the necessities entailed in this approach.

Attention to cognitive functional systems introduces further consequences for the cross-cultural psychologist. Anthropologists have laboured to point out that indigenous classification systems obey rules that are not always congruent with Western schemes (see Tyler, 1969, for total coverage of cognitive anthropology). Domains of colour, kinship, plants, illness for example, have been analyzed from the perspective of the indigenous system itself. These classification systems are translated into our understanding through a meta-language which enables us to discern the rule of classification. In studying various classification systems anthropologists have settled on terminology—how people speak about things—as the target for analysis. Many anthropologists, though not all, have considered that in so analyzing terminology they are revealing something about cognition. Most psychologists would insist that it is not cognitive processes that are being studied by this means; only cognitive products. Nevertheless it is rare to find, in the cross-cultural literature on cognition, instances in which the indigenous scheme of classification has been taken seriously into account when experiments have been designed. One exception is that of Cole and his associates (Cole *et al.*, 1971, Chap. 3), who prefaced their studies of classification among the Kpelle of Liberia with a taxonomy of the Kpelle term for "thing"—this being the most general noun used in that language. Pertinent to this discussion also is Rosch's (1975) distinction of digital versus analogue representation of categories, and her point that analogue processes are a more prevalent mode of categorization in preliterate cultures.

The advantages to the study of cognition from a cross-cultural perspective is that there is thereby revealed significant elements which otherwise elude us if we pay attention only to our own culture. Misunderstanding of the cross-cultural approach ensues if one insists in thinking of it as a separate field of psychology. There is little harm in treating it as a separate field in a purely logistic sense; in terms that some psychologists earn their living by means of this approach, going to other cultures or sub-cultures, and addressing their problems by reference to cultural factors. But so-called cross-cultural psychology is inextricably entangled with theoretical and empirical concerns of both general and social psychology. In some ways it is regrettable that the term "cross" has been conjoined with the term "cultural", as the emphasis is too heavily laid thereby on comparison between groups of people. One could argue that there could be a viable cultural psychology if only one culture was ever inspected. Certainly it is not denied that there are differences between cultures as there are undoubted similarities. The important problem for the cross-cultural *perspective* is the way in which distinct psychological processes are linked with specific socio-cultural factors. From a study of the linkages can emerge the relevant units of comparison.

The necessity for specificity with these socio-cultural factors is a further point that emerges from this analysis. Paradoxically it means for the psychologist a widening of his horizon in order to pin-point such factors. We have already noted a widening into the direction of cognitive anthropology. One might also add, for many parts of the world, that a knowledge of nutritional and medical facts is required : the vague term impoverishment is too generalized to be useful when it comes to cognitive development especially. The same reasoning can be referred to terms like schooling and Westernization. Educational patterns differ sharply across both developed and undeveloped countries (see Thut and Adams, 1964; King, 1973). We need to know precisely what aspect of schooling is integral when the term is used as an explanatory factor in cognitive development. At best such terms as schooling, Westernization, acculturation and the like are vectoring concepts that enable us to look in a certain direction. It is at this point that fusion of cross-cultural psychology and other branches of psychology becomes critical, so that there is a transfer of knowledge from one area of specialization to another. Actually there are signs that this kind of development is emerging. One can point, for example, to the collaboration of cognitive psychologists and nutritionists that has occurred at the Institute of Nutrition of Central America and Panama in Guatemala. Fruitful results have come from the collaboration of educationalists and cognitive psychologists in Africa, for example that of Gay and Cole (1967) or the studies of the Human Development Research Unit in Lusaka, Zambia. Without doubt there are purely methodological problems that bedevil cross-cultural psychologists which are not encountered by their more parochial colleagues. These difficulties persist and remain to be mastered. Substantive problems, on the other hand, are shared equally by both.

REFERENCES

Abiola, E. T. (1965). The nature of intellectual development in Nigerian children. *Teacher Education, 6,* 37–58.

Baratz, S. S. and Baratz, J. C. (1970). Early childhood intervention: the social science base of institutional racism. *Harvard Educational Review, 40,* 29–50.

Barry, H., Child, I. L. and Bacon, M. K. (1959). Relation of child training to subsistence economy. *American Anthropologist, 61,* 51–63.

Berry, J. W. (1966). Temne and Eskimo perceptual skills. *International Journal of Psychology, 1,* 207–29.

Berry, J. W. (1969). On cross-cultural comparability. *International Journal of Psychology, 4,* 119–28.

Berry, J. W. (1971). Ecological and cultural factors in spatial perceptual development. *Canadian Journal of Behavioral Science, 3,* 324–36.

Berry, J. W. (1974). In J. W. Berry and P. R. Dasen (Eds.), *Culture and Cognition: Readings in Cross-Cultural Psychology.* London: Methuen.

Berry, J. W. (1975). An ecological approach to cross-cultural psychology. *Nederlands Tijdschrift Voor De Psychologie, 30,* 51–84.

Berry, J. W. and Annis, R. C. (1974). Ecology, culture and psychological differentiation. *International Journal of Psychology, 9,* 173–93.

Berry, J. W. and Dasen, P. R. (1974). *Culture and Cognition: Readings in Cross-Cultural Psychology.* London: Methuen.

Bonte, M. (1962). The reaction of two African societies to the Müller-Lyer illusion. *Journal of Social Psychology, 58,* 265–8.

Bovet, M. C. (1974). In J. W. Berry and P. R. Dasen (Eds.), *Culture and Cognition: Readings in Cross-Cultural Psychology.* London: Methuen.

Bruner, J. S., Olver, R. R. and Greenfield, P. M. (1966). *Studies in Cognitive Growth.* New York: Wiley.

Castaneda, A. and Ramirez, M. (1975). *Cultural Democracy: Bi-Cognitive Development and Education.* New York: Seminar Press.

Ciborowski, T. (1974). Cultural and cognitive discontinuities of school and home: remedialism revisited. Paper presented at the *Cognition Symposium of the Biennial Meeting of the Australian Institute of Aboriginal Studies,* Canberra, Australia.

Cohen, R. (1969). Conceptual styles, culture conflict and non-verbal tests of intelligence. *American Anthropologist, 71,* 828–55.

Cole, M. (1973). Towards an experimental anthropology of education. Paper presented at *Annual Meeting of the American Anthropological Association,* New Orleans, Louisiana.

Cole, M. (1975). In R. Brislin, S. Bochner and W. J. Lonner (Eds.), *Cross Cultural Perspectives in Learning.* New York: Wiley.

Cole, M. and Bruner, J. S. (1971). Cultural differences and inferences about psychological processes. *American Psychologist, 26,* 867–76.

Cole, M., Gay, J., Glick, J. A. and Sharp, D. W. (1971). *The Cultural Context of Learning and Thinking.* New York: Basic Books.

Cole, M. and Scribner, S. (1974). *Culture and Thought: A Psychological Introduction.* New York: Wiley.

Coleman, J. S. *et al.* (1966). *Equality of Education Opportunity.* Washington, D.C.: U.S. Office of Education.

Dasen, P. R. (1970). Cognitive development in aborigines of central Australia: concrete operations and perceptual activities (unpublished Ph.D. Thesis, Australian National University, Canberra).

Dasen, P. R. (1972). Cross-cultural Piagetian research: a summary. *Journal of Cross-Cultural Psychology, 3*, 23–9.

Dasen, P. R. (1974). In J. W. Berry and P. R. Dasen (Eds.), *Culture and Cognition: Readings in Cross-Cultural Psychology.* London: Methuen.

Dawson, J. L. M. (1967). Cultural and physiological influences upon spatial-perceptual processes in West Africa, Parts 1 and 2. *International Journal of Psychology, 2*, 115–28, 171–85.

Dawson, J. L. M. (1969). Theoretical and research bases of bio-social psychology. An Inaugural Lecture from the Chair of Psychology, University of Hong Kong. Supplement to the *Gazette, 16*(3), 1–10.

Dawson, J. L. M. (1971). Theory and research in cross-cultural psychology. *Bulletin of the British Psychological Society, 24*, 291–306.

Dawson, J. L. M., Young, B. M. and Choi, P. P. C. (1973). Developmental influences on geometric illusion susceptibility among Hong Kong Chinese children. *Journal of Cross-Cultural Psychology, 4*, 49–74.

De Lacey, P. R. (1970). A cross-cultural study of classificatory ability in Australia. *Journal of Cross-Cultural Psychology, 1*, 293–304.

Deregowski, J. B. and Serpell, R. (1971). Performance on a sorting task with various modes of representation: a cross-cultural experiment. *Human Development Research Unit.* University of Zambia, Report No. 18.

De Vos, G. and Hippler, A. E. (1969). In G. Lindzey and E. Aronson (Eds.), *The Handbook of Social Psychology*, 2nd ed., Vol. 4, Ch. 33. Reading, Mass.: Addison-Wesley.

Evans, J. L. and Segall, M. H. (1969). Learning to classify by color and by function: a study of concept-discovery by Gande children. *Journal of Social Psychology, 77*, 35–53.

Fraisse, P. and Vautrey, P. (1956). The influence of age, sex and specialized training on the vertical-horizontal illusion. *Quarterly Journal of Experimental Psychology, 8*, 114.

Furby, L. (1971). A theoretical analysis of cross-cultural research in cognitive development: Piaget's conservation task. *Journal of Cross-Cultural Psychology, 2*, 241–55.

Gallimore, R., Boggs, J. W. and Jordan, C. (1974). *Culture, Behavior and Education: A Study of Hawaiian-Americans*, Vol. II. Sage Library of Social Research. Beverley Hills: Sage Publications.

Gay, J. and Cole, M. (1967). *The New Mathematics and an Old Culture: A Study of Learning among the Kpelle of Liberia. Case Studies in Education and Culture.* New York: Holt, Rinehart and Winston.

Gladwin, T. (1970). *East is a Big Bird: Navigation and Logic in Puluwat Atoll.* Cambridge, Mass.: Harvard University Press.

Goodnow, J. J. (1975). In L. Resnick (Ed.), *New Approaches to Intelligence.* New York: Erlbaum.

Goodnow, J. J. and Bethon, G. (1966). Piaget's tasks: the effects of schooling and intelligence. *Child Development, 37*, 573–82.

Greenfield, P. M. (1966). In J. S. Bruner, R. R. Olver and P. M. Greenfield (Eds.), *Studies in Cognitive Growth.* New York: Wiley.

Greenfield, P. M. (1974). Comparing dimensional categorization in natural and artificial contexts: a developmental study among the Zinacantecos of Mexico. *Journal of Social Psychology, 93*, 157–71.

Greenfield, P. M. and Bruner, J. S. (1969). In D. A. Goslin (Ed.), *Handbook of Socialization Theory and Research,* Ch. 12. Chicago: Rand McNally.

Greenfield, P. M. and Childs, C. P. (1975). Weaving, color terms and pattern representation: cultural influences and cognitive development among the Zinacantecos of Southern Mexico. *Dossiers Pedagogiques* (in press).

Heron, A. (1971). Concrete operations, 'g' and achievement in Zambian children. *Journal of Cross-Cultural Psychology, 2*, 325–36.

Heron, A. and Dowel, W. (1973). Weight conservation and matrix-solving ability in Papuan children. *Journal of Cross-Cultural Psychology, 4*, 207–19.

Hess, R. D. and Shipman, V. C. (1965). Early experience and the socialization of cognitive modes in children. *Child Development, 36*, 869–86.

Hudson, W. (1960). Pictorial depth perception in sub-cultural groups in Africa. *Journal of Social Psychology, 52*, 183–208.

Irvine, S. H. (1970). Affect and construct: a cross-cultural check on theories of intelligence. *Journal of Social Psychology, 80*, 23–30.

Irwin, M. H. and McLaughlin, D. H. (1970). Ability and preference in category sorting by Mano school children and adults. *Journal of Social Psychology, 82*, 15–24.

Irwin, M. C., Schafer, G. N. and Feiden, C. P. (1974). Emic and unfamiliar category sorting of Mano farmers and U.S. undergraduates. *Journal of Cross-Cultural Psychology, 5*, 407–23.

Jahoda, G. (1966). Geometric illusions and environment: a study in Ghana. *British Journal of Psychology, 57*, 193–9.

Kagan, J. and Klein, R. E. (1973). Cross-cultural perspectives on early development. *American Psychologist, 28*, 947–61.

Kellaghan, T. (1968). Abstraction and categorization in African children. *International Journal of Psychology, 3*, 115–20.

King, E. J. (1973). *Other Schools and Ours: Comparative Studies for Today.* London: Holt, Rinehart and Winston.

LeVine, R .A. (1970). In P. H. Mussen (Ed.), *Carmichael's Manual of Child Psychology*, 3rd ed., Vol. 2, Ch. 26. New York: Wiley.

LeVine, R. A. and Price-Williams, D. R. (1974). Children's kinship concepts: cognitive development and early experience among the Hausa. *Ethnology, 13*, 25–44.

Lloyd, B. B. (1971). The intellectual development of Yoruba children: a re-examination. *Journal of Cross-Cultural Psychology, 2*, 29–38.

Lloyd, B. B. (1972). *Perception and Cognition: A Cross-Cultural Perspective.* Harmondsworth: Penguin Books.

Maccoby, M. and Modiano, N. (1969). Cognitive style in rural and urban Mexico. *Human Development, 12*, 22–33.

Morrison, A. and McIntyre, D. (1971). *Schools and Socialization.* Harmondsworth: Penguin Books.

Munroe, R. and Munroe, R. L. (1975). *Cross-Cultural Human Development.* Monterey, Calif.: Brooks/Cole (in press).

Nerlove, S. B., Roberts, J. M. Klein, R. E., Yarbrough, C. and Habicht, J-P. (1974). Natural indicators of cognitive development: an observational study of rural Guatemalan children, *Ethos, 2*, 265–95.

Okonji, O. M. (1971). A cross-cultural study of the effects of familiarity on classificatory behavior. *Journal of Cross-Cultural Psychology, 2*, 39–49.

Oltman, P. K. (1968). A portable rod-and-frame apparatus. *Perceptual and Motor Skills, 26*, 503–6.

Ord, I. G. (1968). *Manual for Pacific Design Construction Test.* Melbourne: Australian Council for Educational Research.

Piaget, J. and Morf, A. (1956). Récherches sur le development des perceptions,

XXX: Les comparaisons verticales à faible intervalle. *Archives de Psychology, 35,* 289–319.

Pollack, R. H. (1963). Contour detectibility as a function of chronological age. *Perceptual and Motor Skills, 17,* 411–17.

Pollack, R. H. and Silvar, S. N. (1967). Magnitude of the Müller-Lyer illusion in children as a function of the pigmentation of the fundus oculi. *Psychonomic Science, 8,* 83–4.

Poole, H. E. (1968). The effect of urbanization upon scientific concept attainment among Hausa children of Northern Nigeria. *British Journal of Educational Psychology, 38,* 57–63.

Price-Williams, D. R. (1961). A study concerning concepts of conservation of quantities among primitive children. *Acta Psychologica, 18,* 297–305.

Price-Williams, D. R. (1962). Abstract and concrete modes of classification in a primitive society. *British Journal of Educational Psychology, 32,* 50–61.

Price-Williams, D. R. (1968). In J. A. Clifton (Ed.), *Introduction to Cultural Anthropology: Essays in the Scope and Methods of the Science of Man.* Boston: Houghton Mifflin.

Price-Williams, D. R. (1969). *Cross-Cultural Studies: Selected Readings.* Harmondsworth: Penguin Books.

Price-Williams, D. R. (1975). *Explorations in Cross-Cultural Psychology.* San Francisco: Chandler and Sharp.

Price-Williams, D. R., Gordon, W. and Ramirez III, M. (1969). Skill and conservation: a study of pottery-making children. *Developmental Psychology, 1,* 769.

Reich, L. (1966). In J. S. Bruner, R. R. Olver and P. M. Greenfield (Eds.), *Studies in Culture and Cognitive Growth,* Ch. 13. New York: Wiley.

Rivers, W. H. R. (1901). In A. C. Haddon (Ed.), *Vision. Reports of the Cambridge Anthropological Expedition to the Torres Straits,* Vol. 2. Cambridge University Press.

Rivers, W. H. R. (1905). Observations on the senses of the Todas. *British Journal of Psychology, 1,* 321–96.

Rosch, E. (1975). In R. W. Brislin, S. Bochner and W. J. Lonner (Eds.), *Cross-Cultural Perspectives on Learning.* Sage Publications. New York: Wiley.

Scribner, S. and Cole M. (1973). Cognitive consequences of formal and informal education. *Science, 182,* 553–9.

Segall, M. H., Campbell, D. T. and Herskovits, M. J. (1966). *The Influence of Culture on Visual Perception.* New York: Bobbs-Merrill.

Serpell, R. (1971). Preference for specific orientation of abstract shapes among Zambian children. *Journal of Cross-Cultural Psychology, 2,* 225–39.

Silvar, R. H. and Pollack, S. N. (1967). Racial differences in the pigmentation of the fundus oculi. *Psychonomic Science, 7,* 159.

Stewart, V. M. (1973). Tests of the 'carpentered world' hypothesis by race and environment in America and Zambia. *International Journal of Psychology, 8,* 83–94.

Strodtbeck, F. (1964). Considerations of meta-method in cross-cultural studies. *American Anthropologist,* Special Publication, *66,* 223–9.

Tajfel, H. (1969). In G. Lindzey and E. Aronson (Eds.). *The Handbook of Social Psychology,* 2nd ed. Vol. 3, Ch. 22. Reading, Mass.: Addison-Wesley.

Tarjan, G. (1970). In H. C. Haywood (Ed.), *Socio-Cultural Aspects of Mental Retardation.* New York: Appleton-Century-Crofts.

Thut, I. N. and Adams, D. (1964). *Educational Patterns in Contemporary Societies.* New York: McGraw-Hill.

Triandis, H. C. (1964). in L. Berkowitz (Ed.), *Advances in Experimental Social Psychology.* New York: Academic Press.

Triandis, H. C., Malpass, R. S. and Davidson, A. R. (1971). In B. J. Siegel (Ed.), *Biennial Review of Anthropology,* Ch. 1. Stanford University Press.

Tyler, S. A. (1969). *Cognitive Anthropology.* New York: Holt, Rinehart and Winston.

Vernon, P. E. (1969). *Intelligence and Cultural Environment.* London: Methuen.

Walter, A. (1942). A genetic study of geometrical-optical illusions. *Genetic Psychology Monographs, 25,* 101–55.

Werner, E. E. (1972). Infants around the world: cross-cultural studies of psychomotor development from birth to two years. *Journal of Cross-Cultural Psychology, 3,* 111–34.

Witkin, H. A. (1967). A cognitive style approach to cross-cultural research. *International Journal of Psychology, 2,* 233–50.

Witkin, H. A. and Berry, J. W. (1975). Psychological differentiation in cross-cultural perspective. *Journal of Cross-Cultural Psychology, 6,* 4–87.

Witkin, H. A., Lewis, H. B., Hertzman, M., Machover, K., Meissner, P. B. and Wapner, S. (1954). *Personality Through Perception.* New York: Harper.

Witkin H. A., Dyk, R. B., Faterson, H. E., Goodenough, D. R. and Karp, S. A. (1962). *Psychological Differentiation.* New York: Wiley.

Witkin, H. A., Price-Williams, D. R., Bertini, M., Christiensen, B., Oltman, P. K., Ramirez, M. and Van Meel, J. (1974). Social conformity and psychological differentiation. *International Journal of Psychology, 9,* 11–29.

Wober, M. (1967). Adapting Witkin's field independence theory to accommodate new information from Africa. *British Journal of Psychology, 58,* 29–38.

Wursten, H. (1947). Récherches sur le development des perceptions, IX. L'évolution des comparaisons de longueurs de l'enfant à l'adulte avec variation d'angle entre la verticle et l'horizontale. *Archives de Psychology, 32,* 1–144.

PART IV

CHAPTER 14

Cognitive Development and Cerebral Dysfunction

S. John Hutt

I. INTRODUCTION

The effects of brain dysfunctions upon cognitive development have engaged the interest of psychologists of widely different theoretical persuasions. These are characterized by three rather different methods of study which may be loosely categorized as psychometric, observational and experimental respectively. By far the largest proportion of studies of brain-behaviour relationships in children has been undertaken within a psychometric framework. The primary aim of such studies is to develop test batteries which are sensitive to the presence of organic dysfunction. Large numbers of tests are administered to children with presumed brain damage. Those tests which reliably discriminate brain-damaged from normal children are retained whilst others which discriminate rather less well are replaced. Ultimately a battery of tests is built up of proven discriminability and this may then be used as part of the diagnostic armoury in further neurological work. The main concern of the psychometrician often appears to be how many sub-tests in a battery discriminate brain-damaged from normal subjects rather than which tests and how.

Where psychometric tests are deemed inappropriate—because the child is unable to understand instructions or is too unco-operative— an observational approach is occasionally employed. Brain-damaged children are studied in a "free-field", that is to say, an environment the physical boundaries of which are fixed, but within which the child is able to move about at will. The physical complexity of the free-field may be varied. Extra stimuli, including adults or other children, may be introduced at predetermined times. A baseline analysis is first made of the child's locomotor, manipulative and visual behaviour, usually in the simplest conditions. By systematically varying the environment it is then possible to examine a number of parameters of the child's attentive behaviour and learning. The impetus for such studies has come primarily from ethology, the biological study of animal behaviour, rather than from experimental psychology.

Relatively fewer in number but potentially of greater theoretical interest are studies formulated within a neuropsychological context. The aim of such studies is the testing of specific hypotheses concerning brain function, by observing the effects of its abnormalities upon behaviour. Whereas the psychometric approach is diagnostic, the neuropsychological approach is experimental. Thus, whilst the psychometrician generally restricts himself to well-established psychological tests, the neuropsychologist must frequently devise new procedures. Study of the adult lesioned patient has contributed greatly to our knowledge of physiological psychology in the last two decades, but relatively little comparable work has been undertaken on children.

The demarcations between the three approaches, psychometric, observational and experimental, are by no means clear-cut and in many instances two approaches are simultaneously employed in the same study. Nevertheless, the approaches are sufficiently distinct to provide a heuristically useful classification and one which will be employed in the present chapter.

II. TYPES OF CEREBRAL DYSFUNCTION

Abnormalities of brain function may follow from at least three causes: structural changes such as those caused by penetrating head wounds, tumours or tissue necrosis; changes in neuronal firing patterns such as epileptic seizures; and abnormalities of brain chemistry, such as phenylketonuria. The distinctions are arbitrary—dysfunctions of all three types may occur in the same individual. Nevertheless, the three categories of dysfunction, anatomical, electrical and biochemical, correspond with the three main classes of independent variable employed in studies of brain damage, and provide a convenient means of subdividing our material.

Within the category of anatomical change we may identify three further subdivisions corresponding with the strength of the evidence from which the diagnosis of brain damage is made. Brain damage may be regarded as *demonstrable* in cases such as penetrating head wounds or brain operations (say, for removal of a cyst) where an actual physical assault is made upon cerebral tissue. Brain damage is *strongly indicated* in cases where, for example, a post-infectious encephalopathy occurred in infancy and positive neurological signs (such as ataxia, hemiparesis) can be elicited at the time of psychological examination. Brain damage is *weakly indicated* in those cases where only so-called soft signs (for instance, minor asymmetries in tone) perhaps with an EEG abnormality are observed (see below). We shall encounter examples, in this chapter, of neurological evidence from each of the three categories.

The distinction we have made between demonstrable and strongly indicated brain damage closely corresponds with a distinction which has been made in practice in a few studies—that between acute and chronic damage. Acute head injuries are generally drawn from the accident wards of general hospitals and are of particular interest because some degree of remission in neurological state will generally take place within a year or so of the injury. Such cases are highly informative if studies of cognitive processes and neurological status are carried out in parallel during the progress of recovery.

Whilst the aetiology of brain injury in acute cases is generally well documented, this may not be so in more chronic cases. The presence of positive neurological signs at the time of psychological examination may reasonably be inferred to be related to certain well documented facts about the child's early history; but in many cases, no such facts may be ascertainable. Conversely, unequivocal evidence of an early brain injury may exist, without any definite neurological signs being demonstrable at the time of psychological examination. In both of these instances we should have to regard the presence of permanent brain damage as being highly probable. Some examples of the kinds of evidence which may be invoked to indicate chronic brain damage are provided by Ernhart et al. (1963) in their study of pre-school children.

In a number of studies, disorders of metabolism have been included amongst groups of children diagnosed as chronically brain-damaged (for example, Ounsted et al., 1966). The most common such disorder is phenylketonuria (PKU). The inclusion of PKU in groups otherwise diagnosed by neurological criteria is based upon the assumption that permanent tissue damage may be caused by the metabolic disturbance if unchecked; and that the effect of PKU upon the brain is global.

In the last decade a considerable amount of research has been devoted to the study of "minimal brain damage" or as it has been more aptly relabelled "minimal cerebral dysfunction" (MCD) (for a recent review see Walzer and Wolff, 1973). Of the three categories of evidence for the existence of brain damage in children—demonstrable, strongly indicated and weakly indicated—the evidence for minimal cerebral dysfunction seldom surpasses uncertain inference. An official publication of the United States Department of Health,

TABLE 14.1

Definitions of brain damage: demonstrable and strongly indicated

Etiology	Neurological symptoms at time of testing	Evidence
I. Prenatal, perinatal, or unknown, but probably not genetic	IA. Pryamidal or extra-pyramidal tract symptoms B. Convulsive symptoms, except petit mal C. Minor or other neurological symptoms	IA. Neurological examination B. Neurological examination C. X-ray evidence of cerebral atrophy or evidence of increased intracranial pressure with cranio-synostosis or hydrocephalus
II. Cerebral cyst or tumour	II. None necessary	II. Operative note
III. Cerebellar cyst or tumour with increased intracranial pressure	III. None necessary	III. Operative note *and* evidence of increased intracranial pressure
IV. Encephalopathy due to: A. Trauma, mechanical B. Intoxication C. Inflammation D. Metabolic etiology E. Vascular etiology	IV. Any definite neurological symptom	IV. Neurological examination; evidence of encephalopathy *and* evidence of etiological agent from hospital record

(*After* Ernhart *et al.*, 1963, p. 191.)

Education and Welfare provides the following definition (Clements, 1967):

> The term "minimal brain dysfunction" refers ... to children of near average, average or above average general intelligence with certain learning or behaviour disabilities ranging from mild to severe, which are associated with deviations of function of the central nervous system. These deviations may manifest themselves by various combinations of impairment in perception, conceptualization, language, memory and control of attention, impulse or motor function.

Among the symptoms most frequently cited are hyperactivity, short attention span, poor concentration, emotional lability, recklessness and poor susceptibility to external controls. In addition, perceptual deficits and disorders such as dyslexia are present in a sizeable proportion diagnosed as MCD. The clinical picture is similar to that generally labelled "the hyperkinetic syndrome" in the earlier neurological literature (Laufer et al., 1957; Ingram, 1956). Whilst it is easy to envisage any of these symptoms leading to learning difficulties, do they necessarily imply brain damage? Benton (1973) has depicted MCD as "a behavioural concept with neurological implications". In other words, whilst a patient may have clear evidence of brain disease without any observable evidence of behavioural abnormality, the constellation of behavioural abnormalities cited above is treated as evidence for an underlying organic dysfunction. There is, however, a real danger that the concept of minimal cerebral dysfunction may become a tautology. A particular syndrome of behavioural difficulties is said to be causally related to a dysfunction of the nervous system, the dysfunction being indicated in part by the presence of behavioural difficulties. The danger of tautology can be avoided if it is demonstrated that the behavioural symptoms are pathognomic of clear-cut neurological disorder. There are, in fact, three possible sources of such evidence (Kornetsky, 1975). In the first place, children with MCD have been shown to have a significantly greater number of the so-called soft signs than matched normal controls (Wikler et al., 1970). Amongst the soft signs thus noted are exaggerated tendon reflexes, choreiform movements, mild ataxia, clumsiness, extensor plantar responses. In the second place, both Wikler et al. (ibid) and Stevens et al. (1968) have reported an excess of abnormalities such as slow waves and spikes in the EEGs of children whose behavioural picture is that of MCD. In the third place, Laufer et al. (1957) have demonstrated that the seizure threshold of hyperkinetic children is lower than that of children with other types of behaviour disorders. Since a lowered seizure threshold is characteristic of both animals and humans who have damage to the diencephalon, this study would seem to indicate that subcortical areas of the brain are damaged in children with the hyperkinetic syndrome. However, all three of these findings—raised frequency of soft neurological signs, EEG abnormalities and lowered seizure threshold—are all characteristic of younger, as opposed to older, normal children. It might be argued therefore that in the absence of gross neurological signs, MCD is at least as likely to be indicative of immaturity of the central nervous system as of actual acquired damage. Kinsbourne (1973) has in fact cogently argued that children of a given age, who are supposedly suffering from minimal brain damage, are merely manifesting a level of neuropsychological maturity commensurate with that of younger normal children. As the minimal brain damage syndrome has recently been the subject of an extensive review (de la Cruz *et al.*, 1973) it will not be necessary to dwell further on the condition in the present chapter.

In a large number of studies of the effects of brain damage in childhood no efforts have been made to distinguish children with generalized abnormalities from those with lateralized ones. One reason why laterality of lesion may have been relatively neglected in children is the difficulty of localization. Where accurate localization may have to depend upon explorations which are even more traumatic for children than they are for adults, such as air-encephalograms, brain-scans, paediatric neurologists may well (quite rightly) have stayed their hands. Certainly such procedures are unjustified if they are unlikely to throw direct light upon possible treatment or rehabilitation.

In general, therefore, information on localization of function in children has come from two sources: studies of gross unilateral neurological abnormalities such as hemiplegia, and studies of focal EEG abnormalities. Such abnormalities provide a rare opportunity to study possible asymmetries of cerebral function in children. We shall refer to a number of studies in which such asymmetries have been studied psychometrically.

The use of EEG data in discussing cerebral dysfunctions introduces two new factors. In the first place, the observation of an abnormality such as a focal spike, a localized sharp wave or a slow wave, gives us no clue as to the state of the underlying tissue (Pennington *et al.*, 1965). Moreover, whilst localized areas of necrotic tissue may be presumed to be continuous in their effects upon cognitive function, this will not necessarily be the case with EEG abnormalities. More often than not, such abnormalities are intermittent, and it is tempting to speculate that any changes in cognitive function associated with the EEG abnormalities are themselves intermittent. Unfortunately (from a neuropsychological point of view) focal abnormalities tend to be of short duration—a focal sharp wave may occupy only a few hundred milliseconds—as well as occurring infrequently. For this reason, very few studies have attempted to compare cognitive functioning during brief localized discharges and during normal EEG background activity.

In contrast, generalized EEG abnormalities such as spike-wave paroxysms tend to be of longer duration (1–10 sec), thus providing samples of neuroelectric activity amenable to experimental analysis. These paroxysmal abnormalities have proved to be of particular interest since impairment in information processing has been demonstrated during them relative to normal "background" activity. The paroxysmal activity may thus be conceptualized as a "reversible lesion" somewhat analogous to short hippocampal after-discharges evoked by intra-cranial stimulation in animals (Flynn *et al.*, 1963).

To sum up, we have identified a number of factors which may be material to our evaluation of the studies cited in the following sections : the strength of the evidence for cerebral dysfunction; the nature of the dysfunction, structural, neuroelectrical or metabolic; and its localization. As will be seen later, these by no means exhaust the factors relevant to consideration of the effects of cerebral dysfunction in children.

The present review is selective rather than comprehensive. Rather than presenting an annotated bibliography, I have chosen to treat in some detail a small number of studies which illustrate particular points of significance. In order to indicate, therefore, the likely generality of the findings, I have thought it necessary to give the numbers of patients being studied in each case as well as their diagnoses.

In the next section findings from studies formulated largely within a psychometric framework will be reviewed, with respect to the effects of both generalized and lateralized brain damage. In the subsequent section, the use of observational techniques will be illustrated by reference to a single behavioural picture frequently associated with brain damage in children, the so-called hyperkinetic syndrome. In the final main section, the experimental approach will be illustrated by reference to hitherto unpublished data we have obtained from children with epilepsy.

III. PSYCHOMETRIC STUDIES

(1) GENERALIZED BRAIN DAMAGE

In the studies to be considered in this section the diagnoses of brain damage, except where otherwise stated, were based upon direct operative information or strong neurological indications.

(i) *Developmental trends.* The study by Graham *et al.* (1962) remains one of the largest-scale investigations of the sequaelae of perinatal complications. One hundred and sixteen children who had suffered perinatal anoxia were psychologically tested at 3 years of age and their performance compared with that of two other groups : eighty children who had suffered other neonatal complications (for instance, prematurity, erythroblastosis fetalis (EBF)), and 159 children whose births had been normal. The psychological examination consisted of : an intelligence test (Stanford-Binet) including an extended version of the vocabulary and definition tests; a concept test; and a battery of perceptual-motor tests. The concepts test consisted of blocks differing in form, colour and size, which had to be employed in tasks of varying levels of difficulty, for instance, matching, sorting by a single dimension, or sorting on two dimensions simultaneously with a third held constant. The perceptual-motor battery comprised four sub-tests: figure-ground discrimination; visual search; two point discrimination of touch; and motor co-ordination. Children who had suffered anoxia were significantly poorer than controls on the test of vocabulary and concepts, but showed no significant impairment in perceptual-motor functions. The children were also poorer on concepts than on vocabulary. Children with severe EBF showed evidence of conceptual impairment, as did prematures. The prematures, however, also showed some impairment of perceptual-motor function. The latter was interpreted by the authors as primarily a developmental lag rather than as impairment. Thus, overall the pattern of impairment which emerges in the 3-year-old, following perinatal complications, is as follows: major decrements on vocabulary and conceptual skills, with sparing of perceptual-motor skills. Since in the present case, damage to the central nervous system occurred at the beginning of life, before normal learning processes have begun, the relative normality of perceptual-motor functions at 3 years is especially interesting. We shall comment on this phenomenon later.

A different pattern of impairment emerges if brain damage occurs somewhat later. Almost all the brain-damaged children in the study by Ernhart *et al.* (1963) received their insults after the neonatal period but within the first three years of life. There were seventy brain-injured children in the sample ranging in age, by six-month steps, from 3 to 5 years exactly. Great care was taken in the definition of "brain damage", ensuring, as the authors indicate, that "the evidence for such a lesion should not be circular, that is, should not depend on behavioural or psychological evidence". The study was preceded by an extensive and carefully conducted cross-sectional study of normal children aged $2\frac{1}{2}$ to $5\frac{1}{2}$ years (Graham *et al.*, 1963). The scores of these children on a battery of psychological tests provided the norms against which the performance of the brain-damaged children could be evaluated. The battery of tests was the same as the one used in the study by Graham *et al.* with the addition of two further perceptual-motor subtests, copying simple visual forms and tracking (drawing between boundaries of two concentric figures). The brain-damaged children were found to be impaired in all areas of performance. The degree of impairment was similar on verbal, conceptual and perceptual-motor tests. The pattern of impairment generally reported in adults—conceptual and perceptual-motor tasks being markedly more impaired than verbal ones—was not obtained.

Studies of brain-damaged children of school age have been carried out by Reitan (1974). Reitan's (1974) sample comprised twenty-nine children aged 5 to 8 years inclusive with a mean age of 7 years 1 month. Each child was matched with a normal control of similar age and sex. The median age at which damage was incurred was estimated as 1 year, the term "brain-damage" covering post-encephalic sequaelae, cerebral palsy and hemiplegia. Three groups of tests were applied : the Wechsler Intelligence Scale for Children (WISC), the Wide-Range Achievement Test (WRAT), and the Reitan-Indiana Neuropsychological Test Battery.* The WRAT is a standard measure of ability in reading, spelling and arithmetic. The Reitan-Indiana Battery is a test especially developed for use with children, based upon the Halstead Neuropsychological Test Battery, and tests primarily perceptual-motor skills. Taking the WISC results first, the most striking difference between the brain-damaged and normal children was in overall IQ, the mean for the former being 78 and that for the latter 104. Both the WRAT and the Reitan Battery proved to be considerably less sensitive in distinguishing the brain-damaged from the normal children than the WISC, and in terms of academic achievement brain-damaged children were not as clearly demarcated from the normals as might have been expected. The apparent insensitivity of the Reitan Tests is also somewhat surprising, since in adults the Halstead Battery has generally proved to be more sensitive to the effects of brain damage than the WAIS. The reversal in children is a further example of a trend already noted in the study by Graham et al. (1962) that verbally-loaded and conceptual tasks (such as the WISC) are impaired by brain damage to a greater extent than are largely perceptual-motor tasks (such as the Reitan).

Reed et al. (1965) compared the psychological test performance of fifty brain-damaged children (degenerative diseases, cerebral tumours, head injuries) with that of fifty matched normal controls. The children were early adolescents, aged 10 to 14 years. The tests employed were the Wechsler-Bellevue Intelligence Scale and a group from the Halstead test battery. The Wechsler IQ of the brain-damaged group was found on average to be 22 points lower than that of the normals. The verbal tests of the Wechsler were consistently more impaired than tests from the performance scale. Tests of the Reitan battery were performed about as well as the Wechsler performance tests. Unfortunately, no attempt was made to partial out the effects of IQ, which raises doubts

---

* For detailed description of the Reitan Indiana Neuropsychological Battery, reference may be made to the recent symposium edited by Reitan and Davidson (1974) which includes considerable information on its validity and correlation with IQ scales. A factorial analysis of the battery is provided by Crockett et al. (1969) and Klonoff (1971).

as to whether the tests were measuring cerebral dysfunction *per se*. Nevertheless, the results are interesting in several respects. First, the overall pattern of dysfunction we have observed in children from 3 years of age is repeated in the adolescent group. Secondly, there is no indication, despite the greater maturity of the children in this study, of a reversal of the pattern of impairment generally found in adults, that is to say, relative sparing of verbal skills and poor performance in problem-solving and perceptual-motor skills. Out of a total of twenty-seven measures, the greatest difference between brain-damaged and normal children was obtained on the Wechsler total weighted score. Interestingly, the second greatest impairment was observed on the Halstead speech sound perception test. In this test subjects are presented with recorded spoken speech sounds from a tape and are required to match the sound heard with one of four visually presented choices. It is tempting to see in this result a possible causative factor in the general verbal dysfunction. Clearly if during the period when language is normally acquired there is damage to the auditory coding apparatus, skills which are primarily mediated by language are likely to be impaired. We might expect children whose brain damage is acquired early in life to be particularly affected. However, it seems unlikely that more than half of the cases in the study by Reed *et al.* (*ibid*) were early injuries—diagnoses, but not durations of injury are given in their paper—which leaves in doubt the degree of homogeneity of the findings in relation to the age at which injury was acquired.

Boll's (1974) study is both a replication and an extension of that of Reed *et al.* (1965). Twenty-seven brain-damaged children were matched for age, sex, race and handedness with normal controls. The mean age of the brain-damaged group was $12\frac{1}{2}$ years. The tests included the Wechsler-Bellevue Form 1, the Halstead Neuropsychological Battery for Children and a number of other tests favoured by the Reitan group, such as tactile form recognition and trail-making. Of a total of forty variables studied, thirty-two significantly discriminated brain-damaged from normal children. On the Wechsler, verbal sub-tests were again generally more impaired by brain damage than performance ones. Sub-tests from the Halstead battery were impaired to approximately the same extent as the performance sub-tests of the Wechsler. Thus the data are consistent with those of Reitan *et al.* in showing that performances involving the use of language and past learning are more impaired in brain-damaged children than are perceptual-motor and visual problem-solving tasks. The speech sounds perception test was somewhat lower in overall ranking in terms of its sensitivity to brain damage than it was in the case of the Reed study; but brain-damaged children still performed significantly worse than controls (p<0.005), and rather worse in the speech sounds test even than on several of the Wechsler verbal sub-tests. Again, as in the study of Reed *et al.* (*ibid*), the crucial variable of age at injury was not considered.

The importance of taking into account age of insult is indicated in a study of Ounsted *et al.* (1966) of 100 children with temporal lobe epilepsy. The children were carefully selected both on the basis of the behavioural pattern of their seizures and by the presence of an unequivocal temporal lobe focal spike in their EEGs. The patients were studied from educational, psychiatric and social points of view. Perhaps the most significant of the large number of findings from this study was that concerning status epilepticus in early life. The authors divided their data into three categories—children who had had a definite cerebral insult (for instance, an injury involving brain tissue, an encephalitis or meningitis); children who had had one or more bouts of status epilepticus (a continuous grand mal seizure lasting 20 min or more), and children who had suffered neither a cerebral insult nor status epilepticus. Table 14.2 shows the median Verbal IQs of the total group of children in relation to the age of onset of their seizures and according to whether the first seizure had been accompanied by either a clear-cut cerebral insult or a bout of status epilepticus.

TABLE 14.2

Median Verbal IQ in relation to age of onset of seizures in children with temporal lobe epilepsy, with or without a history of cerebral insult or status epilepticus

Age of onset of seizures	Temporal lobe epilepsy + cerebral insult	Temporal lobe epilepsy + status epilepticus	Temporal lobe epilepsy alone
Under 1 year	76	74	95
1–3 years	77.5	85	110
Over 3 years	100	100	110

(*After* Ounsted *et al.*, 1966, pp. 63, 66 and 68.)

It can be seen that the earlier dysfunction is manifest, the greater the depression of IQ. The greater the severity of the underlying cerebral dysfunction—as inferred from the overall lower level of performance following a neurological complication, including status epilepticus—the more pronounced the age effect. These data thus go some way to reconciling the findings of Graham *et al.* (1962) and

Ernhart *et al.* (1963) mentioned earlier. It will be recalled that in the former study, where brain damage was attributed to the effects of perinatal anoxia, whilst there was an overall reduction in IQ compared with norms for undamaged children of similar age, verbal and conceptual skills were more adversely affected than performance ones. In the study of Ernhart *et al.* (1963) cerebral insults might have occurred at any time before the age of 3 years and in this case the differential performance on verbal and non-verbal tasks was not observed.

However, it should be noted that even in studies where subjects have been equated for age at cerebral insult, comparisons between brain-damaged children and normal controls may vary according to the age at which testing is carried out. Whilst its relation to tests of cognitive processes may appear somewhat obscure, the study by Teuber and Rudel (1962) of the effects of brain damage upon position sense raises some important and relevant issues. Three different tasks were employed. In the first—the auditory midline task—the subject was required to localize the source of a clicking sound whilst being tilted, in a specially built chair, 28 degrees to the left or to right. The sound source was moved radially in the coronal plane with the subject's occiput as centre. He was required to indicate when he thought the sound was in the midline position. Brain-damaged children aged 5 to 9 years did not differ significantly from normal children of similar age in their ability to pinpoint the sound source correctly. From 11 to 15 years, however, the brain-damaged children became progressively poorer relative to the normals. A second task was designed to assess the magnitude of the so-called starting position effect. With the subject sitting in the upright position, the sound source was gradually brought into the midline position until the subject estimated that it was on the midline. All subjects showed a tendency to localize the sound source on the same side as its starting position. The misalignments for starting positions to the left and right of the subject were summed to give the total starting position error. The magnitude of these misalignments was found to be significantly greater in brain-damaged children than in normals throughout the whole age range. In the third task, subjects were blindfolded and tilted to left or to right, in which position they remained for up to 2 mins. The chair was then rotated back towards the vertical, until the subject said that he felt upright. The normal response is to underestimate slightly the amount by which the chair must be rotated to achieve the vertical—probably due to habituation to the tilted position. The young brain-damaged children showed a considerably greater self-righting error than normal children. With increasing age, however, the gap between brain-damaged and normal children gradually narrowed and after 11 there was no longer any significant difference between them.

It can thus be seen that, using three variants of a simple perceptual-motor task, three quite distinct responses to the effect of brain damage are found. In the case of the starting-position effect, brain damage is associated with a more or less constant level of impairment at each age level tested. On the body-tilt test, the effects of brain damage are not apparent until around 11 years of age. On the self-righting task the exact converse is found, the effect of brain damage being manifest only until age 11, no demonstrable abnormality being found thereafter. The implications of this series of experiments are important. They suggest that in assessing the effects of brain damage, not only must the age at injury be taken into account, but the age at testing. Quite different patterns of impairment may be evinced according as to whether the patient is studied soon after the injury or later. Moreover, such age-dependent effects are task-specific : tasks which are sensitive to the effects of brain damage at one age may not be so at another. Thus, the proposition that brain injuries suffered early in life may have disproportionately more serious consequences for cognitive development than ones suffered later may need further qualification.

(ii) *Severity of lesion.* One variable which has received scant attention is the severity of lesion, both because of the difficulty of providing a suitable criterion of severity and because of the likelihood of confounding severity with acuteness, age at injury, and IQ. A pilot study in this area is that of Reed and Fitzhugh (1966). Brain-damaged children aged 12 to 13 years whose dysfunction was judged as being either mild or moderate were compared on a variety of tests with controls. In addition, two groups of adults, also with either mild or severe lesions, were compared with a control group. The severity of brain damage in this case was based upon long-term prognosis. Children who were judged as requiring long-term hospitalization following traumatic injuries to the brain, degenerative conditions and atrophy, were categorized as "moderately impaired". All patients suffered epileptic seizures. The "mildly impaired" group whilst sharing similar aetiological conditions were not so disabled as to require long-stay care. The same general distinction could be made for the adults. All patients and their controls were tested on the Wechsler Intelligence Scale, the Reitan Trailmaking test and a battery of seven Halstead tests. The patterns of impairment obtained in children and in adults were markedly different. Verbal and conceptual skills were relatively spared in adults compared with perceptual-motor skills. The converse was true for the children. As might be expected, children who were neurologically "moderately" impaired scored consistently worse than those who were only "mildly" impaired. Despite this quantitative difference between moderately and mildly damaged groups the overall pattern of impairment was remarkably similar. Skills which depended upon past learning rather than upon immediate "adaptive" or "problem-solving" ability were most impaired. For example, the Information, Comprehension, Similarities and Vocabulary tests of the Wechsler were very poorly performed in both groups relative to their controls. This group of sub-tests has been held to indicate a "Verbal Comprehension Factor" (Cohen, 1959). Interestingly, speech perception—which in a number of studies already reviewed distinguishes brain-damaged from normal groups—was the most poorly performed sub-test amongst the mildly impaired children and was sixth worse out of twenty sub-tests amongst the moderately impaired. In contrast, the Halstead Tactual Performance Task, in which a version of the Seguin Form Board has to be solved whilst blindfold, showed poor discrimination between normal children and brain-damaged children, irrespective of whether the latter were diagnosed as mildly or moderately impaired. Thus the severity of lesion appears to affect the level at which most tasks are performed, but does not affect their rank order. Neither does severity of lesion apparently affect the child's relative superiority on performance tasks as opposed to tasks of verbal intelligence. However, it should be noted that this generalization holds true only if normal hand control is preserved. As we shall see in the next section, in hemiplegic children a rather different pattern of psychological test performance may be observed.

(2) LATERALIZED LESIONS

So far we have considered only generalized lesions. Studies of children who have suffered lateralized lesions are relatively rarer, but are potentially of great neuropsychological interest, because of the light they may throw upon the development of cerebral dominance and behavioural plasticity. The complexities of the plasticity issue are well illustrated by the studies of Basser (1962) and Annett (1973), in which the effects of laterality of lesion, age of onset and family sinistrality were explored. The importance of taking into consideration the age at which a cerebral insult has been suffered has already been stressed. It is reasonable to suppose that the effects of a cerebral lesion will be different if it is incurred before, rather than during, the sensitive period for the development of a particular cognitive skill. However, in all studies of the effects of cerebral dysfunctions suffered early in life there remains an unanswerable question: to which cerebral hemispheres were particular psychological processes originally allocated? Studies in which not only age of insult but also family sinistrality have been taken into account are therefore of particular interest.

> The best guess that can be made about their (hemiplegic children's) cerebral laterality prior to injury is that the majority would be inclined toward left hemisphere speech, irrespective of familial handedness and that the proportion of cases with potential ambilaterality would be greater in those with familial sinistrality (Annett, 1973).

(i) *Anatomical lesions.* The study by Basser (1962) involved 102 hemiplegics of early onset. Seventy-two of the cases had hemiplegias the onset of which predated the development of speech, generally, ones incurred during the first six months of life. The remainder all suffered insults following the development of speech. The distribution of Verbal IQ scores amongst the sample as a whole was markedly skewed : sixty-eight cases with IQs less than 91; eleven with IQs between 91 and 110; and only ten with IQs of 111 or over. (Not all children were testable.) The distributions of children with left and right hemisphere lesions respectively did not differ significantly from each other. In other words, hemiplegic children, whose injuries might be expected to be fairly lateralized, behaved, as far as verbal intelligence is concerned, very much as children with generalized lesions. Nineteen children (eight, left hemisphere lesions, eleven right) developed either very scanty or no speech and in each of these cases there was a history of continuing seizures, which might point to a more generalized cerebral mischief than the hemiplegia alone would indicate. What is particularly interesting about this sub-group is that fourteen of the children were apparently ones whose hemiplegia was of late onset. The pattern of speech disturbance amongst the late onset group was similar to that found in older children (Alajouanine and L'Hermitte, 1965; McFie, 1961); in general, patients with right hemiplegias were more likely to be impaired in speech than those with left hemiplegias. It may be supposed that in these children speech was becoming, or had become, established in the left hemisphere at the time of injury. The duration of speech disturbance was longer if the lesion causing hemiplegia occurred under 2 years of age than if it occurred over 2 years of age. That is to say, impairment was greater if the cerebral insult occurred when speech would normally begin to develop.

The speech development of children whose hemiplegia was of earlier onset frequently showed an essentially normal pattern of acquisition, irrespective of the side of injury. The early onset cases were divided almost equally between left- and right-sided hemiplegias. There were no significant differences between the two groups with respect to either their age of speech acquisition or their likelihood of chronic speech defects. Since there was nothing in the family histories which indicated an unusual expectation of sinistrality in the children, it seems reasonable to infer that, in the normal course of events, the majority of the children would have been left dominant for speech. We might thus conclude that where injury to the left hemisphere is sustained at the beginning of life, speech can readily be acquired by the intact right cerebral hemisphere. For example, of special interest were a brother and sister, both of whom suffered unilateral lesions— the boy a right hemisphere lesion and the girl a left hemisphere lesion —before speech developed. A right hemispherectomy was performed on the boy, who preoperatively had no speech, at age 4. His sister, who had only a few words preoperatively, received a left hemispherectomy at 20 months of age. Whilst globally each child appears to have performed at only a sub-normal level, both developed clear, simple speech. Referring to the study as a whole, Basser concluded that "speech was developed and maintained in the intact hemisphere and in this respect the left and right hemispheres were equipotential" (p. 451). In a more recent study, however, Annett (1973) has indicated that compensation for left-sided lesions may be severely constrained according to whether or not there is a history of sinistrality in the family of the affected patient.

Annett's (1973) study is probably the most detailed investigation yet undertaken of the intelligence of hemiplegic children. In addition to the effects of laterality of lesion, sex and family sinistrality, Annett also estimated the level of functioning of the hemisphere controlling the less affected hand. The speed with which each child could move a row of pegs from one row of holes to another 8 in. away was measured for both the child's unaffected hand and the affected hand where this proved possible. By comparing performance by the better hand with standards for normal children of similar age, it was thus possible to estimate the degree of damage suffered by the less affected hemisphere. In terms of overall IQ, there were no significant differences between left-sided and right-sided hemiplegics. A factor of far greater importance than laterality of lesion in determining intellectual performance was the integrity of the less affected hemisphere as judged from speed of the better hand. Where performance with the better hand fell within the normal range, that with the affected hand tended to be only moderately impaired. In these cases, IQ was generally near normal, with Performance IQ being consistently higher than Verbal IQ. Where the better hand was adjudged to be slightly or severely impaired, the more affected hand was respectively severely impaired or useless.

In these cases, IQ was in the sub-normal or nearly sub-normal range with Performance IQ being significantly lower than Verbal. From these data we might tentatively infer that where the motor control of either hand is severely impaired, performance skills (as measured by the Wechsler Performance IQ) is severely limited. Where, however, manual dexterity is reasonably preserved, Performance IQ tends to exceed Verbal IQ. We shall return to this possibly important point later.

The incidence of speech defects differed according to both the laterality of the lesion and its age of acquisition. Children whose hemiplegia was acquired after the age of 13 months, when speech normally has begun to develop, showed a pattern of impairment very similar to that found in adults: all but one child with right hemiplegia had a speech defect; only one child with left hemiplegia (believed to have been left-handed prior to insult) showed a speech defect. Amongst children whose hemiplegia was evident at birth or acquired during the first thirteen months of life a much lower incidence of speech defects was observed. Nevertheless, approximately one-third of children with right-sided hemiplegia manifested some disturbance of speech compared with less than one-sixth of children with left hemiplegia. It is thus apparent that whilst some compensation for an early left-sided lesion may be possible in the majority of individuals, there is a nucleus of children for whom this is not the case. It might be expected that these are children in whom genetic factors predisposing towards left hemisphere specialization for speech are especially strong.

To examine this possibility, the Verbal and Performance IQ scores were correlated with speed of hand movement in children with and without a history of familial sinistrality. The findings were in accord with expectation : in right hemiplegics without familial sinistrality both Verbal and Performance IQs were more highly correlated with the speed of the affected hand than with that of the better hand. The opposite was true for groups with familial sinistrality. In other words, it would appear that where genetic factors disposing towards left-sided speech are weaker, intellectual functions are more readily organized in the undamaged hemisphere. However, it would not seem to us to be justified to argue as Annett does that "laterality of lesion is relevant to the motor production of speech but not to the growth of higher language functions and general intelligence" (p. 26). It would appear that where there is strong genetic determination towards left hemisphere specialization for speech, not merely motor production of speech, but other aspects of intellectual performance are localized to the left hemisphere.

The studies by Basser (*op. cit.*) and Annett (*op. cit.*) each indicate that where a cerebral lesion is incurred after the first year of life, a pattern of intellectual deficit is obtained much more like that observed in adults (see for instance, Dennerll, 1964) than like the one seen in children whose lesions occurred in the first year. This finding is in accord with that of an earlier study by McFie (1961) of intellectual impairment and focal lesions in children. McFie's patients, forty children between the ages of 5 and 15 years, had all suffered cerebral insults after the age of 1 year. The majority of the lesions were cerebral tumours which had been verified at operation or necropsy, or by air-encephalography. Whilst the number of patients is small and the results were not always statistically significant, the overall pattern of performance observed by McFie is interesting because of its comparison with adult norms (McFie, 1960). Children with right hemisphere lesions, especially of the right parietal lobe, were significantly impaired on a memory-for-designs task from the Terman-Merrill Scale, a finding identical with that obtained in the adult sample. The overall pattern of scores of children and adults was similar in relation to six other variables: the Digit Span, Similarities, Picture Arrangement and Block Design sub-tests of the Wechsler and the verbal and performance levels of the Terman-Merrill and Koh's Blocks scales respectively. Poor performance on the Digit Span and Similarities tests was associated with left-sided lesions; poor performance on Picture Arrangement and Block Designs was associated with right-sided lesions. Moreover, children with left-sided lesions were more likely to have lower Verbal IQs than Performance IQs, the opposite being true for children with right-sided lesions. One of the main differences between the performances of children and of adults was in respect of the Wechsler Vocabulary sub-test. Children with lesions in either hemisphere were equally impaired, relative to their corresponding age norms. However, by and large, the conclusion is justified that for children whose lesions are acquired after the first year of life, the pattern of deficit appears to reflect an increasing approximation to an adult form of cerebral organization.

(ii) *Neuroelectric lesions.* Comparison of the patterns of impairment found in children and in adults has been studied in relation to minor cerebral dysfunctions indicated by EEG means as well as in relation to demonstrable lesions. In a carefully controlled study of children with epilepsy, Fedio and Mirsky (1969) compared the capacities for sustained attention and for verbal and non-verbal information processing in relation to the site of specific EEG abnormalities. Two of the patient groups consisted of children with "unilateral epilepiform discharges" (presumably focal spikes or spike-wave discharges) localized in either the left or the right temporal lobe. A third group of patients all had bilateral, synchronous and symmetrical 3 Hz spike-wave activity in their EEGs. The latter discharges were presumed to be of "centrencephalic" origin. The three patient groups, each of which contained fifteen children, were carefully matched with each other and with a normal control group by age, education and IQ (WISC and Peabody Picture Vocabulary Test (PPVT)). The mean age of the four groups was approximately $10\frac{1}{2}$ years and their average IQ approximately 100. All children were right-handed. The age of onset of epilepsy in the three patient groups was 3 years or later. Thus, assuming that epileptic discharges of the temporal lobe are indicative of underlying pathology, we should expect a pattern of deficit similar to that found by McFie (1961), that is, one characteristic of adult temporal lobe dysfunction (see for instance Milner, 1967). The expectation was in fact borne out by the data. Whilst there were no significant differences amongst the normal and epileptic groups with respect to Verbal, Performance or Full Scale scores on the WISC, the magnitude and direction of the VIQ–PIQ differences were according to prediction. That is, VIQ was generally lower than PIQ for patients with left temporal foci, whilst the reverse pattern was found in patients with right foci. Moreover, patients with left temporal lesions obtained the lowest scores on the Information, Comprehension, Similarities and Vocabulary sub-tests, which have been identified with a "Verbal Comprehension Factor" (Cohen, 1959). Left temporal epileptics also had lower scores on the PPVT than right temporals or normals.

The pattern of deficits obtained on the tests of verbal and non-verbal memory and learning was exactly as would have been predicted from adult studies. In the verbal memory tasks, series of random words were presented either auditorily or visually. In the auditory version of the task immediate recall was required, whilst in the visual version a reproduction procedure was employed. In each condition two parameters were calculated: memory span, the longest series of items correctly reproduced; and supraspan, the total number of correct responses for all trials which exceeded the patient's immediate memory span. The non-verbal equivalent of the auditory and visual immediate memory tasks consisted of the reproduction of tone sequences and of abstract designs respectively. All groups performed the verbal tasks better than the non-verbal ones and there were no significant differences amongst the various groups on the immediate memory span parameter. The supraspan measure, however, clearly distinguished the two temporal lobe groups from each other. Patients with left temporal foci had the poorest supraspan recall on the verbal task whilst patients with right temporal foci showed the poorest recall for non-verbal material.

Comparable data were obtained for verbal and non-verbal learning tasks. In the verbal task children were required to recall immediately lists of ten unrelated words up to a criterion of two correct repetitions in three trials, followed by a further recall 5 min later. In the non-verbal task, a complex design had to be copied and then drawn from memory after a 3-min interval. The patients with left temporal foci took more trials to achieve criterion on the verbal task and recalled fewer words after a 5-min delay than did the patients with right-sided foci. Conversely, on the non-verbal task, the patients with right-sided foci showed poorer recall.

Patients with centrencephalic epilepsy exhibited no significant memory deficits, but were grievously impaired on the test of sustained attention, in a continuous performance task. This comprised series of letters presented sequentially on a memory drum. The patient's task was to identify prescribed letters or combinations of letters. Significantly fewer signals were correctly identified by the children with centrencephalic epilepsy than by any other patient group. We shall deal in more detail with the impairment of children with centrencephalic epilepsy and tests of sustained attention in a subsequent part of this chapter.

It should be noted that the findings by Fedio and Mirsky (*ibid.*) are not entirely compatible with those of Pennington *et al.* (1965). Pennington *et al.* (1965) correlated the Wechsler Verbal and Performance Scale scores of 158 children with lateralized features in their EEGs. Their sample comprised 158 children aged 6 to 16 years, all of whom were right-handed and divided into five sub-groups : hospitalized patients with left, right and diffuse EEG dysrhythmias; patients with normal EEGs; and non-hospitalized children also with normal EEGs. Extrapolating from findings of Dennerll (1964) and others on adults that left hemisphere dysfunctions generally are associated with Verbal Scale deficits and right hemisphere dysfunctions with Performance Scale deficits, it was hypothesized (i) that a similar pattern of impairment would be found in children with respect to lateralized dysrhythmias; (ii) that children with diffuse dysrhythmias would show similar Verbal and Performance scores. No clear-cut relationship between lateralization or cerebral dysrhythmia and intelligence scores was obtained. In fact, the same pattern of impairment was found in all three groups with EEG dysrhythmias, namely an overall depression in IQ, the Verbal Scale being more adversely affected than the Performance Scale.

The differences between the studies of Fedio and Mirsky (1969) and Pennington *et al.* (1965) can probably be accounted for by reference to two variables: the age of cerebral insult and the specificity of neuroelectric lesions in the two studies. The aetiology of the cerebral dysrhythmias studied by Pennington *et al.* (*ibid.*) is obscure. However, it may have included cases of brain damage acquired before the age of one year. Moreover, the EEG abnormalities appear to have been extremely unspecific, possibly indicating a less clearly localized lesion than that shown in the study by Fedio and Mirsky (*op cit.*). The data are thus in accord with the general pattern of deficit observed in studies of generalized brain damage of early onset.

The relative sparing of performance skills over verbal skills in cases where motor functions themselves are impaired either very little or not at all, has been noted in most of the studies so far reviewed. We shall now examine a study which offers an unexplained and provocative interpretation for this finding.

The obscurely published study by Annett *et al.* (1961) remains one of the most interesting explorations of the relationship between focal EEG abnormalities and cognitive ability. Comparisons were made of the WISC scores of three main groups of children each of which was chosen by EEG criteria only: the EEGs of the first group contained generalized EEG abnormalities only (for instance spikes, slow waves); those of the second group contained unilateral abnormalities only; the EEGs of the third group were normal. Whilst both Verbal and Performance IQs of the group with generalized abnormalities were lower than those of the normal-EEG group, the largest and most interesting differences were observed when children with unilateral EEG abnormalities were compared with normals. On average, such children scored some 15 points lower than normals on both Verbal and Performance Scales. The unilateral foci were classified as ipsilateral or contralateral to the child's preferred hand. Where the child showed no clear hand preference, the EEGs, were classified as "mixed". The WISC Verbal and Performance IQs were then calculated for the three groups thus categorized; the data are reproduced in Table 14.3. Children with focal abnormalities contralateral to the preferred hand were markedly impaired on the WISC Verbal Scale. Those with abnormalities ipsilateral to the preferred hand were impaired to an even greater extent on performance tasks. The mixed group, that is, the ones without any clear-cut hand preference, showed a pattern of impairment which was identical with that in the contralateral group. The authors suggest a novel interpretation of their data, namely, that in children whose cerebral dominance is not yet fully lateralized (the "mixed" group) the undamaged hemisphere assumes control of visuospatial functions with consequent impairment of language. Thus, Annett and her colleagues see the acquisition of visuospatial

gnosis as having precedence in cognitive development over language.
They argue that this would have considerable survival value in that

> the growth of many concepts, including the Object Concept in infants,
> concepts of time, causality and number, depends on an appreciation of
> the changing positions in space of objects and the child's own body . . .
> It seems that an appreciation of spatial relationships may be a basic
> skill upon which a hierarchy of other skills is built (Annett *et al.*, 1961,
> p. 106).

TABLE 14.3

**The mean Verbal and Performance IQs of the normal group compared
with those of groups with unilateral foci**

No.	Verbal mean	Performance mean
Normal		
37	98.95	99.24
Ipsilateral Foci		
19	88.00	78.00
Contralateral Foci		
12	83.08	90.67
Mixed Group		
9	83.44	90.11

(*After* Annett *et al.*, 1961, p. 100.)

According to this argument, if one side of the brain is damaged early
in life, a partial exchange of function between the hemispheres may
occur. The hemisphere predisposed to control speech, if it is undamaged, acquires control of visuo-spatial functions. The damaged
hemisphere acquires control of speech and some manual skills. This
argument adds a new gloss to what we have already discovered, that
generally brain damage in early childhood results in poorer verbal
than perceptual motor ability. If true, the hypothesis of Annett *et al.*
(*idem*) indicates that such impairment follows not because linguistic
skills are more *vulnerable* than perceptual motor ones, but because
they are more *dispensable*.

(3) DISCUSSION

From the majority of studies so far reviewed, one consistent effect
emerges : a global reduction in IQ amongst brain-damaged patients
relative to their normal age peers. This effect is manifest irrespective
of the aetiology of the lesion, its severity, and whether it is identified

by neurological or electroencephalographic means. The one exception to this picture was found amongst children with temporal lobe epilepsy without history of either cerebral insult or status epilepticus, who were of normal average intelligence. In this respect, these children resemble those with Minimal Cerebral Dysfunction, who also tend to be of normal intelligence (Kalverboer, 1975).

Whilst in some instances no differences between the verbal and non-verbal skills of brain-damaged children could be demonstrated (see for instance Ernhart et al., 1963), in the majority of cases discrepancies between verbal and non-verbal performance was observed. The direction of the discrepancy was affected by the age at which the lesion occurred and the estimated extent of brain damage. In general, the earlier the lesion was acquired the more likely that visuo-spatial skills (to the extent that these are measured by the most commonly used tests such as those of the WISC) would be superior to verbal skills. This was seen most clearly in the study by Graham et al. (1962) of the children who suffered perinatal damage. Where lesions are acquired later than the first year of life, an increasing number of children show the pattern of disability usually associated with brain-damaged adults —rather poorer performance overall on visuo-spatial skills than on verbal skills (McFie, 1961). (It is tempting to speculate that studies which show equal impairment of verbal and visuo-spatial skills, and do not indicate the precise age at which brain damage was acquired, may contain equal numbers of children whose age of insult was under 1 year and over 1 year respectively.)

The direction of the discrepancy between verbal and non-verbal performance is apparently affected also by the likely severity of damage. In the study of hemiplegic children by Annett (1973), which we reviewed at length, the severity of cerebral dysfunction was estimated from the relative speed of manipulation of the two hands. If brain damage was associated with poor motor control of both hands— indicated by poor motor performance with the less affected limb— Verbal IQ was superior to Performance IQ (Annett, ibid.) This is perhaps only to be expected, since tests such as the WISC Performance Scale demand a fairly high level of fine manipulative skill for completion of many of the test items, for instance, Koh's Blocks and Digit Symbol sub-tests. Superior Performance IQ over Verbal IQ was obtained by Annett in hemiplegic children whose more affected hand had near normal function and whose less affected hand was wholly normal in function. Thus, provided that there is relative sparing of motor function on at least one side of the body, the more likely pattern remains one in which visuo-spatial tasks are performed more adequately than verbal ones. Moreover, it would appear that where there is no gross motor impediment, the severity of damage (as determined) by clinical assessment) primarily affects the overall *level* of performance, rather than the directional differences between Verbal and Performance Scales (Reed and Fitzhugh, 1966).

The age at which lesions occur appears also to have differential effects upon the motor production of speech and higher language functions. By and large, the earlier the lesion, the less the subsequent speech defect (Basser, 1962; Annett, 1973) but the greater the impairment of verbal intelligence (Ounsted *et al.*, 1966). Conversely, the later the lesion, the more likely it is to affect speech production but leave verbal intelligence relatively intact (McFie, 1961). Again, it would appear that the cut-off point for the differential effects of brain damage upon motor production of speech and upon verbal intelligence is one year of age. It is therefore essential that studies which purport to demonstrate cognitive impairment in children with brain damage should take into account the age at which the lesion is acquired. It should be noted that even when lesions are acquired at more or less the same point in ontogeny, whether they are deemed to have significant effect upon behaviour or not is determined both by the type of test being used and the age at which it is applied (Teuber and Rudel, 1962).

The relative sparing of visuo-spatial as opposed to verbal skills following lesions in the first year of life may be interpreted in relation to the earlier maturation of the left cerebral hemisphere than the right. It might be argued that the left cerebral hemisphere is more functionally active for the first year of life, hence is more vulnerable to the impact of a cerebral insult whatever its aetiology (Taylor, 1969). Interestingly, the recovery of children suffering from phenylketonuria, after treatment from the first months of life with a phenylalamine-free diet, is asymmetric. Whilst such children frequently attain average levels of performance on locomotor and visuo-spatial skills, they may remain relatively retarded in language development (Fuller, 1967a,b).

As we have seen, the left cerebral hemisphere may function not merely to control speech production but also to process verbal material to an extent greater than has hitherto been supposed. This is witnessed by the high correlation found by Annett (1973) between performance with the more affected hand in right hemiplegic children and their performance on both verbal and non-verbal scales of the WISC. Thus, the degree to which reorganization of function is possible following an early cerebral injury is probably considerably less than had been supposed by, for example, Basser (1962). Nevertheless, some reorganization is possible, and what is surprising is that precedence is not given to verbal skills in such reorganization. As we have seen, children with focal EEG abnormalities who have no clear-cut hand preference show a pattern of impairment on the WISC identical with that of children with lesions contralateral to the preferred hand, i.e. poorer Verbal than Performance scale IQ. Annett *et al.* (1961) argue that in such cases where the undamaged hemisphere originally controlled language, the undamaged hemisphere acquires control of visuo-spatial skills. This partial exchange of function, it is argued, is biologically adaptive, since higher level conceptual development depends upon a firm base of sensori-motor skills. It may thus be noted that the plausibility of the hypothesis of Annett and her colleagues depends to a great extent upon the validity of Piaget's (1952) theory of intelligence. Whilst other writers, notably Ayres (1975) have taken a similar viewpoint, it has not gone completely unchallenged. For example, Décarie (1969) was unable to demonstrate any marked impairment of cognitive development amongst thalidomide children with phocomelias or agenesis of arms or legs. It can hardly be doubted that the sensori-motor activity of such children is very peculiar indeed. Thus whilst we are impressed by the biological plausibility of the Annett hypothesis, it must be regarded still as essentially unproven.

IV. OBSERVATIONAL STUDIES

(1) Exploratory behaviour in hyperkinetic children

Many children suffering from severe cerebral dysfunctions are too unco-operative to take part either in psychometric tests or laboratory experiments. A good deal of information may nevertheless be obtained, covering the selective attention, discrimination and memory of such children, by employing a "free-field" approach. The child is observed in an environment the physical dimensions of which are fixed but within which he is free to behave as he pleases. A detailed inventory, which serves as a baseline, is made of the child's behaviour with the free-field empty. Stimuli may then be introduced into the free-field to study their effects upon the child's behaviour. Detailed observation may be made of the amount of visual inspection or manipulation of objects, the amount of locomotion and so on. The observations may be recorded manually either on prepared check-lists or on an event recorder; a verbal commentary may be made on to a tape recorder, using a specially developed telegraphic language; or film or video recordings may be made. Studies of this type have received their impetus from two sources: from studies of exploratory behaviour in animals (for an early summary see Berlyne, 1960); and from the work of animal ethologists (see Hutt and Hutt, 1970). The former group of

21—CP * *

studies has stressed the stimulus selection properties of an animal's behaviour in a free field; the latter have laid somewhat more stress upon variations in animals' response repertoire in relation to environmental changes. The distinction was formalized by Hutt and Hutt (1963), who proposed eight parameters of free-field behaviour which could be derived from analysis of either the child's motor patterns or of the changes wrought in the environment (see Table 14.4).

TABLE 14.4

Measures of behaviour

Measure	Organismal variables	Environmental variables
(1) Frequency	Number of different behaviour patterns recruited in unit time	Number of stimuli engaged in unit time
(2) Total time	Spent in different activities per session	Spent upon each stimulus per session
(3) Mean duration (span)	Duration of activity	Duration of continuous engagement with same stimulus
	e.g. running jumping hitting looking at = Activity span	e.g. blocks light switch sink radiator = Attention span
(4) Rate	Velocity of activity	Rate of change effected in stimulus

(*After* Hutt and Hutt, 1963.)

(2) FREE-FIELD STUDIES OF BRAIN DAMAGED CHILDREN

Using these eight measures in turn Hutt *et al.* (1965) compared the behaviour of a group of brain-damaged children with that of twelve undamaged children, the two groups being matched for age and sex. The age range of the children was 3 to 8 years. Each group was also subdivided into six older and six younger children with a cut-off point at $5\frac{1}{2}$ years. Children were classified as brain-damaged if they had a history of gross cerebral insult (meningitis or encephalitis) and had specific EEG abnormalities (generalized high voltage slow waves or spike-and-wave, with or without fits). The diagnosis of brain damage was made by a neurologist without knowledge of the behavioural observations. The children were studied in a well-lit room which was unfurnished except for a number of fixtures such as a sink and light switches. The floor had a squared covering, each square having a reference number. Children were observed in each of four environments. The basic environment (A) could be modified to give three other environments of varying complexity. In environment B a box of coloured blocks was present in the room. In C, in addition to the blocks, an observer sat in the room but remained passive throughout the session. In D the observer attempted to engage the child in building a design with the blocks. The standard period of observation in each environment was 3 mins. Each child was studied in all four environments, these being presented in four different orders. A second observer watched the child through a one-way screen and recorded

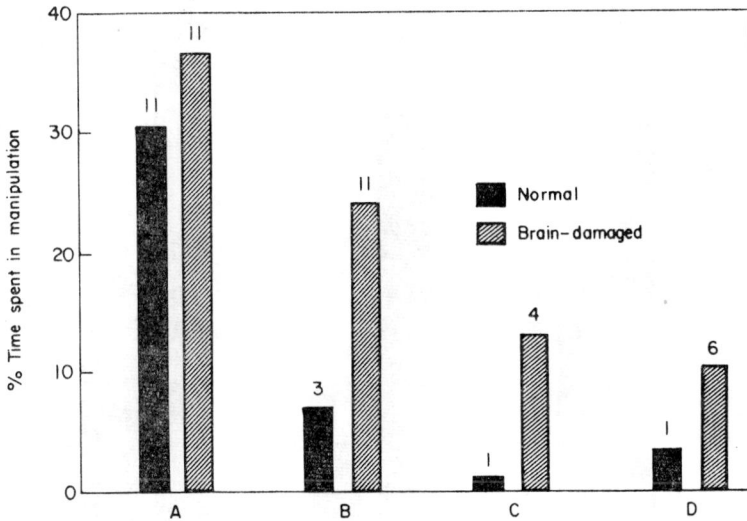

Fig. 14.1. Per cent time spent in manipulating fixtures by brain-damaged and normal children in four environments of increasing complexity. (*After* Hutt *et al.*, 1965, p. 252.)

a behaviour commentary using a standard descriptive language. Five main groups of behaviour were recorded: (i) direction of visual fixation; (ii) manipulation: that is, which part of the environment is being manipulated and the motor pattern deployed; (iii) gestures: these are defined as bodily movements which do *not* bring the child into contact with the environment, for example, rocking, picking the nose, waving the arms; (iv) postures: sitting, standing, etc. and (v) locomotion: changes in the child's position in the room relative to a numbered floor plan. The tape recordings were subsequently transcribed and analysed in terms of the nature and duration of items of motor behaviour, the stimuli engaged, and the time spent in contact with each stimulus.

The contrast between the normal and the brain-damaged children in the ways they explore their environment may be exemplified by their manipulation of the fixtures in the room (Fig. 14.1) and their block play (Fig. 14.2). Once the blocks are provided the normal

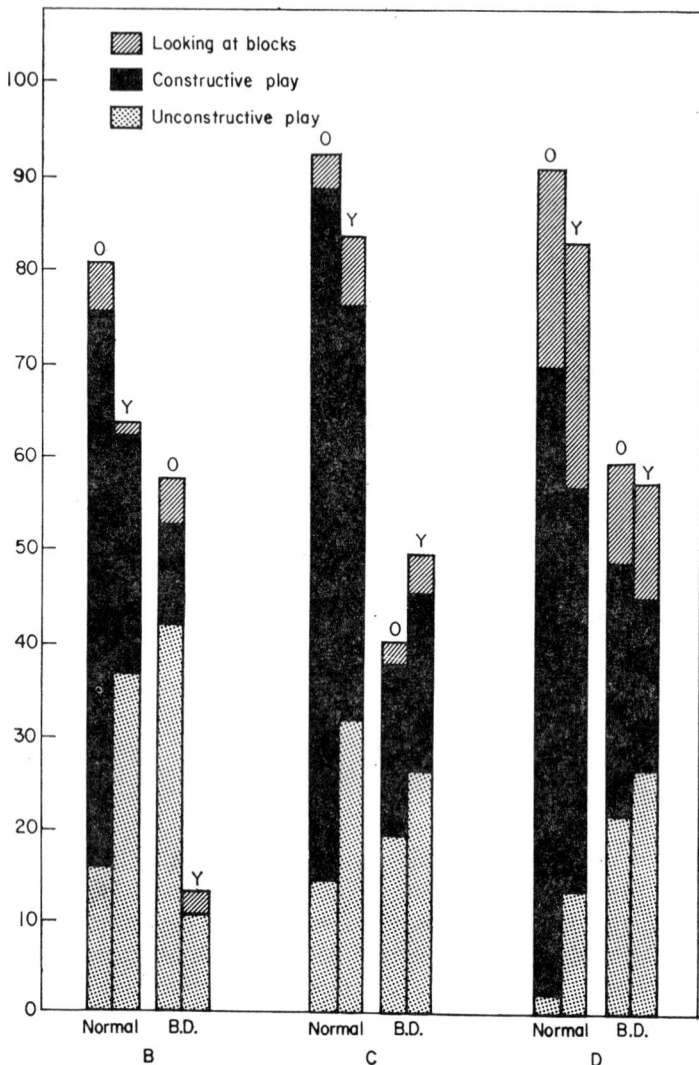

Fig. 14.2. Per cent time spent in three types of block play by older and younger brain-damaged and normal children. (*After* Hutt *et al.*, 1965, p. 256).

children show hardly any manipulation of the fixtures. The provision of the blocks has considerably less effect upon the behaviour of the brain-damaged children. In consequence the total amount of time devoted to block play in the brain-damaged children is less than in the normals. Moreover, the quality of play is different, the brain-damaged children showing a great proportion of unconstructive play (placing blocks singly, hammering them) than constructive play (building a solid structure). The converse is true for the normals. It thus appears that the brain-damaged children show less focused attention than the normals when environmental constraints are increased. Behaviourally, the older brain-damaged children are more similar to the younger normals than to their normal age peers.

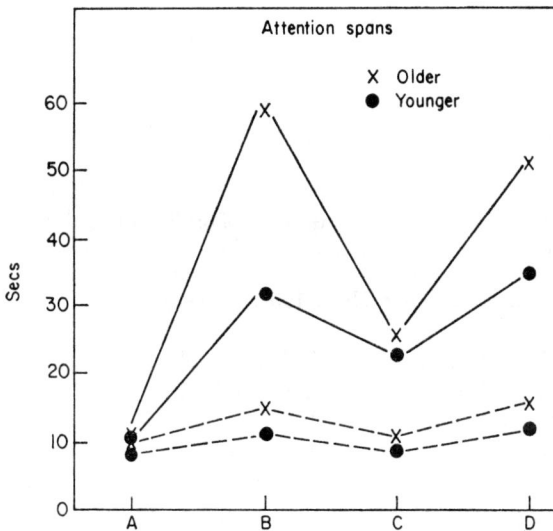

FIG. 14.3. Attention spans of older and younger normal and brain-damaged children in four environments of increasing complexity. (*After* Hutt *et al.*, 1965, p. 258.)

In part, the amount of information gained by the child from its environment is a function of attention span, that is, the length of time during which a specific stimulus is engaged by one or more receptor systems (Hutt and Hutt, 1963). The attention spans of the four sub-groups are shown in Figure 14.3. All sub-groups were very similar in the empty room. In B the older normals, and to a lesser extent the younger normals, fixated largely on the blocks; in C attention was divided between the blocks and the passive observer, the mean duration thus being considerably reduced. In D again, attention was mostly on the blocks, but there was also some watching of the observer. In general, the attention spans of the normal children were flexible and congruous with the complexity of the environment. In the brain-damaged children, on the other hand, attention span remained comparatively inflexible, and in the younger ones, unaffected by any of the environmental changes.

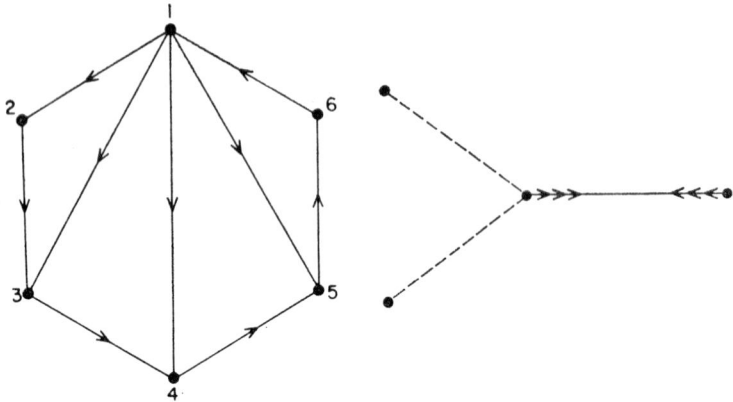

FIG. 14.4. Typical stimulus sampling strategies of brain-damaged children (left) and normal children (right). Brain-damaged children predominantly use a serial sampling stategy and normal children a repetitive sampling strategy in a socially structured environment. (*After* Hutt, 1964, p. 344.)

The meaning of these results is further clarified if we consider the "sampling strategies" of brain-damaged children. In a number of studies we have been interested in the sequence in which various stimuli are sampled by the child. Brain-damaged children, especially the younger ones, explore the environment by a *serial sampling* strategy. That is, they investigate one stimulus for 10 secs, then go on to the second, then the third and so on until all available stimuli have been sampled and then come back to the first and start all over again. This process is repeated continuously, though some stimuli may be omitted in any circuit. Normal children also use this strategy in an unstructured environment, but switch to *repetitive sampling* once the environment is structured. In repetitive sampling, certain crucial stimuli, as in this case the blocks or the social stimulus, are repeatedly sampled to the exclusion of other stimuli. Another interesting feature of the serial sampling behaviour of the brain damaged children was that the motor patterns deployed on each circuit were approximately the same every time the same stimulus was encountered. This unmodifiability of the motor pattern on repeated exposure to the same stimulus led us to hypothesise that these grossly brain-damaged children, in contrast to the normals, were failing to build up a stable memory trace of any stimulus. Thus it was always treated as if it had not been encountered before (see Fig. 14.4). This led us to carry out a further experiment.

Work on nursery school children had shown that if they were exposed to a novel object within a familiar environment for 10 min a day their investigatory behaviour towards the novel object showed a progressive decline on successive days; this decline was described as "habituation" (Hutt, 1966). Our prediction was that if they were impaired in the ability to build up a stable memory trace of the novel object, they would continue to treat it as novel when exposed to it on successive days; that is, they would show a slower rate of habituation than normal children.

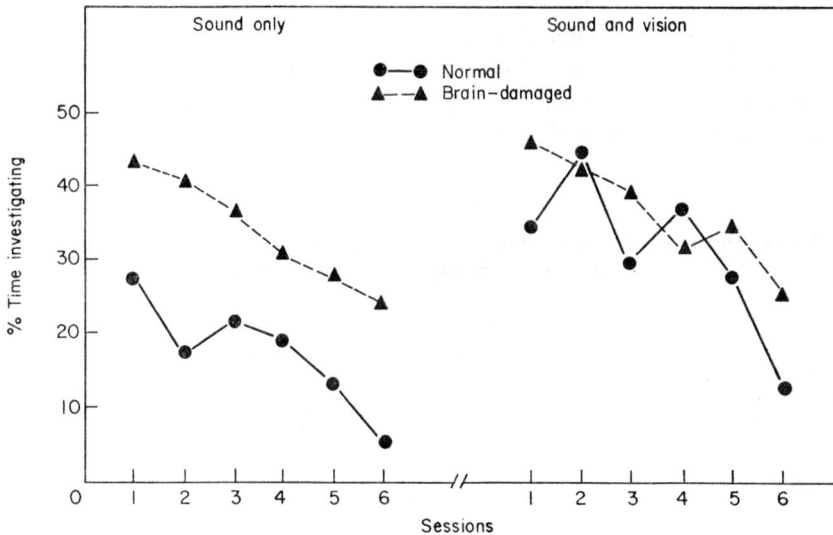

FIG. 14.5. Habituation to a novel object by normal and brain-damaged children during six daily sessions each of 10 min. In the left-hand curves contingent sound only was available, in the right-hand curves both sound and vision. (*After* Hutt, 1968, p. 153.)

The opportunity to test this prediction arose in a study during which children's exploratory behaviour was filmed in a specially constructed playroom (Lee and Hutt, 1964). Ten children, diagnosed as brain-damaged according to the previous criteria, were compared with twelve nursery schoolchildren (Hutt, 1968). The age range of the groups was 3 to 6 years. The children were filmed for 10 min on eight occasions each 48 hr apart. On all days five familiar toys were present in the room. On the third day a novel toy was introduced into the room. This consisted of a red metal box with a lever mounted on top which could be moved in four directions, each movement being registered by a post office counter. Two of the movements could be made to produce sound. In the present study two feedback conditions from the toy were used : (i) with the sound on but the counters covered by a metal plate; (ii) with the counters visible as well as the sound switched on. Results are shown in Fig. 14.5.

If we consider the amount of time spent in behaviour patterns which we classified as investigation of the novel object, we find that the brain-damaged children spend relatively more of their time in investigation than the normals and do indeed show a slower rate of gain of habituation. The difference between slopes is highly significant.

Again on the hypothesis that this slower habituation is due to failure to remember the properties of the novel object from day to day, we would predict that a longer delay between sessions would produce dishabituation of exploratory behaviour. To test this prediction, four normal and four brain-damaged children were exposed to the object two weeks after the sixth session of this experiment.

TABLE 14.5

Mean number of manipulations on sixth session of Study 1 and first session of Study 2 two weeks later

	Study 1 Session 6	Study 2 Session 1	% increase
Normals	37.0	60.75	65.1
Brain-damaged	53.2	100.5	94.5

(*After* Hutt, 1968 p. 156).

Table 14.5 shows the number of manipulations of the object on the sixth session of the study just described and on the first session two weeks later. From the percentage increases in manipulation it is seen that in both groups there was considerable recovery in exploration after two weeks. In the brain-damaged children the increase was almost 100 per cent suggesting that the object was as novel to these children as if it had never been seen before.

(3) Discussion

In recent years a number of important papers formulated within an ethological context have begun to appear from the University of

Groningen in the Netherlands. These are the studies of Kalverboer (1975) of 5-year-old children who were examined neurologically at birth by Prechtl (1961) and his colleagues. A total of fifty-two neurological signs had been evaluated as "optimal" or otherwise according to well-defined criteria. The number of items achieving optimal ratings had then been summed to give an overall "optimality" score. Children were assigned to one of three groups according to whether they had high, medium or low numbers of optimal signs. One hundred and fifty children who had been thus assigned (equal numbers of boys and girls) were examined in a free-field situation as well as being given a battery of psychological tests. In contrast to the studies of Hutt *et al.* (1965), which lasted for a total of 12 min only, those of Kalverboer, took well over 1 hour. In addition to the situation used by Hutt *et al.* (*ibid*)—child alone, with toys alone, with passive observer and with active observer—there was one session with the mother in the empty room and one with the last preferred toy. The data were analyzed separately for boys and girls by a latent profile analysis—a little used method which makes comparison with other studies difficult. The most clear-cut results are given by the boys (though they are to some extent mirrored in the girls). Boys with low neurological scores (i.e. fewest optimal signs) show the highest amounts of exploration and "low-level" play. In contrast the boys with high neurological scores show less exploration, but large amounts of "high-level" play. It is also reported that with low neurological scores "bout lengths" are typically shorter than with high scores. Unfortunately, we were unable to find direct evidence for this statement in Kalverboer's monograph. Nevertheless, the data would appear to be concordant—at least in males— with those of Hutt and Hutt (1963), the majority of whose sample was male. Their brain-damaged epileptic children were also hyperexploratory and possessed of short attention span. The lower the "optimal score" of children in Kalverboer's study the more they might be expected to approximate the neurological state of the children in the Hutts' study.

Disturbances of exploratory behaviour have been extensively reported following lesions in the limbic system. For example, Kimble and Greene (1968) have reported increased exploration of a maze by rats following hippocampal lesions, but without latent learning. Similarly, both Leaton (1965) in rats and Douglas and Pribram (1969) in monkeys have shown that habituation of exploratory behaviour to a novel stimulus is impaired following hippocampal lesions. Amygdalectomy in monkeys has been shown both to produce brief exploratory responses and to reduce recovery of habituation between sessions

(Schwartzbaum *et al.*, 1964). In other studies of monkeys, within-session habituation was not found to be affected by amygdalectomy, but the animals were abnormally distractible. The parallel with the behaviour of the hyperkinetic children observed in the above studies is most suggestive. It is the more so if we consider, in addition, emotional behaviour. Hyperkinetic brain damaged children are often referred to as aggressive, explosive and lacking in fear (Ounsted, 1955). Heightened aggressiveness has been reported in monkeys following amygdaloid lesions (Weiskrantz, 1967) and disruption of conditional fear responses in rats (Myhrer, 1975). The latter report is especially interesting since the lesions were implanted during the first ten days of life and their effects observed in adulthood. It thus appears that there is no amelioration of the reduced fear response with increasing age. Moreover, there is circumstantial evidence that insults to the brain in early life may particularly affect limbic structures in human beings. All children in the study by Hutt and Hutt (1963) were epileptic, as were a substantial proportion in the studies by Hutt *et al.* (1965) and Hutt (1968). In their study of the pathogenesis of temporal lobe epilepsy, Falconer *et al.* (1964) analyzed the resected tissue of 100 patients who had been treated by anterior temporal lobectomy. Amongst the main aetiological factors implicated in the development of epilepsy were birth difficulties, head injury and infections, factors which also played a part in the developmental histories of the patients discussed above. Although nerve cell loss, small tumours and scars were found in the neocortex, by far the most prevalent sites of lesions were the hippocampus and amygdala. Norman (1964), studying whole brains, found these structures to be the most seriously damaged in children who have died following status epilepticus. Again, several of the patients in the above studies had had non-lethal bouts of status epilepticus.

Overall, therefore, there is strong circumstantial evidence that limbic structures such as the hippocampus and amygdala are implicated in the brain dysfunctions of hyperkinetic children. This is not to deny that other brain structures may also be damaged in such cases, but there is nothing inherently implausible in the suggestion that these vulnerable structures may be damaged by a cerebral insult whilst other structures are spared. Thus, a similar pathogenesis could be proposed for both the severe behavioural dysfunctions observed by the Hutts (above) in association with epilepsy and other gross neurological signs, and the disablement of Kalverboer's (1975) patients who neurologically were described as "minimal cerebral dysfunctions" and who, in fact, had normal average IQs. At a behavioural level, the most prevalent features of the children are altered responses to novel stimuli, hyper-exploration, short attention span, distractability, reduced habituation and almost total recovery of response following an increased gap between sessions; all of which, as Rosner (1970) has put it, may point to "an impaired scanning mechanism".

V. EXPERIMENTAL STUDIES

(1) INFORMATION PROCESSING IN CHILDREN WITH EPILEPSY

In children the effects of structural changes in the brain are seldom static. As we have seen, such is the plasticity of the immature brain that profound changes in function may occur with increasing age. Nevertheless, these changes take place over a prolonged period and the ways in which possible recovery processes in the brain interact with later learning experiences remain obscure. In contrast, studies of the inter-ictal EEG activity of children with epilepsy may provide an opportunity to observe the effects of a "reversible lesion" within the course of an experiment lasting only a few minutes. The analogy of a reversible lesion is borrowed from psycho-physiological studies with animals in which the effects of gross alterations in the neuronal firing pattern of the brain have been charted by techniques such as spreading depression or intracranial stimulation. Of particular interest are the so-called after-discharges observable in the electrocortigram after low-frequency stimulation of the hippocampus (Flynn et al., 1963). Such discharges consist of trains of generalized spikes and slow waves similar in appearance to those observed in the inter-ictal EEGs of patients with epilepsy. Often profound changes in attention, learning and memory are observed during such discharges though these changes seldom outlast the stimulation. The hippocampal after-discharge, therefore, with a certain amount of physiological licence, may perhaps be conceptualized as a reversible lesion in the sense that for a few seconds the animal may behave very much as an animal with an anatomical lesion in the hippocampus or related structures, only to return to normal after stimulation has ceased.

A significant number of the children whose behaviour was discussed in earlier sections were suffering from epilepsy usually in association with evidence of either an underlying neuropathological condition or biochemical dysfunction. In some cases the main evidence for an underlying dysfunction was an abnormal EEG containing spike-wave or multiple spike activity. In several studies, the main selection criterion employed was that of an abnormal EEG. We can be fairly sure therefore that a large proportion of the children who have appeared in one or other of the categories already discussed will, in addition to any chronic brain dysfunction which they were suffering, also have suffered intermittent changes in cerebral state of the kind we have described. Moreover, if we accept that generalized spike-wave activity may provide a model in human beings of a reversible lesion, the effects of spike-wave upon information processing will be of general relevance to our understanding of attention processes in children with cerebral dysfunctions.

The conceptual framework within which these studies have been framed is the one proposed by Broadbent (1958, 1971). So far our studies have focused upon three components of Broadbent's model of information processing: immediate memory (Hutt *et al.*, 1963; Hutt, 1968; Gilbert and Hutt, in press); stimulus selection (Hutt, Newton and Fairweather, in press) and perception (Hutt, Denner and Newton, in press). Theoretically, the transient fluctuations of bioelectric activity which we loosely call EEG abnormalities may be regarded as a form of neural "noise" (Hutt and Fairweather, 1971, 1973). Such noise is considered to degrade the information-processing capabilities of that part of the system which is in operation at the same moment.

In the present paper, discussion will be restricted to the perceptual system only. In the simplest case it is assumed that there is only one stimulus demanding access to the P system and that there is a clear translation process to an appropriate response.

A well-tried method of measuring the efficiency of the P system is by the classical choice reaction time experiment (Hick, 1952). Patients are presented with series of random digits on a screen selected from ensemble sizes of 2, 4 or 8 (giving an information load of 1, 2 or 3 bits per stimulus). The patient presses corresponding keys as quickly as possible without making a mistake. Pressing a key triggers the next digit in the series after a 200 msec delay. After training to a 95 per cent correct performance, patients are given ten sessions, all three ensemble sizes being presented at one session. EEG is recorded during performance and reaction times are automatically recorded. A typical performance record is shown in Fig. 14.6. EEG activity is classified into seven categories: localized slow; bilateral slow; generalized slow; localized spike-wave; bilateral spike-wave; generalized spike-wave; and normal "background" activity. The term "bilateral" is used to indicate synchronous discharges from homologous regions of the two cerebral hemispheres which are of limited generalization (two to six EEG leads). Where bilateral discharges occur in eight or more leads they are classified as "generalized". The EEG data are matched to the print-out of performance, indicating which stimulus-response combinations have occurred in association with which type of EEG activity. Reaction times are then computed separately for each category of EEG activity.

In a recent study twenty children with epilepsy, aged 8 to 16, were

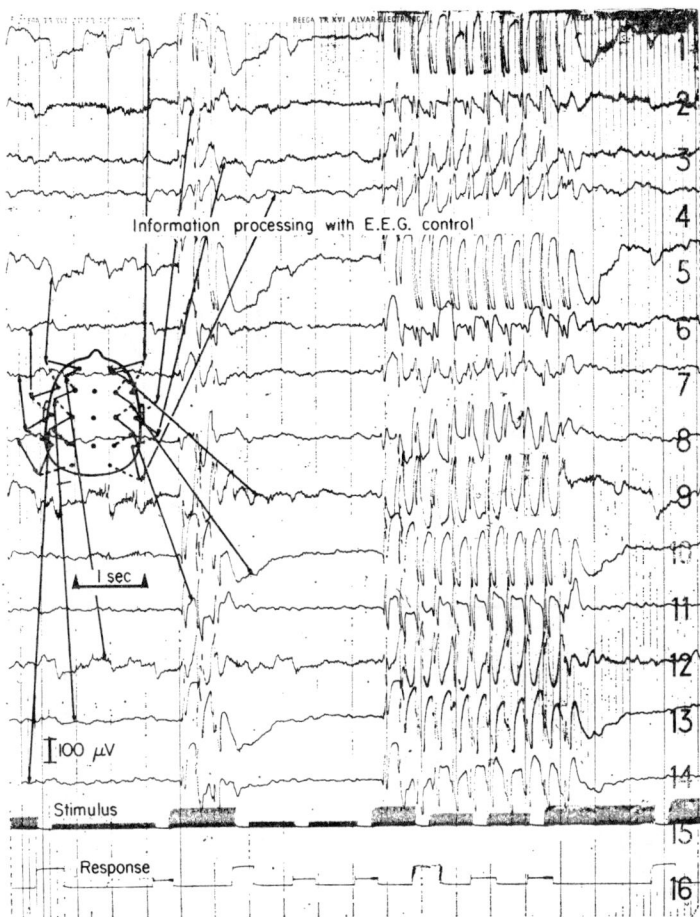

FIG. 14.6. Typical performance record showing fourteen EEG channels together with stimulus and response channels. Bursts of sub-clinical generalized spike-wave lasting 1 sec and $2\frac{1}{2}$ sec respectively are shown. (*After* Hutt *et al.*, in press.)

examined (Hutt, Denner and Newton, in press). Their resting EEGs all showed intermittent bursts of generalized spike-wave activity, which was not accompanied by any observable clinical signs. The spike-wave content of such EEG activity varied from 1 to 5 per cent of the record. Typical individual curves relating reaction time (RT) and task difficulty (in bits per stimulus) during different categories of EEG activity are shown in Fig. 14.7. It is clear that in the majority of cases RT is significantly longer during generalized spike-wave activity than during any other kind of activity. Moreover, the degree of impairment appears to be related to the spread of the spike-wave discharge. Of particular

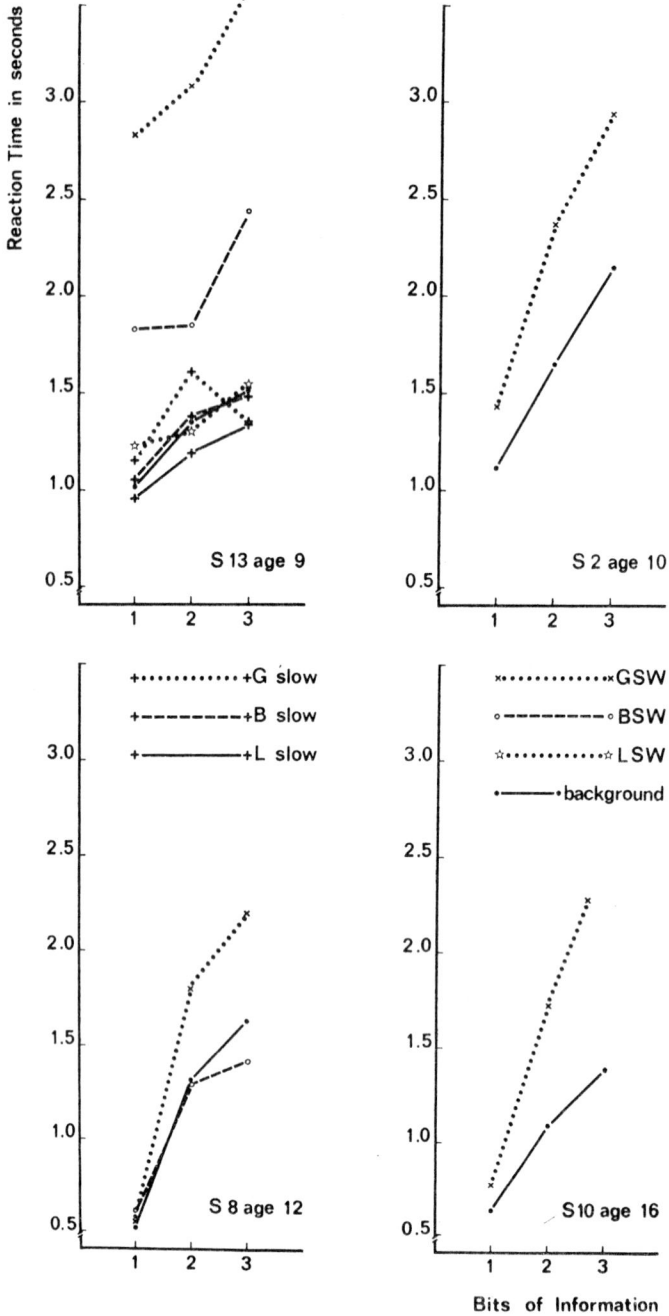

FIG. 14.7. Four typical sets of curves showing effect of different types of EEG activity upon rate of gain of information. (*After* Hutt *et al.*, in press.)

interest, however, is the fact that the spike-wave does not have an all-
or-nothing effect but a differential effect, according to the amount of
information requiring processing. Thus, in the 1-bit task, the difference
between the spike-wave and background activity is generally small.
With increasing information load, the discrepancy between the spike-
wave and normal background activity gradually increases.

The group picture (Fig. 14.8) is similar to the one described for
individuals : significantly longer reaction times during the spike-wave

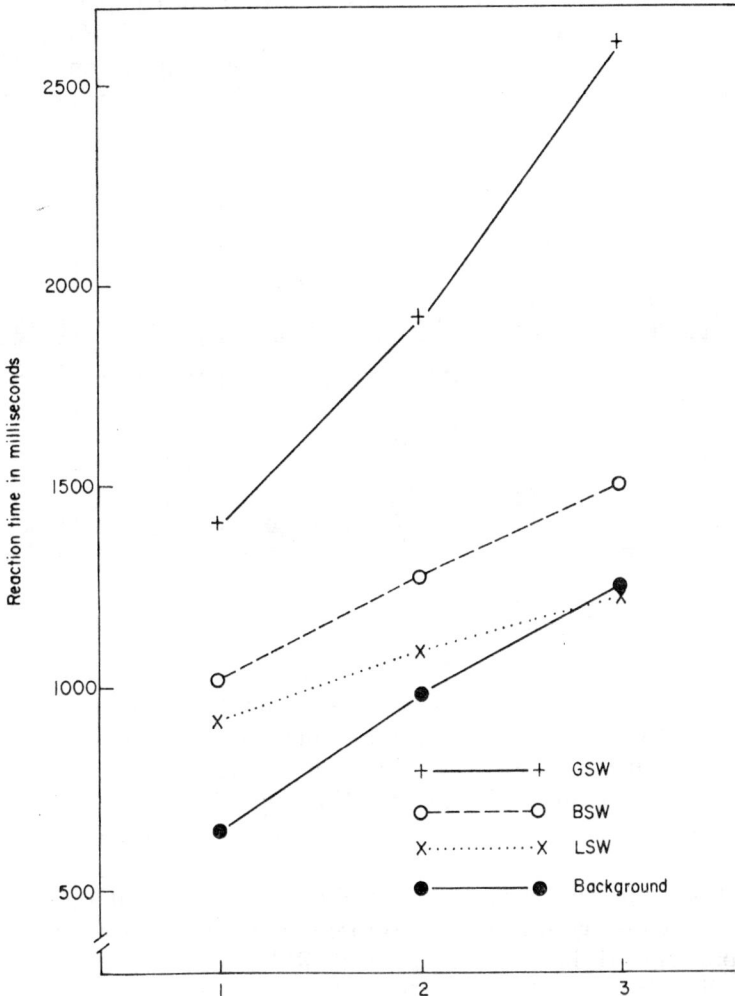

Fig. 14.8. Combined group curves showing effect of different types of EEG
activity upon rate of gain of information. (*After* Hutt *et al.*, in press.)

than during any other type of EEG activity; a stronger effect with increasing cortical generalization; no significant differences amongst slow waves, focal spike-wave and background activity; and a significantly steeper slope for the generalized spike-wave than for the family of non-spike-wave curves. Interestingly, there was no systematic trend in the data for simple reaction times. It appears that the spike-wave has its primary effect upon information processing rather than upon motor activity. (Browne *et al.* (1974), however, have recently reported increases in simple RT to auditory stimuli during the generalized spike-wave.) The effect can be seen most clearly if we compute a single parameter for each patient, "rate of gain of information" (Hick, 1952), that is, the number of bits of information processed per second. Figure 14.9 shows rate of information gain in the twelve subjects whose EEGs

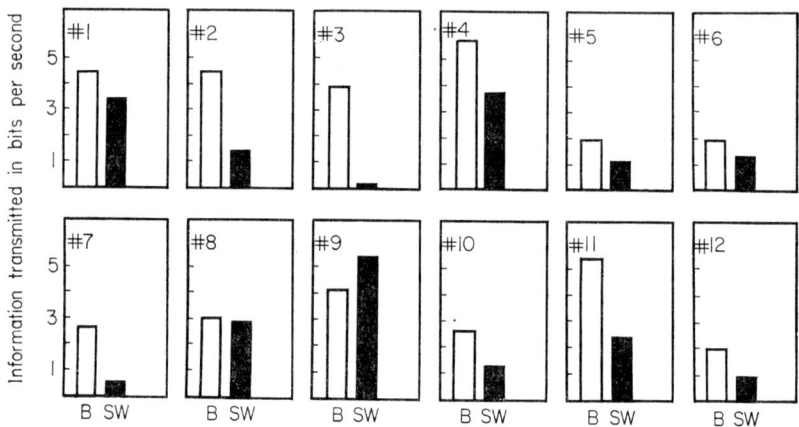

FIG. 14.9. Information processing (in bits per sec) during generalized spike-wave (SW) and normal background activity (B).

contained the greatest abundance of generalized spike-wave. In eleven out of twelve cases the amount of information processed per second is smaller during spike-wave activity than during background activity. It may thus be inferred that the effect of spike-wave activity is to decrease the information handling capacity of the nervous system.

So far we have considered only self-paced tasks. What happens if the task is paced? Providing that RT is short, so that the patient responds correctly to a stimulus before the next one arrives, there are no problems. If, however, the patient's RT exceeds the time between stimuli, difficulties will arise. The patient must now store information about one stimulus whilst making response to another. Where several successive reaction times are of this increased duration, information may have to be stored about a number of stimuli. Under these circumstances, performance is particularly prone to disruption, since recall of items from Primary Memory (Waugh and Norman, 1965) is itself selectively impaired by spike-wave (Gilbert and Hutt, in press). Thus, responses to some stimuli may be omitted entirely.

An idea of how greatly spike-wave may affect paced performance can be gained from a recent study of a 15-year-old epileptic child in

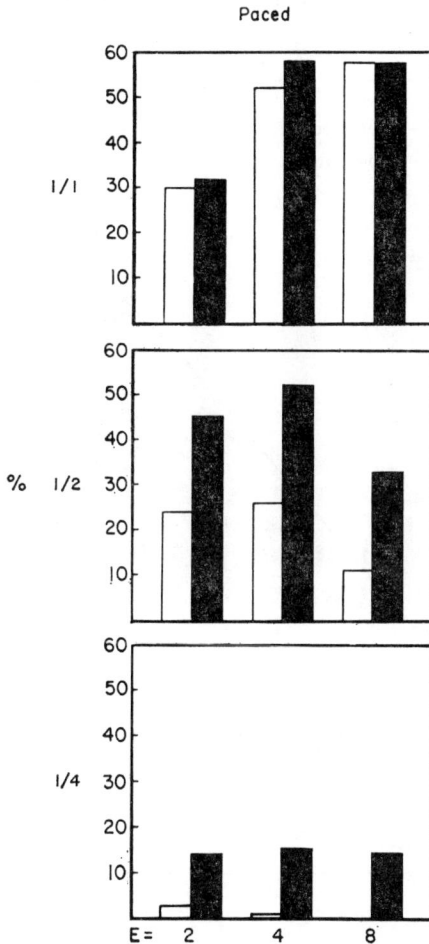

FIG. 14.10. Per cent errors on a paced serial choice response task during spike-wave (SW) and background (B) EEG activity. The task was performed at each of three levels of difficulty (1, 2 or 3 bits per stimulus) and at each of three pacing rates (1 stimulus per sec, 1 per 2 sec or 1 per 4 sec). (*After* Hutt and Fairweather, 1973, p. 89.)

whom some 12,000 reaction times were measured in a number of different conditions (Hutt and Fairweather, 1973). Again three ensemble sizes were used : 2, 4 or 8 keys and three speeds of presentation: 1 stimulus per sec, 1 per 2 sec and 1 per 4 sec. The EEG activity was classified into two main categories : generalized spike-wave and "background". In Fig. 14.10 can be seen the number of errors made under each of the nine speed-ensemble conditions both during spike-wave activity and in its absence. The first striking feature is that if stimuli are presented very fast—1 per sec—almost exactly the same number

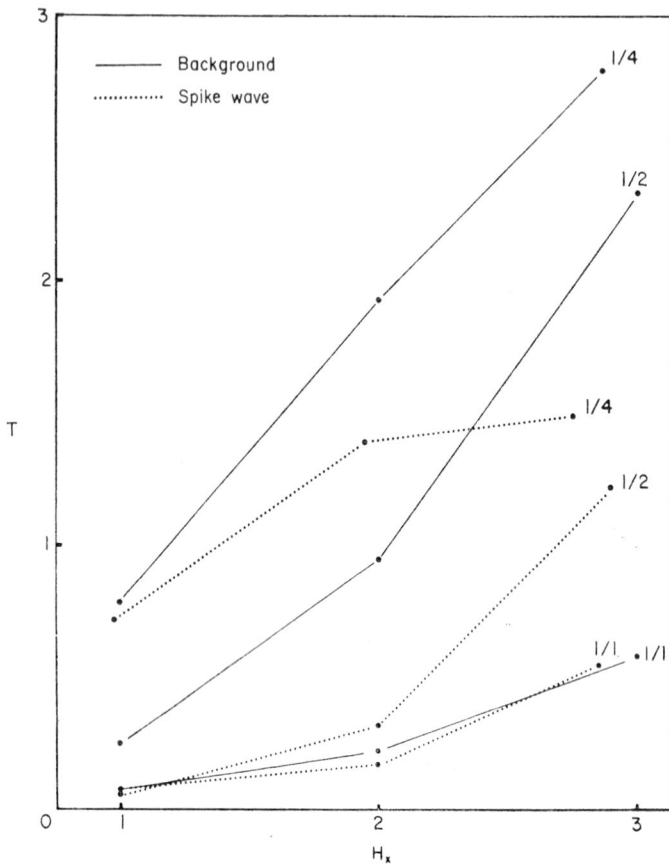

Fig. 14.11. Effects of generalized spike-wave activity upon information processing on a paced serial choice response task, with three levels of difficulty (1, 2 or 3 bits per stimulus) and three rates of performance (1 stimulus per sec, 1 per 2 sec or 1 per 4 sec). The abscissa (Hx) indicates input information and the ordinate (T) the amount of information transmitted. (*After* Hutt and Fairweather, 1971, p. 919.)

of errors occur in each condition. Thus, when the task is impossibly difficult even in normal EEG conditions the spike-wave does not make performance any worse. When the speed of presentation is halved, the number of errors now made in normal EEG conditions is dramatically reduced. In contrast, almost as many errors are now made in the presence of the spike-wave as in the 1 per sec condition. When stimuli are presented at the very slow rate of 1 per 4 sec hardly any errors are made in background EEG conditions. Yet again, however, a substantial number of errors is still made during spike-wave paroxysms.

If we consider not merely the number of errors made but the success with which responses were matched correctly with stimuli, a conventional measure of information processing may be computed (Attneave, 1959). Figure 14.11 compares the amount of information transmitted (T) during spike-wave and during background EEG activity in the nine speed-ensemble conditions (Hutt and Fairweather, 1975). It can be seen that very little information is processed at the fastest presentation rate in either EEG condition. In contrast, as stimuli

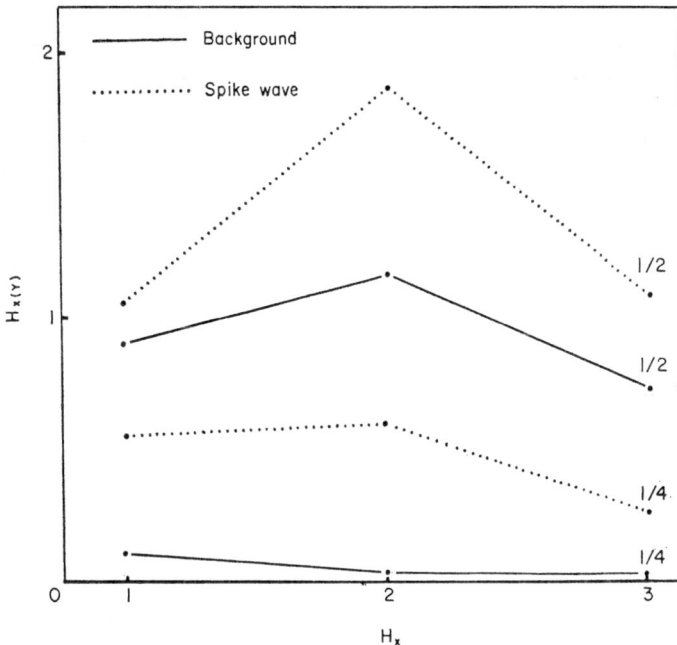

FIG. 14.12. Effects of spike-wave activity upon response ambiguity in a serial choice response task with three levels of difficulty (1, 2 or 3 bits per stimulus) and two rates of presentation (1 stimulus per 2 sec or 1 per 4 sec). The abscissa (Hx) indicates input information and the ordinate $(H_x(Y))$ the "noise" component of response information.

are presented more slowly, a progressively greater discrepancy appears between the amount of information processed in spike-wave and background conditions respectively.

One further parameter may be computed from these data. Response ambiguity is that part of the subject's response which was not made to the original signal. That is, it is gratuitously added by the subject himself and for this reason is generally referred to as "noise". Taking now only the six conditions in which a high level of information transmission was obtained in background condition—the 2 sec and 4 sec presentation rates—it is clear that there is significantly more noise in the subject's response than during background activity. It is on this basis that we have argued (Hutt and Fairweather, 1975) that there may be an isomorphism between the performance and neural levels in children with epilepsy. At a neural level spike-wave may act as noise which in turn reduces "channel capacity" at a behavioural level (see Fig. 14.12).

(2) DISCUSSION

Our data are in accord with other writers (Tizard and Margerison, 1963a,b) in showing that during generalized spike-wave paroxysms RT is significantly increased. However, they go further in two respects. First, our findings go some way in reconciling the apparently contradictory findings of authors who, on the one hand, have found little or no psychological impairment during spike-wave activity (Prechtl et al., 1961), or on the other hand, have found very considerable impairment (Davidoff and Johnson, 1964). Secondly, our data provide some indication of the stages in the information processing tasks which are affected by spike-wave discharges.

We have argued that the nervous system may be conceptualized as an information processing channel of limited capacity whose efficiency is periodically degraded by episodes of neural noise. The effect of such neural noise, for example generalized spike-wave activity, is to decrease channel capacity, the maximum rate at which the nervous system can transmit information. Thus, in the presence of spike-wave activity little impairment may be observed in a simple task which is well within the individual's channel capacity. As task difficulty approaches the individual's maximum rate of transmitting information, the effects of the spike-wave will be progressively more deleterious. In the task employed by Prechtl et al. (1961) and by Tizard and Margerison (1963a,b), patients were required to press buttons serially with one hand to extinguish lights placed adjacent to each finger. There were five such lights (2.3 bits per stimulus) and the task was performed self-paced. Using errors as their measure Prechtl et al. found no significant effect of the spike-wave upon performance (this we would expect on a self-paced task); but Tizard and Margerison obtained significant increases in RT during generalized spike-wave paroxysms exceeding 3 sec. Probably the most complex unpaced continuous performance tasks are ones of serial addition (Ishihara and Yoshii, 1967) and serial subtraction (Davidoff and Johnson, 1964). These tasks demand not only the maintenance of a cognitive set (remembering the arithmetic logic of the task) and short-term memory (of the previous step in the sequence), but also response to a stimulus ensemble which varies after each step. Both groups of authors report "interruptions" of performance during the spike-wave, but it is impossible, from their reports, to determine the basis of these interruptions. However, in the light of our own data, it would seem reasonable to suppose that in the former case the average information to be processed per stimulus is low; in the latter it is high.

We have seen that paced tasks are more vulnerable to the effects of spike-wave activity than are self-paced tasks. This in line with the few other studies which have employed paced tasks in the study of EEG abnormalities. Goode et al. (1970), using a continuously changing input—the pursuit rotor task—found a significant increase in the time "off-target" during spike-wave paroxysms exceeding 3 sec duration compared with normal background activity or paroxysmal slow waves. Similarly, Grisell et al. (1964), using a paced auditory tracking task, found increases in reaction time and in errors during subclinical spike-wave activity. Hutt and Fairweather (1973) have shown that on the serial choice response task described above, there is a monotonic relationship between reaction time to a particular signal and the probability of an error being made to either the next or the next but one signal. As we have surmised above, such errors may occur in situations where information about one signal has to be retained in short-term memory, whilst response is made to the present signal. Gilbert and Hutt (in an unpublished study) have recently shown that items which are held in primary memory (see for instance Atkinson and Shiffrin, 1968) are particularly susceptible to eradication by spike-wave discharges.

Choice RT can be analysed into four sub-units corresponding with each of four successive stages of information processing (Smith, 1968): (i) time for registration of stimulus; (ii) time for recognition of stimulus; (iii) time for organization of response, that is to say, decision time; and (iv) time to execute response. It seems unlikely that stages (i) and (iv) are significantly affected by spike-wave activity. In the first place, we were unable to demonstrate any consistent effect of spike-wave upon simple RT (stages (i) and (iv) combined). In the second place,

Mirsky *et al.* (1973) found no increase in the latency of visual evoked potentials (which may be regarded as a pure measure of stage (i) transmission time) occurring at the same time as evoked spike-wave discharges. This would be consistent with a recent study of our own : using a signal detection paradigm, Hutt, Denner and Newton (*in press*) were unable to demonstrate any significant effect of spike-wave upon auditory detectability (as measured by d') although decision criteria (β) were markedly affected by such discharges. Whilst an effect upon stage (ii) cannot be ruled out, there seems little doubt from these data that stage (iii)—the time for organization of response—is markedly affected by spike-wave activity.

A curious finding in the present study is that the decrease in channel capacity which occurs during spike-wave activity appears to be proportional to the generalization of the discharge. In this respect, the data are reminiscent of the "mass action" effects reported by Lashley (1929). The origins of the discharges remain obscure; morphologically they fall into the category of "centrencephalic" discharges originally described by Penfield and Jasper (1954). It seems likely that such discharges implicate structures at all levels of the brain, both cortically and sub-cortically.

VI. CONCLUSIONS

As was indicated in the Introduction, the majority of studies of the effects of cerebral dysfunction upon cognitive development have been formulated within a psychometric framework. Very few studies to date have examined such dysfunctions within the context of current theories of cognitive development. In consequence, it has not proved possible to relate the material reviewed in this chapter to the more theoretical material presented in preceding chapters. Again, few studies have been directed towards the testing of specific neuropsychological hypotheses. There are exceptions—for instance the studies of Rudel and Teuber (1971) and Rudel, Teuber and Twitchell (1974) on cross-modal functions in brain-damaged children—but these, as yet, are not easily integrated with the main bulk of literature of psychometric origin. We must thus regret the omission of many excellent articles which do not fit readily into the themes chosen for discussion. In this final section we shall merely summarize these main themes without adding to their discussion.

We have seen that cerebral insults in early life may affect the nervous system at any one of several levels. It seems reasonable to suppose that such insults have a disproportionately larger effect upon those systems which are already functionally mature than upon those which have yet to mature. Since sub-cortical structures are considerably more mature at birth than cortical structures, we should expect the former to be particularly at risk. Structures which have been implicated in the control of attention, such as the reticular activating system and limbic system, appear to be particularly vulnerable. Thus, even though a child's IQ may be in the normal range, he may be subject to difficulties in sustaining attention or in filtering salient stimuli from their background. This difficulty in filtering salient and non-salient stimuli was clearly seen in section IV in which we examined the exploratory behaviour of children with gross cerebral lesions. We saw that, in terms of their strategies of exploration, such children show little discrimination amongst the various stimuli available to them. Their abnormally slow habituation to novel stimuli between days and their almost total loss of habituation over a two-week interval suggested that in addition to a possible deficit in the initial filtering of stimuli, children with gross cerebral insults may have fairly major deficits in long-term memory. Unfortunately, it is doubtful whether observational techniques of the kind necessarily employed in the study of children with gross cerebral lesions are of sufficient sensitivity to determine the level of the input–retrieval chain at which the behavioural abnormalities are primarily mediated. We inferred that abnormalities of exploratory behaviour were mediated by sub-cortical structures, most likely the hippocampus, a structure we found to be particularly susceptible to insult in early life, probably by virtue of its early maturation.

The principle that structures undergoing rapid maturation at the time of insult will be most affected functionally, also applies to cortical structures. Consequently, psychological processes which normally are controlled by those structures are likely to be impaired. Since the left cerebral hemisphere should mature earlier than the right, it would not be surprising that verbal skills—which, in the majority of individuals the left hemisphere will control—are particularly susceptible to disruption by such insults. In general, where cerebral insults have been incurred before the first birthday a marked deficit in verbal skills is observed. This deficit appears to embrace the complete gamut of language processing skills from input, organization, and storage to retrieval (Chap. 1 and 2, this volume). For example, we have seen that tests such as the Halstead Test of Speech Sound Perception, and the WISC Digit Memory Information and Vocabulary sub-tests are consistently affected by such early insults. Simple tests of concept formation such as those employed by Graham et al. (1962) or the Similarities sub-test of the Wechsler (see, for instance Reed and Fitzhugh, 1966) are only slightly less impaired and stand in marked contrast to visuo-spatial skills, which to a great extent are spared by insults incurred during the first year of life. Visuo-spatial skills to some extent may be protected by the later maturation of the right cerebral hemisphere, when such insults as serial convulsions are relatively less frequent. Moreover, the left cerebral hemisphere may be more at risk obstetrically than the right (Churchill, 1968). Thus, the later emergence of visuo-spatial skills ontogenetically could in part account for the greater resilience which has been accorded them in the hypothesis of biological advantages of Annett et al. (1961).

In general, the greater the extent of brain damage, the greater the associated dysfunction. This was found in the case of hemiplegic children using level of performance in the less affected hand. A similar picture was found in the case of children with temporal lobe epilepsy, some of whom had suffered cerebral insults in addition to seizures of early onset. It was also found in the case of centrencephalic epileptic discharge, where the greater the generalization of the EEG abnormality, the greater the impairment of sustained attention.

Thus, the earlier an insult is incurred, and the greater the extent of damage, the more severe the resulting impairment. Whilst some plasticity of function is possible, this may be considerably less than has previously been supposed. The bulk of the evidence cited would be compatible with the view of Hebb (1949) that a greater mass of cortex may be required for original learning than for retention of learned material. Such a view would be consonant with recent notions on neural plasticity (Levers, 1975) suggesting that functional reorganization is a biological rarity.

Re-examining the material presented in this chapter, it becomes apparent that much of developmental neuropsychology is divorced from the main-stream of experimental cognitive psychology. A closer collaboration between psychologists working in the fields characterized by Part I and Part IV of this volume can only be to the benefit of both. On the one hand, the more precisely we can identify the stage of information processing impaired by a cerebral insult, the more adequately we can make provision for the education and rehabilitation of the affected child. On the other hand, developmental neuropsychology remains a largely untapped source of information regarding the neural substrates of cognitive development.

REFERENCES

Alajouanine, T. and L'Hermitte, F. (1965). Acquired aphasia in children. *Brain, 88,* 653–62.

Annett, M. (1973). Laterality of childhood hemiplegia and the growth of speech and intelligence. *Cortex, 9,* 1–33.

Annett, M., Lee, D. and Ounsted, C. (1961). Intellectual disabilities in relation to lateralized features of the EEG. *Little Club Clinics in Developmental Medicine,* No. 4. London: Heinemann.

Atkinson, R. C. and Shiffrin, R. M. (1968). Human memory: a proposed system and its control processes. In K. W. Spence and J. T. Spence (Eds.), *Advances in the Psychology of Learning and Motivation: Research and Theory,* Vol. II. New York: Academic Press.

Attneave, F. (1959). *Applications of Information Theory to Psychology.* New York: Holt, Rinehart and Winston.

Ayres, A. (1975). Sensorimotor foundations of academic ability. In W. M. Cruikshank and D. P. Hallahan (Eds.), *Perceptual and Learning Disabilities in Children,* Vol. II. New York: Syracuse University Press.

Basser, L. S. (1962). Hemiplegia of early onset and the faculty of speech with special reference to the effects of hemispherectomy. *Brain, 85,* 427–60.

Benton, A. L. (1973). Minimal brain dysfunction from a neuropsychological point of view. *Annals of the New York Academy of Sciences, 205,* 29–37.

Berlyne, D. E. (1960). *Conflict, Arousal and Curiosity.* New York: McGraw-Hill.

Boll, T. J. (1974). Behavioral correlates of cerebral damage in children aged 9 through 14. In R. M. Reitan and L. A. Davidson (Eds.), *Clinical Neuropsychology: Current Status and Application.* Washington, D.C.: Winston.

Broadbent, D. E. (1958). *Perception and Communication.* Oxford: Pergamon.

Broadbent, D. E. (1971). *Decision and Stress.* London: Academic Press.

Browne, T. R., Penry, J. K., Porter, R. J. and Dreifuss, F. E. (1974). Responsiveness before, during and after spike-wave paroxysms *Neurology, 24,* 659–65.

Churchill, J. A. (1968). A study of hemiplegic cerebral palsy. *Developmental Medicine and Child Neurology, 20,* 453–9.

Clements, S. D. In C. K. Connors (1967). The syndrome of minimal brain dysfunction: psychological aspects. *Pediatric Clinics of North America, 14,* 749–66.

Cohen, J. (1959). The factorial structure of the WISC at ages 7–6, 10–6 and 13–6. *Journal of Consulting Psychology, 23,* 285–99.

Crockett, D., Klonoff, H. and Bjerring, J. (1969). Factor analysis of neuropsychological tests. *Perceptual and Motor Skills, 29,* 791–801.

Davidoff, R. A. and Johnson, L. C. (1964). Paroxysmal EEG activity and cognitive motor performance. *Electroencephalographic Clinical Neurophysiology, 16,* 343–54.

Décarie, T. G. (1969). A study of the mental and emotional development of the thalidomide child. In B. M. Foss (Ed.), *Determinants of Infant Behaviour,* Vol. IV. London: Methuen.

De La Cruz, F. F., Fox, B. H. and Roberts, R. H. (Eds.), (1973) Minimal brain dysfunction. *Annals of the New York Academy of Sciences, 205.*

Dennerll, R. D. (1964). Prediction of unilateral brain dysfunction using Wechsler test scores. *Journal of Consulting Psychology, 28,* 278–84.

Douglas, R. J. and Pribram, K. H. (1969). Distraction and habituation in monkeys with limbic lesions. *Journal of Comparative Physiology and Psychology, 69,* 473–80.

Ernhart, C. B., Graham, F. K., Eichman, P. L., Marshall, J. M. and Thurston, D. (1963). Brain injury in the pre-school child: some developmental considerations. I. Comparison of brain injured and normal children. *Psychological Monographs, 77,* No. 11, 17–33.

Falconer, M. A., Serafetinides, E. A. and Corsellis, J. A. M. (1964). Etiology and pathogenesis of temporal lobe epilepsy. *Archives of Neurology, 10,* 233–45.

Fedio, P. and Mirsky, A. F. (1969). Selective intellectual deficits in children with temporal lobe or centrencephalic epilepsy. *Neuropsychologica, 7,* 287–300.

Flynn, J. P., Wasman, M. and Egger, D. (1963). Behavior during propagated hippocampal after-discharges. In G. H. Glaser (Ed.), *EEG and Behavior.* New York: Basic Books.

Fuller, R. (1967a). In J. Anderson and K. Swaiman (Eds.), *Phenylketonuria and Allied Metabolic Diseases.* Washington, D.C.: U.S. Department of Health, Education and Welfare.

Fuller, R. (1967b). In J. Zubin (Ed.), *Psychopathology of Mental Development.* New York: Grune and Stratton.

Gilbert, S. and Hutt, S. J. Digit memory and evoked discharges in patients with epilepsy (in press).

Goode, D. J., Penry, J. K. and Dreifuss, F. E. (1970). Effects of paroxysmal spike-wave on continuous visual-motor performance. *Epilepsia, 11,* 241–54.

Graham, F. K., Ernhart, C. B., Craft, R. and Berman, P. W. (1963). Brain injury in pre-school child: some developmental considerations. I. Performance of normal children. *Psychological Monographs, 77.*

Graham, F. K., Ernhart, C. B., Thurston, C. and Craft, M. (1962). Development three years after perinatal anoxia and other potentially damaging newborn experiences. *Psychological Monographs, 76.*

Grisell, J. L., Levin, S. M., Cohen, B. D. and Rodin, E. A. (1964). The effects of subclinical seizure activity on overt behaviour. *Neurology, 14,* 133–5.

Hebb, D. O. (1949). *The Organisation of Behavior.* New York: Wiley.

Hick, W. E. (1952). On the rate of gain of information. *Quarterly Journal of Experimental Psychology, 4,* 11–26.

Hutt, C. (1966). Exploration and play in children. *Symposium of the Zoological Society of London, 18,* 61–81.

Hutt, C. (1968). Exploration of novelty in children with and without upper C.N.S. lesions and some effects of auditory and visual incentives. *Acta Psychologica, 28,* 150–60.

Hutt, C and Hutt, S. J. (1963). The study of attentive behaviour in children. *Paper read to Eighth International Ethological Conference,* The Hague, Netherlands.

Hutt, C., Hutt, S. J. and Ounsted, C. (1965). The behaviour of children with and without upper C. N.S. lesions. *Behaviour, 24,* 246–68.

Hutt, S. J. (1964). Hyperactivity in a group of epileptic (and some non-epileptic) brain damaged children. *Epilepsia, 5,* 334–51.

Hutt, S. J., Denner, S. and Newton, J. Auditory thresholds during evoked spike-wave discharges. *Cortex* (in press).

Hutt, S. J. and Fairweather, H. (1971). Spike-wave paroxysms and information processing. *Proceedings of the Royal Society of Medicine, 64*, 918–19.

Hutt, S. J. and Fairweather, H. (1973). Paced and unpaced serial response performance during two types of EEG activity. *Journal of Neurological Science, 19*, 85–96.

Hutt, S. J. and Fairweather, H. (1975). Information processing during two types of EEG activity. *Electroencephalographic Clinical Neurophysiology, 39*, 43–51.

Hutt, S. J. and Hutt, C. (1970). *Direct Observation and Measurement of Behavior*. Springfield, Ill.: Thomas.

Hutt, S. J., Lee, D. and Ounsted, C. (1963). Digit memory and evoked discharges in four light-sensitive epileptic children. *Developmental Medicine and Child Neurology, 5*, 559–71.

Hutt, S. J., Newton, J. and Fairweather, H. Choice reaction time and EEG activity in children with epilepsy. *Neuropsychologica* (in press).

Ingram, T. T. S. (1956). A characteristic form of overactive behaviour in brain damaged children. *Journal of Mental Science, 102*, 550–8.

Ishihara, T. and Yoshii, N. (1967). The interaction between paroxysmal EEG activities and continuous addition work of Uchida-Kraepelin psychodiagnostic test. *Medical Journal of Osaka University, 18*, 75–85.

Kalverboer, A. F. (1975). A neurobehavioural study in preschool children. *Clinics in Developmental Medicine*, No. 54. London: Heinemann.

Kimble, D. P. and Greene, E. G. (1968). Absence of latent learning in rats with hippocampal lesions. *Psychonomic Science, 11*, 99–100.

Kinsbourne, M. (1973). Minimal brain dysfunction as a neurodevelopmental lag. In F. F. De La Cruz, B. H. Fox and R. H. Roberts (Eds.), Minimal brain dysfunction. *Annals of the New York Academy of Sciences, 205*.

Klonoff, H. (1971). Factor analysis of a neuropsychological battery for children aged 9 to 15. *Perceptual and Motor Skills, 32*, 603–16.

Kornetsky, C. (1975). Minimal brain dysfunction and drugs. In W. M. Cruikshank and D. P. Hallahan (Eds.), *Perceptual and Learning Disabilities in Children*, Vol. II. New York: Syracuse University Press.

Lashley, K. S. (1929). *Brain Mechanisms and Intelligence*. Chicago: University of Chicago Press.

Laufer, M. W., Denhoff, E. and Solomons, G. (1957). Hyperkinetic impulse disorder in children's behaviour problems. *Psychosomatic Medicine, 19*, 38–49.

Leaton, R. N. (1965). Exploratory behaviour in rats with hippocampal lesions. *Journal of Comparative Physiology and Psychology, 59*, 325–30.

Lee, D. and Hutt, C. (1964). A play-room designed for filming children. *Journal of Child Psychology and Psychiatry, 5*, 263–5.

Levers, T. E. (1975). Neural stability, sparing and behaviour recovery following brain damage. *Psychological Review, 82*, 344–58.

McFie, J. (1960). Psychological testing in clinical neurology. *Journal of Nervous and Mental Diseases, 131*, 383–90.

McFie, J. (1961). Intellectual impairment in children with localized postinfantile cerebral lesions. *Journal of Neurology, Neurosurgery and Psychiatry, 24*, 361–5.

Milner, B. (1967). Brain mechanisms suggested by studies of temporal lobes. In C. H. Millikan and F. L. Darley (Eds.), *Brain Mechanisms Underlying Speech and Language.* New York: Grune and Stratton.

Mirsky, F. A., Bloch, J. J., Tecce, S., Lessell, S. and Marcus, E. (1973). Visual evoked potentials during experimentally induced spike-wave activity in monkeys. *Electroencephalographic Clinical Neurophysiology 35*, 25–37.

Myhrer, T. (1975). Locomotor, avoidance and maze behavior in rats with selective disruption of hippocampal output. *Journal of Comparative Physiology and Psychology, 89*, 759–77.

Norman, R. M. (1964). The neuropathology of status epilepticus. *Medicine, Science and the Law, 4*, 46–55.

Ounsted, C. (1955). The hyperkinetic syndrome in epileptic children. *Lancet, ii*, 303–5

Ounsted, C., Lindsay, J. and Norman, R. (1966). Biological factors in temporal lobe epilepsy. *Little Club Clinics in Developmental Medicine*, No. 22. London: Heinemann.

Penfield, W. and Jasper, H. (1954). *Epilepsy and the Functional Anatomy of the Human Brain.* London: Churchill.

Pennington, H., Galliani, C. and Voegele, G. (1965). Unilateral encephalographic dysrhythmia and children's intelligence. *Child Develoment, 36*, 539–46.

Piaget, J. (1952). *The Origins of Intelligence in Children.* New York: International Universities Press.

Prechtl, H. F. R., Boeke, P. E. and Schut, T. (1961). The electroencephalogram and performance in epileptic patients. *Neurology, 11*, 296–302.

Reed, H. B. C. Jnr. and Fitzhugh, K. B. (1966). Patterns of deficits in relation to severity of cerebral dysfunction in children and adults. *Journal of Consulting Psychology, 30*, 98–102.

Reed, H. B. C. Jnr., Reitan, R. M. and Klove, H. (1965). The influence of cerebral lesions on psychological test performances of older children. *Journal of Consulting Psychology, 29*, 247–51.

Reitan, R. M. (1974). Psychological effects of cerebral lesions in children of early school age. In R. M. Reitan and L. A. Davidson (Eds.), *Clinical Neuropsychology: Current Status and Applications.* Washington, D.C.: Winston.

Reitan, R. M. and Davidson, L. A. (Eds.) (1974). *Clinical Neuropsychology: Current Status and Applications.* Washington, D.C.: Winston.

Rosner, B. S. (1970). Brain functions. *Annual Review of Psychology, 21*, 555–94.

Rudel, R. G. and Teuber, H. L. (1971). Pattern recognition within and across sensory modalities in normal and brain injured children. *Neuropsychologica, 9*, 389–99.

Rudel, R. G., Teuber, H. L. and Twitchell, T. E. (1974). Levels of impairment of sensori-motor functions in children with early brain damage. *Neuropsychologica, 12*, 95–108.

Schwartzbaum, J. S., Bowman, R. E. and Holdstock, L. (1964). Visual exploration in the monkey following ablation of the amygdaloid complex. *Journal of Comparative Physiology and Psychology, 57*, 453–6.

Smith, E. E. (1968). Choice reaction time: analysis of the major theoretical positions. *Psychological Bulletin, 69*, 77–110.

Stevens, J. R., Sachdev, K. and Milstein, V. (1968). Behavior disorders of childhood and the electroencephalogram. *Archives of Neurology, 18,* 160–77.

Taylor, D. C. (1969). Differential rates of cerebral maturation between sexes and between hemispheres. *Lancet, ii,* 140–2.

Teuber, H. L. and Rudel, R. (1962). Behavior after cerebral lesions in children and adults. *Developmental Medicine and Child Neurology, 4,* 3–20.

Tizard, B. and Margerison, J. H. (1963a). Psychological functions during wave-spike discharge. *British Journal of Social and Clinical Psychology, 3,* 6–15.

Tizard, B. and Margerison, J. H. (1963b). The relationship between generalized paroxysmal EEG discharges and various test situations in two epileptic patients. *Journal of Neurology, Neurosurgery and Psychiatry, 26,* 308–13.

Walzer, S. and Wolff, P. H. (1973). *Minimal Cerebral Dysfunction in Children.* New York: Grune and Stratton.

Waugh, N. C. and Norman, D. A. (1965). Primary memory. *Psychological Review, 72,* 89–104.

Weiskrantz, L. (1967). Emotion. In L. Weiskrantz (Ed.), *Analysis of Behavioural Change.* New York: Harper and Row.

Wikler, A., Dixon, J. F. and Parker, J. B. Jnr. (1970). Brain function in problem children and controls: psychometric, neurological and electroencephalographic comparisons. *American Journal of Psychiatry, 127,* 634–45.

CHAPTER 15

Cognitive Development in Mental Subnormality*†

Penelope H. Odom-Brooks and *Drew J. Arnold*

I. DEFINITION OF MENTAL RETARDATION

Mental retardation or subnormality entails some delay or deficit in cognitive development. To determine the nature of this delay or deficit has been the goal of years and pages of research efforts. It would be an easy task to write a chapter such as this if we could say, as some have, that retarded individuals have an inadequate memory, or incomplete discriminatory powers, or confused organization abilities. As in most areas of inquiry in the behavioural sciences, there is at least a healthy disparity of opinion on most topics, if not open disagreement. Not only is there a wide variety of opinions on what cognitive development is, but there are also diverse ideas about the definition of mental retardation. In this chapter we shall attempt an overview of both these issues, beginning with a discussion of a definition of mental retardation and its influence on research strategies. Most of this chap-

* This work was supported in part by NICHHD Grant No. HD–00973 to the Institute on Mental Retardation and Intellectual Development which is a component of the John F. Kennedy Center for Research on Education and Human Development and also by NIE Grant No. NE–G–00–3–0089. The authors are grateful to Charley McCauley and Al Baumeister for their helpful comments on earlier drafts of this chapter.
† The American Association of Mental Deficiency provides the system of labelling degree of retardation used here. This includes: mild and moderate retardation, classifications based on scores between two and three and three and four standard deviations below the means of standardized intelligence tests. These categories are roughly equivalent to the educational categories, educable mentally retarded (EMR) and trainable mentally retarded (TMR). Categories for those scoring below four standard deviations are not used, reflecting the paucity of basic research with these groups.

ter will be devoted to ways in which theories of cognitive development and their respective data have attempted to account for mental retardation.

For various reasons, the American Association on Mental Deficiency has felt compelled over the years to compile an official definition of mental deficiency. The 1973 version of this definition is as follows: "Mental retardation refers to significantly sub-average general intellectual functioning existing concurrently with deficits in adaptive behavior and manifested during the developmental period." Intellectual functioning is assessed by a standardized test; sub-average refers to performance two or more standard deviations from the mean of the test; adaptive behaviour is typically assessed by a scale of independence and social responsibility (for instance in eating habits, dressing skills). This definition, then, defines mental retardation psychometrically, and as Baumeister and Muma (1975) have noted, inadvertently promotes only one theory of intelligence to the exclusion of others such as in the factorial, structural or developmental approaches. This exclusion is especially crippling because the psychometric model of intelligence is "not sufficiently comprehensive to embrace the wide range of critical variables which are important in understanding the processes of learning, development and social involvement" (p. 8). The IQ score "tells us nothing about internal states of an individual or the processes that mediate socially adaptive behavior" (p. 9).

The narrowness of the IQ approach is also reflected in the correlation of IQ with other indices of cognitive competency. DeVries (1974) compared psychometric (IQ scores) and Piagetian assessments of intelligence and found only slight overlap. She concluded that, to a large extent, the two types of tests measure different aspects of cognitive functioning. Thus, the traditional IQ score is an incomplete index of cognitive ability. This insufficiency has a number of implications; for research purposes, its major influence is a methodological one that, in turn, has far-reaching implications. It is of questionable value to select samples of subjects according to a psychometric criterion while investigating Piagetian-defined intellectual skills, which have very little correlation with the psychometric measure. By accepting the psychometric definition the investigator is confined to the task of seeking what does and does not correlate with IQ and MA.

Another major problem with a psychometrically-based definition of retardation is that it groups otherwise heterogeneous people together, regardless of etiology. People are classified as mentally retarded at some level whether they have suffered brain damage, genetic disorder, or cultural deprivation. This is a procedure much like assigning students to a health and nutrition class on the basis of weight, regardless of how a particular weight was attained by the individual. Such grouping may tend to cover potentially critical effects peculiar to a given etiology. Furthermore, it encourages the tendency to address the common features of the retarded *per se* rather than sub-groups which have more homogeneous cognitive capacities and developmental histories. It is difficult to understand why investigators who seem to have a penchant for analytical approaches, as do those in information-processing, would tolerate an almost arbitrary grouping of their subject population.

There are two perspectives in mental retardation research which differ only subtly, but which make the research difficult to integrate. One suggests that the reference point of research should be mental retardation; the other, cognitive development. Investigators could, on the one hand, seek a cognitive interpretation or description of mental retardation. The outcome of this strategy would be a profile diagramming the relative competence of mentally retarded persons on each of the different processes. Such an index would be similar to a personality inventory, interest scale, or even other tests of mental abilities, except that the strategy would be theoretically motivated rather than empirically determined. As such, the trouble could be diagnosed and intervention procedures could be mechanically specified (for instance, one might see such intervention tactics as attempts to train discrimination, to enhance short-term memory, to increase rehearsal strategies, or to teach conservation). The other view, which has cognitive development as its theme, asks what individual differences are manifested in what cognitive processes. This approach uses research in mental retardation as a means of refining cognitive theory, a role for mental retardation-cognitive development research consistent with Underwood (1975) and recommended by Butterfield (1975). Both views are represented in much of the research concerned with cognitive development and mental retardation but are seldom formally designated. The failure to make this distinction is the source of a great deal of confusion in arguments over appropriate strategies for research and conclusions from research findings. While we have duly noted the distinction, we shall attempt no resolution. The question should be asked about the results of any study, however: do we now know more about retardation or more about cognitive development or both?

To take some stand on the nature of retarded development is automatically to take a stand on the nature of normal development. Two approaches towards normal development have emerged. They are not mutually exclusive, but differ in their underlying assumptions

22—CP * *

concerning the nature of what is learned, and therefore the nature of development. On the one hand, much of the research and many ideas have been contributed by investigators who adopt a traditional information-processing approach. This approach is characterized by an amalgam of verbal learning, memory, and learning research. There is no single basic theory of development or change underlying research except, perhaps, the assumption of a quantitative improvement with maturity or experience. The other approach, best exemplified by Piagetian theory, has rich qualitative assumptions about the nature of change with development, but not such a broad experimental base. The distinction between the two approaches is similar to one made by Reese and Lipsitt (1970) between experimental child psychology and developmental psychology. Followers of the two approaches have produced rather different kinds of research. These will be discussed and reviewed in turn : first, the research resulting from the application of cognitive, information-processing theories followed by that resulting from more developmental approaches. No attempt will be made to review the literature extensively or completely. Just the research that most clearly illustrates the cognitive functioning of retarded children from each of the two approaches is described.

II.   INFORMATION-PROCESSING PERSPECTIVES OF MENTAL RETARDATION

Many investigators have adopted cognitive information-processing approaches as models for mental retardation research. All such models may be characterized as sharing certain epistemological assumptions and theoretical predispositions and limitations which are largely unexpressed, and are, therefore, difficult to axiomatize. Developmentally speaking, the most salient aspects of such models are : (a) an equating of memory of processed units with "knowledge" (that is to say, a child's knowledge about the world equals the total of information that has been processed according to the prescribed sequence), (b) an unwillingness to specify a priori what constitutes information and how past experience influences ongoing processing, and (c) in mental retardation research, the investigator's adoption of some particular level as deficient in functioning, with a resultant deficiency and retardation in later stages of processing. These investigators also tend to adopt a schematic design which reflects a commitment to examine developmental retardation in terms of components and related processes. There are several components that are present in most, if not all, information processing models : a concern for acquisition of information, two or three retention mechanisms (for instance, iconic store, short-term memory (STM) and long-term memory (LTM)), and retrieval mechanisms.

While such approaches have been heuristic and have helped to limit the amount of atheoretical, topographical investigation which has been characteristic of mental retardation research, they can also be misleading. Although components reflect logical constructs and have reference to and require operational definition, breaking a dynamic process up into discrete segments is, in some senses, artificial. A student can be misled into assuming that, because cognitive performance is the result of a continuous chain of operations, the performance of retarded subjects should be investigated only at each stage in the sequence. What is missing in research on the retarded is the recognition that the systems or processes can possibly interact.

There is a basic distinction made available by information process-ing approaches that is relevant to retardation research (that is to say, the distinction between structural features and control processes, Atkinson and Shiffrin, 1968). Structural features are defined as the limits or capacities of behaviour functioning and are usually character-ized as permanently fixed and immutable. For example, the structural features which Fisher and Zeaman (1973) delineate include the number of dimensions to which a child can attend during a learning task, the maintenance of information in STM, the flexibility with which information can be introduced into a rehearsal buffer, and LTM. Control processes, on the other hand, are factors which control the present level of ability and are considered experientially modifiable (for instance, initial probability of attention). By implication, inter-vention would only be possible to the extent that control processes are modifiable; overall cognitive development is determined predomin-antly by the unalterable limitation of the structural components of the model.

Although there is a growing trend towards examining control pro-cesses, most experimenters assume, either tacitly or overtly, that retarda-tion is a structural feature deficit. This assumption is the result of considering intelligence to be a stable trait. There are those who have posited control process theories of intelligence, specifically Hunt (1961). He thought that learning rate is dependent upon the training one gets in learning to learn. This essentially control process theory of intellig-ence is shared by many who use behaviour modification in intervention. The problem in establishing a valid distinction between fixed capacity restrictions and trainable control processes awaits both developmental study and theoretical clarification. This clarification will be necessary if this conceptual system is to be successfully applied to retardation research.

There are two important questions concerning the process-structure distinction that need to be considered. The first is the nature of individual differences as they relate to both structure and process; this will be the focus of the literature reviewed here. Subsuming this, however, is the difficult problem of defining exclusive categories of structure and function when considering a growing organism. While the process-structure distinction was originally intended to describe a static organism, it tends to lose its clarity when considered developmentally because then it is usually assumed that the capacity of structures changes. When change is introduced into the system, the question of modifiability, and *a fortiori* of innate limits of structural change, becomes important in the consideration of individual differences. Since modifiability is a potential characteristic of both structure and process in a developing organism, the problem of structure in this sense becomes isomorphic with the problem of process. Are the capacity differences immutable or will the organism's structures and/or processes continuously evolve and be modified, and if so with what potential for growth?

III. ACQUISITION PROCESSES OF THE RETARDED

Mechanisms of acquisition, retention and retrieval are necessary components of information processing approaches. Of these components, the acquisition stage has been shown to be the most clearly amenable to developmental changes. The acquisition process will be discussed in terms of attention and retention strategies, although the concepts are not entirely independent. Selective attention, for example, may be considered a strategy in the sense that memory load is reduced, thereby facilitating retention.

(1) ATTENTION PROCESSES

Attention is commonly discussed in three ways: as an orienting response (getting one's attention), selective attention (with its concomitant role in learing), and attention in the sense of perseverance in a task. Perseverance in a task, which may reflect levels of functional information input, has received relatively little systematic investigation. Crosby (1972) found more frequent lapses in the attention of retarded subjects to a continuous performance task. Interestingly, retarded and normal subjects were not differentiated by reactions to distracting stimuli. Distractibility, a commonly assumed characteristic of the retarded, is reflected in their greater variability and should not be assumed to show a consistent group difference. There is evidence that these differences are present in neonates (for instance, in Sigman, Kopp, Parmelee and Jeffrey, 1973), although psychometric verification of retardation is difficult at early ages.

The orienting reflex, that is the attaching of signal value to environmental events, has been thought by the Russian psychologists to be related to intelligence. Luria (1963), for example, reviewed the results of habituation studies in which retarded subjects exhibited strong orienting reflexes to intense stimuli that were difficult to habituate, while exhibiting infrequent responses to low intensity stimuli which were relatively easy to habituate. Heal and Johnson (1970), in a review of studies of the orienting reflex of retarded subjects, concluded that the data are very confused and contradictory, enough to warrant the conclusion that there is no relationship between IQ and the orientation reflex. More recent studies of a variety of paradigms (for instance, in Mosley, Bakal and Pilek, 1974; Siddle and Glenn, 1974; Powazek and Johnson, 1973) also have failed to implicate orientation reflex as being associated with retardation.

The literature on selective attention is much less ambiguous. Studies tend to confirm not only developmental delays but differences that retarded children maintain at each stage of their developmental sequence relative to non-retarded children. Although in a general sense a given developmental stage is by definition the same for retarded and non-retarded children, except that the retarded children reach it later, the stages are defined too grossly to detect cumulative effects of differential information processing. The developmental view of intellectual change specifies systems of information treatment that are continuously evolving. Thus, as Inhelder (1968) suggests, it is the closure of such operational systems in mentally retarded children that distinguishes them from non-retarded children. It might be said then that a selective attention deficit is not only a limiting condition at each stage of development, but also that it makes retarded development qualitatively different from normal development.

One method of investigation of the selection of information is through the observation of the orientation of the receptor organs, as distinct from the physiological orienting response. There is evidence that this type of orienting ability is developmental. Vurpillot (1968) studied the eye movements of children at four age levels in a task in which the subjects compared pictures to see if they were identical. For children under 6, picture scanning was limited and judgments were made on the basis of insufficient information. It was concluded that children improve their ability to attend selectively with their eyes to those portions of the visual stimuli which contain the most information. Retarded children seemed to have more difficulty with attending to relevant visual information than normal children of similar abilities. Wilton and Boersma (1974) compared retarded and normal children's eye movements on a conservation task. While eye movement patterns clearly differentiated conservers and non-conservers in both retarded and non-retarded groups, there were fewer conserver–non-conserver differences in retarded subjects in amount of visual scanning activity. This reflects an inefficiency in the searching patterns of retarded children.

While the orientation of receptor organs has not been widely studied with retarded subjects, the results have been consistent (Rosenberg, 1961) and have utilized several different paradigms. Spitz (1969) used retarded and normal subjects matched for CA and MA in a task in which the information level of a target was reduced, thereby depriving subjects of the distinctive properties of the stimulus. It was shown that extreme loss of visual content information was severely but equally deleterious for both the retarded and younger subjects, more so than for the CA-matched normal subjects. This scanning deficiency has also been studied tachistoscopically by Veresotskaya (Shif, 1969). It was found that a short exposure, sufficient to allow non-retarded first grade students to recognize a contour image, caused a different recognition reaction among CA-matched retarded children. A 22 msec exposure was sufficient to allow normal children to identify correctly 57 per cent of the objects presented to them, but at this speed the retarded children could not identify any single object. While this study found a deficiency in information processing capacity, it and others like it lack the power to clarify the manner in which differential processing abilities can make the developmental stages qualitatively different and can delay the acquisition of further behavioural stages.

There have been several studies which have demonstrated qualitative differences between retarded and normal subjects of similar developmental level (that is to say, of equal MA). Winters, Gerjuoy, Crown and Gorrell (1967) found that the correlation between the direction of eye movements and the order of verbal report was higher for normals than for the retarded. In a later study (Winters and Gerjuoy, 1969), subjects were presented with an array of four letters at two exposure durations. While the groups did not differ at the faster duration, at the slower retarded subjects were poorer than MA-matched normals, and both were poorer than CA-matched normals. It was thought that the poorer scanning behaviour of the retarded subjects relative to the MA-matched normals reflected inconsistent scanning behaviour rather than a general inefficiency. The research of Zeaman and House (1963) on the role of selective attention in simple discrimination learning has also shown deficits in the retarded. In their studies they divided the acquisition of correct instrumental responses into a chain of two responses. The first was a central mediating response, identified with attention to the relevant stimulus dimension; and the second was the approach to one of the outcomes of the attentional response. Training was considered successful when the subject consistently selected the stimulus pattern that contained the target cue.

Zeaman and House considered that the difference between fast and slow learners was not in the rate of learning, once the learning started, but in the number of trials that it took for learning to start. They plotted the mean discrimination learning functions for homogeneous groups of subjects; these graphs showed that the performance of the children who took more trials to learn remained near the chance level over a considerable part of the training. When correct responses became greater than chance the percentages of correct choices ascended at, roughly, a rate equivalent to the rate of the children who had reached criterion earlier. Zeaman and House also demonstrated using computer simulation that group differences in learning rate can be explained without assuming individual differences in learning rate parameters; slow learners simply have a low probability of initial attention (see also pp. 130–1).

While the Zeaman and House (1963) studies reflect a delay in development, that is, similar performance in retarded and normal subjects at the same developmental level, other studies reflect differences in attentional processes. This is evident in the work on incidental learning. Hagen (1972a,b) has noted that improvement in memory as a function of age occurs in part because of the ability to attend to certain cues while ignoring others. Especially in information overload conditions, incidental information is ignored in order to maintain performance on the central task. Generally, Hagen found that central memory performance increases with age, while incidental performance does not, and actually declines with age.

Two studies utilizing retarded subjects reflect not only developmental trends but retarded–normal differences. Hagen and Huntsman (1971) found that retarded subjects showed lessened ability to attend to the relevant aspects of a task. The institutionalized retarded subjects also ignored more irrelevant aspects than children of equal mental age. Hagen and West (1970) studied the selective attention of retarded subjects at two age levels. Subjects were asked to learn stimuli and were later tested on both the primary stimuli, the stimuli to be learned, and information incidental to the central stimuli. It was predicted that the number of correct responses would be greater for primary (rewarded) rather than secondary stimuli, and that older subjects would maximize their performance more than younger subjects. Contrary to expectation, the younger retarded individuals showed significant improvement in the last half of the trials compared to the first half; no similar trend was found for the older subjects. These findings are ambiguous since it was not clear whether the older retarded subjects' response patterns were limited by the nature of the task, and hence unrepresentative. However, this does tend to suggest an upper limit on the development of the selective attention abilities of the retarded that needs further examination.

(2) ACQUISITION STRATEGIES

The employment of strategies is basic to the acquisition process and is correlated with intelligence. Strategies may be defined as transformations of input which organize input into manageable, more easily assimilated information units. The research has been consistent in finding that retarded children have difficulty in strategy employment, even when compared to normal subjects of similar developmental level. The implementation of strategies is a process the effectiveness of which varies in degree, and also must be considered in relation to retrieval processes. That is to say, not only must the acquisition strategy and retrieval processes be effective; the interaction of these processes must also be effective (Spitz, 1973; Butterfield, Wambold, and Belmont, 1973). Most of the present research tends towards within-paradigm refinements and does not consider the strategies as they affect the entire information-processing scheme. As a consequence, the literature is more a suggestive exploration than a thorough analysis of task-specific strategies as a precise construct.

One of the most basic distinctions which may be made is between active and passive employment of strategies. Developmental differences found between older and younger children, and between retarded and normal subjects, seem to reflect in part the degree to which strategic behaviours are applied to the task. When a subject is passive and makes little attempt to transform or memorize input, performance is impaired. While there is some suggestion that passive learning by retarded subjects is not notably deficient relative to normal subjects (Butterfield *et al.*, 1973), yet that they as a group fail to institute an active "plan to execute" (Miller, Galanter and Pribram, 1960) has become recognized as a limiting factor in their memory efficiency.

Many studies investigating the activity–passivity dimension with retarded individuals have concluded that they manifest less intent or ability to organize information. Spitz and Nadler (1974) examined the logical problem solving of retarded and normal adolescents. Noting that many studies have shown that retarded subjects do not readily discover redundancy, which would reduce memory load, they studied this basic phenomenon in a logical problem-solving task in which one unit of information was necessary. They found that the retarded subjects were as able to apply given information; however, they did not translate this experience into a principle or logical rule that could be used for subsequent trials. That is, they were capable of using the information but incapable of generating it into a functional applied form. Their results suggest that MA was not always an accurate gauge of performance, and they speculated that MA predicts performance relative to normal ontogenesis when normals are below a certain age, but that this difference becomes acute at MA of 8.

The general failure of retarded subjects to use strategies was demonstrated in a study of Russian children cited by Pinskii (Shif, 1969). Groups of retarded adolescents were given stories to read. One half of the subjects were warned before reading that they would be asked to recall the story. The subjects warned about the impending test recalled 46.6 per cent of "composite semantic units"; those that received no prior warning recalled almost as much (40 per cent). When the same experiment was conducted with normal adolescents of the same age, forewarned subjects recalled 30 per cent more than the uninformed group. Apparently the retarded subjects could not use the warning as a signal to bring memory strategies into play, or else they had no memory strategies to use. The above studies were group studies which looked for retarded–normal differences. When Ellis (1970) analyzed some individual subjects' serial position curves, he found that, when faced with difficult tasks, his retarded subjects developed idiosyncratic and maladaptive rehearsal strategies.

The activity–passivity dimension is implicit in studies of specific strategies, as has been clearly illustrated in the Belmont and Butterfield (1969, 1971) studies of STM. They were able to isolate storage effects from retrieval processes and attention by using hesitation patterns in button pressing during acquisition, thus allowing strategies to be inferred. Hesitation patterns, which were found to be related to recall, were not patterned consistently by retarded subjects. The hesitation patterns of normal subjects led the investigators to believe that they rehearsed the information in chunks. The two curves in Fig. 15.1 comparing college students and sixth graders shows the college students' tendency to chunk the items into two major groupings (indicated by a longer latency on item 4).

A series of studies reported by Ellis (1970) implicates the failure of

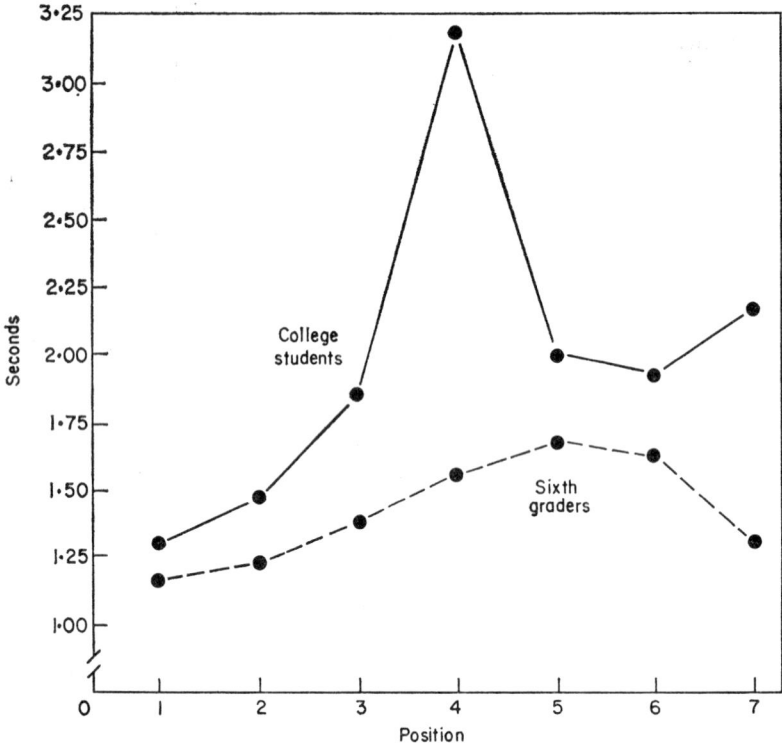

FIG. 15.1. Mean hesitation patterns for college students and sixth graders. (*After* Belmont and Butterfield, 1969, p. 74.)

the rehearsal mechanism in the STM of the retarded. Revising an earlier position (Ellis, 1963), he considered that there were two processes involved in the short-term storage of supra-span information. He postulated a primary memory which remains invariant over a wide range of IQ and is not developmental, and a secondary memory in which rehearsal strategies are important and which varies with intelligence. Ellis, in part, based his conclusions on the differential learning displayed by subjects when the item presentation rate was varied in a serial learning task. While the recall of normal subjects was enhanced at the primacy portion of the serial position curve with longer intervals, presumably due to rehearsal, retarded individuals showed no such improvement. (Figure 15.2 illustrates these findings.) It should be noted that while Ellis used probe recall (that is to say, asking subjects to recall the position in which a single item appeared), Frankel and Tymchuk (1974) used whole list recall and found that faster presentation time facilitated both retarded and normal subjects.

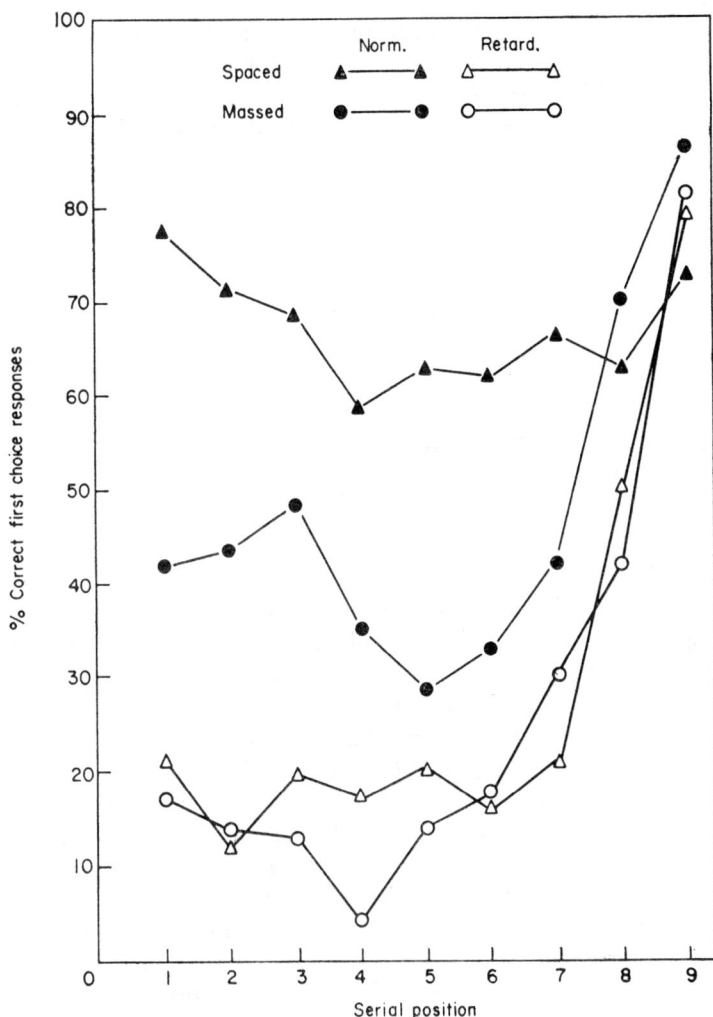

Fig. 15.2. The performance of normal and retarded subjects: under massed (0.0 sec interitem interval) and spaced (2.0 sec interitem interval) conditions on a serial position task. (*After* Ellis, 1970, p. 9.)

Two additional comments upon Ellis's work should be made : first, his studies were done with institutionalized retarded populations, which, as Turnbull (1974) notes, have been shown in similar studies to be a systematically different population. More important, one might be tempted to conclude from this type of model that all one has to do is to insert an effective rehearsal strategy, and memory of retarded individuals will be normalized. This is, perhaps, an empirical question for intervention studies; however, one is left to determine what originally limits the rehearsal process and how this limitation interacts with the total cognitive system.

The data from Belmont and Butterfield's studies indicated that inducing retarded persons to mimic adult pause patterns improved performance, particularly on the primacy portion of the curve. Their finding was suggestive because they gave only pause and not rehearsal instruction. In most studies (for instance, Kellas, Ashcraft and Johnson, 1973) effective rehearsal has not been spontaneously generated by the subjects but introduced through training. This finding might indicate that rehearsal capacity may be a structural feature of memory but that rehearsal use is a control process (McBane, 1972). In contrast, some studies have found that retarded subjects do spontaneously rehearse, but that this rehearsal is not necessarily effective. Glidden (1972) varied meaningfulness in a serially presented paired-associate task and found that, when retention intervals were lengthened, more item rehearsal took place but effectiveness was not improved. This was deduced from the differences in serial position accuracy; longer intervals resulted in more accurate responses but a decrement in the learning of the first position. This finding may, however, reflect retrieval difficulties which are not separated from encoding processes in these experimental manipulations.

Butterfield et al. (1973) found that there were deficiencies, in addition to lack of rehearsal, that hold retarded individuals below their potential capacity in memory studies. They do not properly sequence rehearsal and essential non-rehearsal learning techniques, and they neither co-ordinate multiple retrieval strategies nor co-ordinate these retrieval strategies with strategies of acquisition. This imples that mnemonic deficiencies are much more intricate than were originally supposed. Butterfield et al. (1973) considered that their subjects did not lack the memory processes for accurate performance; what they did lack was spontaneous access to the processes and co-ordination among them. This failure of executive control is trans-situational, a conclusion which would imply that future studies should concern the selecting, sequencing and co-ordinating processes that are in the cognitive repertoire, and not specific processes in isolation.

The several studies in which retarded individuals were trained to use strategies have demonstrated some improvement (for instance, Ellis, 1970; Turnbull, 1974), although this training is more effective with concomitant training in retrieval strategies (for instance, Butterfield et al., 1973). Brown (1972) used a keeping-track task to study rehearsal in the retarded. In this task the number of instances of categories was varied; on each trial the subjects were presented with an inspection set of four items and the subject had to remember the most recent category instance. There are two possible strategies that could be used in this situation; the subject, when asked which instance of a category was displayed in the most recent set, could either search his memory of the states of the inspection set and determine which one is in that category. The other possible strategy entails a search through the possible instances of the category to determine which one is most recently tagged. It was found that adolescent retarded subjects' (CA = 16, MA = 9) performance depended upon the number of states of the probed variables, indicating that they were using the less efficient strategy, searching through the state of the variables in question. The finding that this strategy was similar to that used by pre-school children suggested to Brown that her retarded subjects did not spontaneously adopt a strategy of active rehearsal, although it may suggest only inappropriate rehearsal.

Brown, Campione and Murphy (1974) retested subjects from an earlier study in which some had been trained to use rehearsal strategies in a keeping-track task. They found that the original training remained effective over a six-month period. Similar findings of long term retention of learning strategies have been reported (Allen, 1968; Spitz and Webreck, 1972). These studies of long-term storage do not contain any indication as to how training would permanently alter a retarded person's use of acquisition strategies, nor of the generalizability of specific training techniques. There is little evidence which concerns the scope of generalization of strategy training, but there are indications that, at least with non-schematic techniques such as rehearsal, there is very little generalization; although as Turnbull (1974) noted, this may be a function of the type and method of training and is in need of more thorough study if intervention prescriptions are to be successful.

IV.   RETENTION MECHANISMS OF THE RETARDED

The retention mechanisms of information-processing approaches are analogous to discrete departments with information being processed in sequence through each component. While there may be a shift from this mechanistic approach towards conceptualizing retention in terms of the levels of analysis of information (for instance, Craik and Lockhart, 1972; Brown, 1974), this former approach has been influential in retardation research. The iconic store, a register in which sensory impressions are briefly maintained, is the first retention mechanism in most theories. Visually the icon consists of a more or less photographic image of the stimulus that fades rapidly over a period of several hundred msec. Information passes from the icon to STM and LTM. These mechanisms are usually considered structural features and as a consequence are of great interest to investigators concerned with retardation.

(1) THE ICONIC STORE

Studies of the visual iconic store have demonstrated a relationship between IQ and characteristics of the iconic store. Pennington and Luszcz (1975) have shown that the input of information in sensory storage closely parallels that of normal subjects, although at a slightly lower level. That is, at the same stimulus exposure speed, retarded subjects reported one less letter than normal subjects. Other studies have indicated that the iconic store of the retarded is of longer duration. This implies that once input is established it would interfere with the rapid input of stimulus information; for example, Thor (1971) found that retarded subjects do not process repetitive stimuli as rapidly as normals. The duration of the intervals in which effective masking takes place are developmental and decrease with mental age (Spitz and Thor, 1968). Retarded and normal subjects of the same MA are not necessarily equivalent on these tasks or in their ability to refine their performance in these tasks. For example, normal subjects are found to improve with practice on these tasks while practice has not been shown to be effective with the retarded.

(2) SHORT-TERM MEMORY

From a psychometric point of view, it may be expected that STM would be highly correlated with intelligence. The data on digit span sub-tests, for example, show that it loads substantially on the general factor reported by Wechsler (1958), although it should be noted that lower IQ subjects tend to have a greater variability in digit span scores (Jensen, 1970). Spitz (1973) reviewed his research concerning the amount of information educable retarded adolescents could retain in STM. While Miller (1956) found that normal subjects could process 7 ± 2 chunks of information, data from a variety of paradigms shows that retarded subjects' span of apprehension encompasses 4 ± 1, and even after practice this capacity increased to only 5 ± 2 chunks. Likewise Baumeister (1974) has shown the deficit to be stable across different modalities and with different types of stimuli. (Interestingly Spitz and LaFontaine (1973) found that idiot savants do have an immediate memory span that is within the normal range.) The relatively small STM capacity of the retarded has several implications both in terms of long-term storage of information and also of the reduction of ongoing behavioural capacities. Not only would a limited STM capacity reduce the probability that a given piece of information is stored but, as Farnham-Diggory (1972) has demonstrated, the development of the capacity to synthesize incoming information is contingent upon the memory load relative to STM capacity.

There are several theoretical approaches that have been used to account for the apparent STM deficit in the retarded, including inadequate rehearsal strategies (Belmont and Butterfield, 1969; Ryan, Chivers and Redding, 1969) and memory traces which are more subject to interference (Hawkins and Baumeister, 1965). One of the earliest and perhaps the most influential was the stimulus trace theory Ellis (1963) modified and used to explain the STM deficits of the retarded. For Ellis (1963), as for some information-processing theorists, knowledge is associationistic in nature. If, for some reason, stimulus elements cannot be maintained long enough for associations to occur there would be no incremental improvement in knowledge. Indeed, Ellis's theory would predict deficiencies in a wide range of tasks from reaction time (RT) to paired-associate learning. The strength and duration of the stimulus trace, a transient neural process by which information is maintained, diminishes more rapidly in retarded individuals. The stimulus trace proposed by Ellis was developmental and predicted a change in retention as a function of both IQ and MA. However, it would be considered a structural deficit because the limits of the capacity would not be modifiable.

Conceptually somewhat similar to Ellis's (1963) theory is the neural theory of Spitz (1963) who believed that there is a slowed reaction of the electrochemical processes in the neural cells of the central nervous system, manifested by weak iconic after-effects and fewer reversals of the Necker cube. Like Ellis's, Spitz's theory is structural and would indicate that retarded individuals would fail to make associations because of an inability to establish clear contingencies. However, instead of a quickly reduced signal trace, as Ellis hypothesized, Spitz postulates that once stimuli induce temporary chemical and electrical modification of cortical cells, it takes longer for these calls to return to their previous state (Mosley and McKim, 1973). In summary, both neurological theories make clear predictions that the total information is unlikely to be permanently stored or learned, because information either will never reach LTM or will be disorganized if it does.

Ellis's 1963 theory has been thoroughly studied, with initial mixed reviews giving way to generally unsupportive findings. Holden (1971), for example, chose a series of dot sequences that he thought limited the possibilities of rehearsal strategies, and found little evidence to support and type of stimulus trace theory. Similarly, Mosley and McKim (1973) have found little support for Spitz's (1963) theory with non-organically damaged subjects. The most extensive review of the STM phenomenon in relation to the retarded has been carried out by Belmont and Butterfield (1969). In addition to concluding that a great majority of the studies that had suggested differential forgetting rates of retarded and normal subjects had been confounded by ceiling or floor effects, they also presented methodologically more sophisticated studies which indicated that the rate of forgetting was similar across ability groups. They considered that the more active acquisition strategies employed by older and more intelligent subjects result in the differential attainments in the STM of retarded and normal individuals.

The introduction of rehearsal strategies that have effectively modified the STM capacity of retarded subjects caused Ellis (1970) to revise his original theory. He now includes two discontinuous processes that operate in the retention of supra-span information, one of which is affected by rehearsal strategies and differentiates retarded and normal subjects. Rehearsal is demonstrably a control process effect and interest in it reflects a change from a structural deficit orientation. However, rehearsal processes do not fully explain the STM deficits of the retarded; they suffer additional deficits that may not be reduced to rehearsal deficiencies, or the ability to maintain information in STM. These deficiencies concern the processes employed in the utilization of information that is present in STM.

The search of information being held in STM has been described by Sternberg (1966), and application of his research paradigm to retarded subjects has been illuminating. Sternberg found that the subject's reaction times (RT), in verifying whether an item was in a previously shown display, varied in a linear fashion with memory load (M), in a manner that could be described by the equation $RT = A + B (M)$. He postulated that the constant A represents the time necessary for probe encoding, response decision and response execution, and B represents the time necessary for a probe item to be compared with a single item stored in memory. The linear relationship between RT and memory set size that characterizes the performance of both retarded and normal subjects suggests that search of information is serial and exhaustive. Research with the Sternberg paradigm has been made difficult by the variability of retarded subjects (Baumeister, personal communication); however, this paradigm has yielded some interesting differences between retarded and normal children. There is consistent evidence that the retarded have encoding and/or retrieval difficulties. Silverman (1974) conducted a developmental study in which it was found that children improve with age in the ability to process incoming information, as indicated by lower RTs. This was due to improved stimulus and/or response selection, since there were no differences in the slopes of the curves of children at any age or IQ level. Other investigators (Dugas and Kellas, 1974; Harris and Fleer, 1974), on the other hand, have found deficits in information processing that differentiated retarded and normal subjects, even when the normal subjects had a lower MA. These differences are reflected in the steeper slopes produced by the retarded. As information load increases, it takes them comparatively longer to search their memory. As these studies suggest, the STM of the retarded is not deficit free, they are at a disadvantage both with encoding and retrieval.

(3) LONG-TERM MEMORY

While the deficit in STM is well documented, the nature of the LTM of retarded subjects has been less thoroughly explored. In an early neurological explanation, Spitz (1963) postulated that once stimuli induced permanent changes in the cortical cells, it would be more difficult and take a longer time to switch like or relatively similar stimuli away from particular cell patterns to form new or different trace patterns. This, of course, implies a structural difference between retarded and normal subjects, a difference which has not clearly emerged from other areas of research.

Belmont (1966) is typically cited as presenting data which show that the memory loss of retarded subjects is comparable to that of normal subjects. However, it is often not noted that the Belmont review located only one study (Klausmeier, Feldhusen and Check, 1959) in which the methodological problems were not so great as to invalidate the results. Some later literature (for instance, Prehm and Mayfield, 1970; Goulet, 1968) has shown differential forgetting rates in retarded subjects on rote memorization tasks. It is probable that the methodological problems in their studies also are so complex, especially in equating groups and isolating retrieval rather than retention difficulties, that this issue cannot be considered resolved.

V. CONSTRUCTION PERSPECTIVES ON MENTAL RETARDATION

The other area of research, probably best exemplified by Piaget's large volume of publication and research, characterizes the child as a builder. The child builds or constructs a representation of the world and ways to operate in and on the world. He performs this construction according to two principles, "assimilation" and "accommodation". Assimilation is the process of operating mentally and physically on the world so that it fits already existing knowledge. Assimilation is effective when a child distorts information to fit what he already knows. Two-year-old Wade, when asked if he had a parakeet, repeated back the word "parachute". His father explained that the son knew about parachutes but not parakeets and had not made the auditory distinction. Wade thus "heard" what he already knew, and it would take further efforts at explanation, emphasis, or relevant contact with the bird before he would hear "parakeet". This subsequent change would exemplify the second principle, accommodation, which refers to the ways in which a child changes as a function of new information. Accommodation is the principle which describes intellectual growth. Incoming information is changed by the structure and content of past knowledge and may, in turn, change that same structure and content.

From the interaction of assimilative and accommodative processes, a representation of reality is constructed. Assimilation and accommodation are necessary and sufficient conditions for successful LTM, which in this context is characterized as knowing about space, about time, about movement, and even about remembering. Indeed, it (LTM) constitutes one's knowledge as to how to function in the world at any given moment in development. The principles of assimilation and accommodation provide a framework for discussing another body of literature which has greater breadth and is less analytical than the research discussed in the previous sections. Assimilation is considered a construct synonymous with comprehension and the two terms are used interchangeably.

Whenever activity on the part of the subject is introduced into studies of memory or information processing, the studies can be considered as being of assimilatory processes. Even the studies discussed earlier under the topic of strategies could just as well have been included here because they concern how and when subjects employ old knowledge in the service of incorporating new information. The merger between incoming information and old knowledge is known by various names in the cognitive literature; two of these topics which have been applied to retarded children will be taken up in this section —integration and elaboration.

Integration is said to occur when various diverse kinds of information are combined into a holistic schema or representation. It may be that the learner is subsequently unable to reparcel the schema into its component parts and has difficulty in separating the new and the old information. The conditions determining the occurrence of integration are unknown, although the phenomenon has been demonstrated in two domains, namely spatial and semantic. The development of the capacity to integrate can be investigated within a given domain in that groups of subjects can be compared on a particular task. The task most frequently used involves memory for pictures or sentences. Paris, Mahoney and Buckhalt (1974) read EMR children passages of the following form : (a) John is chasing the dog. (b) The dog is in the schoolyard. (c) The dog is white. The first two premises allowed the inference which was not presented "John is in the schoolyard". A subsequent recognition task including the inference, and other appropriate statements, were given the subjects with the instruction to tell the experimenter whether they had heard that exact sentence before. The results showed that EMR subjects judged the inference as "old" significantly more often than the statements. The finding that the retarded subjects made inferences that required combining two premises is evidence that they do integrate information and make inferences just as non-retarded children do (Paris and Carter, 1973).

Combining in an integrative manner entails detection of thematic similarity (dog, for instance), but it also means that the relationship between "dog", "John", and "yard" was remembered as a single entity which could not be re-partitioned for the recognition task. Thus, the inference, "John was in the yard", was consistent with the integrated representation of the passage and was regarded by the retarded subjects as part of their knowledge. While this study did not directly compare retarded and non-retarded subjects, it did show that the cognitive processes of retarded students operate in ways qualitatively indistinguishable from those of non-retarded counterparts.

A process that exemplifies assimilatory processes is one that also has various names such as mediation, imagery and elaboration. They are all alike in two ways. In the first place, the experimental task is usually some variation of paired-associate learning. Secondly, and more important, the subjects are asked to generate from their knowledge some relationship between the two objects in a pair. Given the paired-associate item "foot-sun", subjects would be asked to make a sentence linking the two, such as "The sun shone on the foot", or to picture in their heads a bizarre relationship like an image of a giant foot stepping on a wincing sun. The result of the subjects' participation in this manner is enhanced recall of items in the task. Why is recall of the items facilitated dramatically once two objects enter into a subjective relationship? At least part of mastering the task consists of remembering which response item is associated with which stimulus item. Successful subjects use some properties of the stimulus item, such as its light projectability or the fact that the foot's flat surface is used as a pivot, to generate a relationship between the foot and the sun. In doing so, the subjects are capitalizing on what they know about feet, what they know about the sun, and what they know about the relationship between their properties. The advantage of this procedure is that it relates the pair of items in an elaborate, unique context which is, apparently, easier to remember. The rule could be stated as follows : the more subjects can apply prior knowledge to learning tasks, the more that learning will be facilitated.

Retardation is, by implication, the condition of having less usable knowledge than those of equivalent CA. Therefore, for comprehending a stimulus, the retarded individual has less to bring to the situation. The retardation becomes cumulative because, in addition to the reduced knowledge, any organic conditions that may have caused the initial lack of knowledge are presumably still operative. This condition would predict that, in a task such as the paired-associate elaboration task just described, retarded subjects would be unable to generate elaborations adequate to facilitate recall, as could non-retarded subjects of the same CA. Such a prediction is consistent with a broader view of development known as the mediation deficiency hypothesis, originally formulated by Maccoby (1964). The mediation deficiency hypothesis has since been further expanded into two parts, adding the possibility of a production deficiency or the failure to produce a mediator at all, or at least one that is potentially effective or objectively adequate. This distinction makes it possible to consider whether a mediator or elaboration is generated by subjects in an experiment (production efficiency), and whether they can employ it appropriately to facilitate recall (mediation efficiency).

There are two ways in which these possibilities have been investigated. Some investigators have attempted to equate retarded subjects and MA- or CA-matched non-retarded subjects on quality of elaboration. Any differences in recall could then be attributed to a mediation deficiency, or an inability to use the mediator efficiently. Subjects are usually equated on elaboration quality by providing them with a mediator or a contextual clue indicating how to incorporate the stimulus (that is to say, giving subjects a sentence containing the two items). This technique has been tried many times by a number of investigators with mixed results. The disadvantage of providing contextual mediators for subjects is that not all elaborations, such as "the foot stepped on the sun", are equally comprehensible or mean the same thing to all subjects. A developmental psychologist who recognizes qualitatively different processes at different stages could criticize the experimenter-provided elaboration studies with the reminder that, because retarded subjects did not benefit as much from the experimenter's mediators as did the CA-matched non-retarded subjects, it does not follow that they cannot benefit from contextual mediators as much as non-retarded subjects. It may be that the retarded subjects did not comprehend those particular elaborations well, but that there exists in the universe of propositions a set which would fit the cognitive structures of retarded individuals and from which they would benefit.

Recall differences between EMR and CA-matched non-retarded children are commonplace. In a recent study, however, Turnure and Thurlow (1975) provided the two groups of children with three types of elaboration: compound sentences (for instance, "His *hat* blew away but finally landed in a wagon"), complex sentences (for instance, "After his *hat* blew away, it landed in a wagon"), and a paragraph (for instance, "His *hat* blew away. It landed in a wagon"). They found no differential recall among the elaboration types, as well as no differences between their subject groups. From the results of this study, it could be concluded that if the retarded subjects are given enough context to ensure comprehension, then there is no recall problem and thus no mediation deficiency. What most elaboration tasks are measuring then is probably not differential mediational proficiency but differential comprehension of the material.

One way of assuring comprehension of the relationship between two items is to induce the subject to express the relationship. The series of studies in which subjects provide their own elaborations, mediators, images or contexts are called subject-generated elaboration studies. One of the first of these studies was conducted by Milgram (1967). He compared 9-year-old retarded and MA-matched non-retarded children on five paired-associate lists, for the second one of which they had to formulate their own sentences relating the items in the pair. The performance of both groups of children benefited significantly from these required self-generated mediators. Only the non-retarded subjects transferred the strategy to later, non-instructed lists. Milgram concluded that the retarded subjects suffered from a production deficiency, or failure to employ verbal statements that were potentially available. He suggested that the decline in spontaneous emission of integrating sentences on the part of the retarded subjects could be due to attitudinal-motivational or cognitive factors. In a related study Turnure, Buium and Thurlow (1975) asked how subjects could be induced to generate verbal mediations or to comprehend the stimulus-response pairs. One method they discovered was to ask the subjects questions about the items (for instance, "Why did the foot step on the sun?"). Apparently, the question format has socially compelling aspects (not unlike the laboratory situation sometimes) which motivates subjects to process the question. Once the question is comprehended, recall is automatically facilitated. The authors compared the performance of EMR and MA-matched non-retarded children in six conditions : labelling, sentence generation, sentence repetition, "what" questions, two kinds of "why" questions. Their data indicated dramatic facilitation of recall in the question conditions (64 to 76 per cent correct in the question conditions v. 6 to 40 per cent correct in the other conditions), and no difference between subject groups. They concluded decisively that the production deficiency hypothesis was inadequate in that it was situation specific; subjects once thought to have a general production deficiency (EMRs) clearly did not. The key to verbal elaboration research lies in the "extent to which the subject is induced by the experimental conditions to integrate the two paired items *via* shared meaning or in a semantic or meaningful relationship" (p. 19).

VI. MOTIVATIONAL APPROACHES

What has been learned about the development of cognitive processes in retarded children from a decade of research on paired-associate elaboration? The consistent finding that experimental attempts to increase comprehension of the stimulus facilitate recall of the items would suggest that the processes used to assimilate information are similar (or have similar ends) in retarded and non-retarded children. There have been so few developmental studies of retarded children, especially ones that systematically investigated structural and semantic aspects of comprehension, that the conclusions regarding the nature of the developmental process are unwarranted. The frequent findings of equivalent performance in retarded and MA- or CA-matched non-retarded subjects suggest that any difference between the two types of subjects arises on occasions when attempts to comprehend are made. When one is forced to account for less frequent occasions rather than lessened ability, one then begins to ask the questions "why the dissimilarity in occasions?" and, "how can the retarded individual be motivated to process and comprehend the stimuli provided by the environment?" These questions have been considered under a number of different names. Haywood and his associates (Haywood and Wachs, 1966; Haywood and Weaver, 1967; Haywood, 1971; Dobbs, 1967) have investigated it under the title of "cognitive motivation". Zigler (1971) and Harter and Zigler (1974) have conducted a number of studies under the name of "effectance motivation" which was first formulated by White (1959).

Haywood's use of the motivational construct, unlike the Harter and Zigler construct, specifies (after Herzberg, Mausner and Snyderman, 1959) two sources of cognitive motivation—intrinsic sources which cause people to explore, learn, and comprehend from an inherent desire to do so, a tendency to acquire knowledge for its own sake, and extrinsic motivation, which causes people to learn for external reasons (for instance, comfort, safety, material gain). Motivational orientation is a significant predictor of performance on many types of learning measures (arithmetic achievement, spelling, reading, simple motor tasks) among mentally retarded children, while it predicts poorly for intellectually superior children. Intrinsically motivated retarded children exceeded IQ-matched children classified as extrinsically motivated by a full grade level. Haywood (1971) points out, however, that it is extremely difficult to find intrinsically motivated retarded individuals, especially in an institution. These observations would suggest that different children learn for different reasons, and that ability *per se* is not always the issue. An important theoretical question therefore concerns what kind of support the environment typically offers and what is the match between the individual's motivational orientation and the environmental demands for adaptation.

Harter and Zigler (1974) attempted to measure effectance motivation in retarded (institutionalized and non-institutionalized) and non-retarded children. They administered several measures to their subjects —variation curiosity, mastery for the sake of competence and preference for challenging tasks. Overall, the normal children possessed greater effectance motivation, obtaining higher scores on the measures, than the non-institutionalized retarded subjects who, in turn, scored better than the institutionalized retarded subjects. The authors attribute the latter difference to different socialization histories, in that institutions provide less opportunity and fewer rewards for exploration and response variation. Effectance motivation then is modifiable to some extent, but there seems to be a deficiency endemic to the condition of mental retardation. Mentally retarded children are not as curious and do not explore as much as normal children.

VII. DEVELOPMENTAL ASPECTS OF RETARDATION

The desire to learn or to adapt must begin much earlier than school age and, thus, we must examine very young retarded children for differences in their attempts to comprehend the world. Such differences would be manifest in the frequency and types of attempts to inquire about the nature of things (that is to say, the degree to which infants explore their world and ways in which they do it). Information-seeking should be considered part of information processing in that the kind of information sought should be an index of the kind of information that the child's cognitive structure can process. Amount of exploration differs from type of exploration, though, because the former is more motivational while the latter has structural-developmental implications. Amount cannot be measured empirically independent of type, however, since there is no way to equate units of exploration (thus, how much mouthing of an object is considered to be the same amount of exploration as 5 sec of visual regard of the same object?). The typical approach (if there is such) has been to examine the frequencies of different types of exploration or curiosity behaviour: What are the kinds of information gained from exploration of different types? What structural changes result from what kinds of exploration? These questions, important as they are, are largely unanswered. The major theoretical, conceptual and research contributions have come from Piagetian theory.

The concepts and the research resulting from Piaget's theory have greatly extended our knowledge concerning the development of cognitive processes. The theory relates to knowledge, how it changes and develops, and how it influences what is learned. It is further concerned with qualitative changes during development as well as quantitative changes. Piaget's theory thus provides insight into the nature of mental retardation through study of the normal development of cognitive processes. It describes not only differences in capacities, but also differences in the structure of effective knowledge and in the ability to perform mental operations upon that knowledge.

Much has been written about the role of Piaget's theory in mental retardation (Wohlwill, 1966; Inhelder, 1968; Stephens, 1966). The theory has been applied to mental retardation research in three ways. It has, for example, been the theoretical basis for the development of assessment instruments that provide alternatives to psychometric intelligence tests (for instance, the Uzgiris-Hunt Scales). Studies with mentally retarded children have also been used as a test of the theory. Woodward (1963) discusses two ways in which the theory can be tested, one being the sequencing of cognitive accomplishments. Should some cognitive milestone appear out of sequence, such a finding might bode ill for the theory of cognitive development. Inhelder (1968) conducted a large-scale study on 150 children who were retarded and found impressive evidence for an invariant sequence of attainment of conservation. Conservation of substance precedes conservation of weight which precedes conservation of volume. Woodward (1959) also found in sixty-five retarded subjects given problems below their level of sensorimotor functioning that sixty of the subjects scored 100 per cent. She concluded that there is evidence for an invariant sequence in the development of cognitive abilities in mentally retarded subjects, and that the sequence is similar to the one found in non-retarded subjects. Chatelanat and Schoggen (1975), however, found one of their retarded children exhibiting behaviour beyond his pre-dominant level of sensorimotor functioning with few in-between behaviours. Their data were recorded in a naturalistic setting and involved eight subjects' interactions with objects. These interactions or action patterns, collected on videotape over a four-week period, were classified as to which of the six sensorimotor stages of development they belonged. The children in the study were diagnosed as Down's Syndrome and the average age was 13 months. The most deviant child displayed stage 3 action patterns most frequently, no stage 4 and 5 patterns, and several stage 6 patterns. These latter patterns were specific to one toy and were not seen in relation to other appropriate objects. The authors concluded that this behaviour was stereotyped in nature but that some caution should be observed in expecting the step-wise sensorimotor sequence from retarded infants.

Piagetian theory has also provided a general approach to the nature of cognitive development, a set of constructs with which to examine cognitive development in mentally retarded children. These constructs have included any of those which are part of the theory, from assimilation-accommodation to classification, class-inclusion and conservation. The investigator's recognition of any of the constructs implies a recognition that information processing is considerably affected by the state of the child's cognitive growth. A child ignores events that cannot be understood and attends only to those aspects of the world that are closely related to structures or knowledge that he already possesses. There are several ways to characterize this approach. One is to say that the real question is "what constitutes 'similarity' between the new and the known?" How disparate do events have to be and in what ways before the child discontinues attempts to comprehend them? Traditionally the investigator's response to this question has been analytical; stimuli have been broken down into smaller and smaller units or simpler properties to discover what the subject detects or responds to. The basis for subdivision is usually physical, for example, wave length, pitch, complexity defined by number of angles, and spatial characteristics. While these properties have some role in cognition, even to consider them in isolation without their ecological relationships (patterns of contrasts in colours and pitches, complexity with respect to what the organism can *do* to the stimulus, position relative to some stationary object) is to make implicit assumptions about what the child apprehends in a given situation; that he is somehow an additive or mathematical function of the physical dimensions acting on him at a given moment.

A much more difficult response but one with more theoretical basis is to consider relational parameters of the entire situation and to examine those with respect to relationships the subject is capable of processing. In a developmental scheme, these relationships have a sensorimotor descriptive base. A young baby's knowledge of anything is based upon his capabilities of operating on the various aspects of the world. A very young child should manipulate and represent objects to the extent that he is capable of motoric interaction with them. This interplay in turn predisposes certain perceptual operations on the objects. A "thing" is defined cognitively as what one can do to it and what stance it presents perceptually (that is to say, whether its functional properties are emphasized in the general context). This means that what he learns about objects is his perceptual and motor relationship with them, what he can do to them and what they do to him. He learns to carry out actions voluntarily that take into account the perceptually available "affordances of objects" (Gibson, in press). These actions are termed "means", their goal, "ends". One of the persistent outcomes of developmental sequences is the separation of means and ends such that the same actions can be directed towards different ends. The separation of means and ends is not a discrete process but undergoes continual refinement. While more general means or actions such as mouthing and shaking (which take into account gross size and depth characteristics) are becoming independent, other actions which take into account more refined characteristics are maturing with respect to a few objects. Very little research with retarded children has been conducted using these concepts. Chatelenat, Henderson, Robinson and Bricker (1971) presented ten developmentally delayed children (24–36 months) with fifteen objects and recorded what the child did with the objects. Compared to a group of non-delayed children, the delayed children used actions which were more general (for instance, mouthing, throwing, hitting the object on the table top). The non-delayed children on the other hand spent more time examining the object visually and tactually, showing the object to another person, and pointing to other functionally related objects. The investigators were led to the conclusion that there is sensorimotor classification of the environment prior to the relevant expressive or receptive language development. Furthermore, the delayed children were manifesting the same sequence of development as the non-delayed children but were somewhat behind them.

Fine motor development with respect to objects in infants has been the subject of a set of studies by Kopp (1975). She identified samples of premature infants (which are high-risk), compared their fine motor behaviour towards objects with that of normal full-term infants of the same age (calculated from expected date of birth), and found the two samples to be qualitatively different. The premature infants made more extraneous movements and spent more time in less mature schemas than the full-term infants at 36 months. Perhaps differences in other grosser movements may be seen even earlier in development.

VIII. SUMMARY

The purpose of this chapter was to provide an overview of the current state of the scientists' knowledge about the development of cognitive processes involved in mental retardation. We chose to divide that know-ledge into two related but non-overlapping sets. One approach to research has been contributed by investigators who take an informa-tion-processing view of cognitive development. Their findings on individual components like the iconic store, short-term memory and long-term memory indicate quantitative but not necessarily qualitative differences between retarded and non-retarded people. The structural feature-control process distinction has added a framework that should help investigators to distinguish the qualitative, permanent disabilities from the modifiable, control processes. One caution was imposed; these processes interact and the nature of the interactions is relatively uninvestigated, especially in retarded people. A second related caution could be added : the relationship between these processes as investi-gated analytically in the laboratory and processes that are used and needed in real-world adaptation is unarticulated. If the nature of mental retardation is to be uncovered, some day we shall have to know what short-term memory has to do with tying shoes, toilet training, arithmetic operations, and giving change. An individual's ineptness in these skills classifies him as mentally retarded, and infor-mation-processing explanations of mental retardation must eventually accommodate themselves to the reasons their population came into existence. Any account of these skills will require some theoretical explanation of how the various components interact.

The second approach to mental retardation discussed in this chapter was broader and more developmental, but less elaborately explored. It emphasized two principles as underlying cognitive growth—assimilation and accommodation. They act in conjunction to deter-mine what the child detects and encodes from his environment and what changes occur within his cognitive structures as a result of new information. From the cognitive literature, the phenomena of integration and elaboration were included as examples of assimilative processes. The constructs of cognitive motivation and effectance motivation were considered as possible ways of explaining why retarded children do not seem to use assimilatory processes. In infancy, motivational concepts are difficult to separate from sensorimotor development because some of the same behaviours are used as indices of each. The Piagetian approach has been suggested as a way to conceptualize the comprehension efforts made by young children.

While it may appear that not a great deal is known about the cognitive processes of mentally retarded children, it is now possible to formulate some meaningful questions :

(a) In what ways should the official definition of mental retardation influence the orientation of mental retardation research?

(b) Is the purpose of mental retardation research to clarify cognitive development or determine the nature of mental retardation?

(c) How can the individual research areas be integrated into a total picture of cognitive functioning in retarded children?

(d) How can developmental research be more consistently and specifically applied to mentally retarded children?

(e) What are appropriate methodologies for investigating the development of cognitive processes in mentally retarded children?

(f) How are the constructs of motivation and cognition to be interrelated in young children?

(g) How can basic research be applied to the problems of intervention?

REFERENCES

Allen, R. M. (1968). Long-term retention of learned visual perception skills by educable mental retardates. *Journal of Mental Deficiency Research, 11,* 254–6.

Atkinson, R. and Shiffrin, R. M. (1968). Human memory: a proposed system and its control processes. In K. W. Spence and J. T. Spence (Eds.), *The Psychology of Learning and Motivation,* Vol. 2. New York: Academic Press.

Baumeister, A. A. (1974). Serial memory span thresholds of normal and mentally retarded children. *Journal of Educational Psychology, 66,* 889–94.

Baumeister, A. A. and Muma, J. (1975). On defining mental retardation. *Journal of Special Education, 9*(3), 293–306.

Belmont, J. M. (1966). Long-term memory in mental retardation. In N. R. Ellis (Ed.), *International Review of Research in Mental Retardation,* Vol. 1. New York: Academic Press.

Belmont, J. M. and Butterfield, E. C. (1969). The relations of short-term memory to development and intelligence. In L. C. Lipsitt and H. W. Reese (Eds.), *Advances in Child Development and Behavior,* Vol. 4. New York: Academic Press.

Belmont, J. M. and Butterfield, E. C. (1971). What the development of STM is. *Human Development, 14,* 236–48.

Brown, A. L. (1972). A rehearsal deficit in retardates' continuous short-term memory: keeping track of variables that have few or many states. *Psychonomic Science, 29,* 373–6.

Brown, A. L. (1974). The role of strategic behavior in retardate memory. In N. R. Ellis (Ed.), *International Review of Research in Mental Retardation,* Vol 7. New York: Academic Press.

Brown, A. L., Campione, J. L. and Murphy, M. D. (1974). Keeping track of changing variables: long term retention of a trained rehearsal strategy by retarded adolescents. *American Journal of Mental Deficiency, 78,* 446–53.

Butterfield, E. C. (1975). Cognitive psychology and mental retardation research. Paper presented at the Gatlinburg Conference on Mental Retardation, Gatlinburg, Tenn.

Butterfield, E. C., Wambold, C. and Belmont, J. M. (1973). On the theory and practice of improving short-term memory. *American Journal of Mental Deficiency, 77,* 654–69.

Chatelanat, G., Henderson, C., Robinson, C. and Bricker, W. (1971). Early classification skills of developmentally delayed toddlers. In D. Bricker and W. Bricker (Eds.), *Toddler Research and Intervention Project Report: Year I,* IMRID Behavioral Science Monograph No. 20, George Peabody College, Nashville, Tenn.

Chatelanat, G. and Schoggen, M. (1975). An observation system of assessment of spontaneous infant behavior-environment interactions. Paper presented at the Gatlinburg Conference on Mental Retardation, Gatlinburg, Tenn.

Craik, F. I. M. and Lockhart, R. S. (1972). Levels of processing: a framework for memory research. *Journal of Verbal Learning and Verbal Behavior, 11,* 671–84.

Crosby, K. G. (1972). Attention and distractibility in mentally retarded and intellectually average children. *American Journal of Mental Deficiency, 77,* 46–53.

DeVries, R. (1974). Relationships among Piagetian, IQ, and achievement assessments. *Child Development, 45,* 746–56.

Dobbs, V. H. (1967). Motivational orientation and programmed instruction achievement gain of educable mentally retarded adolescents. George Peabody College, Nashville, Tenn. (unpublished Doctoral Dissertation).

Dugas, J. L. and Kellas, G. (1974). Encoding and retrieval processes in normal children and retarded adolescents. *Journal of Experimental Child Psychology, 17,* 177–85.

Ellis, N. R. (1963). The stimulus trace and behavioral inadequacy. In N. R. Ellis (Ed.), *Handbook of Mental Deficiency.* New York: McGraw-Hill.

Ellis, N. R. (1970). Memory processes in retardates and normals. In N. R. Ellis (Ed.), *International Review of Research in Mental Retardation,* Vol. 4. New York: Academic Press.

Farnham-Diggory, S. (1972). The development of the equivalence systems. In S. Farnham-Diggory (Ed.), *Information Processing in Children.* New York: Academic Press.

Fisher, M. A. and Zeaman, D. (1973). An attention-retention theory of retardate discrimination learning. In N. R. Ellis (Ed.), *International Review of Research in Mental Retardation,* Vol. 6. New York: Academic Press.

Frankel, F. and Tymchuk, A. J. (1974). Digit recall and mentally retarded and nonretarded children under three presentation rates. *American Journal of Mental Deficiency, 79,* 311–19.

Gibson, J. J. (in press). *An Ecological Approach to Visual Perception.* New York: Houghton Mifflin.

Glidden, L. M. (1972). Meaningfulness, serial position, and retention interval in the recognition short-term memory. *Journal of Experimental Child Psychology, 13,* 154–64.

Goulet, L. R. (1968). Verbal learning and memory research with retardates: an attempt to assess developmental trends. In N. R. Ellis (Ed.), *International Review of Research in Mental Retardation,* Vol. 3. New York: Academic Press.

Hagen, J. W. (1972a). Attention and mediation in children's memory. In W. W. Hartup (Ed.), *The Young Child: Reviews of Research,* Vol. 2. Washington, D.C.: National Association for the Education of Young Children.

Hagen, J. W. (1972b). Strategies for remembering. In S. Farnham-Diggory (Ed.), *Information Processing in Children.* New York: Academic Press.

Hagen, J. W. and Huntsman, J. (1971). Selective attention in mental retardates. *Developmental Psychology, 5,* 151–60.

Hagen, J. W. and West, R. F. (1970). The effects of a pay-off matrix on selective attention. *Human Development, 13,* 43–52.

Harris, G. J. and Fleer, R. E. (1974). High speed memory scanning in mental retardates: evidence for a central processing deficit. *Journal of Experimental Child Psychology, 17,* 452–9.

Harter, S. and Zigler, E. (1974). The assessment of effectance motivation in normal and retarded children. *Developmental Psychology, 10,* 169–80.

Hawkins, W. F. and Baumeister, A. A. (1965). The effect of retroactive inhibition upon the digit-span performance of normals and retardates. *American Journal of Mental Deficiency, 69,* 871–6.

Haywood, H. C. (1971). Individual differences in motivational orientation: a trait approach. In H. I. Day, D. E. Berlyne and D. E. Hunt (Eds), *Intrinsic Motivation: A New Direction in Education.* New York: Holt, Rinehart and Winston.

Haywood, H. C. and Wachs, T. D. (1966). Size discrimination learning as a function of motivation-hygiene orientation in adolescents. *Journal of Educational Psychology, 57,* 279–86.

Haywood, H. C. and Weaver, S. J. (1967). Differential effects of motivational orientation and incentive conditions on motor performance in institutionalized retardates. *American Journal of Mental Deficiency, 72,* 459–67.

Heal, L. W. and Johnson, J. T. (1970). Inhibition deficits in retardate learning and attention. In N. R. Ellis (Ed), *International Review of Research in Mental Retardation,* Vol. 4. New York: Academic Press.

Herzberg, F., Mausner, B. and Snyderman, B. (1959). *The Motivation to Work.* New York: Wiley.

Holden, E. A. (1971). Sequential dot presentation measures of stimulus trace in retardates and normals. In N. R. Ellis (Ed.), *International Review of Research in Mental Retardation,* Vol. 5. New York: Academic Press.

Hunt, J. McV. (1961). *Intelligence and Experience.* New York: Ronald Press.

Inhelder, B. (1968). *The Diagnosis of Reasoning in the Mentally Retarded.* New York: John Day.

Jensen, A. R. (1970) A theory of primary and secondary familial mental retardation. In N. R. Ellis (Ed.), *International Review of Research in Mental Retardation,* Vol. 4. New York: Academic Press.

Kellas, G., Ashcraft, M. H. and Johnson, N. S. (1973). Rehearsal processes in the short-term memory performance of mildly retarded adolescents. *American Journal of Mental Deficiency, 77,* 670–9.

Klausmeier, H. J., Feldhusen, J. and Check, J. (1959). *An Analysis of Learning Efficiency in Arithmetic of Mentally Retarded Children in Comparison with Children of Average and High Intelligence.* Madison, Wis.: University of Wisconsin Press.

Kopp, C. B. (1975). Development of fine motor behaviors: issue and research. In N. R. Ellis (Ed.), *Aberrant Development in Infancy: Human and Animal Studies.* Hillsdale, N.J.: L. Erlbaum.

Luria, A R. (1963). Psychological studies of mental deficiency in the Soviet Union. In N. R. Ellis (Ed.), *Handbook of Mental Deficiency.* New York: McGraw-Hill.

Maccoby, E. E. (1964). Developmental psychology. In P. R. Farnsworth, O. McNemar and Q. McNemar (Eds.), *Annual Review of Psychology,* Vol. 15. Palo Alto, Calif.: Annual Reviews.

McBane, B. M. (1972). Short-term memory and dimensional-independence in retardates. *Dissertation Abstracts, 33*(B), 5544B.

Milgram, N. A. (1967). Retention of mediation set in paired-associate learning of normal children and retardates. *Journal of Experimental Child Psychology, 5,* 341–9.

Miller, G. A. (1956). The magical number seven, plus or minus two: some limits on our capacity for processing information. *Psychological Review, 63,* 81–97.

Miller, G. A., Galanter, E. and Pribram, K. (1960). *Plans and the Structure of Behavior.* New York: Holt, Rinehart and Winston.

Mosley, J. L., Bakal, D. A. and Pilek, V. (1974). Conditioned eyelid response, peripheral vasoconstriction and attention in retarded and nonretarded individuals, *American Journal of Mental Deficiency, 78*, 694–703.

Mosley, J. L. and McKim, M. R. (1973). Developmental view of reversible perspective phenomenon for retarded and nonretarded individuals. *American Journal of Mental Deficiency, 78*, 354–62.

Paris, S. G. and Carter, A. Y. (1973). Semantic and constructive aspects of sentence memory in children. *Developmental Psychology, 9*, 109–13.

Paris, S. G., Mahoney, G. J. and Buckhalt, J. A. (1974). Facilitation of semantic integration in sentence memory of retarded children. *American Journal of Mental Deficiency, 78*, 714–20.

Pennington, F. M. and Luszcz, M. A. (1975). Some functional properties of iconic storage in retarded and nonretarded subjects. *Memory and Cognition, 3*, 295–301.

Powazek, M. and Johnson, J. T. (1973). Heart rate response of novel and signal stimuli in nonretarded and retarded subjects. *American Journal of Mental Deficiency, 78*, 286–91.

Prehm, H. J. and Mayfield, S. (1970). Paired-associate learning and retention in retarded and nonretarded children. *American Journal of Mental Deficiency, 74*, 602–25.

Reese, H. W. and Lipsitt, L. C. (1970). *Experimental Child Psychology*. New York: Academic Press.

Rosenberg, S. (1961). Searching behavior in retarded as a function of stimulus exposure conditions and IQ. *American Journal of Mental Deficiency, 65*, 749–52.

Ryan, J. F., Chivers, J. and Redding, G. (1969). Short-term memory and rehearsal in educable subnormals. *American Journal of Mental Deficiency, 74*, 218–22.

Shif, Z. I. (1969). Development of children in schools for the mentally retarded. In M. Cole and I. Maltzman (Eds.), *A Handbook of Contemporary Soviet Psychology*. New York: Basic Books.

Siddle, D. A. and Glenn, S. M. (1974). Habituation of the orienting response in simple and complex stimuli. *American Journal of Mental Deficiency, 78*, 688–93.

Sigman, M., Kopp, C. B., Parmelee, A. H. and Jeffrey, W. E. (1973). Visual attention and neurological organization in neonates *Child Development, 44*, 461–6.

Silverman, W. P. (1974). High speed scanning of nonalphanumeric symbols in cultural-familially retarded and nonretarded children. *American Journal of Mental Deficiency, 79*, 44–51.

Spitz, H. H. (1963). Field theory in mental deficiency. In N. R. Ellis (Ed.), *Handbook of Mental Deficiency*. New York: McGraw-Hill

Spitz, H. H. (1969). Effects of stimulus information reduction on the search time of retarded adolescents and normal children. *Journal of Experimental Psychology, 82*, 482–7.

Spitz, H. H. (1973). The channel capacity of educable mental retardates. In D. K. Routh (Ed.), *The Experimental Psychology of Mental Retardation*. Chicago: Aldine.

Spitz, H. H. and LaFontaine, L. (1973). The digit span of idiots savants. *American Journal of Mental Deficiency, 77*, 757–9.

Spitz, H. H. and Nadler, B. T. (1974). Logical problem solving by educable retarded adolescents and varying aged normal children. *Developmental Psychology, 10,* 404–12.

Spitz, H. H. and Thor, D. L. (1968). Visual backward masking in retardates and normals. *Perception and Psychophysics, 4,* 245–6.

Spitz, H. H. and Webreck, C. (1972). Effects of spontaneous vs. externally-cued learning on the permanent storage of a schema by retardates. *American Journal of Mental Deficiency, 77,* 163–8.

Stephens, W. B. (1966). Piaget and Inhelder—application of theory and diagnostic techniques to the area of mental retardation. *Education and Training of the Mentally Retarded, 1,* 75–86.

Sternberg, S. (1966). High-speed scanning in human memory. *Science, 153,* 652–4.

Thor, D. H. (1971). Numerosity discrimination of repetitive visual stimuli by mildly retarded adolescents and normal children. *Journal of Abnormal Psychology, 78,* 30–4.

Turnbull, A. P. (1974). Teaching retarded persons to rehearse through cumulative overt labelling. *American Journal of Mental Deficiency, 79,* 331–7.

Turnure, J. E., Buium, N. and Thurlow, M. (1975). The production deficiency model of verbal elaboration: Some contrary findings and conceptual complexities. Research Report No. 82, Project No. 332189, University of Minnesota Research, Development and Demonstration Center in Education of Handicapped Children, Minneapolis, Minn.

Turnure, J. E. and Thurlow, M. (1975). Effects of structural variations in elaboration on learning by EMR and nonretarded children. *American Journal of Mental Deficiency, 79,* 632–9.

Underwood, B. J. (1975). Individual differences as a crucible in theory construction. *American Psychologist, 30,* 128–34.

Vurpillot, E. (1968). The development of scanning strategies and their relation to visual differentiation. *Journal of Experimental Child Psychology, 6,* 632–50.

Wechsler, D. (1958). *The Measurement and Appraisal of Adult Intelligence.* Baltimore: Williams and Wilkins.

White, R. W. (1959). Motivation reconsidered: the concept of competence. *Psychological Review, 66,* 297–333.

Wilton, K. M. and Boersma, F. J. (1974). Eye movements and conservation development in mildly retarded and nonretarded children. *American Journal of Mental Deficiency, 79,* 285–91.

Winters, J. J. and Gerjuoy, I. R. (1969). Recognition of tachistoscopically exposed letters by normals and retardates. *Perception and Psychophysics, 5,* 21–4.

Winters, J. J., Gerjuoy, I. R., Crown, P. and Gorrell, R. (1967). Eye movements and verbal reports in tachistoscopic recognition by retardates and normals. *Child Development, 38,* 1193–9.

Wohlwill, J. F. (1966). Piaget's theory of the development of intelligence in the concrete-operations period. *American Journal of Mental Deficiency, 70* (Monogr. Suppl. 4). 57–78.

Woodward, M. (1959). The behaviour of idiots interpreted by Piaget's theory of sensori-motor development. *British Journal of Educational Psychology, 29,* 60–71.

Woodward, M. (1963). The application of Piaget's theory to research in mental deficiency. In N. R. Ellis (Ed.), *Handbook of Mental Deficiency*. New York: McGraw-Hill.

Zeaman, D. and House, B. J. (1963). The role of attention in retardate discrimination learning. In N. R. Ellis (Ed.), *Handbook of Mental Deficiency*. New York: McGraw-Hill.

Zigler, E. (1971). The retarded child as a whole person. In H. E. Adams and W. K. Boardman (Eds.), *Advances in Experimental Clinical Psychology*. New York: Pergamon.

CHAPTER 16

Cognitive Development in the Neuroses and Schizophrenias

Vernon Hamilton

I. INTRODUCTION

Behavioural science has not yet discovered the *definitive* interacting processes and mechanisms which systematically explain the development of abnormalities of subjective experience, non-rational cognitive responses and social ineptitudes or incongruities which are usually labelled neurotic or psychotic. For this reason and others rigid adherence to traditional models seems to be quite misplaced. Medical disease concepts and classifications are seen more and more clearly as primitive attempts at ordering, and the more recent, carefully controlled studies on the role of genetic transmission produce progressively lower concordance rates for monozygous twins with respect to even the most severe types of dysfunctions (Gottesman and Shields, 1972; Segal *et al.*, 1975). Nineteenth-century conceptualizations of anxiety-inducing human instincts, and *reified* notions of internal censureship and defence continue to detract from some important insights of Freudian theory and its derivatives. Over-simplified concepts of stimulus-response association continue to be cited with lawful implications to account for sequences of responses which have never before been thus combined when elicited by external stimuli which in information content and subjective experience are always unique.

On the other hand, biochemical theorists generally realize that the gap between the demonstrated excess or depletion of various neurotransmitter substances, and complex human skills and subjective experience, is too wide for safe causal inferences. Thus, the recent N.I.M.H. Report on more than a quarter of a century's Institute-supported research states, for example, that "... it is essential that appropriate balance be maintained in . . . support of biologically oriented as contrasted with sociopsychological studies of schizophrenia. The evidence available to date strongly suggests that nonbiological, psychosocial factors play a major pathogenic role . . ." (Segal *et al.*, 1975, p. 179). With respect to neurosis, the same document (pp. 186–7) holds that insufficient research has been done to strengthen any particular theoretical orientation. Since most of the relevant available data on behavioural abnormality are obtained from clinically diagnosed cases, retrospective theorizing will have to be replaced by prospective and extensive longitudinal studies. As will be seen later, these bring awkward (and different) methodological problems in their train.

The title chosen for this chapter has a number of implications representing a particular theoretical stance. It has been the practice to regard neurosis and schizophrenia primarily as disorders of emotionality, mood and personality in which bio-genetic and bio-physiological arousal and activation processes may play a determining role. The emphasis here, however, is on the role of cognitive events which, in the course of individual experience during the acquisition of social skills and exposure to aversively experienced stimulation, result in long-term memory structures with unrealistic and incompletely representational cognitive information content, and restrictive and idiosyncratic processing strategies. Longitudinal studies employing this kind of framework have not been carried out. Therefore, this chapter will concentrate on explanations of the development of adult cognitive deficit. These explanations will have to be clearly tentative and hypothetical.

In order to sustain a cognitive-developmental model of behaviour disorders, four basic assumptions will eventually have to be supported : (1) that adult cognition has a necessary historical relationship to the nature and strategies of cognitive processes in childhood; (2) that hypo- or hyper-active arousal and mid-brain processes play a necessary but *secondary* role in the development of abnormal behaviour; (3) that the neuroses and the schizophrenias may be conceived as cognitive process and information processing disorders; (4) that what is termed anxiety is in the first instance cognitive, involving information about potentially aversive individual experience; and (5) that the cognitive deficits in the neuroses and the schizophrenias may be the result of developmentally early but ultimately unsuccessful attempts in dealing with an overload of simultaneous information, much of it aversive, presented to the components of a central processing system.

The chapter begins with reviews of cognitive deficit theories of anxiety-based neuroses and the schizophenias. In the following section, attention will be directed to studies of the childhood precursors of adult abnormality, while the final section will consider the implications of arousal, of the information content of the environment and of stimulus encoding and retrieval processes for the development of deviant cognitive structures.

In view of the obvious limitations on space, it was decided to confine the cognitive development analysis of the neuroses to those in which anxiety is the major behavioural component. This does not mean that the discussion and subsequent explanatory propositions cannot also be applied to the varieties of hysteria, or to neurotic/reactive depression. Depression especially appears to have suffered from lack of systematic analysis of the cognitive developmental factors involved, particularly in view of the clinically and ethologically respectable concepts of separation, deprivation and loss of attachment (Bowlby, 1973).

Three considerations are responsible for omitting from the following discussion the area of autism. Firstly, the severe behaviour disturbances of early childhood are observationally and functionally different from the adult schizophenias and their precursor characteristics. Secondly, at least one recent study appears to confirm (Goldfarb, 1974) a primarily neurological basis for a majority of child cases labelled autistic or schizophrenic. Thirdly, the classification of schizophrenia specifically excludes organic dysfunctions.

The defining criteria of abnormality adopted here are generally statistical, in terms of the probability that scores or measures or differences in these between groups are due to chance. Deficiencies in the reliability and validity of many of the tests and test situations to be reported are reluctantly accepted. Where they occur, these deficiencies are considered to be modified if replication studies or supportive evidence in sufficient amounts appears to exist. It is thus necessary to consider adult neurotic and schizophrenic deficit in some detail. This will have the additional salutory result of demonstrating the presently existing wide conceptual gap between analytic cognitive processing theory, cognitive deficit theories, current procedures in clinical testing for cognitive deficits in patients, as well as shortcomings in the methodology of precursor studies.

II. COGNITIVE DEFICIT THEORIES OF ANXIETY-BASED NEUROSES

We must distinguish between abnormalities in cognitive processes and cognitive power and skill which it is possible to assess concurrently with clinical assessment, and experimental studies involving patients with differential types of neurosis and degrees of anxiety, in order to elucidate systematic abnormalities in bio-physiological and cognitive factors. The former data are primarily therapy-oriented and are evaluated on criteria of adequacy of social adaptation. The latter are theory-oriented, usually, though not necessarily, unrelated to therapy outcome, and their direction, concepts and procedures are reflections of the priority given to a particular hypothesis concerning pathogenesis.

Considering evidence from the applied orientation first, we must note that objective, systematically controlled data are rare. This is perhaps inevitable because of the greater importance attached to helping rather than research investigation, and because of time pressures on the mental health services. The consensus of data from this area is that neurotics score lower on intelligence tests than normals, but score higher than schizophenics, and that obsessive-compulsives score higher (often significantly) than other neurotics (Payne, 1973). Test performance improves after therapy (for instance, Desai, 1952). These findings apply to adults as well as to children, who most commonly show impairment in their performance respect-ively of occupational and scholastic skills. Constituent cognitive pro-cesses which indicate deficit by observation or self-report include lack of concentration in extended tasks or thought processes; excessively narrow or wide spans of orientation or attention; reluctance or relative inability to acquire new skills; doubts and conflicts in decision-making; and deficits in standardized short-term memory tasks such as digit-span. It is important to note that many of these deficits are generally present in all cases showing non-specific neurotic anxiety or obsessive-compulsive symptoms, but less frequently in phobic patients (particu-larly the mono-symptomatic) in whom anxiety is narrowly focused in one specific person–situation interaction (Endler, 1975). Since there is a general dearth of longitudinal evidence on the cognitive precursors of neurotic anxiety, experimental studies of the concomitants of acute and chronic cases have been the major methods for gathering a systematic body of knowledge which through phenotypic evidence might be able to offer hypotheses concerning genotypical characteristics.

Research data with theory orientation, after an upswing in the 1950s and 1960s, have now somewhat diminished. The majority of more recent studies tend to be carried out on normal populations in which the processes which are held to be abnormal in neurosis are experimentally manipulated. The post-war work may be divided into three major approaches. The first of these represents the application, in the clinical context, of laboratory derived techniques. Retro-spectively considered their importance lay in (i) the introduction of experimentally controlled procedures with apparatus employed to investigate *general* perceptual and other cognitive characteristics; (ii) the resulting *operational* description of some of the concomitants of the neurotic syndrome; and (iii) the associated *quantitative and statistical differentiation* of normal, neurotic, psychotic and brain-damaged groups of patients. These studies were directed at a clearer and finer-grain description of deficit. A recent summary by Payne (1973) concluded that the differences between normal and neurotic subjects were generally small. Neurotics, however, were slower in cognitive tasks, and extravert neurotics particularly had lower persistence. It is interesting to note that while gross abnormalities of thought were absent (as they need to be by definition), over-inclusive thinking, when combining the scores from several tests, showed a greater similarity between neurotics and paranoid schizophrenics than between neurotic and normal subjects. Payne concludes (*op. cit.*) that the demonstrated neurotic deficits are most likely to be the result of interference from neurotic anxiety.

An influential early study yielding data which fit this explanation was carried out by Davis (1948). An analysis of amount and types of errors made by aeroplane pilots showed that those who were neurotic made substantially more errors, and those whose symptoms were mainly of anxiety made errors which were due to over-reacting and over-correction. While cognitive processes would have played a role in terms of criteria of sensitivity and judgmental norms, explanations in terms of psycho-motor disturbances are additionally plausible. This conclusion derives support from studies showing that finger movements of neurotics may become disorganized in conditions of stress, either by the introduction of connotatively emotional material (Luria, 1932), or by fast-paced stimuli requiring a visual discrimination response (Malmo *et al.*, 1951).

The second major approach to the description and explanation of neurosis derived from the general study of learning processes. Since the results of work from this theoretical orientation are so well known and documented, detailed considerations are here unnecessary. We may distinguish between two aims in this approach : to account for the acquisition of neurotic behaviour, and specifically anxiety, by individual differences in conditioning characteristics, and to account for concomitants of this behaviour by differential characteristics of learning processes. The general findings are, firstly, that neurotics with high, questionnaire-demonstrated anxiety establish classical conditioned aversive or avoidance responses more quickly than normal subjects (Spence *et al.*, 1954; Spence and Goldstein, 1961; Spence, 1964; Spence and Spence, 1964). Secondly, interactions between anxiety and the difficulty of a learning task have been demonstrated (for instance, Spence, Farber and McFann, 1956; Spence, Taylor and Kretchel, 1956; Spence, 1958). These interactions assume that anxiety has drive properties which do not differ in their effect on excitation, habit formation and performance from the effects of other drives, and produce the cross-over performance data shown in Fig. 16.1, with drive defined by scores on the Manifest Anxiety Scale (MAS).

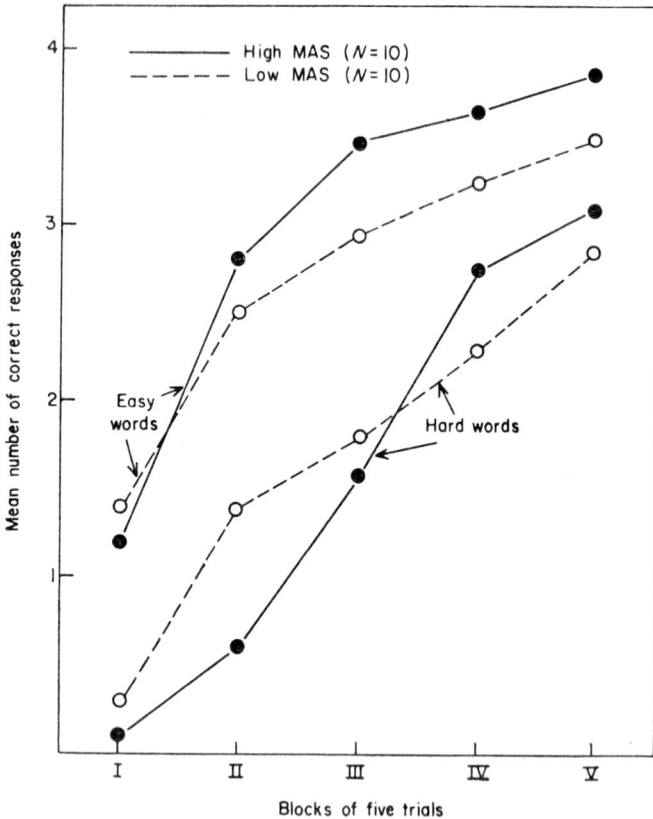

Fig. 16.1. Mean number of correct responses given by a high or low anxiety subject for easy and hard words on successive trial blocks. (*After* Spielberger and Smith, 1966, p. 594.)

The greater speed of conditioning of highly anxious neurotics has been confirmed to only a limited extent through studies on avoidance of shock and of blasts of air directed at the cornea. Generalization from GSR and eyeblink conditioning to other types of autonomically controlled responses has not been successfully demonstrated (Hamilton, 1959a). The drive characteristics of neurotic and non-neurotic high anxiety are also not fully confirmed. This is because of the limited type of tasks in which they have been studied, because of interactions with intelligence not fully accounted for by the theory, and because stimulus and response generalization findings do not fit the theory without elaborations which themselves have not been fully validated. Examples of the latter are early suggestions by Mednick (1958) concerning a positive feedback relationship between anxiety drive and generalization, and Broen and Storms' model (1966) of response ceilings and generalization in conditions of high drive to account for the energizing of inappropriate competing responses in anxiety as well as in schizophrenia. Cogent criticisms of these hypotheses are put forward by, respectively, Buss (1966) and Boland and Chapman (1971). Nevertheless, an unfavourable interaction between learning, memory and problem solving, and high scores on measures of "Test", "State", "Trait" or "Manifest" anxiety by non-neurotics, especially with ego-threatening experimental instructions, appears to be reliably established. This conclusion is strengthened by the results of studies on experienced and novice sport parachutists—a self-evidently realistic anxiety-inducing activity (Epstein and Fenz, 1962; Fenz, 1964, 1975).

Eysenck's variant of learning theory explanations of the development of neurotic states has experienced a number of changes and vicissitudes. These cannot be reviewed here, and the reader is referred to existing material (for instance, H. J. Eysenck, 1957, 1967, 1973; Storms and Sigal, 1958; Hamilton, 1959b; Gray, 1970). The most interesting features are the super-imposition of orthogonal dimensions of introversion–extraversion and neuroticism upon a neurosis or anxiety continuum, and the regularity with which predictions of a relationship between introversion–extraversion (rather than anxiety) and performance levels have been confirmed. The basic feature of the theoretical framework, that introverts and extraverts differ in generating and dissipating autonomic arousal, has remained constant. The Hullian concept of reactive inhibition, to explain I–E differences in conditionability, reminiscence and figural after-effects, has been dropped, however, in favour of a dual arousal-activation mechanism. Introverts are more highly aroused than extraverts, and subjects scoring high on neuroticism are characterized by high levels of limbic system activation. The two systems become interdependent in conditions of high emotionality, yielding high cortical arousal. In conditions of high arousal, trace consolidation (relevant to learning and memory tasks) differs from that of lower arousal in that a highly active process impedes present cognitive skill for the sake of a better skill established after a longer time interval. Thus, the mediating energizing process for the Eysenckians is arousal, while for the Spence group it is anxiety drive; and suboptimal neurotic cognitive perform-ances are due respectively to consolidation and to response competition processes. There is, of course, no reason why consolidation and com-petition need be mutually exclusive, and evaluation of the theory is further complicated by repeated findings of reliable correlations between measures of I–E and anxiety. Any criticism of this stimu-lating but rather rigidly conceived research programme has in the past elicited accusations of inadequate powers of understanding in the critic, and it may be rash to invite these again. It must be suggested, however, that two parallel propositions, namely that introverts con-dition easily *and* that they find the learning of new (that is, difficult) associations initially difficult, may be inconsistent with one another. Also not considered are the interfering cognitive events which are representative of fear of failure. Gray's suggestion (1970), derived from work on animals, that neurotic introverts are specifically suscept-ible to the conditioning of fear and punishment, therefore deserves to be followed up on neurotically anxious subjects. In that case, it might also be worth investigating if arousal, whether related to anxiety, introversion or, say, anger, can remain a unidimensional concept (see for instance, Ax, 1975; M. W. Eysenck, 1974), or whether white noise arousal is in fact identical in its effects to anxiety resulting from assaults on self-esteem.

The third major theoretical attack on the genotypical cognitive deficits in neurosis with anxiety as a major feature considers the primary role of conflict. Two initially separate but converging approaches have emerged : animal studies logically following Pavlov, and human studies conceptually dependent on, or related to, psycho-analytic formulations. Conflict has been defined in various ways: behaviourally by Miller (1944) as counter-posed or mutually exclusive attractions or aversions; and by Maier (1949) and Masserman (1961) as behavioural impasses in the simultaneous presence of conditioned approach and avoidance signals. As is well known, these situations, presented to animals, have elicited respectively oscillating, non-goal directed, substitute or displaced responses, or non-productive, repeti-tive or stereotyped behaviour, frequently terminating in frightened escape or animal panic. The early studies from Miller's laboratory were important, not only because they attempted—and partially succeeded—in demonstrating some validity for a number of Freudian defensive processes (for instance, Murray and Berkun, 1955), but also because of their careful quantitative manipulation of the opposed drives. Their possible inadequacy lay in the behaviouristic narrowness of the definition of conflict in terms of the intensity of the energizing components of drive, which precluded any reference to its cognitive components. That this operational constriction of definition is not strictly necessary even in animal work has been demonstrated by Masserman (1971). His definition of conflict, ". . . in each instance the organism apprehends a failure to predict and control events important to its welfare . . .", has been applied in delayed auditory feedback studies on monkeys which introduced aspects of sequential and temporal uncertainty. The effects of unpredictability and inability to control their own vocal productions led to many of the recognized characteristics of experimental neurosis.

Learned helplessness (Seligman and Maier, 1967) has been cited recently as an example of passive conflict avoidance, and of coping with aversive but unavoidable stimulation. It may well be true that for the paradigmatic canine studies, which employed shock and harness restraints, adopting a supine, motionless posture suggesting relaxation and inhibition constitutes an adaptive rather than a neurotic response (Kimmel, 1971). Learned helplessness as well as the vicious circle behaviour of the "neurotic paradox" at the human level seem to suggest, however, cognitive incapacities in operating upon the restrictive alternatives of simply perceived either-or responses.

The relationship between conflict and neurosis, and conflict and anxiety, has been fully elaborated in the psycho-analytic literature. We shall confine our attention, therefore, to the cognitive restrictions imposed by the hypothesized conflict–anxiety link. Masserman's terms of certainty, predictability and outcome-control (Masserman, *op. cit.*) provide a useful starting point for a consideration of their relevance to human cognitive processes. Conflict can be defined by unresponsiveness, reluctance or inadequacy in a central decision-making process in the presence of equally possible or plausible response alternatives. Anxiety arises if the absence, or the type, of solution is at variance with super-ordinate cognitive and motivational goals. Conflict and anxiety may arise or are exacerbated, therefore, in anxiety type neurosis in the presence of stimulation experienced as emotionally ambivalent or cognitively ambiguous. A person who is already exposed to externally or internally generated mutually exclusive response requirements may be predicted, therefore, to restructure the nature and implications of the cognitive processes required to achieve at least a semblance of adaptiveness in such a manner that objective inadequacies and deficits appear. By definition, stimulus ambiguity implies response conflict, and it may be useful, therefore, in a paper directing attention to cognitive developmental aspects of behavioural abnormality, to refer to Frenkel-Brunswik's (1954) attempt to define the characteristics of ambiguity/conflict avoidance. Conflict, and anxiety in those for whom a conditioned link between the two pre-exists, may be avoided by undue preference for familiarity, symmetry, regularity, stimulus-boundedness, premature closure, over-simplified dichotomizing or tendencies towards black-white solution, unqualified either/or solutions, compartmentalization, perseveration and stereo-typy. The major intermediate stage of avoidance of uncertainty is accomplished by a narrowing of stimulus "meaning", inaccessibility of experience (Memory), mechanical repetition of sets, or by a segmentary randomness and over-emphasis of those aspects of reality which have been preserved. In retrospect, it seems possible to suggest that Frenkel-Brunswik provided an alternative conceptual framework for cognitive control theories (see Chap. 11), and that a present-day re-analysis of the effects of these strategies on information-processing capacity may be fruitful.

This approach to a cognitive appraisal of the role of conflict and anxiety in neurosis has not been popular, even though its relevance to theories of cognitive-affective control and perceptual defence mechanisms is considerable. To date, the only comprehensive attempt to validate this cognitive constriction theory was carried out by Hamilton (1957, 1960). This study has some methodological short-comings, many of them determined by customary problems of working with criterion groups of patients, and by a decision to assess avoidance of cognitive conflict by a wide range of functionally related response situations. The results, however, provided support for the psycho-analytic theory of conflict and anxiety avoidance. They demonstrated that neurotics, and particularly the sub-groups with the postulated greatest need for conflict and anxiety avoidance, showed the greatest avoidance of response categories which would maintain a set of problem-solving, perceptual or conceptual conflict.

III.   COGNITIVE DEFICIT THEORIES OF THE SCHIZOPHRENIAS

Routine as well as hypothesis-directed psychological assessment has contributed a range of systematic data yielded by standardized tech-niques. These have produced more objective and somewhat finer-grain descriptions of cognitive deficit in the schizophrenias than obtained by clinical techniques, and provided a bridge to the more sophisticated experimental investigation of basic cognitive processes and the associated testing of behavioural genotypical theories. The major findings of applied abnormal psychology are : usually reliable differences between verbal and non-verbal measures of intelligence with lower scores on non-verbal tests; impaired speed of problem solving; high variability of scores from tests aimed at different combinations of mnemonic, attentional, symbolic and integrative cognitive processes; and associational looseness as apparent in Rorschach concept contamination, neologisms or tangential or approximate definitions. Probably the most germinal findings are high response latency and conceptual concreteness.

Theory-oriented research projects have accumulated a great many interesting findings, without coming any closer as yet to agreed aetiological explanations for the schizophenias. The major results relate to differences between schizophrenics and non-schizophrenics on stimulus avoidance; attention; classification, generalization and synthesis; motivation; arousal; social stimuli; consistency of performance. While schizophrenics show disturbance to an often abnormal degree in usually more than one of these areas, no single explanatory concept has been accepted as yet as sufficient. The reason for this may well be, as Segal *et al.* (1975) point out, our present inability to consider systematically the interactions between any pair of these variables and their implications for moderating or augmenting processes in one of a pair or any of the others. On the other hand, it may be suggested that although multivariate descriptions of different types of patients are now acceptable, the implications of idiographic uniqueness are not followed up. This would require, of course, a major modification of our experimental methodology in that we should have to control, for example, for attentional strategy, arousal and social withdrawal in order to define independently the extent of over-inclusiveness in classification (Payne, 1973), for instance, or over- or under-constancy in the perception of size-over-distance (Hamilton, 1963, 1966, 1972). The major obstacle—size of available experimental population—may be overcome eventually by new methodological skills in simultaneous measurement.

Drive or arousal theory proposes that perception, learning, thinking and verbal behaviour are disorganized, fragmented and impaired by comparison with neurotics or normals because of abnormally high levels of arousal or activation. The term "drive" has been applied generally to the excitatory functions of anxiety (Mednick, 1958; Broen and Storms, 1966), and more specifically to response strategies for the avoidance of aversive stimulation such as social censure or pain (Rodnick and Garmezy, 1957; Garmezy, 1965). Mednick's analysis of the drive characteristics of anxiety, in addition to effects already discussed earlier, further implies that schizophrenics' inappropriate responses reflect the result of stimulus and associative generalization. These responses are anxiety-reducing; they reinforce avoidance of anxiety-inducing stimulation and assume a dominant position in a response hierarchy. Unequivocal evidence is lacking, however, for all aspects of the theory (Buss and Lang, 1965; Epstein and Coleman, 1970). The utility of re-interpreting drive as cortical arousal has been shown in a number of experiments in which arousal was manipulated by white noise or dynamometer pressing in schizophrenics and normals (Broen, 1968; Broen and Storms, 1967). These investigators hypothesize, like Mednick, that the conceptual distance between dominant and competing responses is smaller for schizophrenics whose response strength ceiling for dominant habits is, additionally, lower. With a rise in arousal level, and assuming that response strength for a dominant habit is already at ceiling value, the probability of generating less veridical or suboptimal competing responses is raised. This is a plausible re-phrasing of drive theory explanations of associative looseness and tangential and approximate responses. It has not contributed at this stage, however, to explanations of why some or any dominant response strength ceilings in schizophrenics are low, and which habits are affected by what kinds of conditions generating arousal. Other criticisms of this approach will be found in Epstein and Coleman (op. cit.), Boland and Chapman (1971) and Salzinger (1973). The idea of the involvement of competing responses may be important, however, in explanations of high response latency, and for cognitive interference theories with quantitative approaches to interference.

Complications for the theory arise when the schizophrenic population is broken down by the application of the acute-chronic, active-withdrawn, reactive–process and paraoid–non-paranoid dimensions, and when necessary distinctions are made between differences in basal or resting arousal level, and intensity of arousal reaction to stimulation. A series of paradigmatic studies by Venables (1958, 1960, 1963, 1964) has been particularly useful. These showed (with varying degrees of reliability) that chronic, withdrawn non-paranoids are highly aroused but relatively unresponsive to stimulation, whereas paranoid, active and acute cases show low arousal but excessive responsiveness. The inverse relationship between behavioural or social and cortical arousal has been confirmed by low thresholds for the perception of small duration intervals between two flashes of light or two mechanical "clicks". Unresponsiveness to stimulation was demonstrated by non-utilization of a change in irrelevant information added to a simple card sorting task. The arousal and responsiveness variables were highly correlated. While this provides evidence for an inverted U type of relationship between arousal and cue utilization in performance (Easterbrook, 1959), it may also reflect the mechanical application of a set, perseveration, primacy, or stereotypy, implying response–selection rather than stimulus–input dysfunctions.

Interference theory refers to a group of processes which may all lead to three related effects: insufficient focusing on relevant aspects of a defined situation, susceptibility to the influence of task-peripheral or irrelevant stimuli, and undiminished focusing even when the skill or habit has become established (Shakow, 1962). Interference with task- or goal-relevant behaviour is held to arise primarily from two sources: inappropriate attentional processes, and distraction from stimuli to which inappropriate attention has been directed. Behaviourally, interference deficits have been demonstrated in a wide variety of settings. They have been defined by long RTs especially with prolonged preparatory intervals (Zahn *et al.*, 1963); by figure–ground confusion in a visual perception/retention task shown by performance differences when manipulating irrelevant distracting features (Weckowicz, 1960); by cross-modal distraction (McGhie *et al.*, 1965); by intrusions in matching stimulus words with multiple-meaning associates or associates of differing associative distance (Chapman, 1958); by excessive centration on a standard object or excessive responsiveness to primary sensory cues in a size constancy task; or by susceptibility to the misleading perceptual features in conservation tasks (Hamilton, 1966, 1972). While Hamilton's studies suggest tendencies towards under-inclusion as the result of a narrowing of external-perceptual and internal-conceptual scanning, the bulk of the interference theory-relevant publications refers to processes of over-inclusion. Substantive reviews of these findings are readily available (for instance in Payne, 1970, 1973), as well as a number of explanatory hypotheses. These were considered to be inconclusive, however, partly because, as over-inclusiveness is defined, it is not only found in schizophrenics, or experimentally prominent even in acute paranoid schizophrenics.

At least one of the attempted theoretical formulations appears to possess considerable plausibility: in terms of scanning and stimulus filtering strategies, which either increase or decrease the number of stimuli made available to a response generating process. Consistent with the evidence that high arousal and reduction in cue utilization may be systematically related, Silverman (1964, 1967) and Neale and Cromwell (1968) suggested that non-paranoid, process schizophrenics are narrow scanners, and paranoid schizophrenics wide scanners, inferring type of scanning-control from size estimation tasks. This strategy could have the effect of stimulus input reduction or excessive filtering for the former, and input augmentation or insufficient filtering for the latter. While the results have been difficult to replicate, partly because tranquillizers tend to inhibt eye-movements, an unpublished study by Hamilton was able to demonstrate that reduced visual scanning was related to the centration effect in size constancy, as well as to low levels of competence in conservation problem solving, for non-paranoid, chronic schizophrenic men, where medication procedures were controlled.

The available data would appear to suggest that the nature of interference differs for the major operationally defined schizophrenic sub-groups. Where external stimulus input is restricted, cognitive interference must necessarily be due, in the main, to self-generated internal cognitive processes. These are likely to be idiosyncratic and subjectively loaded since they are not externally driven, and are not subject to imposed situational constraints. Where external stimulus input is unrestrained and possibly unsystematic, random distraction and stimulus overload make the selection of relevant stimuli and appropriate responses more difficult. It is important to recall at this stage that arousal is said to be high in cases with high input control, from which ongoing internally driven cognitive processes may be plausibly inferred. Thus, while interference theory is often cited as a general explanation of cognitive deficit, a more parsimonious explanation may have to consider the limited capacity of the processing system for which irrelevant stimulation and inappropriate distribution of attention may produce overload conditions.

Processing capacity theory, rarely so named, is a designation that may be applied to explanations of cognitive deficit in schizophrenia based on demonstrations of slowness of cognitive processing, or assumptions that schizophrenics may have too much information to process. Yates (1966) proposed that one of the major cognitive difficulties of schizophrenics resides in the slow rate of processing information in a short-term memory store. Information is inadequately coded for further central processes or channelling into hold or buffer stores, because new information arrives before the earlier operations are completed. The predicted large increases in RT with increasing task complexity have been confirmed (Yates and Korboot, 1970; Court and Garwoli, 1968). While slow processing clearly fits one set of data from relatively simple tasks (Davidson and Neale, 1974), it does not explain the intrusion or selection of irrelevant internal or external stimuli in other settings. The defect may be primarily located at a short-term (or buffer store) memory stage, not because of an intrinsically slow processing, but because preference tends to be given to the most recent immediate input (Salzinger *et al.*, 1970), without simultaneous evocation of conditioned responses which belong to that class of stimuli, or because of the application of idiosyncratic or weak higher-order mnemonic units (Koh *et al.*, 1973) which would adversely affect recall, but not recognition.

Weakness of relevant associative tasks must bring the discussion back to the relationship between arousal or anxiety, and stimulation of competing responses. If low relevance competitive responses are emitted this may be due more to the activation of inappropriate response categories in which past organized experience has been pigeon-holed than to over-inclusive or over-exclusive input filter operations. Moreover, slow processing speed need not be an *a priori* function; it is just as likely to be a reflection of an excessively wide set of search and retrieval processes in response selection determined by poorly structured schemata, undifferentiated conditioned response probabilities (Broadbent, 1958, 1971), or the amount of sifting among remote alternatives in a decision-making process. Interference theory thus requires extension from irrelevant intrusions *per se* to *amount* of intrusion in any given situation; from input strategies in relation to external displays to strategies in *internal response selection processes*; from external to *internal informational complexity*.

There is abundant evidence that there is a heightened level of cognitive activity in all types of schizophrenics. This evidence ranges from the verbal products or self-reports of acute non-paranoid and paranoid schizophrenics (for instance, Bleuler, 1950; Bowers, 1965), to the high reactivity and arousal levels of paranoids and chronic non-paranoids (Venables and Warwick-Evans, 1967; Zahn, 1975). Whilst a high baseline of competing cognitive events and processes may not seriously affect "lower levels" of well-established decision mechanisms and processes (Callaway, 1970; Broadbent, 1971; Hemsley, 1975) —"lower" denoting less active information processing because of solid habit establishment—novel, socially complex or response *choice* tasks may push the information processing beyond its capacity limit. Consistent with this formulation is a set of findings by Hamilton (1972). A size constancy study with objects of different perceptual complexity (a straight white rod and a white square oriented in the diagonal-upright position) showed that operationally defined degrees of over- and under-constancy occurred more frequently with the information-ally more complex object. Similarly, an unpublished study of schizophrenics, with a new instrument for the measurement of conservation of quantity in which informational complexity (task difficulty) was systematically defined and increased (Hamilton and Moss, 1974), showed lower capacity on difficult, compared with easier, items for the same group of chronic, non-paranoid patients. This result is shown in Fig. 16.2, together with the data from children with and without experience of socialization anxiety. For the former reduced information processing capacity had been predicted.

While it may be validly proposed that sensory inhibition centres are defective in the schizophrenias (Lang and Buss, 1965), there is no evidence at present that this is the most fundamental defect, or that it precedes rather than follows acute psychotic disorganization, or that it is unmodifiably bio-genetic. Impairment of sensory inhibition may be consequential upon exposure to early environmental events interpreted as aversive or conflicting, which were accompanied by stress, extremes of arousal or the cognitive data which characterizes anxiety. We shall

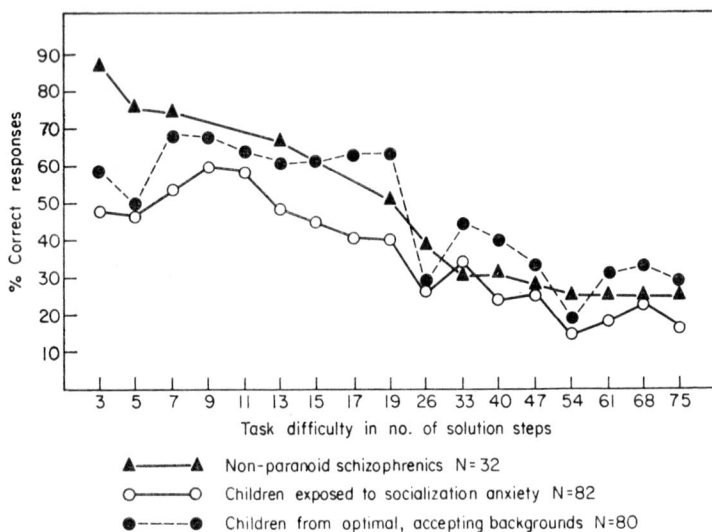

Fig. 16.2. Performance of adult schizophrenics, children exposed to socialization anxiety, and children from optimal, accepting backgrounds, on conservation of quantity problems with increasing information content.

examine briefly, therefore, the evidence of functional disorders in childhood for any evidence, particularly of early cognitive signs, which may be related to the cognitive (as well as behavioural) deficits of adult patients.

IV. PRECURSORS OF ABNORMALITIES

The early identification of behaviour which at a later stage may prove to be disabling for the individual and a strain on society is important for these reasons alone. Controlled studies, however, have an obvious relevance to theories of abnormal development and to the future solution of conflicting theories. The studies to be considered here could not involve the methodology and findings of cognitive process theory because they were initiated too early, and many of their criterion variables, therefore, tend to be observational and clinical rather than physiological or cognitive process-oriented. This applies particularly to the retrospective and concurrent studies which will be mentioned before turning to the more sophisticated "at risk" approach.

(1) RETROSPECTIVE STUDIES

It is clear that problems of the reliability and validity of diagnosis of abnormal behaviour are magnified if data, obtained by differently oriented investigators spread over a period of sometimes many years, are compared for the purpose of finding continuities in the processes of abnormal development. At the same time it is unlikely that children seen by child guidance clinics twenty or thirty years ago were, in fact, normally functioning children. For this reason, the evidence of studies which link adult psychiatric status to evidence previously obtained from the same individuals in child guidance clinics is irreplaceable. Their shortcomings in the light of present-day interests lie mainly in the absence of fine-grain measurements of cognitive processes and physiological reactivity, and in their concentration on precursors of adult schizophrenia. The direction of the results of the investigations convincingly demonstrates that severe childhood behaviour problems have a high probability of becoming or remaining as adult disorders. In terms of sample size and length of follow-up, the St. Louis study is one of the most important. O'Neal and Robins (1959a) showed that 30 per cent of children diagnosed as anti-social in childhood exhibited psychotic reactions as adults. The major precursor symptoms were "truancy", "incorrigibility", "running away" and "fighting". The incidence of adult neurosis in the clinic sample (37 per cent), while showing some continuity, did not differ significantly from that of neurosis in a control group. Furthermore, 30 per cent of child neurotics showed no psychiatric disturbance nearly thirty years later. It is plausible to assume that this latter group did not present serious phobic or obsessive-compulsive characteristics, and that some of the anti-social and delinquent features may have been specific to the situation or to the developmental stage (A. Freud, 1966). A shorter term British follow-up study (Pritchard and Graham, 1966) found similar continuities between child delinquency and adult psychosis (23 per cent), but 51 per cent of child neurotics became adult neurotics. In a more detailed analysis O'Neal and Robins (1958b) showed that former patients now diagnosed as schizophrenic, compared with former patients without psychopathology on follow-up, differed significantly on: physical aggression and lying, over-dependency on mother, worrying or brooding, poor appetite, being emotionally cold and unaffectionate. Studies reviewed by Anthony (1970) cite apathy, shut-in-ness, early peculiarity, but particularly childhood anxiety as significant precursors of adult schizophrenia. A fifteen-year follow-up study on the prediction of adult psychological health (associated with the Berkeley Growth Studies) by Livson and Peskin (1967) found that predictions at pre-adolescence are more reliable than earlier predictions. The authors cite social withdrawal, affective aloofness and poor control over hostility in males, and dependence, self-doubts, lack of intellectual curiosity and eating problems in females, as precursors of later psychological ill-health without, however, categorizing by type.

Fleming and Ricks (1970) compared the childhood emotional precursors of groups of chronic hospitalized and discharged schizophrenics, cases of character disorder and socially adequate control subjects. They found, on the basis of subjects' clinical and retrospective self-reports, that anxiety and feelings of vulnerability, unreality and isolation, differentiated significantly between the groups, and that apparently pre-schizophrenics have more disruptive emotional and disturbing cognitive experiences than any other groups. The exception applied to cases of character disorder: these patients reported more feelings of isolation and alienation. Similar and amplifying pre-schizophrenic behavioural deficits were reported by Ricks and Berry (1970). They confirmed the St. Louis study in respect of delinquent and anti-social early histories accompanied by evidence of physical aggression, low self-esteem, social eccentricity, hyperactivity, incorrigibility, over-reaction to frustration, enuresis, short attention span. A second major pre-schizophrenic group was labelled withdrawn. Two other sub-groups were identified with a better chance of discharge, and with the implication that they exhibited fewer or no "soft neurological signs", that is, activity or co-ordination parameter dysfunctions which might be due to (unvalidated) neurological impairments. In tracing a developmental model for schizophrenia these authors proposed a three-stage process in which the affected individual initially *protests* against unacceptable events and experiences; his responses then move to *despair*, until finally there is *resignation, apathy and detachment*.

The *measurement* of precursor characteristics appears to be confined to intelligence, but has yielded contradictory as well as complex findings. Lane and Albee (1970) revised their earlier findings on intelligence test levels of pre-schizophrenic children in relation to non-pre-schizophrenic sibs and unrelated children. These had suggested that the low IQs often found in schizophrenics are already present in childhood and that significant decreases in IQ can be demonstrated in the early and pre-adolescent school years. While pre-schizophrenics had lower IQs than their siblings in both high and low socio-economic groups, this did not apply to pre-neurotic subjects. Intellectual deterioration during childhood has now been identified as an artifact, but scores lower than those of non-schizophrenic peers and towards the low average range of test normalization data appear to be confirmed for individuals who subsequently become hospitalized schizophrenics (see for instance, Pollack, Woerner and Klein, 1970). Neither the Lane and Albee nor the Hathaway, Monachesi and Salasin (1970) study is able to identify the causal relationship between intelligence level and schizophrenia : whether low IQs are the result of earlier or later abnormal cognitive and affective processes, or whether an *a priori* lower intellectual capacity predisposes towards the major schizophrenic deficits. Hathaway *et al.* (1970) carried out a retrospective analysis of adults from whom as ninth grade children MMPI and intelligence test data had been obtained. High scorers on the Sc(schizophrenia) scale compared with those with average scores were found to have positively skewed distributions for intelligence, scholastic achievement and socio-economic status. These findings for subjects who were unselected for subsequent hospitalization as schizophrenics appear to parallel the findings of ecological studies.

A potentially useful contribution to the identification of the pre-morbid characteristics of schizophrenics comes from an analysis of developmentally important or relevant parameters which distinguish monozygotic twins *discordant* for schizophrenia. Stabenau and Pollin (1967) presented the findings from two subject pools : fourteen pairs studied intensively at the NIMH, and eighty-six pairs studied in other countries. Examination of case histories yielded a list of twenty-six characteristics which were most frequently employed in describing the twins at the pre-schizophrenic stage of the index twin. The differentiating characteristics are shown in Fig. 16.3. While the discriminating items did not always yield between-country matches, and while reliability of twin status and validity of descriptions cannot now be checked, the results from the compound sample match those from the more deliberately conceived NIMH study, and both are consistent with the findings already reviewed above.

(2) CONCURRENT STUDIES

These are distinguished from retrospective studies because they make their own observations and are long-term and continuous, whereas

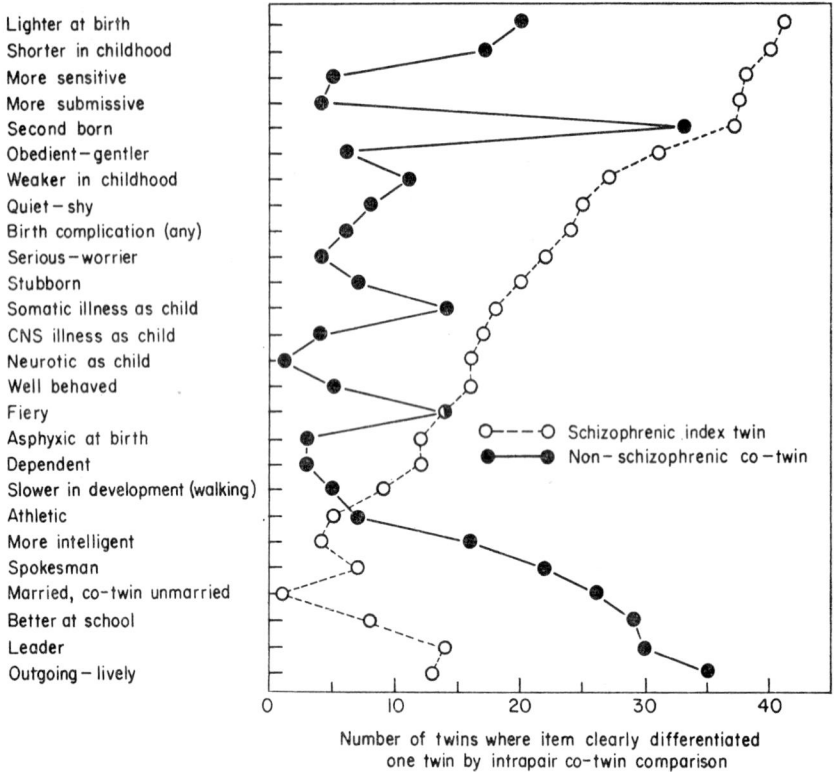

FIG. 16.3. Differentiating characteristics of index and control monozygotic twins discordant for schizophrenia. (*After* Stabenau and Pollin, 1967, p. 725.)

the former are directed from an end state of pathology. However, the concurrent study does depend on its own retrospective data. The best known example of this approach is the New York longitudinal study (Thomas, Chess and Birch, 1968; Chess, Thomas and Birch, 1968). Our discussion will concentrate on their findings because, unlike other concurrent studies at Berkeley (Jones *et al.*, 1971), the Fels Institute (Kagan and Moss, 1962) or Yale (Kris, 1957), this one was specifically oriented towards the development of psychopathological states, and behaviour characteristics were assessed before clinical symptoms became apparent. Thomas *et al.* set out to study the "temperament" of infants beginning with a mean age of 3 months at three-monthly intervals between data-taking in the first 18 months, then six-monthly intervals until the age of 5, followed by yearly intervals. The data were derived from structured interviews with parents, and were factually (rather than interpretatively) oriented. A pilot study provided some evidence of adequate reliability for the observations made by parents in that inter-rater reliability (research staff) was lower than the concordance between observer and parents. Standardized observations during intelligence testing at ages 3 and 6 were also carried out, and parental socialization attitudes and the children's behaviour at school were assessed. Parents were advised that the clinic was available to help them should their children give them cause for concern. Probably because of the care-taking characteristics of the high socioeconomic status sample, the pool of 136 children yielded forty-two clinical cases (two of them brain-damaged) as defined by parental and school report and symptomatic clinical diagnostic procedures. Cases with problems specific as to age, situation and child management were excluded. Symptoms in the clinical group were rated on a four-point mild to severe scale, as a reactive or neurotic behaviour disorder, and as showing "active" or "passive" symptoms.

The temperamental characteristics of all cases were assigned to nine reactivity categories, each with a 3-point rating scale. They were: *Activity level*; *Biological Rhythmicity*; *Approach or Withdrawal* reactions to new stimuli; *Adaptability* of responses in light of circumstances; *Intensity of Reaction*; *Threshold of Responsiveness*; *Quality of Mood*; *Distractability*; *Attention Span and Persistence*. The categories are assumed to reflect children's behavioural style, carry no aetiological inferences and are considered independent of content. The many statistical and sub-group manipulations of the data and subjects are rather difficult to summarize. Both passively and actively responding clinical subjects differed from the non-clinical sample in the combination of biological irregularity, predominantly negative withdrawal responses to new stimuli, non-adaptability or slow adaptability to change, frequent negative mood, and predominantly intense reaction (Chess et al., 1968, p. 338). A factorial index of mood, intensity, approach/withdrawal and adaptability identified the difficult child. Differences in the same direction for persistence and distractability were also found. Of additional interest, in view of the Lane and Albee findings in relation to intelligence, are comparisons between a small number of clinic cases and their sibs. The sibs differed from the control group in the same direction as the clinical group, but to a lesser extent and less consistently, and were near-significantly more non-clinical on negative mood, intensity, rhythmicity and adaptability (Rutter et al., 1964). Thomas et al. (1968) do not hold that a given organization of reactive characteristics is in itself pathognomonic; it may become so, however, by interaction with unfavourably perceived environments. Chess et al. (1968) propose that anxiety and conflict are *secondary* reactions resulting from the stressful experience of an unhealthy temperament—environment interaction. It is likely that this view has emerged as the result of deliberately divorcing stimulus content from the rating of the reaction patterns. Since at an early age perceptual learning proceeds at an accelerating rate with accompanying experiences of satisfaction or aversion, it could be argued that *how* a child reacts cannot really be discussed without reference to *why* and *at what*.

(3) "At-risk" studies

Studies of this type make the basic assumption that the children of parents with a psychopathological history are thereby more likely themselves to develop behavioural abnormalities or inadequacies. The assumptions may be tested in relation to genetic causation or to a genetic/environmental interaction hypothesis. Where theoretical bias favours a genetic determination, existing models permit numerical predictions of the number of children of abnormal parents who will eventually become abnormal to different degrees. An alternative approach predicts abnormalities in children which are concordant with the *severity* of parental symtomatology, but not necessarily in a prospective study. The limitations of the latter approach are clear: while confirmation of predictions in relation to different criterion groups represents one type of validation of a hypothesis, the approach is essentially correlational. There is no requirement, however, that it should necessarily remain so, because a concurrent and systematic variation of relevant independent variables can yield covariance data which now have greater causal implications.

The best known long-term prospective "at risk" study is at present under way in Denmark, with the focus on the fate of the offspring of chronically and severely schizophrenic mothers. A number of published reports have already appeared (for instance, Mednick and Schulsinger, 1968; Mednick, 1970; Mednick, Schulsinger and Garfinkel, 1975), though a follow-up period of twenty-five years is envisaged. The index cases were reliably diagnosed schizophrenic mothers, whose 207 children, aged about 15 at the start of the study, constitute the "at risk" group. It was assumed that this group would eventually yield 100 deviant offspring, thirty of whom would eventually be classified as schizophrenic. The control group consisted of the 104 low risk offspring of mothers without psychopathology, matched for critical variables, including residence of a child in a children's home. As the "at risk" group yields its subjects with developing behavioural disorders, these are compared with matched control subjects and with a matched sub-group of the high risk group which has not yielded evidence of behavioural deviancy. The latest available analyses are based on two groups, each with $N = 20$ of high risk subjects, one of them containing those who had been admitted to hospital with behaviour disorders, including schizophrenia. These groups were compared (and with the control group) on fourteen experimental measures which had been obtained at the beginning of the study and before any breakdown in a subject had occurred. We shall confine our summary of the findings to parameters which are more directly relevant to cognitive factors. On GSR the high risk deviant group responded too quickly and too much and recovered too quickly from a 96 dB noise. There were no significant differences in basal rates, but the high risk deviant group showed more conditioning, more generalization and a relative lack of autonomic response habituation. The investigators suggest that the experimental group exhibits insufficient ANS inhibitory control (Mednick, Schulsinger and Garfinkel, 1975). Their previous report (Mednick and Schulsinger, 1968) indicated that the experimental group had non-significantly lower intelligence test scores, but significantly higher scores on two critical indices of a continuous word association test. The presence of genetic/environmental interaction is indicated by the greater incidence of maternal separation and perinatal complications in the experimental group. Also important is the confirmation of aggressive, hostile and self-control traits discussed in (1) above.

In view of the findings of the New York study (Thomas et al., op. cit.), it is likely that the Danish children were already far too old to permit a tough approach to the nature/nurture problem. This disadvantage may be overcome, however, by investigations currently under way in Mauritius (Bell et al., 1975). A further inevitable shortcoming of the Danish work is the absence of social parameters, since it might be predicted that the presence of over-reaction and aggression might lead to social isolation which in turn might affect cognitive development and subjective preoccupation. There is at least one study (Rolf, 1972) which shows that the vulnerable offspring of schizophrenic mothers (both traced through centralized records) were socially less mature, competent and popular than any other children except those who exhibited as part of their behaviour disturbance a dominant aggressive mode of social interaction.

All the precursor studies considered so far appear to have assigned insufficient importance to fundamental cognitive processes and skills which develop early in life. The discussion presented in Chap. 11, however, suggests that early cognition–motivation–personality interactions do occur, and that they may exercise long-term influence on the structure, direction and adaptiveness of adult cognitive processes.

One study is available, however (Anthony, 1968), where this approach
has been adopted. Unfortunately, its major clinical orientation adversely affected methodology, and the systematic selection and manipulation of cognitive development-relevant variables. As in the Danish
study, the investigations were concerned with the comparison of the
children of schizophrenic and non-psychotic parents, and succeeded
in supplying supportive evidence of autonomic lability and generalization, plethysmographically and electrodermally, for the "at risk"
group. Scores on cognitive tests indicated initially lower scores (under
9 years old), but subsequently higher scores (over 9 years old) for
high risk subjects. The tests were the Children's Embedded Figures test
and two Piagetian tests: "Three Mountains" and "Broken Bridge".
These results were influenced by the higher intelligence test levels
of the experimental group. At the same time, Anthony notes that the
higher scores on the cognitive tests by the high risk group were accompanied by *unusual* verbalizations. The potentially interesting underlying aim of this investigator has been an attempted synthesis between
psycho-sexual/psycho-social and cognitive stages of development
(Anthony, 1970), but the absence of rigorous, operationally defined
predictions has diminished the conceptual utility of a series of only
partially integrated studies.

A considerable number of studies initiated more recently is now
under way in different countries. Garmezy (1975) has presented a
general overview of largely prospective projects on children at risk for
schizophrenia and related disorders. An assessment of most of these
must be deferred, however, until fuller accounts beyond the preliminary follow-up stages become more generally available.

(4) Summary

The consensus of studies that have been reviewed suggests that future
schizophrenics may show early signs of later maladaptation. The
major indicators may be summarized as arousal functions, physiological lability, intra-personal and social conflict, anxiety, and sub-
optimal intellectual competence. In the absence of critical studies one
can only hypothesize that the precursor syndromes and characteristics
may be the outcome of initially external stimulation which, through
bio-physiological sensitivity and non-inhibition by internal cognitive
appraisal and identification of stimulus content, leads to a progressive
development of incomplete, unrepresentational, unintegrated or
aversive schemata, anxiety, withdrawal and aggression.

While few cognitive or bio-physiological precursors of neurosis have
been identified, it seems likely that the basic coping resources of future

neurotics and schizophrenics differ quantitatively, and that they may differ particularly in anxiety avoidance strategies, and in the capacity to modulate cognitive processes more integratively and thereby more economically.

V. DEVELOPMENT OF DEVIANT COGNITIVE PROCESSES

(1) INTRODUCTION

Of considerable importance to a cognitive developmental approach is the growing evidence that genetic influences in the schizophrenias appear to be weaker than previously thought (Stabenau and Pollin, 1967; Gottesman and Shields, 1972). The types of general vulnerability shown to be present in some high risk groups of children (Anthony, 1968; Mednick and Schulsinger, 1972), and in a proportion of a relatively unselected sample of younger children (Thomas *et al.*, 1968) support the proposition, however, that in some future patients, general or specific bio-physiological hyper- or hypo-sensitivities may have been present from birth. This possibility is strengthened by fairly recent findings that institutionalized and non-institutionalized chronic schizophrenics may be subdivided on the basis of responding and non-responding to an orienting stimulus as shown by SCR (Gruzelier and Venables, 1972; Gruzelier, 1973). The habituation and lability characteristics of the responding group appear to be similar to the results obtained before breakdown from the deviant high risk group of the Danish study. Venables, Gruzelier, and also Mednick, are now suggesting that the demonstrated over-reaction abnormalities implicate limbic or hippocampal dysfunction which have developed as the result of anoxia at birth. Although contrary arguments have been raised (Kessler and Neale, 1974), the suggestions are in line with assumptions often made in the literature that the variations in schizophrenic syndromes may be partly due to some organic dysfunctions with generalized effects.

Only a small minority of neonates with a history of birth complications appears to become schizophrenic or neurotic and, therefore, a functional explanation for the vast majority of cases still seems more plausible. This conclusion forms the basis of the remainder of this chapter. Vulnerability to physiological stress and anxiety will be considered as a single dimension, which, together with differences in type and onset of cognitive adaptive strategies, themselves strongly influenced by patterns of socialization experiences, determine a neurotic or psychotic outcome. In this context behavioural abnormalities are considered not as a sudden or regressive loss of skill, but rather as evidence of sub-optimal early cognitive development which, through a combination of subsequent unfavourable experience, has prevented the emergence of those higher order structural units which are required for optimal functioning in the more complex adult social setting.

While arousal and other energizing systems are a basic requirement of all responses, this phylogenetically more primitive energy system of man does not react in the absence of sensory information or cognitive operations upon it. The degree of over- or under-reaction depends not only on the threshold and lability characteristics, nor necessarily on stimulus intensity, but in the first instance on the identification of degrees and types of pleasantness or aversiveness which central code analysers attach to stimuli. The adaptive skill represented by this operation will show improvements which are concurrent with the development of perceptual differentiation. Where a stressfully *experienced* environment contains an excess of unmodulated, over-simplified information, a small number of global, relatively undifferentiated cognitive structures and behavioural or mood schemata develops. Where stress is engendered by early stimulus complexity and premature demands for discrimination learning, an excessively large number of structures and schemata with a fine-grain degree of differentiation may result. The structures may additionally vary in internal consistency, elaboration and inter-communication, by means of which they mediate those processes which we term obsessional doubt and uncertainty, inability to concentrate on any one task as in anxiety, or associative looseness or incongruent responding, as in one or the other types of schizophrenia. The developmental outcome is either that which at some stage has occasioned the greatest drop in stressful experience, or the persistence of a response repertoire which has become prematurely stereotyped but is maintained because, for reasons not yet fully understood, alternative responses or a change in strategy cannot be generated. It is proposed that three influences combine to bring about this situation : unadaptive bio-physiological sensitivity, the information content of the socializing environment, and the cognitive processes which internalize, interpret, manipulate and store selected features of the information made available to an information processing system.

A considerable number of hypothetical statements will be required to formulate a set of models of neurotic and schizophrenic development. In the absence of established functional relationships between early and later cognitive processes no other course is open. Essentially, an attempt must be made to bridge the wide gap between the symptoms and cognitive deficits of confirmed adult patients, and the evidence from analytic, narrowly focused studies of stimulus encoding and retrieval, and attentional, perceptual and conceptual skills and strategies. In the final analysis, unrealistic fears, autonomous perseverative acts and thoughts and incongruous behaviour are the product of unadaptive cognitive structures with low evidential thresholds, retrievable from long-term memory systems.

(2) Bio-physiological sensitivity

Comprehensive electro-physiological data accompanying childhood disorders as part of a precursor study are not available. Consideration of the case history data from the New York and Danish studies suggests, however, that SCR characteristics which reflects arousal in adult patients might show similar types of deviations in children—allowing, of course, for differences due to neurological immaturity. This conclusion is drawn from the "temperamental" problems of children who were subsequently taken into treatment. Thus, Case 5, aged 36 months (Thomas et al., 1968, p. 36), resisted going to sleep, had tantrums at bedtime, and awoke at night screaming. Case 13, aged 42 months (p. 38), stole and lied, was judged as under-achieving in the nursery, was easily frustrated and attached great importance to objects and situations representing status. Although a "temperament profile" is not given, it is plausible to suggest that activity level, adaptability, intensity and threshold of responsiveness were deviant, and sympathetic ANS involvement high—customary findings in neurosis and anxiety. High arousal in adult neurotic patients is reflected in high resting levels, fluctuations and variability of skin conductance and a low habituation rate for all types of anxiety except specific phobias (Lader, 1975). These data are supported by high sedation thresholds for patients with a major symptom of anxiety (Claridge, 1975), and for normal, high-anxious subjects (Katkin, 1975). A study by Hirschman and Katkin (Katkin, op. cit.) is particularly interesting in that it showed high non-specific SCR responsiveness to stimulation which was of *personal relevance* to a subject.

Excessive arousal interferes with performance. This effect is amply demonstrated when arousal is equated with drive (see Section II above), when it is equated with emotionality or anxiety (see for instance, Broadhurst, 1959; Malmo, 1959; Kahneman, 1973), or when manipulated by noise, sleeplessness, heat, air pressure or diurnal rhythms (Broadbent 1971). The reason for the effects, as argued by Easterbrook (1959), is a postulated narrowing of the range of cue utilization. Considering emotionality, drive and arousal as analogous, this range is defined as the number of environmental cues in any situation that an organism observes, maintains an orientation towards, responds to, or associates with a response. The supportive studies cited by Easterbrook indicate that the cues referred to are primarily external/perceptual on different points of a spatial peripheral/central axis. With high arousal, attention shrinks towards central cues, excluding first irrelevant and finally task, or behaviour-relevant, stimuli. The most recent support for this proposition (Bacon, 1974) indicates that decrements are limited, however, to a diminution in sensitivity to stimulation (d') for peripheral tasks which *initially* attracted less attention. This suggests that stimuli internal to the subject (subjective decisions in task evaluation and on attention deployment) may play a more important role in arousal-related decrements. Narrowing of the range of cue-utilization as conceived by Easterbrook also appears to be too non-specific to be able to account for more recent conceptions of attentional characteristics without (Wachtel, 1967) or with the involvement of threat (Wachtel, 1968; Cornsweet, 1969).

A more plausible explanation of the adverse effects of high arousal on optimum performance is Kahneman's suggestion (1973) that arousal impairs the orientation reaction and fine-grain discrimination and performance strategies through strains on the allocation of effort in central processing operations. Kahneman's model, which shows the relationship between arousal, information content of stimuli and selective attention, is shown in Fig. 16.4. The greater the externally driven demands on the system, the greater the processing efforts required. Increased effort from effort reserves would be required if the enduring dispositions are interpreted as including attention to task-irrelevant stimuli.

While effort may be unproductively employed to counteract the unpleasant physiological components of emotionality or anxiety, it is also required to deal with task-irrelevant associations which contain information about the effects of previously experienced unfavourable events. If there is a large LTM store with low retrieval thresholds of this type of information, the effects of arousal may also be defined by a broadening of the utilization range of *internal* cues. In non-phobic anxiety states this would account for the wide range of aversive events or situations the patient reports, the lack of concentration and the impairment of STM. In phobias, however, the increase in internal information is reflected in the broadening of stimulus generalization by which objects, events and situations only remotely associated with the phobic nucleus affect behaviour. Some of the differences in the cognitive content of anxiety neurosis and phobia are amplified by Beck and Rush (1975). In obsessive-compulsive neurosis the effect of arousal on internal information stores is shown primarily by a pathological degree of doubt and indecisiveness in response selection, where, due to rigid and over-elaborated multiple classifications, no response is experienced as fully adequate. In acute and particularly in paranoid schizophrenia, the heightened level of responsiveness would lead to an exacerbation of the effects of long-term unadaptive associations through input from too wide a range of external stimuli which are poorly discriminated, while yet being cognitively searched for relevance

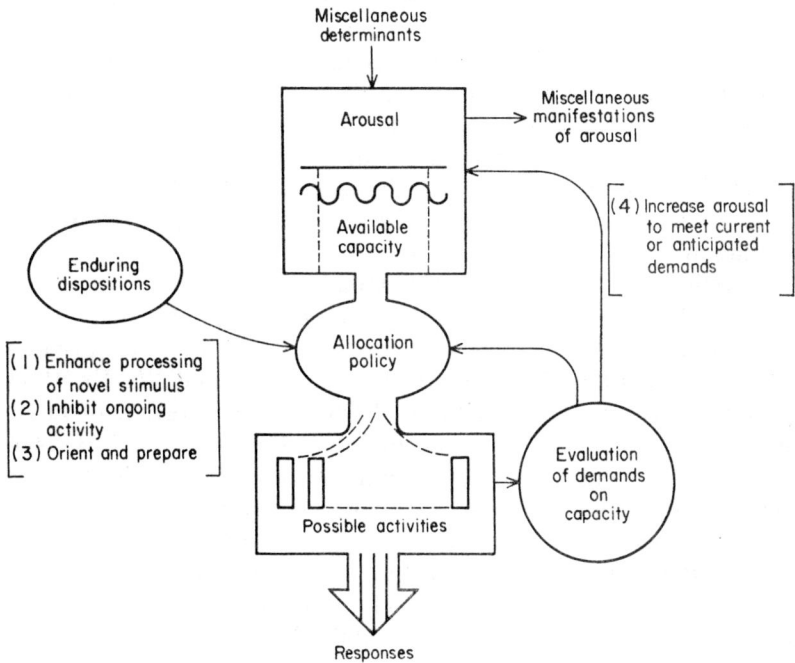

FIG. 16.4. Components of the orientation reaction. (*After* Kahneman, 1973, p. 47.)

to dominant subjective preoccupations or enduring dispositions. Non-paranoid, process schizophrenics, by comparison, could be said to channel the main effect of arousal towards the manipulation of internal cues. One can only infer on the basis of some of the evidence discussed earlier (see Section III) that external cue sampling in schizophrenics has become progressively more unsystematic or inhibited because of its aversively experienced implications. The *effects* of arousal, therefore, appear to be more important than arousal *per se*, and clearly depend on the type of external and internal stimulus input on which it can operate (see Fig. 16.1).

(3) The informational environment

Given a general behavioural basis in arousal, reactivity thresholds and labilities, specific anxieties and disturbance of reality-related thought processes can occur only because objects and their attributes, events and situations and their learnt or expected implications, are part of the informational data banks of a cognitive system. While it is important to know how the data banks are acquired through developmental periods of increasing organizing and coding capacity, the *sources* of information are equally important. The environment presents at least four of these : objects and events eliciting, stimulating or encouraging interaction *per se*; reciprocal manipulation of the environment by caretaker and child; socialization and child-rearing strategies and attitudes of parents; and, less frequently considered, the informational representation of the immediate and wider environment within the caretaker, usually the mother. The most frequently studied in relation to abnormal development is the third source, usually by an investigation of the parental, but mainly maternal, characteristics of schizophrenic, neurotic and control offspring. The literature is extensive and cannot be reviewed here in any detail (see for instance, Bateson *et al.*, 1956; Fisher *et al.*, 1959; Mishler and Waxler, 1968; Quay and Werry, 1972; Heilbrun, 1973). A recent review of family interaction studies aimed at the differential presence and types of dominance, conflict, affect or communication was carried out by Jacob (1975). This suggests that many investigations contain disabling methodological inadequacies, and many of them do not show the hypothesized differences in the predicted direction of greater family pathology for disturbed or schizophrenic children. Interaction analysis studies are notorious for the difficulty of isolating the role of the investigator, however, and, therefore, these findings need not invalidate the major proposition.

The relationship between parent-child interaction and cognitive development has been fairly fully discussed already in Chap. 11, and the conclusion was drawn that sub-optimal mothering is likely to result in sub-optimal child cognition. Too little or too much attention-giving, intrusion, protective care, affection, dominance or control have been shown to be related to inhibition on dependent variables ranging from exploration to achievement seeking, from conserving capacity to intelligence. The methods adopted by parents in guiding the activities of their offspring convey information. This can be ordered on a number of dimensions such as simple–complex, verbal–non-verbal, factual–personalized, unequivocal–ambiguous, internally consistent–contradictory, child-paced–parent-paced, reward-linked–censure-linked, physically mediated–verbally mediated, affection-oriented –rejection-oriented and democratic–autocratic. The examples can be multiplied, of course, particularly with amount, intensity, variability, and sex of parents as additional dimensions.

There does not seem to be any *direct* evidence of the relationship between dimensions of parental stimulation such as these and the development of *neurotic cognition,* though Harvey *et al.* (1961) and Harvey and Felknor (1970) have demonstrated the implications of some of these for the development of non-pathological cognitive systems (see Chap. 11). It may, however, be possible that a combination of complex, ambiguous, censurious and rejecting communication does not enable the child to learn easily responses which will be accompanied by rewards of pleasure or acceptance. Because of their unreliable expectancy or uncertainty of outcome, response conflict will occur instead. If the conflict is insoluble, but a response must be made, anxiety will occur because important child needs can only be met by responding. The type of parental behaviour described here is itself evidence of maladjustment, neurosis or anxiety, either in both parents (Fisher *et al.*, 1959) or in one of them (Becker *et al.*, 1959; Jenkins, 1968). The greater the number of dimensions involved in parental stimulation, the demands in terms of amount and intensity, and the implications for the potential loss of affectional attachment needs, the greater the pressure on the child to simplify perceptual and conceptual information to enable him to make a response. In view of the evidence for the development and presence of super-ordinate cognitive control processes (see Chap. 11), and the studies on intolerance of ambiguity referred to above (Section II), anxiety can be partially controlled by semantic, pictorial or other symbolically representational categories which are either few in number, over-comprehensive and imprecise, or numerous, over-precise and non-integrated.

The evidence on the relationship between parental stimulation and *schizophrenic cognition* is similarly inconclusive. Rodnick and Garmezy's original findings (1957) that schizophrenics are sensitive to any form of criticism and censure have not been replicated, but Garmezy (1965) rephrased his proposition so that perceptual and learning deficits are now linked only to a developmental history during which censure was irrelevant to task performance and could not be avoided. This appears to be the essential feature of the "double-bind" hypothesis (Bateson *et al.*, 1956) which has engendered so much criticism. Much of this may be considered irrelevant because inappropriate and irrelevant paradigms were tested (see for instance Schuham, 1967). A relevant objection might be that "meta-meta-messages" can be conceptualized only by intelligent future patients.

24—CP * *

Heilbrun, in a recent review of the literature (1973), suggests that 79 per cent of the studies considered contain some evidence of the presence of high control in the mothers of schizophrenics, but emotional rejection appears much less implicated. After completion of a long series of integrated experiments on normal subjects varying on high and low control and nurturance in their self-report socialization experience, Heilbrun presents evidence of contrasting open or closed adaptive cognitive styles. Both styles are defensive against *aversively experienced maternal communication*. At the pathological end the closed style may lead insidiously to process schizophrenia through its avoidance of censure, failure or rejection experiences mediated by social withdrawal, and with its additional effects of stimulus input control and subjectively steered cognitive processes. The pathological end of the open style adaptation is linked by Heilbrun to paranoid schizophrenia, and preceding excessive input of stimulation through broad external scanning and premature categorization. Although considerable support has emerged for the relationship between the dichotomized socialization experiences and the postulated styles, the analogue status of the studies with respect to the schizophrenias is admittedly tenuous as yet.

An interesting light on the familial informational environments of schizophrenics has been cast by a number of studies relating evidence of irrationality and thought disorder in patients to that of their non-hospitalized parents (Lidz et al., 1958; Wynne and Singer, 1963; Singer and Wynne, 1965). Many of the parents appeared emotionally vulnerable, requiring sharply circumscribed conditions to maintain their integration. In such settings, facts are often altered to suit parental emotional needs, and symbiotic relationships develop between mother and child in which the latter is used to meet the needs of the former (Lidz, 1968). One might almost say that the parents teach the child to become psychotic as the result of their own disturbance. Some evidence for this assumption comes from results obtained with an Object Sorting test originally designed by Vygotsky with a scoring technique devised by Lovibond (1954). McConaghy (1959) had found that the parents of schizophrenics obtained high (poor) scores which were similar to those obtained by their schizophrenic offspring, and significantly different from those of a control group of non-patients. These results were replicated by Lidz et al. (1963), both experiments concluding that there was thus evidence favouring dominant genetic transmission. A rather better controlled study by Schopler and Loftin (1969), however, permitted a different interpretation. These investigators also found non-normal results in Object Sorting test scores for mothers of psychotic or autistic patients when they were tested in the

clinic which they were attending with their psychotic child for conjoint therapy. A further experiment indicated, however, that the poor
performance of the mothers of patients was more validly accounted
for in terms of the effects of test anxiety elicited by concern over the
child in treatment. Explaining either the development or the adult
presence of schizophrenic deficits as plausibly related to anxiety has
remained unpopular, however, following Mednick's (1958) somewhat
premature, over-simplified learning theory approach.

The susceptibility of schizophrenic social behaviour, perception and
thinking to interference from goal- or task-irrelevant intrusions
appears to be fully established (see Section III). While there is no
longitudinal evidence linking anxiety, as traditionally defined, with
the development of non-paranoid process schizophrenia, it seems
entirely plausible to link a history of progressive decline in rational
interaction and increasing social withdrawal to what may be the only
protective strategy for a particular type of bio-physiological vulnerability. If the growth in input dysfunction is seen as an attempt to
protect a poorly organized and integrated cognitive system from
further disorganizing stimulation, it would be disingenuous to suggest
that this protective avoidance behaviour *excludes* a similar reaction
to stimulation that is aversive, by virtue of containing some kind of
threat or danger for the person. There is every reason to suppose that
the more inefficiently structured cognitive system is anything but
immune from ambivalent, equivocal, over-protective or rejecting
parental communication, or the intellectual incongruities of schizo-
typic or schizoprone parents (Meehl, 1962). All of these would tend
to increase the number of cognitive identifying, matching and search
processes necessary to select a relatively conflict-free response. Similarly, there are few reasons for excluding from the development of
paranoid or reactive schizophrenics a substantial role for anxiety since
they possess all the bio-physiological equipment for labile over-
reaction, and thus for excessive input and internal operations upon it.

Parents, as socializers, reflect the rules and habit systems of their
culture. Interaction with children reflects not only parental affect,
intelligence, patience or a child-centred orientation, but also attempts
to be consistent with the child-rearing expectation of the social group
or sub-groups. These expectations vary in degree of rigidity, elaboration and severity, as do parents in the extent to which they need to
conform. Parental guidance and control thus reflect society's informational complexity, as well as parental capacity to assimilate it and to
resist the conflicts and feelings of inadequacy they may engender.
The parent who responds with frustration or anxiety to the perceived
stereotypical child-rearing assumptions of the larger social groups is

less likely to be child-oriented, and may engage in strategies along some of the dimensions of interaction mentioned earlier, which the child will perceive as aversive. Unfavourable mothering need not be considered, therefore, as either the cause or the effect of abnormal child development, but as the result of informational complexity reflecting maternal conformity strategies interacting with the child's bio-physiological sensitivity. It is of interest to note that the New York precursor study could not differentiate at its inception between the mothers of children who subsequently become patients and those who did not (Thomas *et al.*, 1968). Only at the symptom stage did the largely middle-class parents seem to interact unfavourably with their temperamentally unstable offspring.

(4) SOME DETERMINANTS OF UNADAPTIVE COGNITIVE STRUCTURES

In the present context, and in view of the preceding discussion, greater logical force attaches to a historical cognitive development approach to deviant cognition than to a behavioural regression concept of *pre-morbid adequacy*. Spontaneous deterioration of behavioural skills may follow on acute stress, of course, but is unlikely to occur without biological vulnerability in early stages of development having provided the basis in insecurely established conceptual structures, and often a tenuous integration of motoric, affective and cognitive components. Three salient hypothetical determinants of developmental inadequacy will be examined : amount of information, type of information, and ensuing inadequacies of encoding, identifying and storage processes.

(i) *Amount of information.* Our analysis will assume that at any given point in time and development, the processing capacity for amounts of information is limited. Wickens (1974) reviewed the evidence in relation to temporal limits for children above 3 years of age. His tentative conclusions are *inter alia* : practice, motivation, incentive and attentiveness affect children's maximum information processing rate to a greater extent than that of adults; age is related to latency of perceptual processing, and to efficiency and speed of response selection mechanisms; children have greater limitations than adults in co-ordinating the release of simultaneously compatible responses. A vulnerable response system thereby must become increasingly inefficient in conditions of distraction from within or without, with excessive stimulus information content represented either by simultaneous stimuli, or by a rapid sequence of different stimuli, or by the perceptual and conceptual complexity of stimulus designation.

Since one of the major tasks of child development is to make sense

of the surrounding world and to create a satisfying response repertoire, stimulus complexity may be increased in environments deficient
in object, situation or communication experience. The latter would
occur if parental and mainly maternal stimulation is poorly structured,
contradictory, incongruent or unpredictable in content or periodicity.
In such situations, approved responses may become difficult or
impossible, and age appropriate schemata required for the development of adult discrimination and generalizing abilities would remain
suboptimal. Instead, situation-specific, unintegrated mental work may
ensue to assist the process of making sense, but with inadequate
facilities for classifying the experience there would be an impairment
of processing economics (see Chap. 9). Furthermore, in the face of an
unpredictable environment, passivity and dependence or hyperactivity
and lack of behavioural control may result. We cannot say with any
degree of conviction which child would respond with which style in
which conditions of processing and response-generating difficulty.
The deficits in constancy and conservation discussed above with
reference to non-paranoid schizophrenia (see Section III), and the
early, suboptimal intelligence of this group (Lane and Albee, 1970)
suggest, however, that future non-paranoid schizophrenics may have
experienced information overload conditions early in life. These conditions may have prevented the development of integrative strategies.

(ii) *Type of information.* Turning to the role of type of information
made available during major socialization stages, we distinguish two
general types: pleasant and unpleasant. The first engenders approach,
the second avoidance. Consistent with the interpretation of anxiety in
terms of uncertainty, unpredictability and non-avoidability of noxious
stimulation (see above), unpleasant information conveys general
expectations of negative reward contingencies. These features of a
stimulus situation are compounded with the negative poles of the
dimensions of parental interaction and communication considered
earlier. Together they provide a basis for early primitive concepts of
good and bad which are applied to external objects and situations,
and to self-perception. While it is plausible to hold that total, protective parental care may retard and distort cognitive development
through the development of over-dependent passivity, our discussion
will focus on aversive experience, aversively interpreted parental
stimulation and aversive self-perception.
    Depending on the sensitivity of the bio-physiological reactivity
mechanisms and parental need-oriented socialization strategies,
children structure differentially elaborated schemata of aversiveness
with respect to themselves and their needs, to external objects and

situations, and to their caretakers. Under the influence of positive as well as negative feedback interactions with arousal mechanisms, structures encoding aversive experience become unobjectively differentiated as well as over-generalized. Anxiety, as the most representative type of aversive experience, may thus be interpreted as information or cognitive data. In a limited capacity processing system, this information competes for space and time with the physical objective cognitive data presented by the environment, and its objective response requirements. The kind of interference referred to here is difficult to elicit from young children verbally. It may be inferred, however, from some of the behavioural descriptions of the New York study, or from items of, for instance, Sarason's Test Anxiety Scale for Children (Sarason, 1972), such as "When you are taking a hard test, do you forget some things you knew very well before you started taking the test?" Representative questionnaire items given to adults indicate that experiences of inadequacy, fear of failure or personal unacceptability become elaborated in relation to more demanding social settings. For example: "I constantly seem to feel that I have offended someone", or "I usually feel awkward with strangers" (Dixon et al., 1957). The aversive *type* of information has implications for the *amount* of information presented to an information-processing system at any given time. This is not only because the questionnaire terms "constantly" or "usually" yield an affirmative response from very anxious people, but because the social situations referred to elicit imaginary, trial-and-error stimulus and potential response situations which reflect the low thresholds as well as the degree of uncertain classification and excessive elaboration attaching to such situations. For children, content and complexity of interference depend, of course, on the developmental stage reached, but then the tasks or processes interfered with are also simpler.

A quantitative model to account for the well-documented problem-solving deficits associated with anxiety in schoolchildren, students and adults has been proposed recently (Hamilton, 1975). Assuming the availability of a limited capacity multiple component information-processing system to which cognitively interpreted anxiety adds task-irrelevant, internally generated additional information, the model demonstrates how increases in task complexity, high basal levels and concurrently increasing levels of aversive or self-threatening information, can together exceed the processing capacity of the system, probably through over-loading some of its components. The model is illustrated in Fig. 16.5. In the notation, APC is average processing capacity, SPC is the effort reserve of spare capacity, I_{ev} is primary external task information, $I_{i(c)}$ is internally generated competing information elicited by the external task, and $I_{i(A)}$ is internally generated aversive information connotating anxiety. The latter differs quantitatively for people differing in self-report anxiety and/or through the manipulation of ego threat, and primarily by virtue of over-elaborated aversive LTM structures activated by response requirements.

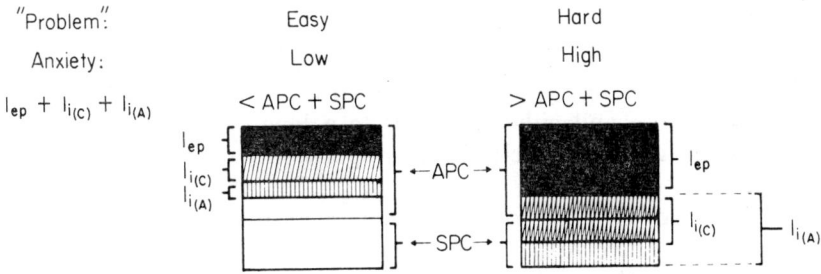

"Problem":	Easy	Hard
Anxiety:	Low	High
$I_{ep} + I_{i(C)} + I_{i(A)}$	< APC + SPC	> APC + SPC

Fig. 16.5. The effects of anxiety—cognitively interpreted—on the processing capacity of an information processing system.

Once again we are in ignorance concerning the role of excessive information with aversive and conflict-inducing content in the development of specific disorders in given individuals. It seems plausible to suggest, however, that object- and person-specific anxieties and conflicts occur primarily in individuals possessing systems of well-structured basic schemata. In neurosis these have either established non-veridical links, or a high probability of such links is always present as part of a response-selection process. This must mean, however, that a basic representation of the objective environment has become established pre-morbidly, and that early processing capacity was adequate for this development. If this argument is acceptable, it would follow that the best defence against schizophrenic non-integrative cognitive structures is the development of a large number of stimulus and response categories. These are particularly characteristic of the obsessional person, and are significantly absent in all types of schizophrenias except nuclear paranoids.

(iii) *Sub-optimal encoding and storage.* The development of cognitive structures and processes is achieved as the result of appropriate coding and integrated storing of, at first, primarily externally presented information. Let us now briefly examine a set of hypothetical relationships between external stimuli and their utilization, and internally generated stimuli elicited by them.

Only a portion of sensory input can pass from iconic to more durable storage for further processing. At the same time, volitional activities may affect the persistence of iconic data for the purpose of conveying information from a more difficult task to a longer term memory store. Input of a rapid succession of stimuli will either summate with the first set of icons or erase it, while storage capacity of the first durable store is limited and may be disturbed by new inputs (see Chap. 1). Encoding proceeds by a hierarchical assigning of initially phonemic or graphemic codes which become symbolic, lexical, semantic or pictorial memories. Verbal or graphical recognizer, or addressing systems, after serial search, identify data in a temporary store and either assign it to a long-term memory system or employ it immediately in a response-generating process (see Chap. 2).

If it could be experimentally established that the precursors of abnormal cognitive skills appear to involve an inability in dealing with subjectively and/or objectively excessive stimulus input, then a developmental basis would be available for the encoding of information-deficient and/or objectively unrepresentative or false inputs. The effects of this would persist in long-term storage and, in the absence of early correction, would provide inadequate early schemata, chunks or structures which would prevent the subsequent development of veridical, efficient and rational systems for the classification and integration of percepts.

From the earlier discussion (see Sections (i) and (ii)) it might be proposed that this sequence of events reflects the characteristic precursors of the more fundamental cognitive deficits of the schizophrenias, in whom aversive, response-irrelevant information accumulates primarily as a *consequence* of cues derived from an inadequate response. The effects of encoding of hypo- or hyper-reactivity are likely to be similar to each other. In the former, a small input may be excessive and inimical to categorical encoding. In the latter, sustained, focused attention appears to be low and selective discrimination of signals is impaired so that encoding and schematizing are likely to be tenuous (see Chap. 3). This formulation, while clearly speculative, is nevertheless consistent with the previously discussed evidence of sub-optimal constancy and conservation. It was argued that these early skills were impaired in schizophrenics because responses were based on sensory/perceptual data rather than on conceptual operations which require the integration of a number of firmly established cognitive structures. Some support of this proposition is available from a study by Anthony (1970) who found greater under-constancy in children exhibiting micropsia—experiences of visual perception in which objects in space assume sizes close to their subtended visual angle.

The degree of structural cognitive integrity in neurosis suggests a much later start for sub-optimal processes and less extreme arousal or reactivity in early life. It is plausible, therefore, to propose that aversive, response-irrelevant informational content accumulates only at the stage at which parental intentions and socializing strategies can be adequately coded and identified. From this, it would follow that the perception of the environment and the handling of its response requirements would become sub-optimal only at the stage when it becomes socially complex. The increase in complexity, however, is a conjoint function of behavioural mobility, parental expectations of behavioural skill, and parental communications concerning the child's acceptability.

We have now identified two possible pathogenic cognitive components: unstructured or weak categories, and irrelevant, aversive categories. The extent to which these categories are used in responding would depend on their proportional presence in long-term memory stores, and their retrieval thresholds. The greater the presence of weak or affectively aversive structures, the greater their influence on short-term memory operations and, consequently, on central co-ordinating processes which precede response selection. A gross model representing this analysis is shown in Fig. 16.6.

It is easier to propose a model to demonstrate how weak or poorly structured concepts are maintained in development than to show how they first arose. A weak concept or schema is an inadequate basis for generalization and it is occasion-specific because it is very dependent on sensory data. When this kind of cognitive system is exposed to stimulation, sensory or concrete rather than conceptually analytic semantic recognizers would be prominent in scanning stimuli which have entered a more durable buffer store. In the absence of strong, conceptual data-scanning operations, a much larger number of specific and conceptually primitive operations are required for the identification of input (see Fig. 16.7). To use the language of Miller *et al.* (1960), the number of TOT operations is unadaptively increased. Even if the time consuming matching operation could be completed before trace decay occurs either through lack of reactivation or through a succession of new incoming stimuli, the ensuing response would continue to reflect weak conceptual identification. The process of permanent concreteness can be interrupted, however, by helping the child to recognize higher order relationships in his stimulus field, as occurs in teaching, or in a supportive, relatively intelligent and communicative parental home.

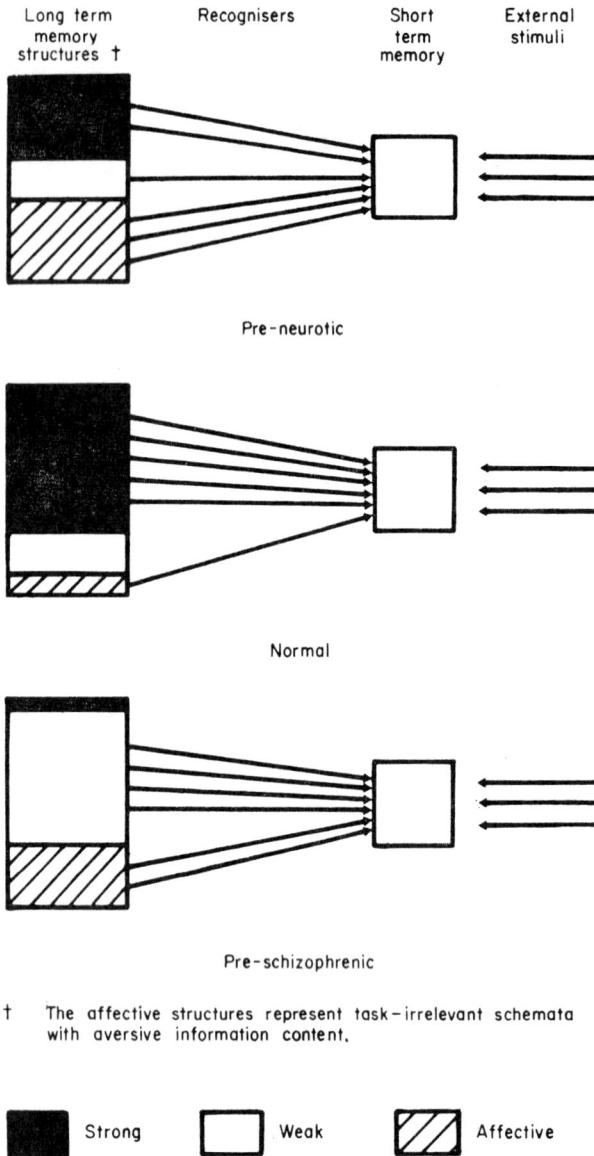

FIG. 16.6. The differential role of weak and affective LTM structures in STM identifying operations.

If a response setting is interpreted as aversive because of its subjective complexity, because it is a source of potential incompetence, or if personally aversive outcomes are expected as a consequence and with a high degree of uncertainty, these constitute sources of additional information. As was suggested earlier (Fig. 16.5), task-irrelevant information may exhaust the processing capacity of the system. Interference with task- or response-relevant operations may occur at two interfaces: when recognizers are applied at a first durable buffer store stage, or at more central pigeon-holing or response-integrating stages. It is easier to conceptualize what may happen in short-term memory processes as the result of irrelevant anxiety associations elicited by a task or social situation, particularly if a child admits to being anxious. Such a report of self-awareness, we may propose, is

Memory stores

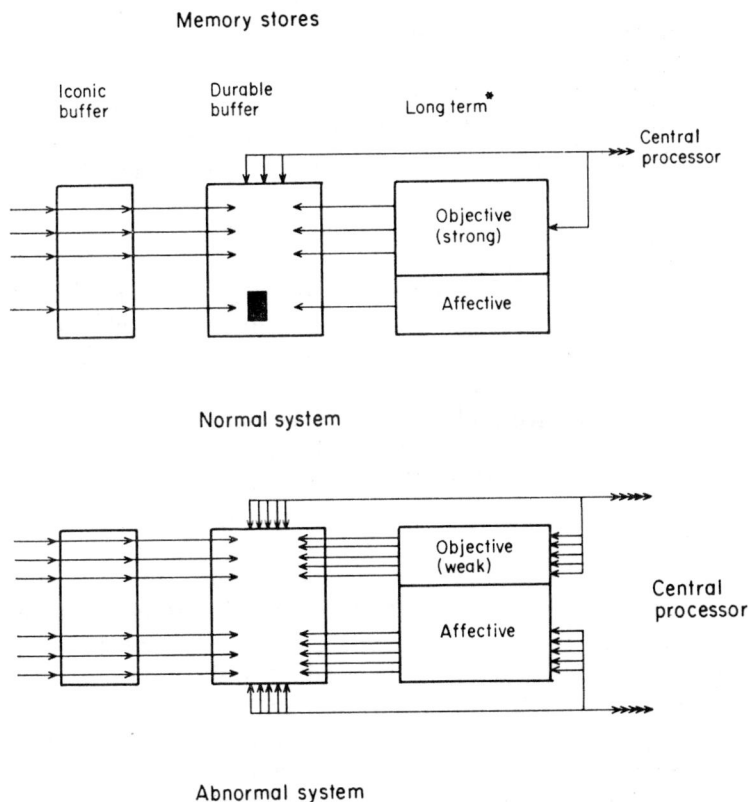

Normal system

Abnormal system

*The affective component represents task-irrelevant structures with aversive information content.

FIG. 16.7. Differences in cognitive processing loads engendered by differences in LTM structures and content.

possible only because the information subsumed by it has entered at least one component of a STM system. Three related events would interfere with optimal cognitive operations: internally generated expectancies of aversive outcomes for responses, an irrelevantly large number of weak recognizers, and excessive attentional scanning triggered by uncertain event identification and probability of aversive experience. As a consequence input into iconic and durable buffer stores would increase not only through irrelevant external inputs, but as the result of LTM recognizers with dual functions of evaluating objective as well as affective data. A tentative model illustrating the quantitative difference between strong and weak and anxiety-free and anxiety-present STM operations is shown in Fig. 16.7. It may be added that if the hypothesized kind of interference starts at an early developmental stage, its effect might be similar, though not identical, to the effects previously related to subjective surfeits of external stimulus input. Thus it is conceivable that the development of perception and identification of forms and objects (see Chap. 4 and 5) might be adversely affected by interference from early anxiety, and provide a basis for later misinterpretation and misperception.

(5) Conclusions

Our cognitive analysis offers a possible conceptual basis for Werner's (1948) and Witkin's (1965) propositions of individual differences in the development of behavioural and structural differentiation. It appears to be particularly relevant to the re-interpretation of some of the validated subjective and defensive operations of psycho-dynamic theories. These have been conceptualized already as ongoing cognitive processes (Peterfreund, 1971). We must reiterate the importance of a fundamental role for anxiety, interpreted as aversive cognitive information, because the evidence suggests that all types of therapy, behavioural or dynamic, aimed at anxiety types of neurosis or schizophrenia achieve their best results by a manipulation of anxiety-inducing features of the environment, as well as by restructuring or minimizing the information content of adaptive situations.

It has not been possible to present new evidence to account for the differential development of neurosis and schizophrenia, but a number of testable propositions are implicit in the models of differential cognitive processing presented above. In neurosis there is greater evidence of reportable anxiety and conflict, a longer history of successful self-regulation and self-monitoring of behaviour in relation to socially approved goals, and greater evidence of social and conceptual learning vis-à-vis people, objects and situations. The two types of disorder are likely to differ, therefore, with respect to the developmental phase in which aversive experience and excessive information loads first interfered with the establishment of objectively engendered response categories. If this were true, then it could be postulated that the significant differences between neurosis and schizophrenia, and their sub-categories, reside in the structures, contents and integration of long-term memory storage systems.

In the absence of relevant reality testing and behavioural feedback, the future neurotic will elaborate his aversive cognitive structures by internally driven processes so that they achieve a hierarchical precedence and low evocation thresholds. This will increase their readiness to intrude irrelevantly, and reduce the person's capacity to operate adaptively upon objective, affectively neutral input.

The future schizophrenic is unable to overcome early deficiencies in representational codes and structures. The inefficient economy of his cognitive system makes him more generally vulnerable to information suggesting personal incompetence, failure and unacceptability, especially when this is presented through the controlling strategies of a vulnerable caretaker. As in the developmental stages of the anxiety neuroses, the major solution to an unacceptable social situation is an avoidance of external information input, but it is more far-reaching. Since the internally generated processes operate on less differentiated, weaker concepts, the future schizophrenic's elaborations of his cognitive structures are necessarily more reality-remote and incongruent and often only subjectively logical. Cognitive process development is more deviant than in neurosis because the expectations of aversive experience involve unrepresentative or false basic concepts. Adaptive responding shows progressively increasing deficits because the increasing informational complexity of the social environment elicits an increasing prominence of internally generated irrelevant and inconsistent data-matching processes. These reflect aversive sensitivity as much as existing incomplete conceptual structures.

724   THE DEVELOPMENT OF COGNITIVE PROCESSES

REFERENCES

Anthony, E. J. (1968). The developmental precursors of adult schizophrenia. In D. Rosenthal and S. S. Kety (Eds.), *The Transmission of Schizophrenia.* Oxford: Pergamon.

Anthony, E. J. (1970). The behaviour disorders of childhood. In P. H. Mussen (Ed.), *Carmichael's Manual of Child Psychology,* 2nd ed. New York: Wiley.

Ax, A. F. (1975). Emotional learning deficiency in schizophrenia. In M. L. Kietzman, S. Sutton and J. Zubin (Eds.), *Experimental Approaches to Psychopathology.* New York: Academic Press.

Bacon, S. J. (1974). Arousal and the range of cue utilization. *Journal of Experimental Psychology, 102,* 81–7.

Bateson, G., Jackson, D. D., Haley J. and Weakland, J. (1956). Toward a theory of schizophrenia. *Behavioral Science, 1,* 251–64.

Beck, A. T. and Rush, A. J. (1975). A cognitive model of anxiety formation and anxiety resolution. In I. G. Sarason and C. D. Spielberger (Eds.), *Stress and Anxiety, 2.* Washington, D. C.: Hemisphere Publishing Corporation.

Becker, W. C., Shoemaker, D. J., Peterson, D. R., Quay, H. C. and Hellmer, L. A. (1959). Factors in parental behavior and personality as related to problem behaviour in children. *Journal of Consulting Psychology, 23,* 107–18.

Bell, B., Mednick, S. A., Raman, A. C., Schulsinger, F., Sutton-Smith, S. and Venables, P. H. (1975). A longitudinal psychophysiological study of three-year-old Mauritian children; preliminary report. *Developmental Medicine and Child Neurology, 17,* 320–4.

Bleuler, E. (1950). *Dementia Praecox or the Group of Schizophrenias.* New York: International Universities Press.

Bleuler, M. (1968). A 23-year longitudinal study of 208 schizophrenics and impressions in regard to the nature of schizophrenia. In D. Rosenthal and S. S. Kety (Eds.), *The Transmission of Schizophrenia.* Oxford: Pergamon.

Boland, T. B. and Chapman, L. J. (1971). Conflicting predictions from Broen's and Chapman's theories of schizophrenic thought disorder. *Journal of Abnormal Psychology, 78,* 52–8.

Bowers, M. (1965). The onset of psychosis—a diary account. *Psychiatry, 28,* 346–58.

Bowlby, J. (1973). *Attachment and Loss, II: Separation, Anxiety and Anger.* London: Hogarth Press.

Broadbent, D. E. (1958). *Perception and Communication.* London: Pergamon.

Broadbent, D. E. (1971). *Decision and Stress.* London: Academic Press.

Broadhurst, P. L. (1959). The interaction of task difficulty and motivation: the Yerkes-Dodson Law revived. *Acta Psychologica, 16,* 321–8.

Broen, W. E., Jnr. (1968). *Schizophrenia—Research and Theory.* New York: Academic Press.

Broen, W. E., Jnr. and Storms, L. H. (1966). Lawful disorganization: the process underlying a schizophrenic syndrome. *Psychological Review, 73,* 265–79.

Broen, W. E., Jnr. and Storms, L. H. (1967). A theory of response interference in schizophrenia. In B. A. Maher (Ed), *Progress in Experimental Personality Research,* Vol IV. New York: Academic Press.

Buss, A. H. (1966). *Psychopathology.* New York: Wiley.

Buss, A. H. and Lang, P. J. (1965). Psychological deficit in schizophrenia, I: affect, reinforcement and concept attainment. *Journal of Abnormal Psychology, 70,* 2–24.

Callaway, E. (1970). Schizophrenia and interference: an analogy with a malfunctioning computer. *Archives of General Psychiatry, 22,* 193–208.

Chapman, L. J. (1958). Intrusion of associative responses into schizophrenic conceptual performance. *Journal of Abnormal and Social Psychology, 56,* 374–9.

Chess, S., Thomas, A. and Birch, H. G. (1968). Behaviour problems revisited: findings of anterospective study. In S. Chess and A. Thomas (Eds.), *Annual Progress in Child Psychiatry and Child Development.* New York: Bruner/Mazel.

Claridge, G. S. (1975). Psychophysiological indicators of neurosis and early psychosis. In M. L. Kietzman, S. Sutton and J. Zubin (Eds.), *Experimental Approaches to Psychopathology.* New York: Academic Press.

Cornsweet, D. M. (1969). Use of cues in the visual periphery under conditions of arousal. *Journal of Experimental Psychology, 80,* 14–18.

Court, J. H. and Garwoli, E. (1968). Schizophrenic performance on a reaction-time task with increasing levels of complexity. *British Journal of Social and Clinical Psychology, 7,* 216–23.

Davidson, G. S. and Neale, J. M. (1974). The effects of signal-noise similarity on visual information processing of schizophrenics. *Journal of Abnormal Psychology, 83,* 683–6.

Davis, R. D. (1948). *Pilot Error.* London: Air Publications 3139a, H.M.S.O.

Desai, M. M. (1952). Test-retest reliability of the Progressive Matrices Test. *British Journal of Medical Psychology, 25,* 48–53.

Dixon, J. J., de Monchaux, C. and Sandler, J. (1957). Patterns of anxiety: an analysis of social anxieties. *British Journal of Medical Psychology, 30,* 107–12.

Easterbrook, J. A. (1959). The effect of emotion on cue-utilization and the organization of behavior. *Psychological Review, 66,* 183–201.

Endler, N. S. (1975). A person-situation interaction model for anxiety. In C. D. Spielberger and I. G. Sarason (Eds.), *Stress and Anxiety,* I. Washington, D.C.: Hemisphere Publishing Corporation.

Epstein, S. and Coleman, M. (1970). Drive theories of schizophrenia. *Psychosomatic Medicine, 32,* 113–40.

Epstein, S. and Fenz, W. (1962). Theory and experiment on the measurement of approach-avoidance conflict. *Journal of Abnormal and Social Psychology, 64,* 97–112.

Eysenck, H. J. (1957). *The Dynamics of Anxiety and Hysteria.* London: Routledge and Kegan Paul.

Eysenck, H. J. (1967). *The Biological Basis of Personality.* New York: C. C. Thomas.

Eysenck, H. J. (1973). Personality, learning and "anxiety". In H. J. Eysenck (Ed.), *Handbook of Abnormal Psychology,* 2nd ed. London: Pitman.

Eysenck, M. W. (1974). Extraversion, arousal and retrieval from semantic memory. *Journal of Personality, 42,* 319–31.

Fenz, W. (1964). Conflict and stress as related to physiological activation and sensory, perceptual and cognitive functioning. *Psychological Monographs, 78,* 1–33.

Fenz, W. (1975). Strategies for coping with stress. In I. G. Sarason and C. D. Spielberger (Eds.), *Stress and Anxiety*, II. Washington, D.C.: Hemisphere Publishing Corporation.

Fisher, S., Walker, D., Boyd, I. and Sheer, D. (1959). Parents of schizophrenics, neurotics and normals. *Archives of General Psychiatry, 1,* 149–66.

Fleming, P. and Ricks, D. F. (1970). Emotions of children before schizophrenia and before character disorders. In N. Roff and D. F. Ricks (Eds.), *Life History Research in Psychopathology.* Minneapolis: University of Minnesota Press.

Frenkel-Brunswik, E. (1954). Further explorations by a contributor to *"The Authoritarian Personality".* In R. Christie and M. Jahoda (Eds.), *Studies in the Scope and Method of "The Authoritarian Personality"—Continuities in Social Research.* New York: Free Press.

Freud, A. (1966). *Normality and Pathology in Childhood.* London: Hogarth Press.

Garmezy, N. (1965). The prediction of performance in schizophrenia. In P. H. Hoch and J. Zubin (Eds.), *Schizophrenia.* New York: Grune and Stratton.

Garmezy, N. (1975). The experimental study of children vulnerable to psychopathology. In A. Davids (Ed.), *Child Personality and Psychopathology: Current Topics,* Vol. 2. New York: Wiley.

Goldfarb, W. (1974). *Growth and Change of Schizophrenic Children: A Longitudinal Study.* New York: Wiley.

Gottesman, I. I. and Shields, J. (1972). *Schizophrenia and Genetics: A Twin Study Vantage Point.* New York: Academic Press.

Gray, J. A. (1970). The psycho-physiological basis of introversion-extraversion. *Behaviour Research and Therapy, 8,* 249–66.

Gruzelier, J. H. (1973). Bilateral asymmetry of skin conductance orienting activity and levels in schizophrenics. *Biological Psychology, 1,* 21–41.

Gruzelier, J. H. and Venables, P. H. (1972). Skin conductance orienting activity in a heterogeneous sample of schizophrenics. *Journal of Nervous and Mental Diseases, 155,* 277–87.

Hamilton, V. (1957). Perceptual and personality dynamics in reactions to ambiguity. *British Journal of Psychology, 48,* 200–15.

Hamilton, V. (1959a). Theories of anxiety and hysteria—a rejoinder to Hans Eysenck. *British Journal of Psychology, 50,* 276–80.

Hamilton, V. (1959b). Eysenck's theories of anxiety and hysteria—a methodological critique. *British Journal of Psychology, 50,* 48–63.

Hamilton, V. (1960). Imperception of phi: some further determinants. *British Journal of Psychology, 51,* 257–66.

Hamilton, V. (1963). Size constancy and cue responsiveness in psychosis. *British Journal of Psychology, 54,* 25–39.

Hamilton, V. (1966). Deficits in primitive perceptual and thinking skills in schizophrenia. *Nature, 211,* 389–92.

Hamilton, V. (1972). The size constancy problem in schizophrenia: a cognitive skill analysis. *British Journal of Psychology, 63,* 73–84.

Hamilton, V. (1975). Socialization anxiety and information processing: a capacity model of anxiety-induced performance deficits. In I. G. Sarason and C. D. Spielberger (Eds.), *Stress and Anxiety*, II. Washington D.C.: Hemisphere Publishing.

Hamilton, V. and Moss, M. (1974). A method of scaling conservation of quantity problems by information content. *Child Development, 45,* 737–45.

Harvey, J. O. and Felknor, C. (1970). Parent-child relations as an antecedent to conceptual functioning. In R. A. Hoppe, G. A. Milton and E D Simmel (Eds.), *Early Experiences and the Process of Socialization.* New York: Academic Press.

Harvey, J. O., Hunt, E. E. and Schroder, H. M. (1961). *Conceptual Systems and Personality Organization.* New York: Wiley.

Hathaway, S. R., Monachesi, E. and Salasin, S. (1970). A follow-up study of MMPI high 8 schizoid children. In M. Roff and D. F. Ricks (Eds.), *Life History Research in Psychopathology.* Minneapolis: University of Minnesota Press.

Heilbrun, A. B., Jnr. (1973). *Aversive Maternal Control: A Theory of Schizophrenic Development.* New York: Wiley.

Hemsley, D. R. (1975). A two-stage model of attention in schizophrenia research. *British Journal of Social and Clinical Psychology, 14,* 81–9.

Jacob, T. (1975). Family interaction in disturbed and normal families: a methodological and substantive review. *Psychological Bulletin, 82,* 33–65.

Jenkins, R. L. (1968). The varieties of children's behaviour problems and family dynamics. *American Journal of Psychiatry, 124,* 1440–5.

Jones, M. C., Bayley, N., Macfarlane, J. W. and Honzik, M. P. (Eds.) (1971). *The Course of Human Development.* Waltham: Xerox College Publishing.

Kagan, J. and Moss, H. A. (1962). *Birth to Maturity.* New York: Wiley.

Kahneman, D. (1973). *Attention and Effort.* New Jersey: Prentice-Hall.

Katkin, E. S. (1975). A psychophysiological analysis of individual differences in response to stress. In I. G. Sarason and C. D. Spielberger (Eds.), *Stress and Anxiety,* II. Washington, D. C.: Hemisphere Publishing Corporation.

Kessler, P. and Neale, J. M. (1974). Hippocampal damage and schizophenia: a critique of Mednick's theory. *Journal of Abnormal Psychology, 83,* 91–6.

Kimmel, H. D. (1971). Pathological inhibition of emotional behaviour. In H. D. Kimmel (Ed.), *Experimental Psychopathology: Recent Research and Theory.* New York: Academic Press.

Koh, S. D., Kayton, L. and Berry, R. (1973). Mnemonic organization in young nonpsychotic schizophrenics. *Journal of Abnormal Psychology, 81,* 299–310.

Kris, M. (1957). The use of prediction in a longitudinal study. *Psychoanalytic Study of the Child, 12,* 175–89.

Lader, M. (1975). *The Psychophysiology of Mental Illness.* London: Routledge and Kegan Paul.

Lane, E. A. and Albee, G. W. (1970). Intellectual antecedents of schizophrenia. In M. Roff and D. F. Ricks (Eds.), *Life History Research in Psychopathology.* Minneapolis: University of Minnesota Press.

Lang, P. J. and Buss, A. H. (1965). Psychological deficit in schizophrenia: II. Interference and activation. *Journal of Abnormal Psychology, 70,* 77–106.

Lidz, T. (1968). The family, language and the transmission of schizophrenia. In D. Rosenthal and S. S. Kety (Eds.), *The Transmission of Schizophrenia.* Oxford: Pergamon.

Lidz, T., Cornelison, A., Terry, D. and Fleck, S. (1958). Intrafamilial environment of the schizophrenic patient: VI. The transmission of irrationality. *Archives of Neurology and Psychiatry, 79,* 305–16.

Lidz, T., Wild, C., Schafer, S., Rosman, B. and Fleck, S. (1963). Thought disorders in the parents of schizophrenic patients: a study utilizing the Object Sorting test. *Journal of Psychiatric Research, 1,* 193–200.

Livson, N. and Peskin, H. (1967). The prediction of adult psychological health in a longitudinal study. *Journal of Abnormal Psychology, 72*, 509–18.

Lovibond, S. (1954). The Object Sorting test and conceptual thinking in schizophrenia. *Australian Journal of Psychology, 6*, 52–70.

Luria, A. R. (1932). *The Nature of Human Conflict.* New York: Liveright.

Maier, N. R. F. (1949). *Frustration: The Study of Behavior without a Goal.* New York: McGraw-Hill.

Malmo, R. B. (1959). Activation: a neuropsychological dimension. *Psychological Review, 66*, 367–86.

Malmo, R. B., Shagass, C., Belanger, D. J. and Smith, A. A. (1951). Motor control in psychiatric patients under experimental stress. *Journal of Abnormal and Social Psychology, 46*, 539–47.

Masserman, J. H. (1961). *Principles of Dynamic Psychiatry.* Philadelphia: Saunders.

Masserman, J. H. (1971). The principles of uncertainty in neurotigenesis. In H. D. Kimmel (Ed.), *Experimental Psychopathology: Recent Research and Theory.* New York: Academic Press.

McConaghy, N. (1959). The use of an Object Sorting test in elucidating the hereditary factor in schizophrenia. *Journal of Neurology, Neurosurgery and Psychiatry, 22*, 243–6.

McGhie, A., Chapman, J. and Lawson, J. S. (1965). Effect of distraction on schizophrenic performance. *British Journal of Psychiatry, 111*, 383–98.

Mednick, S. A. (1958). A learning theory approach to research in schizophrenia. *Psychological Bulletin, 55*, 316–27.

Mednick, S. A. (1970). Breakdown in children at high risk for schizophrenia: behavioral and autonomic characteristics and possible role of perinatal complications. *Mental Hygiene, 54*, 50–63.

Mednick, S. A. and Schulsinger, F. (1968). Some premorbid characteristics related to breakdown in children with schizophrenic mothers. In D. Rosenthal and S. S. Kety (Eds.), *The Transmission of Schizophrenia.* Oxford: Pergamon.

Mednick, S. A. and Schulsinger, F. (1972). A learning theory of schizophrenia: thirteen years later. In M. Hammer, K. Salzinger and S. Sutton (Eds.), *Psychopathology.* New York: Wiley.

Mednick, S. A., Schulsinger, F. and Garfinkel, R. (1975). Children at high risk for schizophrenia: predisposing factors and intervention. In M. Kietzman, S. Sutton and J. Zubin (Eds.), *Experimental Approaches to Psychopathology.* New York: Academic Press.

Meehl, P. E. (1962). Schizotaxia, schizotypy, schizophrenia. *American Psychologist, 17*, 827–31.

Miller, G. A., Galanter, E. and Pribram, K. H. (1960). *Plans and the Structure of Behavior.* New York: Rinehart and Winston.

Miller, N. E. (1944). Experimental studies of conflict. In J. McV. Hunt (Ed.), *Personality and the Behavior Disorders.* New York: Ronald.

Mishler, E. G. and Waxler, N. E. (1968). *Interactions in Families.* New York: Wiley.

Murray, E. J. and Berkun, M. M. (1955). Displacement as a function of conflict. *Journal of Abnormal and Social Psychology, 51*, 47–56.

Neale, J. M. and Cromwell, R. J. (1968). Size estimation in schizophrenics as a function of stimulus-presentation time. *Journal of Abnormal Psychology, 73*, 44–8.

O'Neal, P. and Robins, L. N. (1958a). The relation of childhood behaviour problems to adult psychiatric status: a 30-year follow-up study of 150 subjects. *American Journal of Psychiatry, 114,* 961–9.

O'Neal, P. and Robins, L. N. (1958b). Childhood patterns predictive of adult schizophrenia. *American Journal of Psychiatry, 115,* 385–91.

Payne, R. W. (1970). Disorders of thinking. In C. G. Costello (Ed.), *Symptoms of Psychopathology—A Handbook.* New York: Wiley.

Payne, R. W. (1973). Cognitive abnormalities. In H. J. Eysenck (Ed.), *Handbook of Abnormal Psychology,* 2nd ed. London: Pitman.

Peterfreund, E. (1971). Information systems and psychoanalysis: an evolutionary biological approach to psychoanalytic theory. *Psychological Issues, 7,* Monographs No. 25–6.

Pollack, M., Woerner, M. G. and Klein, D. F. (1970). A comparison of childhood characteristics of schizophrenics, personality disorders and their siblings. In M. Roff and D. F. Ricks (Eds.), *Life History Research in Psychopathology.* Minneapolis: University of Minnesota Press.

Pritchard, M. and Graham, P. (1966). An investigation of a group of patients who have attended both the child and adult departments of the same psychiatric hospital. *British Journal of Psychiatry, 112,* 487–603.

Quay, H. C. and Werry, J. S. (Eds.) (1972). *Psychopathological Disorders of Childhood.* New York: Wiley.

Ricks, D. F. and Berry, J. C. (1970). Family and symptom patterns that precede schizophrenia. In N. Roff and D. F. Ricks (Eds.), *Life History Research in Psychopathology.* Minneapolis: University of Minnesota Press.

Rodnick, E. H. and Garmezy, N. (1957). An experimental approach to the study of motivation in schizophrenia. In M. R. Jones (Ed.), *Nebraska Symposium on Motivation, 1957.* Lincoln: University of Nebraska Press.

Rolf, J. E. (1972). The social and academic competence of children vulnerable to schizophrenia and other behavior pathologies. *Journal of Abnormal Psychology, 80,* 225–43.

Rutter, M., Birch, H. G., Thomas, A. and Chess, S. (1964). Temperamental characteristics in infancy and the later development of behaviour disorders. *British Journal of Psychiatry, 110,* 651–61.

Salzinger, K. (1973). *Schizophrenia: Behavioral Aspects.* New York: Wiley.

Salzinger, K., Portnoy, S., Pisoni, D. and Feldman, R. S. (1970). The immediacy hypothesis and response-produced stimuli in schizophrenic speech. *Journal of Abnormal Psychology, 76,* 258–64.

Sarason, I. G. (1972). Experimental approaches to test anxiety: attention and the use of information. In C. D. Spielberger (Ed.), *Anxiety: Current Trends in Theory and Research.* New York: Academic Press.

Schopler, E. and Loftin, J. (1969). Thinking disorders in parents of young psychotic children. *Journal of Abnormal Psychology, 74,* 281–7.

Schuham, A. I. (1967). The double-bind hypothesis a decade later. *Psychological Bulletin, 68,* 409–16.

Segal, J., Boomer, D. S. and Bouthilet, L. (1975). *Research in the Service of Mental Health.* Report of the Research Task Force of the National Institute of Mental Health, N.I.M.H., Rockville, Maryland.

Seligman, M. E. P. and Maier, S. F. (1967). Failure to escape traumatic shock. *Journal of Experimental Psychology, 74,* 1–9.

Shakow, D. (1962). Segmental set: a theory of the formal psychological deficit in schizophrenia. *Archives of General Psychiatry, 6,* 17–33.

Silverman, J. (1964). The problem of attention in research and theory in schizophrenia. *Psychological Review, 71*, 352–79.

Silverman, J. (1967). Variations in cognitive control and psychophysiological defence in the schizophrenias. *Psychosomatic Medicine, 29*, 225–45.

Singer, M. T. and Wynne, L. C. (1965). Thought disorder and family relations of schizophrenics: IV. Results and implications. *Archives of General Psychiatry, 12*, 201–12.

Spence, K. W. (1958). A theory of emotionally based drive (D) and its relation to performance in simple learning situations. *American Psychologist, 13*, 131–41.

Spence, K. W. (1964). Anxiety (drive) level and performance in eyelid conditioning. *Psychological Bulletin, 61*, 129–39.

Spence, K. W., Farber, I. E. and McFann, H. H. (1956). The relation of anxiety (drive) level to performance in competitional and non-competitional paired-associates learning. *Journal of Experimental Psychology, 52*, 296–305.

Spence, K. W., Farber, I. E. and Taylor, E. (1954). The relation of electric shock and anxiety to level of performance in eyelid conditioning. *Journal of Experimental Psychology, 48*, 404–8.

Spence, K. W. and Goldstein, H. (1961). Eyelid conditioning as a function of emotion-producing instruction. *Journal of Experimental Psychology, 62*, 291–4.

Spence, K. W. and Spence, J. T. (1964). Relation of eyelid conditioning to manifest anxiety, extraversion and rigidity. *Journal of Abnormal and Social Psychology, 68*, 144–9.

Spence, K. W., Taylor, J. A. and Kretchel, R. (1956). Anxiety (drive) level and degree of competition in paired-associates learning. *Journal of Experimental Psychology, 52*, 306–10.

Spielberger, C. D. and Smith, L. H. (1966). Anxiety (drive) stress and social position effects in serial-verbal learning. *Journal of Experimental Psychology, 72*, 589–95.

Stabenau, J. R. and Pollin, W. (1967). Early characteristics of monozygotic twins discordant for schizophrenia. *Archives of General Psychiatry, 17*, 723–34.

Storms, L. H. and Sigal, J. J. (1958). Eysenck's personality theory with special reference to *The Dynamics of Anxiety and Hysteria. British Journal of Medical Psychology, 31*, 228–46.

Thomas, A., Chess, S. and Birch, H. G. (1968). *Temperament and Behavior Disorders in Children.* New York: New York University Press.

Venables, P. H. (1958). Stimulus complexity as a determinant of the reaction time of schizophrenics. *Canadian Journal of Psychology, 12*, 187–90.

Venables, P. H. (1960). The effect of auditory and visual stimulation on the skin potential response of schizophrenics. *Brain, 83*, 77–92.

Venables, P. H. (1963). Selection of attention, withdrawal, and cortical activation. *Archives of General Psychiatry, 9*, 74–8.

Venables, P. H. (1964). Input dysfunction in schizophrenia. In B. A. Maher (Ed.), *Progress in Experimental Personality Research*, Vol. I. New York: Academic Press.

Venables, P. H. and Warwick-Evans, L. A. (1967). Cortical arousal and two-flash threshold. *Psychonomic Science, 8*, 231–7.

Wachtel, P. L. (1967). Conceptions of broad and narrow attention. *Psychological Bulletin, 68,* 417–29.

Wachtel, P. L. (1968). Anxiety, attention and coping with threat. *Journal of Abnormal Psychology, 73,* 137–43.

Weckowicz, T. E. (1960). Perception of hidden pictures by schizophrenic patients. *Archives of General Psychiatry, 2,* 521–7.

Werner, H. (1948). *Comparative Psychology of Mental Development.* Chicago: Follett.

Wickens, C. D. (1974). Temporal limits of human information processing: a developmental study. *Psychological Bulletin, 81,* 739–55.

Witkin, H. A. (1965). Psychological differentiation and forms of pathology. *Journal of Abnormal Psychology, 70,* 317–36.

Wynne, L. C. and Singer, M. T. (1963). Thought disorder and family relations of schizophrenics: I. A research strategy. *Archives of General Psychiatry, 9,* 191–8.

Yates, A. J. (1966). Psychological deficit. *Annual Review of Psychology, 17,* 111–44.

Yates, A. J. and Korboot, P. (1970). Speed of perceptual functioning in chronic nonparanoid schizophrenics. *Journal of Abnormal Psychology, 76,* 453–61.

Zahn, T. P. (1975). Psychophysiological concomitants of task performance in schizophrenia. In M. L. Kietzman, S. Sutton and J. Zubin (Eds.), *Experimental Approaches to Psychopathology.* New York: Academic Press.

Zahn, T. P., Rosenthal, D. and Shakow, D. (1963). Effects of irregular preparatory intervals on reaction time in schizophrenia. *Journal of Abnormal and Social Psychology, 67,* 44–52.

General Conclusions

M. D. Vernon

The initial chapters in this book by Coltheart and Seymour on information processing in adults demonstrate that a high degree of detail and precision has been achieved in specifying, formulating and investigating the successive stages which are hypothesized to occur in the input, storage and utilization of certain types of information. The processes of coding and the earlier and later stages of storage have been differentiated according as to whether the input is visual or auditory/verbal; and the two forms of processing are considered to be to some extent independent, though linked and integrated within the dominant coverage of semantic processing. However, other variations in type of information are not considered extensively. The discussion and the evidence cited demonstrate the extreme subtlety and complexity attributed to the successive stages of information processing. It is perhaps not surprising therefore that little has so far been achieved in fitting knowledge about adult information processing at all precisely to investigation of the emergence of information processing procedures in children and to the part these play in their general cognitive development. This failure is due in part to the emphasis placed by so many adult studies on the symbolic processes which are not extensively developed in young children who are more concerned with objects. Moreover, it seems probable that information processing procedures develop in children only gradually, in a piecemeal and fragmented fashion. Also they may vary greatly according to the type of information and the total situation, as well as to the children's ages and cognitive abilities.

Clearly, as age increases, processing increases in speed, complexity and integration, and the permanent data store also grows in range and complexity. But also the manner of processing may change qualitatively. In the pre-operational child processing is related principally to immediate perception and action feedback, and storage is relatively impermanent. All stages in processing are partially fragmented and unintegrated. Although as noted the precise details of these procedures have not been investigated, it is nevertheless interesting to consider what evidence there is as to their nature and development.

The infant's primary need in obtaining information is to discover the nature and functions of real objects in his immediate surroundings, and their relation to his actions. Indeed, Odom-Brooks and Arnold (Chap. 15) have suggested that an important factor in mental retardation is a deficiency in "intrinsic cognitive motivation" to explore and discover the nature of the surroundings. Mentally retarded children appear to exhibit no deficiency in the innate process of orientation towards primary sources of information. But in all children these sources may at first be impressive physical characteristics such as intensity and high contrast which initially "catch" and hold attention. This orientation is then supplemented by selective attention, occurring after habituation to repeated stimulation, to novel stimuli which need to be investigated in order to widen the range of knowledge (Mackworth, Chap. 3; M. D. Vernon, Chap. 4). However, in early infancy objects may not be perceived as such, and attention seems to be directed towards certain qualities of form. The somewhat surprising observations of Fantz (1958), and of many others after him, indicated that from birth patterned fields are discriminated from and attended to rather than unpatterned. Moreover, as age increases attention is increasingly directed towards patterns of greater complexity which provide more information and therefore require more prolonged investigation.

Nevertheless, perception and identification of objects are fundamental to the child's cognitive development. These involve attention to and discrimination of essential invariant characteristics (Gibson, 1969), their iconic representation and their filtering into the short-term memory store. Later of course they also pass into long-term memory; but habituation studies have shown that this is not persistent in infancy. Young children have difficulty in deciding which aspects of objects are invariant, and which invariants are essential for identification. In time certain form characteristics are selected which appear to be similar to those observed by adults (M. D. Vernon, Chap. 4); and indeed rules of invariance may be built up (Vurpillot, Chap. 5). Yet these rules may differ from those of adults, and may be largely affected by actual experiences. Also certain qualities such as brightness and colour may have undue influence.

The development of concepts of objects as integrated wholes would seem to necessitate some kind of schematization of invariant characteristics; and this appears to begin at an early age. Piaget has maintained that early schemata are based on the child's own actions with and responses to objects. Yet it would seem that some types of schema may be based solely on perception and perceptual scanning, and from these are constructed discrete "chunks" which constitute objects (Donaldson, Chap. 7). Essential to an understanding of the nature of objects is the acquisition by the infant of the concept of object permanence. The important experiments of Bower (1974) and others, discussed by Vurpillot (Chap. 5) and Donaldson (Chap. 7), have indicated, however, that this acquisition is not an all-or-none process, as Piaget suggested, but that it proceeds piecemeal, and passes through successive stages which may appear strange to adults, such as the failure to attribute permanent identity to displaced objects though not to stationary objects. Thus the infant appears to acquire, encode and organize information which has meanings peculiar to his understanding and which may be employed in the prediction of future events, although it may differ qualitatively from that which would seem significant to adults. Again, Walk's discussion (Chap. 6) indicates that the types of information processed in the perception of and reaction to depth may differ from those utilized by adults.

Vurpillot differentiates between the early identification of particular objects which the child has previously encountered, and the subsequent categorial identification of objects as belonging to a class of similar objects. This again is based on the emergence of rules for selecting the essential invariant characteristics of the class. Vurpillot hypothesizes that for each class of familiar objects children construct a "figurative invariant" which is simple and unambiguous and is composed of a few characteristic details; and the presence or absence of these determines categorical identification. It is likely that at first the child's own experiences and actions are essentially involved, though they may be increasingly supplemented and refined by adult naming and explanation. Not surprisingly the selection of relevant invariants and the organizing of information to construct class concepts are difficult to perform, and errors are frequent. As Donaldson shows (Chap. 7), children tend to incorporate in their concepts irrelevant information from the total situation and what they expect its meaning to be, including the implications of the experimenter's instructions. Indeed, the intrusion of situational aspects may for long confuse children's conceptual judgments. Thus an essential function of maturation in selective attention is the suppression and omission of the irrelevant, in which selective scanning of the field is integrally involved (Mackworth, Chap. 3; M. D. Vernon, Chap. 4).

It is not until the concrete operational stage has been reached in cognitive development that children acquire more advanced and generalized concepts such as those involved in conservation (Farnham-Diggory, Chap. 9). Until then children tend to direct attention towards and base their judgments on irrelevant perceptual qualities such as height, area, etc. But also they clearly fail to understand the invariance of certain general characteristics of objects such as substance, weight, etc., which are unaffected by situational change. However, recent experiments by Bryant (1974) and others have shown that conservation is acquired gradually and fragmentally, and that its understanding may depend on the total situation. So also the principles involved in understanding relations such as those of seriation, class inclusion, etc., are only gradually acquired (Donaldson, Chap. 7). Farnham-Diggory has outlined several information-processing models applicable to these developments, and some of the rules which seem to function in problem solving behaviour at the pre-operational and operational stages. However, it is obviously difficult to fit general models based on adult information processing to the former stage because of the fragmented and illogical nature of young children's information processing.

Similar developments occur in the learning processes, as discussed by Reese and Porges (Chap. 10). In early infancy, involuntary associative learning is conditioned to innate reflexes. But during later infancy, and increasingly as age increases, associative learning is supplemented and replaced by cognitive learning proceeding from voluntary attention, though associative learning does persist even into adult life. Reese and Porges discuss the successive appearance of early cognitive learning in operant and classical conditioning. By about seven years learning is largely cognitive, as exemplified in discriminative learning and transfer and in discrimination learning sets. Presumably it is during these later developments that information processing functions with increasing effectiveness.

Mentally retarded children exhibit several deficiencies in information processing procedures (Odom-Brooks and Arnold, Chap. 15). Selective attention is impaired and scanning inefficient; hence there is less ability to discover redundancy and to perceive the relevant aspects of the field. The organization of information is also deficient by comparison with that of normal children. There is failure to construct and operate plans actively, to integrate relevant information, to utilize the memory store effectively and retrieve information from it in an efficient manner. But it would appear that these children do eventually reach the stage of concrete operations, and that the order of attainment of various types of conservation is similar to that occurring in normal children.

In some respects the effects of brain damage on cognitive development are similar. As might be expected, intelligence is generally impaired, but naturally the effects vary in nature and amount with severity of lesions and the age of their occurrence. Hutt (Chap. 14) hypothesizes that it is the functions of the cortical structures maturing at any particular age which are most affected by injury at that age. Though in many cases verbal and conceptual skills are more impaired than non-verbal, yet performance in free play situations at 3–8 years is also affected, and differs from that of normal children. There is a narrow span of attention and inadequate maintenance of attention, with a high degree of distractability. Children tend to view objects in the field sequentially and non-selectively, rather than directing attention towards its significant and interesting aspects. But their brief memory span reduces habituation, and makes them react to every object as if it were novel. There appears to be a particularly marked effect on the organization of information processing during generalized spike-wave activity in epileptic children. The effects are greatest when information load is high and when short-term memory is additionally involved. Thus it would seem that certain types of brain injury may impair several information processing procedures, though, as Hutt points out, little is known as to the precise effects of brain injury on these.

Although undoubtedly the more advanced forms of information processing are affected by linguistic functions, it appears now to be generally agreed that the development of certain linguistic functions is closely related to operational maturation (Donaldson, Chap. 7; Farnham-Diggory, Chap. 9). However, some linguistic functions obviously precede the concrete operational stage. Cromer (Chap. 8) points out that the differentiation of speech sounds from other sounds begins as early as 4 weeks. Classification of speech sounds in accordance with certain distinctive phonological features also occurs at an early age, and governs subsequent production of speech sounds. Certain purely linguistic rules operate in the construction of sentences as soon as these appear. Nevertheless the content and meaning, and in part the structure, of sentences spoken and understood are related to the child's understanding of his experiences, and the expectations of event probabilities which these engender; and also to his own actions. It would seem therefore that information processing in the auditory discrimination of invariants begins at an age comparable with that of visual discrimination, and that the memory storage of phonological representations must develop during the first year of life. Later forms of linguistic conceptualization parallel those employed for visually acquired information. Similar types of erroneous conceptualization also occur, though they are accompanied and modified by purely linguistic errors.

It seems probable that the various types of information processing in cognitive development as discussed above have some form of structural basis. Such structures must exist in the central nervous system. But it has also been hypothesized that there exist psychological intervening variables, in the form of a hierarchy of "abilities" of which general intelligence is considered to be the most significant. The information processing skills which appear at successive stages of cognitive development, culminating in conceptualization at the concrete and formal operational stages, are presumably based on intelligence, which exhibits marked individual differences, as illustrated in mentally retarded children. It is commonly found that these skills are related together, and that children who perform well in one also perform well in others (P. E. Vernon, Chap. 12). Nevertheless, adult proficiency may not be very closely related to that of young children. It is likely that children concentrate on the development of particular sets of skills at certain ages and then move on to others. Moreover, the operation of innate ability, the so-called "Intelligence A", is undoubtedly modified from infancy upwards by reinforcement through favourable environmental conditions or inhibition by unfavourable conditions, resulting in the actually operative "Intelligence B". It is probable that many of the information processing skills have an innate and indeed a hereditary basis, and are therefore included in "Intelligence A". A poor natural endowment appears to underlie the subnormal and restricted processing of mentally retarded children; though more for some of the processing functions than for others.

It has been maintained that there exist within the total personality, and independently of intelligence, certain cognitive "styles" or "controls", which considerably affect the manner in which information is processed (Hamilton, Chap. 11). These are considered to be enduring personality dispositions to handle information in particular ways, which have been extensively investigated by Witkin, Gardner and their colleagues. Of special interest are the individual differences, studied by Witkin et al. (1962), in the development of the capacity for differentiation and subsequent articulation and integration, in attention deployment, in perception and in conceptual processing. However, they have not been much studied in young children. It is not clear whether they have an innate basis, such as that of intelligence, but they are probably affected by environmental conditions.

Gardner and his colleagues have attempted to relate cognitive controls to motivational factors in the personality, though not very successfully. There is however abundant evidence that certain types of environmentally affected motivation are influential in the functioning of information processing skills, as discussed by Hamilton (Chap.

11). He argues that optimal cognitive capacity is related in the first place to children's selective attention, response to novelty and exploration, as encouraged or discouraged by adults, notably by maternal stimulation or by restriction in socialization procedures. So also is further conceptual development, particularly in the formation of conceptual schemata. Anxiety generated during socialization, especially by maternal coldness or rejection, may inhibit exploration and attention to novelty; and may produce disturbance in response to ambiguous or conflicting situations in which information is inadequate. Even such information processing capacities as the child possesses may not be effectively utilized, for instance in conservation tasks, because internal aversive information may generate self-evaluatory information processing and hence distract attention from task performance, producing over-simplification of task-related information processing. P. E. Vernon (Chap. 12) also discusses the effects of maternal attitudes and practices on intelligence. But he notes that the type of linguistic interchange between mother and child may be of paramount importance to cognitive development. Hamilton also suggests that in turn type of motivation and strategies of goal-seeking may be mediated by cognitive processes and data.

In Chapter 16 Hamilton develops further, in relation to schizophrenia and the neuroses, his hypotheses as to the causes and effects of inadequate information processing. He postulates the possible existence in these disorders of unadaptive biological sensitivity, interacting with maternal stimulation which is too complex, ambiguous and aversive; thus there results a lack of differentiation and over-generalization of information processing, and failure to develop appropriate higher order structures. Hence there arises an avoidance of external objective inputs and an incapacity to adapt to the environment, which are greater in schizophrenia than in neurosis because they originate at an earlier and more immature stage of development. It is to be hoped that the models which Hamilton has devised for these processes may be filled out through future experimental investigation.

It seemed to the Editors of this book that it would be a matter of considerable interest to discover whether the cognitive development of children in other societies differed from that of children in our own. It is clear, however, from Price-Williams's discussion (Chap. 13) that there are formidable difficulties in investigating and establishing the existence and nature of such differences and their possible causes. Genetic variations may be involved, and also a variety of environmental factors. Moreover, the cognitive processes studied have often been inadequately analysed and operationally defined. Investigations of differences in intelligence test scores have most frequently been studied (see P. E. Vernon, Chap. 12). The cognitive processes involved in these and in various Piagetian tasks are undoubtedly affected to a greater or less extent by numerous environmental conditions such as Western acculturation, education, type of language, socialization practices, differences in social conformity, etc., as well as by economic and nutritional conditions. Differences in socialization practices may be related to variations in cognitive differentiation, as in Western children (see Hamilton, Chap. 11). Perhaps the most interesting conclusion is that of Cole and Scribner (1974) that though the basic cognitive processes are similar in different cultures, they are differently organized in a variety of complex functional systems. Quite clearly the experiences and knowledge involved must differ substantially.

Thus it may be concluded that much further investigation is needed of the manner in which children gradually acquire the capacity to attend selectively to and derive information from different types of input. We may suppose that as this information is increasingly coded and stored semantically, feedback, in the form of developing expectations, directs attention appropriately to significant invariants, while inhibiting it to the irrelevant. Modification of information processing becomes increasingly effective as conceptual organization develops, and as the semantic store expands in range, complexity and relevance. It is important that there should be more extensive investigation of the manner in which the actual information processing procedures of infancy and early childhood differ qualitatively from those of adult life; and of the circumstances in which the former fail to reach their optimum potential.

REFERENCES

Bower, T. G. R. (1974). *Development in Infancy.* San Francisco: Freeman.

Bryant, P. (1974). *Perception and Understanding in Young Children.* London: Methuen.

Cole, M. and Scribner, S. (1974). *Culture and Thought: A Psychological Introduction.* New York: Wiley.

Fantz, R. L. (1958). Pattern vision in young infants. *Psychological Record, 8,* 43–7.

Gibson, E. J. (1969). *Principles of Perceptual Learning and Development.* New York: Appleton-Century-Crofts.

Witkin, H. A., Dyk, R. B., Faterson, H. F., Goodenough, D. R. and Karp, S. A. (1962). *Psychological Differentiation.* New York: Wiley.

AUTHOR INDEX

Numbers in italics refer to pages in References at the end of each chapter.

Graham, K. K., 120, *149*
Graham, N. C., 319, *356*
Graham, P., 697, *729*
Grandstaff, N. W., 127, 128, *151*
Gratch, G., 202, *233*, 283, *301*
Gray, C. R., 174, *185*
Gray, J. A., 477, 492, *500, 503*, 687, 688, *726*
Gray, W., 98, *106*
Green, J., 17, *40*
Greenbaum, C., *544*
Greenberg, D. J., 119, *149*, 158, 159, 162, *185*, 262, *272*
Greene, E. G., 623, *641*
Greenfield, P. M., 321, 323, 324, 338, 339, 340, 341, 342, 345, *356*, 551, 552, 554, 564, 568, 569, 570, 571, *584, 585*
Greenough, W. T., 419, *443*
Greenwood, A., 119, *151*
Gregg, L. W., 395, *406*
Gregg, V. H., 80, 85, 86, 98, *103*
Grice, H. P., 296, *301*
Grisell, J. L., 635, *640*
Grober, E. H., 391, *408*
Grobstein, R., 156, *186*
Gross, C. G., 248, *272*
Grusec, J., 474, *504*
Gruzelier, J. H., 705, *726*
Guilford, J. P., 43, 44, *104*, 513, 514, *544*
Gummerman, K., 174, *185*
Gurin, G., *505*
Gutierrez, S., *274*
Guzman, R., 217, *234*

H

Haaf, R. A., 165, 166, *185*
Haber, R. N., 16, 20, 21, 22, 24, *40*, 453, *500*
Habicht, J. P., *586*
Hagen, J. W., 429, *443*, 653, *676*
Hague, B., 238, *271*
Haith, M. M., 118, 121, 122, *149, 151, 186, 188*, 219, *235*
Halcombe, C. G., 135, *148*
Hale, G. A., 216, 217, *233*
Haley, J., *724*
Hall, V. C., 208, *232*
Halle, M., 344, *354, 356*

Halperin, M., 390, *406*
Hamacher, J. H., 313, 314, 315, *358*
Hamilton, L. W., 418, 422, *447*
Hamilton, V., 6, 7, 401, 402, *406*, 451, 455, 458, 462, 467, 477, 484, 487, 489, 490, 495, *500*, 681, 686, 687, 690, 691, 693, 694, 695, 716, *726*, 738, 739, 740
Hammond, J., 18, 19, *39*
Harlow, H. F., 372, *406*, 454, *500*, 512
Harlow, M. K., *500*
Harrell, R. F., 529, *544*
Harrington, D. M., *497*
Harris, G. T., 58, *104*, 663, *676*
Harris, M., 334, *356*
Harris, P. L., 202, *233*, 283, *301*
Harter, M. R., 158, *185*
Harter, S., 668, 669, *676*
Hartmann, D. P., *501*
Hartup, W. W., 489, *500*
Harvey, O. J., 464, 468, 469, 470, *500*, 711, *727*
Hasher, L., 390, *406*
Hathaway, S. R., 699, *727*
Hatton, H. M., *443*
Hawkins, H. L., 83, *104*
Hawkins, W. F., 661, *676*
Hayes, J. R., 289, *301*
Haynes, H., 155, *185*, 245, 250, *272*
Haywood, H. C., *504*, 668, 669, *677*
Head, H., 509
Heal, L. W., 651, *677*
Hebb, D. O., 453, *501*, 508, 509, 510, 511, 523, 528, 533, *544*, 638, *640*
Heber, R., 532, 533
Heckhausen, H., 456, *501*
Heft, H., 485, *505*
Heilbrun, A. B., 456, 487, *501*, 710, 712, *727*
Hein, A., 254, 255, *272*
Heinis, H., 522, *544*
Held, R., *185*, 243, 245, 250, 254, 255, *272, 275*
Hellmer, L. A., *724*
Helmstatter, G. C., 456, *501*
Hemsley, D. R., 695, *727*
Henderson, C., 672, *675*
Henderson, L., 30, 31, *40*
Henderson, S. E., 30, *40*
Henle, M., 295, *302*
Henley, N. M., 71, *104*

J

Jackendoff, R. S., 317, *356*
Jackson, D. D., *724*
Jackson, J. C., 417, *443*
Jackson, P. W., 514, *543*
Jacob, T., 710, *727*
Jacobson, J. Z., 62, *104*
Jacobson, L., 535, *545*
Jahoda, G., 556, 557, *586*
Jakobson, R., 343, 344, *356*
James, C. R., 262, *273*
James, C. T., 68, *104*
Janikoun, R., 216, *233*
Jankowski, J. J., *506*
Jarvik, L. F., 533, *543*
Jasper, H., 636, *642*
Jaynes, J., 474, *498*
Jeffrey, D. B., 489, *501*
Jeffrey, W. E., 161, *185*, 217, 219, *233*,
    368, 390, *407, 409*, 428, 434, *443*,
    651, *678*
Jeffreys, D. A., 262, *273*
Jencks, C., 540, *544*
Jenkins, R. L., 711, *727*
Jennings, J. R., 138, *150*
Jensen, A. R., 526, 529, 535, 537, 538,
    539, 540, 541, *544*, 660, *677*
Jinks, J. L., 539, 540, *544*
Johnsen, A. M., 57, *102*
Johnson, D., 98, *106*
Johnson, J. T., 651, *677, 678*
Johnson, L. C., 634, 635, *639*
Johnson, M. K., 391, *404*
Johnson, N. S., 658, *677*
Johnson-Laird, P. N., 295, *302*, 360,
    361, 377, 394, 398, *407, 411*
Jonasson, J. T., 35, *39*
Jones, A., 454, 474, 487, *501*
Jones, E. C., 153, *185*
Jones, H. E., 531, 533, *542, 544*
Jones, M. C., 475, *501*, 517, 525, 531,
    544, 700, *727*
Jones, M. H., *271*
Jones, P., *232*
Jones, S., 140, *150*
Jones-Molfese, V. J., 157, *185*
Jordan, C., 573, *585*
Juola, J. F., 65, 71, 74, 100, *102, 104,*
    105
Just, M. A., 83, *102*, 361, *407*

K

Kagan, J., 117, 118, 119, 120, 136,
    150, 151, 163, 164, 167, *185, 186,*
    188, 219, *233, 235*, 388, *410*, 423,
    444, 455, 461, 464, 465, 480, 485,
    501, 504, 529, 530, *544, 545*, 574,
    586, 700, *727*
Kahneman, D., 15, *40*, 495, *502*, 707,
    708, 709, *727*
Kail, R. V., 429, *443*, 487, *502*
Kalafat, J., *186*
Kalhorn, J., 530, *542*
Kalil, K., 376, *407*
Kalverboer, A. F., 613, 623, 624, *641*
Kantowitz, S. R., *443*
Kaplan, A., 413, *444*
Kaplan, B. E., 139, *150*
Karmel, B. J., 158, 159, *185*, 245, 260,
    262, *273*
Karp, S. A., 463, *500, 502, 505, 588,*
    741
Kasatkin, N. I., 425, *444*
Kaszor, P., 377, *404*
Katkin, E. S., 707, *727*
Katz, I., 538, *544*
Katz, J. J., 317, 318, 319, 320, 321,
    325, *356*
Katz, J. M., 465, *502*
Kaye, H., 122, *150*, 422, *443*
Kayton, L., *727*
Kear, J., 256, *273*
Keasey, C. B., 388, *411*
Keating, D. P., 387, *407*
Keele, S. W., 153, *187*
Keen, R., 121, *150*
Keiffer, K., 286, *301*
Kellaghan, T., 565, *586*
Kellas, G., *105*, 658, 663, *676, 677*
Kendler, H. H., 433, 434, 435, *444*
Kendler, T. S., 426, 428, 433, 434,
    435, *444*
Kent, N., 530, *545*
Keogh, B. K., 177, *186*
Kessen, M., 128, *151*
Kessen, W., 128, *151*, 156, *185, 186,*
    187, 192, *235*
Kessler, P., 705, *727*
Kilpatrick, F. P., 241, *273*
Kimble, D. P., 623, *641*
Kimmel, H. D., 689, *727*

SUBJECT INDEX

A

Accommodation, 374, 457, 664, 671
Activation, 682, 687, 707
    infant, 471–81
Anxiety, 681–723
    and achievement motivation, 456,
        491–2
    and ambiguity avoidance, 455, 467,
        487
    and arousal, 486
    and attention, 484–6
    as aversive information, 489–91, 682,
        716–22
    and concept formation, 712
    and conservation, 489–90
    excitatory function of, 691
    and generalization, 687
    and information processing, 696,
        706, 708–9, 711, 716–23
    and information processing capacity,
        464, 484, 486, 490–6
    and intelligence, 481–4, 529
    and learning processes, 685–90
    psychoanalytic theory of, 690, 722
    quantitative model of, 490–1,
        716–17
    "test", "state", "trait", 687
Arousal, 111, 120, 126, 136, 137, 139,
        454, 457, 486, 487, 494, 512, 682,
        687, 688, 691–2, 704, 707, 719
    and cue utilization, 707–8, 716
    and performance, 692, 695, 707–9
Assimilation, 374, 457, 664, 665, 668,
        671, 674
Attachment, 471–81
Attention, 111, 113, 114, 129–35, 144,
        145, 157, 217, 220, 365, 381, 384,
        387, 431–2, 436, 463, 465, 484–6,
        487, 494, 512, 567–9, 576, 608,
        610, 615–25, 649, 650–5, 684, 691,
        693, 707–9

B

Behaviorism, 413–14
Berkeley Growth Studies, 480, 482,
        517, 530, 698, 700

Autonomic nervous system responses
    cardiac, 118, 120, 138, 417, 422–3
    GSR (skin conductance), 125, 137,
        138, 139, 146, 703–5, 707
    parasympathetic, 416, 418
    sympathetic, 416, 418
Aversive stimulation, 495, 682, 686,
        691

C

Categories, categorization
    dominance of, 69–71, 92
    of faces, 214
    frequency of co-occurrence of, 69–71
    iconogenic, 78
    internal structure of, 72
    of names, 98
    pictorial, 86
    refinement of, 208
    relatedness in, 69–72, 86, 101
    semantic, 65–77, 98
    of words, 65, 66
Centration, decentration, 178, 281, 693
Cerebral dominance, 604–7, 610, 611,
        613, 614–15
Cerebral dysfunction
    and age of insult, 597–605, 607, 608,
        611, 613, 614
    anatomical, 605–8
    and attention, 608, 610, 615–25
    in brain-damaged children, 616–24
    in cognitive development, 591–638
    and exploration, 615–25
    and general lesions, 597–604
    in hyperkinetic children, 136–7, 595,
        615–16, 624